Motivation, Emotion, and Goal Direction in Neural Networks

Motivation, Emotion, and Goal Direction in Neural Networks

Edited by

Daniel S. Levine
University of Texas at Arlington

Samuel J. Leven
Radford University and For a New Social Science

LEA LAWRENCE ERLBAUM ASSOCIATES, PUBLISHERS
1992   Hillsdale, New Jersey   Hove and London

Lawrence Erlbaum Associates, Inc., Publishers
365 Broadway
Hillsdale, New Jersey 07642

Library of Congress Cataloging-in-Publication Data

Motivation, emotion, and goal direction in neural networks / Daniel S.
  Levine and Samuel J. Leven, editors.
      p. cm.
  Papers presented at a workshop held in Dallas, 1988, sponsored by
the Metroplex Institute for Neural Dynamics.
  Includes bibliographical references and index.
  ISBN 0-8058-0447-1
  1. Motivation (Psychology)—Congresses. 2. Emotions—Congresses.
3. Classical conditioning—Congresses. 4. Neural circuitry-
-Congresses. 5. Goal (Psychology)—Congresses. I. Levine, Daniel
S. II. Leven, Samuel J. III. Metroplex Institute for Neural
Dynamics.
  BF199.M67 1991
  153—dc20   91–12950
                                                           CIP

Printed in the United States of America
10 9 8 7 6 5 4 3 2 1

Contents

Preface

Emotion used to be a dirty word in science. The late 1800s and the first half of the 1900s were dominated by a profound belief in the ultimate triumph of rationality over ignorance (and, by extension, over emotion). The attempt to rationalize, to quantify, to make things precise spread from the traditional natural sciences to newer disciplines. As academic psychologists strove to be more scientific, they took their cues from the older natural sciences such as physics and chemistry, restricting their attention to phenomena that were easily and cleanly measurable. Hence, the behaviorist, or stimulus–response, school of psychology came to a position of ascendancy. Social scientists in other fields—sociology, political science, management theory, economics—likewise set out to explain the human phenomena they studied by positing rational actors seeking to maximize some measurable quantity. Hence, in all these fields, there has been some tendency to regard emotion as either not worth serious study, or worth serious study because it is undesirable.

The articles gathered in this volume represent examples of a quite different approach to the study of mental phenomena. They represent a blend of theory and experiment, informed not just by easily measurable laboratory data but also by human introspection. Approach and avoidance, desire and fear, novelty and habit are studied as natural events, which may not exactly correspond to but at least correlate with some (known or unknown) electrical and chemical events in the brain.

Whenever there are patterns in nature with any sort of regularity, the temptation arises to look for scientific understanding of the phenomena involved. In the realms of motivation, emotion, and goal direction, the science of brain and behavior is still at any early stage of grappling with problems, but already, from a combination of experimental and theoretical work, some underlying principles are starting to be visible.

Some philosophers of science (e.g., Young, 1951; Stich, 1983; Churchland, 1986) suggested that the precise concepts of neurobiology, as they emerge, will actually replace the more vague concepts of folk psychology. Our belief, rather, is that *some* concepts from folk psychology will be replaced, but others will prove useful in suggesting organizing principles for understanding the brain. In particular we reject the extreme reductionist position that questions of motivation and emotion will be side-stepped as brain science progresses. Further progress in brain science, rather, depends on the courage to use recent technological and theoretical advances to confront these very questions of motivation and emotion.

Obviously part of the problem has been the lack of precise definitions for terms like "emotion." Several recent researchers have made promising attempts at definition. Gray and Baruch (1987) discussed an approach that "treats the emotions as central states elicited by reinforcing events—that is, events, unconditioned or conditioned, that are capable of increasing or decreasing the probability of instrumental responses on which they are made contingent." Similarly Buck (1988, p. 6) viewed motivation as "a potential for the activation and direction of behavior that is inherent in a system of behavior control; then he went on (Buck, 1988, p. 9) to say: "I define emotion as the process by which motivational potential is realized, or 'read out,' when activated by challenging stimuli." Although we are not adhering strictly in this volume to any definition of terms, the articles contained herein all relate to manifestations in natural or artificial neural networks of "motivation" or "emotion" as Gray and Baruch or Buck defined them.

Understanding the roles of emotion in cognition and behavior has an obvious future potential for application to the understanding and treatment of psychiatric disorders. It also has more immediate applications to the industrial uses of neural networks. For, as the previous definitions suggest, the problem of emotion is intimately connected with the problem of goal direction and planning in either a living organism or an intelligent machine. Hence, the subject of study of this volume bears directly on the incorporation of planning and goal direction into artificial neural systems. These capabilities will be particularly important in the use of such systems for control, as in robotics, which is likely to be a major, future growth area for neural network technology. The study of emotion, motivation, and goal direction is also important for the design of better human–computer interfaces, because such design must be based on an accurate portrayal of human decision processes.

The 1970s and 1980s have seen rapid growth in our understanding of brain function and the relations of brain to behavior. Exciting progress in experimental neurobiology has been paralleled by explosive development of computer and mathematical models of neural networks (see, for example, Grossberg, 1982a, 1987, 1988; Levine, 1983; in press; McClelland & Rumelhart, 1987; Rumelhart

& McClelland, 1986). Neural networks are often thought to be mainly of interest to the study of pattern recognition and categorization. The fact is that neural network studies have already begun to address, without yet definitely solving, a wide range of other issues in cognition and behavior. As the chapters in this volume (particularly those of Aparicio and Strong, Grossberg et al., Hestenes, Leven, Levine et al., and Ricart) make clear, this includes issues of motivation, emotion, and goal direction.

Now some rationalists might argue that, sure, emotions are part of functioning, but are they part of *optimal* functioning? Is not the most efficient behavior characterized by the triumph of reason over emotion? Academic psychologists, by and large, supported this notion until the mid-1950s and 1960s, when the explanation of positively reinforcing events as *drive reducing* (Hull, 1943) yielded in part to the alternative explanation of positively reinforcing events as *drive inducing* (Mowrer, 1960).

The drive reduction notion has some intuitive plausibility; after all, eating reduces hunger; drinking reduces thirst; and sexual intercourse reduces lust. Hence, drive reduction has remained popular in some circles despite an apparent telling blow from neurophysiology: the discovery by James Olds (1955) of "pleasure centers" in the hypothalamus of the rat's brain. Olds found that, if rats could press a lever to stimulate certain brain regions, they chose lever pressing over more conventional satisfactions like food and sex. Moreover, the drive for brain stimulation did not satiate in the manner of the hunger or sexual drives; the rats kept pressing the lever on and off for hours.

Further physiological discoveries hinted that strong drive can sometimes be associated with pleasure rather than pain. Although the lateral hypothalamus is one area whose stimulation is pleasurable (Olds, 1977), it has also been found that stimulation of the same area can lead to increased eating (Delgado & Anand, 1953)! From the point of view of understanding brain organization, that a pleasure center is also a hunger center might seem to be a paradox (if it is not the result of sloppy experimentation). Yet the paradox disappears, if we remember, with Maslow (1971) and Grossberg (1982b), the times we have been on the verge of eating a delicious meal or making love with a desirable partner. The experience is one of high drive combined not with pain but with pleasurable anticipation.

The experimental results of Olds, Delgado, Anand, and others suggest that positively reinforcing events are not those events that reduce drive but rather are those events that *induce* drive (i.e., that activate a positive feedback loop in the brain that consummates drive). Hence, stimulation of the lateral hypothalamus does not produce "hunger" in the sense of physiological signs like stomach contractions and low blood sugar. Such stimulation *mimics* the effect of hunger by activating consummatory feedback in the absence of physiological signs that are normally necessary for this feedback to occur. Loops of drive-related neural activity have been studied in neural networks since the early 1970s.

Klopf (1982) attempted to formalize, in neural network terms, the idea that organisms actively seek stimulation. He contrasted the seeking of maximum stimulation with the tendency to seek a balanced or steady-state condition in other respects (such as blood sugar or hormone levels). The seeking of a steady-state condition is called homeostasis (Cannon, 1929); thus, Klopf coined the opposing word *heterostasis* for the seeking of a maximum condition.

In Klopf's theory, all parts of the brain are independently seeking positive stimulation (the analog of "pleasure") and avoiding negative stimulation ("pain"). In other words, brain areas are goal-seeking devices: They respond electrically to stimuli elsewhere in the brain and test the consequences of their own responses. If responding to a given stimulus leads to "pleasure," the given brain area will respond more frequently to that stimulus in the future, just like a miniature version of rats pressing a lever that has previously yielded them food (Skinner, 1938). If responding to that stimulus leads instead to "pain," the brain area will respond less frequently to that stimulus in the future.

Yet Klopf's work also contains an implicit suggestion that there is a single organizing criterion (maximum stimulation of the brain's reticular formation, in this case) by which people and animals make all of our decisions. Levine (1983, p. 64), listed some evidence from experimental psychology that argues against a single decision criterion. Solomon et al. (1953), for example, found an experimental model of learned helplessness. They trained dogs to make a particular motor response to avoid electric shock, then later shocked the animals for making that very same response.. The result was a great deal of confusion and some self-punitive behavior on the part of the dogs. Gray and Smith (1969) and others have found that animals, under many conditions, will perform a response more reliably if it is intermittently reinforced with food than if it is reinforced every time they do it. The comparison with human gambling is obvious.

The controversy over whether there is an all-encompassing human decision criterion rages not only in psychology but also in economics. The orthodox view among economists (e.g., Lancaster, 1966; Weintraub, 1979) is that there is some expected measure of happiness or "utility" that both consumers and producers are maximizing at all times. An opposing view (Heiner, 1983, 1985; Leven, 1988) is that much economic behavior is predictable without being rational. For example, consumers will often stick with the "tried and true" even after a demonstration that a new product is superior in some way—as happened when "new Coke" was rejected and "old Coke" had to be reintroduced, even though the new taste had been preferred by a two-to-one margin over the old one in blind taste tests. Paradoxically, some other products sell just because they are novel and for no other substantive reason.

More pernicious issues may underlie assumptions made about choice processes. Do the ghetto poor, for example, *prefer* their current schedule of leisure and early death to work and education? Implicit suggestions that people are always *optimizing* (and doing so *rationally*) reinforce social agendas that should be viewed with a certain scientific skepticism, and not only conservatives but liberals as well have at times been informed, or rather misinformed, by excessive belief in rationality. Programs for urban renewal in the 1950s and 1960s, for example, tended to emphasize "rational" factors such as space and cleanliness but ignore "affective" factors such as community. Affect and habit are intrinsic in neural function; thus, our models of human behavior must consider them integrally.

Grossberg (1971, 1975, 1982b) addressed some of these decision issues in neural networks designed to explain conditioning data. His networks included some subsystems that coded sensory events, or the memories of those events. The networks also included other subsystems that coded motor actions or the intentions to perform them, but he found that the data could best be explained by the inclusion, in addition to sensory and motor representations, of what he called *drive representations*. That is, there were neural subsystems that simultaneously coded the level of a drive and the possibility of satisfying it. The hunger drive representation, for example, was highly active whenever the organism was hungry *and* there was either available food or some cue that signified future availability of food. Thus, in the classic experiment of Pavlov (1985) where the sound of a bell is repeatedly followed by presentation of meat powder to a dog until the dog salivates to a bell, the association the animal makes is not "bell to meat powder." Rather it is "bell sound representation activation to hunger drive representation activation."

Positive feedback between sensory and drive representations plays many important roles. Such feedback determines which stimuli and which actions a person or animal will find rewarding or punishing. (In addition to representations of "positive" drives like hunger, Grossberg's neural networks also contain representations of "negative" drives like fear.) It also strongly influences which events in a complex environment will be attended to.

In the artificial neural networks developed by Klopf, Grossberg, and many others, reason is in no way "superior" to emotion. Rather, in such networks, reason and emotion perform separate functions, and both are necessary for cognition and memory. Emotion provides the sense of what organisms need and want, whereas reason provides the techniques and strategies for achieving those needs.

The movement in academic psychology toward a more favorable view of human needs and desires has been paralleled by an analogous movement in psychotherapy. Maslow (1968, p. 28) set out to challenge the common notion (shared by a gamut running from theologians to economic theorists) that "good or happiness or pleasure is essentially the consequence of amelioration of this unpleasant state-of-affairs of wanting, of desiring, of needing." Indeed (Maslow, 1968, p. 30) "different basic needs are related to each other in a hierarchical order such that gratification of one need and its consequent removal from the center of the stage brings about not a state of rest or Stoic apathy, but rather the emergence into consciousness of another 'higher' need." In other words, there are *biological* needs not just for survival but for fulfillment, for richness in life, for connected-ness. Maslow contrasted this view with a traditional view informed by naive Freudianism, that natural human impulses are almost all toward satisfying base, "animalistic" urges and that a superego of elaborate social codes is required to suppress such destructive urges.

The separate but interacting nature of rational and emotional functions also informs the qualitative notion of the "triune brain" (for example, MacLean, 1970). From extensive behavioral studies of the stimulation or lesion of different brain areas, MacLean developed a theory that the human brain is divided into three "layers" that arrived at different stages of evolution. At the deepest levels is the midbrain reticular formation and other areas forming the "reptilian brain" that has changed little from reptiles to higher mammals to humans. The reptilian brain is responsible for species-specific, almost automatic instinctive behavior. Such behavior is needed for the basic maintenance of the organism but also extends to habitual patterns such as dominance hierarchies. Above the reptilian brain is the limbic system, which is the center of the "old mammalian brain." It is responsible, in this scheme, for emotions such as fear, love, and anger that attend the needs for survival of the individual and survival of the species. Finally, at the top, is the cerebral cortex, which is called the "new mammalian brain" (because it is poorly developed in vertebrates other than mammals, and some of it—the frontal area—is only well developed in primates). The new mammalian brain is the "thinking cap" over the rest of the brain, the part that is responsible for our rational strategies and our extensive verbal and intellectual capacities.

MacLean's scheme is open to, and has received, significant criticism on scientific grounds (e.g., Pribram, 1984). His assignment of functions to specific subregions of the brain is not always correct in detail. Neither is his association of brain regions with species accurate; the hippocampal area of the limbic sys-tem, for example, is well developed in reptiles. Yet MacLean made a major contribution to cognitive psychology by adding to the reason–emotion dichoto-my a third category for instincts or habits.

The distinction between emotions and habits is also supported by results of recent experiments performed on macaque monkeys (Mishkin & Appenzeller, 1987; Mishkin, Malamut, & Bachevalier, 1984). Mishkin and his co-workers showed that extensive damage to the limbic system prevented monkeys from being able to remember the emotional importance of sensory events, for use in future cognitive tasks. The same limbic damage did not, however, interfere with a more primitive capacity, the learning of an invariant motor response to a previously rewarded stimulus. Seemingly these monkeys remembered the motor response they had developed on the basis of reward while forgetting about the reward itself. These researchers concluded that there are two separate neural systems for encoding memories and habits. The memory system, centered in the hippocampus and amygdala (both parts of the limbic system), stores representa-tions of how rewarding or punishing are specific sensory stimuli or motor actions. The habit system, centered in the basal ganglia, stores representations of the motor actions themselves regardless of their reinforcement value.

In the brain, the interplay of reason, emotion, habit, and novelty is controlled by complex control circuits with extensive feedback. Several of the articles in this volume (those of Banquet et al., Hestenes, Leven, Levine et al., and Pribram) show that the barest beginnings of a system understanding of these control circuits has been achieved. Damage to different regions in this control circuit can lead to various kinds of cognitive defects. Further insights should be obtained from building analogs of these brain regions out of suitable concatenations of artificial networks previously designed to perform simpler functions (such as perception and learning).

The work that is edited here heralds some profound changes in the landscape of our understanding of psychological function. Some of the past and anticipated future intellectual history of our field is discussed by Pribram (1985):

> The transition from behaviorism, especially stimulus-response behaviorism, to cognitive psychology, was characterized by an increasing difficulty to operationalize such concepts as effort and attention. I believe that the next revolutionary turn in psychology will, in a similar way, be characterized by an increasing difficulty in operationalizing concepts we now hold dear, such as information processing, and by an increasing ability to operationalize such concepts as meaning and intuition. (p. 6)

The articles in this volume, while diverse and highly interrelated, fall naturally into three major sections. The first section consists of articles on the theory of Pavlovian (classical) conditioning. This is one of the richest current areas of contact between neurophysiology, psychology, and neural modeling. Further, Pavlovian conditioning studies can illuminate the study of more complex forms of learning that involve motivational influences.

The second section consists of both theoretical and experimental studies on complex brain control circuits and their disruption. Such circuits involve a coordination of cortical areas such as the frontal lobes with subcortical areas such as the limbic system, hypothalamus, and basal ganglia. Computational studies of these brain regions are still in their infancy, but the work discussed herein suggests that encouraging progress may occur in the next several years. Neural network principles are starting to make some order out of the dizzying profusion of regions, connections, and chemical transmitters in these more "central" areas of the brain, areas that are not directly sensory or motor.

The third and last section of this book consists of artificial neural network studies designed with applications in mind. Preliminary efforts to include "plans" or "goals" in industrial systems are apparent here. This is a step toward opening up the promise (or specter, depending on your viewpoint) of building machines with genuine, biological cognitive capabilities.

This book arose from a workshop of the same title, with close to a hundred participants, that was held at the Infomart in Dallas over Memorial Day weekend, 1988. This workshop was sponsored by the Metroplex Institute for Neural Dynamics (M.I.N.D.), a Dallas–Fort Worth area-wide neural networks interest group, with assistance from two local computer companies. Several of the first authors (Aparicio, Leven, Levine, Pribram, Ricart) gave talks at the conference, and others (Cruz and Grossberg) sent material to be presented at the conference in absentia. The remaining first authors (Banquet, Dawes, Hestenes, Kehoe, and Killeen) could not be fit into the conference program but were subsequently invited to submit chapters, because they were working in areas compatible with the theme of the conference.

As coeditors of this volume, and coorganizers of the conference from which it arose, we wish to thank all the contributing authors and many other people who helped make this volume possible. The membership of M.I.N.D. gave the workshop its enthusiastic support, in both time and money. The executive committee of M.I.N.D. and the staff of Martingale Research Corporation (Robert Dawes, its President; David Davis, and others) worked tirelessly to organize the program, invite speakers, put together brochures, and publicize it both locally and nationally. The staff at the Infomart provided unparalleled facilities for the conference. Rockwell International, Defense Communications and Sequent Computer Systems, Incorporated, gave financial assistance to the conference, which enabled us to rent those facilities. Two graduate students active in M.I.N.D., Paul Prueitt (also a co-author on Chapter 9) and Wesley Elsberry, provided invaluable assistance at many stages of the conference and the subsequent organization of the book, including the careful notes that Wesley took at the conference. Harry Klopf and Elliott Ross gave two very stimulating talks at the conference, both of which included videotapes, and unfortunately were not able to contribute to the volume itself because of other time commitments.

We owe a debt of thanks to the staff at Lawrence Erlbaum Associates, Inc.— Julia Hough and Judi Amsel, our editors at different stages; Hollis Heimbouch, our editorial assistant; and Lawrence Erlbaum, president. Julia and Judi in particular realized the importance of the subject at an early stage, and energetically and cheerfully saw the book project through many changes and slow starts.

Finally we would like to thank our wives, Lorraine and Nina. Their support, encouragement, and perspective helped make the project of organizing this book considerably smoother than it would have been otherwise.

Daniel S. Levine
Arlington, TX

Samuel J. Leven
Radford, VA

References for Preface

Buck, R. (1988). *Human motivation and emotion*. New York: Wiley.

Cannon, W. B. (1929). Organization for physiological homeostasis. *Physiological Review, 9*, 399–431.

Churchland, P. S. (1986). *Neurophilosophy*. Cambridge, MA: MIT Press.

Delgado, J. M. R., & Anand, B. K. (1953). Increase of food intake induced by electrical stimulation of the lateral hypothalamus. *American Journal of Physiology, 172*, 162–168.

Gray, J. A., & Baruch, I. (1987). Don't leave the "psych" out of neuropsychology. *The Behavioral and Brain Sciences, 10*, 215–216.

Gray, J. A., & Smith, P. T. (1969). An arousal-decision model for partial reinforcement and discrimination learning. In R. M. Gilbert & N. S. Sutherland (Eds.), *Animal discrimination learning* (pp. 243–272). New York: Academic Press.

Grossberg, S. (1971). On the dynamics of operant conditioning. *Journal of Theoretical Biology, 33*, 225–255.

Grossberg, S. (1975). A neural model of attention, reinforcement, and discrimination learning. *International Review of Neurobiology, 18*, 263–327.

Grossberg, S. (1982a). *Studies in mind and brain: Neural principles of learning, perception, development, and motor control*. Boston: Reidel.

Grossberg, S. (1982b). A psychophysiological theory of reinforcement, drive, motivation, and attention. *Journal of Theoretical Neurobiology, 1*, 286–369.

Grossberg, S. (1987). *The adaptive brain* (Vols. I and II). Amsterdam: Elsevier.

Grossberg, S. (1988). *Neural networks and natural intelligence*. Cambridge, MA: MIT Press.

Heiner, R. (1983). The origin of predictable behavior. *American Economic Review, 73*, 560–585.

Heiner, R. (1985). The origin of predictable behavior: Further modeling and applications. *American Economic Review, 75*, 391–396.

Hull, C. L. (1943). *Principles of behavior*. New York: Appleton.

Klopf, A. H. (1982). *The hedonistic neuron: A theory of memory, learning, and intelligence*. Washington, DC: Hemisphere.

Lancaster, K. (1966). A new approach to consumer theory. *Journal of Political Economy, 74*, 131–157.

Leven, S. J. (1988). *Choice and neural process*. Unpublished doctoral dissertation, Institute of Urban Studies, University of Texas at Arlington.

Levine, D. S. (1983). Neural population modeling and psychology: A review. *Mathematical Biosciences, 66,* 1–86.

Levine, D. S. (in press). *Introduction to neural and cognitive modeling.* Hillsdale, NJ: Lawrence Erlbaum Associates.

MacLean, P. D. (1970). The triune brain, emotion, and scientific bias. In F. Schmitt (Ed.), *The Neurosciences Second Study Program* (pp. 336–349). New York: Rockefeller University Press.

Maslow, A. H. (1968). *Toward a psychology of being.* New York: Van Nostrand.

Maslow, A. H. (1971). *The farther reaches of human nature.* New York: Viking.

Mishkin, M., & Appenzeller, T. (1987, June). The anatomy of memory. *Scientific American,* 80–89.

Mishkin, M., Malamut, B., & Bachevalier, J. (1984). Memories and habits: Two neural systems. In G. Lynch, J. L. McGaugh, & N. M. Weinberger (Eds.), *Neurobiology of learning and memory* (pp. 65–77). New York: Guilford.

Mowrer, O. H. (1960). *Learning theory and behavior.* New York: Wiley.

Olds, J. (1955). Physiological mechanisms of reward. In M. Jones (Ed.), *Nebraska Symposium on Motivation.* Lincoln, NE: University of Nebraska Press.

Olds, J. (1977). *Drives and reinforcements: Behavioral studies of hypothalamic functions.* New York: Raven.

Pavlov, I. P. (1985). *Conditioned reflexes* (V. Anrep, Trans.). London-Oxford University Press.

Pribram, K. (1984). Emotion: A neurobehavioral analysis. In K. Scherer & P. Ekman (Eds.), *Approaches to emotion* (pp. 13–38). Hillsdale, NJ: Lawrence Erlbaum Associates.

Pribram, K. H. (1985). Holism could close the cognition era. *APA Monitor,* Vol. 16, pp. 5–6.

Rumelhart, D. E., & Mc Clelland, J. L. (1986). *Parallel distributed processing.* Cambridge, MA: MIT Press.

Skinner, B. F. (1938). *The behavior of organisms.* New York: Appleton.

Stich, S. (1983). *From folk psychology to cognitive science.* Cambridge, MA: MIT Press.

Weintraub, E. R. (1979). *Microfoundations.* New York: Cambridge University Press.

Young, J. Z. (1951). *Doubt and certainty in science: A biologist's reflections on the brain.* Oxford: Clarendon Press.

List of Contributors

Manuel Aparicio, International Business Machines Corporation, Internal Zip 030440, 5 West Kirkwood Boulevard, Roanoke, TX 76299-0001.

Jean-Paul Banquet, Hôpital de la Salpétrière, Laboratoire d'Électrophysiologie et de Neurophysiologie Appliquée, CNRS, 47 Boulevard de l'Hôpital, 75651 Paris, France and Center for Adaptive Systems, Boston University, 111 Cummington St., Boston, MA 02215.

Claude A. Cruz, Plexus Systems, Inc., 139 Coburn Woods, Nashua, NH 03063.

Robert L. Dawes, Martingale Research Corporation, 100 Allentown Pkwy., Suite 211, Allen, TX 75002.

Stephen Grossberg, Director, Center for Adaptive Systems, Boston University, 111 Cummington Street, Boston, MA 02215.

W. Guenther, Psychiatric Hospital, Munich, Federal Republic of Germany.

David Hestenes, Department of Physics, Arizona State University, Tempe, AZ 85287.

E. James Kehoe, School of Psychology, The University of New South Wales, P. O. Box 1, Kensington, NSW 2033, Australia.

Peter R. Killeen, Department of Psychology, Arizona State University, Tempe, AZ 85287.

Samuel J. Leven, Center for Brain Research and Informational Sciences, Radford University, Radford, VA 24142.

Daniel S. Levine, Department of Mathematics, University of Texas at Arlington, Arlington, TX 76019.

Karl Pribram, Director, Center for Brain Research and Informational Sciences, Radford University, Radford, VA 24142.

Paul S. Prueitt, Department of Physics, Georgetown University, Washington, DC 20057.

Lt. Richard Ricart, 2711 State Route 235, Xenia, OH 45385.

Nestor Schmajuk, Department of Psychology, Northwestern University, Evanston, IL 60201.

Mark Smith, Hôpital de la Salpétrière, Laboratoire d'Électrophysiologie et de Neurophysiologie Appliquée, CNRS, 47 Boulevard de l'Hôpital, 75651 Paris, France.

Paschal N. Strong, Jr., Department of Psychology, University of South Florida, Tampa, FL 33620.

THEORIES OF PAVLOVIAN CONDITIONING

1 Propagation Controls for True Pavlovian Conditioning

Manuel Aparicio IV
International Business Machines Corporation

Paschal N. Strong
University of South Florida

The architectures and mechanisms of learning are becoming more important to the design of machines that will work on more complex and open problems. Biological systems are being studied as the prior art for such designs, but several controversies still remain about the role of habituation in conditioning, the generation of responses that cannot be defined a priori, and the reality of a new computational rubric within actual nervous systems. As a bridge between recent discoveries in both computer and neural sciences, this work presents a quantitative model of habituation and sensitization, most notably found in the mollusc *Aplysia,* but as part of a larger dynamics analogous to connectionism's computation of energy contours and their control by simulated annealing. Pavlovian conditioning is modeled as the control of propagation through laterally connected reflex arcs. These arcs pass through two layers: The alpha layer computes temporal contingencies according to activity-dependent sensitization and habituation. The beta layer stores an energy contour similar to a dominant focus. Feeding forward to the beta layer, the alpha layer controls both stimulus propagation through the contour and the formation of the contour itself by potentiation. Negative feedback from the beta layer provides the control function analogous to simulated annealing. This model demonstrated habituation, classical conditioning, extinction, and spontaneous recovery. Both alpha and beta conditioning were produced, but, in contrast to alpha conditioning, the beta response learning curve showed initial positive acceleration and much higher final asymptote. Extinction and spontaneous recovery were demonstrated as properties of habituation. The model's limitations are considered for the future elaboration of a more complete and general mechanics.

CROSSDISCIPLINARY BRIDGES

The resurgence of neural modeling within recent years is the resurgence of a very simple idea: Study extant neural systems as the prior art for machine design. Although our understanding of learning is still at the forefront of research, there is an enormous prospect for using this knowledge for the design of adaptive systems. This is especially true of learning when more precisely defined as "conditioning," the strategy by which animals infer the causal structure of their environment for competitive survival in real time and real space. Understanding how animals make such inferences will allow the design of machines that are able to do the same.

Motivation, emotion, and goal direction are integral parts of learning, making neural systems much more intricate than learning simple association matrixes. The past several decades of neuroscience have provided insight into both the function and physiology of how attention, drive, incentive, and instinct are related to learning; yet several principles of design remain underrepresented in the neural network literature. For instance, Premack's Principle (1962) refutes any notion of specialized reinforcers; all stimuli have the potential to reinforce each other. On the other hand, some associations are more difficult to learn than others; Seligman's concept of preparedness (1970) indicates a continuum of instinctive reflexes and learned ones. Such a continuum is necessary for survival.

Our model incorporates such principles and moreover, demonstrates motivation as a set of control processes. Motivation is a determinant in stimulus attention and the initial storage of memory, but, in addition, motivation and emotion are important components in the expression of memory. We use the phenomenon of spontaneous recovery from extinction to show how such controls determine whether or not a learned memory is in fact expressed.

Learning research has many strong traditions across many different fields, but, for further progress in neural modeling of learning, stronger bridges must be built across the fields of information and neural sciences. In the conclusions of Sejnowski, Koch, and Churchland (1988), "we expect future brain models to be intermediate types that combine the advantages of both realistic and simplifying models" (p. 1305). Realistic models include as much detail as possible; simplifying models abstract the important principles. Our model presents one such bridge between the rubric of gradient descent, energy contours, and simulated annealing and the known facts of neuroscience. Simplifying models too easily lose touch with biology; thus, our bias is more strongly toward neuroscience. We do not adopt any computation simply for the sake of its correct function. On the other hand, realistic models by themselves can fail to describe the overall functions of a system. This is why we use the mechanics of energy contours (Hopfield, 1982) and simulated annealing (Kirkpatrick, Gelatt, & Vecchi, 1983) to understand conditioning across its many levels of investigation: physiology, architecture, and behavior.

2

As an intermediate between realistic and simplifying types, our model is not of any particular neural system. Every component is based not so much on any specific data but on known neuroscientific fact, law, or principle. Just as principles are validated across a range of systems, we present a general model of Pavlovian conditioning based on the larger body of learning and motivational theory. We hope this establishes a bridge between the detailed mechanisms described in the present section of this book and the global brain dynamics to be described in the next section. Our full model will have implications for cerebrocortical processing and simultaneous input for potentiation, but we begin with an invertebrate, a "soft underbelly" to establish the physiological detail of simple conditioning.

BACKGROUND MODELS

Aplysia, a gastropod mollusc, has been a major biological system in the search for the engram. Several decades of work have elucidated the elemental mechanisms of habituation and sensitization and how these mechanisms operate in simple conditioning. Fig. 1.1A shows one of the more complete models to date as proposed by Hawkins and Kandel (1984). Tactile stimulation to the siphon or mantle shelf represents a conditioned stimulus (CS), which activates the appropriate sensory neuron and its monosynaptic connection to the motor neuron. Habituation, the most elemental form of learning, is an intrinsic governor of the sensory neuron terminals; through some mechanism for calcium channel dysfunction, habituation decreases the efficacy of the sensory neuron synapse as a function of repeated low-intensity stimulation. Calcium is required for the release of neurotransmitter; thus, calcium channel dysfunction decreases the synapse's efficacy.

However, if a CS is followed by an unconditioned stimulus (UCS), the UCS activates a facilitatory interneuron responsible for presynaptic modulation of the sensory-motor neuron synapse. In contrast to habituation, this extrinsic governor is called activity-dependent sensitization. Sensitization by the UCS is dependent on just-prior activity within the CS pathway; therefore, repeated presentation of a CS1 followed by the UCS will selectively increase the motor neuron's response to only the predictive CS1 (not the CS2). Such a mechanism has been implemented in simplifying neural networks, such as Sutton and Barto's (1981) use of an eligibility trace, and in realistic models of calcium influx and buffering in *Aplysia* (Byrne, Gingrich, & Baxter, 1989). This calcium trace mechanism also produces the interstimulus-interval (ISI) effect at the behavioral level of conditioning; there is some delay in the accumulation of intracellular calcium caused by the CS, and, because UCS facilitation is amplified by intracellular calcium, conditioning is best when the CS is presented just before the UCS. Simultaneous stimuli produce poor conditioning.

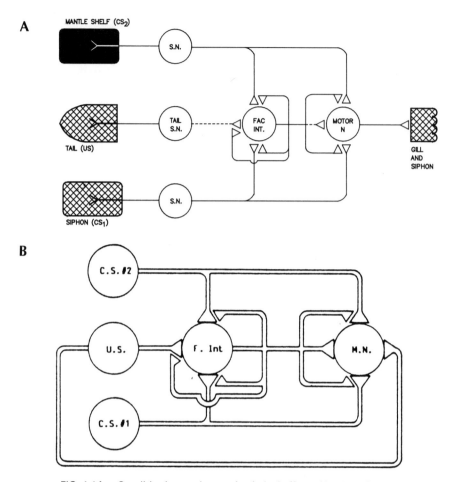

FIG. 1.1A. Conditioning pathways in *Aplysia* (from Hawkins & Kandel, 1984). The sensory neurons (S.N.) of conditionable stimuli (CS1 and CS2) make monosynaptic connections with the motor neuron. All stimuli, including the unconditioned stimulus (US), excite a facilitatory interneuron (FAC.INT.) that presynaptically modulates all sensory connections, both to the motor neuron and to itself. Furthermore, because the CSs are already connected to the motor neuron, and this is the only response in the associative repertoire, this circuit is capable only of alpha conditioning; pairing-specific enhancement produces a larger response in the motor neuron to which it is already connected, not a new response. FIG. 1.1B. Circuit for computational model of conditioning in *Aplysia* (from Gluck & Thompson, 1987). This circuit is identical to the Hawkins–Kandel configuration, but with the addition of a direct US connection to the motor neuron. This addition allows the facilitatory neuron to become refractory after CS activation, for blocking, but still allows an unconditioned response to the US. Again this allows only alpha conditioning; there is only one response in the repertoire and all stimuli are innately connected to its motor neuron. (Both reprinted by permission of American Psychological Association.)

Kandel's earlier representations of this circuit showed only the feedforward connections of the facilitatory interneuron to the sensory-motor neuron synapses, but when Hawkins and Kandel argued that these elemental mechanisms form an alphabet for the construction of several conditioning effects, they added feedback. In order to explain such phenomena as secondary reinforcement, they added sensory-facilitatory neuron synapses and feedback modulation of the facilitatory neuron to synapses on itself. In this manner, CS1 can also access the facilitatory machinery to act like a UCS during secondary reinforcement of the CS2. Hawkins and Kandel's qualitative speculation about this alphabet was followed by Gluck and Thompson's (1987) quantitative model. Fig. 1.1B shows their model, identical to that of Hawkins and Kandel except for additional stimulus symmetry, a monosynaptic connection from every stimulus pathway (including the UCS) to the motor neuron.

Our model is highly indebted to the Hawkins and Kandel consolidation, but there are several remaining concerns with *Aplysia* models in general that we hope to resolve. First, we will incorporate complete stimulus symmetry according to Premack's principle (Premack, 1962). Any stimulus can reinforce any other stimulus; definitions of the CS and UCS cannot be a priori established by asymmetrical circuit design. Hawkins also included such complete symmetry in his most recent model (Hawkins, 1989). Second, *Aplysia* models demonstrate only alpha conditioning, the enlargement of an already established response. In contrast, true Pavlovian conditioning does not assume an a priori connection between the CS and its eventual conditioned response (CR). As illustrated by a bell coming to elicit salivation in Pavlov's dogs, true Pavlovian conditioning can establish a CR not initially elicited by the CS. Third, there is still a need to bridge the detailed physiology of learning in *Aplysia* with the abstract analogies of energy contours and simulated annealing, central to the new computational rubric of parallel distributed processing (PDP).

The resurgence of neural modeling over the last several years is in large part due to this new rubric—in large part due to Hopfield's (1982) model and its notion of neural "energy terrains." By including in his model several significant features (reciprocal feedback among them), Hopfield established a powerful gradient descent mechanism for neural networks. If there are locally stable states within such a neural system, the system will move "down-hill" in state space until it rests in a stable state, called a local minimum.

As with gradient descent mechanisms in general, Hopfield networks get stuck in local minima instead of finding the one global minimum across an entire state space. Fortunately an optimization method (Kirkpatrick et al., 1983) overcomes such problems by analogy to the Metropolis Procedure for annealing a perfect crystal. Simulated annealing will find the global minimum of a system, if there exists some output that measures whether or not the system is approaching the minimum, and (in an abstract sense) the system can be heated and cooled by negative feedback based on this output. If the system is not approaching the minimum, heat can be added to the system to help move it from its current local minimum. As it enters a more global minimum, negative feedback removes the heat, therefore, cooling the system in such an optimized configuration.

This annealing method was originally used to find the global minimum of a static optimization problem, but biasing the weights themselves, adjusting the memory contour itself, can be assumed to constitute learning. As specific weights increase, this stronger basin of attraction will become an even more preferred output. One such combination of simulated annealing and Hopfield's prescription for a content-addressable memory is the Boltzmann Machine (Ackley, Hinton, & Sejnowski, 1985). These new conceptions are very powerful, but the simplistic definition of learning as weight change is still too general and far-removed from the real physiology of conditioned change. There are also many outstanding problems in neural network theory, such as linear scaling, which could be helped by an infusion of neurobiology. To bridge the gap, our model casts these abstract computations within the elemental terms of learning theory, a subdiscipline of psychology that has a long history of very close ties to neurophysiology and architecture.

CONSOLIDATION

Our hypothesis for true Pavlovian conditioning is very similar to the concept of neural thermodynamics. We use the name "Pavlovian" conditioning rather than "classical" conditioning to emphasize this particular tradition from Pavlov. He established the concept of reflex centers on the cerebral cortex and studied how these centers interact during conditioning, which he described as the pairing of a weak CS center and a strong UCS center. The UCS forms a strong center, because it tends to be of greater strength or significance, and, by this property, is defined as a reinforcer. Its strong activation produces an area of lowered resistance called a dominant focus. Subsequent CS activation flows to this UCS area to produce the CR. This idea of a dominant focus has been controversial but has a very important tradition in both the Russian and Western literatures (Livanov, 1977; Morrell, 1961; Pribram, 1971).

Dominant foci are obviously very similar to attractive energy basins, but, more significantly, simulated annealing is similar to the reflexology of stimulus types and the general theory of their interaction. There are two types of reflexes: positive feedback and negative feedback (Kosak & Westerman, 1966). A positive feedback reflex such as the orienting or scratching reflex tends to be weak and habituable; if it were not, its positive sign would lead to explosive buildup. In contrast, a negative feedback reflex, such as withdrawal from any noxious stimulus, is strong and nonhabituable. Noxiousness or strong biological relevance implies that the organism should not ignore the stimulus by means of habituation but should continue to exercise its innate avoidance response. The UCS elicits the negative feedback UCR in an attempt to remove the source of activation. If this is successful, the innate reflex has served its purpose, but, if the stimulus again presents itself, the nonhabituable reflex will tend to sensitize, subsequently producing a more vigorous response.

This property of the UCS provides the crucial component of simulated annealing—a negative feedback signal—but the complete analogy to conditioning is given by understanding how this feedback works for the adaptive interaction of reflexes. Conditioning is most readily formed by the pairing of a weak, habituable CS and a strong, nonhabituable UCS (Kimmel, 1973; Kosak & Westerman, 1966). The nonhabituable reflex will try to remove a repetitious, noxious stimulus by making a more vigorous response, but, if the UCR by itself fails to remove such a stimulus, the UCS will then "employ" any weak stimulus that comes before the UCS. The UCS employs the CS to act as its substitute, producing the (CR) earlier in time. This anticipatory CR gives preparatory control of the UCS when its own innate reflex strategy is insufficient.

The concept of employment, as discussed by Kosak and Westerman (1966), is very well described by the terms of energy contours and simulated annealing in neural networks. With repeated stimulation, the strong UCS enlarges its UCR by reducing local resistance, and in so doing forms a deeper and wider basin of attraction, a dominant focus. If the reflexive response to the UCS is ineffective, the source of activation continues until it employs another stimulus (the CS) that propagates its own activation to the UCS–UCR reflex (the CR). The predictive CR generates the negative feedback response in avoidance of the UCS. Avoiding the source of the activation thereby freezes the system in the state that maintains the CS–CR pathway.

These terms of employment also necessitate habituability of the CS (Kimmel, 1973). The UCS can make the CS's activation large enough to produce the CR, but the CS must not be intrinsically strong. If it were, it would be a UCS itself, enlarging its own local minimum to employ some other stimulus for negative feedback. All weak stimuli tend to habituate, reducing their own local focus and activation, except as needed for conditioning. Therefore, the term *habituability* emphasizes the controllability of weak stimuli. They are malleable, able to either decrease or increase their activation as needed for homeostasis of the entire system.

This approach highlights many incorrect assumptions in the current literature. First, habituation has been largely neglected in the computations of the PDP approach, but it was certainly important to Pavlov and has been a major component of more recent Pavlovian theorizing. As Levine (1983) pointed out in his landmark review of neural modeling, the typical definition of habituation as weight reduction is not truly synonymous with the behavioral and physiological phenomenon that neuroscience calls habituation. Biological habituation has a set of peculiar properties (Thompson & Spencer, 1966). For instance, the habituation paradox is one of the most significant parameters and yet, being a paradox, is difficult to model; weaker stimuli habituate faster and to lower asymptotes. Stimulus strength is an important parameter for sensitization as well. Moreover, the strength functions for habituation and sensitization together define what will be the CS and UCS of Pavlovian conditioning. By defining such stimulus types as functions of stimulus strength, a priori definitions of asymmetrical pathways are not necessary.

Second, computational models of learning frequently connect their layers with complete crossbars, whereas biological interneurons are local and limited in their connection pattern. Where global connection patterns are used, their functions tend to be diffuse and modulatory and do not represent specific point-to-point associative paths. The complete crossbar, connecting everything to everything else, is no more a model of true Pavlovian conditioning than the alpha conditioning models of *Aplysia;* the stimulus–response connections are just as much defined a priori (in this case, for all possible combinations). It is doubtful that the sound of a bell is biologically prestructured to elicit salivation or leg withdrawal. The real architecture of nervous systems is a substrate for learning—a structure that allows functional associations—not a structural preconnection to suit every possible contingency in the life of an organism.

Third, there are several good exceptions (e.g., the articles of Levine, Leven, & Prueitt, chapter 9 in this volume; Hestenes, chapter 7 in this volume; and Ricart, chapter 5 in this volume), but neural modeling in general has not incorporated well the role of neuromodulation, of ubiquitous importance across all nervous systems. Central to the topic of motivation and emotion, modulation is important for understanding not only how memory is created but also how its expression is controlled. The use of nonsignaling neurotransmitters is well established for controlling the formation of contour weights, but a good deal of synaptic activity is subliminal or biasing rather than activating. By further analogy to simulated annealing, subliminal neuromodulation will be used as a control signal—to determine if activation can flow "up-hill" to escape the local minima of the CS.

Despite these weaknesses of neural modeling when compared to real nervous systems, the established direction of artificial intelligence toward a neural style of computation is to be cheered and further developed. This means combining previously developed models into more powerful, higher level combinations, with special emphasis on binding the neural and information sciences. We bring together two separate areas by the incorporation of two layers. The first, or alpha layer, is primarily indebted to the mechanisms from *Aplysia.* The second, or beta layer, is a network for energy contours across laterally connected interneurons. We do not model simulated annealing as the exact formalism given by Kirkpatrick and others; however, the analogy between simulated annealing and Pavlovian conditioning has been critical to our development of the following mechanics. As such, we call the entire network *Aplysia vitriformis* (*vitri* = glass + *formis* = like).

MODEL CONSTRUCTION

Alpha Layer

Fig. 1.2A shows how the alpha layer is mostly equivalent to the previous *Aplysia* models. The three sensory neurons make monosynaptic connections to the motor system, except that each sensory neuron is connected to its own motor neuron. As the model of Cruz (chapter 11 in this volume) also does, *A. vitriformis* emphasizes the reflex arc as a basic architectural element. The entire set of responses is visualized as a continuous sheet with an isomorphic mapping between every sensory and motor unit.

The alpha layer performs two basic calculations as found in *Aplysia*. Habituation is found in the sensory neuron terminal, and activity-dependent sensitization is found in the presynaptic modulation of the sensory neuron by the facilitatory neuron. The arrangement of the facilitatory neuron in Fig. 1.2A is functionally identical to the previous schematics for *Aplysia*, but the reciprocal synapses between the facilitatory and sensory neurons simplify the diagram. Reciprocal synapses also simplify the connectivity of real nervous systems (Bennett & Goodenough, 1978), although the specific implementation is inconsequential for this general model.

With emphasis on a modularized and repetitive architecture, every reflex module is treated equally. Showing full stimulus symmetry, this network avoids definitions of the CS and UCS according to network design. The previous models of *Aplysia* gave habituation to the CS and not the UCS synapses, but here the physiology of habituation and sensitization is only a function of stimulus strength. Every stimulus pathway has the potential to habituate, but weak stimuli habituate more readily than stronger ones, which tend not to habituate. Likewise every module has access to the facilitory neuron's machinery according to stimulus strength, not a priori connections or connection strengths.

The circuitry of *A. vitriformis* is similar to that of previous *Aplysia* models, but there is one, most important way in which the formal equations are different. The Gluck–Thompson model includes two separate functions for habituation and sensitization; however, these two functions are not dual processes as described by Groves and Thompson's theory (1970), because both functions operate on a single weight. Habituation and sensitization drive the single weight in different directions, undoing each other in direct violation of the dual process theory. In contrast, we model separate weights according to known physiology; habituation lowers the number of active calcium channels, whereas sensitization lengthens the duration that the active calcium channels are opened (see Appendix).

Even with these refinements, the alpha layer by itself is incapable of modeling true Pavlovian conditioning, because only one response is available to each sensory neuron. The typical solution of learning neural networks is to form a complete crossbar, connecting every stimulus input pathway with every possible

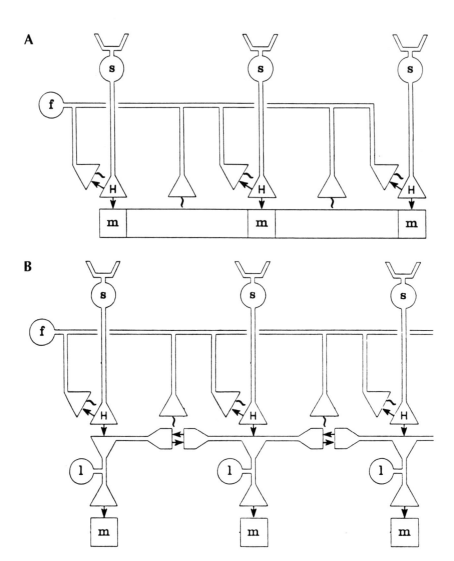

FIG. 1.2A. Alpha layer of *Aplysia vitriformis*. Three sensory neurons transmit information from their receptive structures (concave polygon) to the motor neuron (bottom rectangle). The facilitatory interneuron (*f*) makes presynaptic connections on the sensory neuron (*s*) terminals and direct connections to the motor system (*m*). (*H:* habituation in sensory neuron terminals, → : excitatory signal transmission, ~ : modulating transmission). This circuit is functionally equivalent to the Gluck–Thompson and Hawkins–Kandel circuits but with some modification. First, the relationship between sensory neurons and the facilitatory neuron is simplified to an equivalent microcircuit for diagrammatic convenience. Beyond this geometric transformation, *A. vitriformis* maintains complete symmetry between all stimuli by adding presynaptic facilitation to the US–MN connection of the Gluck–Thompson model. Finally the motor system rectangle emphasizes the

output for behavioral completeness (e.g., Gelperin, Hopfield, & Tank, 1985; Hampson & Kibler, 1983; Sutton & Barto, 1981). Again, this is no better than alpha conditioning and no less an a priori solution for the case in which all associations are predefined. It is true that these networks will not demonstrate a CR prior to conditioning when the connection weights are initially set below some threshold, but such a distinction between alpha and beta conditioning based on whether a response is initially above or below some threshold is trivial. Real nervous systems are more conservative of their connections, indicating that our models could be more elegant.

Beta Layer

Fig. 1.2B shows the addition of interneurons between the sensory and motor neurons. These interneurons transmit sensory-motor reflex activation, but they also transmit horizontal propagation through their lateral processes. Reciprocal synapses are again used for diagrammatic convenience, but their functional attributes of bidirectional flow and feedback may be implemented by a variety of means: by reciprocal synapses as shown here, by pairs of collaterals, or by field effects.

Activation from a sensory neuron propagates through the interneurons according to their lateral connection weights. This activity also alters the weights, establishing a different contour for subsequent activity. Although not explicitly a model of long-term potentiation (LTP), this process is called potentiation, because it has some similarity to LTP. LTP is an attractive physiology for the use of Hebb's rule in neural network theory, but the physiology's specific relationship to conditioning is still unclear (Brown, Chapman, Kairiss, & Keenen, 1988).

Potentiation is distinguishable from the weight modification rules already discussed. As given in the alpha layer, activity-dependency calculates the contingency between two stimuli; the CS must occur before the UCS in order to be predictive, and in fact simultaneous presentations of the CS and UCS produce very poor conditioning. Contingency is given by the correlation of UCS sensitization with the CS's calcium trace, not by the CS signal itself. Contingency has already been calculated; therefore, the beta layer does not repeat it. Instead the beta layer must create the energy contour for which the correlational or

---

physical extension of a response surface. The motor neurons are not explicitly drawn in order to emphasize that the motor system of this model is incomplete and can be greatly elaborated. FIG 1.2B. Beta layer interneurons. These interneurons (I: lateral interneuron) pass sensory signals to the motor neuron but also allow the lateral spread of activation through reciprocal synapses. Like the presynaptic microcircuit, this reciprocal configuration may or may not be used in reality, but the diagrammatic convenience represents reciprocal positive feedback by whatever anatomy.

Hebbian synapse is used. However, such memory formation is not the correlation of a CS ad UCS. The UCS need not reinforce CS activation again but must reinforce itself to form the dominant focus. UCS activity is autoassociative through two paths: Through the beta layer, the UCS signal propagates inversely as distance from the UCS neuron. Through activation of the facilitatory neuron, the UCS also sends a modulatory signal to couple with and, therefore, to remember the beta layer's activation.

Potentiation forms the energy depression around the UCS center, but subsequent CS activity cannot propagate into the UCS basin unless the reciprocal synapses between interneurons include feedback (are not rectified). Slope is a relational calculation between two points, and reciprocal feedback is needed for gradient descent as an interaction of connection weights. There are other types of propagation that use amplifying chemical transmission, but *A. vitriformis* represents a more primitive scheme such as through electrotonic synapses, using fractional transmission weights. In this case, as demonstrated by reciprocal feedback in Hopfield networks, propagation along the memory contour emerges as the effective computation.

However, we also found that the dominant focus effect worked too well. Signal amplification due to feedback was so attractive toward the dominant focus that any stimulus delivered to the beta layer produced virtually the same level of output. Activation became more dependent on the beta layer weights and lost sensitivity to any alpha layer calculations of habituation and sensitization. Even when the alpha layer discriminated a large difference between a predictive CS and a control stimuli, both would elicit the same pseudoconditioned response after propagating through the beta layer. Hence, it was necessary to add more inhibition to the network.

Additional Controls

Fig. 1.3 shows the complete circuitry of *Aplysia vitriformis* that includes two additional inhibitory functions. First, the inhibitory feedforward connections from the alpha to the beta layer were added to control the expression of the beta layer memory. Going back to known Aplysia circuitry, we noticed an inhibitory neuron that receives input from the distal entry of sensory neurons (Kandel, 1979). Its input is before the additions of habituation and sensitization; its output is feedforward. *A. vitriformis* uses this inhibition to put the brakes on propagation. Producing an opposite force, the facilitatory neuron not only participates as a neuromodulator for weight adjustment, but, in some similarity to the strong input pathway for LTP, it also provides subliminal depolarization to the interneuron's postsynaptic membrane. Together the difference between these inhibitory and facilitatory factors contains the alpha layer's calculations of habituation and sensitization. This difference is distributed to the beta layer interneurons as a subliminal factor called coupling, which variably controls lateral propagation.

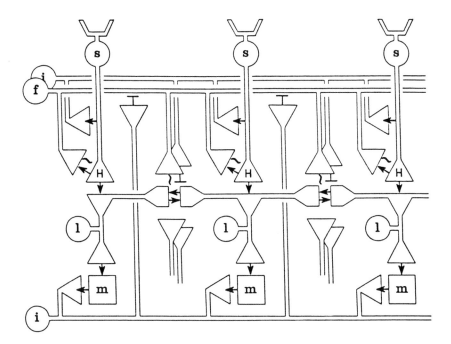

FIG. 1.3.   Complete circuit of *Aplysia vitriformis.* Other global circuitry is added. An inhibitory interneuron (*i*) takes distal signals from the sensory neuron and terminates as a modulator of the beta layer (⊥ : inhibitory transmission). Another inhibitory interneuron takes signals from the motor neurons and delivers refractory inhibition to the facilitatory neuron. The terminals of two other systems are included in this circuit but are not actually modeled; they indicate the possibility of other systems that could modulate beta layer propagation.

Coupling has an interesting property for the mechanics of gradient descent. In this particular case, given two sources of lateral input, a connection weight of 0.5 will differentiate whether propagation will increase or decrease across a reflex module. Incremental propagation by reflected feedback requires a weight that is at least the reciprocal of the number of lateral inputs. More interestingly, beta layer propagation is now controlled by two weights: the intrinsic weights of the interneurons, and the coupling bias. In this case, the product of the two factors reaching the 0.5 threshold will determine whether or not propagation will increase or decrease across the module. In general, an arbitrary number of factors can be used to control propagation, which is functionally similar to local minima trapping and hill climbing. If the coupling factor is insufficient for incremental propagation, stimulus activity remains trapped in its own focus. Sufficient coupling is necessary to propagate to a more dominant focus.

Finally another inhibitory neuron completes the circuitry. The analogy to simulated annealing requires negative feedback to freeze the system at the point when the CR is produced. This is thought to be mediated by environmental feedback; the CR is preparatory and gives at least partial avoidance of the UCS. However, the explicit avoidance properties of Pavlovian conditioning are not universally accepted. Explicit avoidance properties can be demonstrated in many conditioning paradigms, but we use internal inhibition to be more theoretically conservative and give closure to the model's circuitry in and of itself. Production of the predictive CR provides negative feedback to the facilitatory neuron and any further sensitization and potentiation by the UCS.

Physiological Detail

Detail has been excluded from the previous presentation, but an Appendix provides the complete algorithm and some discussion of its physiological justification. Aparicio (1988) provided a more complete discussion of the relevant neuroscience.

All of the following simulations were run with the same algorithm and parameter set. Based on the final circuitry already shown in Fig. 1.3, the complete network used for simulation included 20 structures in an one-dimensional array. Unless otherwise noted, the CS was presented as a weak stimulus to reflex module 5; the UCS was presented as a strong stimulus to reflex module 10.

SIMULATION RESULTS

Habituation

Before *A. vitriformis* established the role of habituation in conditioning, it first had to establish the proper functions for habituation itself. The habituation paradox was the most important characteristic we wished to model. Fig. 1.4A demonstrates these properties in *A. vitriformis,* whereas Fig. 1.4B shows similar properties in a study of the cat's hindlimb reflex by Thompson and Spencer (1966). Habituation to weaker stimuli was more rapid and to lower asymptotes. Incidentally both sets of curves show the same ratio relationships between the levels of stimulation.

Fig. 1.5A shows the effect of habituation on propagation through 20 reflex modules as used in our simulations. The spread of activation was small, because the stimulus was weak, and this spread became even smaller as the reflex habituated. Fig. 1.5B shows the effect of sensitization. In this case, a strong stimulus produced a strong response, and rather than habituate across repeated trials, this strong stimulus increased both its reflexive response and its lateral propagation.

A

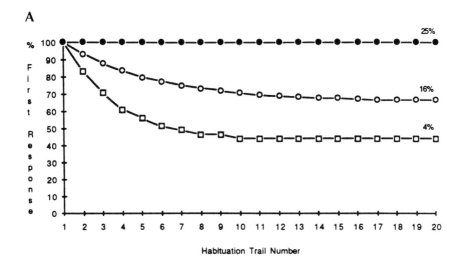

Habituation Trail Number

B

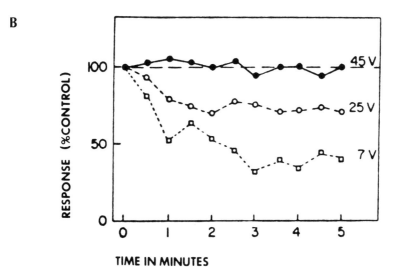

TIME IN MINUTES

FIG. 1.4A. Simulated habituation as a function of stimulus strength. Reflexive response strength is reported as relative to the response strength of the first trial. The raw measurement was firing frequency of the motor neuron. Stimulus strength was defined as percent of maximum sensory neuron firing frequency. Weaker stimuli habituated more readily and to lower asymptotes. FIG. 1.4B. Habituation of hindlimb flexion reflex in a spinal cat as a function of stimulus strength (from Thompson & Spencer, 1966). Voltages refer to stimulator output. Weaker stimuli habituated more readily and to lower asymptotes. (Reprinted by permission of American Psychological Association.)

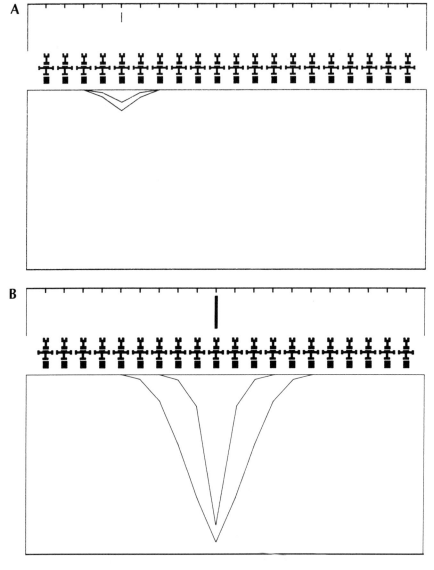

FIG. 1.5A. Simulated response surface for a habituable stimulus. The two depressions around unit 5 show the response on trial 1 and its reduced size on trial 20. This graph shows the raw size of responding to such a relatively weak stimulus (9% of sensory neuron Maxfrequency). Stimulus strength and position are shown above the neural network; response strengths are given below the network as distance away from the network. This 9% stimulus at unit 5 was used as the CS for conditioning. FIG. 1.5B. Response surface for a nonhabituable stimulus. The spread of activation became larger from trial 1 to trial 20 due to potentiation in the beta layer. The widened stimulus bar at top indicates that this stimulus activated the global modulator.

Pavlovian Conditioning

Fig. 1.6 demonstrates Pavlovian conditioning as the interaction of these two stimuli when contingently presented. When the CS was followed by the UCS, the CS did not habituate but instead amplified to produce both an alpha and beta CR. Alpha conditioning is the enlargement of the CS's reflexive response. However, the major component of true Pavlovian conditioning, beta conditioning, was demonstrated by CS propagation to the UCS–UCR reflex.

Both the alpha and beta response learning curves can be seen in Fig. 1.7 and 1.8 respectively. The alpha response curve began at the initial, nonzero level of the CS's reflexive response. Its subsequent increase was negatively accelerating and limited to an asymptote of 200%–300% of the initial response. These properties are typical of alpha conditioning in *Aplysia* (Fig. 1.7B) in which the acquisition curve accelerates negatively to an asymptote slightly above 200% of the initial response (Hawkins, Abrams, Carew, & Kandel, 1983). This simulated alpha learning was shown to be associative; when the CS and UCS were presented unpaired, the CS's reflexive response showed the typical pattern for CS habituation.

Although the conditioned alpha response is associative, the learning curve for true Pavlovian conditioning is different from alpha conditioning in three respects. First, the beta-conditioned response is initially nonexistent; there is no a priori

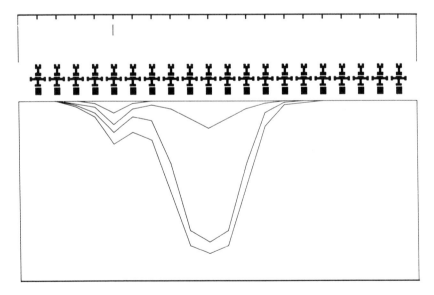

FIG. 1.6.   Progression of response surface during classical conditioning. This composite graph of responses to the CS in trials 1, 10, 20, and 40 shows development of both the alpha- and beta-conditioned responses at units 5 and 10 respectively.

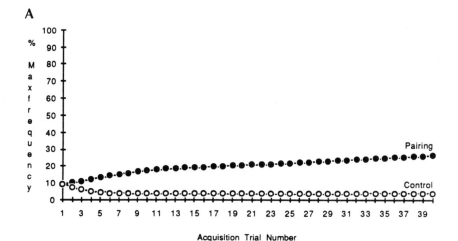

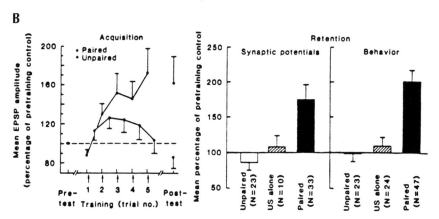

FIG. 1.7A. Alpha response conditioning as a function of paired- and unpaired-stimulus trials. The paired-stimulus curve shows negative acceleration to an asymptote, approximately 200–300% of the first response. This negative acceleration began from trial 1. In the unpaired-stimulus condition, the reflex immediately began to habituate. The response is given as percent of the motor neuron's maximum firing frequency (% Maxfrequency). FIG. 1.7B. Alpha response conditioning in *Aplysia* withdrawal response (from Hawkins et al., 1983). The excitatory postsynaptic potential (EPSP) increases with paired-stimulus trials; the unpaired condition shows some nonspecific sensitization (not included in *A. vitriformis*) over the first few trials, which drops back to baseline and to a slight habituation level at posttest. For both the physiology of the synaptic potential and the resulting conditioned behavior, the relative increase of this alpha conditioning mechanism is only about 200% of the initial baseline. (Reprinted by permission of American Association for the Advancement of Science.)

A

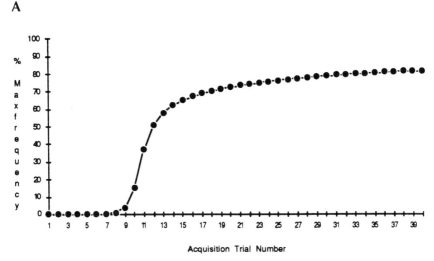

Acquisition Trial Number

B

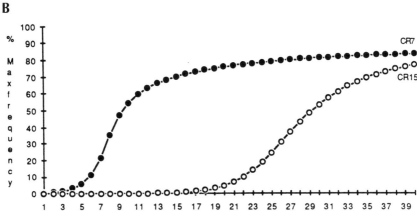

Acquisition Trial Number

FIG. 1.8A.   Beta response acquisition as a function of paired-stimulus trials. Consistent with the typical learning curve, this curve shows initial positive acceleration followed by negative acceleration to an asymptote. There was virtually no beta response for the control condition; the CS habituation immediately developed and no facilitation accrued. FIG. 1.8B. Beta response acquisition as a function of interstimulus distance and paired-stimulus trials. In both cases, the CS was positioned at unit 5, but the US was at unit 7 in one case and at unit 15 in another. The greater interstimulus distance slowed the speed of acquisition.

association between the CS and UCR/CR. Second, early trials tend to show an initial positive acceleration of the learning curve before acceleration turns negatively toward an asymptote. Third, this asymptote is typically high; to fulfill the terms of its employment (Kosak & Westerman, 1966), the CR must be relatively large, mimicking the action of the UCR in order to provide strong negative feedback.

Such positive acceleration of the learning curve is not generally included in the performance of neural networks such as the *Aplysia* models, or in formal learning models such as that of Rescorla and Wagner (1972). In neural networks, the CS is anatomically preconnected to its eventual CR (even if the initial connection strength is zero), and CS–CR strength grows against its limit from the very first trial. Even in purely formal models, the CS and UCS are predefined terms, so again the preconnection is assumed by the theorist. There is also another reason for negative acceleration; associative strength is typically modeled as only one component. There are exceptions; the Frey and Sears (1978) model demonstrates initial positive acceleration in learning due to the growth of two associative components, stimulus specific attention and associative strength per se. Learning curves with positive initial acceleration also occur in the models of Klopf (1988) and Grossberg, Levine, and Schmajuk (chapter 2 in this volume).

Like the Frey and Sears model, *A. vitriformis* also demonstrated the typically ogive learning curve (Fig. 1.8A). The network must enlarge two components: stimulus specific sensitization in the alpha layer and potentiation of the energy contour in the beta layer. The beta response started at zero but quickly accelerated by the synergism of these two growth components and finally decelerated when the CR produced its negative feedback. Furthermore, because the associative strength is made of two components, and one of these, potentiation, acts through distance in the energy contour, *A. vitriformis* demonstrated the concept of preparedness (Seligman, 1970). Some associations are more easily learned than others. Fig. 1.8B shows this concept of preparedness as a factor of interstimulus distance; nearer interstimulus distances produced faster learning.

This factor of distance is critical to understanding conditioning as a mechanism for detecting cause and effect. The temporal relationship between cause and effect is defined as contingency (Rescorla, 1967), but the physical relationship is defined as proximity. In the topography of virtually all sensory systems, the network is superficially presented to the environment where the spatial juxtaposition of cause and effect are impressed upon the neural sheet. *A. vitriformis* assumes a physical continuity between reflex units, which in turn assumes that closer stimuli are more likely to have a causal relationship.

Extinction and Spontaneous Recovery

Opponent process and frustration theories elaborate many complex aspects of extinction, but learning theory since Pavlov has held that extinction is basically a

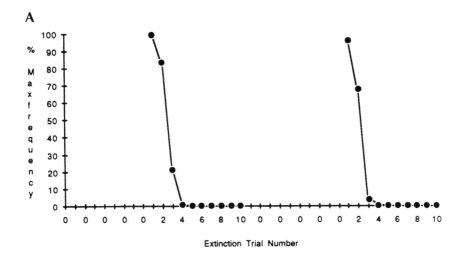

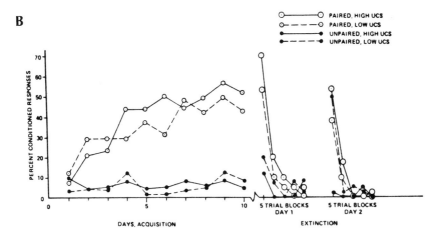

FIG. 1.9A. Extinction and spontaneous recovery as a function of CS-only trials and rest. Ten extinction trials were given 5 min after conditioning. This was followed by another 5 min rest period, followed by another set of extinction trials. The response on the very first extinction trial is slightly larger than the last acquisition trial, because a small amount of CS habituation decayed during the 5 min rest after conditioning. Habituation again decayed during the 5 min rest after extinction, allowing spontaneous recovery of the CR in the next extinction cycle. FIG. 1.9B. Extinction and spontaneous recovery after conditioned acquisition in the leech (from Henderson & Strong, 1972). The initial responses to extinction are slightly larger than during conditioning; otherwise extinction is very rapid. Spontaneous recovery after rest is seen on the next day of extinction trial blocks.

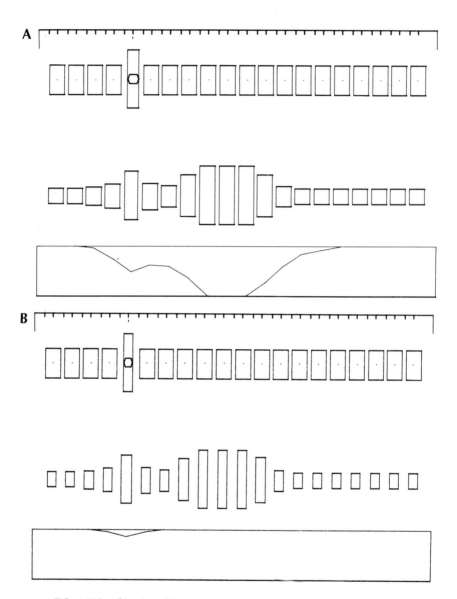

FIG. 1.10A. Simulated internal physiology at extinction trial 1. The top tier of rectangles represents habituation and sensitization in the sensory neurons; the rectangle of each unit becomes thinner with increased habituation and/or longer with increased sensitization. All show the standard configuration (no habituation or sensitization) except unit 5, which shows maximum sensitization by its increased length and no habituation by its standard width. The second tier of rectangles represents potentiation and coupling as length and width respectively. This graph shows that the global coupling factor was near 1 (the bottom tier widths are all the maximum standard). The lengths demonstrate the potentiation built around the CS at unit 5 and

process of habituation. Extinction and habituation have many properties in common such as trial frequency effects, disinhibition, and spontaneous recovery. However, habituation has not been fully represented in neural and formal models of learning. Extinction is typically modeled as unlearning due to nonreinforcement, but learning theory strongly contradicts this; spontaneous recovery indicates that extinction cannot be a process of forgetting, because the memory can be reelicited by rest. Opponent process models add other dynamics such as conditioned inhibition during extinction (not demonstrated by *A. vitriformis*), but *A. vitriformis* is the first neural model to properly demonstrate extinction and spontaneous recovery (Fig. 1.9A) as a function of habituation, according to the more elemental components of Pavlovian theory and the behavior of real organisms (Fig. 1.9B).

Being a physiological model, *A. vitriformis* allows further exploration of the differences as well as the similarities between habituation and extinction. In our simulations, habituation was relatively gradual and proceeded to a nonzero asymptote, yet extinction was much more rapid and proceeded to zero. Fig. 1.10A shows the physiological state for *A. vitriformis* on the first extinction trial, five minutes after conditioning. The alpha layer physiology for the CS shows maximum sensitization and very little habituation. The beta layer shows the potentiation levels that defined the energy contour and the coupling between interneurons that was virtually complete.

Fig. 1.10B shows the internal physiology at trial 4. There were two changes: In the alpha layer, the presentation of the CS alone caused its sensory neuron's habituation. In the beta layer, this habituation globally reduced the interneuron's coupling, which in turn disallowed the CR's propagation. Therefore, extinction was caused by habituation, but such habituation of the CR was different from habituation of the CS's own reflexive response. The CS–CR connection was much more tenuous, requiring the appropriate thresholds for beta layer propagation. As habituation moved the coupling factor towards and then below this threshold, the CR was dramatically extinguished.

The most important fact is that the conditioned association itself remained. Fig. 1.10B shows the continued presence of sensitization and potentiation as established by conditioning. For this reason, rest gave time for habituation to decay, which in turn allowed repropagation of the CR. Further presentation of the

the UCS at unit 10. Stimuli and responses are shown at the top and bottom respectively. The circle in the top tier at unit 5 represents the size of the calcium trace (the dots in the other sensory neurons represent zero intracellular calcium). FIG. 1.10B. Internal physiology at extinction trial 4. The reduced width of unit 5 (top tier) shows the development of stimulus habituation. The reduced widths of all units in the second tier show the global effect of this habituation on coupling. Although the beta CR did not propagate, the conditioned changes of sensitization and potentiation had not decayed.

CS alone again caused habituation, and this was again responsible for reextinction.

ELABORATIONS

Increasing the network's size is the most trivial elaboration, but the architecture of *A. vitriformis* has excellent scaling properties. Such properties are not trivial. As discussed, many learning networks use a complete crossbar for interlayer connections, but this leads to an exponential increase in connections as these networks include more units. *A. vitriformis* adds connections only in direct linear proportion to its growth. Good scaling properties are crucial for the application of neural networks. Good scaling properties also validate models of real neural architecture, which likewise cannot afford a complete crossbar.

As demonstrated in *A. vitriformis,* real neural networks rely on functional, not structural, connections by spreading activation. However, because propagation in *A. vitriformis* takes place through an unidimensional array, all reflex units between two stimuli are elicited by the interstimulus propagation. Adding more dimensions to the architecture helps; propagation between two points involves proportionally fewer units in a higher dimensional matrix. However, it is also possible to use a temporal rather than a physical dimension. For vertebrates systems at least, frequency, phase, and coherence are characteristic properties of spreading activation.

The most important elaborations may come from the properties of interneuron coupling. An arbitrarily large number of modulators can be used to control propagation, thus, controlling the expression of memory. *A. vitriformis* implements only the simplest case, one global signal, but more intricate arrangements are also possible. Pribram and McGuinness (1975) described the topography of the human cerebral cortex according to its rostral/caudal polarities for activation and arousal. Subcortical control mechanisms project differentially across these continua and, therefore, can bias propagation to one pole or another.

Even more intricately, it should also be possible to project one energy contour onto another. One contour can modify another, for instance, to establish a different context. Such contextual control is essentially demonstrated by extinction and spontaneous recovery, but the projection of context as an intricate map of biases would be much more powerful. Touretzky and Hinton (1986) described something very similar for a connectionist production system; several Boltzman Machine networks interact with each other for variable binding. Teyler and DiScenna (1986) suggested another similar function for the hippocampus; it contains not just a cognitive map of the physical world but builds a control map for the rest of the cortex. By subliminal projection of its own activity pattern across the rest of the cortex, the hippocampus can conform the cortex and shift it from one context to another. These complexities are currently far beyond *A. vitriformis* but are suggested by the performance of extinction and spontaneous recovery and the additional connections in Fig. 1.3 that do not yet have any function.

Fig. 1.3 suggests another needed elaboration; the motor system is very much underrepresented. This is adequate for modeling the impoverished environments used in real animal conditioning, but a more complete model of adaptive behavior should describe motor actions through a more complete environment. Positive feedback to the CS has been ignored, but more complete theories of Pavlovian conditioning (Bindra, 1978) make heavy emphasis of incentive motivation toward stimuli. In moving to such an elaboration, the major position of *A. vitriformis* should be maintained; positive and negative feedback reflexes should not be structured a priori but should be a function of stimulus strength. As demonstrated in Braitenberg's vehicles (1984), a positive feedback motor system can orient animals toward weak stimuli, but beyond limits set by negative feedback, stimulation becomes too strong, and animals withdraw.

Similar to incentive theories of conditioning, propagation control systems and positive feedback responses would allow *A. vitriformis* to show operant conditioning. Pavlovian conditioning, as idealized in Fig. 1.11A, presents an isomorphic configuration between eliciting stimuli, internal activations, and appropriate responses. The more difficult mapping needed for operant conditioning is shown in Fig. 1.11B. In this case, activation must flow from its stimulus source to any response that can control the stimulus activation. This mapping may not be isomorphic; thus, any means for increasing the contingent response (by wise selection of the discriminative stimulus, for instance) will help operant conditioning (Kimmel, 1973). Just as the CS and UCS are experimenter constructs, not a priori connections, the distinction between Pavlovian and operant conditioning is only procedural. It is very important to understand the nervous system as one powerful architecture that operates across a range of procedures.

Therefore, it is most important to continue binding various models together. The 1 sec unit time of *A. vitriformis* is very crude, but a more realistic model of calcium's role in ISI such as Byrne, Gingrich, and Baxter's (1989) may serve to consolidate *A. vitriformis* with the other ISI models presented in this volume (especially chapter 5 in this volume by Ricart). Additionally the beta layer is still too far removed from the terms of cerebrocortical function. Other models (Bear, Cooper, & Ebner, 1987; Bienenstock, Cooper, & Munro, 1982; Freeman, 1979; Yao & Freeman, 1989) are more representative and include such needed properties as lateral inhibition, normalization, wave propagation, and chaos, which are not yet in *A. vitriformis*. Our model demonstrates some basic principles that are otherwise underrepresented in neural modeling, but additional properties must be included for *A. vitriformis* to become a truer and more applicable system.

The compromises between simplifying and realistic models will always remain, but there is a growing need to overcome the differences of individual approaches and generate a common theory of neural mechanics. The hope is to develop a general architecture based on well established facts, laws, and prin-

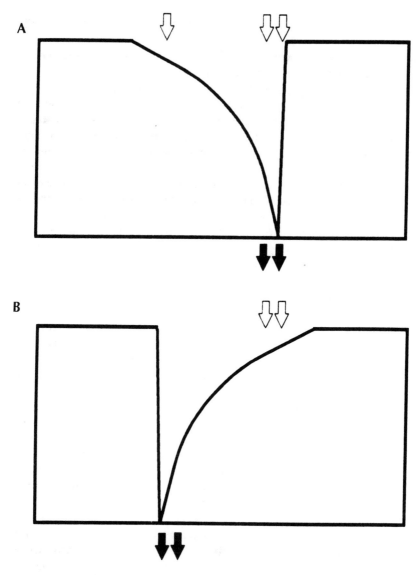

FIG. 1.11A. Idealized Pavlovian conditioning. The patterns of input, propagation, and output are isomorphic to each other. The CS and UCS are represented by single and double input arrows respectively. The UCS's dominant focus elicits the CS's propagation to produce the CR (double output arrow). FIG. 1.11B. Idealized operant conditioning. The reinforcer's activation must be directed to an arbitrary other output; the input, propagation, and output patterns are no longer isomorphic. A discriminative stimulus (equivalent to the CS of Pavlovian conditioning) is not shown, because it is not essentially required for operant conditioning. However, a discriminative stimulus can ease conditioning, if it is well selected to produce the contingent response as its own reflexive response. Otherwise operant conditioning is best when such a stimulus is sensitized.

ciples—both as a model of our own brains and for powerful applications of this renewed computational style.

ACKNOWLEDGMENTS

This work was supported in part by a National Science Foundation Minority Fellowship to the first author, under the direction of the second author, while at the University of South Florida.

APPENDIX

General

The simulator was built in BASICA. The state calculation subroutine is given in Listing 1 and described following. U is an integer pointer to designate the 20 reflex units in array. This subroutine is accessed once for each unit time of 1 SECOND. Although a more efficient algorithm could be used, we maintained heavy detail to better represent the physiology.

Sensory Neuron

Two factors are used to calculate the final release of sensory neuron neurotransmitter, SRELEASE: the number of times that calcium channels are opened by the action potential, SFREQUENCY, and the duration of each action potential, ACTIONTIME. The product of these factors, OPENTIME, is the total amount of time the calcium channels are open for the entire unit time of 1 second. ACTIONTIME is a function of the parameter NORMTIME, the standard duration of the action potential, and the effect of sensitization, which lengthens its duration through potassium channel dysfunction (Klein, Shapiro, & Kandel, 1980). The effective number of potassium channels, ACTIVEPOTASS, is the normal number, the parameter NORMPOTASS, minus those DYSFUNCTIONED by sensitization. The other factor of OPENTIME, SFREQUENCY, is defined as a fraction of the neuron's maximum signal capacity, the parameter MAXFREQUENCY. STIMULUS is that fraction defined by the experimenter for every U and every SECOND of a 60 second stimulation cycle. Our formulas for sensitization are very similar to those of Hawkin's (1989).

Neurotransmitter release is caused by the INFLUX of calcium; therefore, INFLUX is a function of calcium channel OPENTIME and the number of ACTIVECALCIUM channels, which can be inactivated by habituation (Klein et al., 1980). HABITUATED calcium channels are subtracted from the normal number of calcium channels, the parameter NORMCALCIUM. The constants of proportion, INRATE for calcium and OUTRATE for transmitter, give the sensory neuron's final output, SRELEASE.

Inhibitory Neuron

Inhibition from the alpha layer is a disjunctive function, because the inputs from each sensory neuron to the inhibitory neuron are relatively distant from each other (Feldman & Ballard, 1982). INHIBITOR takes its value from the largest SFREQUENCY of all 20 sensory neurons. The inhibitory neuron takes its input before the sensory neuron adds sensitization and habituation; thus, SFREQUEN-CY rather than SRELEASE is used as the sensory neuron output.

Facilitatory Neuron

The facilitatory neuron uses a function similar to the inhibitory neuron except that FACILITOR is a function of SRELEASE, which includes sensitization and habituation. FACILITOR and INHIBITOR are similar in order to be used reciprocally for COUPLING. MODULATOR is another release of the facilitatory neuron, which also controls synaptic weight adjustment. MODULATOR is a much more critical function and requires a higher threshold for release. We model such a threshold based on the notion of a B stimulus from Lara (Lara, Tapia, Cervantes, Moreno, & Trujillo, 1980). In their model of habituation, they established a critical level of stimulation above which no habituation occurs. We have generalized its use for the entire network; B is the point that separates weak and strong stimuli. Stimulation stronger than B is nonhabituable, but as well it is the critical level at which MODULATOR begins to be released.

Finally MODULATOR can be blocked by negative feedback from the inhibitory neuron in the beta layer. Mathematically similar to INHIBITOR and FA-CILITOR, REFRACTOR takes its value from the largest motor neuron response, MFREQUENCY. REFRACTOR is a feedback signal; therefore, the current refractory period is a function of motor neuron output from the previous simulation second.

Coupling

FACILITOR increases coupling, whereas INHIBITOR decreases it. Contrary to the typical PDP formalism, excitation and inhibition are not additive and subtractive. Instead division is a closer approximation to the shunting action of inhibition described by the Goldman equation. The parameters NORMPOTASS/ MIN-POTASS determine the range of sensitization's action and are used here to adjust the range of COUPLING to match that of sensitization's possible effect on it.

Habituation

The function for habituation is similar to Lara's (Lara et al., 1980) and the use of a B–level stimulus. Habituation is inversely proportional to stimulus strength, which, at the sensory neuron terminal, means the action potential frequency, SFREQUENCY. Taking into account the B-level stimulus, the percent of calcium channels habituated is a function BFREQUENCY–SFREQUENCY; a smaller SFREQUENCY yields more habituation. According to the definition of B, there is no habituation when SFREQUENCY > BFREQUENCY. Stimulus strength adds newly habituated channels, NEWHABITUATE, to those that are already HABITUATED. Therefore, NEWHABITUATE works only on the residual number of channels, the ACTIVECALCIUM that excludes HABITU-ATED channels.

As empirically discovered very recently, the physiology of habituation is even more complex. Marcus, Nolen, Rankin, and Carew (1988) demonstrated that habituation and sensitization are separate processes according to the dual process theory (Groves & Thompson, 1970), and yet the two processes can also interact; the delivery of a strong stimulus just after habituation can reverse habituation. This process of dishabituation is separate from sensitization. Contrary to sensitization, dishabituation is an intrinsic reversal rather than an external countereffect to habituation; sensitization can increase synaptic efficacy beyond naive levels, but dishabituation cannot. This empirical discovery is a theoretical imperative; habituability of the CS implies its controllability by the UCS. Unpredictive stimuli are irrelevant and, therefore, are allowed to habituate, but the predictive CS is important, and the UCS should not allow it to habituate. The UCS must dishabituate it.

The mechanism of dishabituation has not been found yet, but *A. vitriformis* assumes a PENDING status for newly habituated calcium channels. NEW-HABITUATE channels enter the PENDING status except for those that DIS-HABITUATE by the action of FACILITOR. This subliminal output of the facilitatory neuron was discussed for its action in the beta layer, but to maintain symmetry, it here too subliminally depolarizes the sensory neuron terminal, effectively reducing the habituation caused by weak stimuli. The UCS can DIS-HABITUATE those calcium channels that are in the PENDING status. Channels are added to this status as a function of NEWHABITUATE and are removed from the status by DISHABITUATE or by the autonomous rate of decay, DEL-TA. DISHABITUATE returns the channels to normal, but otherwise DELTA is the rate at which PENDING channels become fully HABITUATED. Once fully HABITUATED, calcium channels are independent of the facilitatory neuron and can return to normal only through the decay rate for habituation, AL-PHA.

Facilitation

Facilitation lengthens the action potential duration because of DYSFUNC-TIONED potassium channels (Klein et al., 1980). Limits on this dysfunction are set by the parameters NORMPOTASS and MINPOTASS, the normal and minimum number of active potassium channels in the sensory neuron terminal respectively. The assumption is that, of all the potassium channels used for membrane repolarization, only a fraction are sensitive to the effects of MODULATOR. NEWDYSFUNCTION, the number of channels that are newly DYSFUNC-TIONED, is a joint function of MODULATOR and the intracellular calcium trace. This trace provides the predictive relationship between the CS and UCS, because the CS's ELIGIBILITY is based on calcium INFLUX to the sensory neuron from the previous simulation seconds. This INFLUX builds a trace of calcium, STRACE, which decays according to DELTA. This same decay rate serves both STRACE and PENDING; in both cases, DELTA represents the terms of the interstimulus interval. This is an exponential decay of the UCS's ability to interact with previous CS activity.

The *B* stimulus level again comes into play. The CS is weak and is the source of the stimulus trace, the sensitivity of ELIGIBILITY is set to the range of weak stimuli. ELIGIBILITY is a ratio of the STRACE to BTRACE, the level of calcium influx corresponding to BSTIMULUS. As with HABITUATED, potassium channel dysfunction is possible only on the RESIDUAL, those potassium channels that can be but are not yet DYSFUNCTIONED. DYSFUNC-TIONED channels are returned to normal status by the decay rate BETA.

Interneuron Spreading Activation

Each interneuron receives three inputs: direct reception of the sensory neuron's neuromodulator and postsynaptically weighted inputs from the left and right interneurons. These inputs are called *S* (sensory), *L* (left), and *R* (right) respectively. Using the addition law for probabilities, these excitatory inputs are summed against the limit of the neuron's maximum firing frequency, MAXFRE-QUENCY. *S* is taken as SRELEASE without any postsynaptic weight modification. *L* and *R,* on the other hand, include each interneuron's postsynaptic WEIGHT and the global, extrinsic COUPLING factor.

WEIGHT is a function of potentiation. The parameters NORMRECEPTOR and MAXRECEPTOR define its range. Of all the postsynaptic receptors included in MAXRECEPTOR, a portion of them are always active as NORM-RECEPTOR. The rest are present in the membrane but are normally covered and, therefore, inactive. When these receptors become POTENTIATED, they are uncovered and become active in the postsynaptic WEIGHT.

Although the simulation unit time is 1 second, the calculation of interneuron feedback requires finer iterations. The unit second is divided in 50 time slices, *T*. These 50 iterations of feedback across 20 modules closely approach asymptotic propagation. IFREQUENCY and NEWFREQUENCY are used as the interneuron firing rates, for recording the old and new rates across the iterations.

Potentiation

Potentiation is very similar to sensitization except that ELIGIBILITY is a function of IFREQUENCY. This is similar to LTP's postsynaptic voltage-dependency, which, along with MODULATOR dependency, determines receptor activation called NEWPOTENTIATE. BETA is the autonomous rate of decay for both sensitization and potentiation.

Motor Neuron

There is no motor system processing. Motor neuron frequency, MFREQUENCY, is simply taken from the corresponding IFREQUENCY.

Parameter Values

Again, many of the parameters are completely inconsequential and, although nominally included to describe the biochemical steps, could be reduced to a more efficient algorithm. For instance, INRATE and OUTRATE could be combined; MAXFREQUENCY and NORMTIME are reciprocals, and MAXRELEASE is calculated from other parameters such as MAXFREQUENCY and NORM-CALCIUM. Furthermore, the parameters do not have to be explicitly valued for one particular neural system; specific systems vary across several orders of magnitude. The model is extremely robust and allows for such range. However, important relationships remain between some of the parameters: in particular, for three rate constants, the B level, and two limits.

DELTA, = 0.2, is the rate of calcium trace decay due to membrane pumps, internal sequestering, and diffusion. Connor and Nikolakopoulou (1982) reported a half-time recovery on the order of 1 to 3 sec. Zucker and Stockbridge (1983) suggested a time constant of a few seconds.

ALPHA, = 0.005, is the decay rate of habituation due to the return of inactive calcium channels to an operational state. Gingrich and Byrne (1985) modeled a 15.6 sec time constant of recovery for short-term habituation. ALPHA tries to account for such short-term habituation and a longer term component as one lumped rate constant.

BETA, = 0.0, is the decay rate of sensitization and potentiation. We model sensitization and potentiation as a long-lasting, conditioned association. Across the less than one-half hour simulation times, this memory is virtually without autonomous decay.

Stimulus levels were 1%, 4%, 9%, 16%, 25%, 36%, 49%, 64%, and 81% of the sensory neuron's MAXFREQUENCY. BSTIMULUS was simply set at the central value (25%) to make roughly half of the stimuli habituable and the other half sensitizing.

Two limits are important for sensitization and potentiation respectively. Sensitization in *Aplysia* is limited to a doubling of the action potential's duration (Carew, Walters, & Kandel, 1981). This limit is included by setting MIN-POTASS = 0.5 * NORMPOTASS. Potentiation is more arbitrarily defined; MAXRECEPTOR = 4 * MINRECEPTOR establishes a naive propagation resistance that is 0.25 of its maximum potential. This is speculative, but all the parameters are robust; in this case of potentiation, changing the receptor densities only determines the initial ease of propagation and the rate of learning as this initial level grows to its maximum. The essential operations of the network remain.

In any case, the entire algorithm is only a first approximation. We have included terms for membrane channels to draw attention to the neuron's rich internal state space as given in the real neurochemistry, but subsequent development should include more realistic nonlinearities as given by the Goldman equation or equivalent electrical circuits.

Listing 1. State calculation subroutine

```
REM Sensory Neuron
FOR U = 1 TO 20
 LET SFREQUENCY(U) = STIMULUS(U,SECOND%) * MAXFREQUENCY
 LET ACTIVEPOTASS = NORMPOTASS - DYSFUNCTIONED(U)
 LET ACTIONTIME = NORMTIME * NORMPOTASS/ACTIVEPOTASS
 LET OPENTIME = ACTIONTIME * SFREQUENCY(U)
  IF OPENTIME > 1 THEN LET OPENTIME = 1
 LET ACTIVECALCIUM = NORMCALCIUM - HABITUATED(U)
 LET INFLUX(U) = INRATE * ACTIVECALCIUM * OPENTIME
 LET SRELEASE(U) = OUTRATE * INFLUX(U)
NEXT U
'

REM Inhibitory Neuron
LET INHIBITOR = 0
FOR U = 1 TO 20
 IF SFREQUENCY(U)/MAXFREQUENCY > INHIBITOR THEN INHIBITOR=SFREQUENCY(U)/MAXFREQUENCY
NEXT U
'

REM Facilitatory Neuron
LET FACILITOR = 0: LET REFRACTOR = 0
FOR U = 1 TO 20
 IF SRELEASE(U)/MAXRELEASE > FACILITOR THEN FACILITOR = SRELEASE(U)/MAXRELEASE
 IF MFREQUENCY(U)/MAXFREQUENCY > REFRACTOR THEN REFRACTOR=MFREQUENCY(U)/MAXFREQUENCY
NEXT U
LET MODULATOR = (FACILITOR-BRELEASE/MAXRELEASE) / (1-BRELEASE/MAXRELEASE)
 IF MODULATOR < 0 THEN LET MODULATOR = 0
LET MODULATOR = MODULATOR * (1 - REFRACTOR)
'

REM Coupling
LET COUPLING = FACILITOR / (INHIBITOR * NORMPOTASS/MINPOTASS)
'

REM Habituation
FOR U = 1 TO 20
 LET ACTIVECALCIUM = NORMCALCIUM - HABITUATED(U)
 LET NEWHABITUATE(U) = ACTIVECALCIUM * (BFREQUENCY-SFREQUENCY(U))/MAXFREQUENCY
  IF SFREQUENCY(U) = 0 OR SFREQUENCY(U) > BFREQUENCY THEN NEWHABITUATE(U) = 0
 LET DISHABITUATE = FACILITOR * PENDING(U)
 LET HABITUATED(U) = HABITUATED(U) - DISHABITUATE
 LET PENDING(U) = PENDING(U) - DISHABITUATE
 LET NEWHABITUATE(U) = (1-FACILITOR) * NEWHABITUATE(U)
 LET HABITUATED(U) = HABITUATED(U) - ALPHA*HABITUATED(U) + NEWHABITUATE(U)
 LET PENDING(U) = PENDING(U) - DELTA*PENDING(U) + NEWHABITUATE(U)
NEXT U
'

REM Facilitation
FOR U = 1 TO 20
 LET RESIDUAL = NORMPOTASS - MINPOTASS - DYSFUNCTIONED(U)
 LET ELIGILITY = STRACE(U) / BTRACE
 LET NEWDYSFUNCTION = MODULATOR * ELIGIBILITY * RESIDUAL
 LET DYSFUNCTIONED(U) = DYSFUNCTIONED(U) - BETA*DYSFUNCTIONED(U) + NEWDYSFUNCTION
```

```
LET STRACE(U) = STRACE(U) - DELTA*STRACE(U) + INFLUX(U)
 IF STRACE(U) > BTRACE THEN LET STRACE(U) = BTRACE
NEXT U
REM Spreading Activation
FOR T = 1 TO 50
FOR U = 1 TO 20
LET WEIGHT = (NORMRECEPTOR+POTENTIATED(U)) / MAXRECEPTOR
LET S = SRELEASE(U)  /MAXRELEASE
LET L = IFREQUENCY(U-1)/MAXFREQUENCY * WEIGHT * COUPLING
LET R = IFREQUENCY(U+1)/MAXFREQUENCY * WEIGHT * COUPLING
LET NEWFREQUENCY(U) = (S + L + R - S*L - S*R - L*R + S*L*R) * MAXFREQUENCY
NEXT U
FOR U = 1 TO 20
LET IFREQUENCY(U) = NEWFREQUENCY(U)
NEXT U
NEXT T
'

REM Potentiation
FOR U = 1 to 20
LET RESIDUAL = MAXRECEPTOR - NORMRECEPTOR - POTENTIATED(U)
LET ELIGIBILITY = IFREQUENCY(U) / MAXFREQUENCY
LET NEWPOTENTIATE = MODULATOR * ELIGIBILITY * RESIDUAL
LET POTENTIATED(U) = POTENTIATED(U) - BETA*POTENTIATED(U) + NEWPOTENTIATE
NEXT U
'

REM Motor Neuron
FOR U = 1 TO 20
LET MFREQUENCY(U) = IFREQUENCY(U): LET IFREQUENCY(U) = 0
NEXT U
```

REFERENCES

Ackley, D. H., Hinton, G. E., & Sejnowski, T. J. (1985). A learning algorithm for Boltzmann machines. *Cognitive Science, 9,* 147–169.

Aparicio, M. (1988). *Neural computations for true Pavlovian conditioning: Control of horizontal propagation by conditioned and unconditioned reflexes.* Unpublished doctoral dissertation, University of South Florida, Tampa.

Bear, M. F., Cooper, L. N., & Ebner, F. F. (1987). A physiological basis for a theory of synaptic modification. *Science, 237,* 42–48.

Bennett, M. V. L., & Goodenough, D. (1978). Gap junctions. *Neuroscience Research Program Bulletin, 16,* 373–486.

Bienenstock, E. L., Cooper, L. N., & Munro, P. W. (1982). Theory for the development of neuron selectivity: orientation specificity and binocular interaction in visual cortex. *Journal of Neuroscience, 2,* 32–48.

Bindra, D. (1978). How adaptive behavior is produced: a perceptual-motivation alternative to response-reinforcement. *The Behavioral and Brain Sciences, 1,* 41–92.

Braitenberg, V. (1984). *Vehicles: Experiments in synthetic psychology.* Cambridge, MA: MIT Press.

Brown, T. H., Chapman, P. F., Kairiss, E. W., & Keenan, C. L. (1988). Long-term synaptic potentiation. *Science, 242,* 724–728.

Byrne, J. H., Gingrich, K. J., & Baxter, D. A. (1989). Computational capabilities of single neurons: Relationship to simple forms of associative and nonassociative learning in *Aplysia.* In R. D. Hawkins & G. H. Bower (Eds.),*Computational models of learning in simple neural systems* (pp. 31–64). New York: Academic Press.

Carew, T. J., Walters, E. T., & Kandel, E. R. (1981). Classical conditioning in a simple withdrawal reflex in *Aplysia californica. Journal of Neuroscience, 1,* 1426–1437.

Connor, J. A., & Nikolakopoulou, G. (1982). Calcium diffusion and buffering in nerve cytoplasm. *Lectures on Mathematics in the Life Sciences, 15,* 79–101.

Feldman, J. A., & Ballard, D. H. (1982). Connectionistic models and their properties. *Cognitive Science, 6,* 205–254.

Freeman, W. J. (1979). Analysis gives model of neural template-matching mechanism for sensory search with olfactory bulb. *Biological Cybernetics, 35,* 221–234.

Frey, P. W., & Sears, R. J. (1978). Model of conditioning incorporating Rescorla–Wagner associative axiom, a dynamic attention process, and a catastrophe rule. *Psychological Review, 85,* 321–340.

Gelperin, A., Hopfield, J. J., & Tank, D. W. (1985). The logic of *Limax* learning. In A. Selverston (Ed.), *Model neural networks and behavior* (pp. 237–261). New York: Plenum Press.

Gingrich, K. J., & Byrne, J. H. (1985). Simulation of synaptic depression, posttetanic potentiation, and presynaptic facilitation of synaptic potentials from sensory neurons mediating gill-withdrawal reflex in *Aplysia*. *Journal of Neurophysiology, 53,* 652–669.

Gluck, M. A., & Thompson, R. F. (1987). Modeling the neural substrates of associative learning and memory: a computational approach. *Psychological Review, 94,* 176–191.

Groves, P. M., & Thompson, R. F. (1970). Habituation: a dual-process theory. *Psychological Review, 77,* 419–450.

Hampson, S., & Kibler, D. (1983). A Boolean complete neural model of adaptive behavior. *Biological Cybernetics, 49,* 9–19.

Hawkins, R. D. (1989). A simple circuit model for higher-order features of classical conditioning. In J. H. Byrne & W. O. Berry (Eds.), *Neural models of plasticity: Experimental and theoretical approaches* (pp. 73–93). New York: Academic Press.

Hawkins, R. D., Abrams, T. W., Carew, T. J., & Kandel, E. R. (1983). A cellular mechanism of classical conditioning in *Aplysia:* activity-dependent amplification of presynaptic facilitation. *Science, 219,* 400–405.

Hawkins, R. D., & Kandel, E. R. (1984). Is there a cell-biological alphabet for simple forms of learning? *Psychological Review, 91,* 375–391.

Henderson, T. B., & Strong, P. N. (1972). Classical conditioning in the leech *Macrobdella ditetra* as a function of CS and UCS intensity. *Conditional Reflex, 7,* 210–215.

Hopfield, J. J. (1982). Neural networks and physical systems with emergent collective computational abilities. *Proceedings of the National Academy of Sciences, 79,* 2554–2558.

Kandel, E. R. (1979). Small systems of neurons. *Scientific American, 241,* 66–76.

Kimmel, H. D. (1973). Reflex "habituability" as a basis for differentiating between classical and instrumental conditioning. *Conditioned Reflex, 8,* 10–27.

Kirkpatrick, S., Gelatt, C. D., & Vecchi, M. D. (1983). Optimization by simulated annealing. *Science, 220,* 671–680.

Klein, M., Shapiro, E., & Kandel, E. R. (1980). Synaptic plasticity and the modulation of the Ca + + current. *Journal of Experimental Biology, 89,* 117–157.

Klopf, A. H. (1988). A neuronal model of classical conditioning. *Psychobiology, 16,* 85–125.

Kosak, K., & Westerman, R. (1966). Basic patterns of plastic change in the mammalian nervous system. *Symposium of Experimental Biology, 20,* 509–544.

Lara, R., Tapia, R., Cervantes, F., Moreno, A., & Trujillo, H. (1980). Mathematical models of synaptic plasticity: I. Habituation. *Neurological Research, 2,* 1–18.

Levine, D. S. (1983). Neural population modeling and psychology: a review. *Mathematical Biosciences, 66,* 1–86.

Livanov, M. N. (1977). *Spatial organization of cerebral processes.* New York: Wiley.

Marcus, E. A., Nolen, T. G., Rankin, C. H., & Carew, T. J. (1988). Behavioral dissociation of dishabituation, sensitization and inhibition in *Aplysia:* evidence for a multi-process view of nonassociative learning. *Science, 241,* 210–213.

Morrell, R. (1961). Effect of anodal polarization on the firing pattern of single cortical cells. *Annals of the New York Academy of Science, 92,* 860–876.

Premack, D. (1962). Reversibility of the reinforcement relation. *Science, 136,* 255–257.

Pribram, K. H. (1971). *Languages of the brain: Experimental paradoxes and principles in neuropsychology.* Englewood Cliffs, NJ: Prentice-Hall.

Pribram, K. H., & McGuinness, D. (1975). Arousal, activation, and effort in the control of attention. *Psychological Review, 82,* 116–149.

Rescorla, R. A. (1967). Pavlovian conditioning and its proper control procedures. *Psychological Review, 74,* 71–80.

Rescorla, R. A., & Wagner, A. R. (1972). A theory of Pavlovian Conditioning. Variations in the effectiveness of reinforcement and nonreinforcement. In A. H. Black & W. F. Prokasy (Eds.), *Classical conditioning II: Current research and theory* (pp. 64–99). New York: Appleton-Century-Crofts.

Sejnowski, T. J., Koch, C., & Churchland, P. S. (1988). Computational neuroscience. *Science, 241,* 1299–1306.

Seligman, M. E. P. (1970). On the generality of the laws of learning. *Psychological Review, 77,* 406–418.

Sutton, R. S., & Barto, A. G. (1981). Toward a modern theory of adaptive networks: expectation and prediction. *Psychological Review, 88,* 135–171.

Teyler, T. J., & DiScenna, P. (1986). The hippocampal memory indexing theory. *Behavioral Neuroscience, 100,* 147–154.

Thompson, R. F., & Spencer, W. A. (1966). Habituation: a model phenomenon for the study of neural substrates of behavior. *Psychological Review, 73,* 16–43.

Touretzky, D. S., & Hinton, G. E. (1986). *A distributed connectionist production system.* CMU–CS–86–172: Carnegie-Mellon University.

Yao, Y., & Freeman, W. J. (1989). Pattern recognition in olfactory systems: modeling and simulation. In *Proceedings of International Joint Conference on Neural Networks, 1,* 699–704.

Zucker, R. S., & Stockbridge, N. (1983). Presynaptic calcium diffusion and the time courses of transmitter release and synaptic facilitation at the squid giant synapse. *Journal of Neuroscience, 3,* 1263–1269.

2

Associative Learning and Selective Forgetting in a Neural Network Regulated by Reinforcement and Attentive Feedback

Stephen Grossberg
Boston University

Daniel Levine
University of Texas at Arlington

Nestor Schmajuk
Northwestern University

ABSTRACT

A real-time neural network model is described in which reinforcement helps to focus attention upon and organize learning of those environmental events and contingencies that have predicted behavioral success in the past. The same mechanisms control selective forgetting of memories that are no longer predictive. Computer simulations of the model reproduce properties of attentional blocking, inverted-U in learning as a function of interstimulus interval, primary and secondary excitatory and inhibitory conditioning, anticipatory conditioned responses, attentional focusing by conditioned motivational feedback, and limited-capacity short-term memory processing. Qualitative explanations are offered of why conditioned responses are forgotten, or extinguish, when a conditioned excitor is presented alone but do not extinguish when a conditioned inhibitor is presented alone. These explanations invoke associative learning between sensory representations and drive, or emotional, representations between sensory representations and learned expectations of future sensory events, and between sensory representations and learned motor commands. Drive representations are organized in opponent positive and negative pairs (e.g., fear and relief), which are modeled by recurrent gated dipole, or READ, circuits. Cognitive modulation of conditioning is regulated by adaptive resonance theory, or ART, circuits that control the learning and matching of expectations and the reset of sensory short-term memory in response to disconfirmed expectations. Disconfirmed expectations interact with opponent mechanisms to regulate selective forgetting. Unless expectations are disconfirmed, memory does not passively decay, yet does not saturate due to cumulative learning over successive learning trials. To achieve selective forgetting, the read-in and read-out of learned memories are functionally dissociated within the opponent READ circuit. Such dissociation may be achieved by using dendritic spines as a site of associative learning. The selective forgetting mechanism is called *opponent extinction.*

INTRODUCTION AND SUMMARY

A key problem in biological theories of intelligence concerns the manner in which external events interact with internal organismic requirements to trigger learning processes capable of focusing attention upon motivationally desired goals. The results reported herein further develop a neural theory of learning and memory (Grossberg, 1982, 1987) in which sensory-cognitive and cognitive-reinforcement circuits help to focus attention upon and organize learning of those environmental events that predict behavioral success and regulate selective forgetting of reinforcement contingencies that no longer predict behavioral success.

The first set of results (Grossberg & Levine, 1987) describe computer simulations that show how the model reproduces properties of attentional blocking, inverted-U in learning as a function of interstimulus interval, anticipatory conditioned responses, secondary reinforcement, attentional focusing by conditioned motivational feedback, and limited-capacity short-term memory processing. Conditioning occurs from sensory to drive representations ("conditioned reinforcer" learning), from drive to sensory representations ("incentive motivational" learning), and from sensory to motor representations ("habit" learning). The conditionable pathways contain long-term memory traces that obey a non-Hebbian associative law. The neural model embodies a solution of two, key design problems of conditioning, the synchronization and persistence problems. This model of vertebrate learning has also been compared with data and models of invertebrate learning. Predictions derived from models of vertebrate learning have been compared with data about invertebrate learning, including data from *Aplysia* about facilitator neurons and data from *Hermissenda* about voltage-dependent Ca^{++} currents.

In the second set of results (Grossberg & Schmajuk, 1987), representations are expanded to include positive and negative opponent drive representations, as in the opponency between fear and relief. This expanded real-time neural network model is developed to explain data about the learning and forgetting, or acquisition and extinction, of conditioned excitors and inhibitors. Systematic computer simulations have been performed to characterize a READ circuit, which joins together a mechanism of associative learning with an opponent processing circuit, called a *recurrent gated dipole*. READ circuit properties clarify how positive and negative reinforcers are learned and forgotten during primary and secondary conditioning. Habituating chemical transmitters within a gated dipole determine an affective adaptation level, or context, against which later events are evaluated. Neutral *CS*s can become reinforcers by being associated either with direct activations or with antagonistic rebounds triggered within a previously habituated dipole. Neural mechanisms are characterized whereby learning can be selectively forgotten, by a process called *opponent extinction,* although no passive memory decay occurs.

Active regulation of recognition learning by reinforcement learning may be achieved by joining READ circuit mechanisms to mechanisms for associative learning of incentive motivation; for activating and storing internal representations of sensory cues in a limited-capacity short-term memory (STM); for learning, matching, and mismatching sensory expectancies, learning to the enhancement or updating of STM; and for shifting the focus of attention toward sensory representations whose reinforcement history is consistent with momentary appetitive requirements. This architecture has been used to explain conditioning and extinction of a conditioned excitor; conditioning and extinction of a conditioned inhibitor; properties of conditioned inhibition as a "slave" process and as a "comparator" process, including effects of pretest deflation or inflation of the conditioning context, of familiar or novel training or test contexts, of weak or strong shocks, and of preconditioning US-alone exposures (Grossberg & Schmajuk, 1987). The same mechanisms have also been used (Grossberg, 1982, 1987) to explain phenomena such as unblocking, overshadowing, latent inhibition, superconditioning, partial reinforcement acquisition effect, learned helplessness, and vicious-circle behavior. Alternative models have been unable to explain an equally large data base, because they omit explicit descriptions of such cognitive-emotional feedback interactions.

NEURAL NETWORK MACROCIRCUITS

Two types of macrocircuits control learning within the theory.

Sensory-Cognitive Circuit

Sensory-cognitive interactions in the theory are carried out by an Adaptive Resonance Theory (ART) circuit (Carpenter & Grossberg, 1985, 1987a, 1987b, Grossberg, 1976, 1987). The ART architecture suggests how internal representations of sensory events, including conditioned stimuli (CS) and unconditioned stimuli (US), can be learned in stable fashion (Fig. 2.1). Among the mechanisms used for stable self-organization of sensory recognition codes are top–down expectations that are matched against bottom–up sensory signals. When a mismatch occurs, an arousal burst acts to reset the sensory representations of all cues that are currently being stored in STM. In particular representations with high STM activation tend to become less active, representations with low STM activation tend to become more active, and the novel event that caused the mismatch tends to be more actively stored than it would have been had it been expected.

Cognitive-Reinforcement Circuit

Cognitive-reinforcer interactions in the theory are carried out in the circuit described in Fig. 2.2. In this circuit, there exist cell populations that are separate

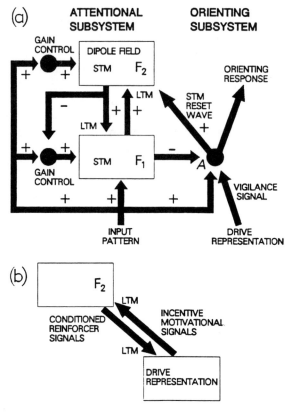

FIG. 2.1. Anatomy of an adaptive resonance theory (ART) circuit: (a) Interactions between the attentional and orienting subsystems. Code learning takes place at the long-term memory (LTM) traces within the bottom–up and top–down pathways between levels F_1 and F_2. The top–down pathways can read-out learned expectations, or templates, that are matched against bottom–up input patterns at F_1. Mismatches activate the orienting subsystem A, thereby resetting short-term memory (STM) at F_2 and initiating search for another recognition code. Subsystem A can also activate an orienting response. Sensitivity to mismatch at F_1 is modulated by vigilance signals from drive representations. (b) Trainable pathways exist between level F_2 and the drive representations. Learning from F_2 to a drive representation endows a recognition category with conditioned reinforcer properties. Learning a drive representation to F_2 associates the drive representation with a set of motivationally compatible categories. (Adapted from Carpenter & Grossberg, 1990)

from sensory representations and related to particular drives and motivational variables (Grossberg, 1972a, 1972b, 1987). Repeated pairing of a *CS* sensory representation S_{cs} with activation of a drive representation D by a reinforcer causes the modifiable synapses connecting S_{cs} with D to become strengthened. Incentive motivation pathways from the drive representations to the sensory representations are also assumed to be conditionable. These $S \rightarrow D \rightarrow S$ feedback pathways shift the attentional focus to the set of previously reinforced, motivationally compatible cues (Fig. 2.2). This shift of attention occurs because the sensory representations, which emit conditioned reinforcer signals and receive incentive motivation signals, compete among themselves for a limited-capacity short-term memory (STM) via a shunting on-center off-surround anatomy. When incentive motivational feedback signals are received at the sensory representational field, these signals can bias the competition for STM activity towards motivationally salient cues.

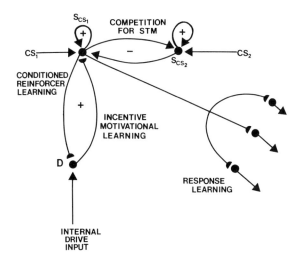

FIG. 2.2. Schematic conditioning circuit: Conditioned stimuli (CS_i) activate sensory representations (S_{cs_i}) that compete among themselves for limited-capacity short-term memory activation and storage. The activated S_{cs_i} elicit conditioned signals to drive representations and motor command representations. Learning from an S_{cs_i} to a drive representation D is called *conditioned reinforcer learning.* Learning from D to S_{cs_i} is called *incentive motivational learning.* Signals from D to S_{cs_i} are elicited when the combination of external sensory plus internal drive inputs is sufficiently large. In the simulations reported herein, the drive level is assumed to be large and constant.

ATTENTIONAL BLOCKING AND
INTERSTIMULUS INTERVAL

The attentional modulation of Pavlovian conditioning is part of the general problem of how an information processing system can selectively process those environmental inputs that are most important to the current goals of the system. A key example is the blocking paradigm studied by Kamin (1969) (Fig. 2.3). First, a stimulus CS_1, such as a tone, is presented several times followed at a given time interval by an unconditioned stimulus US, such as electric shock, until a conditioned response, such as fear, develops. Then CS_1 and another stimulus CS_2, such as a light, are presented simultaneously followed at the same time interval by the US. Finally CS_2 is presented alone, not followed by a US, and no conditioned response occurs. Intuitively the CS_1 "blocks" conditioning of the simultaneously presented CS_2, because the CS_1 by itself perfectly predicts its consequence, the US.

The blocking property may be explained in terms of four key properties of selective information processing during learning:

1. Pairing of a CS_1 with a US in the first phase of the blocking experiment endows the CS_1 cue with properties of a conditioned, or secondary, reinforcer.
2. Reinforcing properties of a cue shift the focus of attention towards its own processing.
3. The processing capacity of attentional resources is limited so that a shift of attention towards one set of cues can prevent other cues from being attended.
4. Withdrawal of attention from a cue prevents that cue from entering into new conditioned relationships. A computer simulation of these processes is summarized below.

$$1. \quad CS_1 \quad \text{---} \quad US$$
$$CS_1 \quad \longrightarrow \quad CR$$

$$2. \quad CS_1 + CS_2 \quad \text{---} \quad US$$
$$CS_2 \quad \nrightarrow \quad CR$$

FIG. 2.3. A blocking paradigm. The two stages of the experiment are discussed in the text.

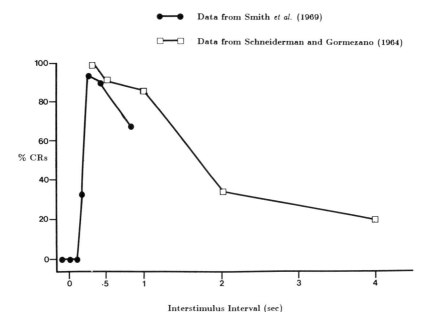

FIG. 2.4. Experimental relationship between conditioned response strength (measured by percentage of trials on which response occurs) and interstimulus interval in the rabbit nictitating membrane response. (Reprinted with permission from Sutton & Barto, 1981).

The explanation of blocking also leads to an explanation of the inverted-U relationship between strength of the conditioned response (measured in one of several ways) and the time interval (ISI) between conditioned stimulus and unconditioned stimulus. Fig. 2.4 summarizes experimental data on the effects of ISI from studies of Smith, Coleman, and Gormezano (1969) and Schneiderman and Gormezano (1964) of the rabbit nictitating membrane response.

A unified explanation of blocking and ISI data is suggested below. Such an explanation is noteworthy, because Sutton and Barto (1981) claimed that the ISI data pose a difficulty for any network with associative synapses, that is, synapses whose efficacy changes as a function of the correlation between presynaptic and postsynaptic activities. They argued that a network with associative synapses should, to a first approximation, have an optimal ISI of zero, because cross-correlation between two stimulus traces is strongest when the two stimuli occur simultaneously. To avoid this difficulty, other modelers introduced a delay in the CS pathway that was equal to the optimal ISI. However, such a delay would delay the CR by an equal amount and, hence, is incompatible with the so-called anticipatory *CR* that occurs before *US* onset. To overcome this difficulty, Sutton and Barto (1981) suggested that a different type of learning law was needed.

Our simulations contradict the Sutton and Barto claim by reproducing the ISI data and the anticipatory *CR* without invoking a long delay in the *CS* pathway. Poor conditioning with a small ISI is, moreover, explained by a mechanism identical to the mechanism of attentional blocking. In the blocking paradigm, a conditioned reinforcer CS_1 blocks conditioning of a simultaneously presented CS_2. In the ISI paradigm, a *US* blocks conditioning of a simultaneously presented *CS*. In both cases, the stimulus with more motivational significance inhibits the processing of the stimulus with less motivational significance. Poor conditioning with *CS* and *US* at a large ISI occurs, simply because, by the time the *US* arrives, the *CS* representation has decayed in short-term memory to a level that is below the threshold for affecting efficacy of the appropriate synapses.

The properties (1) to (4), listed above, arise within a network that includes modifiable associative links between sensory and drive representations (in both directions) and competitive links between different sensory representations (Fig. 2.2). Associative learning within these pathways does not obey the classical Hebb (1949) postulate that requires associative strength to increase with every conditioning trial. Instead, as illustrated in equations (11) and (12) below, associative learning is balanced by gated memory decay, which permits synaptic strength to either increase or decrease due to pairing of presynaptic and postsynaptic activities (Grossberg, 1968, 1969, 1982). Such an associative law has recently received direct neurophysiological support (Levy, Brassel, & Moore, 1983; Levy & Desmond, 1985; Rauschecker & Singer, 1979; Singer, 1983).

The drive representations (Fig. 2.2) are network loci where reinforcement signals and homeostatic signals converge to regulate the network's motivational decisions. Such a representation was introduced into the neural network modeling literature in Grossberg (1971). Grossberg (1971, 1972a, 1972b) used drive representations to analyse a variety of data about Pavlovian and instrumental conditioning, and showed that their properties could be derived as part of the solution of a fundamental problem, called the *synchronization problem* of conditioning; that is, of how a stable conditioned response can develop, even if variable time lags occur between the *CS* and the *US*, as they typically do in a real-time learning environment. Subsequently a number of authors invoked representations that play a role analogous to the drive representations. Bower called them *emotion nodes* (Bower, 1981; Bower, Gilligan, Monteiro, 1981) and Barto, Sutton, and Anderson (1983) called them *adaptive critic elements*.

A *US* unconditionally activates its drive representation, if the drive input to the node is sufficiently large. Repeated pairing of a *CS* with, for example, a food *US*, causes correlated activation of the *CS* sensory representation, denoted S_{CS}, with that of the drive representation corresponding to hunger, denoted D_H. As a result, associative learning occurs in the synapses of pathway $S_{CS} \rightarrow D_H$, thereby enabling subsequent activation of S_{CS} to activate D_H, if the drive input to D_H is also large. This is how a CS becomes a conditioned, or secondary, reinforcer, which clarifies the first of the four properties needed to analyse blocking.

Property (2) concerns the manner in which reinforcing properties of a sensory event shift the focus of attention towards its own processing. This property utilizes the fact that synapses in the incentive motivational pathway $D_H \to S_{CS}$ are also strengthened by conditioning. When the sensory representation S_{CS_1} is activated by the conditioned reinforcing cue CS_1, it enhances its own activation via the positive feedback loop $S_{CS_1} \to D_H \to S_{CS_1}$. Other sensory representations, such as S_{CS_2}, are placed at a competitive disadvantage, because the synapses in their feedback pathways $S_{CS_2} \to D_H \to S_{CS_2}$ are weak. The enhanced activation of S_{CS_1} causes the suppression of activation at representations such as S_{CS_2}, because the competition between representations limits the possible total activation, or capacity, across all the sensory representations S. The same competitive property attenuates conditioning of a CS to a US, if the ISI is small,

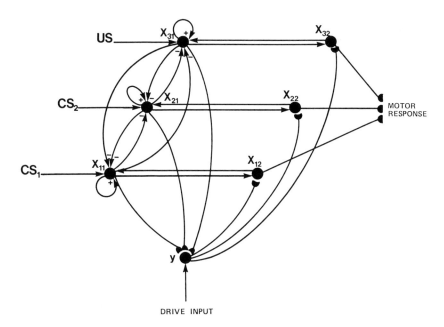

FIG. 2.5.   Simulated network: Each sensory representation possesses two stages with STM activities x_{i1} and x_{i2}. A CS or US input activates its corresponding x_{i1}. Activation of x_{i1} elicits unconditionable signals to x_{i2} and conditioned reinforcer signals to D, whose activity is denoted by y. Incentive motivational feedback signals from D activate second stage potentials x_{i2}, which then send feedback signals to x_{i1}. Conditionable long-term memory traces are designated by hemidisks.

because the *US* activates a strong feedback pathway $S_{US} \rightarrow D \rightarrow S_{US}$ corresponding to its own sensory representation S_{US}.

The limited capacity of short-term memory, which is needed to achieve property (3), is a property of shunting on-center off-surround feedback networks. The limited capacity property follows from more basic capabilities of this class of networks: their ability to process and store in STM spatially distributed input patterns without distorting these patterns due to either noise or saturation (Ellias & Grossberg, 1975; Grossberg, 1982; Grossberg & Levine, 1975). Fig. 2.2 schematizes a network with modifiable sensory-to-drive and drive-to-sensory association links and on-center off-surround feedback interactions between sensory representations.

Our computer simulations, reported more completely in Grossberg and Levine (1987), modeled the behavior of the network illustrated in Fig. 2.5, which is a variant of the network in Fig. 2.2. Fig. 2.5 includes three sensory representations, CS_1, CS_2, and *US*, and one drive representation, *D*. The $US \rightarrow D$ and $D \rightarrow US$ synapses are fixed at high value. The $CS_i \rightarrow D$ and $D \rightarrow CS_i$ synapses are strengthened by appearance of the *US* while the CS_i short-term memory representation is active. In this variant of the network, sensory representations are divided into two successive stages. The activity x_{i1} of the first stage of S_{CS_i} can activate conditioned reinforcer pathways $S_{CS_i} \rightarrow D$. The activity x_{i2} of the second stage of

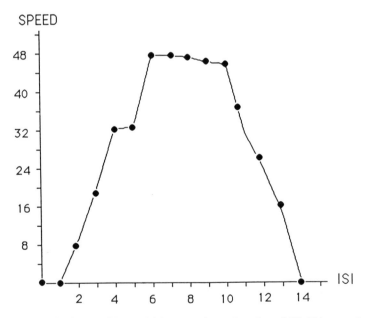

FIG. 2.6.   Plot of *CR* acquisition speed as a function of ISI. This speed was computed by the formula 100 × (number of time units per trial)/(number of time units to first *CR*).

S_{CS_i} receives conditioned incentive motivational signals $D \to S_{CS_i}$ from D, which can thereupon activate x_{i1} to enhance the activation of S_{CS_i}. Activation of x_{i2} can also generate output signals to motor control pathways.

The same set of network parameters was used to simulate both the ISI inverted-U curve and attentional blocking. In both cases, the CR anticipated the US.

The simulated ISI curves (Fig. 2.6) are qualitatively compatible with experimental data on the rabbit's conditioned nictitating membrane response shown in Fig. 2.4. For ISIs of fewer than 2 time units in the numerical algorithm, competi-

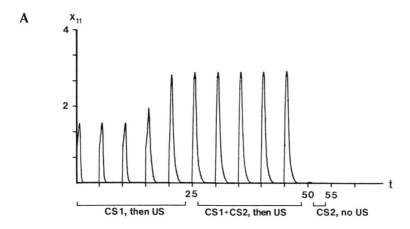

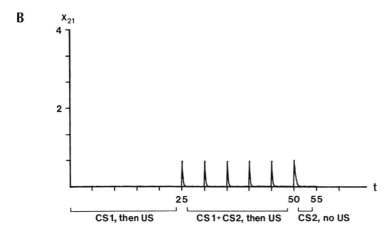

FIG. 2.7.   Blocking simulation: In (a)–(d), the ISI = 6 between CS_1 and US onset. Five trials of $CS_1 - US$ pairing are followed by five trials of $(CS_1 + CS_2) - US$ pairing. Then CS_2 is presented alone for one trial. (a) Activity x_{11} of S_{CS_1} through time; (b) Activity x_{21} of S_{CS_2} through time; (c) LTM trace z_{11} from S_{CS_1} to D through time; (d) LTM trace z_{21} from S_{CS_2} to D through time.

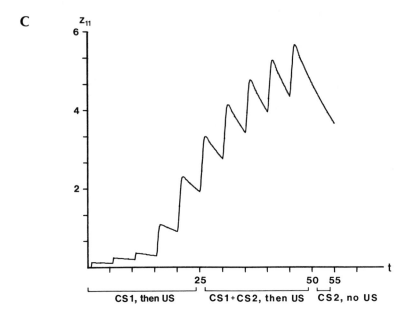

C

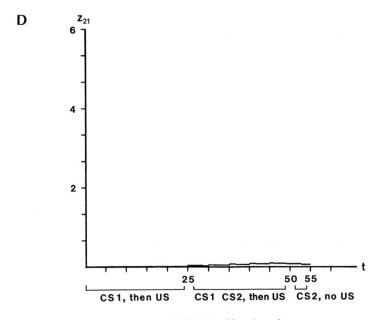

D

FIG. 2.7. (*Continued*)

tion from the US representation prevented CS activity from staying above the S_{CS} $\rightarrow D$ pathway's threshold long enough to appreciably increase the pathway's strength during the time interval when D was activated by the US. At long ISIs, the prior decay of the CS's short-term memory trace prevented the $S_{CS} \rightarrow D$ pathway from sensing the later activation of D by the US.

In the blocking simulation (Figs. 2.7a through 2.7d), pairing of CS_1 with a delayed US enabled the long-term memory trace of the $CS_1 \rightarrow D$ pathway to achieve an S–shaped cumulative learning curve (Fig. 2.7c). After CS_1 became a conditioned reinforcer, it enhanced its own short-term memory storage (Fig. 2.7a) by generating a large $S_{CS_1} \rightarrow D \rightarrow S_{CS_1}$ feedback signal. As a result, when CS_1 and CS_2 were simultaneously presented, the short-term memory activity of S_{CS_2} was quickly suppressed by competition from CS_1 (Fig. 2.7b). Consequently the long-term memory of $S_{CS_2} \rightarrow D$ pathway did not grow in strength (Fig. 2.7d), thereby "blocking" CS_2 and preventing it from becoming a conditioned reinforcer or eliciting a CR.

COMPARISON WITH *APLYSIA* CONDITIONING MODEL

An alternative explanation of blocking, due to Hawkins and Kandel (1984), involves habituation of transmitter pathways. Based on invertebrate evidence, these authors developed a model whereby each US activates a *facilitator neuron* that presynaptically modulates CS pathways. They explained blocking by saying that "the output of the facilitator neurons decreases when they are stimulated continuously" (p. 385). Thus, after a CS_1 is paired with a US on a number of trials, subsequent presentation of a compound stimulus $CS_1 + CS_2$ with a US does not condition CS_2, because the facilitator neuron cannot fire adequately. Hawkins and Kandel's explanation, however, is incompatible with the fact (Kamin, 1969) that blocking can be overcome ("unblocked"), if $CS_1 + CS_2$ is paired with either a higher or lower intensity of shock than CS_1 alone. Recent evidence (Matzel, Schachtman, & Miller, 1985) indicates that unblocking can also occur if the response to CS_1 is extinguished.

In our framework, the explanation for unblocking depends on *gated dipole* opponent processes that link together "positive" and "negative" drive representations (Fig. 2.8). Positive and negative opponent channels allow for a comparison between current and expected levels of positive or negative reinforcement. The more complete theory of Grossberg (1982, 1987) that includes gated dipoles has been used to explain unblocking data.

In the remainder of the article, some of our computer simulation results using gated dipoles are summarized. A more systematic development is provided in Grossberg and Schmajuk (1987). Gated dipoles are needed because, in the cognitive-reinforcement circuit, CSs may be conditioned to either the onset or the offset of a reinforcer. In order to explain how the offset of a positive (or negative) reinforcer can generate an antagonistic rebound in an opponent negative (or

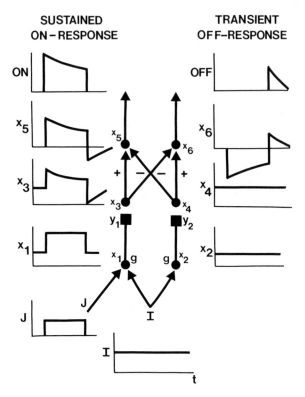

FIG. 2.8.   Example of a feedforward gated dipole: A sustained habituating on-response (top left) and a transient off-rebound (top right) are
elicited in response to onset and offset respectively of a phasic input J
(bottom left) when tonic arousal I (bottom center) and opponent processing (diagonal pathways) supplement the slow gating actions
(square synapses). See text for details.

positive) channel to which a simultaneous *CS* can be conditioned, gated dipoles
were introduced in Grossberg (1972a, 1972b). A gated dipole is a minimal neural
network that is capable of generating a sustained but habituative on-response to
onset of a cue as well as a transient off-response, or antagonistic rebound in the
opponent channel, to offset of the cue (Fig. 2.8).

THE READ CIRCUIT: A SYNTHESIS OF
OPPONENT PROCESSING AND ASSOCIATIVE
LEARNING MECHANISMS

Although several versions of a gated dipole circuit can be used to model associative learning between a *CS* and the onset or the offset of a reinforcer, a
specialized gated dipole is needed to explain secondary inhibitory conditioning.

Secondary inhibitory conditioning consists of two phases. In phase one, CS_1 becomes an excitatory conditioned reinforcer (e.g., a source of conditioned fear) by being paired with a US (e.g., a shock). In phase two, the offset of CS_1 generates an off-response that is used to condition a subsequent CS_2 to become an inhibitory conditioned reinforcer (e.g., a source of conditioned relief). In order to explain how this happens, a gated dipole circuit must contain internal feedback pathways (i.e., it should be recurrent) (Grossberg, 1975, 1987). In addition, such a recurrent gated dipole must be joined to a mechanism of associative learning. The total circuit that we have developed to embody both of these requirements is called a READ circuit, as a mnemonic for REcurrent Associative gated Dipole (Fig. 2.9).

The equations for the READ circuit are as follows:

Arousal + US + Feedback On-Activation:

$$\frac{d}{dt}x_1 = -A_1 x_1 + I + J + T(x_7) \tag{1}$$

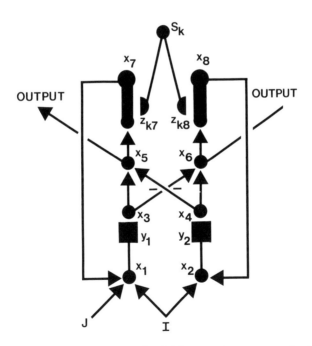

FIG. 2.9.   A READ I circuit: This circuit joins together a recurrent gated dipole with an associative learning mechanism. Learning is driven by signals S_k from sensory representations S_k activate long-term memory (LTM) traces z_{k7} and z_{k8} that sample activation levels at the on-channel and off-channel, respectively, of the gated dipole. See text for details.

Arousal + Feedback Off-Activation:

$$\frac{d}{dt}x_2 = -A_2x_2 + I + T(x_8) \tag{2}$$

On-Transmitter:

$$\frac{d}{dt}y_1 = B(1 - y_1) - Cg(x_1)y_1 \tag{3}$$

Off-Transmitter:

$$\frac{d}{dt}y_2 = B(1 - y_2) - Cg(x_2)y_2 \tag{4}$$

Gated On-Activation:

$$\frac{d}{dt}x_3 = -A_3x_3 + Dg(x_1)y_1 \tag{5}$$

Gated Off-Activation:

$$\frac{d}{dt}x_4 = -A_4x_4 + Dg(x_2)y_2 \tag{6}$$

Normalized Opponent On-Activation:

$$\frac{d}{dt}x_5 = -A_5x_5 + (E - x_5)x_3 - (x_5 + F)x_4 \tag{7}$$

Normalized Opponent Off-Activation:

$$\frac{d}{dt}x_6 = -A_6x_6 + (E - x_6)x_4 - (x_6 + F)x_3 \tag{8}$$

Total On-Activation:

$$\frac{d}{dt}x_7 = -A_7x_7 + G[x_5]^+ + L \sum_{k=1}^{n} S_k z_{k7} \tag{9}$$

Total Off-Activation:

$$\frac{d}{dt}x_8 = -A_8x_8 + G[x_6]^+ + L \sum_{k=1}^{n} S_k z_{k8} \tag{10}$$

On-Conditioned Reinforcer Association:

$$\frac{d}{dt}z_{k7} = S_k[-Hz_{k7} + K[x_5]^+] \tag{11}$$

Off-Conditioned Reinforcer Association:

$$\frac{d}{dt} z_{k8} = S_k[-Hz_{k8} + K[x_6]^+]$$ (12)

On-Output Signal:

$$O_1 = [x_5]^+$$ (13)

Off-Output Signal:

$$O_2 = [x_6]^+,$$ (14)

where the notation $[x_i]^+$ denotes a linear signal above the threshold value zero; that is, $\max(x_i, 0)$.

In the equations, I denotes the tonic arousal level, J the US input, S_k the kth CS, z_{k7} and z_{k8} the association of the kth CS with the on- and the off-response, respectively. A, B, C, D, E, F, G, H, K, and L are parameter values, which were kept constant for all simulations. When $E = F$, x_5 and x_6 compute an opponent process and a ratio scale. In particular, at equilibrium, equation (7) implies that

$$x_5 = \frac{E(x_3 - x_4)}{A_5 + x_3 + x_4}.$$ (15)

This property of the READ circuit enables the circuit to achieve the property of *associative averaging* rather than of simple summation.

OPPONENT EXTINCTION BY DISSOCIATING
LONG-TERM MEMORY READ-IN AND
READ-OUT AT DENDRITIC SPINES

A second key property of the READ circuit has been called *opponent extinction*. Passive memory decay does not occur in the parameter ranges that we used. A network in which passive memory decay does occur cannot achieve a large memory capacity, because all associations must be actively practiced before they are forgotten, but only a limited number of events can be practiced within a fixed amount of time.

An active process of selective forgetting is achieved by opponent extinction. In particular, when the net signals in the on- and off-channels are balanced, then, by equation (15), $x_5 = 0 = x_6$. Consequently, by equations (11) and (12), the conditioned reinforcer associations z_{k7} and z_{k8} from sensory representation S_k to the on- and off-drive representations approach 0. By a similar argument, it can be seen that these associations continually readjust themselves to the *net imbalance* of activation between the on- and off-channels. Opponent extinction hereby avoids the simultaneous saturation at maximal values of both z_{k7} and z_{k8}.

Opponent extinction requires the third key property of the READ circuit for its realization. This property is a dissociation between read-in and read-out of associative memories. For example, in the on-channel, read-out is proportional to $[x_7]^+$, whereas read-in is proportional to $[x_5]^+$. The read-out signals $\Sigma_k S_k z_{k7}$ and $\Sigma_k S_k z_{k8}$ in equations (9) and (10) are fed back via the signal pathways $x_7 \rightarrow x_1 \rightarrow x_3 \rightarrow \{x_5, x_6\}$ and $x_8 \rightarrow x_2 \rightarrow x_4 \rightarrow \{x_6, x_5\}$ to compete via opponent interactions. These interactions generate a consensus, or competitive decision, as in equation (15), which provides the data read-in to associative memory via equations (11) and (12).

Grossberg (1975) proposed that such a dissociation between read-in and read-out can be physiologically implemented by assuming that synaptic plasticity occurs at the dendritic spines of neural cells. As in Fig. 2.10, signal $[x_5]^+$ is

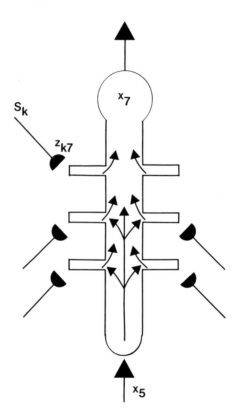

FIG. 2.10.   A possible microarchitecture for dissociation of LTM read-in and read-out: Individual LTM-gated sensory signals $S_k z_{k7}$ are read-out into local potentials that are summed by the total cell body potential x_7 without significantly influencing each other's learned read-in. In contrast, the input signal x_5 triggers a massive global cell activation that drives learned read-in at all active LTM traces abutting the cell surface. Signal x_5 also activates the cell body potential x_7.

assumed to cause a global potential change that invades all the spines, thereby inducing learned changes at all synapses throughout the dendritic column as in equation (11). However, due to the geometry and electrical properties of the dendritic tree, a sensory input S_k that activates a particular dendritic branch may not be influenced by inputs that activate different dendritic branches. Activation at a particular dendritic branch would produce local potentials that do not in themselves cause learning. These local potentials propagate to the cell body where they influence axonal firing via potential x_7 in equation (9). Potential x_7 activates x_5 via the competitive feedback loop, and x_5 can influence learning, as in equations (15) and (11).

COMPUTER SIMULATIONS OF PRIMARY AND SECONDARY CONDITIONING

This section summarizes computer simulations of several classical conditioning paradigms. Although the simulations show the competence of the READ circuit in these paradigms, additional neural machinery (such as the ART circuit in Fig. 2.1) is also necessary to explain conditioning data.

Excitatory Primary Conditioning

The *CS* is presented in the presence of the *US;* therefore, it becomes associated with the on-response. Variable CS_1-ON describes conditioning of the LTM trace z_{17} within the pathway from the sensory representation of CS_1 to the READ on-channel. After 10 acquisition trials, presentations of CS_1 alone do not cause extinction of the CS_1-ON association (Fig. 2.11). As explained later in the text, forgetting of CS_1-ON associations is due to the acquisition of CS_1-OFF associations.

Inhibitory Primary Conditioning

The *CS* is presented after *US* offset; thus, it becomes associated with the off-response that is generated by an antagonistic rebound within the READ circuit. Variable CS_1-OFF describes conditioning of the LTM trace z_{18} within the pathway from the sensory representation of CS_1 to the off-channel. After 10 acquisition trials, presentations of CS_1 alone cause the CS_1-OFF association to relax to a persistent remembered value (Fig. 2.12). As explained later in the text, forgetting of the CS_1-OFF association is due to the acquisition of CS_1-ON associations.

In Grossberg and Schmajuk (1987), the following additional types of secondary conditioning phenomena are also simulated:

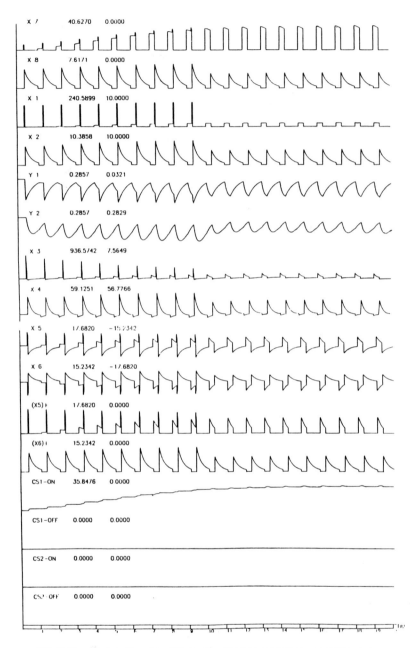

FIG. 2.11. Computer simulation of primary excitatory conditioning and extinction with slow habituation and large feedback in a READ I circuit: CS_1 is paired with the US during the first 10 simulated trials, and CS_1 is presented in the absence of the US in the next 10 simulated trials. The numbers above each plot are the maximum and minimum values of the plot. Parameters follow: $A = 1$, $B = .005$, $C = .00125$, $D = 20$, $E = 20$, $F = 20$, $G = .5$, $H = .005$, $K = .025$, $L = 20$, $M = .05$.

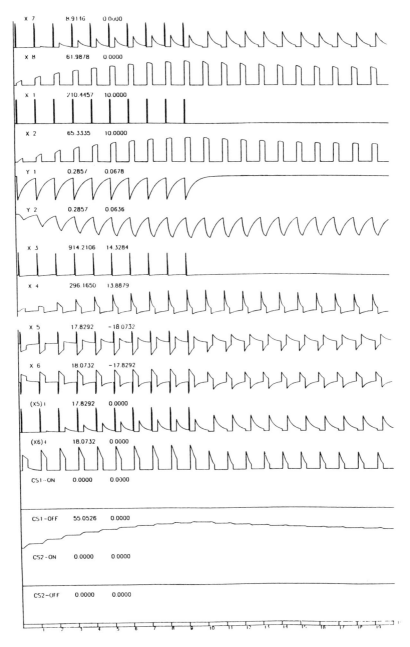

FIG. 2.12. Computer simulation of primary inhibitory conditioning and extinction with slow habituation and large feedback in a READ I circuit: CS_1 is presented after the US offset during the first 10 simulated trials, and CS_1 is presented in the absence of the US in the next 10 simulated trials. The same parameters were used as in FIG. 2.11.

57

Excitatory Secondary Conditioning

The LTM trace CS_1-ON grows during the first 10 trials and is then used to induce the growth of the LTM trace CS_2-ON during the next 10 trials.

Inhibitory Secondary Conditioning

The LTM trace CS_1-ON grows during the first 10 trials and is then used, by presenting a CS_2 after CS_1 offset, to induce the growth of the LTM trace CS_2-OFF during the next 10 trials.

QUALITATIVE EXPLANATIONS OF SELECTIVE FORGETTING DATA

This section presents qualitative explanations for some difficult conditioning data that require the additional neural machinery of an ART circuit, notably STM reset due to expectancy mismatch.

Excitatory Conditioning and Extinction

When a CS is paired with an aversive US on successive conditioning trials, the sensory representation S_1 of CS_1 is conditioned to the drive representation D_{on} corresponding to the fear reaction, both through its conditioned reinforcer path $S_1 \rightarrow D_{on}$ and through its incentive motivational path $D_{on} \rightarrow S_1$. As a result, later presentations of CS_1 tend to generate an amplified STM activation of S_1 and, thus, CS_1 is preferentially attended. Due to the limited capacity of STM, less salient cues tend to be attentionally blocked when CS_1 is presented.

As the cognitive-motivational feedback loop $S_1 \rightarrow D_{on} \rightarrow S_1$ is strengthened during conditioning trials, S_1 is also associated to a sensory expectation of the shock within an ART circuit. During extinction, S_1 is presented on unshocked trials. Parameters of the READ circuit are chosen to prevent passive decay of LTM traces from occurring on these trials. However, when the expected shock does not occur, a sensory mismatch occurs with the learned expectation that is read-out by S_1. The mismatch causes STM to be reset. In particular, the STM activity of S_1 is reduced by the STM reset. This reduction in S_1 causes a reduction in the total input to D_{on}, as in equation (11). An antagonistic rebound consequently occurs in the off-channel D_{off} of the READ circuit. As a result, S_1 becomes associated with the antagonistic rebound at D_{off}. S_1 is smaller after reset than before; therefore, $S_1 \rightarrow D_{off}$ associations take place at a slower rate than during conditioning. After several learning trials, however, the pathway $S_1 \rightarrow D_{off}$ can become as strong as the $S_1 \rightarrow D_{on}$ pathway. Due to opponent extinction, the associative weights to both D_{on} and D_{off} are selectively forgotten. Thus, a conditioned excitor does extinguish.

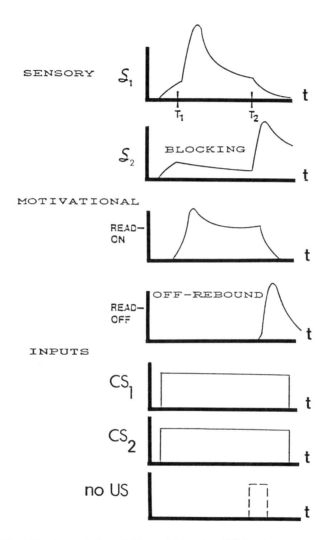

FIG. 2.13. Presentation of CS_1 and CS_2 when CS_1 has become a conditioned excitor, and the compound stimulus is followed by no-shock: During the no-shock interval between times T_1 and T_2, S_1 is actively amplified by positive feedback, and S_2 is blocked. Nonoccurrence of the expected shock causes both S_1 and S_2 to be reset. S_1's STM activity decreases, and S_2's STM activity increases. Due to S_1's increase, D_{on} also decreases, thereby causing a rebound at D_{off}. This rebound becomes associated with the increased activity of S_2.

Inhibitory Conditioning and Nonextinction

Suppose that CS_1 has become a conditioned excitor by being paired with the US, and that CS_1 and CS_2 are then presented together in the absence of the US. When CS_1 and CS_2 are simultaneously presented (Fig. 2.13), S_1's activity is amplified by positive feedback through the strong conditioned $S_1 \rightarrow D_{on} \rightarrow S_1$ pathway. As a result of the limited capacity of STM, the STM activity of S_2 is blocked at time T_1 in Fig. 2.13. When the expected US does not occur at time T_2, the mismatch with S_1's sensory expectation causes both S_1 and S_2 to be reset, and S_1's STM activity decreases, whereas S_2's STM activity increases. Due to S_1's decrease, a rebound occurs at D_{off}. Consequently the unexpected nonoccurrence of the shock enables S_2 to become associated with D_{off} in both the pathways $S_2 \rightarrow D_{off}$ and $D_{off} \rightarrow S_2$. These learned changes turn CS_2 into a conditioned inhibitor. In addition, S_2 is conditioned to a sensory expectation of situational cues that do not include the occurrence of shock.

Due to properties of the READ circuit, when CS_2 is subsequently presented alone, the conditioned value of $S_2 \rightarrow D_{off}$ does not passively decay. In addition, S_2 activates a sensory expectation that predicts the absence of the US. Since this sensory expectation is not disconfirmed, S_2's STM activity is not reset. Consequently no antagonistic rebound occurs within the READ circuit, and no opponent extinction occurs. Thus, a conditioned inhibitor does not extinguish.

CONCLUSION

At least four types of learning processes are relevant in the present paper: learning of conditioned reinforcement, incentive motivation, sensory expectancy, and motor command. These several types of learning processes, which operate on a slow time scale, regulate and are regulated by rapidly fluctuating limited capacity STM representations of sensory events. The theory suggest how nonlinear feedback interactions among these fast information processing mechanisms and slow learning mechanisms actively regulate learning and memory to generate predictive internal representations of external environmental contingencies.

ACKNOWLEDGMENTS

Stephen Grossberg was supported in part by the Air Force Office of Scientific Research (AFOSR F49620–86–C–0037 and AFOSR F49620–87–C–0018) and the National Science Foundation (NSF IRI–84–17756 and NSF IRI–87–16960).

Nestor Schmajuk was supported in part by the National Science Foundation (NSF IRI–84–17756).

We wish to thank Cynthia Suchta and Carol Yanakakis for their valuable assistance in the preparation of the manuscript and illustrations.

REFERENCES

Barto, A. G., Sutton, R. S., & Anderson, C. W. (1983). Neuron-like adaptive elements that can solve difficult learning control problems. *IEEE Transactions, SMC–13,* 834–846.

Bower, G. H. (1981). Mood and memory. *American Psychologist, 36,* 129–148.

Bower, G. H., Gilligan, S. G., & Monteiro, K. P. (1981). Selectivity of learning caused by adaptive states. *Journal of Experimental Psychology: General, 110,* 451–473.

Carpenter, G. A., & Grossberg, S. (1985). Category learning and adaptive pattern recognition: A neural network model. *Proceedings of the Third Army Conference on Applied Mathematics and Computing, ARO Report 86–1,* 37–56.

Carpenter, G. A., & Grossberg, S. (1987a). A massively parallel architecture for a self-organizing neural pattern recognition machine. *Computer Vision, Graphics, and Image Processing, 37,* 54–115.

Carpenter, G. A., & Grossberg, S. (1987b). ART 2: Self-organization of stable category recognition codes for analog input patterns. *Applied Optics, 26,* 4919–4930.

Carpenter, G. A., & Grossberg, S. (1990). Neural dynamics of category learning and recognition: Structural invariants, reinforcement, and evoked potentials. In M. L. Commons, R. J. Herrnstein, S. M. Kosslyn, and D. B. Mumford (Eds.), *Computational and Clinical Approaches to Pattern Recognition and Concept Formation.* Hillsdale, NJ: Lawrence Erlbaum Associates.

Ellias, S., & Grossberg, S. (1975). Pattern formation, contrast control, and oscillations in the short term memory of shunting on-center off-surround networks. *Biological Cybernetics, 20,* 69–98.

Grossberg, S. (1968). Some physiological and biochemical consequences of psychological postulates. *Proceedings of the National Academy of Sciences, 60,* 758–765.

Grossberg, S. (1969). On learning and energy-entropy dependence in recurrent and nonrecurrent signed networks. *Journal of Statistical Physics, 1,* 319–350.

Grossberg, S. (1971). On the dynamics of operant conditioning. *Journal of Theoretical Biology, 33,* 225–255.

Grossberg, S. (1972a). A neural theory of punishment and avoidance, I: Qualitative theory. *Mathematical Biosciences, 15,* 39–67.

Grossberg, S. (1972b). A neural theory of punishment and avoidance, II: Quantitative theory. *Mathematical Biosciences, 15,* 253–285.

Grossberg, S. (1975). A neural model of attention, reinforcement, and discrimination learning. *International Review of Neurobiology, 18,* 263–327.

Grossberg, S. (1976). Adaptive pattern classification and universal recoding, II: Feedback, expectation, olfaction, and illusions. *Biological Cybernetics, 23,* 187–202.

Grossberg, S. (1982). *Studies of mind and brain: Neural principles of learning, perception, development, cognition, and motor control.* Boston: Reidel.

Grossberg, S. (Ed.). (1987). *The adaptive brain, I: Cognition, learning, reinforcement, and rhythm.* Amsterdam: Elsevier/North-Holland.

Grossberg, S., & Levine, D. S. (1975). Some developmental and attentional biases in the contrast enhancement and short term memory of recurrent neural networks. *Journal of Theoretical Biology, 45,* 341–380.

Grossberg, S., & Levine, D. S. (1987). Neural dynamics of attentionally-modulated Pavlovian conditioning: Blocking, inter-stimulus interval, and secondary reinforcement. *Applied Optics, 26,* 5015–5030.

Grossberg, S., & Schmajuk, N. A. (1987). A neural network architecture for attentionally-modulated Pavlovian conditioning: Conditioned reinforcement, inhibition, and opponent processing. *Psychobiology, 15,* 195–240.

Hawkins, R. D., & Kandel, E. R. (1984). Is there a cell-biological alphabet for simple forms of learning? *Psychological Review, 9,* 375–391.

Hebb, D. O. (1949). *The organization of behavior.* New York: Wiley.

Kamin, L. J. (1969). Predictability, surprise, attention, and conditioning. In B. A. Campbell and R. M. Church (Eds.), *Punishment and aversive behavior* (pp. 279–298). New York: Appleton-Century-Crofts.

Levy, W. B., Brassel, S. E., & Moore, S. D. (1983). Partial quantification of the associative synaptic learning rule of the dentate gyrus. *Neuroscience, 8,* 799–808.

Levy, W. B., & Desmond, N. L. (1985). The rules of elemental synaptic plasticity. In W. B. Levy, J. Anderson, & S. Lehmkuhle (Eds.), *Synaptic modification, neuron selectivity, and nervous system organization* (pp. 105–121). Hillsdale, NJ: Lawrence Erlbaum Associates.

Matzel, L. D., Schachtman, T. R., & Miller, R. R. (1985). Recovery of an overshadowed association achieved by extinction of the overshadowing stimulus. *Learning and Motivation, 16,* 398–412.

Rauschecker, J. P., & Singer, W. (1979). Changes in the circuitry of the kitten's visual cortex are gated by postsynaptic activity. *Nature, 280,* 58–60.

Schneiderman, N., & Gormezano, I. (1964). Conditioning of the nictitating membrane response of the rabbit as a function of the CS–US interval. *Journal of Comparative and Physiological Psychology, 57,* 188–195.

Singer, W. (1983). Neuronal activity as a shaping factor in the self-organization of neuron assemblies. In E. Basar, H. Flohr, H. Haken, & A. J. Mandell (Eds.), *Synergetics of the brain* (pp. 89–101). New York: Springer-Verlag.

Smith, M. D., Coleman, S. R., & Gormezano, I. (1969). Classical conditioning of the rabbit's nictitating membrane response at backward, simultaneous, and forward CS–US intervals. *Journal of Comparative and Physiological Psychology, 69,* 226–231.

Sutton, R. S., & Barto, A. G. (1981). Toward a modern theory of adaptive networks: Expectation and prediction. *Psychological Review, 88,* 135–170.

3 Versatility in Conditioning: A Layered Network Model

E. James Kehoe
University of New South Wales

No situation ever repeats itself exactly, even in the most tightly controlled laboratory (Hilgard & Marquis, 1940, pp. 176–177; Pavlov, 1927, p. 111). Thus, a key requirement for the success of any adaptive organism is its ability to transfer what has been learned in one situation to another situation. Transfer of learning not only permits the organism to tolerate random variation across reoccurring situations but also permits the organism to capitalize on previous experience to deal effectively with more novel situations as they arise.

The present chapter is intended to show how a layered network of adaptive units can explain a wide variety of transfer phenomena, some of which have defied conventional theoretical approaches. It is well recognized that networks with parallel but interconnected inputs are highly tolerant to random variation. However, it is less widely recognized that the layering of units confers additional transfer abilities on an adaptive network (Kehoe, 1986, 1988). As its empirical base, the present chapter will describe experimental and modelling efforts that have been directed at transfer in classical conditioning of the rabbit nictitating membrane (NM) response.

TYPES OF TRANSFER

The textbook design for a demonstration of transfer contains two groups. The "experimental" group receives initial training on one task (A) and then is switched to a second task (B). The "control" group ideally receives no programmed initial training, the so-called "rest" condition, before it too receives training in the second task (B). Frequently, however, the control group is not

63

allowed to rest. Rather, it receives some other training regime that minimizes the type of learning that occurs in Task A while matching the exposure that the experimental group receives to the stimuli in Task A. A comparison of the performances by the experimental and control groups in Task B is used to identify the degree of transfer from Task A (Ellis, 1965). Among the large number of transfer effects, they fall roughly into two classes, *immediate transfer* and *general transfer*.

Immediate transfer is said to have occurred when, after training in Task A, the performance of the experimental and control groups differs on the very first presentations of the stimuli in Task B. In conditioning research, the most familiar example of immediate transfer is *stimulus generalization*. Typically, the experimental group shows graded reductions in responding to stimuli in Task B as their physical differences from the training stimulus in Task A are progressively increased (e.g., Moore, 1972). In contrast, a rest control group shows little or no responding to either the training stimulus (A) or any of the test stimuli (B). In more elaborate stimulus generalization experiments, a control group that has received some previous training will show relatively uniform levels of responding to both the A and B stimuli (Thomas, 1970; Mackintosh, 1977).

Immediate transfer and particularly stimulus generalization have proved amenable to a variety of theoretical approaches. In all cases, physically similar stimuli are thought to produce overlapping representations. For example, Pavlov (1927, p. 154), who first experimentally demonstrated stimulus generalization, argued for spatial "irradiation" over cortical fields as the basis for immediate transfer. More behavioristic theories have dropped the neural speculation but have retained a spatial metric (Blough, 1972; Cross, 1965; Spence, 1936). Connectionist models have readily captured those notions by assuming that any individual stimulus activates a number of parallel inputs, and physically similar stimuli activate many but not all of the same inputs (e.g., Desmond, 1988; Hawkins & Kandel, 1984).

General transfer is said to have occurred when initial training on Task A alters the rate of learning in Task B. A clear example of general transfer is *learning to learn*, which denotes a progressive increase in the rate of learning across a series of tasks that are similar in structure but differ dramatically in their superficial stimuli (Ellis, 1965, p. 32). In animal conditioning, learning to learn has been repeatedly demonstrated using stimuli in Task A and Task B that differ in their sensory modalities. For example, Thomas, Miller, and Svinicki (1971) found that rats given initial discrimination training between two light intensities acquired a discrimination between two tone frequencies faster than control rats given initial training with one light intensity (cf. Holt & Kehoe, 1985).

Unlike immediate transfer, general transfer has been relatively intractable to a broad theoretical solution. There have been two alternative strategies, both of which have had only limited success. First, a number of theorists have argued that initial training not only produces acquisition of a specific association but also neutralizes interference from irrelevant stimuli (Mackintosh, 1977, Seraganian, 1979; Tennant & Bitterman, 1975) or from nonfunctional responses (Harlow, 1959). Where appropriate control conditions have been used, neutralization of potential interference does not appear sufficient to explain general transfer in classical conditioning (Kehoe, Morrow, & Holt, 1984; Westbrook & Homewood, 1982). Second, other theorists have argued for superordinate learning in which the animal acquires a sensitivity to the structural relations among stimuli, responses, and reinforcers (Behar & LeBedda, 1974; Holt & Kehoe, 1985; Levine, 1959; Rodgers & Thomas, 1982; Thomas, 1970). Although hypotheses of superordinate learning allow for predictions concerning the range of tasks over which general transfer will occur, those hypotheses provide little insight into the mechanism by which the subject extracts the key structural relations among tasks.

As will be shown in the remainder of this chapter, a layered network model does provide an insight into the mechanism of general transfer. Rather than dividing the consequences of initial learning into a hierarchy of specific and superordinate components, the proposed layered network model divides initial learning into a sequence of two associative linkages. One linkage is specific to the conditioned stimulus (CS). The other is an interior linkage specific to the response and is available in subsequent learning tasks.

BASIC MODEL FOR GENERAL TRANSFER

Fig. 3.1 shows a schematic for what may be the simplest layered network (Barto, 1985; Kehoe, 1986, 1988). An input for a notional "tone" CS (T) and a separate input for a notional "light" CS (L) projects to one adaptive unit (X), and that X unit projects to a second adaptive unit (R), which generates the observable

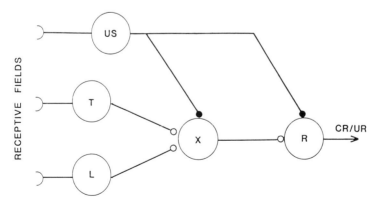

FIG. 3.1. The minimal network that can explain general transfer in classical conditioning. It contains three sensory elements (T, L, US) and two adaptive elements (X, R).

response output. The T–X, L–X, and X–R connections are all assumed to be subject to alteration. In addition, both the X unit and R unit receive a fixed input from an unconditioned stimulus (US). This US input has the capacity to trigger both the X and R unit in an all-or-none fashion.

The learning and performance rules for the X and R units in the network are as follows: The change in the value ΔV_{ij}, of a connection between the ith input and jth unit is assumed to follow a delta learning rule (Gluck & Bower, 1988; Sutton & Barto, 1981; Rescorla & Wagner, 1972):

$$\Delta V_{ij} = a_j (\lambda_j - V'_{ij}) \tag{1}$$

where the following occur:

1. a_j is the rate parameter for the target unit of the connection ($0 < a_j < 1$). On nonreinforced trials, a_j is reduced by the parameter B_0 ($0 < B_0 < 1$).
2. λ_j is the total connection value that can be supported by the US on any given trial. ($\lambda_j = 1.0$ on reinforced trials. $\lambda_j = 0.0$ on nonreinforced trials.)
3. V'_{ij} is the net sum of the connection values of all currently eligible inputs to the jth unit.

Both the sensory inputs and the output of each unit are either 1 or 0. In the simulations the sensory inputs T, L, and US are specified on a trial-by-trial basis. The output of each unit is determined by a comparison of V'_{ij} to a noisy threshold value between 0 and 1. Thus, the firing of both X and R is all-or-none and is determined by a normally distributed random threshold variable. Thus, on a given trial, X fires in response to an input from T, only if the T–X connection value exceeds the threshold on that trial. Likewise, R fires, only if the X–R connection value exceeds the current threshold.

As may be apparent, the establishment of a conditioned response (CR) to, say, a tone CS, requires that both the T–X and X–R connections be strengthened. Thus, the conditioning pathway is effectively wired in series. The appearance of series wiring seems curious, for, as anybody who has ever tried to fix an old-fashioned string of Christmas lights knows, series wiring is highly failure-prone. Nevertheless the series wiring feature is the essential ingredient to effective transfer. The consequences of a failure in series wiring are minimized in larger layered networks through their inbuilt redundancy in the form of interconnected, parallel connections.

HYSTERESIS AND SUCCESSIVE ACQUISITIONS

Before considering the application of the model to learning to learn, there is a more basic form of general transfer that occurs when sessions of CS–US pairings are alternated with sessions in which the CS is presented alone. Thus, the demands of the tasks are constantly being reversed. As the cycle of CS–US pairings and CS-alone presentations is repeated, the speed of CR acquisition during the CS–US pairings becomes progressively faster, and the speed of CR extinction also becomes progressively faster (e.g., Hoehler, Kirschenbaum, & Leonard, 1973; Scavio & Thompson, 1979; Schmaltz & Theios, 1972; Smith & Gormezano, 1965). In very broad terms, the organism's learning system shows hysteresis, that is to say, the system preserves a residue of previous learning even when the demands of the task change dramatically. As will be shown following, a layered network provides some degree of hysteresis.

Initial CR Acquisition

At the beginning of training with a naive animal, only the outputs from the US to X and R are effective. That is to say, only the US unit can trigger an all-or-none firing of X and R. Initially the T input is unable to trigger the X unit, but the T input does render its connection with X eligible for modification by the US input should it occur during a brief period that follows CS onset (Sutton & Barto, 1981). Thus, as the T–X connection strengthens over successive CS–US pairings, T will begin to trigger X. Then the X–R connection will become eligible for change by the US's input to R. Observable CRs to the tone will only begin to appear when the intervening connections become strong enough so that T triggers X and then X triggers R. Fig. 3.2, left-hand column of panels, shows the changes across blocks of CS–US trials in the following: (a) the T–X connection, (b) the X–R connection, and (c) the percent CR measure produced by a computer simulation. As can be seen in the bottom panel of that column, it is possible to reproduce a typical acquisition curve.

Extinction and Subsequent Acquisitions

In its remaining panels, Fig. 3.2 shows the simulated changes for T–X, X–R, and percent CR across an initial extinction, a reacquisition, and a reextinction. During the initial extinction, the T–X connection declines at a steady rate, whereas the X–R connection declines to an asymptotic level of .70. As the T–X connection weakens, and X's frequency of firing declines, the X–R connection becomes eligible for modification less and less often. In this way, the X–R connection is largely protected from extinction and remains intact. It can be seen that CR frequency reaches a negligible level, whereas both the T–X and X–R connections are still appreciable. Consequently, during reacquisition in the third stage, both the T–X and X–R connections need relatively few reinforcements to regain their asymptotic levels, yielding a rapid reappearance of the CR.

The second extinction in the simulation does not appear particularly more rapid than the first extinction. To some extent, this simulated outcome is accurate; the available data indicate that changes in extinction rate emerge more

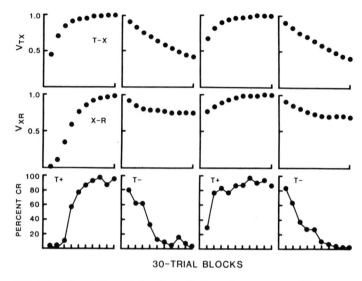

FIG. 3.2. Simulation of the T–X, X–R, and percentage CRs in successive acquisitions and extinctions.

slowly than changes in acquisition rate across alternations of the training conditions. Thus, this version of the model appears to be accurate to a first approximation.

Additional parallel linkages may be needed to further accelerate later acquisitions as well as later extinctions. For example, Klopf (1988) proposed a single unit model in which there are parallel excitatory and inhibitory connections for each CS. Specifically the former can take on only positive values, and the latter can take on only negative values. During CS-alone presentations, the value of the excitatory connection declines toward zero, and the inhibitory connection becomes increasingly negative in value. According to Klopf (1988), the two values stabilize when the negative value of the inhibitory connection balances the residual positive value of the excitatory connection, thus, protecting the excitatory residual from further extinction. In this way, a parallel network can also yield hysteresis. A hybrid of the present layered architecture combined with Klopf's parallel excitatory and inhibitory connections may yield the additional versatility needed for progressively accelerating successive acquisitions and extinctions.

LEARNING TO LEARN

Learning to learn has been most widely studied in humans and primates. It is often viewed as a quasicognitive function (e.g., Cameron, 1979, 1981; Harlow, 1949, 1959; Levine, 1959; Medin, 1972), and comparisons of learning to learn across species have been proposed as a phylogenetic scale of "intelligence" (Warren, 1965). However, even in basic associative tasks, learning to learn is a large and robust phenomenon. In classical conditioning of the rabbit NM response, initial training with a CS in one sensory modality dramatically accelerates subsequent CR acquisition to a new CS in another sensory modality. This facilitation in CR acquisition occurs although the animals clearly distinguish the two CSs (Holt & Kehoe, 1985; Kehoe & Holt, 1984; Kehoe et al., 1984; Schreurs & Kehoe, 1987).

Empirical Demonstration

Figures 3.3, 3.4, and 3.5 show the details of learning to learn as observed in the rabbit NM preparation (Kehoe & Holt, 1984). In Stage I, one group of rabbits (Group 4-8) received presentations of either a tone or light CS that was paired with an electrotactile US presented 400 ms later. Two other groups served as "no learning" controls. One group (28-8) was given exposures to the CS and US but separated by an interval of 2,800 ms. The third group (R-8) was a rest control that did not receive presentations of either the CS or US. As can be seen in Fig. 3.3, Group 4-8 showed rapid CR acquisition to the CS that reached a terminal level of 98% CRs, Group 28-8 showed modest CR acquisition that reached only

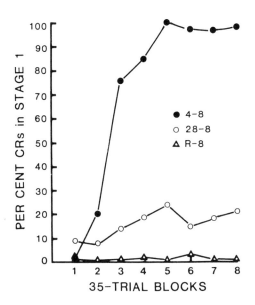

FIG. 3.3. Stage I of learning to learn. Group 4-8 received CS–US pairings at a 400 ms CS–US interval; Group 28-8 received pairings at a 2,800 ms CS–US interval, and Group R-8 received no pairings (Kehoe & Holt, 1984).

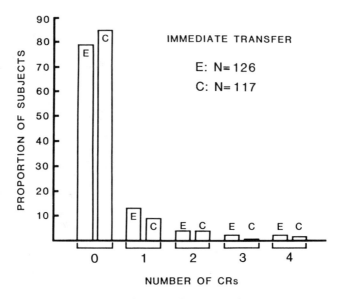

FIG. 3.4. Tests for immediate transfer across CS modalities. The proportion of subjects showing either 0, 1, 2, 3, or 4 responses during four
test presentations to a new CS following previous training with a CS in
another sensory modality. Subjects designated as E had received previous training at a short CS–US interval, whereas subjects designated
as C had received either widely separated presentations of the CS and
US or no exposure to either stimulus.

20% CRs, and Group R-8 showed a few spontaneous responses that never exceeded 2%.

At the start of Stage II, all three groups received four presentations of an
alternative CS. For example, animals that had been exposed to a tone CS in Stage
1 were tested with a light CS in Stage 2. The four tests with the new CS were
conducted to determine the level of immediate transfer between auditory and
visual modalities. In fact no immediate transfer between the auditory and visual
CSs has been detected. Fig. 3.4 summarizes the results of the generalization tests
collated across the rabbit NM studies conducted in my laboratory. Specifically
Fig. 3.4 depicts the proportion of subjects that showed either 0, 1, 2, 3, or 4
responses on the four test presentations. The subjects are divided into two
groups. One group includes those "experimental" subjects (E) that received
Stage I training that produced CR acquisition, as in Group 4-8. The second group
includes control subjects (C) that received either widely spaced presentations of
the initial CS and US, like Group 28-8, or no Stage I training at all, like Group
R-8. As can be seen, the vast majority of subjects in both groups showed no
response to the new CS. Any apparent differences in the distributions failed to
reach statistical significance.

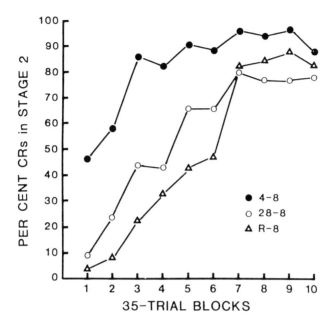

FIG. 3.5. Stage II of learning to learn. CR acquisition to a new CS at an 800 ms CS–US interval. Earlier, during Stage I, Group 4-8 had received CS–US pairings at a 400 ms CS–US interval, Group 28-8 had received pairings at a 2,800 ms CS–US interval, and Group R-8 had received no pairings (Kehoe & Holt, 1984).

Although there was no discernible immediate transfer, learning to learn appeared soon after CS–US training with the new CS commenced. In Stage II, a CS–US interval of 800 ms was used; this longer value ensured a moderate rate of CR acquisition that allowed detection of either positive or negative transfer. As can be seen in the acquisition curves for Stage II shown in Fig. 3.5, the pretrained group (4-8) showed extremely rapid CR acquisition to the new CS. For example, Group 4-8 achieved a mean CR likelihood of 46% CRs within the first block of CS–US trials. In comparison, the control groups, 28-8 and R-8, achieved a mean CR likelihood less than 10% CRs within the first block of trials. In this and other studies, the degree of transfer between tone and light has been symmetric.

Simulation of Learning to Learn

Fig. 3.6 shows the results of simulations for learning to learn. The simulation of initial CR acquisition with the tone proceeded in the same way as seen in Fig. 3.2. In particular, observable CRs to the initial CS required the successive strengthening of the T–X and X–R connections. In subsequent transfer training

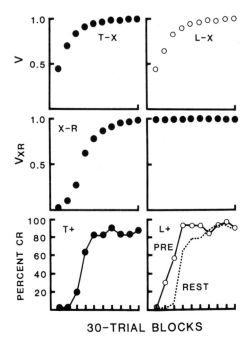

FIG. 3.6. Simulation of the learning-to-learn effect. The panels show the changes in the value of the connections (T–X, L–X, X–R) and the simulated CR acquisition curves.

with the L input, immediate transfer did not appear, because the L–X connection initially had a value of zero. However, once L–US pairings began, and the L–X connection started to strengthen, the earliest firings of X by L were translated immediately into CRs via the previously established X–R connection, thus, facilitating CR acquisition to L. In summary, CRs to the first CS (T) waited upon the strengthening of the T–X and X–R connections, but CRs to the second CS (L) required only the establishment of the L–X connection, which then capitalized on the existing X–R connection. In Fig. 3.6, this facilitation can be seen in the lower right-hand panel, specifically in the simulated acquisition curve labeled as PRE, which denotes pretraining. For purposes of comparison, a simulated learning curve for a rest control condition is also displayed, labeled as REST.

By relying on a common connection and the convergent CS inputs, a layered network can explain learning to learn. Whereas the hysteresis seen in successive acquisitions could arise from either a parallel network like Klopf's or a layered network like mine, learning to learn appears to be a unique product of a layered network. Parallel architectures, as noted previously, provide a natural method for producing immediate transfer by means of overlapping activation of inputs by different stimuli. Together layered and parallel structures provide a powerful means for promoting the transfer of previous learning.

Learning to Learn After Extinction

Learning to learn in classical conditioning shows the same kind of hysteresis as seen in successive acquisitions to the same CS. Fig. 3.7 shows the results from an experiment in which subjects were trained with a CS (A) and then underwent an extinction procedure with the same CS (A). However, rather than retraining with the same CS, a new CS (B) from another modality was introduced to determine whether learning to learn would still appear—which it did (Kehoe et al., 1984).

As in the demonstration experiment previously described, the key experimental groups (4-E and 4-H) received initial training with one CS (A) at a short, 400 ms CS–US interval. Two control groups (28-E and 28-H) also received exposure to CSA and the US but at a long, 2,800 ms CS–US interval. Examination of the left-hand panel of Fig. 3.7 reveals that Groups 4-E and 4-H showed high levels of CR acquisition, whereas Groups 28-E and 28-H showed negligible levels of responding. Following CSA–US training, Groups 4-E and 28-E received a CSA-alone extinction procedure, whereas Groups 4-H and 28-H remained in their home cages. The middle panel shows that Group 4-E displayed considerable extinction of the CR to CSA, whereas Group 28-E continued to display little responding. Finally all groups received transfer training with a second CS (CSB–US). The right-hand panel reveals that, despite the near elimination of the initial conditioned reflex (CSA–CR) in Group 4-E, those animals acquired the new conditioned reflex (CSB–CR) as rapidly as did Group 4-H, both of which showed positive transfer relative to the control groups, 28-E and 28-H.

Computer simulations, which are shown in Fig. 3.8, reproduced the ability of learning to learn to survive extinction of the initial CR (Kehoe, 1988). According to the simulations depicted in Fig. 3.8, learning to learn survives for exactly the same reason that reacquisition after extinction is more rapid than initial acquisition. Namely, during extinction, the reduction of the T–X connection largely shields the X–R connection from reduction. Subsequently pairings of CSB (L) with the US can still take advantage of the X–R connection and rapidly produce CRs as the L–X connection begins to strengthen. The lower right-hand panel of Fig. 3.8 shows two simulated CR acquisition curves. The solid line represents acquisition to the CSB (L) in the group that received CSA pretraining followed by CSA extinction (i.e., Group 4-E). The dotted line represents the simulated curve from a pretrained group that did not undergo extinction of the original CR (i.e., Group 4-H). In agreement with the behavioral data, the two curves overlap perfectly.

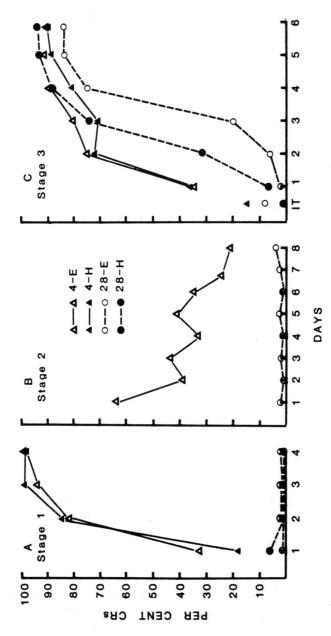

FIG. 3.7. Learning-to-learn survives extinction of the initial CR. Panel A shows the results of initial CS–US training at either a 400 ms CS–US interval (Groups 4-E and 4-H) or a 2,800 ms CS–US interval (Groups 28-E and Groups 28-H). Panel B shows the results of extinction training for Groups 4-E and 28-E. Panel C shows the results of CS–US training with an alternate CS at an 800 ms CS–US interval (Kehoe, Morrow, & Holt, 1984).

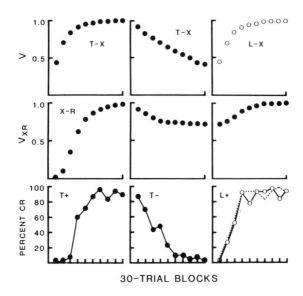

FIG. 3.8. Simulation results for initial CR acquisition to a tone CS, extinction of the CR to the tone CS, and subsequent transfer to a light CS.

Real-Time Hysteresis

Although my basic model represents the CR as an all-or-none event, a real CR is nothing like a stereotyped "reflexive" response. Instead the CR is a finely graded, temporally controlled response that reaches its maximum at the time of maximal promise or threat. In the rabbit NM preparation as well as other classical conditioning preparations, the initiation of the CR anticipates the onset of the US, but the maximal CR (peak CR amplitude) tends to occur shortly after the onset of the US (Gormezano, Kehoe, & Marshall, 1983; Kimmel & Burns, 1975; Millenson, Kehoe, & Gormezano, 1977). Thus, the time course of the CR is highly attuned to the CS–US interval.

To determine whether or not there was any hysteresis in the time course of the CR during the learning to learn paradigm, Kehoe and Napier (in press) trained separate groups of animals with CSA–US intervals of 200, 400, or 600 ms. In those three groups, the peak of the CR appeared dutifully around 250, 450, and 650 ms following CS onset. In the second phase of training, all animals were switched to a new CS (B) in another sensory modality at a CSB–US interval of 400 ms. During CSB–US training, one in every four trials was a presentation of CSB alone so that the peak of the CR could be detected without intrusion by the UR. Fig. 3.9 depicts the temporal distribution of CR peaks on the CSB-alone presentations. As can be seen on the first day of CSB–US training, there were systematic differences among the groups in the timing of their CR peaks. Specifi-

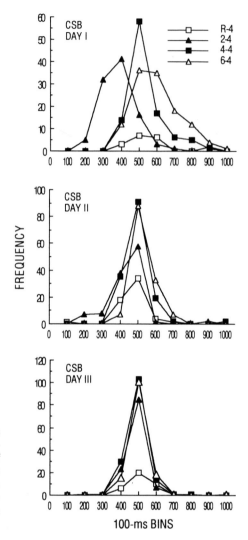

FIG. 3.9. Frequency polygons depicting the temporal distribution of CR peaks during CSB of groups trained with a 400 ms CSB–US interval following initial training with CSA–US intervals of 200, 400, and 600 ms (Kehoe & Napier, in press).

cally Group 400, for which the CSA–US and CSB–US intervals were identical, showed a sharply defined distribution centered at 450 ms following CSB onset. In contrast, Groups 200 and 600 showed broader distributions that tended to be displaced toward the 200 ms and 600 ms points respectively. Over the subsequent days, the distributions for Groups 200 and 600 converged on that of Group 400. A rest control group also placed its CR peaks around the 450-ms point. In summary, there was hysteresis in transfer of the CR across sensory modalities from CSA to CSB, which, however, was overcome by CSB–US training.

The time course of the CR has been a special concern of real-time models of conditioning (e.g., Desmond & Moore, 1988; Sutton & Barto, 1987; Zipser, 1986). In my basic network model, the learning rule applies at the trial level. That is to say, the rule assumes that connection weights are updated only once per trial, and no account is taken of the temporal relation between the CS and US or between the CS and CR. There is nothing, however, to prevent a real-time model from being implemented within the framework of a series-wired network.

If both the X and R units were to operate as independent real-time units, some adjustments would probably be necessary in both the structure and learning rules of the network. On the structural side, the available real-time models assume that each CS generates multiple, parallel connections with the adaptive unit. Accordingly both the X and R units would each need to be elaborated into small networks with multiple weights. Thus, there would be multiple X–R connections. Depending on assumptions regarding time lags in the network, adjustments in the rules for each unit would be needed to generate an appropriately timed CR based on the aggregate operation of the X unit, the R units, and their interconnections.

In the just-described results, there is evidence that the X–R connection and R unit operate according to real-time principles. Specifically the initial bias in the temporal distribution of CRs to CSB indicates that the weights for generating the CR's time course are located—at least in part—downstream from the point of convergence between CSA and CSB. In the basic model, that point corresponds to the X–R connection.

It remains to be determined whether or not the connections between the CS inputs and the counterpart to the X unit operate on a real-time basis. They probably do. If the X–R connection entirely determined the time course of the CR, then it would be impossible for the animal to generate different CRs to different CSs at any given time. In fact, Kehoe, Graham-Clarke, and Schreurs (1989) recently demonstrated that the animals can differentiate between CSs in terms of their CS–US intervals. Two CSs, a tone and a light, were each paired with the US at CS–US intervals of 600 ms and 1,600 ms respectively. Trials with the tone and light were intermixed on a quasirandom basis. Fig. 3.10 shows the time course of the CRs on test presentations of the tone and light on the last day of training. As can be seen, the animals clearly placed the peak of the CR for each CS near to the time at which the US had been presented.

In summary, the examination of the CR's time course indicates several directions for further development of any model of conditioning. On the one hand, the animal clearly displays hysteresis in that it can capitalize on previous training at one CS–US interval to generate CRs to a new CS at a different CS–US interval. On the other hand, the animal has enough versatility so that it can adjust the timing of CRs to changing demands. Specifically the animal can adjust the timing of CRs to a new CS–US interval across modalities (Kehoe & Napier, 1989) and also within modalities (Coleman & Gormezano, 1971). Moreover, the animal can acquire appropriately timed CRs to two different CSs at their respective CS–US intervals (Kehoe et al., 1989).

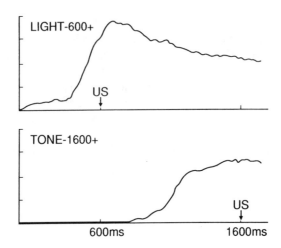

FIG. 3.10. The time course of CRs during light and tone test trials after training with CS–US intervals of 600 ms and 1,600 ms respectively (Kehoe, Graham-Clarke, & Schreurs, 1989).

LATENT LEARNING

It is a truism that experience often has an impact that does not immediately manifest itself through a change in behavior. This disjunction is most commonly expressed in terms of the distinction between learning and performance. Experimentally the latent effects of experience are usually demonstrated by means of a transfer procedure. In classical conditioning of the rabbit NM response, there have been recent demonstrations that the first few CS–US pairings can produce large transfer effects. Moreover, these latent effects would appear to be explainable by a layered network model. A reexamination of the previously described simulations reveals that there are large associative changes well before any CRs appear. Specifically the T–X connection rises to a high level before the X–R connection shows any substantial change. Thus, manipulations very early in training would be expected to have profound effects on later CR acquisition.

Within-CS Transfer

Ross and Scavio (1983) demonstrated that the CS–US interval during brief initial training can dramatically alter the subsequent rate of CR acquisition to the same CS. In their experiment, subjects were given 15 trials at a CS–US interval ranging from 0 ms to 4,000 ms. During those 15 trials, no CR acquisition was observed. Subsequently all subjects were shifted to a common CS–US interval of 500 ms. During CR acquisition at the 500 ms CS–US interval, there were sustained savings for groups initially exposed to CS–US intervals around 250 ms, the optimal value for rabbit NM conditioning. Savings tailed off systematically for groups initially given shorter or longer intervals.

According to the present model, the savings following the initial CS–US trials reflect the early growth in the T–X connection as governed by the initial CS–US interval. To simulate the effects of CS–US interval, the learning rate parameters for the T–X and X–R connections were varied on the basis of parameter fits for data from independent manipulations of the CS–US interval. Fig. 3.11 shows simulations for the T–X, X–R, and percent CRs as a function of the nominal CS–US interval during the initial 15 trials. Each curve in each panel represents

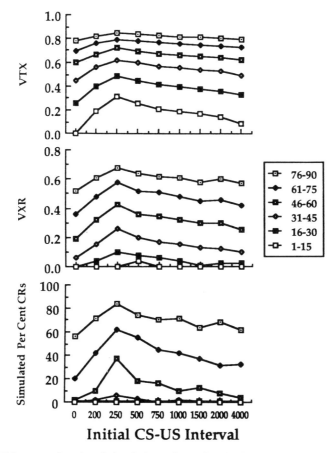

FIG. 3.11.   Results of simulations directed at the findings of Ross and Scavio (1983). In their experiment, the animals received 15 CS–US pairings at CS–US intervals ranging from 0 ms to 4,000 ms. Thereafter, all pairings were conducted at a uniform CS–US interval of 500 ms. Each curve represents successive blocks of 15 trials.

successive blocks of 15 trials. Thus, the curve labeled 1-15 represents the initial 15 trials in which the learning rate parameters were manipulated, and all subsequent blocks represent training at the 500 ms CS–US interval, for which the learning rate parameters were the same for all simulated groups. As can be seen in Fig. 3.11, the initial 15 trials produced large differences in the T–X connection without producing any growth in the X–R connection. During the subsequent training, the initial increments in the T–X connection for the optimal CS–US intervals gave them a persistent lead in reaching the threshold for firing X, incrementing the X–R value, and ultimately producing CRs.

Cross-Modality Transfer

Schreurs and Kehoe (1987) provided converging evidence for the acquisition of considerable associative strength during the first few CS–US pairings. As part of a larger experiment, three groups of rabbits received either 0, 15, or 30 initial CSA–US pairings at an interval of 300 ms, where CSA was a tone for half the subjects and a light for the other half. As Ross and Scavio (1983) found, 15 pairings produced no CRs. The group that received 30 initial pairings showed CRs in only 5% of their trials. Subsequently all three groups received transfer training with the alternative CS (B). They were given no further CSA–US pairings, but test presentations of CSA were interspersed among the CSB–US trials. All three groups showed similar rates of CR acquisition to CSB. The tests with CSA, however, revealed the effects of the initial CSA–US pairings. On the one hand, the group given zero CSA–US pairings never showed any CRs to CSA. On the other hand, as CR acquisition to CSB occurred, the groups given 15 and 30 CSA–US pairings showed progressive increases in responding on CSA test trials from baserate levels less than 6% CRs to asymptotes of 34% and 62% CRs respectively. Responding to CSB reached an asymptote of 100% CRs in all three groups.

The results of Schreurs and Kehoe (1987) had been predicted from the layered network model. According to the model, the initial CSA–US pairings partially strengthened an outer connection between the appropriate CS input and the X unit. Notionally consider it to be the T–X connection. By truncating initial training after a few trials, the X–R connection remained largely unstrengthened. During subsequent CSB–US training, the alternate connection (L–X) was strengthened, and, more importantly, the X–R connection was strengthened. As the X–R connection strengthened, presentations of CSA (T) would begin to evoke CRs via the previously established T–X connection and the newly established X–R connection. Consequently the emergence of CRs on CSA test trials was expected to parallel the acquisition of CRs on CSB–US trials. Moreover, responding to CSA in the 15- and 30-pairing groups reached asymptotic levels that were considerably less than 100% CRs. These low asymptotic levels presumably reflect the limit of CR evocation imposed by the partial strengthening of the T–X connection during the initial CSA–US pairings.

Parallel Model of Configural Learning

A final and somewhat different form of versatility in conditioning is configural learning, which requires the animal to differentiate a compound of two CSs, say tone (A) + light (B), from its separate components (Kehoe & Gormezano, 1980). Configural learning can be seen as a simple example of the representation problem that arises whenever the output mapping for a combined set of inputs is not a linear combination of the mappings for the separate inputs (e.g., Anderson, 1986; Barto, Anderson, & Sutton, 1982; Minsky & Papert, 1969). It is possible to concoct a nonlinear discrimination with as few as two inputs, namely the exclusive-OR problem (XOR) in which the learner is to respond to each of two inputs separately but *not* to their joint occurrence (Barto, 1985, p. 35; Rumelhart, Hinton, & Williams, 1986, p. 319). Within conditioning, the chief example of the XOR problem is the negative patterning schedule in which the animal is presented a mixture of three, following types of trials: (a) one stimulus that is paired with the US (A+), (b) a second stimulus that also is paired with the US (B+), and (c) a compound stimulus that is always presented alone (AB−) (Pavlov, 1927, p. 144; see Bellingham, Gillette-Bellingham, & Kehoe, 1985; Kehoe & Graham, 1988; Woodbury, 1943).

In the connectionist modeling literature of course, considerable effort has been devoted to solving nonlinear discriminations by synthesizing representations of compound inputs as the need arises. This effort has centered on layered networks (e.g., Anderson, 1986; Rumelhart & McClelland, 1986). Recently I examined the applicability of a layered network with a minimal number of units to configural learning phenomena (Kehoe, 1986, 1988). The intent was to extend the basic X–R network and its learning rules in the most economical fashion. Fig. 3.12

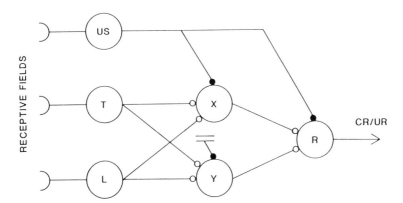

FIG. 3.12. A parallel network for solving simple nonlinear discrimination problems in classical conditioning. It contains three sensory elements (T, L, US) and three adaptive elements (X, Y, R).

shows the extended network. As can be seen, it entails the addition of an extra hidden unit (Y) with connections to the sensory inputs (T, L, US) and the response unit (R). In other words, the new network is two parallel instances of the basic network.

According to the model, configural learning arises, because the network synthesizes a representation of the compound by allowing either the X or Y unit to be triggered only by the joint occurrence of the two CS inputs. In turn the key to that synthesis lies in the delta rule by which each unit operates. According to the delta rule, if two inputs to either the X, Y, and/or R units occur simultaneously, then those inputs compete for the available connection weight supported by the US input (λ). Thus, in compound training, simultaneous T and L inputs to, say, the X unit, will divide the available connection weight between them. If only the summated T–X and L–X connections are strong enough to trigger the X unit, then the X unit effectively constitutes a representation of the compound (cf. Barto, 1985, pp. 36–40; Kehoe 1986, 1988; Rumelhart et al., 1986, pp. 332–333).

A series of simulations using the expanded network and a constant set of parameters was able to reproduce a large variety of conditioning phenomena involving compound stimuli (Kehoe, 1988). Specifically successful, following simulations were obtained when: (a) the X unit had a higher mean threshold than the Y unit ($T_x = .70$, $T_y = .15$) and (b) the X unit had a higher learning rate than that of the Y unit ($\alpha_x = .050$, $\alpha_y = .001$). The high threshold for the X unit made it very sensitive to the effects of any competition between the T and L inputs. When T and L divided the weights evenly ($V_{TX} = V_{LX} = .50$), then X was only triggered in response to the compound. Conversely, the low threshold of the Y unit made it insensitive to the effects of competition between the T and L inputs. The Y unit was reliably triggered in response to either the T or L input at all but the lowest connection weights. The difference in the learning rates between the X and Y units give the X unit an advantage in competing with the Y unit for access to the R unit. With its high learning rate, the X unit would begin to trigger earlier in training and, thus, ensure that the X–R connection started to strengthen before the Y–R connection became eligible for alteration. The R unit had an intermediate learning rate ($\alpha_r = .010$) and an intermediate threshold ($T_r = .50$).

Hysteresis in Configural Learning

The parallel model relies on the same connections and same units as the transfer phenomena described previously in this chapter. Therefore, I have begun to test how well the parallel model predicts transfer between different schedules of training involving compound stimuli, for example, transfer from conditioned inhibition to negative patterning. Whereas conditioned inhibition entails a differentiation between the compound (TL−) and only one of its components (L+), negative patterning entails a differentiation between the compound (TL−) and both its components (T+, L+). That small operational difference between the two schedules yields distinctive patterns of connection weights in the parallel model.

Fig. 3.13 shows the terminal connection weights for conditioned inhibition and negative patterning; both simulations were based on the parameter values described for configural learning. In the case of conditioned inhibition, the X and Y units function in parallel. The T input develops inhibitory connections with both the X and Y units, while the L input develops excitatory connections. Hence, on TL− trials, the net sum of the inputs to both intermediate units falls

CONDITIONED INHIBITION

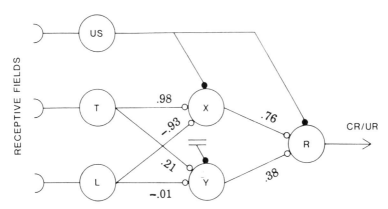

NEGATIVE PATTERNING

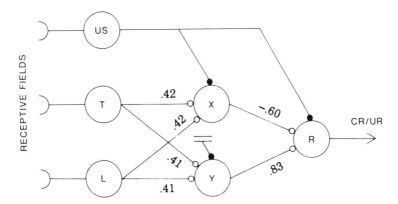

FIG. 3.13.   The terminal weights from the simulations of conditioned inhibition and negative patterning (Kehoe, 1989).

below the value of their thresholds, thus, failing to activate the excitatory X–R and Y–R connections. On L+ trials, the excitatory L–X and L–Y connections operate in an unimpeded fashion to trigger both intermediate units and ultimately the R unit.

In the case of negative patterning, the X unit becomes tuned solely to the compound and in turn acquires an inhibitory connection with the R unit. That is to say, the simulated T+ and L+ trials yield excitatory connections in the first layer, namely T–X, L–X, T–Y, and L–Y. Furthermore, because of X's high threshold, only the summated T–X and L–X connections can trigger X. As a result, the X input to the R unit occurs only on TL− trials, and the X–R connection weight is driven into the negative range ($V_{XR} = -.61$) in contrast to the excitatory Y–R connection ($V_{YR} = .82$). Hence, on compound trials in which both X and Y units are triggered by the combined T and L inputs, the opposing weights of the X–R and Y–R connections largely cancel each other and preclude CRs to the compound. On component trials, the separate T and L inputs are insufficient to trigger X but are high enough to trigger Y. Hence, only the strongly excitatory Y–R connection activates the R unit with the consequent generation of a CR.

The distinctive connection weights produced by conditioned inhibition and negative patterning provided an opportunity to test the model on a within-subjects basis. By conducting conditioned inhibition training and then estimating the appropriate parameters, it was possible to test whether the model could predict the course of transfer to a subsequent negative patterning schedule. Fig. 3.14 shows the results of the behavioral experiment in the left panel (Kehoe, 1989) and those of the simulations in the right panel. The results for three of eight animals are shown. They represent the animal that showed the largest differentiation between B+ and AB− at the termination of the conditioned inhibition schedule ("Fastest S"), the animal that showed the median level of differentiation ("Median S"), and the animal that showed the least differentiation ("Slowest S"). For each animal, curves were fitted to its performance during the conditioned inhibition schedule by conducting an extensive search across combinations of the learning rate parameters for the X, Y, and R units. Other parameters were fixed uniformly for all three animals at the values used to simulate configural learning. The estimated parameter values for each animal were then used to conduct a simulation of transfer to the negative patterning schedule.

A comparison of the actual and simulated responding reveals a moderate correspondence in negative patterning. Both the rabbits and the simulation displayed successful transfer from conditioned inhibition to negative patterning. However, as the reader may have noted, the abscissa for the simulated negative patterning is compressed from two-day to six-day blocks. That is to say, the attainment of negative patterning in the simulations required approximately three times as long as the rabbits did. Thus, the model overpredicted the hysteresis in transfer from conditioned inhibition to negative patterning.

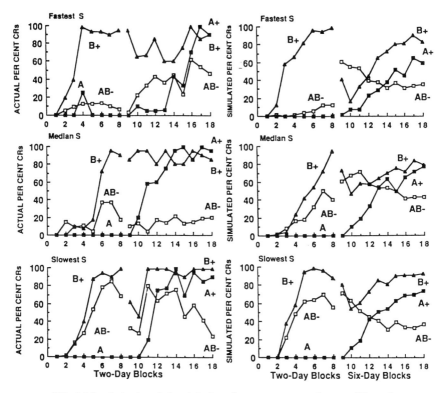

FIG. 3.14. Actual and simulated performance curves for conditioned inhibition followed by negative patterning in three representative subjects (Kehoe, 1989).

In examining the simulated curves, a similar pattern appeared for all three parameter sets, namely as follows: (a) a dip in responding to B+ immediately following the introduction of the negative patterning schedule and a subsequent recovery in the level of responding, (b) an abrupt rise in responding to AB− followed by a gradual decline, and (c) a steady rise in responding to A+. In comparing the simulated curves to those of the rabbits, it becomes clear that there is considerable room for improvement in capturing the individual differences among the subjects. The best agreement between the simulated and actual subjects appeared in the "Slowest S," which showed the initial dip in responding to B+, the gradual decline in responding to AB−, and the steady rise in responding to A+. The next best agreement appeared in the "Fastest S," which showed the dip in responding to B+ and the rise in responding to A+ but showed a slow rise rather than a decline in responding to AB−. In the "Median S," there was very little agreement between the actual and simulated curves.

The foregoing exercise clearly indicates that individualized within-subjects prediction provides a rigorous test for the proposed network model, exposing potential shortcomings that are not apparent in between-subjects assessments (Kehoe, 1986, 1988). These shortcomings can be used to advantage in guiding further development and testing of the model. Rather than relying on individual differences to generate a spread of parameter estimates, a delineation of the parameters can be more readily accomplished by a systematic manipulation of the schedules' independent variables, for example, the proportion of reinforced to unreinforced trials.

CONCLUSIONS

My investigations indicate that multiple adaptive connections wired in series as in a layered network play a critical role in fulfilling functions in associative learning, functions that have remained largely unexplained by conventional theories. My particular model has been kept as simple as possible, in terms of both its structure and its learning rules. Nevertheless the simulations revealed that even a minimal layered network has considerable scope for explanation and prediction. It now remains to be determined how far the insights provided by the present model can be extended to other conditioning preparations, other conditioning phenomena, and more massive networks.

The versatility in learning conferred by a layered network can be viewed in two ways that might otherwise seem contradictory. As can be seen in learning to learn phenomena, a layered network yields some *productivity,* that is, capitalization on past experience in novel situations (Agostino, 1984, p. 86; Reynolds & Flagg, 1977, p. 241). At the same time, a layered network provides *hysteresis,* that is the preservation of past experience even when current demands are in an opposite direction. The rapid reacquisition following extinction is a clear example of the hysteresis inherent in a layered network.

Although mathematical proof is not available, the properties of productivity and hysteresis appear to be general features of any layered network, large or small, as long as it possesses convergent stimulus inputs. Likewise these properties should appear under a huge range of learning rules. There certainly should be no difficulty in using other versions of the delta rule. In particular the delta rule in the present model was chosen to maximize its compatibility with already existing models of conditioning (viz. Rescorla & Wagner, 1972), including "real time" models directed at the moment-by-moment features of CR generation (e.g., Klopf, 1988; Sutton & Barto, 1981, 1987). Furthermore, the network's productivity and hysteresis should not require the delta rule's competitive apparatus. Thus, other learning rules could be substituted for the delta rule (e.g., Mackintosh, 1975; Schmajuk & Moore, 1988; Pearce & Hall, 1980). For example, preliminary investigations in my laboratory using a commercial demonstration package for the Boltzman machine readily reproduced the basic learning to learn effect. For hysteresis to appear, it may only be necessary to assume that the interior connections (e.g., X–R) change more slowly than the connections from the stimulus inputs to the hidden units (e.g., T–X).

ACKNOWLEDGMENTS

Preparation of the manuscript was supported by Grant A28315236 from the Australian Research Council. The author thanks Renee Napier for her assistance in preparation of this manuscript.
Correspondence should be sent to E. James Kehoe, School of Psychology, University of New South Wales, Kensington, NSW 2033, AUSTRALIA.

REFERENCES

Agostino, F. (1984). Chomsky on creativity. *Synthese, 58,* 85–117.
Alkon, D. L., & Farley, J. (Eds.). (1984). *Primary neural substrates of learning and behavioral change.* New York: Cambridge University Press.
Anderson, C. W. (1986). *Learning and problem solving with multilayer connectionist systems.* Unpublished doctoral dissertation, University of Massachusetts, Amherst, MA.
Barto, A. G. (1985). *Learning by statistical cooperation of self-interested neuron-like computing elements.* (COINS Tech. Rep. 85–11). Amherst, MA: University of Massachusetts, Department of Computer and Information Science.
Barto, A. G., Anderson, C. W., & Sutton, R. S. (1982). Synthesis of nonlinear control surfaces by a layered associative search network. *Biological Cybernetics, 43,* 175–185.
Behar, I., & LeBedda, J. M. (1974). Effects of differential pretraining on learning-set formation. *Journal of Comparative and Physiological Psychology, 82,* 277–283.
Bellingham, W. P., Gillette-Bellingham, K., & Kehoe, E. J. (1985). Summation and configuration in patterning schedules with the rat and rabbit. *Animal Learning & Behavior, 13,* 152–164.
Blough, D. S. (1972). Recognition by the pigeon of stimuli varying in two dimensions. *Journal of the Experimental Analysis of Behavior, 18,* 345–367.
Cameron, C. A. (1979). Trials per problem and age as factors in learning set formation of children. *Journal of Experimental Child Psychology, 27,* 410–422.
Cameron, C. A. (1981). Stimulus factors in children's learning set performance. *Journal of Experimental Child Psychology, 31,* 245–255.
Coleman, S. R., & Gormezano, I. (1971). Classical conditioning of the rabbit's (*Oryctolagus cuniculus*) nictitating membrane response under symmetrical CS–US interval shifts. *Journal of Comparative and Physiological Psychology, 77,* 447–455.
Cross, D. V. (1965). Metric properties of multidimensional stimulus generalization. In D. I. Mostofsky (Ed.), *Stimulus generation* (pp. 72–93). Stanford, CA: Stanford University Press.
Desmond, J. E. (1988). *Temporally adaptive conditioned responses: Representation of the stimulus trace in neural-network models.* (COINS Tech. Rep. 88–80). Amherst, MA: University of Massachusetts, Department of Computer and Information Science.
Desmond, J. E., & Moore, J. W. (1988). Adaptive timing in neural networks: The conditioned response. *Biological Cybernetics, 58,* 405–415.
Ellis, H. (1965). *The transfer of learning.* New York: Macmillan.
Gluck, M. A., & Bower, G. H. (1988). Evaluating an adaptive network model of human learning. *Journal of Memory and Language, 27,* 166–195.

Gormezano, I., Kehoe, E. J., & Marshall, B. S. (1983). Twenty years of classical conditioning research with the rabbit. In J. M. Sprague & A. N. Epstein (Eds.), *Progress in psychobiology and physiological psychology* (Vol. 10, pp. 197–275). New York: Academic Press.

Harlow, H. F. (1949). The formation of learning sets. *Psychological Review, 56,* 51–65.

Harlow, H. F. (1959). Learning set and error factor theory. In S. Koch (Ed.), *Psychology: A study of a science* (Vol. 2, pp. 492–537). New York: McGraw-Hill.

Hawkins, R. D., & Kandel, E. R. (1984). Is there a cell-biological alphabet for simple forms of learning? *Psychological Review, 91,* 375–391.

Hilgard, E. R., & Marquis, D. G. (1940). *Conditioning and learning,* New York: Appleton.

Hoehler, F. K., Kirschenbaum, D. S., & Leonard, D. W. (1973). The effects of overtraining and successive extinctions upon nictitating membrane conditioning in the rabbit. *Learning and Motivation, 4,* 91–101.

Holt, P. E., & Kehoe, E. J. (1985). Cross-modal transfer as a function of similarities between training tasks in classical conditioning of the rabbit. *Animal Learning & Behavior, 13,* 51–59.

Kehoe, E. J. (1986). A layered network model for learning-to-learn and configuration in classical conditioning. *Proceedings of the Eighth Annual Conference of the Cognitive Science Society* (pp. 154–175). Hillsdale, NJ: Lawrence Erlbaum Associates.

Kehoe, E. J. (1988). A layered network model of associative learning: Learning to learn and configuration. *Psychological Review, 95,* 411–433.

Kehoe, E. J. (1989). Connectionist models of conditioning: A tutorial. *Journal of the Experimental Analysis of Behavior, 52,* 427–440.

Kehoe, E. J., & Gormezano, I. (1980). Configuration and combination laws in conditioning with compound stimuli. *Psychological Bulletin, 87,* 351–378.

Kehoe, E. J., & Graham, P. (1988). Summation and configuration in negative patterning of the rabbit's conditioned nictitating membrane response. *Journal of Experimental Psychology: Animal Behavior Processes, 14,* 320–333.

Kehoe, E. J., Graham-Clarke, P., & Schreurs, B. G. (1989). Temporal patterns of the rabbit's nictitating membrane response to compound and component stimuli under mixed CS–US intervals. *Behavioral Neuroscience, 103,* 283–295.

Kehoe, E. J., & Holt, P. E. (1984). Transfer across CS–US intervals and sensory modalities in classical conditioning of the rabbit. *Animal Learning & Behavior, 12,* 122–128.

Kehoe, E. J., Morrow, L. D., & Holt, P. E. (1984). General transfer across sensory modalities survives reductions in the original conditioned reflex in the rabbit. *Animal Learning & Behavior, 12,* 129–136.

Kehoe, E. J., & Napier, R. M. (in press). Temporal specificity in cross-modal transfer of the rabbit nictitating membrane response. *Journal of Experimental Psychology: Animal Behavior Processes.*

Kimmel, H. D., & Burns, R. A. (1975). Adaptational aspects of conditioning. In W. K. Estes. (Ed.), *Handbook of learning and cognitive processes.* (Vol. 2., pp. 99–142). Hillsdale, NJ: Lawrence Erlbaum Associates.

Klopf, A. H. (1988). A neuronal model of classical conditioning. *Psychobiology, 16,* 85–125.

Levine, M. (1959). A model of hypothesis behavior in discrimination learning sets. *Psychological Review, 66,* 353–366.

Mackintosh, N. J. (1975). A theory of attention: Variation in the associability of stimuli with reinforcement. *Psychological Review, 82,* 276–298.

Mackintosh, N. J. (1977). Stimulus control: attentional factors. In W. K. Honig & J. E. R. Staddon (Eds.), *Handbook of operant behavior* (pp. 481–513). Englewood Cliffs, NJ: Prentice-Hall.

Medin, D. L. (1972). Role of reinforcement in discrimination learning sets in monkeys. *Psychological Bulletin, 77,* 305–318.

Millenson, J. R., Kehoe, E. J., & Gormezano, I. (1977). Classical conditioning of the rabbit's nictitating membrane response under fixed and mixed CS–US intervals. *Learning and Motivation, 8,* 351–366.

Minsky, M. L., & Papert, S. (1969). *Perceptrons: An introduction to computational geometry.* Cambridge, MA: MIT Press.

Moore, J. W. (1972). Stimulus control: Studies of auditory generalization in rabbits. In A. H. Black & W. F. Prokasy (Eds.), *Classical conditioning II: Current research and theory.* New York: Appleton-Century-Crofts.

Pavlov, I. P. (1927). *Conditioned reflexes: An investigation of the physiological activity of the cerebral cortex* (G. V. Anrep, trans.). London: Oxford University Press.

Pearce, J. M., & Hall, G. (1980). A model for Pavlovian conditioning: Variations in the effectiveness of conditioned but not of unconditioned stimuli. *Psychological Review, 7,* 532–552.

Rescorla, R. A., & Wagner, A. R. (1972). A theory of Pavlovian conditioning: Variations in the effectiveness of reinforcement and nonreinforcement. In A. H. Black & W. F. Prokasy (Eds.), *Classical conditioning II* (pp. 64–99). New York: Appleton-Century-Crofts.

Reynolds, A. G., & Flagg, P. W. (1977). *Cognitive psychology.* Cambridge, MA: Winthrop.

Rodgers, J. P., & Thomas, D. R. (1982). Task specificity in nonspecific transfer and in extradimensional stimulus generation in pigeons. *Journal of Comparative and Physiological Psychology, 73,* 314–319.

Ross, R. T., & Scavio, M. J., Jr. (1983). Perseveration of associative strength in rabbit nictitating membrane response conditioning following ISI shifts. *Animal Learning & Behavior, 11,* 435–438.

Rumelhart, D. E., Hinton, G. E., & Williams, R. J. (1986). Learning internal representations by error propagation. In D. E. Rumelhart & J. L. McClelland (Eds.), *Parallel distributed processing: Explorations in the microstructure of cognition: Volume 1. Foundations* (pp. 318–362). Cambridge, MA: MIT Press.

Rumelhart, D. E., & McClelland, J. L. (Eds.). (1986). *Parallel distributed processing. Volume 1. Foundations.* Cambridge, MA: MIT Press.

Scavio, M. J., Jr., & Thompson, R. F. (1979). Extinction and reacquisition performance alternations of the conditioned nictitating membrane response. *Bulletin of the Psychonomic Society, 13,* 57–60.

Schmajuk, N. A., & Moore, J. W. (1988). The hippocampus and the classically conditioned nictitating membrane response: A real-time attentional-associative model. *Psychobiology, 16,* 20–35.

Schmaltz, L. W., & Theios, J. (1972). Acquisition and extinction of the classically conditioned response in hoppocampectomized rabbits (*Oryctolagus cuniculus*). *Journal of Comparative and Physiological Psychology, 79,* 328–333.

Schreurs, B. G., & Kehoe, E. J. (1987). Cross-modal transfer as a function of initial training level in classical conditioning with the rabbit. *Animal Learning & Behavior, 15,* 47–54.

Seraganian, P. (1979). Extradimensional transfer in the easy-to-hard effect. *Learning and Motivation, 10,* 39–57.

Smith, M., & Gormezano, I. (1965). Effects of alternating classical conditioning and extinction sessions on the conditioned nictitating membrane response of the rabbit. *Psychonomic Science, 3,* 91–92.

Spence, K. W. (1936). The nature of discrimination learning in animals. *Psychological Review, 43,* 427–449.

Sutton, R. S., & Barto, A. G. (1981). Toward a modern theory of adaptive networks: Expectation and prediction. *Psychological Review, 88,* 135–171.

Sutton, R. S., & Barto, A. G. (1987). A temporal difference model of classical conditioning. *Proceedings of the Ninth Conference of the Cognitive Science Society* (pp. 355–378) Hillsdale, NJ: Lawrence Erlbaum Associates.

Tennant, W. A., & Bitterman, M. E. (1975). Extradimensional transfer in the discriminative learning of goldfish. *Animal Learning & Behavior, 3,* 201–204.

Thomas, D. R. (1970). Stimulus selection, attention, and related matters. In J. H. Reynierse (Ed.), *Current issues in animal learning* (pp. 311–356). Lincoln: University of Nebraska Press.

Thomas, D. R., Miller, J. T., & Svinicki, J. G. (1971). Nonspecific transfer effects of discrimination training in the rat. *Journal of Comparative and Physiological Psychology, 74,* 96–101.

Warren, J. M. (1965). Primate learning in comparative perspective. In A. M. Schrier, H. F. Harlow, & F. Stollnitz (Eds.), *Behavior of nonhuman primates* (Vol. 1, pp. 249–275). New York: Academic Press.

Westbrook, R. F., & Homewood, J. (1982). The effects of a flavour toxicosis pairing upon long-delay, flavour aversion learning. *Quarterly Journal of Experimental Psychology, 34B,* 139–149.

Woodbury, C. B. (1943). The learning of stimulus patterns by dogs. *Journal of Comparative Psychology, 35,* 29–40.

Zipser, D. (1986). A model of hippocampal learning during classical conditioning. *Behavioral Neuroscience, 100,* 764–776.

4 Behavioral Geodesics

Peter R. Killeen
Arizona State University

In this chapter, I recast some of the phenomena of conditioning into the language of dynamic systems. In that mapping, reinforcers and UCSs are cast as fixed-points, or attractors, thus respecting the defining attribute of such stimuli—that they attract (or in the case of aversive stimuli, repel) behavior. Such goal direction occurs in a landscape dimpled with the potential wells of appetitive stimuli and the potential hills of aversive stimuli. Conditioning involves moving neutral stimuli (including those issuing from the animal's own behavior) from ground level close to the tops or bottoms of these features. Behavior is viewed as the trajectory of a marker as it rolls through this landscape, avoiding hills, veering toward wells, and occasionally being captured by them. The relief of the landscape is determined by the organism's motivation and may be affected by emotional manipulations, with arousal steepening the features (and forcing behavior to the nearest attractor), and relaxation leveling the features (and freeing behavior to meander). Asymptotic conditioning generates geodesics: paths of minimum length that move away from hills and into wells. Because there is no more direct path than a geodesic, further conditioning is impossible, unless the elevation of the relevant well/hill is affected by manipulations of the reinforcer. This dynamic metaphor accommodates the notions of associative strength, surprise minimization, species-specific defense, and appetitive behaviors; it treats various types of conditioning from a unified perspective. The dynamic systems approach to conditioning is consistent with neural models of attention and categorization and may provide a common language for behavioral and cognitive phenomena.

S. S. Stevens introduced his audience to the *Handbook of experimental psychology* (Stevens, 1951) by discussing the notion of invariance and its relevance to psychology. By invariance, he meant observations, categories, and laws that did not change as the context in which they occur varied:

> The scientist is usually looking for invariance whether he knows it or not. When-ever he discovers a functional relation between two variables his next question follows naturally: under what conditions does it hold? . . . under what transforma-tions is the relation invariant? The quest for invariant relations is essentially the aspiration toward generality. . . . (p. 20)

Stevens was strongly influenced by Mach, as this passage shows: Mach viewed science as efficient codification of data. Invariant relations are more efficient than variant ones because fewer parameters must be used to code for specificity of context. Such a spirit of parsimony underlies Stevens development of the theory of scale types. When we map observations into the number sys-tem—when we measure things—the resulting numerical "model" may permit manipulations or predictions that do not make sense in terms of the original observations. The full-blown system of real numbers is stronger than necessary for many modeling jobs. A model language must preserve the invariances that existed in the original observational language but should not assert invariances that do not exist in the data. Stevens' theory of scale types categorized the various levels of invariances at which mathematics may be used in the process of model-ing.

In this article, I shall explore the generality of the concept *attractor* and attempt to make a case for it as a fundamental invariant for psychology. In using this model system, we must respect the different strengths of data in the various domains of psychology. In some areas, the full range of "ratio scale" predictions from nonlinear dynamical analysis is appropriate; in others, which we shall start with, only ordinal relations may be reflected in the data. We may hope to move from the weaker to the richer scale types as the theory is developed.

PHYSICAL ATTRACTION: DYNAMICS

Dynamics tell us how things change over time as a function of applied forces; its standard model language involves differential equations. Consider the following fundamental equation of classical mechanics, force (F) equals mass (m) times acceleration (the second derivative of position, x):

$$F = m\frac{d^2x}{dt^2} \tag{1}$$

If the force is generated by a spring and is proportional (k) to the distance the spring has been stretched from the origin, the following is true:

$$F = -kx. \tag{2}$$

Setting these equations equal to one another generates the equation of motion for the particle. The potential energy function for this system is defined as that function whose negative derivative equals Equation 2:

$$U = \frac{1}{2}kx^2 \tag{3}$$

This is a parabola, concave up and centered on the origin (see Fig. 4.1A). It is unique up to an additive constant (i.e., potential energy constitutes an interval scale). The force acting on a particle along the x–axis is given by Equation 2. Obviously there is no force acting on the particle when $x = 0$. A particle at rest at $x = 0$ will stay there: When velocity is zero, $x = 0$ is a *steady state* of the system. A particle released anywhere else along the x–axis will be forced to $x = 0$, around which it will oscillate. Dissipative forces such as friction are represented by adding to the equation of motion the product of the coefficient of friction and the velocity of the particle ($k'dx/dt$). If $k' > 0$, the particle will eventually come to rest at $x = 0$. That position is therefore a *stable* steady state, or *fixed point* of the system. It is an *attractor*.

Now consider a system (from Haken, 1977) whose force function is as follows:

$$F = -kx - k''x^3 \tag{4}$$

The potential function for this system follows:

$$U = \frac{1}{2}kx^2 + \frac{1}{4}k''x^4 \tag{5}$$

When $k = 0$, and $k'' = 1$, it takes the form shown in Fig. 4.1B, for our purposes not very different than the parabola described by Equation 3. But when k goes negative, the picture changes radically: Figure 4.1C shows the potential surface for $k = -20$ and $k'' = 1$. There is no force exerted on the particle when the derivative of Equation 5 is zero, which occurs at three locations: $x = 0$ and $x =$

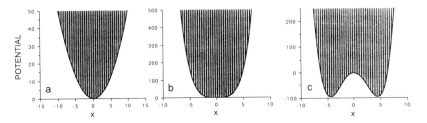

FIG. 4.1. Potential surfaces corresponding to: (a) Equation 3, with $k = 1$; (b) Equation 5, with $k = 0$ and $k'' = 1$; (c) Equation 5, with $k = -20$ and $k'' = 1$.

$\pm\sqrt{|k|/k''}$, which are the steady states of the system. However, we see from the figure that these steady states are not all the same. At $x = 0$, minor changes in the position of the particle will accelerate it away from the origin. At the other locations, minor changes in position of the particle will engender restoring forces that will tend to return it to its steady state. The point $x = 0$ is an *unstable equilibrium*, whereas the other steady states are stable equilibria. Values of $x > 0$ are in the *basin of attraction* of the fixed point $x = \sqrt{20}$; this means that the particles will oscillate around that attractor and, if there is any friction, will come to rest there. Values of $x < 0$ are in the basin of attraction of the fixed point $x = -\sqrt{20}$.

Representation

The abscissae in these figures represent the positions of a particle, but the analysis remains appropriate when the position of the particle is itself an indicator of some other variable. We may take Fig. 4.1A as the potential function for the core temperature of a homeotherm such as a horse. Deviations from a setpoint temperature, due, say, to running, engage mechanisms that will force the temperature back to its steady state. In Fig. 4.1C, where $k \ll 0$, we may take the abscissae as the speed of the horse. The figure then shows a stable state around a speed corresponding to one gait and another stable state around a speed corresponding to another gait. The unstable state at the origin corresponds to a speed where both gaits are equally attractive—a Buridan's ass in motion. Any spur, however minuscule, will speed it to the right; any impediment, however trivial, will slow it to the left. Once settled into one of the gaits, a considerable amount of energy will be required to carry it up out of the potential wells centered at $\pm\sqrt{20}$. The values of surface parameters such as k may be affected by training or by motivational and emotional manipulations. Early imprinting may make an improbable figure such as Konrad Lorenz an object of lifelong attraction to geese, whereas changes in hormonal levels may convert a strong attractor such as found at $x = 0$ in Fig. 4.1B into a very unstable state, as in Fig. 4.1C, within the course of seconds or minutes.

BEHAVIORAL ATTRACTION

What attractors might we look for in behavior? In his discussion of invariants, Stevens cited the work of Beach (1951) and others on instinctive behavior in herring gulls and noted the invariance of their approach to "eggs" for a large class of objects that are taken to be eggs by gulls. Only a few special features of artificial eggs (e.g., sharp contours) will give them away. Tinbergen (1960) drew another picture of instinctive maternal behavior in birds. Once a tern sees an egg outside the nest, the following occurs:

The bird walks over from the nest until it is almost but not entirely above the egg. It will then sit down, at the same time making the normal egg-shifting movement: that is, reaching with the bill beyond the egg, and shovelling it under the breast, thereby moving the egg a little distance towards the nest. It remains sitting on this single egg only a short time, and walks back to the nest as soon as this catches its eye. Back on the nest, the sight of the exposed egg will again stimulate the bird to go over towards it and shovel it under its breast as soon as it can reach it. But again the bird will see the nest and walk back towards it. Thus it is torn back and forth between nest and egg. When walking towards the single egg, it leaves the accustomed nest-site only reluctantly, and goes only just as far as is absolutely necessary, . . . it employs the normal shifting reaction, and its attachment to the nest-site causes it to do this as soon as it can reach the egg. In coming back to the nest, there is nothing compelling it to draw the egg towards it. In this way, the unequal competition between nest-plus-two-eggs, and one-egg-outside-the-nest, combined with egg-shifting movements, results, after some time, in the egg being rolled back into the nest. (p. 142)

Thus, a single instinctive pattern—approach eggs and shift them underbody to brood—is creatively extended to solve the loose egg problem. Picture the hen at any point on the x-axis of Fig. 4.1A, with the only visible eggs at the origin. It is forced to the eggs and places them under its center of gravity. Then it sees the nest it left, to which it is attracted and returns. The cycle repeats until the loose egg has been returned to the nest. Tinbergen (1960) wrote:

In watching such clumsy attempts one is struck by the restrictiveness of instinctive behavior. It would be so easy to roll the egg back with an extended wing, or by using one of the webbed feet! Yet it does not "occur" to the gull to try it; it is rigidly confined to one type of action. The executive organs are there, but the central nervous mechanisms to use them in these circumstances are absent. . . this remarkable restrictedness [is] a character of all instinctive behavior" (p. 140)

As Tinbergen suggested, examples of simple reflexes, concatenated to generate adaptive behavior, are ubiquitous in lower organisms. The *Sphex* wasp moves captured prey to the mouth of the burrow containing her eggs, enters the burrow (to check the eggs?), and then returns to drag the prey into the burrow for her offspring (Fabre, 1915). Apparently the wasp has never learned to go straight in with the prey but only to back in with it when it is available contiguous to the burrow. If the prey is moved a few inches, the wasp repeats the inspection routine. On one occasion, the experiment was replicated 40 times with the same wasp, each time with the same results—39 redundant checks of the burrow (reported in Wooldridge, 1968). In both of these examples, the animals oscillate between two attractors: The tern between two sites of eggs; the Sphex, between the burrow when nearby with a cricket, and the cricket when exiting from its burrow.

Hofstadter (1985) cited such behavior as the epitome of thoughtlessness (and the eponym of it: "I propose to call the quality here portrayed *sphexishness,* . . . and then I propose that consciousness is the possession of *antisphexishness* to the highest possible degree" (p. 529). Where does such "mindless" behavior leave off and "intelligent" behavior begin? Weiss (1941; reprinted in Gallistel, 1980) concluded that, for organisms at and below the level of amphibians, basic response topographies are modified only by selective facilitation or inhibition of classes of existing motor patterns but that there is a "tremendous efflorescence of the ability to 'invent' coordination patterns on the way from rat to man" (p. 271; also see Yates, 1984). Of course there will be no one point at which "antisphexishness" emerges. Romanes (1882) extended Darwin's arguments for the continuity of mind by documenting numerous instances of animal behavior that could be explained in terms of complex intellectual procedures. Later investigators preferred a more parsimonious explanation of the continuity of behavior in terms of the concatenation of simple reflexes in both man and beast. Even rats can on occasion manifest behavior that appears quite intelligent, whereas some waspish *Homo sapiens* will return to their bungalow multiple times to ensure that it was left in order. I argue that the ability of humans to be more consistently thoughtful than wasps is due to their ability to control the (reflexive) forces that draw them to the dominant attractors in their environment (Killeen, 1989). This ability is based on their unparalleled knack for modifying the local character of their potential landscape through mentation, which brings other attractors not immediately present in their environment to bear on their behavior, and their ability to modulate the emotions that determine the relief of the landscape (Levine, Leven, & Prueitt, chapter 9 in this volume).

A Mathematician's Apology: Metaphor or Model?

In what sense should we treat the behaviors exemplified previously as responses to attractors? Are we not guilty of being too literal, of making some sort of nominal fallacy in equating the physical attraction of particles with the behavioral attraction of organisms? The animals are hardly simple particles attracted toward points according to equations such as (2) and (4); they are not forced toward their eggs by stretched springs. However, we need not hypothesize about the nature of the force drawing a mother to her brood; it is necessary only to develop a plausible model that will capture the phenomenon and perhaps make a few novel predictions about it. What after all is the nature of our understanding of the force binding two atoms together that justifies our use of the harmonic oscillator as a model of their behavior? Our knowledge of the force is little more than our knowledge of the dynamic behavior of a particle in its grasp—whether the particle is an atom, a pendulum, or a planet. At the level of gross physical movements, it has long been known that factors such as momentum and "centrifugal swing" affect the choice behavior of rats in mazes (Ballachey & Buel, 1934). The motion of rats through runways may be captured by modeling them as uniformly accelerated particles, with the recovered parameters of acceleration and point of deceleration providing more concise and efficient parameters than the speed profiles previously used (Killeen & Amsel, 1987). There is no reason that more refined and covert actions cannot also be treated in a physicalistic manner, and that is what is attempted here. Although the discussion starts metaphorically, it becomes a model as it ascends the scale from ordinal to interval representation.

The treatment of complex behavior as a trajectory through a state space makes contact with current neural modeling at several points. Boltzmann machines (Hinton & Sejnowski, 1986) and Harmony theory (Smolensky, 1986) both posit a potential space in which the categorization of stimuli occurs in such a way as to minimize the deviations between the input and categorical prototypes. The identification process involves adding noise to the position of the object in state space and reducing the noise as the quality of the match improves. This "simulated annealing" (Kirkpatrick, Gelatt, & Vecchi, 1983) is isomorphic with treatment of the potential landscape as having continually variable relief, with aroused organisms existing in heavily contoured landscapes, strongly attracted to the steepest local potential well, and with calm organisms existing in smooth landscapes where the multiplicity of attractors bear on them with only mildly differentiated forces. Adaptive Resonance Theory (e.g., Grossberg, Levine, & Schmajuk, chapter 2 in this volume) posits a mismatch arousal, which potentiates the strongest potential match on a field of candidate prototypes. If the stimulus representation can "approach" this attractor adequately closely (i.e., if its pattern of synapse activity matches that of the candidate within some error given by a "vigilance" parameter), the arousal is quenched and an identification effected. If the match is not within tolerance, that attractor candidate is reset to remain inactive for a while, giving the field over to the next candidate. Organisms under high drive have lax criteria for a match, whereas less aroused organisms sample many candidate attractors before settling, just as a point in state space may roll through many shallow attractors before settling in any particular potential well. It is possible that the executive function that modulates arousal/relief may be mediated by the frontal lobes (Levine, Leven, & Pruett, Chapter 9 in this volume).

The dynamic analysis sketched here thus resonates with descriptions of behavior both on the physical level, and with theories of behavior deriving from neural models. In the following paragraphs I develop the former set of relationships, saving the latter for a future publication.

UNCONDITIONED ATTRACTORS

When we step on a tack there is an immediate withdrawal of the wounded foot and a compensatory increase in muscle tonus in the opposite leg. Such reflexes were originally thought to be a "reflection" of the stimulating energy through the spinal cord to the effectors. This cannot be the case for most reflexes, as the violence of a sneeze is out of proportion to the mote of dust that elicited it. Stimuli must be viewed as triggers for the responses. Among the many reflexes that have been cataloged are salivation and other gastrointestinal secretions to dry food, withdrawal from shock, blocking of the EEG alpha rhythm to light, the pupillary reflex to light, vasomotor reactions to shock, the knee jerk to a patellar blow, and so on (Kimble, 1961).

Many of these are relatively fixed in that the effective stimuli are limited in number, and that number cannot be increased. However, a few of the reflexes— in particular movement away from noxious stimuli or toward pleasant stimuli— are subject to extensive elaboration. This is important for those who see the reflex as the fundamental unit of behavior, because the short list of the basic reflexes is uncharacteristic of the majority of behavior of higher organisms. The process of elaboration brought about by associating a response with a stimulus is called conditioning, because the responses engendered by that procedure become "conditional" upon the presentation of the appropriate stimuli.

CONDITIONED ATTRACTORS

The literature on conditioning paints a large and complex picture (see, e.g., Mackintosh, 1974, 1983; Honig & Staddon, 1977), one whose fundamental images are sometimes lost in the welter of data now available. There are said to be two major types of conditioning, classical and instrumental. Classical conditioning is the pairing of one stimulus—the (to be) conditioned stimulus, CS— with another, biologically significant unconditioned stimulus (the US), with the effect that some of the responses normally emitted to the second stimulus are also emitted in response to the first. Instrumental conditioning is the pairing of a response with a reinforcer (i.e., a US), causing an increase in the frequency of similar responses.

As noted previously, one of the most potent responses elicited by a US is approach or withdrawal (Schneirla, 1959, held that "*approach* and *withdrawal* are the *only* empirical, objective terms applicable to *all* motivated behavior in *all* animals" p. 1.) This fundamental effect is not always obvious in experimental paradigms where animals are kept harnessed or confined to small enclosures (Zener, 1937). The conditioning of approach responses to a CS became a *cause célèbre* when Brown and Jenkins (1968) found that the prototypical operant response of key pecking was as easily established by classical conditioning as it was by operant shaping. This conditioned approach has been christened sign-tracking (Hearst & Jenkins, 1974; Locurto, Terrace, & Gibbon, 1981), and it has been shown to occur even when it interferes with the receipt of reward: Peden, Browne, and Hearst (1977) found that pigeons would run to the south end of a long box to peck at a conditioned stimulus, although the food that it signaled would be available at the north end for only a few seconds. The trip south made it impossible to get to the food in time; nonetheless signtracking continued until the inability to get food ruined the correlation between the signal and food. Of course, once the animals stopped approaching the sign, the correlation between stimulus and food was strengthened, and then signtracking reemerged. Many other instances of the persistence of elicited approach behavior, despite contingencies that should discourage it, are available in the literature. It is impossible for many lower organisms to retreat from signs of reinforcement, and such behavior in higher organisms depends on the motivational level of the subject, with a highly aroused subject finding retreat difficult or impossible (Birch, 1945).

Normally signs for USs or reinforcers are close to those stimuli, and approach thus strengthens conditioning rather than weakening it. Even the molecular acts comprising instrumental behavior, behavior that typically moves the animal closer to the unconditioned attractor, serve as catalysts to incite additional instances of that behavior. Hanson and Killeen (1981) and Keller (1980) independently found that the responses occurring during "Fixed Interval" reinforcement schedules were best modeled as autocatalytic functions. The same autocatalysis underlies association of external stimuli and attractors: As an animal pays more attention to a CS, that stimulus is better able to be conditioned to the US. In recognition of this fact, Frey and Sears (1978) modified Rescorla and Wagner's (1972) model of conditioning to include a positive feedback effect of conditioning on the attention parameter. (Such loops are potentially unstable; Frey and Sears included a threshold to moderate the feedback.) However, because of this autocatalytic aspect of conditioning, small differences in attention at the beginning of conditioning may easily trap the animals into responding to different aspects of the stimulus. Just such differences in the idiosyncrasies of conditioning have been demonstrated by Lashley (1942), Reynolds (1961), and others. Theoretical attempts to cope with such variability have employed constructs such as "pure stimulus acts," "behavioral oscillation," "receptor-exposure acts," and models such as stimulus sampling theory (Terrace, 1966). But those approaches succeeded only in labeling the phenomenon. It is this sensitivity to initial conditions, mediated by attention and its vagaries, that reduces our precisely administered independent variables to the probabilistic spread of actions from which we must marshal our dependent variables.

INSTRUMENTAL BEHAVIOR AS TAXIS

Let us proceed by recognizing that most of an animal's instrumental behavior consists of approach to signs of reinforcement (or retreat from signs of punishment). This was also a fundamental assumption of Deutsch (1960) and of Bindra (1974). Some of the apparent exceptions to this generalization are mitigated by the following important qualification: The signs of reinforcement must be from the perspective of an animal's own posture and behavior. A lever viewed from the left part of the chamber is different than one viewed from the right part of the chamber. Because it is not *very* different, there will be a strong tendency for generalization among the various perspectives of the lever. If reinforcement is only given when a paw is on the lever, the animal will move to the lever and eventually place its paw to the lever, because that is the only way it can recreate the paw-on-the-lever stimulus. It will be attracted to any position that leads to this posture, and thus is its behavior "shaped" to press the lever. With the recognition that the animal's own behavior is part of the sign, signtracking then becomes a viable candidate for the basic law of instrumental learning.[1] Types of actions not easily associable with approach/withdrawal, or parts of the anatomy not easily incorporated as parts of a sign, will not be instrumentally trainable. The important distinction then becomes not the one between instrumental and classical conditioning paradigms but between appetitive and consummatory responses (Craig, 1918), with "instrumental" conditioning being the (classical) conditioning of appetitive approach (or withdrawal) behavior, and consummatory responses being relatively fixed reflexes or "fixed action patterns" that are elicited when the organism is in close contiguity with an attractor.

This reconstruction permits us to treat appetitive behavior as movement toward an attractor. But what are the axes: In what space do we study that movement? If we mark the important effectors of an organism—the beak and wings of pigeons, the snout and paws of rats, the hands of primates, and so forth, then clusters of actions that we typically categorize as "responses" would give rise to dense tracings in certain vicinities—paws near levers, beaks near hoppers, hands near switches. Devices are commercially available to construct such maps (Eldridge & Pear, 1987). Of course animals orient to specific objects in the environment, not to arbitrary spatial coordinates. However, unless the objects are moved, the descriptions are isomorphic, as we may always center the origin of our coordinates on the reinforcer or sign of it. Other behaviors such as grooming, scratching, and sneezing would not be recognizable in these coordinate axes, because they are directed at a movable part of the environment, the organism

---

[1]Mackintosh (1983) reported studies where external stimuli are unavailable to guide behavior. "Learning is relatively difficult under these circumstances, a finding consistent with the assumption that learning to approach such stimuli is the normal way for the rat to solve the problem, but it is by no means impossible" (p. 40). Our assumption that the effective stimulus is compound and includes the rats position and posture will handle many, though perhaps not all, of those data. That assumption is further reinforced by a study by Garrud, Goodall, & Mackintosh (1981) cited by Mackintosh, showing that "classical conditioning suffers if the reinforcer is better predicted by the subject's own responses than by the external CS" (Mackintosh, 1983, p. 93). Although he allowed the classical conditioning of rats' approach responses to the lever, he felt that the present theory "will not easily explain how the instrumentally trained rat ends up lever-pressing with economy and efficiency" (1983, p. 77). But they will not always end up that way: "Unless the lever has the thick, stubby, rounded front end found in most commercial levers, rats frequently will bite, shake, push under with their nose, and gnaw it rather than press it" (Timberlake & Lucas, 1989, p. 240).

itself. To represent such responses in this schema would require a coordinate transformation to center the origin on the animal. Such transformations have been described by Pellionisz and Llinas (1979). O'Keefe and Nadel (1978) and Foreman and Stevens (1987) suggested that egocentric representation is the rule in some parts of the nervous system (e.g., the superior colliculus) and allocentric representation the rule in other part (e.g., the hypothalamus). The laws governing intrinsically organism-centered responses may differ, however, as they are often difficult or impossible to condition (Konorski, 1967; Morgan & Nicholas, 1979; Shettleworth, 1975, 1981; Turner & Solomon, 1962). For instance, Pearce, Colwill, and Hall (1978) could maintain rats' scratching of themselves as an instrumental response only when they fitted the rats with a collar that itself elicited scratching. It is primarily when the effectors of the animal are part of an external frame of reference that contains other approachable signs of reinforcement that instrumental conditioning proceeds rapidly. This may in part be due to the overshadowing of egocentric responses, because they are generally available in all contexts and, therefore, not differentially associated with the context of reinforcement.

HIERARCHIES OF RESONANCE

There are many levels of analysis in the brain, each with its own attractors and in resonance with levels above and below it; therefore, attention to one minor stimulus may lead to a strong resonance that can retune the whole system. A consummatory well for eating may be displaced by one for sex, or one for escape. Consider the picture of a landscape dimpled with many large basins, corresponding to congeries of appetitive behaviors such as foraging, mating, and so forth (cf. Fig. 4.2). Within each basin, we find deeper basins corresponding to more specific acts, such as lying in wait, stalking, chasing, and so on. At the lowest levels are consummatory acts such as pouncing, grabbing, and biting. The larger, shallower potential basins correspond to higher neural fields whose activation then potentiates more specific discriminations and responses in the fields below them. Movement into any of the basins may be elicited by stimuli at lower levels—releasers or unconditioned stimuli (USs)—stimuli whose efficacy is primed by motivational states corresponding to activation of the higher levels (Gould and Marler, 1984).

> Egg rolling, for instance, is a behavioral unit which appears about a week before incubation begins and lasts until about a week after hatching. The drive or "motivation" to respond to the sign stimulus for eggs in this way appears to be absent at other times. It is easy to think of behavioral units of this sort as subroutines whose availability is controlled endogenously by day-length, hormone level, social signals, or what have you. Hence, the long-term responsiveness to particular cues is

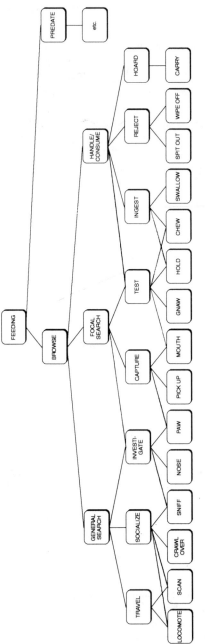

FIG. 4.2. A hierarchy of appetitive and consummatory behavior in the rat (redrawn from Timberlake & Lucas, 1989, with permission of authors). The descent to specific action patterns is also a descent into lower potential wells, with variants of the approach behaviors that lead most readily to the lowest modes being the ones that become conditioned. Similar elaboration of the predation system and reciprocal inhibitory lines between the browsing and predation systems are not redrawn here.

shifted in a predictable and adaptive way as an animal's needs change on the basis of innately recognized "priming stimuli." (Gould & Marler, 1984, pp. 51–52).

Activation of an animal's defense system has been shown to bias both perceptions (Bolles & Fanselow, 1980) and response tendencies (Masterson & Crawford, 1982).

Once a motivational field has become activated, specific movements become more predictable: Teitlebaum, Schallert, and Whishaw (1983) found that "when we break down the systems involved in motivated, operant behavior . . . in every case we reveal reflexive behavioral subcomponents. Apparent spontaneity becomes when analysed, mere reflex action" (p. 60). Loeb (1973), after recognizing the mediating role of goal images, went further:

> Our conception of the existence of "free will" in human beings rests on the fact that our knowledge is often not sufficiently complete to account for the orienting forces . . . due to the sheer endless number of possible combinations and mutual inhibitions of the orienting effect of individual memory images. (p. 172)

PERCEPTUAL-BEHAVIORAL SPACES: THE *UMWELT*

Objects require more than four dimensions to describe them completely—not only are they located in space and time, they also have colors and odors and shapes associated with them, and these features may be even more critical to an animal than the stimulus, arbitrary spatiotemporal coordinates (Rescorla & Furrow, 1977). Were all of these potential dimensions to bear equally on a conditioning procedure, we could embed our data in a dynamic representation only at the price of a very thinly populated data space of inordinate dimensionality (Ballard, 1986). However, in any one experiment, not all of these features are varied. More importantly, there are privileged routes through this space. Only one or a few dimensions may come to bear on an organism's performance, insofar as its attention is brought to bear on that dimension. For instance, Yaginuma and Iwai (1986) showed that, during the initial stage of learning a discrimination, monkeys do not attend to cues if there is even a small separation between the cue and its response site. von Uexkull (1909) referred to this functional space of an organism as its *Umwelt*. I shall defer treatment of the perceptual paths through this *Umwelt* to another chapter (Killeen, 1990) and focus here on behavioral paths.

RULES OF ASSOCIATION

What does the dynamic metaphor permit us to say about the course of associations? Our notion has been that motivation and conditioning warp the animal's potential surface, much as changing the value of k warped it in Fig. 4.1. Conditioning makes a novel stimulus(/response) an attractor, because it permits approach to a major unconditioned attractor—consummatory behavior of some sort. How are the dimensions selected, and how do they control behavior? We know that spatial, temporal, and perceptual contiguities are important and that they interact in lawful ways (e.g., Blough, 1972; Wilkie, 1989). Our current representation permits us to treat the concept of contiguity in a novel and continuous way—as a geodesic path through the organisms's *Umwelt*.

A geodesic is the shortest path between two points along a surface: On a plane, it is a straight line; on a sphere, it is a great circle. Many physical laws may be subsumed under a few principles of least action involving geodesics. Fermat's principle states that light follows the path that minimizes the time of travel—its geodesic will depend on the speed of light in the materials through which it travels. Hamilton's principle states that a geodesic is the route through a potential field that minimizes the difference between the potential and kinetic energy integrated over time (Feynman, Leighton, & Sands, 1963, I.26). Familiar laws of refraction, mechanics, and electrodynamics may be derived from these optimality principles, although the actual determination of the ideal path is often a nontrivial problem in the calculus of variations (Boas, 1966). In our case, the problem is compounded by the uncertainty concerning which features of which stimuli will be attended to and how they are perceived by the organism. Preliminary work in identifying such features has been accomplished by Thinus-Blanc and associates (1987). Retrospective evaluation of the dimensions on which similarity is based (Shepard & Arabie, 1979) may give us additional cues to the nature of the dimensions, if not their order of evaluation.

One of the most important dimensions in the formation of associations is time. An arbitrary stimulus may be readily associated with a US, if they are temporally contiguous.[2] It is as though the conditioning process created a gully that would channel behavior toward a deep potential well of consummatory behavior controlled by the US. In creating such a channel, the course that behavior takes depends on both the field around the potential well and on the contour of the channel itself. If one wishes to move behavior quickly, what is the best contour of the channel? Clearly, it is neither a horizontal reach followed by a sudden drop nor a sudden drop followed by a horizontal reach. To determine the unique contour that minimizes some action requires a clear specification of the forces at work and then application of the calculus of variations to determine which one of the many possible trajectories is a geodesic. Of course these are difficult to

---

[2]Hinde & Stevenson-Hinde (1973) provided examples of constraints on conditioning where this is not always the case. Such constraints may be represented as dimensions of greater or lesser salience, routes of more or less accessibility. Taste aversion learning may withstand long delays, because the dimension of taste is intrinsically primed by (and, thus, "closer to" that of) gastrointestinal distress than are other dimensions. The degree of focusing on a few, salient dimensions depends on the level of arousal, with increasing levels of arousal being correlated with "narrower" behavioral maps that exclude alternative paths.

provide in general, as the perceptual dimensions along which stimuli are judged are only approximately known, and the forces at work are a subject of conjecture.[3] However, we may approach the problem by varying a single dimension for which we have some confidence of the subjective metric, temporal contiguity between CS and US.

Hanson (1977) developed a candidate model of the temporal geodesic that underlies conditioning. Hanson analyzed the standard conditioning paradigm in which a CS is presented for several seconds before the US is delivered. He decomposed the CS into a sequence of epochs and assumed that the overall change in "expectancy" of the US (the subjective temporal proximity to the US—the abscissae of Fig. 4.1) during conditioning equalled the sum of the changes during each of these epochs. He then asked how the expectancy at each of these epochs should change as a function of time so as to maximize the overall predictability of the US. The solution was constrained by assuming a ceiling on the total amount of association possible, with conditioning being a function of the distance from that ceiling. This is the same assumption that underlies both the Rescorla–Wagner Law of Association (Rescorla & Wagner, 1972; which in turn grew out of Kamin's, 1969, Expectancy-Based Theory of Conditioning), and the PDP connection modification scheme called the Delta Rule (Rumelhart, Hinton, & McClelland, 1986). In the dynamic framework, this constraint merely restates the obvious: The potential for conditioning an organism is the distance from where the animal's expectations/knowledge currently are to the bottom of the relevant potential well. Hanson used the calculus of variations to find the appropriate geodesic, which turned out to be the difference of two exponential functions. In the case of minimal control by the background (i.e., when the field is not already sloping steeply toward the attractor), this equation predicts an exponentially decaying expectancy throughout the duration of the cue, one whose slope and intercept depend on both the time between trials and the duration of the CS. As control by the background increases, the function predicts a positively skewed curve rising from zero to a maximum and then slowly decaying. By assuming further that expectancy was correlated with general arousal, Hanson

---

[3]In the approach known as "Behavioral Economics" (see, e.g., Staddon, 1980) the force of attraction is assumed to vary as the square (or, in some models, as a power function with a positive exponent) of the distance between an attractor and a global well called the "bliss point." Although inverse-square or constant force assumptions might seem more reasonable, auxiliary assumptions of the models make them not particularly sensitive to the nature of the forcing function over the range of variables studied. Behavioral equilibria are determined by assuming that the subject's behavior itself warps the topography, such that the high response rates often necessary to maximize proximity with the bliss point reduce the attractiveness of that point. By varying the experimentally determined tradeoffs between behavior and the quantities maximized, values for the force parameters may be estimated, or they may be assumed while the scale values for the rewards are estimated. According to these models the dynamic properties of the behavior interact with the potential field; thus, they are intrinsically more complex than the approach outlined in this chapter. To extend our physics metaphor, they are to the current treatment as electrodynamics is to mechanics.

successfully used the geodesic to describe the change in activity through the course of a CS.

' Perhaps more important than the particular form of Hanson's equation is the ingenious model he provided us for dealing with behavioral attraction in a quantitative manner. The insight that a CS may be decomposed into a number of epochs, each subject to limitations on association (also see Ayres, Albert, & Bombace, 1987) is also seminal. Killeen and Fetterman (1988) predicated a theory of timing on the existence of such epochs and identified them with successive periods of adjunctive behaviors during the CS. If CSs are generally decomposed by the animal in such a fashion, then the total association strength of the US must be apportioned among each segment. As the number of such units increase with the duration of the CS, the average strength conferred on each epoch will decrease, rendering conditioning poorer for longer-duration CSs. Those adjunctive behaviors closer in time to the US are at a relatively low potential and, therefore, should support conditioning of other responses to gain access to the opportunity to perform them. Short intertrial intervals (ITIs) permit alternate features of the environment to predict the US almost as well as does the CS, and, if those features are favored on other accounts (e.g., spatial proximity to the US), they may overshadow the nominal CS (i.e., capture the trajectory). If Killeen and Fetterman's version is correct, the number of epochs within a CS will vary with the rate of reinforcement in real time. For long ITIs, there will be fewer epochs within the CS, thus, facilitating conditioning. These notions are of course speculative but reflect only a few of the new perspectives possible from the dynamic systems view of behavior.

EROSION OF THE "IDEAL" GULLEY

Even after successful discriminations have been established or effective behavior patterns constructed, we may find regression to instinctive or habitual paths, even though, given the constraints imposed by the experimenter, they seem less than optimal. The Brelands noted a strong tendency for motor patterns "invented" by a trainer to drift toward more innate forms, a tendency that they labeled *instinctive drift* (Breland & Breland, 1966; cf. Timberlake, Wahl, & King, 1982). Norman (1981) noted a similar drift, which he called *action slips*, toward habitual patterns in humans. Segal (1972) suggested that "the ease of rendering a topography operant [i.e., subject to instrumental conditioning] may be related to the ease with which the topography can free itself of control by its inducing stimuli" (p. 25). Attraction to a conditioned stimulus or response may pull a subject into the basin of attraction of a more powerful reflex more readily associated with a different consummatory well (Boakes, Poli, Lockwood, & Goodall, 1978). Continual energy must be expended to keep the behavior in the desired but unstable channel. "Tuning" an experimental paradigm (Timberlake & Lucas, 1989) is the process of putting these natural trajectories in the service of the goals of the experimenter (Biederman, D'Amato, & Keller, 1964). In the long run, it may be easier to condition new responses outside powerful instinctive basins or to reroute using existing reflexes as a detour, as Pearce and associates did with the scratch collar, as the Brelands did for their circus animals, and as mother nature did for the sooty terns.

PARASITIC ATTRACTORS

Biologically significant events not only elicit reflexes but also drive organisms to engage in displacement behavior apparently unrelated to the US. In one of the first reports of adjunctive behavior, Falk (1961) noted that hungry rats, fed periodically, consumed inordinate amounts of water—100 g might be drunk by a rat weighing only 200 g in the course of a three-hour session. Since then a variety of other schedule-induced or adjunctive behaviors have been reported (see, e.g., Gilbert & Keehn, 1972), such as schedule-induced attack, pica, and general activity. Adjunctive behavior shares characteristics with other dissipative structures such as turbulent flow (Prigogine, 1984). It is "parasitic" upon an extreme energy gradient—periods of reward alternating with periods of extinction. Its onset is not immediate but may require dozens of cycles to become established. The form and sequencing of adjunctive behaviors depends heavily on the nature of the environment. Although adjunctive behaviors are adamant to intrinsic punishment—hemodilution resulting from polydipsia, wounds resulting from schedule-induced attack—they are easily modified by manipulating the likelihood of their onset, which might be accomplished for "psychogenic" polydipsia simply by moving the water source away from the pellet dispenser. Like plumes of turbulence, adjunctive behaviors are easily deterred at inception but powerful once established.

How may we characterize the path among these adjunctive attractors? If the USs are delivered on a periodic schedule, the probabilities of engaging in one or another adjunctive behavior is a smooth function of the time through the interval (Staddon, 1977), with some adjunctive behaviors more likely early in the interval and others late in the interval. Hanson's (1977) geodesic provides a decent mathematical model of the average probabilities as a function of time through the interval. However, during any one episode, animals shift between different behaviors in an unpredictable, stochastic way. Iverson (1986) recorded transition probabilities between bouts of wheel-running for different behaviors of rats and found that the transitions were path-dependent: The probability of exploring after a lever-press following a run was 0.31, after a lever-press following exploration was 0.90, and after a lever-press following other activities was 0.65. It may be these very path dependencies are fundamental, and the probability distributions for the various adjunctive behaviors derivative from them. In turn, the path dependence may arise through positive and negative feedback from the performance of the activities (Houston & Sumida, 1985; Reid & Staddon, 1987;

Toates, 1980), which may be the source both of periodicities and of the potential for aperiodic (chaotic) sequences.

Whereas most biological systems are designed to avoid chaotic responses, for an organism with no access to the US, complete exploration of the repertoire in novel sequences is an ideal way to maximize the variability and thus, the creativity of its response to a frustrating environment. The utility of having a chaotic regime available may be further enhanced, if evolutionarily robust activities such as exploration retain larger (if shallower) basins of attraction.

Falk (1986) noted that, in some cases, adjunctive behaviors may act to defer choice by moving the organism off a saddlepoint:

> When the behavioral vectors for the primary, crucial behavior appropriate to the situation and escape behavior are approximately equal, the conflict constitutes an unstable equilibrium. Even momentary dominance of one vector would probably occlude the other one. . . . Since this choice could be of fateful importance to an animal, it had better not be a hasty one. . . . A conflict situation which diversifies into displacement activities or adjunctive behavior will be buffered with respect to a too precipitous resolution of its unstable equilibrium. (pp. 338–339)

Not only may adjunctive behavior defer a decision, and in the meantime constitute a novel "coping" response to frustration, it may also provide the material out of which more effective responses to the environment are selected by contiguity with reinforcement—that is, by conditioning (Staddon & Simmelhag, 1971; Falk, 1971).

TRAJECTORIES, GEODESICS, & SPACES

The gist of these discussions is that we may represent behavior as a trajectory through an organism's behavioral-perceptual space, its *Umwelt*. This space is not necessarily metric; whenever features are separable, the organism minimizes its information-processing load by focusing on one feature after another (Killeen, 1990). The selection of features is determined in large part by higher-order prototypes such as prey, motivated by needs or primed by context. Some attractors that fill this space are fixed from birth and are called reflexes. Others are acquired early in life; under special circumstances, these are stabilized quickly, and the stabilization is called imprinting. Others acquired throughout life are more malleable and are called habits. However, as such habits continually channel behavior, they become set, and unless the environment undergoes radical change, it is unlikely that the stream of behavior will find new routes (Waddington, 1957).

The ability to evaluate a large number of features and modify one's trajectory by attention to some goal is contingent on a relatively low level of arousal correlated with a relatively smooth potential surface; higher levels lock the organism into whichever pattern is at the moment dominant, just as a phasic increase in arousal may precipitate a likely but intemperate response (Hestenes, chapter 7 in this volume). Previous experience may buffer arousal- or drug-induced stereotypy (DeVietti, Pellis, Pellis, & Teitelbaum, 1985), but it can rarely eliminate it. Just as the potential wells of habit attract variant behaviors toward old patterns, the confusion and clumsiness that attend new ways of seeing and doing are potential barriers against innovation, and trap behavior in local minima. Modulation of the potential landscape by manipulation of our arousal is instrumental in transcending this deterministic fate (cf. Banquet, Smith, & Guenther, chapter 6 in this volume).

The forces that drive the organisms are not "in" the world, so much as in their evolutionary and life histories in the world. When a habitual attractor becomes suddenly unavailable, organisms continue to strive for it as though its potential well still existed, a perseverance that one theorist has treated as behavioral momentum (Nevin, 1988). Conversely, if the goal object is simply moved closer, the animal may pass by it (or even over it; Stolz & Lott, 1964) in the search for it in its usual location. The dynamic metaphor must, therefore eventually be reinterpreted in terms of the attractions between representations of stimuli on one neural field and the templates of attractor stimuli/responses existing on other neural fields. In the meantime, it may serve as a language that will permit us to reformulate the laws of motivation, emotion, and goal direction from a perspective that is congenial to models of neural networks.

Whereas a trajectory is a path through space, a geodesic is a trajectory that minimizes certain constraints. We saw in Hanson's work the possibility of treating conditioning as the transformation of a trajectory into a geodesic. We may generalize that result and treat all conditioning as the creation of a geodesic through an animal's *Umwelt,* a path that minimizes the spatiotemporal distance between need and its satisfaction, image and its realization. Whereas a trajectory may wander under the influence of attention, a geodesic conforms to some minimal and relatively fixed surface between the organism's current position in its *Umwelt* and the position that has regularly satisfied the current needs. This surface is determined by species-specific perceptual and behavioral abilities, by histories of reinforcement that have created familiar paths, and by levels of arousal that will permit or preclude alternate routes to the goal.

A geodesic is the "shortest" path to the goal; therefore, once it is established, further conditioning is impossible. What has traditionally been spoken of as "habituation of the reinforcer" may be seen as the formation of a geodesic. It is only when there are precipituous drops into the wells of attractors that the dynamo of conditioning can empower new learning, learning that serves to undermine the precipice by leading attention or behavior more directly to the attractor. Many of the existing laws of conditioning are illuminated by this treatment. For instance, "associative potential" in Rescorla and Wagner's (1972) theory corresponds to deepness of the well, with additional learning becoming possible when the depth is increased by motivational manipulations. Blocking is the deflection of attention or behavior by an already existing trajectory that is closer to a geodesic than that offered by the new stimulus, and so on. At this point, reinterpretations are easy. However, each time they are made, the theory gains texture and, thus, moves from metaphor to model. Eventually predictions become possible, while at the same time, the structure becomes increasingly recalcitrant to the accommodation of new data. The dynamic approach is itself a "trajectory" in theory-space; it is now relatively simple for meanders in its route to embrace various fields of data. Whether it eventually becomes a geodesic—a better approach than other extant theories—depends on whether it will get us closer to our goal of understanding behavior and whether it will provide a deeper understanding than that available from other approaches.

ACKNOWLEDGMENT

The writing of this article was supported in part by NIMH Grant R01 MH39496.

REFERENCES

Ayres, J. J. B., Albert, M., & Bombace, J. C. (1987). Extending conditioning stimuli before versus after unconditioned stimuli: Implications for real-time models of conditioning. *Journal of Experimental Psychology: Animal Behavior Processes, 13,* 168–181.

Ballachey, E. L., & Buel, J. (1934). Centrifugal swing as a determinant of choice-point behavior in the maze running of the white rat. *Journal of Comparative Psychology, 17,* 201–223.

Ballard, D. (1986). Cortical connections and parallel processing: Structure and function. *Behavioral and Brain Sciences, 9,* 67–120.

Beach, F. A. (1951). Instinctive behavior: Reproductive activities. In S. S. Stevens (Ed.), *Handbook of experimental psychology* (pp. 387–434). New York: Wiley.

Biederman, G. B., D'Amato, M. R., & Keller, D. M. (1964). Facilitation of discriminated avoidance learning by dissociation of CS and manipulandum. *Psychonomic Science, 9,* 229–230.

Bindra, D. (1974). A motivation view of learning, performance, and behavior modification. *Psychological Review, 81,* 199–213.

Birch, H. G. (1945). The role of motivational factors in insightful problem-solving. *Journal of Comparative Psychology, 38,* 295–317.

Blough, D. S. (1972). Recognition by the pigeon of stimuli varying in two dimensions. *Journal of the Experimental Analysis of Behavior, 18,* 345–368.

Boakes, R. A., Poli, M., Lockwood, M. J., & Goodall, G. (1978). A study of misbehavior: Token reinforcement in the rat. *Journal of the Experimental Analysis of Behavior, 29,* 115–134.

Boas, M. L. (1966). *Mathematical methods in the physical sciences.* New York: Wiley.

Bolles, R. C., & Fanselow, M. S. (1980). A perceptual-defensive-recuperative model of fear and pain. *Behavioral and Brain Sciences, 3,* 291–323.

Breland, K., & Breland, M. (1966). *Animal behavior.* New York: Macmillan.

Brown, P. L., & Jenkins, H. M. (1968). Auto-shaping of the pigeon's key-peck. *Journal of the Experimental Analysis of Behavior, 11,* 1–8.

Craig, W. (1918). Appetites and aversions as constituents of instincts. *Biological Bulletin, 34,* 91–107.

Deutsch, J. A. (1960). *The structural basis of behavior.* Chicago: University of Chicago Press.

DeVietti, T. L., Pellis, S. M., Pellis, V. C., & Teitelbaum, P. (1985). Previous experience disrupts atropine-induced stereotyped "trapping" in rats. *Behavioral Neurosciences, 99,* 1128–1141.

Eldridge, G. D., & Pear, J. J. (1987). Topographical variations in behavior during autoshaping, automaintenance, and omission training. *Journal of the Experimental Analysis of Behavior, 47,* 319–333.

Fabre, J. H. (1915). *The hunting wasps.* New York: Dodd, Mead.

Falk, J. L. (1961). Production of polydipsia in normal rats by an intermittent food schedule. *Science, 133,* 195–196.

Falk, J. L. (1971). The nature and determinants of adjunctive behavior. *Physiology and Behavior, 6,* 577–588.

Falk, J. L. (1986). The formation and function of ritual behavior. In T. Thompson & M. D. Zeiler (Eds.), *Analysis and integration of behavioral units* (pp. 335–355). Hillsdale, NJ: Lawrence Erlbaum Associates.

Feynman, R. P., Leighton, R. B., & Sands, M. (1963). *Lectures on physics.* London: Addison-Wesley.

Foreman, N., & Stevens, R. (1987). Relationships between the superior colliculus and hippocampus: Neural and behavioral considerations. *Behavioral and Brain Sciences, 10,* 101–152.

Frey, P. W., & Sears, R. J. (1978). Models of conditioning incorporating the Rescorla–Wagner associative axiom, a dynamic attention process, and a catastrophe rule. *Psychological Review, 85,* 321–340.

Gallistel, C. R. (1980). *The organization of action: A new synthesis.* Hillsdale, NJ: Lawrence Erlbaum Associates.

Garrud, P., Goodall, G., & Mackintosh, N. J. (1981). Overshadowing of a stimulus-reinforcer association by an instrumental response. *Quarterly Journal of Experimental Psychology, 33B,* 123–135.

Gilbert, R. M., & Keehn, J. D. (1972). *Schedule effects: Drugs, drinking and aggression.* Toronto: University of Toronto Press.

Gould, J. L., & Marler, P. (1984). Ethology and the natural history of learning. In P. Marler & H. S. Terrace (Eds.), *The biology of learning* (pp. 47–74). New York: Springer-Verlag.

Haken, H. (1977). *Synergetics: An introduction; nonequilibrium phase transitions and self-organization in physics, chemistry and biology.* New York: Springer-Verlag.

Hanson, S. J. (1977). *The Rescorla–Wagner model and the temporal control of behavior.* Unpublished masters thesis, Arizona State University, Tempe.

Hanson, S. J., & Killeen, P. R. (1981). Measurement and modelling of behavior under fixed-interval schedules of reinforcement. *Journal of Experimental Psychology: Animal Behavior Processes, 7,* 129–139.

Hearst, E., & Jenkins, H. M. (1974). Sign tracking: The stimulus reinforcer relation and directed action. *Monograph of the Psychonomic Society.* Austin, TX.

Hinde, R. A., & Stevenson-Hinde, J. (Eds.). (1973). *Constraints on learning.* New York: Academic Press.

Hinton, G. E., & Sejnowski, T. J. (1986). Learning and relearning in Boltzmann machines. In D. E. Rumelhart & J. L. McClelland (Eds.), *Parallel distributed processing: Explorations in the microstructure of cognition* (Vol. 1, pp. 282–317). Cambridge, MA: MIT Press.

Hofstadter, D. R. (1985). *Metamagical themas: Questing for the essence of mind and pattern.* New York: Basic.

Honig, W. K., & Staddon, J. E. R. (1977). *Handbook of operant behavior.* Englewood Cliffs, NJ: Prentice-Hall.

Houston, A., & Sumida, B. (1985). A positive feedback model for switching between two activities. *Animal Behaviour, 33*, 315–325.

Iverson, I. H. (1986). Time allocation, sequential, and kinematic analyses of behaviors controlled by an aperiodic reinforcement schedule. *The Psychological Record, 36*, 239–255.

Kamin, L. J. (1969). Predictability, surprise, attention, and conditioning. In M. R. Jones (Ed.), *Miami Symposium on the Prediction of Behavior*. New York: Appleton-Century-Crofts.

Keller, K. J. (1980). Inhibitory effects of reinforcement and a model of fixed-interval performances. *Animal Learning & Behavior, 8*, 102–109.

Killeen, P. R. (1989). Behavior as a trajectory through a field of attractors. In J. R. Brink & C. R. Haden (Eds.), *The computer and the brain: Perspectives on human and artificial intelligence*. North-Holland: Elsevier.

Killeen, P. R. (1990). *Perceptual geodesics*. Unpublished manuscript.

Killeen, P. R., & Amsel, A. (1987). The kinematics of locomotion toward a goal. *Journal of Experimental Psychology: Animal Behavior Processes, 13*, 92–101.

Killeen, P. R., & Fetterman, J. G. (1988). A behavioral theory of timing. Psychological Review, 95, 274–295.

Kimble, G. A. (1961). *Hilgard and Marquis' conditioning and learning* (2nd ed.). New York: Appleton-Century-Crofts.

Kirkpatrick, S., Gelatt, C. D., & Vecchi, M. D. (1983). Optimization by simulated annealing. *Science, 220*, 671–680.

Konorski, J. (1967). *Integrative activity of the brain*. Chicago: University of Chicago Press.

Lashley, K. S. (1942). An examination of the "continuity theory" as applied to discrimination learning. *Journal of General Psychology, 26*, 241–265.

Locurto, C. M., Terrace, H. S., & Gibbon, J. (1981). *Autoshaping and conditioning theory*. New York: Academic Press.

Loeb, J. (1973). *Forced movements, tropisms, & animal conduct*. New York: Dover. Original work published 1918.

Mackintosh, N. J. (1974). *The psychology of animal learning*. New York: Academic Press.

Mackintosh, N. J. (1983). *Conditioning and associative learning*. Oxford: Oxford University Press.

Masterson, F. A., & Crawford, M. (1982). The defense motivation system: A theory of avoidance behavior. *Behavioral and Brain Sciences, 5*, 661–696.

Morgan, M. J., & Nicholas, D. J. (1979). Discrimination between reinforced action patterns in the rat. *Learning and Motivation, 10*, 1–22.

Nevin, J. A. (1988). Behavioral momentum and the partial reinforcement effect. *Psychological Bulletin, 103*, 44–56.

Norman, D. A. (1981). Categorization of action slips. *Psychological Review, 88*, 1–15.

O'Keefe, J., & Nadel, L. (1978). *The hippocampus as a cognitive map*. Oxford: Clarendon.

Pearce, J. M., Colwill, R. M., & Hall, G. (1978). Instrumental conditioning of scratching in the laboratory rat. *Learning and Motivation, 9*, 255–271.

Peden, B. F., Browne, M. P., & Hearst, E. (1977). Persistent approaches to a signal for food despite food omission for approaching. *Journal of Experimental Psychology: Animal Behavior Processes, 3*, 377–399.

Pellionisz, A., & Llinas, R. (1979). Brain modelling by tensor network theory and computer simulation. The cerebellum: Distributed processor for predictive coordination. *Neuroscience, 4*, 323–348.

Prigogine, I. (1984). Nonequilibrium thermodynamics and chemical evolution: An overview. In G. Nichols (Ed.), *Advances in chemical physics Volume LV* (pp. 43–62). New York: Wiley.

Reid, A. K., & Staddon, J. E. R. (1987). Within-session meal-size effects on induced drinking. *Journal of the Experimental Analysis of Behavior, 48*, 289–301.

Rescorla, R. A., & Furrow, D. R. (1977). Stimulus similarity as a determinant of Pavlovian conditioning. *Journal of Experimental Psychology: Animal Behavior Processes, 3*, 203–215.

Rescorla, R. A., & Wagner, A. R. (1972). A theory of Pavlovian conditioning: Variations in the effectiveness of reinforcement and nonreinforcement. In A. H. Black & W. F. Prokasy (Eds.), *Classical conditioning II: Current research and theory* (pp. 64–99). New York: Appleton-Century-Crofts.

Reynolds, G. S. (1961). Attention in the pigeon. *Journal of the Experimental Analysis of Behavior, 4,* 203–208.

Romanes, G. J. (1882). *Animal intelligence.* London: Keegan, Paul, Trench.

Rumelhart, D. E., Hinton, G. E., & McClelland, J. L. (1986). A general framework for parallel distributed processing. In D. E. Rumelhart & J. L. McClelland (Eds.), *Parallel distributed processing: Explorations in the microstructure of cognition* (Vol. 1, pp. 45–76). Cambridge, MA: MIT Press.

Schneirla, T. C. (1959). An evolutionary an developmental theory of biphasic processes underlying approach and withdrawal. In M. R. Jones (Ed.), *Nebraska Symposium on Motivation* (pp. 1–42).

Segal, E. F. (1972). Induction and the provenance of operants. In R. M. Gilbert & J. r. Millenson (Eds.), *Reinforcement: behavioral analyses* (pp. 1–34). New York: Academic Press.

Shepard, R. N., & Arabie, P. (1979). Additive clustering: Representations of similarities as combinations of discrete overlapping properties. *Psychological Review, 30,* 87–123.

Shettleworth, S. J. (1975). Reinforcement and the organization of behavior in golden hamsters: Hunger, environment and food reinforcement. *Journal of Experimental Psychology: Animal Behavior Processes, 1,* 56–87.

Shettleworth, S. J. (1981). Reinforcement and the organization of behavior in golden hamsters: Differential overshadowing of a CS by different responses. *Quarterly Journal of Experimental Psychology, 33B,* 241–255.

Smolensky, P. (1986). Information processing in dynamical systems: Foundations of harmony theory. In D. E. Rumelhart & J. L. McClelland (Eds.), *Parallel distributed processing: Explorations in the microstructure of cognition* (Vol. 1, pp. 194–281). Cambridge, MA: MIT Press.

Staddon, J. E. R. (1977). Schedule-induced behavior. In W. K. Honig & J. E. R. Staddon (Eds.), *Handbook of operant behavior* (pp. 125–152). Englewood Cliffs, NJ: Prentice Hall.

Staddon, J. E. R. (Ed.). (1980). *Limits to action: The allocation of individual behavior.* New York: Academic Press.

Staddon, J. E. R., & Simmelhag, V. L. (1971). The "superstition" experiment: A re-examination of its implications for the principles of adaptive behavior. *Psychological Review, 78,* 3–43.

Stevens, S. S. (1951). Mathematics, measurement, and psychophysics. In S. S. Stevens (Ed.), *Handbook of experimental psychology* (pp. 1–49). New York: Wiley.

Stolz, S. B., & Lott, D. F. (1964). Establishment in rats of a persistent response producing a net loss of reinforcement. *Journal of Comparative and Physiological Psychology, 57,* 147–149.

Teitelbaum, P., Schallert, T., & Whishaw, I. Q. (1983). Sources of spontaneity in motivated behavior. In E. Satinoff & P. Teitelbaum (Eds.), *Handbook of behavioral neurobiology* (Vol. 6, pp. 23–65). New York: Plenum.

Terrace, H. S. (1966). Stimulus control. In W. K. Honig (Ed.), *Operant behavior: Areas of research and application* (pp. 271–344). New York: Appleton-Century-Crofts.

Thinus-Blanc, C., Bouzouba, L., Chaix, K., Chapuis, N., Durup, M., & Poucet, B. (1987). A study of spatial parameters encoded during exploration in hamsters. *Journal of Experimental Psychology: Animal Behavior Processes, 13,* 418–427.

Timberlake, W., & Lucas, G. A. (1989). Behavior systems and learning. In S. B. Klein & R. R. Mowrer (Eds.), *Contemporary learning theories: Instrument conditioning theory and the impact of biological constraints on learning* (pp. 237–275). Hillsdale, NJ: Lawrence Erlbaum Associates.

Timberlake, W., Wahl, G., & King, D. (1982). Stimulus and response contingencies in the misbehavior of rats. *Journal of Experimental Psychology: Animal Behavior Processes, 8,* 62–85.

Tinbergen, N. (1960). *The herring gull's world: A study of the social behavior of birds.* New York: Basic.

Toates, F. M. (1980). *Animal behavior—A systems approach.* New York: Wiley.

Turner, L. H., & Solomon, R. L. (1962). Human traumatic avoidance learning: Theory and experiments on the operant–respondent distinction and failures to learn. *Psychological Monographs, 76* (40, Whole No. 559).

von Uexkull, J. (1921). *Umwelt und innenwelt der tiere.* [*The outer- and inner-world of animals*]. Berlin: Springer-Verlag.

Waddington, C. H. (1957). *The strategy of the genes: A discussion of some aspects of theoretical biology.* London: Allen & Unwin.

Weiss, P. (1941). Self-differentiation of the basic patterns of coordination. *Comparative Psychology Monographs, 17* (Whole No. 4).

Wilkie, D. M. (1989). Evidence that pigeons represent Euclidean properties in space. *Journal of Experimental Psychology: Animal Behavior Processes, 15,* 114–123.

Wooldridge, D. E. (1968). *Mechanical man; the physical basis of intelligent life.* New York: McGraw Hill.

Yaginuma, S., & Iwai, E. (1986). Effects of small cue-response separation on pattern discrimination in Macaques (Macaca fuscata and M. mulatta). *Journal of Comparative Psychology, 100,* 137–142.

Yates, F. E. (Ed.). (1984). *Self-organizing systems: The emergence of order.* New York: Plenum Press.

Zener, K. (1937). The significance of behavior accompanying conditioned salivary secretion for theories of the conditioned response. *American Journal of Psychology, 50,* 384–403.

5 Neuromodulatory Mechanisms in Neural Networks and Their Influence on Interstimulus Interval Effects in Pavlovian Conditioning

Richard Ricart, 1Lt, USAF
Wright Research and Development Center,
Wright-Patterson Air Force Base

The effects of the interstimulus interval (ISI) in Pavlovian conditioning are reexamined in this chapter due to the controversy that remains regarding the observable effects attributable to the ISI and the lack of current theory's ability to account for recent experimental results. According to the prevailing view, backward conditioning (negative ISI) and simultaneous conditioning (zero ISI) are incapable of producing conditioned responses. However, the author presents behavioral and recent neurophysiological experimental evidence suggesting the conditions under which excitatory backward and simultaneous conditioning are possible. The author concludes that the negative and positive effects attributable to backward and simultaneous conditioning are due to contrasting experimental procedures.

Computer simulations of a neural network model analogous to certain limbic areas are performed that exhibit the effects of backward and simultaneous conditioning consistent with the experimental evidence reviewed. The neural network model, called the READ circuit, was originally developed by Grossberg. In this study, a mechanism is added to the circuit that modulates the analog of potassium channels of the model neurons via a center analogous to the *locus ceruleus*.

The ISI in Pavlovian conditioning, or classical conditioning, has been considered to be one of the important variables determining the associative strength that may be obtained between the conditioned stimulus (CS) and the unconditioned stimulus (US). The ISI is the interval between the CS onset and the US onset. Although the effects of ISI have been perused since the early part of this century by many investigators, including Pavlov himself, there remains a controversy as to what exactly are the observable effects attributable to ISI and, more significantly, whether existing theory can account for these effects.

In this chapter, the view held is that the ISI variable alone, without considering the internal state of the animal and other environmental information, is insufficient to determine how stimuli will be associated in a given classical conditioning experiment. This is particularly true in the case of backward and simultaneous conditioning. Contrary to the prevailing view, excitatory simultaneous and backward conditioning are accepted as true phenomena. To support this position, the contrasting experimental data will be reviewed in Part I of this chapter. In Part II, a neural network model incorporating opponent processing, spatial pattern learning, and neuromodulation is proposed that explains the conditions under which excitatory simultaneous and backward conditioning are possible. Computer simulations of this model are shown that exhibit behavior consistent with observed experimental behavior. In addition, this model, which is a crude analog of the limbic system, is able to demonstrate the effects of long-term potentiation and depotentiation.

PART I

The ISI Curve

The prevailing view specifies a concave-down curve associated with the relationship between the conditioned response (CR) strength and the ISI as shown in Fig. 5.1. This relationship precludes conditioned excitation with ISIs less than 50 msecs or so, has a maximum CR strength at an ISI between 250–500 msecs (sometimes referred to as the optimal ISI), and has a monotonically decreasing CR strength as the ISIs increase beyond this "optimal" point. This relationship has been supported by extensive research in Pavlovian conditioning of the rabbit's nictitating membrane by Schneiderman and Gormezano (1964); Schneiderman (1966); Smith, Coleman, and Gormezano (1969); Gormezano (1972); and Gormezano, Kehoe, and Marshall (1983). Similar results in invertebrate studies have been reported by Hawkins, Carew, and Kandel (1986) suggesting common underlying learning mechanisms across species. Siegel and Domjan (1971) and Moscovitch and LoLordo (1968), studying the effects of backward and simultaneous conditioning in other mammals, reported either no conditioning or inhibitory effects.[1] Backward conditioning has also been used as a control in other invertebrate conditioning studies (Lukowiak & Sahley, 1981) because of the *inability* of the backwardly paired stimuli to produce CRs. Forward, simultaneous, and backward conditioning are defined in terms of the ISI (see Mahoney & Ayres, 1976, footnote 2). Forward conditioning is equated with a positive ISI, simultaneous conditioning is equated with an ISI of zero, and backward conditioning is equated with a negative ISI.

---

[1]For a recent treatise on conditioned inhibition, see Miller & Spear (1985).

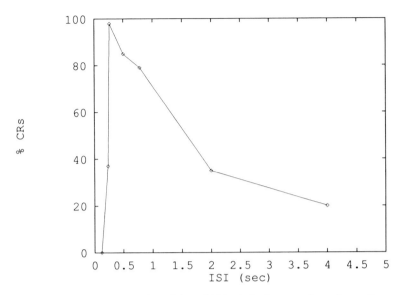

FIG. 5.1.   Representation of the rabbit's nictitating membrane's conditioned response strength versus the interstimulus interval. (Adapted
from Sutton & Barto, 1981)

Most theories of conditioning do indeed predict the associative relationship between the CS and the US described previously. Hull (1952) proposed that the CS develops a stimulus trace with an initial onset latency of approximately 100 msec and a maximum strength at approximately 450 msec after CS onset. Furthermore, the associative strength developed between the CS and the US depends on CS trace and US contiguity and is proportional to the CS trace strength at the time. Thus, the CS trace and ISI–CR function curves approximate each other.

The most prevalent accounts of conditioning emphasize the information the CS must provide of the impending reinforcer (Moscovitch & LoLordo, 1968; Kamin, 1969; Rescorla & Wagner, 1972; Mackintosh, 1974, 1983; Dickinson & Mackintosh, 1978; Pearce and Hall, 1980; Cantor, 1981). When a CS is conditioned to a shock US, for example, that CS becomes a predictor of impending danger. However, when the CS immediately follows the shock, the CS predicts relatively long periods of safety and becomes an inhibitor of fear (Moscovitch & LoLordo, 1968). As one can see, thus, the informational aspects attributable to the CS and the ISI effects go hand in hand in the theory.

Several models of classical conditioning or associative learning that have been developed recently (Sutton & Barto, 1981; Gluck & Thompson, 1987; Klopf, 1988; Schmajuk & Moore, 1988) have incorporated the informational aspects of current conditioning theory as well as Hull's CS trace. Each of these models is capable of predicting varied phenomena observed in Pavlovian conditioning, including, most importantly, the ISI effects discussed previously. The following comment made by Gluck and Thompson (1987) illustrates how important many consider the ISI variable to be: "In our view, the effect of the interstimulus onset interval on conditionability is perhaps the most fundamental property of basic associative learning" (p. 178).

However, there also exists a large body of empirical data confirming the existence of excitatory backward and simultaneous conditioning. Spetch, Wilkie, and Pinel (1981) called for a reevaluation of backward conditioning and its properties due to the preponderance of evidence confirming the ability of that procedure to produce conditioned excitation. They argued that the existence of a phenomenon should be based on empirical criteria alone and not whether the phenomenon supports theory. If one accepts the validity of excitatory backward and simultaneous conditioning, then one must question the validity of the ISI, *taken by itself,* as a dependable variable in conditioning. More importantly, due to the inability of the informational theories of conditioning to account for excitatory simultaneous and backward conditioning, these theories should be reevaluated, modified, or new ones developed.

Excitatory Backward Conditioning

In this section and in the section that follows, the evidence for excitatory backward and simultaneous conditioning will be presented. Afterwards a theory is formulated that can account for these phenomena. For a more detailed review, see Spetch et al. (1981), and, for an opposing view, see Hall (1984).

As noted by Spetch, et al. (1981), the controversy as to what is observed behaviorally in backward conditioning began with Pavlov himself. Pavlov (1927/1960) initially stated:

> Further, it is not enough that there should be overlapping between the two stimuli; it is also and equally necessary that the conditioned stimulus should begin to operate before the unconditioned stimulus comes into action.
>
> If this order is reversed, the unconditioned stimulus being applied first and the neutral stimulus second, the conditioned reflex cannot be established. (p. 27)

Later, in the same book, in a section entitled *New Interpretations,* he modified his initial conclusions:

> . . . repeated this combination [backward CS–US configuration] only a very few times, to avoid the development of the inhibitory process. In many cases the expected result was obtained. The hitherto neutral stimulus when now tested alone revealed undoubted conditioned properties. (p. 393)

In the latter quote, a major difference in experimental procedure, resulting in seemingly paradoxical observations, is implied. Pavlov's earlier observations resulted after numerous US–CS presentations. In the experiments where excitatory backward conditioning was reported, only a few stimulus pairings were administered. Indeed most investigators who have reported the ability of backward conditioning to produce unmistakable CRs did so upon single or very few US–CS presentations (Mowrer & Aiken, 1954; Matsumiya, 1960; Champion & Jones, 1961; Heth & Rescorla, 1973; Keith-Lucas & Guttman, 1975; Wagner & Terry, 1975; Mahoney & Ayres, 1976; Heth, 1976; Burkhardt, 1980a, 1980b; Shurtleff & Ayres, 1981; Ayres, Haddad, & Albert, 1987; Van Willigen, Emmett, Cote, Ayres, 1987). On the other hand, those who have reported on either no conditioning or inhibitory backward conditioning (see above) usually subjected the experimental animals to numerous stimulus pairings over a period of several days.

A pattern emerged over the years, suggesting an initial excitatory phase that degrades into an inhibitory phase with repeated training trials. This *transient* phenomenon was investigated in at least two studies. Although the final interpretation of the data differed, Spooner and Kellogg (1947) and Heth (1976) developed experiments whereby the transient effects of backward conditioning were shown. Heth used the conditioned emotional response (CER)[2] procedure popularized by Kamin (1968) and developed by Estes & Skinner (1941). Heth showed that animals that were subjected to 10 backward conditioning trials exhibited strong excitatory responses when tested with the CS alone, whereas the subjects that received 160 trials exhibited inhibitory behavior upon testing. Spooner and Kellogg (1947) used the finger withdrawal reflex paradigm with humans and showed similar results. Shock to the finger was used as the US, and the sound of a buzzer was the CS. Fig. 5.2 shows the result of the experiment. The evidence shows, therefore, a propensity for excitatory conditioning in the initial stimulus pairings and inhibitory or no conditioning after many conditioning trials. As Spetch et al. (1981) pointed out, Pavlov's (1932) final conclusion acknowledged the "double effect" of the backward conditioning paradigm.

Smith et al. (1969) and Siegel and Domjan (1971) tested for excitatory backward conditioning throughout their training but found no evidence of it. A closer look at their data reveals that any excitatory tendencies could have been easily missed. Smith, Coleman, and Gormezano trained their animals with 8 blocks of 80 conditioning trials for a total of 640 trials. The result of conditioning was

---

[2]The typical CER procedure is composed of two phases. In the first phase, the subjects, usually rats, are instrumentally conditioned to press a bar for food. In the second phase, the conditioning phase, the CS is paired with a shock usually delivered to a floor grid. The CR is measured as a *suppression ratio* of the bar pressing. The suppression ratio is $A/A + B$, where A is the amount of bar pressings during the CS, and B is the amount of bar pressings during the interval just prior to the onset of the CS and equal to the CS duration. A suppression ration of 0.5 means the CS resulted in no CR, and one of 0.0 corresponds to total suppression. A more direct measure of conditioned suppression, suppression of licking behavior, has been incorporated by Ayres and his colleagues in their work (see text).

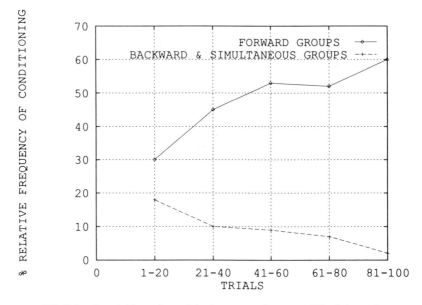

FIG. 5.2.   Acquisition of conditioning strength over a 100 trial conditioning session. Three forward groups combined tested at ISIs of 1.5, 1.0, and 0.5 sec, produced a typical acquisition curve. Two backward groups and a simultaneous group combined produced an acquisition curve that highlights an early excitatory process that degrades with continuing conditioning. (Adapted from Spooner & Kellogg, 1947)

tested with a CS alone every four conditioning trials. However, the data were averaged together in the 80 trial blocks (i.e., the 20 data points acquired during CS alone tests in each block were averaged together). The chances for any excitatory tendencies to be buried in the data are high during the first block of conditioning trials. From Spooner and Kellogg's (1947) and Heth's (1976) results, no excitatory tendencies should be expected in subsequent data blocks. A similar situation arises in Siegel and Domjan's experiment.

Note that, because of the *transient* effects of backward conditioning, many have not considered this phenomenon as true learning but as pseudoconditioning or sensitization (Underwood, 1949; Osgood, 1953; Terrace, 1973; Mackintosh, 1974). Champion and Jones (1961) explicitly tested for this possibility by comparing forward, backward, and pseudoconditioning in galvanic skin reaction (GSR) conditioning experiments and concluded that the backward procedure resulted in true learning. More recent backward conditioning experiments including, Ayres et al. (1987); Burkhardt (1980a, 1980b); Heth and Rescorla (1973); Keith-Lucas and Guttman (1975); Mahoney and Ayres (1976); Shurtleff and Ayres (1981); Van Willigen et al. (1987); and Wagner and Terry (1975) were provided with controls for pseudoconditioning and sensitization (see Spetch et al., 1981). Furthermore, evidence exists suggesting that excitatory backward and forward conditioning are due to the same learning process. Shurtleff and Ayres (1981) showed that backward conditioning exhibits the phenomena of acquisition, extinction, spontaneous recovery, and long-term retention in much the same manner as forward conditioning. Also, like forward conditioning, backward excitatory conditioning exhibits the phenomena of blocking (Burkhardt, 1980a) and of increase in excitatory strength with US intensity (Burkhardt, 1980b).

With all the evidence supporting the validity of excitatory backward conditioning, one may wonder at the continued reluctance of some to accept its existence. For example, in another recent review, Hall (1984) concluded that backward conditioning is unable to produce a CR. Hall did not consider any backward conditioning data, accepted by Spetch et al. (1981), which was obtained using the CER or GSR paradigms due to questions raised on these experimental procedures' means of measuring the CR. More recently, Ayres et al. (1987) rejected the basis of the CER data exclusion used by Hall (1984). Based on newer evidence, Ayres and his colleagues supported the contention that the CS does become conditioned to fear and is, therefore, a true example of excitatory backward Pavlovian conditioning.

Based on the inordinate amount of data produced on backward conditioning since Pavlov's days, the conclusion here mirrors that of Spetch et al. (1981) following:

> Regardless of the particular theoretical framework in which backward conditioning is considered, the empirical evidence for its existence can no longer be ignored. Thus the time for disputing whether [excitatory] backward conditioning is possible is past; it is time, instead, for systematic exploration of the conditions under which it occurs and the variables that affect the magnitude and duration of the effect. (p. 174)

To accept the validity of excitatory backward conditioning is not to reject the validity of inhibitory backward conditioning. If one accepts what the empirical evidence bears out and is not hampered by theoretical biases, then both of these phenomena can be accepted. A theory that explains both of these seemingly paradoxical behaviors will be developed a step at a time in the following sections of this article, beginning with the next one.

Variables Affecting Backward Conditioning

Thus far, one of the variables affecting backward conditioning has been identified: the number of conditioning trials. Why does the number of conditioning trials have such a significant effect on backward conditioning? Wagner and Terry (1975) suggested that it is the unexpected or surprising effect of the US during the initial conditioning trials that accounts for the CS–US association.

Wagner and Terry (1975) developed a theoretical explanation that includes processes internal to the animal and is central to the major thesis of this article.

> . . . we have proposed that CS–[US]UCS association depends upon the postepisodic rehearsal of the two events in short-term memory, and that UCS rehearsal varies with the degree to which the UCS is predicted by the aggregation of cues which precede it. . .
>
> We shall need to assume that the net associative tendency accruing to a CS during any interval of time embracing a CS and UCS will depend upon the amount of joint CS and UCS rehearsal and the amount of CS alone rehearsal that is afforded: Joint rehearsal should increase the tendency for the CS to be acted toward as a signal for the UCS while CS-alone rehearsal should decrease this tendency. According to this view, a forward CS–UCS pairing is more likely to produce conditioned responding than is a backward UCS–CS pairing, as in the latter case CS-alone rehearsal is likely to continue after UCS rehearsal has been terminated. However, it also suggests that any manipulation which changes the duration of UCS rehearsal should influence the degree of backward conditioning: The more protracted is UCS rehearsal, the more likely it should overlap with CS rehearsal to promote association between CS and UCS and deny CS-alone rehearsal that would diminish the association.
>
> If it is assumed (e.g., Terry & Wagner, 1975; Wagner, 1971; Wagner, Rudy, & Whitlow, 1973) that the same UCS will be rehearsed longer when it is "surprising" than when it is "expected," it is possible to account for a transient phase of conditioning. The initial UCS–CS pairings should involve a surprising UCS, favoring associative learning. As the UCS comes to be expected on the basis of contextual cues, further UCS–CS pairings should more principally induce CS-alone rehearsal as opposed to joint CS and UCS rehearsal and lead to extinction (and eventually inhibitory tendencies). This analysis would lead to a further expectation. That is, that more persistent backward conditioning should be producible by maintaining the surprisingness of the UCS over the course of the UCS–CS trials. (pp. 370–371)

Wagner and Terry (1975) developed an experiment to test their hypothesis of the effect of a surprising versus an expected US. The experiment was quite elaborate, with numerous controls for pseudoconditioning and sensitization. A simplified version will be described here: There were basically two groups of rabbits given eyelid conditioning with shock as the US. During the first phase of the training, one group of animals, called CS+, was trained to predict the US by conditioning a CS(+) in the typical forward manner. The other group, called CS−, was presented with an unreinforced CS(−) in each training trial during this first training phase. In the second and last phase of the experiment, both groups were subjected to a total of 24 backward conditioning trials using new CSs. During each training trial, the US was preceded by either a CS+ or CS− (depending on the group) and followed by the new CS. Therefore, the CS+ group expected the US during training, whereas the CS− group did not. Conditioning was tested by embedding 24 test trials within the training trials. The CS−group produced substantially stronger CRs than the CS+ group throughout the experiment. These findings support the hypothesis that the unexpected US in the initial backward conditioning trials is responsible for developing the association between the CS and the US.

Wagner and Terry predicted that excitatory backward conditioning can be maintained, if the US remains surprising. This prediction is confirmed by a series of experiments. Dostálek (1972, 1973) reported persistent excitatory backward conditioning, even after 200 training trials. At first glance, these results appear to be inconsistent with all previously cited work. After analyzing Dostálek's experimental procedure and evaluating the results in light of Wagner and Terry's theory, one may better accept and understand maintainable excitatory backward conditioning.

The one discriminating feature in Dostálek's backward conditioning procedure is the use of a random intertrial interval (ITI). This interval ranged between 10 sec and 3 min. All other researchers cited previously used a fixed ITI. The use of a fixed ITI establishes a pattern and rhythm that may be easily perceptible to the animal. As a result, the occurrence of the next stimulus pair may be readily predicted during the course of training. On the other hand, the use of a random ITI may create an environment in which the onset of the US is always *surprising*. Even though the US may be anticipated, the animal can never know *when* to expect it. This can lead to increased fear and anxiety. These internal events add to the confusion of the animal and help maintain the surprising effects of the stimuli. Consequently, as predicted by Wagner and Terry's hypothesis, excitatory backward conditioning can be kept regardless of the number of conditioning trials as long as the US is maintained surprising.

There may be alternative explanations that can account for Dostálek's results. Woody (1982, p. 78) suggested that Dostálek's (1972) use of a light US may produce "retinal afterimages" that can last long enough to overtake the CS. This could be sufficient to produce forward conditioning. However, in a later experiment, Dostálek (1973) used an air puff US and reported similar results. If the afterimage explanation is accepted, one cannot then discount internal afterimages of other sensory modalities that may or may not be consciously experienced by the animal during conditioning. These afterimages could be the internal replay of the CS and US as Wagner and Terry (1975) suggested.

Another explanation for Dostálek's results may be that forward conditioning resulted when the ITIs were around 10 secs. In other words, the CS of one trial became associated with the US of the following trial, when the ITI was relatively short. This explanation is suspect, because Dostálek (1973) also trained a forward group with an ISI of 440 msec and found that the acquisition curve for the backward and forward group did not differ significantly. In contrast, Schneiderman and Gormezano (1964) showed significant differences between subjects trained with an ISI 500 msec and those trained with an ISI of 4 sec (see Fig. 5.1).

An additional six seconds added to the ISI should produce even larger differences between the two groups. Therefore, a forward conditioning account of the experiment is highly unlikely.

The explanation used in this article that accounts for backward conditioning requires the prolonged, internal replay of the US when that US is surprising. Only when the internal representations of the US and CS are coactive can learning take place. As will be discussed later, the hypothesis is made that midbrain monoaminergic centers are, at least in part, responsible for modulating these internal representations. This explanation is supported by the seeming lack of evidence for excitatory backward conditioning in invertebrate studies (Lukowiak & Sahley, 1981; Hawkins et al., 1986; Byrne, 1987; Grover & Farley, 1987). It is assumed that the invertebrates used in these studies do not have the necessary neuromodulatory mechanisms, comparable to those of higher order animals, responsible for modulating and prolonging internal US replay. Therefore, before excitatory backward conditioning can be established, the animal must have acquired, in the process of phylogenetic development, the neural mechanisms sufficient for modulating the short-term memory (STM)[3] of reinforcing signals.

The theory so far suggests that excitatory backward conditioning could still be exhibited by any species under extreme stimulus conditions. Considerable CS–US overlap could still be accomplished with a negative ISI, if the CS and the US durations are long enough. If the CS is not extended far beyond the US in this situation, then *persistent* excitatory backward conditioning should be attainable. We will now see evidence of this. Earlier we saw that Heth (1976) found evidence for a biphasic backward conditioning process. In Experiment 4, the US was a 4 sec shock, and the CS was a 2 sec tone whose onset followed US offset by .5 sec. He also performed a similar test for what he called *simultaneous* conditioning in Experiment 3 (i.e., simultaneous conditioning was tested for transient effects). The experimental paradigm was CER training using a 4 sec, 5 ma shock US and a 2 sec compound tone-light CS. Although the CS–US configuration was labeled simultaneous, shock onset preceded CS onset by 2 sec with both signals terminating simultaneously. By our definition, this is backward conditioning. The result ran counter to what the ISI curve predicts. Although there was attenuation of suppression, suppression persisted even after 160 trials. This result differed from the other backward conditioning case (where CS onset followed US offset), where inhibitory tendencies were found after 160 conditioning trials. These results suggest that another important variable must be considered in backward conditioning studies: the amount of CS–US overlap.

Heth's results are significant, for they provide direct support for Wagner and Terry's hypotheses suggesting that it is the total amount of simultaneous CS–US

---

[3]Short-term memory in this chapter refers to neuronal activity. Long-term memory (LTM) refers to synaptic effectiveness characterized as synaptic weights. A mathematical definition for STM and LTM will be provided later in the Part II.

STM internal replay versus CS-alone STM replay that determines whether an association between the CS and the US will be produced. This can be accomplished in two ways: (a) if there is sufficient duration of CS–US overlap to begin with, or (b) the internal US replay is protracted through a modulatory mechanism when the US is surprising. In addition to the surprisingness of the US and the duration of CS–US overlap, all variables associated with forward conditioning should apply to backward conditioning. This hypothesis is based on the results of Shurtleff and Ayres (1981) and Burkhardt (1980a, 1980b) mentioned earlier. These results suggest that excitatory backward and forward conditioning result from the same learning process. In conclusion, the ISI variable by itself is insufficient for determining the outcome of a backward conditioning experiment.

Simultaneous Conditioning and Hebbian Learning

As mentioned on numerous occasions, Wagner and Terry's (1975) position requires joint rehearsal of the conditioning stimuli before the CS can be associated with the US. This is by no means a unique position. In fact modern neurobiology's conceptual framework was developed in part by Hebb (1949), who first proposed this (Shepherd, 1988, p. 86). Hebb hypothesized that memory or thought was due to neuronal activity. Long-term memory, according to the theory, resides in the synapse, which can become more effective only with sufficient coactive postsynaptic and presynaptic activity. Hebb's hypotheses were also very influential to many neural network modelers who have developed a wide range of associative learning systems over the years. These researchers include Marr (1969); Grossberg (1969, 1972c); von der Malsburg (1973); Anderson, Silverstein, Ritz, and Jones (1977); Kohonen (1977); and Cooper, Liberman, and Oja (1979), to name some of the earlier investigators. The 1980s have brought a proliferation of neural network theoretical studies incorporating Hebbian or Hebbian-like learning.

In this section, behavioral and neurophysiological evidence for Hebbian learning, as it relates to simultaneous conditioning, will be presented. If Hebbian learning is valid, then one would expect simultaneous presentation of the CS and the US to produce learning, but, as previously mentioned, conflicting results have been reported. After evaluation of the evidence, the conclusion will be made that the simultaneity of events is the important factor in learning. This position demands a perspective internal to the animal (i.e., the cellular level), not at the level at which the stimuli are being presented.

As was mentioned previously, Smith et al. (1969) reported no existence of CRs after conditioning the rabbit's nictitating membrane with simultaneous presentations of a 50 msec, 1000 Hz tone CS and a 50 msec, 4 ma shock US. Hawkins et al. (1986) suggested they produced similar results when they classically conditioned the sea mollusk *Aplysia californica*. Siegel and Domjan (1971) reported that 50 presentations of a 500 msec, 1 ma shock simultaneously paired with a 2 min, 1400 Hz tone (although they called it backwardly paired), produced subsequent inhibition of suppression in CER training. These results along with the results reporting inhibitory backward conditioning support Hull's trace and signal contiguity theory as well as the informational theories of learning discussed earlier.

Burkhardt and Ayres (1978), on the other hand, suggested that the long CS extending so far beyond the US, in Siegel and Domjan's experiment, was equivalent to a CS-alone extinction trial, diminishing any excitatory tendencies that might be produced in the early overlap of the signals. Burkhardt and Ayres tested this hypothesis with a single, simultaneous presentation of a 4 sec US and a 0, 1, 4, 64, or 128 sec CS. They found that the 4 sec CS group exhibited significantly more suppression of licking than any other group and that the 0 and 128 sec CS groups produced minimal suppression and did not differ from one another.

No modulatory mechanisms of STM nor any additional attentional mechanisms are needed to explain excitatory simultaneous conditioning, as implied in Heth's (1976) findings (see previous section). This suggests that phylogenetically older animals should be able to exhibit learning after receiving simultaneous CS–US pairings. A closer look at Hawkins et al. (1986) data reveals that some learning occurred with an ISI of zero, although the investigators reported that the learning was statistically insignificant. It is predicted here that, if longer lasting stimuli than the ones used by Hawkins and his associates in their experiment (.5 sec CS and 1 sec US) are used in similar conditioning experiments on *Aplysia,* more pronounced CRs will be detected. This prediction is based on the results obtained by Alkon and his associates over the last decade in studying associative learning in another mollusk, *Hermissenda crassicornis* (for a review, see Byrne, 1987, pp. 374–382). Alkon (1984, 1987), Crow and Alkon (1978), Farley and Alkon (1982, 1987), and Grover and Farley (1987) showed conditioned suppression of phototaxic behavior, or a simulation of this in an in vitro preparation, when simultaneously pairing light (CS) with rotation (US). The CS and US duration was 30 sec in most cases.

A similar prediction can be made for nictitating membrane conditioning experiments similar to the ones conducted by Gormezano and his colleagues. Longer duration stimuli should produce measurable CRs upon testing regardless of the number of conditioning trials. Burkhardt and Ayres (1978), Heth (1976), Heth and Rescorla (1973), and Mahoney and Ayres (1976) reported significant excitatory simultaneous conditioning in rats, using stimuli lasting between 2–8 sec. Furthermore, Burkhardt and Ayres (1978) suggested that the CS–US associative strength increases as a function of the duration of CS–US overlap (Experiment 3). A CS duration of 2, 4, or 8 sec simultaneously presented with a US duration of 2, 4, or 8 sec produced respectively stronger CRs. This provides yet further evidence for Wagner and Terry's position. A possible explanation for why very short duration stimuli presented simultaneously will not result in learning whereas longer duration stimuli will result in learning will be presented later. Before this explanation, further evidence for Hebbian learning will be offered.

Evidence supporting Hebbian learning can also be found in studies of another type of associative learning: long-term potentiation (Byrne, 1987, pp. 389–403; Eccles, 1983; Kelso, Ganong, & Brown, 1986; Levy, 1985; LTP). Although it is still not clear exactly what role LTP plays in memory and learning, LTP exhibits enough similarities to classical conditioning, especially at the cellular level, to suggest common underlying mechanisms. LTP is the long-lasting enhancement of postsynaptic activity due to brief, high-frequency electrical stimulation of presynaptic pathways. The hippocampus has been the main target in LTP investigations, although other preparations have been studied as well. It has been found that, upon presynaptic stimulation, postsynaptic activity is necessary before LTP is possible (Dunwiddie, Madison, & Lynch, 1978; Levy & Steward, 1979; Eccles, 1983; Scharfman & Sarvey, 1984; Levy, 1985). Presynaptic stimulation must also be strong enough and *persist long enough* before LTP is evoked (McNaughton, Douglas, & Goddard, 1978; Levy, 1985). Yet further evidence for Hebbian-like learning Rauschecker and Singer (1979) and Singer (1983) presented in their studies of the cat's visual cortex. These findings are consistent with the findings of the previous paragraph and lend further support to the ongoing argument.

A possible link between LTP and Pavlovian conditioning at the behavioral level was recently found. Berger (1984) potentiated the perforant pathway of the hippocampus in one group of rabbits prior to classically conditioning the nictitating membrane. Berger found that the potentiated group learned significantly faster than a control group of animals that had not been potentiated. However, the most important correlation between the two forms of associative learning can be found at the cellular and subcellular level. There is widespread evidence showing that changes in synaptic plasticity are mediated by second messenger systems[4] (Byrne, 1987). More importantly, these changes in synaptic plasticity are associated with observed behavioral changes during classical conditioning and LTP. Walters and Byrne (1985), studying LTP in *Aplysia,* suggested the same second messenger system involved in the enhancement of transmitter release (cyclic AMP combined with accompanying synergistic effects of calcium) is the same one observed when *Aplysia* is classically conditioned (Hawkins, Abrams, Carew, & Kandel, 1983; Kandel, Abrams, Bernier, Carew, Hawkins, & Schwartz, 1983; Byrne, 1987).

---

[4]Second messengers are molecules that are indirectly activated by first messengers: the neurotransmitters such as glutamate and acetylcholine (see Woody, 1982; Nestler & Greengard, 1984; Shepherd, 1988). These second messengers in turn are catalysts for chemical processes that either enhance neurotransmitter release (Kandel & Schwartz, 1982), increase the number or effectiveness of the neurotransmitter receptors (Eccles, 1983), or change ionic channel conductances (Alkon, 1987), to name some of the better understood systems.

The ubiquitous role of calcium (Ca^{2+}) as a second messenger in synaptic plasticity has been suggested in LTP studies of the hippocampus (Turner, Baimbridge, & Miller, 1982; Dingledine, 1983; Eccles, 1983; Lynch, Larson, Kelso, Barrionuevo, & Schottler, 1983; Lynch & Baudry, 1984; Malenka, Kauer, Zucker, & Nicoll, 1988). The role of Ca^{2+} in conditioning *Aplysia* was mentioned earlier. In the mollusk *Hermissenda,* intracellular influx of Ca^{2+} is believed to lead to the phosphorylation of membrane potassium (K$^+$) channels or their associated proteins (Alkon, 1987). This phosphorylation leads to a reduction in the K$^+$ currents, resulting in the enhancement and protraction of the cell's excitability.

Gingrich and Byrne (1987) proposed a single-cell neuronal model for associative learning that reflects the subcellular mechanisms of the tail withdrawal reflex in *Aplysia.* In this model, the ISI function is related to the time course of intracellular influx and subsequent buffering of Ca^{2+}. Increase in transmitter release in this model (the presynaptic process of enhanced synaptic efficacy) depends on the chemical cascade initiated by the neuromodulator serotonin that is triggered by the US. This chemical cascade is effective only in the presence of a sufficient concentration of intracellular Ca^{2+}. Stronger and longer lasting CS stimulation will result in an increased influx of and a subsequent higher intracellular concentration of Ca^{2+}. In this model, the effects of ISI were simulated and resulted in the characteristic ISI curve (Fig. 5.3). However, as can be seen in

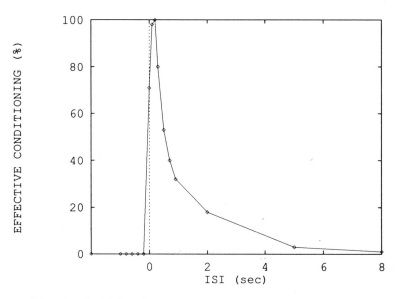

FIG. 5.3. ISI–CR function curve that resulted from computer simulations of a neuronal model of the tail withdrawal reflex in *Aplysia.* (From Gingrich & Byrne, 1987)

Fig. 5.3, an ISI of zero resulted in very effective conditioning. A CS of 400 ms and a US of 200 ms was used in this simulation. The model predicts that longer duration stimuli will result in even more effective conditioning when these stimuli are presented simultaneously. Furthermore, if the CS and US were 4 sec in duration, for example, the conditionability of an ISI of 0 or 500 msec would be virtually indistinguishable. This model, therefore, reflecting neurophysiological evidence, is consistent with the argument that the coactivity of the conditioning stimuli is responsible for establishing an association between the stimuli.

There is still much to be learned about the electrical and chemical processes leading to changes in synaptic efficacy. In LTP studies of the hippocampus, for example, changes in synaptic plasticity appear to be largely due to postsynaptic processes (Eccles, 1983; Scharfman & Sarvey, 1984; Malenka et al., 1988), but presynaptic and even retrograde (postsynaptic to presynaptic) trophic processes have also been observed (see Eccles, 1983; Byrne, 1987). However, there appears to be a growing consensus that a few second messenger systems are responsible for these varying changes in synaptic efficacy. There is evidence suggesting that it is the electrical and chemical results of the coactivity of the CS and the US STM replay that trigger these second messengers. The empirical evidence at the behavioral level in classical conditioning and LTP studies is consistent with this view.

As has been seen in this section, the empirical evidence suggests that CS–US associative strength is governed by the amount of CS–US overlap. Very short duration CSs and USs, as the ones used by Smith et al. (1969), seem incapable of producing learning. On the other hand, much longer CSs and USs are capable of producing excitatory simultaneous conditioning. A possible explanation for this will now be provided. The CR strength is also affected by CS and US intensity, but, in this discussion, it will be assumed the CS and the US are sufficiently strong to produce learning.

There are two factors to consider: intracellular biochemical processes and neuronal circuitry. As discussed previously, several second messenger systems have been identified as being responsible for changes in synaptic efficacy. Whether the process is a presynaptic or a postsynaptic one, after initial cell stimulation, a chemical cascade leads to the phosphorylation of proteins. Depending on which protein is acted on, changes in transmitter release, in ionic conductances, in the effectiveness of neurotransmitter receptors, or in the morphology of the lipid membrane (i.e., changes in the number of ionic channels or receptors) is believed to occur. All this takes time. Exactly how much time will depend on the system (see Gingrich & Byrne, 1987, for one possibility). It suffices to say that a short delay exists between the time CS and US signaling occur and synaptic changes occur.

Even more significant delays arise from the neural circuitry to be conditioned. Simple, monosynaptic systems will result in short delays between initial cellular stimulation and synaptic stimulation. Complex, multisynaptic systems will result in relatively long delays between initial stimuli and conditioning locus (synapse or cell) stimulation. This is due to the electrotonic or cable properties of neurons. These properties are due in part to the size of the fibers and whether or not they are myelinated (Shepherd, 1988, p. 117).

These delays then can account for why very short duration stimuli presented simultaneously, as used by Smith et al. (1969), are unable to elicit learning in such complex systems as the neural circuitry involved in the conditioning of the rabbit's nictitating membrane (Byrne, 1987, pp. 407–413). If these stimuli do not last long enough to account for the CS transmission line delay to the conditioning loci, US transmission line delay to same loci, and the intracellular biochemical delay discussed previously, then insufficient or no correlated presynaptic and postsynaptic activity will occur. On the other hand, if the CS and the US last long enough to account for these delays, then presynaptic and postsynaptic coactivity will occur long enough to elicit synaptic changes. Evidently the 2–8 sec duration conditioning stimuli used by Heth and Rescorla (1973), Heth (1976), Mahoney and Ayres (1976), and Burkhardt and Ayres (1978), in their conditioned suppression experiments in rats, were long enough to account for these delays in the very complex neuronal system investigated.

Evidence has been presented in this section supporting the validity of excitatory simultaneous conditioning and Hebbian or Hebbian-like learning. As in the backward conditioning case, the ISI variable is an insufficient indicator of the associability of stimuli in simultaneous conditioning. According to the argument presented in the last two sections, the duration of the CS–US overlap is as important as the ISI. This follows from the hypothesis, supported by neurophysiological evidence, that the STM replay of the CS and the US must be coactive at the locus of conditioning.

Conditioning Theory

The arguments that have been presented, thus far, lead to the proposition that the characteristic ISI curve is an artifact of an experimental procedure. This procedure includes the repetitive presentation of short duration (tens of milliseconds) conditioning stimuli at a fixed ITI. As a differing view, it is not *when* signals are presented that is important but *how much* coactivity of the internal CS and US representations occurs over time versus CS alone internal replay. According to this view, the backward presentation of the CS and the US can lead to learning, if the resultant internal representation of these signals are simultaneously rehearsed. This is possible when a surprising US triggers a neuromodulator that protracts the US rehearsal. As mentioned previously, the ISI variable is but one that must be considered in a given classical conditioning experiment. Other variables suggested for consideration include the CS and US durations, the duration of the CS–US overlap, whether the ITI is fixed or random, the number of training trials utilized, the emotional state of the animal, the complexity of the neuronal circuitry, the phylogenetic development of the animal, and whether the experimental preparation is in vitro or in vivo.

In Part II of this article, a theoretical framework is presented that incorporates Wagner and Terry's (1975) postulates, and has aspects reminiscent of Jones' (1962) two-principle theory of classical conditioning and Mowrer's (1960) two-factor theory. It is also very similar to the theory of opponent-process developed by Solomon and Corbit (1974) and espoused by Shurtleff and Ayres (1981) and Wagner and Larew (1985). The most important aspect of the theory was presented by Grossberg (1972a, 1972b) where he developed a quantitative model of opponent-processing that he called the *gated dipole*. This model was later refined by Grossberg and Schmajuk (1987) and was named the *recurrent associative gated dipole,* or READ circuit (for a distinction between the Solomon–Corbit opponent-process and the Grossberg opponent-process, see Grossberg and Schmajuk, 1987). The READ circuit also incorporates a spatial pattern learning rule. Like the Hebbian postulate, this rule specifies that the synaptic strength increase as a function of presynaptic and postsynaptic coactivation. However, unlike the Hebbian postulate, this rule specifies conditions under which this synaptic strength diminishes as well. Finally a mechanism for neuromodulation will be added to this model. This revised model of conditioning will be able to exhibit the observed behavioral phenomena attributable to backward and simultaneous conditioning.

PART II

Theoretical Framework

An addition to the model of drive, reinforcement, attention, and motivation Grossberg and his associates developed over the last two decades (Grossberg, 1972a, 1972b, 1975, 1982a, 1982b, 1983c, 1987a, 1987b; Grossberg & Levine, 1987; Grossberg & Schmajuk, 1987) is being proposed in this investigation. This addition is in the form of a neuromodulator locus analogous to the locus ceruleus, the major noradrenergic center of the brain. Addition of this center will produce modulation of the drive representations in STM as a result of unexpected noxious events such as shock. This STM regulation is the key that gives the modified model the capability to exhibit both excitatory and inhibitory backward conditioning consistent with observed behavioral data.

Within the theoretical foundation being exercised here, the diverse phenomena observed in Pavlovian conditioning can only be explained at the system level. That is not to say that micromechanisms are not important. This theoretical framework utilizes the formal language of nonlinear mathematics to develop fundamental dynamical laws of STM, LTM, and depletable transmitters. These dynamical laws are in turn the basis of the building blocks of neural architectures used to explain a wide range of cognitive and behavioral data (Grossberg, 1982c,

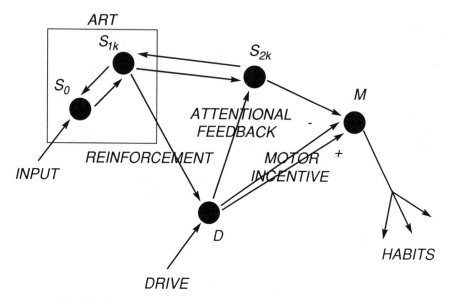

FIG. 5.4. Neural network architecture for drive, reinforcement, attention, and motivation. Sensory information (CS) is preprocessed at level
$S_0 - S_{1k}$. The preprocessed CSs become associated with drive representations at drive centers D. The drive centers in turn produce attentional feedback signals and positive or negative motor incentive signals used in learning and eliciting approach and avoidance behavior.
(Adapted from Grossberg, 1975, 1982a)

1987a, 1987b, 1988). The emphasis, therefore, is on the emergent properties of
hierarchical and heterarchical systems. This approach is quite different from the
classical approaches, relying on formal and single cell models, used to explain
Pavlovian conditioning (for a discussion of this distinction, see Grossberg,
1982b). A full treatment of this theoretical framework is not feasible here, but the
parts most relevant to this paper will be presented following.

Grossberg's model for drive, reinforcement, attention, and motivation is
shown in Fig. 5.4. Each of the major centers shown in Fig. 5.4 (S_0, S_{1k}, S_{2k}, D,
and M) represents a multiple cell structure. The higher-order sensory representations ($S_{1k}(t)$), or the CSs, are associated with drive representations ($D(t)$) such as
hunger, thirst, sex, pain, and their associated emotional responses, or the USs,
along conditionable *reinforcement* pathways. For example, the sounds of a met-
ronome can be associated with pleasurable food morsels along these pathways
(Pavlov, 1927/1960). The drive representations also provide two types of
arousal: attentional feedback and *motor incentive*. These two types of arousal
help explain how and what sensory information is attended to and how habits can
be formed. One of the strengths of this model is that it provides an unambiguous

connection between classical and instrumental conditioning. For a complete description of the system, see Grossberg (1975, 1982a).

In this chapter, concentration will be focused on the interaction between the sensory representations at the S_{1k} level and the drive centers at D. A detailed analysis of the circuits comprising the drive centers follows. An additional neuromodulatory center and its interaction with the drive centers will also be presented. More detailed anatomical and neurophysiological considerations will be addressed later.

The drive centers at D in Fig. 5.4 are comprised of READ circuits. The dipole is a neural mechanism for rebound, subserving positive and negative incentive motivation, and is central to Grossberg's theory of classical and instrumental conditioning. Grossberg (1972a, 1972b) indicated the necessity for a rebound mechanism in order to provide positive incentive (relief) from the termination of

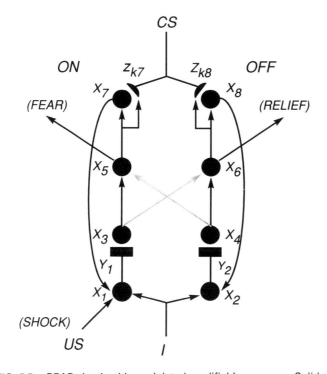

FIG. 5.5.   READ circuit with modulated modifiable synapses. Solid arrows represent excitatory connections, open arrows represent inhibitory connections, and the triangles (z_{k7} and z_{k8}) represent the modifiable synapses. The excitatory lower-level connections to the synapses represent on-response (US) modulation and off-response (US-rebound) modulation. The square synapses represent the depletable transmitters. CS stimulation comes from the sensory representations at S_{1k}.

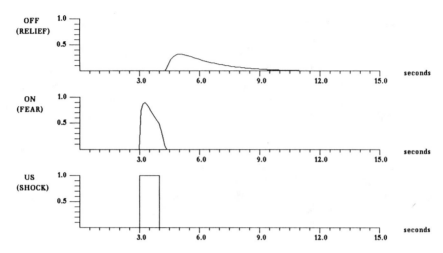

FIG. 5.6.   A computer simulation of the on-response and off-response dynamics of the READ circuit. A sustained on-response is produced during US stimulation, and a transient off-response or rebound results from US termination.

noxious stimuli such as shock. Grossberg and Schmajuk (1987) described how conditioned excitation and conditioned inhibition result in their analysis of the READ circuit (Fig. 5.5). A summary will be provided in the following.

The READ circuit has two main channels for processing information: the on-channel and the off-channel. The on-channel responds to the drive input or US. In the case shown in Fig. 5.5, the US is shock. The off-channel produces a transient response upon the reduction or termination of the drive input. The output of the system is at level x_5 (on-response) and x_6 (off-response). The on-response and off-response dynamics are shown in Fig. 5.6.

When the US is active, a sustained on-response is produced. This on-response will result in the attentional feedback and motor incentive signals previously mentioned (see Fig. 5.4 and 5.5). As can be seen in Fig. 5.5, the on-response also activates cell x_7 and modulates the synapses z_{k7}. The effects here are very similar to the ones Gingrich and Byrne (1987) modeled. The first modification to Grossberg's model is also encountered here. When the CS representations ($S_{1k}(t)$) are active at the same time an on-response both activates x_7 and modulates the synapses z_{k7}, the synaptic strengths (LTM traces) z_{k7} increase. This increase of synaptic efficacy results in conditioned excitation. After learning, a CS alone will excite x_7, which will in turn excite x_1 via the feedback pathway shown in Fig. 5.5, and subsequently produces an on-response. Conditioned inhibition occurs in a similar fashion. LTM traces z_{k8} increase only when CS representations are coactive with an off-response that resulted from the termination of a US. A CS alone tested after an increase of synaptic strengths z_{k8} will result in an off-response much like in the conditioned excitation case.

If the US is shock (see Fig. 5.5), the on-response of fear will produce a negative motor incentive signal and suppress motor activity, as in the CER conditioning paradigm. As may be recalled, conditioned excitation in this form of conditioning procedure was measured by how much a feeding behavior was suppressed. Any CS conditioned to the on-channel, or fear, will, therefore, also suppress motor activity when the CS is presented alone. The off-response relief signal will produce a positive motor incentive signal that will support motor activity. A CS conditioned to the off-channel, or relief, will signal safety and will not suppress motor activity, or feeding as in the CER conditioning paradigm.

The READ circuit described previously is, therefore, capable of producing conditioned excitation during forward and simultaneous presentations of the CS and the US. Conditioned inhibition occurs as a result of backwardly paired CSs and USs. In order for this model to exhibit excitatory backward conditioning, a mechanism that modulates US rehearsal in STM must be incorporated within the READ circuit. This mechanism is introduced in the following section.

Neuromodulatory Mechanism and Modification of READ Circuit

The proposed modulatory mechanism results in a modification of the READ circuit and an addition of a neuromodulatory center as shown in Fig. 5.7. Neuromodulator n is released whenever an unexpected US is experienced. This has the effect of prolonging the STM representation of the US. Further presentations of the US will result in less and less neuromodulator release as the US becomes expected. As this occurs, STM replay of the US will contract. It is the prolonged replay of the US in the initial backward conditioning trials that accounts for the excitatory backward conditioning phenomenon (see Part I, previous). On latter trials, as the STM replay of the US diminishes, the CS becomes a conditioned inhibitor.

As seen in Fig. 5.7, NC effects an added node to the READ circuit. This new node, x_0, is the relay between the US and the READ circuit on-channel. Neuromodulator n prolongs the US STM replay by decreasing the ionic (K^+) channel conductance that brings the cell activity (potential) back to its resting state. The lower this conductance is, the more enhanced and prolonged the cell activity $x_0(t)$ will become upon stimulation. Therefore, on-channel activity, representing US STM replay, is maintained after the actual termination of the US by the effects of neuromodulator n on x_0's ion channels.

Up to this point, a qualitative description of the READ circuit, its proposed modification, and the neuromodulatory mechanism has been provided. The dynamic equations for each of these will now be presented in the following. The

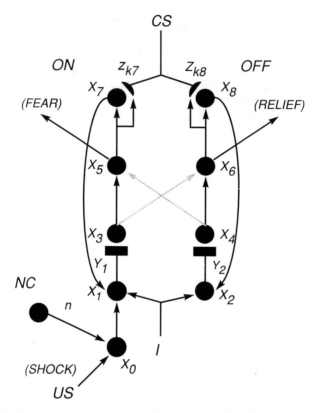

FIG. 5.7.   Addition of neuromodulatory center *NC*. *NC* releases neuro-transmitter *n* when a surprising US is experienced. *n* reduces the passive decay term of an added US relay node, x_0, to the READ circuit. This causes protraction of the US STM replay after the termination of the US.

reader is encouraged to compare these equations with the ones for the READ I equations Grossberg and Schmajuk (1987) introduced. The most significant changes are the additions to the model (Equations 1–3) and the altered LTM dynamics (Equations 14 and 15). For compatibility, the same nomenclature will be used for most of the equations following as the one used for the equations in Grossberg and Schmajuk (1987).

Neurotransmitter Release

$$\frac{d}{dt}n = -A_2 n + (n_{max} - n)P \tag{1}$$

US Activation

$$\epsilon_1 \frac{d}{dt} x_0 = -A_1 x_0 + (1 - x_0)J \tag{2}$$

Ion Channel Modulation

$$\frac{d}{dt} A_1 = (A_{max} - A_1) + (A_{min} - A_1)h(n) \tag{3}$$

Tonic Arousal + US + Feedback On-Activation

$$\epsilon_1 \frac{d}{dt} x_1 = -x_1 + I + f(x_0) + Mf(x_7) \tag{4}$$

US + Feedback Off-Activation

$$\epsilon_1 \frac{d}{dt} x_2 = -x_2 + I + Mf(x_8) \tag{5}$$

On-Transmitter

$$\frac{d}{dt} y_1 = B(2 - y_1) - Cg(x_1)y_1 \tag{6}$$

Off-Transmitter

$$\frac{d}{dt} y_2 = B(2 - y_2) - Cg(x_2)y_2 \tag{7}$$

Gated On-Activation

$$\epsilon_1 \frac{d}{dt} x_3 = -x_3 + Dg(x_1)y_1 \tag{8}$$

Gated Off-Activation

$$\epsilon_1 \frac{d}{dt} x_4 = -x_4 + Dg(x_2)y_2 \tag{9}$$

Normalized Opponent On-Activation

$$\epsilon_1 \frac{d}{dt} x_5 = -x_5 + (E - x_5)x_3 - (E + x_5)x_4 \tag{10}$$

Normalized Opponent Off-Activation

$$\epsilon_1 \frac{d}{dt} x_6 = -x_6 + (E - x_6)x_4 - (E + x_6)x_3 \tag{11}$$

On-Activation by CS Inputs

$$\epsilon_1 \frac{d}{dt} x_7 = -x_7 + (1 - x_7)(G[x_5]^+ + H \sum_k S_{1k} z_{k7}) \qquad (12)$$

where $[x]^+ = max(x,0)$

Off-Activation by CS Inputs

$$\epsilon_1 \frac{d}{dt} x_8 = -x_8 + (1 - x_8)(G[x_6]^+ + H \sum_k S_{1k} z_{k8}) \qquad (13)$$

Modulated On-Conditioned Reinforcer Learning

$$\epsilon_2 \frac{d}{dt} z_{k7} = g(x_7)(-K_1 z_{k7} + L_1 S_{1k}[x_5]^+) \qquad (14)$$

Modulated Off-Conditioned Reinforcer Learning

$$\epsilon_2 \frac{d}{dt} z_{k8} = g(x_8)(-K_2 z_{k8} + L_2 S_{1k}[x_6]^+) \qquad (15)$$

On-Response Signal

$$O_1 = [x_5]^+ \qquad (16)$$

Off-Response Signal

$$O_2 = [x_6]^+ \qquad (17)$$

Equation 1 describes the neuromodulator n release from the neuromodulatory center NC. NC is triggered by a short-duration event-related potential P originating from the Adaptive Resonance Theory (ART, Grossberg, 1984; Carpenter & Grossberg, 1987) circuit at the $S_0 - S_{1k}$ level (see Figs. 5.4 and 5.8). P triggers n release at a concentration level approaching n_{max}. The neuromodulator n decays slowly at rate A_2 after initial release. Therefore, when an unexpected US is experienced, P is produced and triggers the neuromodulatory release. When ART experiences an unexpected event, an event-related potential is produced and resets ART's recognition codes (Grossberg, 1984; Banquet & Grossberg, 1987). For now, it will be assumed that an ART (not explicitly simulated here) at the level shown in Fig. 5.4 also signals the NC. The focus in this investigation is on the effects of neuromodulation on the READ circuit and how these effects influence conditioning. For simplicity, it will be assumed that, on the first occurrence of the US, the P signal will be generated and produce n release. Further US presentation will not result in additional event-related potentials nor further neuromodulator release.

Equation 2 describes the initial stage of the US activation of the on-channel. J

is a rectangular pulse function corresponding with the US input. Equation 2 is in the form of the following equation describing the membrane potential V of neurons (Hodgkin, 1964; Grossberg & Schmajuk, 1987; Shepherd, 1988):

$$C\frac{dV}{dt} = (V^p - V)g^p + (V^+ - V)g^+ + (V - V)g^- \qquad (18)$$

C relates to a constant lipid membrane capacitance. The constants V^p, V^+, and V^- relate to the passive, excitatory, and inhibitory membrane potential saturation points respectively. In the Hodgkin and Huxley (1952) model, these saturation points indicate the equilibrium potential of specific ions. The terms g^p, g^+, and g^- are the passive, excitatory, and inhibitory ionic conductances respectively. In Equation 2, the inhibitory portion of the membrane equation is missing, and V^p is 0. In reality, there are many more ionic conductances than those shown in Equation 18 (see Shepherd, 1988), but these can be grouped functionally into the three main types of conductances: passive conductances, to bring the cell back to its resting potential; excitatory conductances; and inhibitory conductances.

Term A_1 in Equations 2 and 3 is analogous with g^p or the various K^+ channel conductances of neurons. It is known that all K^+ channels act to bring the cell back to its polarized resting state (Shepherd, 1988). In this model, n (assumed to be norepinephrine) modulates A_1 (the K^+ channels) as described by Equation 3. When n is released, n drives A_1 to its minimum value A_{min}. In the absence of n, A_1 recovers to its maximum value A_{max}. Direct neurophysiological evidence for this type of modulation will be presented later.

Equations 4 and 5 describe the on-channel and off-channel activation resulting from US input via x_0, tonic input I, and READ circuit feedback. M critically damps positive feedback to avoid sustained oscillations in the circuit (see Grossberg, 1987a, for the use of gated dipoles as oscillators and pacemakers). Equations 6 and 7 describe transmitter depletion, at constant rate C, and transmitter recovery, at constant rate B. Equations 8 and 9 describe the effects of the gated on-channel and off-channel signals. When there is no inhibition and the total excitatory input can be controlled to a small value, an additive approximation of the shunting membrane equation may be used as in Equations 4, 5, 8, and 9.

Equations 10 and 11 describe opponent-processing through a competitive mechanism. Notice that Equations 10 and 11 contain the three major parts of the membrane equation: passive decay, excitation, and inhibition. Terms E and $-E$ define the excitatory and inhibitory saturation points in these equations.

The last processing stage of the READ circuit is described in Equations 12 and 13. The higher-level sensory stages make synaptic connections (z_{k7} and z_{k8}) with nodes x_7 and x_8 as shown in Fig. 5.4 and 5.7. On-activation of x_7 is produced by the combination of on-response $[x_5]^+$ and CS (S_{1k}) signaling. It will be assumed in this model that a given CS will correspond with an individual kth sensory representation term S_{1k}. This S_{1k} signal is gated by the LTM trace, or synaptic strength z_{1k}, and combined with other contextual sensory information in the sum

$H \Sigma S_{1k}z_{k7}$. Off-activation of x_8 is produced similarly and is described in Equation 13. Grossberg and Schmajuk (1987, p. 204) defined the relationship

$$\sum S_{1k}z_{k7} > \sum S_{1k}z_{k8} \tag{19}$$

as a *positive conditioned reinforcer context* and

$$\sum S_{1k}z_{k8} \; S_{1k}z_{k7} > \tag{20}$$

as a *negative conditioned reinforcer context*. A *positive conditioned reinforcer context* is equivalent to a conditioned excitor and will elicit an on-response from the READ circuit. On the other hand, a *negative conditioned reinforcer context* is equivalent to a conditioned inhibitor and will elicit an off-response from the READ circuit.

Associative learning is described in Equations 14 and 15. In equation 14, LTM traces z_{k7} grow, if presynaptic activity S_{1k}, synaptic on-response modulation $[x_5]^+$, and postsynaptic activity $g(x_7)$ are coactive. The decay term $-K_1z_{k7}$ ensures that the LTM traces record possible decreases in modulated paired presynaptic and postsynaptic activity as well. This associative learning rule correlates modulated presynaptic cell activity, coded as spatial patterns, with postsynaptic activity. In other words, LTM traces z_{k7} tend to match the modulated spatial pattern produced by S_{1k}. In a similar fashion, LTM traces z_{k8} encode the spatial pattern produced by S_{1k} when modulated by $[x_6]^+$ in Equation 15.

The unmodulated version of this learning rule (i.e., without on-response or off-response modulation) was introduced by Grossberg (1969) and has played a leading role in the development of his theories and architectures (Grossberg, 1982c, 1987a, 1987b, 1988; Grossberg & Kuperstein, 1986). Direct neurophysiological evidence for this learning law has been reported by Levy and Steward (1979) and Levy (1985), in their investigations of LTP in the hippocampus, and Rauschecker and Singer (1979) and Singer (1983), in their studies of the cat's visual cortex. Indeed the unmodulated versions of Equations 14 and 15 can be used in this model without causing any significant differences in how and what is learned. The unmodulated versions of Equations 14 and 15 are shown following.

Unmodulated On-Conditioned Reinforcer Learning

$$\frac{d}{dt}z_{k7} = g(x_7)(-K_1z_{k7} + L_1S_{1k}) \tag{21}$$

Unmodulated Off-Conditioned Reinforcer Learning

$$\frac{d}{dt}z_{k8} = g(x_8)(-K_2z_{k8} + L_2S_{1k}) \tag{22}$$

A third alternative was introduced by Grossberg and Schmajuk (1987) in their analysis of conditioned reinforcement and conditioned inhibition in READ circuit dynamics. Equations 23 and 24 describe their on-conditioned reinforcer learning and off-conditioned reinforcer learning respectively.

On-Conditioned Reinforcer Learning

$$\frac{d}{dt} z_{k7} = S_{1k}(-K z_{k7} + L[x_5]^+) \qquad (23)$$

Off-Conditioned Reinforcer Learning

$$\frac{d}{dt} z_{k8} = S_{1k}(-K z_{k8} + L[x_6]^+) \qquad (24)$$

Now z_{k7} computes a time average of $[x_5]^+$ at a rate proportional to S_{1k} (Grossberg & Schmajuk, 1987, p. 206). In other words, what is learned is the on-response signal in the presence of an active S_{1k}, not the S_{1k} spatial pattern. Similarly z_{k8} learns the off-response signal in the presence of an active CS. This distinction is not important in the simple experiments simulated in Grossberg and Schmajuk (1987) and in this chapter, because the final results are very similar. This is because each given CS is processed through a distinct input pathway S_{1k}. When a CS is coactive with an on-response, for example, the LTM trace for that CS pathway grows and results in an easily identifiable conditioned excitor regardless of whether Equations 14–15, 21–22, or 23–24 is used.

However, if the neural network becomes much more complex than in these simulations, the problem that arises in using the learning in Equations 23 and 24 becomes apparent. Say, for example, various READ circuits or drive centers compete for activation in order to elicit an appropriate emotional response. If the CSs and other environmental contextual cues produce complex spatial patterns along the reinforcement pathway shown in Fig. 5.4, then the various READ circuits must be able to learn and distinguish these spatial patterns. Otherwise the environmental signals would be meaningless and the system would not be able to function appropriately. In the much more complex case just described, equations in the form of Equations 23 and 24 cannot be used, because these do not encode the spatial pattern produced by S_{1k}.

In this section, the dynamic equations for the neuromodulatory mechanism and the modified READ circuit were presented. For a more in-depth analysis of the gated dipole and the READ circuit, see Grossberg (1972b, 1984), and Grossberg and Schmajuk (1987). The computer simulations of this system follow.

Computer Simulations

As Grossberg commented on numerous occasions, the full extent of observed behavioral phenomena can neither be explained with single equations nor with simple systems. Grossberg and his colleagues have shown how the READ circuit, within the architecture described in the Theoretical Framework section, can explain a wide range of behavioral phenomena in previous work (Grossberg, 1982b, 1984; Grossberg & Levine, 1987; Grossberg & Schmajuk, 1987). The purpose of the simulations described in this section is to examine how the modified READ circuit handles simultaneous and backward conditioning. For this purpose, the entire architecture described previously need not be implemented. The results of these simulations are consistent with observed behavior. As far as this author knows, this has not been achieved by any other neural network model. In addition, LTP of cell x_7, an analog of hippocampal cells, is shown.

The dynamics and learning capabilities of the modified READ circuit, described by Equations 1–17, will be examined and the results shown in Fig. 5.8–5.22. In these simulations, a passive extinction process is assumed (see Grossberg & Schmajuk, 1987, for a distinction between passive and active extinction processes). This process is controlled by the interaction of parameters K_i and L_i in learning Equations 14 and 15. Parameters K_1 and L_1 are chosen to allow excitatory weights z_{k7} to decay towards zero during CS-alone extinction trials, and parameters K_2 and L_2 are chosen to provide inhibitory weights z_{k8} with a resistance to passive extinction during CS-alone trials. The appendix shows the values of all parameters used in these simulations.

In each simulation, the dynamics of selected elements along the on-channel and on-response and off-response dynamics are shown to illustrate the important characteristics of the system. In each of the figures that follow, a series of graphs shows, in order from bottom to top, the synaptic weights after each training trial, the US and CS configuration in time, and selected element dynamics. The element dynamics shown in each figure are those associated with the last trial shown in the synaptic weight graph. In each of the simulations shown, a CS-alone extinction session follows each conditioning session. A CS of magnitude .25 was used in the simulations shown in Fig. 5.8–5.16. The units of time and magnitude are arbitrary; however, in these simulations, the unit of time is assumed to be the second.

Figures 5.8–5.11 show the results of a simulated backward conditioning experiment. Figure 5.8 exhibits the results of the first trial of conditioning. As explained earlier, the assumption is made that, on the first trial of conditioning, the unexpected US results in the signaling of NC, which in turn produces the release of neuromodulator n. One can see this initial neuromodulator release, in the graph labeled n, at the same time of US onset. Notice the slow rate of decay of n over time. The effects of n on parameter A_1 (the K^+ channel conductance) are quite dramatic as can be seen in the figure. The sudden increase of n causes a very rapid reduction of the decay term A_1 of cell x_0. Although the dynamics of x_0 are not shown, notice the effects of x_0 on x_1. The $x_1(t)$ activity reflects the protracted STM replay of the US. One can see that this activity extends beyond the actual US offset. The on-response and off-response (recall these reflect the positive activity of x_5 and x_6 respectively) are shown in the top two graphs of

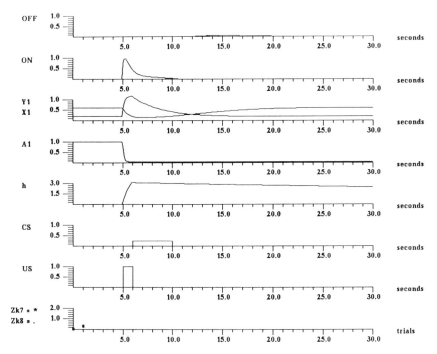

FIG. 5.8.   The first trial of a computer simulation of backward conditioning showing an increase of the excitatory weight. The ordinate of
each graph is shown to the left of the graph and the abscissa to the
right. From bottom to top, the synaptic weight strengths, the CS–US
configuration, and selective components of the READ circuit are
shown to illustrate the important dynamics of the system. The STM
and element dynamics shown in this and all subsequent figures represent the dynamics after the last session shown in the weight graph
labeled Z_{ki}.

Fig. 5.8. The on-response gradually decreases over time; thus, very little off-
response results. Cells x_7 and x_8 are directly stimulated by the on-response and
off-response respectively. The activity of these elements are not shown in the
figure. The increase of the excitatory weight z_{k7}, at the end of the first trial,
reflects the simultaneous coactivation of presynaptic CS activity, postsynaptic x_7
activity (not shown), and synaptic on-response modulation.

   Fig. 5.9 shows the results of the backward conditioning session after the
eighth trial. Neuromodulator n has now decayed, or dissipated, to a very low
level. This in turn has allowed the decay term A_1 to increase. Notice how much
the US STM replay, reflected by the $x_1(t)$ activity, has contracted compared to the
same activity in the first trial as shown in Fig. 5.8. The contracted on-response
reflects the contracted US STM replay. The opponent-processing is now produc-

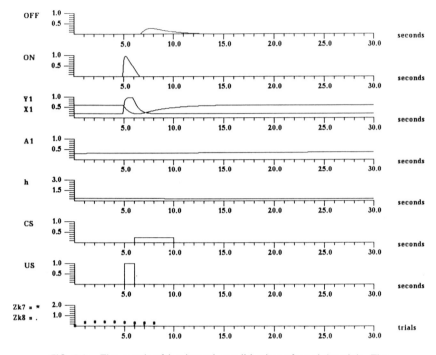

FIG. 5.9. The result of backward conditioning after eight trials. The excitatory strength produced in the first few trials has weakened as conditioning progresses.

ing a strong rebound as depicted by the off-response. We turn our attention now to the synaptic weights. Notice there was an increase of the excitatory weight z_{k7} over the first few trials, then a slight decrease by the eighth trial. Although it is difficult to discern in the figure, the inhibitory weight z_{k8} has begun to increase. This reflects the CS sampling of the off-response at cell x_8 that is now occurring.

Fig. 5.10 shows how learning has progressed by the 30th trial. The increase of the inhibitory weight is now clear by this time. The neuromodulator has completely decayed, and the x_1 cell decay term A_1 has reached its unmodulated high level. Compare the on-response and off-response dynamics shown in Fig. 5.10 with the same dynamics shown in Fig. 5.8. The on-response in Fig. 5.8 lasts over five seconds, whereas the on-response in Fig. 5.10 lasts just slightly over one second, nearly the same duration as the US. In Fig. 5.8, very little rebound is seen after on-response; however, in Fig. 5.10, a strong rebound is observed. Figure 5.11 shows where the inhibitory weight z_{k8} asymptotes after 60 trials of backward conditioning. The scale on the weight graph has changed in this figure.

Figs. 5.8–5.11 have shown the transient effects attributable to backward conditioning. The initial trials produced an excitatory tendency as a result of the

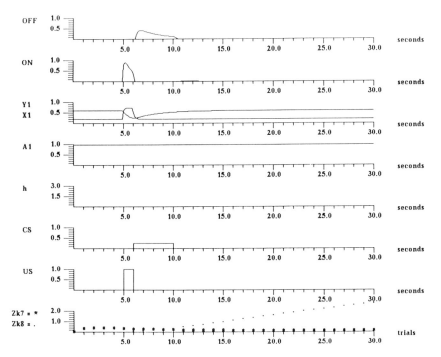

FIG. 5.10. Learning after 30 trials of backward conditioning, in this computer simulation, shows the biphasic behavior attributable to this learning paradigm. An early excitatory phase gives way to a sustained inhibitory phase with repeated training.

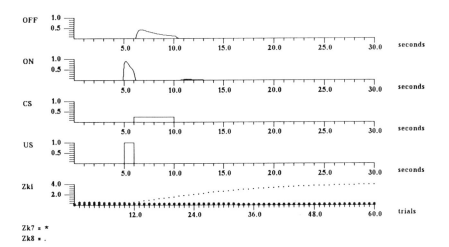

FIG. 5.11. The same backward conditioning stimulus configuration shown in FIGS. 5.8–5.10 exhibits the inhibitory weight asymptote after 60 simulated conditioning trials. The weight magnitude scale was increased in this figure.

145

protraction of the US STM replay. This STM protraction was caused by the release of neurotransmitter n, which in turn reduced the K^+ channel conductance analog (A_1) of cell x_0. As training progressed, the US STM replay contracted to approximately the same duration of the US pulse itself as n decayed. As the US STM replay contracted, the off-response rebound became more prominent, and the CS sampled less of the on-response and more of the off-response. For this reason, the initial excitatory tendency gave way to sustained inhibition. Figure 5.12 shows a 10-trial, CS-alone extinction session with the weights obtained in the 60 trial backward conditioning session. As Fig. 5.12 illustrates, the inhibitory weight decreases somewhat throughout the session; however, the conditioned inhibition is resistant to extinguishment. This will become more apparent in the next two simulations.

Figs. 5.13–5.18 show the simulation results of three different simultaneous conditioning experiments using different sets of CS and US durations. Figs. 5.13, 5.15, and 5.17 show only the synaptic weights after each training trial, the CS–US configuration, and the on-response and off-response dynamics of the last training trial. Figs. 5.14, 5.16, and 5.19 show CS-alone extinction trials for the three experiments. Fig. 5.13 describes the result of a 30-trial, 60 sec CS paired with a 1 sec US. This is similar to Siegel and Domjan's (1971) experiment where a very long CS and a very short US were paired. As can be seen, negligible conditioned excitation was produced. On the other hand, inhibition was established after the fifth trial and was maintained throughout the remainder of the session. This result is consistent with Siegel and Domjan's findings. As Burkhardt and Ayres (1978) suggested, the CS extending so far beyond the US acted

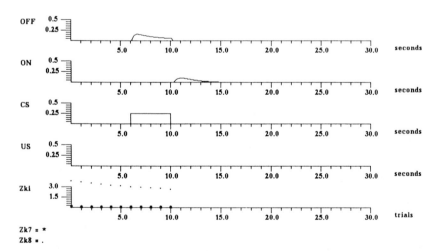

FIG. 5.12. Computer simulation of a ten-trial CS-alone extinction session after the learning achieved in the conditioning session described in FIG. 5.11.

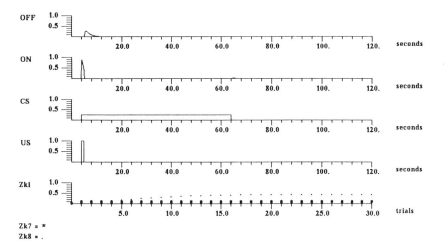

FIG. 5.13. Computer simulation results of a 30-trial simultaneous conditioning experiment. A 60 sec CS is paired with a 1 sec US. Minimal conditioned excitation is produced even in the first few trials when the US STM replay is protracted. Conditioned inhibition is the final outcome.

as a CS-alone extinction trial. Even with the effects of the neuromodulator in the first few trials, any excitatory tendencies were counteracted by the very long CS. Fig. 5.14 again shows that the inhibitory weight obtained during the conditioning experiment depicted in Fig. 5.13 is resistant to extinguishment during a CS-alone session.

A CS of four seconds is used in the simulation depicted in Fig. 5.15. Although the final outcome is similar to that of the previous simulation, the initial trials show very different results. During the first few trials, when the US STM is protracted, the CS becomes a conditioned excitor. As the US STM contracts with time, the inhibitory weight overtakes the excitatory weight, making the CS a conditioned inhibitor. The CS-alone extinction session shown in Fig. 5.17 is consistent with the simulations of the other two extinction sessions showing that the inhibitory weight is maintained after ten trials. However, one can see that the conditioned excitation initially established is rapidly extinguished during the extinction session.

In the simulated experiments that have been described so far, the READ circuit has been directly stimulated with rectangular pulse CSs and USs. It has also been assumed that no transmission line delays nor intracellular biochemical delays exist or, equivalently, that the CS and US durations in each experiment account for these delays. These delay assumptions will be maintained in the conditioning and extinction sessions described in Fig. 5.17 and 5.18; however, in the simulation shown in those figures, the READ circuit was stimulated by the

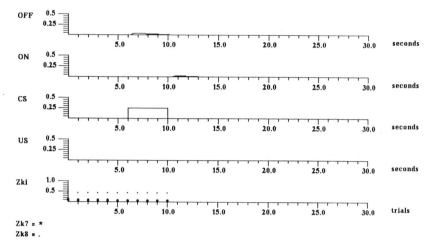

FIG. 5.14. Computer simulation of a ten-trial CS-alone extinction session after the learning achieved in the conditioning session described in FIG. 5.13. Consistent with observed experimental behavior, the conditioned inhibition is resistant to extinguishment.

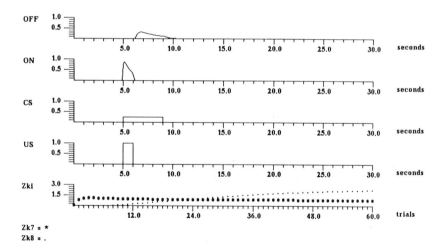

FIG. 5.15. Results of another simulation of a simultaneous conditioning session. The CS duration in this simulation is 4 sec. Although the final outcome is similar to the result shown in FIG. 5.13, the initial trials show a significant increase in the excitatory weight.

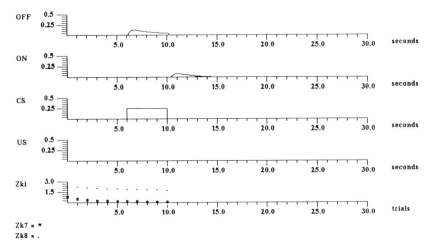

FIG. 5.16. This CS-alone extinction session again shows the inhibitory weight's resistance to extinguishment. The excitatory weight, on the other hand, rapidly extinguishes during the CS-alone trials.

CS via a sensory s_1 node. In other words, a CS rectangular pulse excited s_1 and in turn produced a CS STM signal (see Fig. 5.17). This CS STM signal then excited the z_{k7} and z_{k8} synapses. This arrangement is similar to that depicted in Figs. 5.4 and 5.5. Equation 25 describes the $s_1(t)$ activity.

$$\epsilon_1 \frac{d}{dt} s_1 = -s_1 + (1 - s_1)S \tag{25}$$

S in Equation 25 is a rectangular pulse function corresponding to the CS input.

The simulation in Fig. 5.17 is of the final simultaneous conditioning experiment presented here. In this experiment, a .5 magnitude, 4 sec CS and a .5 magnitude, 4 sec US were paired. The result shown is consistent with what Heth (1976) demonstrated in the 160-trial CER simultaneous conditioning experiment. As may be recalled, Heth reported that the suppression (measure of CR strength) observed in the initial trials was attenuated at the end of the session; however, suppression was maintained even after 160 trials. The need for the inclusion of the s_1 node in the circuit may now be apparent. As can be seen in Fig. 5.17, the relatively slow decay of the CS STM allowed for a small amount of coactive CS STM activity and off-response rebound. This accounts for the small increase of the inhibitory weight after the 12th trial and for the suppression of the overall excitatory strength, or the *positive conditioned reinforcer*, by the end of the conditioning session. If the READ circuit would have been directly stimulated by the CS pulse, the conditioned excitation produced would not have been attenuated by the end of the conditioning session. Thus, the s_1 node was included to give the circuit the capability to exhibit more realistic behavior. The extinction

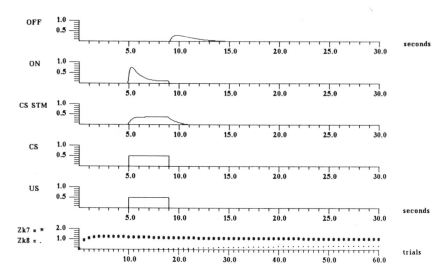

FIG. 5.17. In this simultaneous conditioning simulation, a relay node between the CS and the READ has been added in order to introduce CS STM replay. In this simulation, the CS and US duration is 4 sec. Although the total *positive conditioned reinforcer* strength is attenuated after 60 trials, the CS is established as a conditioned excitor in this simultaneous CS–US configuration. This is consistent with Heth's (1976) experimental findings.

session described in Fig. 5.18 shows the extinguishment of the excitatory weight after CS-alone trials.

In the simulations described so far in this section, the modified READ circuit exhibited behavior consistent with the experimental evidence presented in Part I. The neural network model employed here is also consistent with Wagner and Terry's (1975) proposition that the [positive] CS–US association depends upon the degree of "postepisodic rehearsal of the two events in STM," that US STM rehearsal depends on how surprising the US is and that any positive association established decreases during CS-alone rehearsal. This position has also been supported by others, especially Burkhardt and Ayres (1978), and Dostálek (1972, 1973). This hypothesis is extended in this article by adding that a negative CS–US association depends on the postepisodic rehearsal of CS STM and the rebound STM of the US. This rebound STM has an emotional value opposite to that of the US STM, such as in the case of relief from fear. Whether the CS becomes a conditioned excitor (positive conditioned reinforcer context) or a conditioned inhibitor (negative conditioned reinforcer context) depends on the total positive and negative association established as described in the relationships in Equations 19 and 20.

One final set of simulations was performed in order to test the modulated

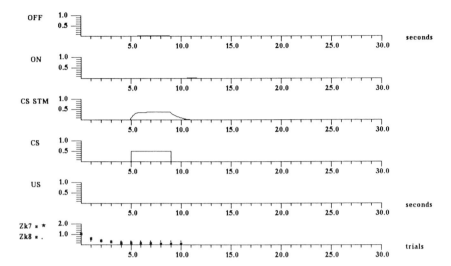

FIG. 5.18. Consistent with observed behavioral phenomena, this extinction session shows the extinguishment of the excitatory strength produced in the simulation described in FIG. 5.17.

conditioned reinforcer learning rule (Equations 14 & 15) in the READ for LTP. As previously mentioned, Levy (1985) and Levy and Steward (1979) found direct evidence for the unmodulated form of Equations 14 and 15 in their studies of LTP in the hippocampus. As will be discussed in the next section, cells x_7 and x_8 are analogous to the hippocampus. This mock-hippocampus should be able to be potentiated and depotentiated similarly to what has been observed experimentally. As discussed in Part I, evidence shows that the presynaptic stimulation must be strong enough and persist long enough in order to produce LTP. Hence, neither strong, short pulse trains nor weak, long pulse trains should be able to potentiate the READ. These conditions were examined in the simulations. The simulations consist of direct pulse stimulation of cells x_7 and x_8 along the monosynaptic CS pathway used in the simulations described in Figs. 5.8–5.16. A small initial weight of .05 was assigned to z_{k7} and z_{k8}. This is a completely valid assumption based on the experimental evidence.

Fig. 5.19 shows the result of a 10-trial potentiation session using a .8 magnitude, 4 sec presynaptic stimulus (CS). As illustrated by the rise in z_{k7}, potentiation was established by the 5th trial. Levy (1985) and Levy and Steward (1979) demonstrated that, after LTP had been established, subsequent depotentiation could be produced by strong postsynaptic stimulation. Fig. 5.20 exhibits this phenomenon. A strong postsynaptic activity was produced by a 1 magnitude, 4 sec US signal applied to x_0, stimulating the on-channel and subsequently x_7. Figs. 5.21 and 5.22 show that neither weak, long pulses nor strong, short pulses are sufficient to produce LTP. This predicts behavior observed experimentally.

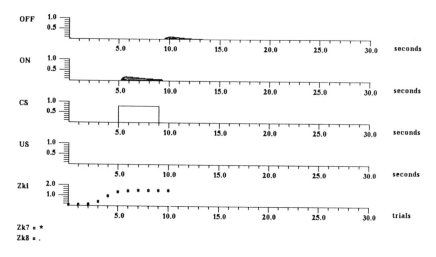

FIG. 5.19. Computer simulation of LTP of the READ. A 4 sec, .8 magnitude presynaptic stimulus (CS) was sufficient to potentiate the mock-hippocampal synapses z_{k7}.

In summary, the simulations described in this section have shown the conditions under which backward and simultaneous conditioning are possible. In addition, these simulations have shown that the neural network model can predict the conditions under which LTP and depotentiation in the hippocampus can occur. These findings are consistent with the experimental evidence introduced in Part I.

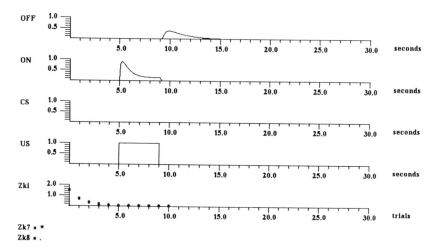

FIG. 5.20. Consistent with experimental evidence, depotentiation results from strong postsynaptic stimulation. In this case, the postsynaptic stimulus (US) is a 4 sec, 1 magnitude pulse.

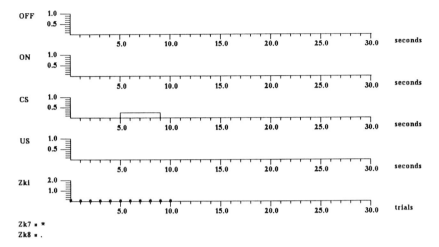

FIG. 5.21.   Computer simulation of a 4 sec, .25 magnitude presynaptic stimulus is insufficient to produce LTP.

Anatomical and Neurophysiological Analogs

As was mentioned in the first section of Part II, each drive center D (see Fig. 5.4) is made up of a READ circuit. It was also suggested that center D is representative of the hypothalamus and various other limbic system structures. In this

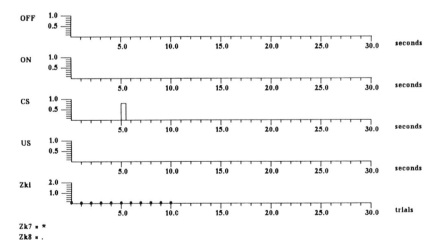

FIG. 5.22.   Computer simulation of a 1 sec, .8 magnitude presynaptic stimulus is insufficient to produce LTP. This result and the results shown in FIGS. 5.19–5.21 are consistent with the experimental evidence suggesting that the presynaptic stimulus must be strong enough and persist long enough before LTP is established.

section, we will consider the originally suggested analogs of this system in greater detail and, based on more current data, suggest revisions of the earlier position. In addition, neurophysiological and anatomical analogs of the proposed neuromodulatory center will be provided at the end of this section. Adding a cautionary note, the READ circuit and its individual elements were never meant to be exact replicas of real anatomies (Grossberg, 1975). Instead the analogies are meant to provide possible insight into the functional interrelationships of real anatomical systems.

Grossberg (1972b) proposed that the channel processing noxious or painful information in the gated dipole, such as the on-channel in Figs. 5.5 and 5.7, is analogous to the ventromedial hypothalamus (VMH) and that the relief pathway is analogous to the lateral hypothalamus (LH). Later Grossberg (1975) revised and extended the model. He proposed that the circuit up to the level of x_5 and x_6 (the gated dipole) is a "mock-septum" and that cells x_7 and x_8 comprise a "mock-hippocampus." He further suggested that the source of the drive input is from the hypothalamus and the source of the tonic input from the reticular formation. Still later Grossberg (1982a) proposed that neurophysiological data suggested that the READ circuit is analogous to the circuitry joining the hypothalamus, septum, amygdala, and hippocampus. He also referenced his original position reflecting the dipole's analogy to the hypothalamus, the x_7 and x_8 cells' analogy to hippocampal cells, and the feedback pathway's analogy to the medial forebrain bundle. Finally, as was mentioned in the Theoretical Framework section, the mock-hippocampus has bidirectional communication with the mock-neocortex along the reinforcement and attentional feedback pathways.

Although the READ circuit is an obvious oversimplification of the system it models, the anatomic analogs assigned to it appear to be quite good ones in light of emerging neurobiological data and theories. Stellar, Brooks, and Mills (1979) and Stellar (1982) reported further evidence that the LH is associated with reward and pleasantness, whereas the VMH is associated with punishment and unpleasantness. This supports Grossberg's earlier suggestions relating to the hypothalamic centers. The dipole as an analogy of the septum also appears to be a valid one. Thomas (1988) recently presented ample evidence for the lateral septum's (LS) role in relief from fear or anxiety, and inhibition of emotional behavior. Thomas also suggested that the medial septum (MS) is involved in producing anxiety. Even more interestingly, Thomas presented evidence of rebound effects in the MS following the electrical stimulation of the LS. Taken together, the evidence suggests a dual channel motivational system with the ability to process complementary emotional signals of opposite sign or meaning, and with rebound capabilities. It appears that the VMH in conjunction with the MS is associated with anxiety and punishment, whereas the LH in conjunction with LS is associated with relief and reward. This is certainly reminiscent of the dipole.

With the information available thus far, a revision of the earlier analogies can be suggested and made somewhat more specific. It is suggested that the lower portions of the gated dipole, up to the level of y_1 and y_2, are analogous with the hypothalamus and the portions responsible for opponent-processing, up to x_5 and x_6, with the septum. This may be too specific; therefore, alternatively and closer to the original analogy, one can simply consider that the gated dipole is analogous to the combination of the hypothalamus and the septum. It is also necessary to clarify the situation further. As one may recall, center D in Fig. 5.4 is representative of a drive hierarchy that includes thirst, hunger, sex, pain, and so on. Therefore, the VMH/VS processes the negative aspects of the previous drives, whereas the LH/LS processes the positive aspects of the same drives.

The drive input and tonic input analogies to the READ or mock-limbic system must now also be revised. Based on recent findings, it is now known that the hypothalamus receives [drive] input from at least two sources: the nucleus of the solitary tract in the medulla oblongata, and various nuclei in the reticular formation, possibly the nucleus pontis caudalis and the nucleus gigantocellularis (Nauta & Feirtag, 1986; Shepherd, 1988; Vertes & Miller, 1976). The nucleus of the solitary tract receives afferents from various chemoreceptors and baroreceptors of the body including the mouth, digestive tract, respiratory tract, heart, and blood vessels. Therefore, the hypothalamus receives important visceral information via the nucleus of the solitary tract. The mesencephalic reticular formation is responsible for relaying somatosensory information to the hypothalamus. This is done via the spinoreticular tract, which in turn is a branch of the spinothalamic tract: the main channel for somatosensory information. Therefore, the drive input to the READ is analogous to afferents from the nucleus of the solitary tract and afferents from somatosensory nuclei in the reticular formation. Grossberg suggested that the tonic input drive originated from the reticular formation as well. This analogy is probably a good one, albeit a more speculative one. This input may be a tonic serotonergic input from the raphé medianus. It is also possible that the tonic input is a combination of serotonin (or 5–HT) and norepinephrine released from the raphé medianus and the lateral tegmentum respectively (Foote & Morrison, 1987; Hestenes, chapter 7 in this volume).

Based on well known anatomical facts, the analogy of the associative part of the READ to the hippocampus also appears to be a good one, although again oversimplification is evident. The septum communicates with the hippocampus via the medial forebrain bundle (MFB). The hippocampus communicates with the mammillary body of the hypothalamus also along the MFB. For the functional role assigned to x_7 and x_8, the emerging theories of Mishkin, Malamut, and Bachevalier (1984) suggest that a more appropriate analogy is one of the hippocampus and the amygdala combined.

Attention is now directed to the proposed addition of the neuromodulatory center. As stated previously, center NC shown in Fig. 5.8 is analogous to the locus ceruleus (LC), the main source of norepinephrine (NE) in the brain. In support of this analogy, some of the established LC properties and the putative effects of NE on target neurons will be reviewed. As with the previous analogies, the functional role assigned to the effects of NE on the READ circuit, or mock-limbic system, is vastly oversimplified. Foote and Morrison (1987) established the modulatory role of NE and the other monoamines (5–HT, dopamine, and acetylcholine). Foote and Morrison (1987) summarized the LCs functional role in this manner:

> Taken together, the data concerning LC projections, the activity of source neurons, and the effects of the transmitter on target neurons indicate that the LC is activated during alerting or arousal and releases noradrenaline onto target neurons in many brain regions, including the neocortex. This transmitter then acts to enhance the selectivity and vigor of responses to subsequent sensory stimuli or other synaptic input to the target neurons. The LC may well also play a role in more tonic behavioral state changes, such as the sleep-wake cycle. It has been proposed that the function of LC could best be described as altering behavioral modes from internally oriented and generated states, such as sleep, grooming, and food consumption, to an externally oriented mode that involves active matching of appropriate behaviors with novel, stressful, or informative stimuli. (p. 74)

Madison and Nicoll (1982) found direct evidence for NE's modulatory effects on the K^+ channels suggested in the previous section. They found that perfusing hippocampal slices with NE resulted in the blocking of K^+ conductance. Spike activity was greatly increased upon subsequent electrical stimulation.

The role $NC-n$ (mock-LC-NE) has been assigned in the READ circuit, is but a subset of what the experimental findings suggest. This is a preliminary position. As previously stated, the LC projects to most areas of the brain including the neocortex, thalamus, amygdala, hippocampus, septum, and hypothalamus. This implies that NC efferents should project to all portions of the READ circuit (see Fig. 5.7). In this study, the effects of NE on US STM replay have been isolated from other possible effects of NE by restricting NC efferent projections to node x_0: the initial relay station of US stimulation for the on-channel of the READ. As was seen in the last section, this is sufficient to give the READ circuit the ability to exhibit behavior consistent with the observed behavior associated with backward and simultaneous conditioning. In a future study, the effects of $NC-n$ on the mock-hippocampus may also be analyzed. This will have the effect of protracting CS STM replay as well as US STM replay. This may be required to reproduce all the data Burkhardt and Ayres (1978) reported on the CS and US duration effects in simultaneous conditioning. Another possibility to consider is the addition of frontal lobe mechanisms Leven & Levine (1987) suggested. See also Levine, Leven, and Prueitt (chapter 9 in this volume), which might enhance mock-hippocampal STM activity during unexpected events.

The analogies presented thus far have been made primarily on anatomical and neurophysiological considerations. The functional role ascribed to the READ circuit in the previous sections does indeed appear to be converging with emerging theories of the limbic system and its role in motivation, memories, and habits. Mishkin et al. (1984) proposed that two distinct neural systems are involved in the development of memories and habits. According to these researchers, the cortico-limbo-thalamic system is involved in the more cognitive aspects of learning, such as the acquisition of information or knowledge (e.g., assigning meaning to things and events). The other system is the cortico-striatal system (the striatal system refers to the more general basal ganglia), and is responsible for the formation of habits or motor output. Based on more recent considerations (Hestenes, chapter 7 in this volume), the latter system should be enlarged to include the limbic areas, thereby making it the cortico-limbo-striatal system. Stellar (1982) also made theoretical suggestions that mirror those Grossberg proposed. Stellar proposed that the limbic system is responsible for generating motivated behaviors such as eating, drinking, thermoregulation, and sexual behavior. Stellar also concluded that the limbic system contains "dual mechanisms, responsible for arousal and satiation, approach and withdrawal, and positive and negative reinforcement" (p. 403). He speculated that dual mechanisms he ascribed to the limbic system might be the substrates of Solomon and Corbit's (1974) opponent-process, a much less developed cousin of this theory.

The functional properties given to the interaction of the limbic system, neocortex, reticular formation, and basal ganglia in this theory have not been proven nor is there any global consensus suggesting such functionality. However, neurobiological data and theories are emerging that coincide with these propositions.

CONCLUSION AND FINAL DISCUSSION

In summary, the addition of the proposed neuromodulatory mechanism to an already powerful model of conditioning and attention, which incorporates opponent-processing and spatial pattern learning, is able to explain some of the most paradoxical and controversial empirical data observed in classical conditioning experiments: the excitatory and inhibitory effects attributable to backward and simultaneous conditioning. From the experimental evidence and the theoretical position taken here, the conclusion is that the ISI variable, taken by itself, does not provide enough information to determine the outcome of a given Pavlovian conditioning experiment, especially in the case of simultaneous and backward conditioning. Other variables suggested for consideration include the CS and the US duration, the duration of the CS and the US overlap, whether the ITI is fixed or random, the number of training trials utilized, the emotional state of the animal, the complexity of the neuronal circuitry, the phylogenetic development of the animal, and whether the experimental preparation is in vitro or in vivo. This list of variables suggested is probably not exhaustive and some of the variables suggested are interrelated.

In this article, there are two divergences from the original theory Grossberg and Levine (1987) and Grossberg and Schmajuk (1987) developed. The first divergence is in the choice of the learning equation as discussed in the Neuromodulatory Mechanism and Modification of READ Circuit section of Part II. The other divergence is in the explanation of ISI effects. In an alternative view, Grossberg and Levine (1987) suggested that the ISI effects result from the competition that occurs at the S_{1k} level (see Fig. 5.4) or mock-neocortex. In this explanation, the US produce drive input to the READ as well as input to the sensory representation stage at level S_{1k}. This is supported by the anatomical analogies of this theory. Sensory representations compete for activation at the S_{1k} level. By the very nature of the US, this signal has motivational and sensory significance to the animal. According to the model, this means that there are strong synaptic weights along the reinforcement and attentional feedback pathways associated with US representations at level S_{1k} and S_{2k}. If a neutral CS is presented simultaneously with a US, strong US STM activity at the S_{1k} level, enhanced by S_{2k} feedback, will rapidly inhibit the relatively weaker CS STM activity. Only if a CS precedes the US will the CS produce enough STM activity at the S_{1k} level to slow the inhibition produced by the onset of US STM activity. Only then will there be enough coactive CS STM activity and READ circuit on-response activity to produce learning before CS STM is inhibited by the gaining US STM activity. Grossberg and Levine showed through computer simulations how the concave-down ISI curve could result from this explanation. By replacing the US with previously conditioned CSs, the model can explain blocking, secondary and higher-order reinforcement, and overshadowing.

In the version of the model used in this article, the assumption is that the US sensory representations are just part of the overall contextual information available. Prior to training, US pathways should not be biased as suggested by Grossberg and Levine (1987) since any given previously unexperienced US has no meaning within the experimental context. In addition, if the US would be biased as suggested, excitatory backward and simultaneous conditioning would be difficult to explain. Of course one may add a neuromodulatory mechanism, similar to the one proposed here, to Grossberg and Levine's version of the model. This other mechanism would decrease the inhibitory gain as well as protract STM activity at the S_{1k} level. However, this runs counter to the putative effects of NE on target cells, especially on cortical cells. Foote, Bloom, and Aston-Jones (1983) indicated that NE works synergistically with GABA to *increase* the inhibitory effects of neurons.

Some would consider these inconsistencies in the theory to reflect a weakness of the approach. I believe rather this brings out the strength of the theory, not its weakness. The theory is flexible enough to test a variety of hypotheses within a strong theoretical foundation. What specifics are settled within this general framework will depend upon our understanding of neurobiology and the behavioral phenomena these models can predict. Additions and revisions of specifics can build upon the model while leaving the general framework intact. For example, the previous explanations for how the READ circuit exhibits conditioned excitation, conditioned inhibition, blocking, secondary conditioning, and overshadowing (Grossberg & Levine, 1987; Grossberg & Schmajuk, 1987); and how the READ circuit in conjunction with ART can explain many more behavioral phenomena (Grossberg, 1982b), still hold after the addition of the proposed neuromodulator. The revised model can now also explain the observable behaviors attributable to forward and backward conditioning without altering the theoretical foundation.

Arguably other strengths of this theoretical approach lie with its neurobiological plausibility consistent with emerging theories of thalamo-corticolimbo-reticular function and cortico-limbo-striatal function. This theory, thus, becomes a strong link between neurobiology and psychology, and as suggested by Hestenes' chapter in this volume, also a link between neurobiology and psychiatry. Within this framework, the model can be expanded to test hypotheses of how other brain structures are involved in learning, cognition, and behavior. This article is an example of such hypothesis testing.

To conclude this chapter, a few pertinent words from Pavlov's (1927/1960) seminal work are offered:

> On the whole, looking back upon this new field of physiological research I find it full of fascination, especially since it satisfies two of the fundamental cravings of the human intellect-striving to realize ever new and new truths, and to protest against the pretension of finality in truth we have already gained. In this domain there will for long remain an immense breadth of uncharted ocean compared with the small patches of the known. (p. 394)

APPENDIX: NUMERICAL METHODS AND PARAMETERS

The simulations in this article were performed on an LMI Lisp machine using Zetalisp and Flavors. Euler's method was used to approximate the solutions of the differential equations. That is, given the differential equation

$$\epsilon \frac{da}{dt} = f(a) \tag{26}$$

the discrete time approximation of (26) is

$$a(t + 1) = a(t) + \tau/\epsilon[f(a)] \tag{27}$$

where τ is the positive time increment of a.

The parameter values used in the simulations described are $\epsilon_1 = .167$, $\epsilon_2 = 4$, $\tau = .1$, $A_{max} = 1$, $A_{min} = .001$, $A_2 = .01$, $B = .125$, $C = .5$, $D = 3$, $E = 3$, $G = 1$, $H = 1$, $I = .25$, $K_1 = 3$, $K_2 = .15$, $L_1 = 50$, $L_5 = 10$, $M = .1$, $n_{max} = 5$. In addition, the following define the signal functions used in Equations 4–20:

$$f(x) = x \qquad (28)$$

$$g(x) = x^2/\alpha + x^2 \qquad (29)$$

where $\alpha = .25$

$$h(x) = x \qquad (30)$$

REFERENCES

Alkon, D. L. (1984). Persistent calcium-mediated changes of identified membrane currents as a cause of associative learning. In D. L. Alkon & J. Farley (Eds.), *Primary neural substrates of learning and behavioral change* (pp. 291–324). London: Cambridge University Press.

Alkon, D. L. (1987). *Memory traces in the brain.* London: Cambridge University Press.

Anderson, J. A., Silverstein, J. W., Ritz, S. A., & Jones, R. S. (1977). Distinctive features, categorical perception, and probability learning: Some applications of a neural network model. *Psychological Review, 84,* 413–451.

Ayres, J. J. B., Haddad, C. & Albert, M. (1987). One-trial excitatory backward conditioning as assessed by conditioned suppression of licking in rats: Concurrent observations of lick suppression and defensive behaviors. *Animal Learning and Behavior, 15,* 212–217.

Banquet, J., & Grossberg, S. (1987). Probing cognitive processes through the structure of event-related potentials during learning: an experimental and theoretical analysis. *Applied Optics, 26,* 4931–4946.

Berger, T. W. (1984). Long-term potentiation of hippocampus synaptic transmission affects rate of behavioral learning. *Science Washington, DC, 224,* 627–630.

Burkhardt, P. E. (1980a). *Attenuation of conditioned suppression in rats: The role of forward and backward conditioning during element and compound training.* Unpublished master's thesis, University of Wisconsin at Osh Kosh.

Burkhardt, P. E. (1980b). One-trial backward fear conditioning in rats as a function of US intensity. *Bulletin of the Psychonomic Society, 15,* 9–11.

Burkhardt, P. E., & Ayres, J. J. B. (1978). CS and US duration effects in one-trial simultaneous fear conditioning as assessed by conditioned suppression of licking in rats. *Animal Learning and Behavior, 6,* 225–230.

Byrne, J. H. (1987). Cellular analysis of associative learning. *Physiological Review, 67,* 329–439.

Cantor, M. B. (1981). Information theory: A solution to two big problems in the analysis of behavior. In P. Harzem & M. D. Zeiler (Eds.), *Predict ability, correlation, and contiguity* (pp. 287–320). Chichester, UK: Wiley.

Carpenter, G. A., & Grossberg, S. (1987). ART2: Self-organization of stable category recognition codes for analog input patterns. *Applied Optics, 26,* 4919–4930.

Champion, R. A., & Jones, J. E. (1961). Forward, backward, and pseudoconditioning of the GSR. *Journal of Experimental Psychology, 62,* 58–61.

Cooper, L. N., Liberman, F., & Oja, E. (1979). A theory for the acquisition and loss of neuron specificity in visual cortex. *Biological Cybernetics, 33,* 9–28.

Crow, T. J., & Alkon, D. L. (1978). Retention of an associative behavioral change in *Hermissenda. Science, 201,* 1239–1241.

Dickinson, A., & Mackintosh, N. J. (1978). Classical conditioning in animals. *Annual of Review Psychology, 29,* 587–612.

Dingledine, R. (1983). N–methyl asparate activates voltage-dependent calcium conductance in rat hippocampal pyramidal cells. *Journal Physiology London, 343,* 385–405.

Dostálek, H. K. (1972). Backward conditioning: one-session vs. ten-session experiment. *Activitas Nervosa Superior, 14,* 58–59.

Dostálek, H. K. (1973). The role of unconditional stimulus intensity in backward conditioning. *Activitas Nervosa Superior, 15,* 239–240.

Dunwiddie, T. V., Madison, D., & Lynch, G. (1978). Synaptic transmission is required for initiation of long-term potentiation. *Brain Research, 150,* 413–417.

Eccles, J. C. (1983). Calcium in Long-term potentiation as a model for memory. *Neuroscience, 10,* 1071–1081.

Estes, W. K., & Skinner, B. F. (1941). Some quantitative properties of anxiety. *Journal of Experimental Psychology, 29,* 390–400.

Farley, J., & Alkon, D. L. (1982). Long-term associative neural and behavioral change in *Hermissenda:* Consequences of nervous system orientation for light- and pairing-specificity. *Journal of Neurophysiology, 48,* 785–807.

Farley, J., & Alkon, D. L. (1987). In vitro associative conditioning of *Hermissenda:* Cumulative depolarization of Type B Photoreceptors and short-term associative behavioral changes. *Journal of Neurophysiology, 57,* 1639–1668.

Foote, S. L., Bloom, F. E., & Aston-Jones, G. (1983). Nucleus Locus Ceruleus: New evidence of anatomical and physiological specificity. *Physiological Reviews, 63,* 844–914.

Foote, S. L., & Morrison, J. H. (1987). Extrathalamic modulation of cortical function. *Annual Review of Neuroscience, 10,* 67–95.

Gingrich, K. J., & Byrne, J. H. (1987). Single-cell neuronal model for associative learning. *Journal of Neurophysiology, 57,* 1705–1715.

Gluck, M. A., & Thompson, R. F. (1987). Modeling the neural substrates of associative learning and memory: A computational approach. *Psychological Review, 94,* 176–191.

Gormezano, I. (1972). Investigations of defense and reward conditioning in the rabbit. In A. H. Black & W. F. Prokasy (Eds.), *Classical conditioning II: Current research and theory* (pp. 151–181). New York: Appleton.

Gormezano, I., & Kehoe, E. J. (1975). Classical conditioning: Some methodological-conceptual issues. In W. K. Estes (Eds.), *Handbook of learning and cognitive processes. Volume 2: Conditioning and behavior theory* (pp. 143–179). Hillsdale, NJ: Lawrence Erlbaum Associates.

Gormezano, I., Kehoe, E. J., & Marshall, B. S. (1983). Twenty years of classical conditioning research with the rabbit. In J. M. Sprague & A. N. Epstein (Eds.), *Progress in psychobiology and physiological psychology* (pp. 198–274). New York: Academic Press.

Grossberg, S. (1969). On learning the energy–entropy dependence in recurrent and nonrecurrent signed networks. *Journal of Statistical Physics, 1,* 319–350.

Grossberg, S. (1972a). A neural theory of punishment and avoidance, I: Qualitative theory. *Mathematical Biosciences, 15,* 39–68.

Grossberg, S. (1972b). A neural theory of punishment and avoidance, II: Quantitative theory. *Mathematical Biosciences, 15,* 253–285.

Grossberg, S. (1972c). Neural expectation: Cerebellar and retinal analogs of cells fired by learnable or unlearned pattern classes. *Kybernetik, 10,* 49–57.

Grossberg, S. (1975). A neural model of attention, reinforcement, and discrimination learning. *International Review of Neurobiology, 18,* 263–327.

Grossberg, S. (1982a). A psychophysiological theory of reinforcement, drive, motivation, and attention. *Journal of Theoretical Neurobiology, 1,* 286–369.

Grossberg, S. (1982b). Processing of expected and unexpected events during conditioning and attention: A psychophysiological theory. *Psychological Review, 89,* 529–572.

Grossberg, S. (1982c). *Studies of mind and brain: Neural principles of learning, perception, development, cognition, and motor control.* Boston: Reidel.

Grossberg, S. (1984). Some psychophysiological and pharmacological correlates of a developmental, cognitive, and motivational theory. In R. Karrer, J. Cohen, & P. Tueting (Eds.), *Brain and Information: Event Related Potentials, 425,* 58–151.

Grossberg, S. (Ed.). (1987a). *The adaptive brain, I: Cognition learning, reinforcement, and rhythm.* Amsterdam: Elsevier/North-Holland.

Grossberg, S. (Ed.). (1987b). *The adaptive brain, II: Vision, speech, language, and motor control.* Amsterdam: Elsevier/North-Holland.

Grossberg, S. (Ed.). (1988). *Neural network and natural intelligence.* Cambridge, MA: MIT Press.

Grossberg, S., & Kuperstein, M. (1986). *Neural dynamics of adaptive sensory-motor control: Ballistic eye movements.* Amsterdam: Elsevier/North-Holland.

Grossberg, S., & Levine, D. S. (1987). Neural dynamics of attentionally modulated Pavlovian conditioning: Blocking interstimulus interval, and secondary reinforcement. *Applied Optics, 26,* 5015–5030.

Grossberg, S., & Schmajuk, N. A. (1987). Neural dynamics of attentionally modulated Pavlovian conditioning: Conditioned reinforcement, inhibition, and opponent processing. *Psychobiology, 15,* 195–240.

Grover, L. M., & Farley, J. (1987). Temporal order sensitivity of associative neural and behavioral changes in *Hermissenda. Behavioral Neuroscience, 101,* 658–675.

Hall, J. F. (1984). Backward conditioning in Pavlovian type studies: Reevaluation and present status. *Pavlovian Journal of Biological Sciences, 19,* 163–168.

Hawkins, R. D., Abrams, T. W., Carew, T. J., & Kandel, E. R. (1983). A cellular mechanism of classical conditioning in *Aplysia:* Activity-dependent amplification of presynaptic facilitation. *Science Washington DC, 219,* 400–405.

Hawkins, R. D., Carew, T. J., & Kandel, E. R. (1986). Effects of interstimulus interval and contingency on classical conditioning in *Aplysia* siphon withdrawal reflex. *Journal of Neuroscience, 6,* 1695–1701.

Hebb, D. O. (1949). *The organization of behavior.* New York: Wiley.

Heth, D. C. (1976). Simultaneous and backward fear conditioning as a function a number of CS–UCS pairings. *Journal of Experimental Psychology: Animal Behavior Processes, 2,* 117–129.

Heth, D. C., & Rescorla, R. A. (1973). Simultaneous and backward fear conditioning in the rat. *Journal of Comparative and Physiological Psychology, 82,* 434–443.

Hodgkin, A. L. (1964). *The conduction of the nervous impulse.* Liverpool: Liverpool University Press.

Hodgkin, A. L., & Huxley, A. F. (1952). A quantitative description of membrane current and its application to conduction and excitation in nerve. *Journal of Physiology (London), 117,* 500–544.

Hull, C. L. (1952). *A behavior system.* New Haven: Yale University Press.

Jones, J. E. (1962). Contiguity and reinforcement in relation to CS–UCS intervals in classical aversive conditioning. *Psychological Review, 69,* 176–186.

Kamin, L. J. (1968). "Attention-like" processes in classical conditioning. In M. R. Jones (Ed.), *Miami symposium on the Prediction of Behavior: Aversive stimulation.* Miami: University of Miami Press.

Kamin, L. J. (1969). Predictability, surprise, attention and conditioning. In B. A. Campbell & R. M. Church (Eds.), *Punishment and aversive behavior* (pp. 9–31). New York: Appleton-Century-Crofts.

Kandel, E. R., Abrams, T. W., Bernier, L., Carew, T. J., Hawkins, R. D., & Schwartz, J. H. (1983). Classical conditioning and sensitization share aspects of the same molecular cascade in *Aplysia. Cold Spring Harbor Symposium on Quantitative Biology, 48,* 821–830.

Kandel, E. R., & Schwartz, J. H. (1982). Molecular biology of learning: Modulation of transmitter release. *Science Washington DC, 218,* 433–443.

Keith-Lucas, T., & Guttman, N. (1975). Robust single-trial delayed backward conditioning. *Journal of Comparative and Physiological Psychology, 88,* 468–476.

Kelso, S., Ganong, A., & Brown, T. H. (1986). Hebbian synapses in hippocampus. *Proceedings of the National Academy of Sciences USA, 83,* 5326–5330.

Klopf, A. H. (1988). A neuronal model of classical conditioning. *Psychobiology, 16,* 85–125.

Kohonen, T. (1977). *Associative memory: A system-theoretical approach.* New York: Springer-Verlag.

Leven, S. J., & Levine, D. S. (1987). Effects of reinforcement on knowledge retrieval and evaluation. In M. Caudill & C. Butler (Eds.), *Proceedings of the IEEE First International Conference on Neural Networks, II* (pp. 269–277). Piscataway, NJ: IEEE Press.

Levy, W. B. (1985). Associative changes at the synapse: LTP in the hippocampus. In W. B. Levy, J. A. Anderson, & S. Lehmkuhle (Eds.), *Synaptic modification, neuron selectivity, and nervous system organization.* Hillsdale, NJ: Lawrence Erlbaum Associates.

Levy, W. B., & Steward, O. (1979). Synapses as associative memory elements in the hippocampal formation. *Brain Research, 175,* 233–245.

Lukowiak, K., & Sahley, C. (1981). The in vitro classical conditioning of the gill withdrawal reflex of *Aplysia californica. Science, 212,* 1516–1518.

Lynch, G., & Baudry, M. (1984). The biochemistry of memory: a new and specific hypothesis. *Science Washington DC, 224,* 1057–1063.

Lynch, G., Larson, J., Kelso, S., Barrionuevo, G., & Schottler, F. (1983). Intracellular injections of EGTA block induction of hippocampal long-term potentiation. *Nature, 305,* 719–721.

Mackintosh, N. J. (1974). *The psychology of animal learning.* New York: Academic Press.

Mackintosh, N. J. (1983). *Conditioning and associative learning.* Oxford, UK: Oxford University Press.

Madison, D. V., & Nicoll, R. A. (1982). Noradrenaline blocks accommodation of pyramidal cell discharge in the hippocampus. *Nature, 299,* 636–638.

Mahoney, W. J., & Ayres, J. J. B. (1976). One-trial simultaneous and backward fear conditioning as reflected in conditioned suppression of licking in rats. *Animal Learning and Behavior, 4,* 357–362.

Malenka, R. C., Kauer, J. A., Zucker, R. S., & Nicoll, R. A. (1988). Postsynaptic calcium is sufficient for potentiation of hippocampal synaptic transmission. *Science, 242,* 81–84.

Marr, D. (1969). A theory of cerebellar cortex. *Journal of Physiology, 202,* 437–470.

Matsumiya, Y. (1960). The effects US intensity and CS–US pattern on conditioned emotional response. *Japanese Psychological Research, 2,* 35–42.

McNaughton, B. L., Douglas, R. M., & Goddard, G. V. (1978). Synaptic enhancement in fascia dentata: Cooperativity among coactive afferents. *Brain Research, 157,* 277–298.

Miller, R. R., & Spear, N. E. (Eds.). (1985). *Information processing in animals: Conditioned inhibition.* Hillsdale, NJ: Lawrence Erlbaum Associates.

Mishkin, M., Malamut, B., & Bachevalier, J. (1984). Memories and habits: Two neural systems. In G. Lynch, J. L. McGaugh, & N. M. Weinberger (Eds.), *Neurobiology of learning and memory* (pp. 65–77). New York: Guilford.

Moscovitch, A., & LoLordo, V. M. (1968). Role of safety in the Pavlovian backward fear conditioning procedure. *Journal of Comparative and Physiological Psychology, 66,* 673–678.

Mowrer, O. H. (1960). *Learning theory and behavior.* New York: Wiley.

Mowrer, O. H., & Aiken, F. G. (1954). Contiguity vs. drive-reduction in conditioned fear: Temporal variations in conditioned and unconditioned stimulus. *American Journal of Psychology, 67,* 26–38.

Nauta, W. J. H., & Feirtag, M. (1986). *Fundamental neuroanatomy.* New York: Freeman.

Nestler, E. J., & Greengard, P. (1984). *Protein phosphorylation in the nervous system.* New York: Wiley.

Osgood, C. E. (1953). *Method and theory in experimental psychology.* New York: Oxford University Press.

Pavlov, I. P. (1932). The reply of a physiologist to psychologists. *Psychological Review, 39,* 91–127.

Pavlov, I. P. (1960). *Conditioned reflexes: An investigation of the physiological activity of the cerebral cortex* (G. B. Anrep, Ed. and trans.). New York: Appleton. (Original work published 1927)

Pearce, J. M., & Hall, G. A. (1980). A model for Pavlovian learning: Variations in the effectiveness of conditioned but not of unconditioned stimuli. *Psychological Review, 87,* 532–552.

Rauschecker, J. P., & Singer, W. (1979). Changes in the circuitry of the kitten's visual cortex are gated by postsynaptic activity. *Nature, 280,* 58–60.

Rescorla, R. A., & Wagner, A. R. (1972). A theory of Pavlovian conditioning: Variations in the effectiveness of reinforcement and nonreinforcement. In A. H. Black & W. F. Prokasy (Eds.), *Classical conditioning II: Current research and theory* (pp. 64–99). New York: Appleton-Century-Crofts.

Scharfman, H. E., & Sarvey, J. M. (1985). Postsynaptic firing during repetitive stimulation is required for long-term potentiation in hippocampus. *Brain Research, 331,* 267–274.

Schmajuk, N. A., & Moore, J. W. (1988). The hippocampus and the classically conditioned nictitating membrane response: A real-time attentional-associative model. *Psychobiology, 16,* 20–35.

Schneiderman, N. (1966). Interstimulus interval function of the nictitating membrane response of the rabbit under delay versus trace conditioning. *Journal of Comparative and Physiological Psychology, 62,* 397–402.

Schneiderman, N., & Gormezano, I. (1964). Conditioning of the nictitating membrane of the rabbit as a function of CS–US interval. *Journal of Comparative and Physiological Psychology, 57,* 188–195.

Shepherd, G. M. (1988). *Neurobiology* (2nd ed.). New York: Oxford University Press.

Shurtleff, D., & Ayres, J. J. B. (1981). One-trial backward excitatory fear conditioning in rats: Acquisition, retention, extinction, and spontaneous recovery. *Animal Learning & Behavior, 9,* 65–74.

Siegel, S., & Domjan, M. (1971). Backward conditioning as an inhibitory procedure. *Learning and Motivation, 2,* 1–11.

Singer, W. (1983). Neuronal activity as a shaping factor in the self-organization of neuron assemblies. In E. Basar, H. Flohr, H. Haken, & A. J. Mandell (Eds.), *Synergetics of the brain* (pp. 89–102). New York: Springer-Verlag.

Smith, M. C., Coleman, S. R., & Gormenzano, I. (1969). Classical conditioning of the rabbit's nictitating membrane response. *Journal of Comparative and Physiological Psychology, 69,* 226–231.

Solomon, R. L., & Corbit, J. D. (1974). An opponent-process theory of motivation: I. Temporal dynamics of affect. *Psychological Review, 81,* 119–145.

Spetch, M. L., Wilkie, D. M., & Pinel, J. P. J. (1981). Backward conditioning: A reevaluation of the empirical evidence. *Psychological Bulletin, 89,* 163–175.

Spooner, A., & Kellogg, W. N. (1947). The backward conditioning curve. *American Journal of Psychology, 60,* 321–334.

Stellar, E. (1982). Brain mechanisms in hedonic processes. In D. W. Pfaff (Ed.), *The physiological mechanisms of motivation* (pp. 377–407). New York: Springer-Verlag.

Stellar, J. R., Brooks, F. H., & Mills, L. E. (1979). Approach and withdrawal analysis of the effects of hypothalamic stimulation and lesions in rats. *Journal of Comparative and Physiological Psychology, 83,* 446–466.

Sutton, R. S., & Barto, A. G. (1981). Toward a modern theory of adaptive net works: Expectation and prediction. *Psychological Review, 88,* 135–170.

Terrace, H. S. (1973). Classical conditioning. In J. A. Nevin & G. S. Reynolds (Eds.), *The study of behavior: Learning, motivation, emotion, and instinct.* Glenview, IL: Scott, Foresman.

Terry, W. S., & Wagner, A. R. (1975). Short-term memory for "surprising" vs. "expected" USs in Pavlovian conditioning. *Journal of Experimental Psychology: Animal Behavior Processes, 1,* 122–133.

Thomas, E. (1988). Forebrain mechanisms in the relief of fear: The role of the lateral septum. *Psychobiology, 16,* 36–44.

Turner, R. W., Baimbridge, K. G., & Miller, J. J. (1982). Calcium-induced long-term potentiation in the hippocampus. *Neuroscience, 7,* 1411–1416.

Underwood, B. J. (1949). *Experimental psychology.* New York: Appleton-Century-Crofts.

Van Willigen, F., Emmett, J., Cote, D., & Ayres, J. J. B. (1987). CS modality effects in one-trial backward and forward excitatory conditioning as assessed by conditioned suppression of licking in rats. *Animal Learning and Behavior, 15,* 201–211.

Vertes, R. P., & Miller, N. E. (1976). Brain stem neurons that fire selectively to a conditioned stimulus for shock. *Brain Research, 103,* 229–242.

von der Malsburg, C. (1973). Self-organization of orientation sensitive cells in the striate cortex. *Kybernetik, 14,* 85–100.

Wagner, A. R. (1971). Elementary associations. In H. H. Kendler & J. T. Spence (Eds.), *Essays in neobehaviorism: A memorial volume to Kenneth W. Spence.* New York: Appleton-Century-Crofts.

Wagner, A. R., & Larew, M. B. (1985). Opponent processes and Pavlovian inhibition. In R. R. Miller & N. E. Spear (Eds.), *Information Processing in Animals: Conditioned Inhibition* (pp. 233–265). Hillsdale, NJ: Lawrence Erlbaum Associates.

Wagner, A. R., Rudy, J. W., & Whitlow, J. W. (1973). Rehearsal in animal conditioning. *Journal of Experimental Psychology, 97,* 407–426.

Wagner, A. R., & Terry, W. S. (1975). Backward conditioning to a CS following an expected vs. a surprising UCS. *Annual Learning & Behavior, 3,* 370–374.

Walters, E. T., & Byrne, J. H. (1985). Long-term enhancement produced by activity-dependent modulation of *Aplysia* sensory neurons. *Journal of Neuroscience, 5,* 662–672.

Woody, C. D. (1982). *Memory learning, and higher function.* New York: Springer-Verlag.

II COMPLEX MOTIVATIONAL-COGNITIVE CIRCUITS IN THE BRAIN

Top-Down Processes, Attention, and Motivation in Cognitive Tasks

J. P. Banquet
M. Smith
W. Guenther
LENA-CNRS, Hôpital de la Salpêtrière, Paris, Psychiatric University Hospital, Munich

Event-related Potentials (ERP) were associated to behavioral indices to explore cognitive and attentional processes in normal and depressed subjects. Specifically contextual effects on single event processing were tested by a probability learning paradigm.

Effects of the probability context were found in the preparatory and identification stages of the event processing in normals. Depressed patients exhibited a dissociation between probability processing that was normal and anticipatory use of probability that was deficient. This deficit was related to a perturbation of phasic and tonic attention processes.

These results are interpreted in the framework of the Adaptive Resonance Theory (ART), which includes a two-way circulation of information (bottom–up and top–down) between two processing stages.

Gestalt psychology proposed that percepts result from fusion between bottom–up external sensory inputs and top–down internal expectancies, thus integrating present experience and memories. ART (Grossberg, 1976a, 1976b, 1980, 1982a, 1982b, 1986; Carpenter & Grossberg, 1987), among other theories, attributes an important role to top–down information transfers during cognitive processes. Grossberg suggested (1980) that gestalt fusion of two inputs (external–internal) arises from a pattern matching process leading to code formation in neural networks. A percept is regarded as a state of resonant activation among different modules, reflecting consistent encoding of sensory input.

Here we extend this bottom–up/top–down mechanism to higher-order cognitive processes, and in particular to contextual processing. Evidence is presented, in terms of specific electrical activity, for two types of top–down information transfers in normal subjects (Ns), during probability learning: *feed-forward an-*

ticipation-preparation and *feed-back contextual conditioning*. This latter process means association of a contextual probability valence to previously neutral stimuli. These results suggest the existence of at least two loci of stimulus probability effects, pre-stimulus and poststimulus delivery, corresponding to two different modalities of top–down processes.

The specific purpose of the investigation was to test the hypothesis, suggested by previous results (Banquet & Lesèvre, 1980), that contextual probability effects (top–down influence of probability context on single-trial processing strategies) could account for the existence of high and low performance levels in a group of normal subjects responding to frequent stimuli of an auditory discrimination task. To test this hypothesis, a *probability learning paradigm* was used, and three experimental conditions were separately analyzed: (a) a *prelearning phase* occurring either in naive subjects with no previous experience of probability context or in trained subjects just after shift from one probability condition to other; (b) a *postlearning* phase at end of practice of a fixed probability condition; (c) an *overlearning phase* involving a long-term practice effect.

We then studied *depressed* patients (Ds) as a pathological model of *motivational-emotional deficit*. These subjects are supposed to have deficits of right hemisphere functions (Flor-Henry, 1988) and motivation. Attentional disorders were found as well as deficits in both anticipatory and conditioning processes, although stimuli and probability context were normally processed. They will be discussed in terms of the different varieties of attention identified by neurophysiologists (Pribram & McGuiness, 1975) or cognitive psychologists (Posner & Presti, 1987).

The methodology employed involved combination of behavioral (Reaction Time, RT) and electrical indices (Event-Related Potentials, ERP).

HYPOTHESIS AND METHODS

Hypothesis

The prevailing methodology of *additive factors* in cognitive psychology, as adapted by Sternberg (1969), supposes a serial model of information processing. An experimental factor is assumed to modulate preferentially or specifically a single processing stage. Therefore, two distinct factors are supposed to affect different stages, if they produce additive effects on a specific dependent variable, and conversely to affect the same stage, if they produce interactive effects. In this approach, emphasis is on indirect individualization of stages through the analysis of global chronometric effects of experimental factor manipulations. Several caveats, however, must be taken into consideration:

1. This method becomes inoperant, or at the very least insufficient, if the serial hypothesis is not verified. Evidence from neurophysiology of sensorimotor

systems (e.g., feature extraction of visual stimuli, motor preparation) and from cognitive psychophysiology rather suggests massive parallelism. Overlapping of different ERP components (exogenous–endogenous, motor–cognitive) could be a manifestation of such parallelism. Nevertheless this does not necessarily exclude seriality at higher processing levels.

2. The additive factors assumption does not take into consideration the possibility that *superfactors* could affect (either directly or indirectly) several processing stages. For instance, event probability affects at least three ERP components and probably three different stages.

3. This approach attaches little or no importance to *information transfer*. Bottom–up discrete or continuous interstage transfers (Coles, Gratton, Bashore, Eriksen, & Donchin, 1985) have up to now been the central object of study in experimental psychology. However, a wealth of classical (e.g., perceptual illusions) and recent experimental results suggest the importance of top–down information transfer in mental activity and particularly in cognitive processes. Top–down information transfers between processing stages are either self-initiated, such as in anticipation, or secondary, in reaction to bottom–up processes. In connectionist theory (for a review see Levine, 1983), and in particular in ART, information transfers performed by adaptive filters actively participate in information processing because of the modulation of the transferred signals by Long Term Memories (LTM) of the synaptic weights.

In electrophysiological studies, ERP components can be considered as objectifying the hypothetical construct of processing stages. ERPs vary with diverse experimental factors and reflect corresponding cognitive functions. The use of continuous electrical variables enables the mapping of neural activity in terms of electrical fields, emphasizing *spatiotemporal dynamics* of processes. The combination of a dense electrode coverage of the scalp, mathematical modeling of electrical signal transfer functions, and increasingly accurate models of skull and brain anatomy give a relatively satisfactory solution to the *reciprocal problem* of locating ERP component generators. Spatiotemporal mapping of ERP sequences referred to underlying brain structures has now become possible in information processing tasks. The advantage of these electromagnetic methods over more recent approaches of cerebral imagery (Guenther et al., 1986) lies, in the present state of the art, in their very short time constant (on the order of msec), thus, monitoring cognitive processes in quasireal time.

Our ERP paradigm presents three main advantages over a simple behavioral procedure. It enables segmentation of the time window between stimulus and response into several *subwindows,* each delineated by ERP components and corresponding to different information-processing operations: feature extraction, stimulus identification and categorization, and context processing. Moreover, it provides direct insight into activity occurring during the time window between the response and the onset of next stimulus, which is of course not directly accessible to a pure behavioral approach. This time window spans the locus of contextual updating, equivocation and ambiguity resolution, statistical weightings, and expectancy-preparation processes. Finally it is possible to analyse covariations of these different ERP components and, therefore, to test both bottom–up and top–down influences of different stages on each other.

Event-Related Potentials

ERPs are brain electrical activities time-locked to external stimuli. Fast (10 msec), middle (50 msec) and slow (200 msec) components reflect brainstem, thalamic, and cortical activity respectively. Two subclasses of them reflect different functions:

1. *Exogenous* evoked potentials are obligatory potentials reflecting physical characteristics of stimuli. The most explored exogenous component, $N1$, seems to be related to the detection phase of perception.

2. *Endogenous,* slow, event-related potentials are elicited only when a cognitive task has to be performed. Here the term ERP will only refer to endogenous ERPs. They can be present in response to stimulus omission in a series, provided that this omission conveys information to subjects. This result strongly suggests that they reflect activation of memory registers. The term *wave* or *deflection* refers to different possible morphologies of an ERP. The term *component* is attributed to one of several independent sources of variability or generators of the ERP waveform.

An early component (100 ms) labeled *Nd* (negative displacement) was first demonstrated by Hillyard, Hink, Schwent & Picton (1973) and Hansen and Hillyard (1984) in a dichotic listening task with short (100–800 ms) random interstimulus intervals (ISI). Attended stimuli elicited an enhanced $N1$ negativity at 100 ms from stimulus onset, compared to the $N1$ elicited by an identical but unattended stimulus to other ear. The authors interpreted this effect as a selective increase in the activity of $N1$ generators and related it to stimulus-set mechanisms of early stimulus selection (McCallum, Curry, Cooper, Pocock, & Papakostopoulos, 1983; Picton, Campbell, Baribeau-Braun, & Proux, 1978) based on physical features, first proposed by Broadbent (1970).

With longer and constant ISIs (800 ms), Näätänen, Gaillard & Mantysalo (1978), and Näätänen (1982) observed a selective attention effect extending for several hundred milliseconds, beyond the time window of the $N1$ component. These authors proposed that this negative shift constitutes a different endogenous ERP component ($N1$ being exogenous), which they labeled *processing negativity* (PN). Donald and Young (1982) made an important contribution by demonstrating the dynamic evolution of these ERPs during practice. PN is elicited by relevant and irrelevant stimuli, but its amplitude is a function of the physical similarity of the eliciting stimulus to the relevant stimulus and is, therefore, maximal for the relevant target. Our paradigm is not a situation of dichotic listening; the same stimuli are delivered to both ears, and the two channels have to be attended. Only one template can be matched by the stimulus; therefore, the PN-like component found in our results, conversely to PN, probably results from a combination of match and mismatch.

A second negativity, the $N200$, has been one of the most difficult to interpret, largely because it reflects multiple components. We will mention here only the two most widely accepted components of the $N200$ deflection. The *mismatch negativity*, MMN (Näätänen et al., 1978, 1982), occurs in response to stimuli physically deviant from immediately preceding standard stimuli, with about the same amplitude whether the stimuli are attended or unattended. MMN represents, therefore, an automatic process, not influenced by selective attention. MMN topography is modality-specific (Simson, Vaughan, & Ritter, 1977), and this component is sensitive to physical changes in stimuli, such as pitch or intensity, and to the magnitude of the change. In the attented condition, it precedes or overlaps a $P165–N200–P300$ complex, which is more centrally located. It could reflect short-duration memory processes, such as sensory registers or preattentive memory storage taking place in the sensory cortex (Näätänen & Picton, 1986).

$N2b$ (Renault & Lesèvre, 1978; Näätänen et al., 1982) is a negative component that precedes $P300$. Its central location seems independent of stimulus modality, and it is elicited by temporally unexpected or rare stimuli. Its occurrence depends not only on the degree of stimulus change but also on the orientation of focal attention to the stimulus source. $N2b$ could reflect transient activation of subcortical centers releasing the orienting reflex (Näätänen & Gaillard, 1983).

A later negative component named $N400$ (Kutas & Hillyard, 1980) was discovered in response to incongruent words embedded in a meaningful sentence and has since been interpreted as a reflection of word expectancy and semantic association (Kutas & Hillyard, 1984; Neville, Kutas, Chesney, & Schmidt, 1986).

In a first, rough approximation, it can be said that negative components are dominant in the first, early part of the time window of analysis of a trial, and the positive components later on. Somewhere between the two, usually on the positive side of the window, occurs the RT. The positive components are essentially made of the $P300$ complex. $P300$ has been one of the most explored ERP deflections ever since its discovery by Sutton, Braren, Zubin & John (1965). First explained in terms of different psychological constructs (task relevance, expectancy, Roth, 1973; subjective probability, Duncan-Johnson & Donchin, 1977) or theories (information theory, signal detection theory), it was later explored for its specific role as a scalp manifestation of various information transactions in the brain (Desmedt, 1980; Desmedt & Debecker, 1979; Donchin, 1981).

$P300$ soon appeared as a nonunitary, composite wave. Squires, Squires, & Hillyard (1975), examining $P300$s in response to occasional shifts in ongoing trains of tones, in attentive and nonattentive conditions, found components of different latency and topography during nonattended ($P3a$) and attended ($P3b$) conditions. Courchesne (1978) and Courchesne, Hillyard & Galambos (1975) further investigated the dynamics of various $P300$ components in situations of novelty. Kutas, McCarthy & Donchin (1977) showed how $P300$ could enrich *mental chronometry* by demonstrating its correlation with RT under accuracy but not speed instructions to perform the task. McCarthy and Donchin (1981) defined $P300$ as a reliable index of the end of perceptive processes and not directly involved in motor response stages.

The $P3a$ component reflects processes distinct from $P3b$. $P3a$ was elicited by an unpredictable shift in an ongoing train of auditory stimuli, although sounds were task-irrelevant or not attended (Squires et al., 1975). Courchesne (1978) showed that $P3a$ amplitude response to novel events shifts from frontal to parietal maximum with repeated presentations. More recently, it has been demonstrated that this component is less sensitive to prior probability of events than $P3b$ (Banquet, Baribeau, & Lesevre, 1984; Banquet & Guenther, 1985; Banquet, Renault & Lesevre, 1981). Munson, Ruchkin, Ritter, Sutton, and Squires (1984) described a similar component, $P300E$, which does not react to prior probability. Frontocentral $P3a$, thus, occurs not only for attended task-relevant events but also for unattended, task-irrelevant intermittent stimuli. Its amplitude is related to immediately preceding probability rather than prior probability per se. Similarities in the eliciting conditions of $N200$ and $P3a$ led several authors to regard $N2b$–$P3a$ complex as an aspect of a single process, relating it to an orienting reaction consecutive to the activity of a mismatch detector (Donchin et al., 1984; Rosler, Hasselman, & Sojka, 1987; Snyder & Hillyard, 1976; Squires, Squires, & Hillyard, 1975). This complex could be a sign of an attention-switching mechanism and reflect the breakthrough of the unattended into consciousness.

On the contrary, $P3b$ is a later component elicited by attended, task-relevant target stimuli. Subjective probability, stimulus meaning, and information transmission are the three parameters of the model of Johnson (1986) linked to variations in $P3b$ amplitude. $P3b$ covaries with many different variables; thus, it has also been suggested that it represents a general subroutine invoked in different cognitive operations, such as *context updating* (Donchin, Ritter, & McCallum, 1978; Donchin, 1981) and postdecision *closure mechanism* (Desmedt, 1980). Grossberg (1975, 1978, 1984) postulated the existence of two parallel output pathways from the orienting subsystem (A) whose effects on their target networks may be compared with data about $P3a$ and $P3b$. One branch, from (A) to the attentional subsystem, causes short-term memory (STM) reset. The other branch of (A) activates processes associated with the orienting response, including processes that gate the release of orienting movements. The relationship between *P3b* amplitude and the quality of subsequent recall seems to confirm the association of *P3b* to short- or medium-term memory processes (Karis, Fabiani, & Donchin, 1984).

A later component, *P600* or slow wave, which follows *P3b*, combines a negative deflection in anterior regions with a positivity in posterior regions of the scalp. It has been extensively studied by Ruchkin, Sutton, Kietzman, & Silver (1980); Ruchkin, Sutton, & Stega (1980); Ruchkin, Johnson, Mahaffey & Sutton (1988) and seems to be related to the need for further processing either of the stimulus or of the cognitive aspects of the task. In a study manipulating automatic and controlled factors of the task, we have found it to covary with the factor of control (Banquet, in press).

Little is known on *underlying mechanisms* of ERP generation, because very few studies have been conducted in animals. Scalp-recorded ERPs essentially reflect cortical activity, although ERPs can be recorded from other brain structures, such as the thalamic nuclei and hippocampus (Halgren et al., 1980). It has been suggested that cortical ERPs originate from two generators, located in apical dendrites and neuronal somata respectively (Caspers, Speckman, & Lehmenkulher, 1980). Scalp-recorded surface potentials of identical polarity may reflect either excitatory or inhibitory states of neuronal populations, according to different dipole configurations.

Unlike exogenous evoked potentials and spontaneous EEG activities, *endogenous* ERPs may result from synchronization of a particular type of postsynaptic potentials: *Slow inhibitory or excitatory postsynaptic potentials* (sIPSP or sEPSP). The sPSPs have been mainly studied in mammalian sympathetic ganglia (Libet, 1984) and also in the hippocampus and the granular frontal cortex. According to Libet, their synaptic delay and duration range from 25 msec to 1000 msec and 1 sec to more than 1000 sec respectively.

The slow dynamics of sPSPs extend the impact of punctual events in time. Excitability changes associated with sPSPs can last from some seconds up to several minutes, within a single postsynaptic component. These sPSPs constitute, therefore, a means for the nervous system to mediate interactions between successive inputs occurring during this slow time course. Brain modelers have introduced loops and reverberating circuits to cope with the maintenance of short-term altered neuronal responsiveness, beyond the short range (tens of msec) of fast PSPs. Slow PSPs do not preclude the existence of such circuits, although they are candidates to perform the same function.

Thus, the increased excitability of the postsynaptic neuron, induced by sPSPs, holds for any synaptic site of this neuron. This widespread facilitation increases the range of possible *heterosynaptic interactions* at the cost of a loss of specificity. Conversely *homosynaptic facilitation* (e.g., long-term potentiation, LTP), as a model of induction and storage of memory trace, is strictly local, limited to the synaptic junction between two coactivated cells. Therefore, homosynaptic and heterosynaptic models of memory consolidation are not mutually exclusive but rather complementary. ERPs may reflect both of these processes.

Experimental Paradigm

Our experimental procedure has been described in detail elsewhere (Banquet & Grossberg, 1987; Banquet, Guenther, & Smith, 1987). We will just outline the main, relevant features of it here. In order to separate situations without and with knowledge of a probability context (a necessary condition to test our hypothesis of a contextual effect on single-trial processing strategies), we used a passive learning procedure in an *odd-ball paradigm* with a discrimination task. In this odd-ball paradigm, subjects received Bernoulli series of high and low tones of complementary probability. One of the tones was frequent or standard, the other rare. Subjects had to release a motor response for either frequent or rare target stimuli (*go-no-go*). Thus, two complementary tasks had to be performed: (a) the *explicit* task of motor response to targets, and (b) the *implicit,* automatic task of probability context evaluation. Our central hypothesis was that contextual knowledge about probability relations between events will differentially affect single-trial processing strategies, according to stimulus frequency. It was further hypothesized, on behalf of preliminary behavioral results, that depressed subjects (Ds) will not process probability context.

Three probability conditions (20%–80%, 50%–50%, 80%–20%) were tested in five consecutive sequences (80 stimuli) for each condition. A second session was a replication of the first session, one week later. *Learning* effects were detected by a *within-condition* analysis for each session. RTs and ERPs averaged separately during first and last two runs of each unequal probability condition were compared. A *between-session* analysis compared grand averages across the five runs of unequal probability conditions. Three experimental factors, were, thus, explored: probability, practice, and task.

Having established the learning paradigm in normal subjects (Ns), we attempted to separate *cognitive and motivational* dimensions of information processing by applying it to a pathological group of subjects known to show highly decreased motivation with little disturbance of purely cognitive functions. Most cognitivists simply ignore drive-motivation dimensions of information processing because of the difficulty of controlling for such factors in experimental designs. Depression is an interesting model of decreased motivation, as it is usually considered to involve a deficit in right hemisphere functions and also possibly in limbic system structures that are at the base of emotional-motivational drives.

Data Recording and Analysis

EEG was recorded from six electrodes referred to linked ears, spaced at intervals of 10% of the nasion–inion distance, starting from Fz and including Cz and Pz.

Supraorbital and suborbital electrodes around the right eye monitored ocular potentials. The nominal bandpass of the system was 0.7 Hz–150 Hz. A/D conversion was performed at a rate of 500 Hz for a sampling epoch of 750 msec, including 200 msec prestimulus baseline. Trials contaminated by EOG artifacts were manually rejected from the analysis.

RTs and ERPs were averaged separately for the different experimental conditions. Endogenous ERPs were measured both by subtracting ERPs to the frequent stimuli from ERPs to the infrequent stimuli (Ritter, Simson, Vaughan & Macht, 1982; Simson, Vaughan & Ritter, 1977), and by subtracting the (exogenous) auditory evoked potential recorded in a passive situation (no task) with purely random stimuli, from ERPs to both rare and frequent stimuli in the task situation (Näätänen, 1982). The main purpose of both subtraction techniques is to neutralize the overlapping of N100 and P200 exogenous evoked potentials on the early endogenous ERPs, PN and N200.

Peaks were identified as the highest amplitude values detected on spatiotemporal maps of the ERPs, relative to the prestimulus baseline. N200 was taken as the most negative peak between 160 msec–240 msec; P3a and P3b were the most positive peaks between 250 msec–350 msec at frontocentral sites and 350 msec–550 msec at parietal sites respectively. Mathematical analysis on the results included ANOVA, plus a specific Student t–test and Principal Component Analysis (PCA).

RESULTS

Three learning stages could be distinguished in normals (Ns), whereas no learning at all was manifested by behavioral indices for depressed patients (Ds), in spite of electrical evidence of quasinormal automatic cognitive processes. One of the most striking features of these results is the consistency for Ns, and inconsistency for Ds, between the variations in behavioral and electrical indices.

Prelearning

The *prelearning phase* initiated the practice of a probability condition. The task was correctly performed by Ns, and behavioral responses were not significantly shorter for frequent than for rare events (Fig. 6.1). Significant negative and positive ERP components were elicited. However, only the positive complex, and more specifically the P3b component, showed an amplitude difference in response to rare and frequent stimuli (Fig. 6.3). This *real time* indexing of prior probability held not only when subjects encountered a prior probability condition for the first time but also after the shift from the first probability condition to the next. These results taken together suggest that systems generating the P300 complex actually participated in probability processing. Further investigations have clarified the functional significance of previously individualized subcompo-

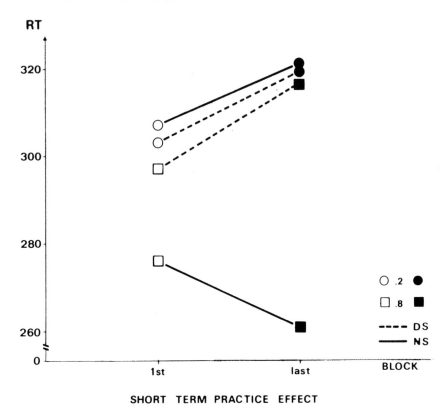

SHORT TERM PRACTICE EFFECT

FIG. 6.1. Time course of RTs from first (prelearning) to last (postlearning) runs of the first session in Normals (Ns) and Depressed (Ds).

nents (Banquet et al., 1981, 1984, 1985): Frontally located *P3a* reflected the local probability of a sequence of at most five stimuli (Fig. 6.2). Parietal *P3b* indexed both local and global probability. This functional difference is interpreted as evidence of bottom–up information transfer between two systems with memory registers of different time constants: The *P3b* system processes the same type of information (contextual probability) as the *P3a* system, but over a longer time span. Munson et al. (1984), Ruchkin, Sutton & Mahaffey (1987) showed comparable results on *P3b* and *P3e* components, the latter probably being the same as our *P3a*.

The *N200* component, which is known to be related to stimulus identification, in spite of a significantly large amplitude, did not show any amplitude difference in response between rare and frequent events at learning onset (Fig. 6.3). This negative result suggests that the *N200* generating system is not directly involved in probability context processing. Furthermore, in this specific probability context (20%–80%), a pitch difference between high and low stimuli did not result in significant amplitude differences of the *N*200 complex, composed of MMN and *N2b*.

Finally *timing* of the PN onset, at about 40 msec poststimulus delivery, indicated that information processing was triggered by stimulus detection and, therefore, that ascending bottom–up processes were predominant at this phase.

Ds performed the task correctly, although their responses to frequent events were slower than Ns'. More importantly, their RT was not different in response to rare or frequent events (Fig. 6.1). Considering these behavioral results alone, one is tempted to conclude that Ds did not process probability. However, this hypothesis, which can be construed as a defect of procedural memory, was not supported by ERP averages over the first session. *P3b* amplitude response to prior probability was quasinormal, with a significant difference between responses to rare and frequent events (Fig. 6.4). This dissociation between behavioral and electrical data constitutes a *first paradox* between ERP and RT results. It is also a good example of the specific contribution of ERPs in evaluating cognitive processes. More precisely, this result indicates that basic *automatic* cognitive processes of stimulus and probability context evaluation were quasinormal. Never-

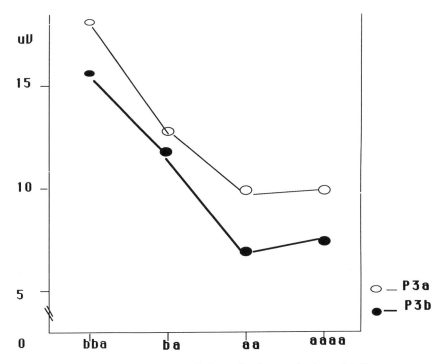

FIG. 6.2. Average *P3a* and *P3b* amplitudes on the last trial *N* as a function of the structure of the preceding *a* or *b* type stimuli.

theless the *P3a* component of the positive complex, which is often interpreted in association with *N2b* as a reflection of conscious orienting reaction, was significantly decreased in Ds.

The nonconfirmation of our working hypothesis of a defect of prior probability context processing did not give any indication as to the actual processing deficits responsible for the counterperformance of Ds. Negative component analysis combined with the dynamic study of probability learning nevertheless gave us important clues.

In contrast to normal *P3b* and in conformity with decreased *P3a* in Ds, negativities, and in particular *N200*, showed a large decrease in amplitude (Banquet, Guenther, & Smith, 1987), mainly when no motor response was required (no-go) (contamination from motor preparatory components made such amplitude comparisons more difficult in the go condition). This result was confirmed in a dichotic listening paradigm, by El Massioui and Lesèvre (1988). This result was notably different from the significantly high and equal amplitudes of *N200* in Ns to high and low probability stimuli at the beginning of a probability condition, during the first session (Fig. 6.3). The result on the Ds group was interpreted as a defect in focal attention and/or orienting reaction. We were, thus, confronted with a *second paradox* between behavioral and ERP results: RT suggested that Ds reacted as if all stimuli were rare and unexpected (slow RT even to frequent stimuli), but *N200* indicated that there was no startle or orienting reaction, even when events were rare. A parsimonious interpretation supposes an *absence of specific expectations* for a particular type of stimulus, a kind of indifference to events, and particularly to nontargets. As a result, there is no learning and improved performance, because of the absence of preparation; there cannot be surprise or orienting, because no specific stimulus is expected. This interpretation is consistent with the result that not only *N200*, but also *P3a*, decreased in our type of Ds. Nevertheless we will also see in the discussion that this interpretation is not sufficient.

Taken together, these results suggest that probability processing functions, which rely on procedural memory, are robust, automatic, bottom–up, acquired early in psychogenesis, and operational without need for any further learning. Furthermore, this process is robust enough to resist emotional-motivational perturbations such as those occurring in severely depressed subjects. Conversely different varieties of attention, in particular automatic phasic orienting and controlled tonic focal attention, seem to be highly sensitive to this motivational dimension.

Postlearning

The *postlearning phase* corresponded to the end of practice of a fixed probability condition, after subjects had received about 400 stimuli over approximately ten minutes of practice, in the first session. Both behavioral responses and ERP profiles changed considerably after learning in Ns.

1. The most dramatic behavioral result (Fig. 6.1) concerned diverging time courses of RTs to frequent events (decreased) and to rare events (increased). This result is interpreted as evidence of a *biased preparation* in favor of frequent stimuli. This biased preparation accelerates or slows down processing according to whether or not it is congruent with the delivered stimulus.

2. ERPs showed an emergent *prestimulus negativity* about 100 msec prior to stimulus delivery. Due to constant interstimulus intervals (1.5 sec), subjects can anticipate stimulus delivery time and type, at least for frequent ones, and prepare themselves. Hence, this prestimulus negativity is interpreted as an equivalent of late components of the *contingent negative variation* (CNV, Tecce, 1972; Walter, Cooper, Aldridge, McCallum & Winter, 1964). Late CNV, according to recent results (Damen & Brunia 1987; Gaillard, 1977; Rohrbaugh, Syndulko, & Lindsley, 1976; Ruchkin, Sutton, Mahaffey & Glaser, 1986) is best interpreted as a composite wave combining motor Bereitschaftpotential and perceptual *stimulus preceding negativity* (SPN).

3. This prestimulus negativity is in continuity with subsequent poststimulus negativities (i.e., *PN* and *N*200 components). The major change with the pre-learning stage comes from *divergence in amplitude* of these negative components according to stimulus probability (Fig. 6.3):

a. In the case of a frequent expected stimulus, an early negative peak (50 ms poststimulus) was followed by rapidly decaying negative and then positive (*P*300) activity. Maximum activity was early and followed by an early motor response. This early peak corresponded, therefore, to stimulus identification.

b. Conversely, in case of rare, unexpected events, an early positive reversal of activity (*P*120) was followed by maximal late activity for both negative (*N*200) and positive (*P*300) components. RT was delayed in this situation. Not only ERP amplitudes, studied here, but also latencies (Banquet et al., 1986) followed this diverging time course according to stimulus probability. Hence, the positive *P*300 as well as the negative *N*200 components reacted to probability by the end of the first learning session. This delayed diverging course of *N*200 amplitude and latency is remarkably parallel to that of RT latency. This confirms that *N*200 represents the stimulus identification stage, the last necessary and sufficient step before elicitation of a motor response (Renault, Ragot, Lesevre & Rémond, 1982; Ritter, Simson, Herbert, Vaughan & Friedman, 1979).

Whereas most evident learning effects in Ns were located in the *N*200 complex and in preparatory activity, the most salient results in Ds, besides evidence of normal stimulus and probability processing (implying normal procedural memory), were negative.

Behavioral responses did not show evidence of task learning from the beginning to the end of a probability condition in first session. Rather performance deteriorated for both types of events (Fig. 6.1) suggesting a fatigue factor taking over the learning process. Whereas Ns dramatically reduced RT in response to

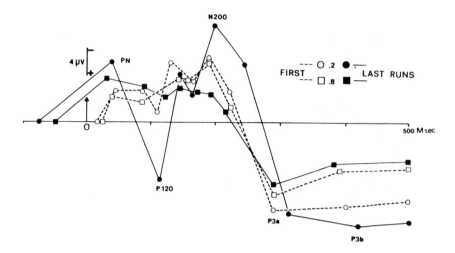

FIG. 6.3.   Mean amplitudes of ERP components over all subjects. ERP amplitudes (in microvolts) are displayed as a function of time (unit scale, 100 ms), stimulus probability (squares, high probability, circles, low probability), and runs (dotted lines, first two runs; full lines, last two runs). The peaks were measured on interpolated maps at their maximum amplitude value, in different locations. Therefore, the diagram does not represent a unique electrode site. Four experimental conditions are superimposed: (a) frequent and rare stimuli in *first sequences:* dotted lines with squares and circles respectively; and (b) frequent and rare stimuli in *last sequences:* full lines with squares and circles respectively. The main advantage of this representation is to eliminate the smoothing of the peaks due to intersubject latency jitter for the different components. (Reproduced by permission of the Optical Society of America)

frequent events and just as dramatically increased RT in response to rare ones, as a consequence of biased preparation, Ds did not present this diverging pattern. Rather, by the end of a probability condition in the first session, they maintained similar responses to rare and frequent stimuli. They reacted, at least on behavioral grounds, to both types of events as if they were rare, surprising, and unexpected, that is, with an absence of preparation. Their performance deterioration in the postlearning condition (Fig. 6.1), was probably for reasons different from the biased preparation that caused a slowing down of RT to rare stimuli in Ns, because this deterioration equally affected responses to rare and frequent stimuli. RT variability was larger for Ds than for Ns, even without taking into account the extremely slow (beyond 1 sec) responses, in the average. This variability was interpreted as a confirmation of focal attention fluctuations.

For technical reasons, and at variance with RT, ERPs were not averaged separately at the beginning (prelearning) and end (postlearning) of a probability condition. Yet first-session ERP averages of Ds were very different from first session either prelearning or postlearning patterns of Ns. In Ns, there was little or no task (motor response) effect: Cognitive potentials to target (go) and nontarget (no-go) stimuli were similar, once motor potentials were appropriately controlled (Banquet et al., 1981). Indeed both type of stimuli were task-relevant and, therefore, equally processed, in a task where processing demands were not overwhelming. Conversely Ds displayed a *task effect:* no-go $N200$ was small, even for rare stimuli (Fig. 6.4), clearly indicating a defect in either "contextual conditioning" or orienting reaction (or both). These defects in orienting could

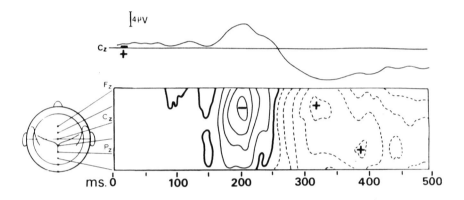

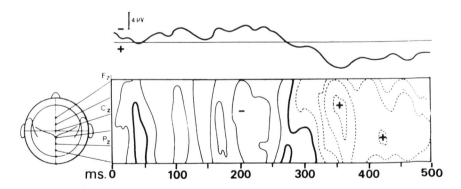

FIG. 6.4.   Grand-mean auditory ERPs (across subjects) in Ns and Ds for the first session, in response to rare no-go stimuli. These spatiotemporal maps result from the subtraction of the auditory evoked potentials in a passive situation from the no-go ERP responses. There is an increment of 1.6 uV from one isopotential line to the next. The Cz monopolar recording is presented above each map.

explain deficiencies in expectancy and preparation, indirectly demonstrated here by similar RTs to rare and frequent stimuli, and directly manifested as a decreased terminal CNV in a majority of depressive states (Timsit-Berthier, Mantanus, Poncelet, Marissaux & Legros, 1987). Nevertheless $N200$ amplitude of Ds was closer to that of Ns, in the go situation, when they had to emit a motor response. This result could explain why motor retardation, as expressed by RT, was slight compared to clinical scales rating major psychomotor retardation. This discrepancy between *spontaneous* and *reactive* behavior seems to be common observation in Ds who in particular preserve abilities for automatic behaviors (e.g., driving a car).

Thus, in this task, the probability dimension was automatically processed by Ds, although not expressed behaviorally in the RT results. Deficits in motivational aspects of cognition were most reflected by the ERP components indexing focal attention (PN) and orienting reaction ($N2b$). Such dysfunctions could cause deficits in more controlled processes such as expectancies, anticipation, and preparation, that appear to be the main factors of behavioral learning in this paradigm.

Overlearning

In the overlearning phase of Ns, during a second session identical to the first, one week late, different ERP–RT alterations occurred:

1. ERP *amplitude gradients,* which differentiated $N200$–$P300$ responses to rare and frequent stimuli by the end of the first session, remained present although at a lower level at second session onset. This suggests consolidation of first-session learning in LTM. The reduced amplitude of these gradients evokes two plausible explanations.

a. In second session, subjects had learnt a more realistic model of probability context: To different degrees, not only frequent but also rare events were expected and were, therefore, no longer much of a surprise. Accordingly the orienting reaction to rare events decreased.

b. An alternative interpretation, which is not exclusive of the previous one, supposes task automatization and, therefore, less drawing upon of controlled cognitive resources. This explanation holds only for $N2b$ and part of $P300$ reflecting controlled processes but not for MMN, which corresponds to a fully automatic process. Similarly prestimulus anticipatory electrical activity was present right from the beginning of the second session.

2. Direct signs of task *automatization* (Kramer, Schneider, Fisk, & Donchin, 1986) were manifested by RT floor values to frequent stimuli, at the beginning of the second session. This behavioral result was associated with dramatic changes in $P300$ component topography: Frontal $P3a$ and parietal $P3b$ converged and lined up to a central location. This was taken as an indication of the potential

plurality of *P300* generators, their activation depending on task learning stage and strategies adopted by the subjects.

3. An alteration in "baseline" levels of ERP components varied similarly for both types of stimulus frequency, but the negative and positive components varied in opposite directions in this second session. For negative components, a *decrease* in baseline amplitude occurred that was interpreted as a result of *habituation* (Woods & Elmasian, 1986) and/or automatization of perceptual aspects of the task. For positive components (Fig. 6.5), there was an *increase* in *P3a–P3b* baseline amplitude, greatest for the responses to frequent stimuli. This phenomenon, evident in second session, was possibly present at postlearning stages of the first session but masked by opposite amplitude evolutions of *P300* responses to rare and frequent stimuli. This increase in baseline *P300* amplitude is considered as an equivalent of *long-term potentiation* (LTP) occurring in animal conditioning (Banquet, Smith, Spinakis & El Ouardirhi, 1989). This LTP reflecting a synaptic facilitation with strict topological specificity (limited only to the activated synapses in the conditioned circuits) is thought to reflect the process of

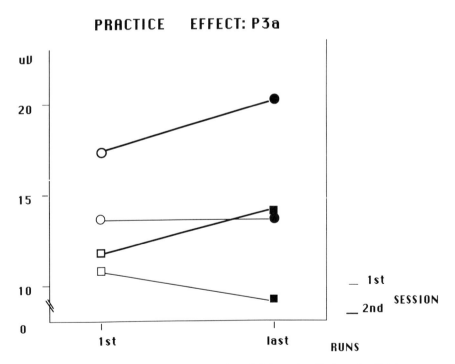

FIG. 6.5.   *P3a* amplitude as a function of: (a) *session,* first session light lines, second session, heavy lines; (b) *sequences* in each session, empty and full figures represent first and last sequences respectively; and (c) *probability:* circles rare and square frequent events.

LTM *engram formation* in animals. That LTP is manifested, in animal neuronal recordings, as an increased EPSP amplitude is neither in favour or against this interpretation for a positive component, because, as already mentioned, the polarity of scalp ERPs depends not only on the neuronal activation or inhibition but also on the depth of the generators and dipoles' configuration.

This second session in Ds came after a short course of pharmacotherapy. Behavioral and electrical courses closely fitted responses to treatment: (a) Patients not improved clinically after a week of treatment further deteriorated behavioral and electrical responses during the second session, and (b) conversely clinically improved patients tended to normalize both types of indices, and in particular *PN*, which is assumed to reflect focal aspects of attention (Näätänen et al., 1978; Hillyard, Hink, Schwent, & Picton, 1973). Nevertheless improved RTs did not discriminate between rare and frequent events, suggesting that global levels of activation were restored but that more subtle inferential processes of expectancy, anticipation, and preparation were not fully normalized.

DISCUSSION

Results will be interpreted in the framework of adaptive resonance theory (ART), which will be adapted to fit peculiarities of the data. Results in Ds will be further interpreted in terms of possible defects of monoamine neurotransmitter systems (cf Hestenes, chapter 7 in this volume).

Normals

Electrical evidence demonstrates the importance of top–down processes as a dominant strategy in event recognition, once subjects (who do not need to learn probability processing) have decoded probability contexts. This does not preclude the possibility of top–down information transfers in other processing conditions. However, the magnitude of the top–down effect seems to vary, as a function not only of existence or nonexistence of a previous recognition code (category) of the input but also of the degree of knowledge of the probability context in which the events take place. In this experiment, two types of top–down processes can be differentiated. They can be seen in ERPs after probability learning. The first type of top–down process is automatic in response to a bottom–up input. The second type of top–down attended process is self-generated and supposes *expectancy* and, therefore, a LTM trace of *subjective probability*.

The first type is an *automatic feed-back, top–down* process that we call *contextual conditioning:* Physical characteristics of stimuli, previously affected with neutral contextual probability valence before assessment of probability context, become weighted by or associated with a defined probability. This interpretation is based on the variable $N200$ amplitude reaction to probability during learning. It is closely linked to our more general interpretation of $N200$ and in particular its *MMN* component. Yet other possible hypotheses must also be reviewed.

In an attended odd-ball paradigm like the one used here, $N200$ deflection has been shown to have two major components: *MMN* and *N2b*. Näätänen's hypothesis concerning the mechanisms of *MMN* generation is directly inferred from experimental results but is nevertheless not fully convincing because of the ad hoc nature of the assumptions (Banquet, Smith & Renault, 1990). For example, he proposed (Näätänen, 1990), for the tone frequency *MMN,* that some highly frequency-specific neuronal population (in sensory memory) is in a state of homogeneous *inhibition* during presentation of the first stimulus, because no *MMN* is elicited. This first stimulus releases from inhibition the neurons specific to other frequencies but not those specific to the frequency of the stimulus. Therefore, the next stimulus elicits a *MMN* only if it differs from the first. The repetitions strengthen the stimulus-specific inhibition pattern whereas increasing *excitability* elsewhere in the system. Thus, according to this interpretation, an island of specific inhibition is surrounded by an ocean of activation.

Our results, however, as well as the parsimony principle, suggest a different mechanism. We suppose that two mechanisms *compete* for *MMN* and indirectly induce *N2b* when attention is voluntarily or automatically oriented to the stimulus. The input's model in sensory or working memory is composite (Sams, Alho, & Näätäanen, 1984), including not only standard but deviant stimuli templates. It is also unstable, modulated by short sequences of the most recent stimuli. There is neither template selection nor inhibition in automatic stimulus processing. Hence, any input induces a combination of match (predominant in case of standards) and mismatch (predominant in case of deviant stimuli) in the primary auditory cortex. As suggested by the ART, a dominant match induces a *reinforcement* of the nodes' activity (which gives a deflection of a few microvolts, such as in PN). Conversely a dominant mismatch induces a *decrement* of the nodes' activity. In the case of dominant mismatch, this modality-specific generator of the auditory cortex alerts a second nonspecific generator in the right frontal cortex (Giard, Perrin, Pernier & Peronnet, 1988). This second generator is the main determinant of *MMN* and $N200$ amplitude. It gives a "call" for attention that is at the origin of a patent-orienting reaction, if the "call" gets through. This interpretation presents at least two advantages, besides its being coherent with the known experimental results. First, the supposed dominance of the right frontal generator over the specific generator accounts for the topographical dominance of *MMN* in the frontal regions and the right hemisphere (Näätänen, 1990). Secondly this interpretation gives a parsimonious and unified explanation of the mechanisms of production of *MMN* and *PN*. In this framework, *PN* results from a pure match due to a preset top–down inhibition (by the process of selective feature filtering) of the nodes coding the template features that are not relevant. This match would be the *only process* reflected in the amplitude of *PN*. Indeed there is no need for a "call" for attention and orienting, because attention is already focalized in a selective attention paradigm. This match is maximal for relevant and only partial for irrelevant stimuli as a function of similarity to the relevant stimulus. Hence, *PN* seems to reflect an island of activation surrounded by an ocean of inhibition.

According to this hypothesis, three possible interpretations, not equally plausible, of delayed *N*200 reactivity to probability once learning has occurred can be proposed. There is little chance that this delayed *N*200 reaction to stimulus frequency actually reflects prior *probability processing* by the *N*200 system. This type of processing was indexed right from the beginning by the *P*300 wave. According to the principle of parsimony, there is no reason to believe that the two systems perform the same function. An even more serious argument is the short time span of a few seconds of *MMN* memory registers (Näätänen & Picton, 1986), which is not sufficient to monitor a probability context (requiring several, consecutive stimuli to be evaluated) with interstimulus intervals of 1.5 sec. A delayed response of *N*200–*MMN* system to *physical characteristics* of the stimuli (i.e., recomposition in short-term memory of a model of physical characteristics of the stimuli from previously extracted features) is also untenable. This is indeed one of the functions attributed to the *MMN* system. However, experimental evidence (Sams et al., 1984) shows that the dynamics of this function are much faster than that of the process observed here. Such a physical model is rapidly constructed after a few inputs and very closely monitors changes in stimulus physical characteristics. Physical parameters per se were not systematically manipulated in this experiment but rather fixed at two levels, high and low pitch, thus, allowing for early tuning of the *MMN* system. Nevertheless such a rapid amplitude difference, in response to physically distinct stimuli, due to the *MMN* component of *N*200 (Näätänen, Simpson, & Loveless, 1982), was not significant at unequal probability condition onset. The difference wave that was computed in this experiment (by subtracting the passive random condition from active odd-ball paradigm) probably favored the expression of the *N2b* component of *N*200 more than the *MMN* component, because there is a small *MMN* even in the passive equiprobable condition (Näätänen, 1990). A *N2b* component preponderant over *MMN* could have masked small *MMN* differences. Thus, progressive changes over several hundred stimuli must be due to other mechanisms.

This delayed reactivity of *N*200 to stimulus probability reflects a mechanism requiring time to build up and, therefore, involving recent long term memory (LTM). One of the most plausible interpretations is *contextual conditioning:* Whereas, in the prelearning phase, stimuli were neutral as regards event probability, in postlearning, they acquired probabilistic valence. Thus, an association between stimulus physical characteristics and specific probability conditions was created. The term *conditioning* (which refers to both behavioral and structural changes) is used here to refer to the association between physical CS and contextual information, which plays the role of the US, for the $P300$ amplitude response. The term conditioning is justified, because a stimulus (here a given sound), as a consequence of consistent association with a complex contextual information (probability), inherits the property to elicit a response ($N200$ amplitude modulation as a function of prior probability) that does not belong to the natural register of the $N200$ system activated by this stimulus. The natural register of the $N200$ system is in fact automatic response to physical differences between consecutive stimuli. This system does not react to prior probability per se and in particular does not need an *odd-ball* paradigm to be elicited. This indicates that *MMN* responds to local variations of stimuli but not to prior probability. However, this response to probability corresponds to the natural register of another system ($P300$ system), and, therefore, prior probability considered as a complex stimulus has the status of an unconditioned stimulus (US) for this system and of conditioning stimulus for the $N200$ system. The conditioned response (CR) is not behavioral and patent in this case but rather a covert delayed $N200$ amplitude response as function of stimulus probability. Existence of a delay both in *onset* and *extinction* of $N200$ amplitude modulation by probability (CR) further justifies assimilating this learning process to conditioning. Indeed, after the first shift from unequal to equal probability, the $N200$ system keeps on responding as in the previous condition (Banquet & Grossberg, 1987). Adaptation to a new probability requires the same delay as was required to adapt to the first probability condition, whereas the $P300$ system adapts, in real time, to the new probability.

At the *neurophysiological* level, this conditioning could correspond to the *weighting* of previously neutral physical models or templates by a probability valence (Banquet, Smith & Renault, 1990). This top–down information transfer constitutes a *reactive* top–down process and corresponds, in the framework of ART, to template read-out in a LTM register of a specific probability context and not in the LTM register of the code or category of an event. In terms of ART theory, the F_n processing level affects (by the process of top–down template readout) not only the F_{n-1} level but also the F_{n-2} level. F_n may, thus, represent the probability context processing level (i.e., the level of rule formation). F_{n-1} represents the recognition code or the categorization level. F_{n-2} corresponds to the stimulus physical identification level.

The *functional consequence* could be as follows.

1. At the *preidentification* stage, stimuli seem to be given a *priority rank,* such that a higher priority template is permanently subactivated in working memory and mobilizes few processing resources when the corresponding input is presented. The lower priority template is less or not at all activated, hence, requiring a larger amount of processing resources at the presentation of the corresponding infrequent stimulus.

2. At the *postidentification* stage, a new *composite* LTM is created that associates, in a single memory pattern, information issued from two different processing levels and thus from two memory patterns (i.e., recognition code and prior probability). The recognition code memory has, thus, been weighted by the "probability" memory.

The *strategic significance* of this conditioning is subject to diverse interpretations. In the context of this experiment, it can be considered that this conditioning allows the subject to automatically assign probabilities to stimuli at their identification stage. Probability is contextual information that, to be evaluated normally, requires maintenance of some kind of memory trace during a train of stimuli. Contextual conditioning could be an efficient way of performing two operations at once: stimulus-set identification (low pitch–high pitch) and response-set categorization (rare–frequent). Frequent and rare responses were associated, in this experiment, to frequent and rare events; therefore, an effective processing strategy may have been to substitute the criterion of frequency (probability) for that of pitch (proposed by instructions) in the response selection stage. This association would spare subjects any reference to working or long-term memory for (re)activating the rule of stimulus–response association announced in the instructions. This association of a context to stimulus physical characteristics is not so far from *complex conditioning* situations in animals where it has been shown that not only two stimuli are associated but also stimulus and context. This strategy supposes, to be operational, probability context stability.

This seems to be a sufficient strategy for correct task performance, assuming that prior probability of events is unequal and does not change. Yet, on the automatic level, systems maintain the ability to rapidly detect probability changes (Johnson & Donchin, 1982). Therefore, this strategy must be purely "local" for fast stimulus–response association: It aims to accelerate stimulus categorization and, thus, response selection on the basis of a relation between stimulus frequency and response type. For local tactical purposes, the system automatically associates a probability to any incoming stimulus, on the basis of previous experience. Yet effective probability context updating must be going on for longer-range strategic purposes and in particular for detecting an eventual probability shift.

In our results, at the first probability shift from unequal to equal probabilities, the $N200$ system persisted in reacting according to an obsolete, previous probability context. The $N200$ amplitude kept on being large or small according to stimulus type in spite of equal stimulus probability, whereas the longer-range strategic system of context updating, reflected by $P300$, adapted in real time to the new probability context. This functional paradox had no behavioral consequence in our paradigm, in which response choice was linked due to the instructions, to stimulus pitch consistently throughout the experiment. One can suppose that the "executive controller" was vigilant enough to make this rule predominate. However, one can wonder what would have occurred, if response choice had been linked to stimulus probability. It is not hazardous to suppose that $N200$ systems and subjects would have gone on responding according to previous frequency patterns, although stimuli had gained equal probability, thus, logically making it impossible to decide response choice on grounds of probability criteria.

Thus, contextual conditioning can be considered as evidence of top–down feedback processes of a special kind in that they associate information concerning a context with information concerning stimulus type. This process manifests only after learning, because, in prelearning phase, recent LTM information concerning probability context is not available to the system. It can be considered for the initial condition that each stimulus is equally weighted. This delayed manifestation of the process seen with ERPs does not imply that reactive top–down, feed-back process did not exist right from beginning of practice. It just implies that, at task onset, this top–down feedback did not convey information or was not detectable by ERPs.

One can imagine different specific situations in which stimulus identification takes place without the help of top–down processes or with top–down processes that do not bring further relevant information than that provided by bottom–up input. This should take place for completely *new events* that have never previously been encountered. In this case, there is no corresponding recognition code or category in LTM. A *new class* is then created that is momentarily represented by a unique sample. It is hardly possible to speak of a probability context. In this specific case, the part played by top–down processes in event identification is minimal or nil. The identification itself amounts to simply recognizing a radical difference with all that was previously memorized. This occurrence must be particularly frequent in early infancy. It has been explored by Courchesne (1978) for unique visual patterns interspersed with trains of repetitive stimuli. These patterns give rise to a specific frontal $P3a$ whose topography changes to more posterior locations when the original stimulus is repeated. We relate this topographical change to the movement of $P3a$ towards central locations during the task automatization stage of our experiment. It remains to be determined whether this frontal $P3a$ corresponds to the creation of a new recognition code or reflects nonspecific processes related to orienting.

The second type of process can be characterized as a *top–down, feed-forward controlled* process, although it is difficult to determine respective parts of control and automaticity in anticipation-preparation. It is no longer a reactive process directly related to stimulus input. However, it retains the essence of a top–down process, because a complex contextual level of probability processing, inducing expectancies, affects lower levels of stimulus identification and motor response, by the bias of anticipation and preparation. This strategy of expectancy-anticipation-preparation has the advantage of short-cutting a part of the processing chain. It, thus, enhances performance when successful (i.e., in case of a match between expected and delivered events). However, there is a price to pay for improved performance. A major drawback of such a strategy occurs in case of expectancy failure, (i.e., in case of mismatch between expected and actually delivered events). Then need to reset inappropriately activated neural nets wastes time and results in reinstating a bottom–up strategy. This is the most parsimonious interpretation of degraded performance of Ns in response to rare events after learning. Therefore, net benefits of these anticipatory strategies depend on frequency and cost of rare failures. According to tasks, subjects must decide, if benefits of enhanced performance are larger than losses due to infrequent failures. Obviously solutions to this dilemma depend on types of task and subjects' priorities.

In the framework of ART (Carpenter & Grossberg, 1987), this feed-forward, top–down information transfer corresponds to a *self-initiated* process. This top–down process is not in reaction to a specific input but anticipates, by subliminal activation of lower levels F_i, a forthcoming specific input. Gain control systems in ART affect top–down processes with a negative gain; thus, the ⅔ rule (which states that at least two out of three inputs must be active on a node to turn it on supraliminally) is not fulfilled. Therefore, a F_i level receiving top–down priming inputs is turned on only when the bottom–up input matches the top–down template. At the functional level, there could be identity or simple relation between this top–down, feed-forward process and the priority status granted to the frequent stimulus at the preidentification stage of the reactive top–down process. The most important difference would be the character of automaticity of the latter versus the aspect of control and anticipation of the former.

The question whether stimulus identification may result from a simple bottom–up sweep of the whole processing neural system or whether it also depends upon total or partial top–down processes is closely related to the *states of memory* registers involved in processing task-relevant information. If there is a preexisting recognition code or prototype of an input, LTM registers of this adequate recognition code will gate the top–down signals. Consequently LTMs will be strengthened, if there is congruence between activated template and stimulus, or altered, if the congruence is only partial, in order to incorporate the characteristics of the new sample in the category. When there is no preexisting recognition code in LTM, a new one is then created, and event identification could be performed by reference to a model created in working memory by stimulus repetition. This is the only possibility Näätänen acknowledges to account for *MMN* elicitation (Näätänen, 1990). In our paradigm, this last possibility could correspond to the strategy used before overlearning phase and explain why the *N*200 component: either did not differ in amplitude for the two types of stimuli in prelearning phase, because their models in working memory were then randomly or equally weighted; or did differ widely in early postlearning phase, as a result of an all or nothing response, because the repetition was frequent enough to create an enduring template only for the most probable stimulus. Differences between STM and LTM dynamics explain how modifications can take place in STM (in particular several hypothesis testing cycles for stimulus identification) before any permanent LTM trace is imprinted (Banquet & Grossberg, 1987).

The third type of problem, previously mentioned, concerns the *modality* and the *range* of top–down processes. Are they limited to two levels (e.g., at the stage of stimulus identification), or do they extend between several or even all F_i levels of processing? Are they *backpropagation* processes or processes *bypassing* intermediate levels? We bring some evidence that several levels appear to be concerned.

Delayed $N200$ amplitude response to prior probability, during the first session, has been interpreted as evidence of a top–down information transfer from context to stimulus physical identification stages of processing. $P3a$ showed a similar delayed response to prior probability during the second session. It was shown, in the first session, that $P3a$ reacted to local probability, and $P3b$ reacted both to local and global probability. This was interpreted as a sign of bottom–up transfer of information from the $P3a$ to the $P3b$ system, this latter memory register being able, because of a longer time constant, to integrate information on a longer span of time. Nevertheless plots of $P3a$ amplitude responses to prior probability during the second session showed not only an increase in baseline amplitude, as earlier mentioned, but also an amplitude difference between responses to rare and frequent stimuli that had become largely significant, whereas it was at the limit of significance in the first session (Fig. 6.5).

This course of $P3a$ reaction to prior probability parallels that of $N200$, except that its dynamics are slower: $N200$ becomes reactive to probability by the end of the first session, whereas $P3a$ does so only during the second session. If these results are confirmed, they corroborate that top–down processes operate not only between two specific processing stages (e.g., category code formation level and physical identification level) but are between several, if not all, levels of different complexity. In the ERP literature, there is other evidence of interaction between global and local probability (Squires, Wickens, Squires, & Donchin, 1976), reflected only by the $P3b$ component. For identical sequences (5 stimuli maximum) of two types of complementary probability stimuli, $P3b$ amplitude to the last stimulus of the sequences depends not only on specific sequence structures (i.e., local probabilities) but also on the prior probability law responsible for these specific sequences.

Researchers working on the visual system in monkeys have provided arguments against the existence of top–down, feed-back processes in early identification. The main argument put forward is evidence of specific neuron firing in the inferotemporal cortex, related to face recognition (Rolls, 1987), as early as 140 msec poststimulus. Face recognition is high-level processing, supposing more than 10 previous relays in visual pathways. With an average firing frequency of 100 Hz for these neurons and an estimated delay of 5 msec to 10 msec per relay, they conclude that identification must be consecutive to a simple bottom–up sweep of the whole processing circuit. However, these chronometric arguments are not fully convincing, because top–down information transfers do not need to be a *full sweep* all the way down to receptor level. They can remain local (e.g., between two terminal stages involved in stimulus identification). Furthermore, the possibility that higher levels bypass intermediate levels in order to influence lower levels cannot be excluded. Further, top–down processes may not be involved in an early identification (sufficient to emit a response) but rather play a role in confirming stimulus identification in a later *control* stage. Experimental psychology has well-documented response decisions taken on the basis of different levels of certainty, in particular depending on instructions. If error is detected at this controlled processing stage, then either a response has not yet been emitted, and some correction of the motor preparatory stages reflected by ERP changes (Coles, Gratton, & Donchin, 1988) is possible in order to give out a correct behavioral response, or the neural command of behavioral response has already been emitted, and some top–down, feed-forward process, akin to error *backpropagation* in multilayer neural networks or more plausibly similar to a reward–penalization type of signal, can be considered. In this case, the more elaborated and accurate identification could play the role of reference (teacher) for early inaccurate identification. This correction mechanism in error situations must be distinguished from top–down processes taking place during successive *hypothesis testing cycles* (Banquet & Grossberg, 1987), which are more like a progressive tuning mechanism for event identification. In the case of the backpropagation type of top–down process, which is a controlled process with a teacher, differences are computed at the higher level of the processing chain and retropropagated by independent pathways to the lower levels. In the case of automatic top–down processes of the hypothesis testing cycles, and in the ART model in general, differences are computed at the lower end of the chain (match–mismatch) and fed forward to the higher level. In both cases, comparisons and differences are computed, but the latter process is no longer dependent on a teacher but on the learning of a recognition code or rule.

Depressed Subjects

Results from depressed patients (considered as a pathological model of selective impairment of the motivational-emotional aspect of cognition) yielded two apparently contradictory results. The task was correctly performed, although more slowly and with a larger number of errors than normals. Yet the large RT variance indicated defects in the focus of attention. ERPs showed basic automatic steps of stimulus evaluation and probability context processing to be quasinormal, thus, providing Ds with the necessary information for task performance. These results confirm that systems processing complex contextual information can function correctly, although attention systems are deficient, suggesting that the two types of systems are anatomically separated but functionally related because of the modulation of information processing by the attentional system. Main defects were located on subtler levels and could be globally characterized as follows: (a) defects in different varieties of attention, and (b) deficiency in top–down feedback or feed-forward information transfers and blocking of information transfers between automatic and controlled processes as well as impediment of secondary automatization of the task, and (c) motor retardation.

Defects in attention were documented both by behavioral (large RT variance) and electrical indices. Consider the following:

1. The defect in *PN*, just like *RT* variability, expressed perturbations in the focal, controlled, *tonic* component of attention (activation). This is a voluntary, self-initiated process, which certainly depends closely on the motivation dimension. Decreased *PN* amplitude is improved by successful pharmacotherapy, making *PN* a possible index of patient recovery.

2. The *phasic* aspect of attention represented by orienting seems to originate in more automatic and possibly cognitive processes. It is reflected by the *N*200 component of the ERPs. The *N*200 defect seems more complex and difficult to explain. As mentioned earlier, *N*200 has two components: (a) a modality-specific *MMN* with modality-specific temporal and nonspecific frontal generators, reflecting stimulus physical identification; and (b) nonspecific *N2b*, assumed to reflect a cortical orienting reaction. These components are superimposed, in the auditory modality of the attended odd-ball paradigm, and both of them could be altered in depression.

As a *first hypothesis,* an absence or weakness of contextual conditioning (i.e., of template weighting by a probability factor), would result, at the functional level, in an absence of priority for a specific type of stimulus and, therefore, an absence of clear-cut matches or mismatches. This could account for poorly differentiated *N*200s as a function of stimuli probability. According to this hypothesis, Ds would permanently react as do Ns in the prelearning stage. Yet *N*200 responses of Ns, in that stage, were identical for the two types of stimuli but of a consistently large amplitude. Conversely in Ds, there was a consistently low amplitude *N*200. Therefore, another mechanism, not necessarily different, but consecutive to the absence of template weighting, must be involved.

The *second hypothesis,* not exclusive of the first, but more plausible, supposes weakness of both the response of the frontal *MMN* generator and the *N2b* generator, which seem to be the support of the orienting reaction at automatic and controlled levels respectively. This would represent a deficiency of the *phasic* aspect of attention. The deficiency of *N2b* reaction is supported by the fact that *P3a*, at variance with *P3b*, had a significantly smaller amplitude in Ds than in Ns. *N2b* and *P3a* seem to react, at least partially, to the same experimental factors and have been related to the "breakthrough of the unattended in consciousness." Recent results (A. Pierson et al., in prep.) show that Ds with a small (orienting) *P3a* and a normal (cognitive) *P3b* belong to the "blunted affect" type of depression, whereas subjects with a normal *P3a* and a small *P3b* belong to the "impulsive" type of depression, with higher scores of anxiety. This pattern of ERP reactivity is constant across task conditions and could, therefore, correspond to preexisting traits in predepressive subjects, which could condition the type of depression such patients fall into. An absence or decrease in the usual frontal and right hemispheric dominance of *MMN* would be in favor of a deficit of the frontal generator. This weak reactivity to orientation would be partially overcome in response to target stimuli as a consequence of an external solicitation to respond via instructions.

3. Evidence for a perturbation of *alertness or diffuse attention* is only indirect in this experiment. It comes from the defect of high-level inferential cognitive processes (expectancy, anticipation) supported by this type of attention, which we have called feed-forward, top–down processes. This evidence comes from the uniform response (same RT) to rare and frequent stimuli, persisting in Ds even after practice or successful short therapy. Indeed the respective shortening and lengthening of *RT* to frequent and rare stimuli was the most obvious manifestation of a preparation in Ns. However, there is direct evidence of poor anticipation-preparation in Ds, manifested as a decreased terminal CNV, although this decrement is not constant (Timsit-Berthier et al., 1987).

Therefore, three ERP "windows" are the spatiotemporal loci of perturbations in Ds: preparatory activity, *PN,* and *MMN*. These components are mostly frontal and central in the auditory modality. Nevertheless they are in favor of an attentional system that is not based on a single center or on a holistic system of the brain but rather on interconnected centers carrying on specialized functions. We will, therefore, attempt to integrate these specific deficits in the framework of the more global dysfunction of the right hemisphere, which we have postulated as a characteristic of Ds and/or as a dysfunction of the frontal lobes.

Indications of the attentional functions more specifically supported by the right hemisphere (and, therefore, presenting a higher risk of perturbation in Ds) can be found in these extreme cases of dysfunction that constitute the lesions of the right hemisphere. The most commonly encountered neglect of the opposite spatial hemifield in right hemisphere lesions does not necessarily imply that spatial attention is under control of the right hemisphere. Experiments based on heart rate or galvanic skin response to warning stimuli (Heilman, Watson, & Valenstein, 1985) show that right hemispheric patients have difficulty with alerting, associated with impaired performance in vigilance tasks (Wilkins, Shallice, & McCarthy, 1987). The complementary experiment of right hemisphere lesions provided by selective stimulation of one hemisphere can be performed in split-brain patients. When information is delivered to the isolated left hemisphere, these patients present lower vigilance levels than when the information is delivered to the right hemisphere (Dimond & Beaumont, 1973). These results suggest that the right hemisphere includes the structures that sustain the mechanisms of the maintenance of an alert state. They provide an interpretation for the lack of expectancy, anticipation, and preparation found in our results. This failure to get prepared does not result from a lack of information on the probability context but rather from an inability to sustain a state of alertness, or diffuse attention, in the absence of a specific target.

Obviously this system of alerting must be in close functional relation with the system of *target detection* and *focused attention*. In particular, in case of an alert state, the threshold of stimulus detection should be lower than in a situation of nonexpectancy. A potentiation of the target detection system by the alerting system is plausible. In our results with normal subjects, the electrical activity related to the successive activation of the two systems (alertness and focal attention) encompass the stimulus delivery, the prestimulus preparatory activity merging into the poststimulus processing negativity. In Ds, the alerting deficit is associated with a focal attention deficit reflected by a decreased *PN,* which recovers a larger amplitude after successful pharmacotherapy. *PN* could, therefore, be an index of recovery. *PN* presents at least two components, one of them being nonmodality-specific and frontally located. There is, therefore, partial agreement between these electrophysiological results and cerebral blood flow studies (Peterson, Fox, Rosner, Mintum, & Raichle, 1988), which have located a system reacting to the detection of targets in anterior *cingulate gyrus* and a nonspecific system active in tasks involving both language and spatial imagery in the *lateral superior frontal area.* The demonstration by Posner and Presti (1987) of the importance of engaging the focal attention system in the production of widespread interference between signals supports the existence of a unified system hierarchically organized and involved in detection of signals whatever their source. The hallmark of this focal attention system is awareness and voluntary control. Its dysfunction is easily understandable in depression in which motivational deficit plays a major role.

It is more unexpected that the system called *involuntary orienting* by Luria (1973) and *posterior attention system* by Posner and Presti (1987) is also disturbed. This system, reflected by *N200,* is (according to the hypothesis of Näätänen concerning the auditory modality) triggered into activity by an automatic mismatch, indexed by the *MMN* component of *N200.* In our interpretation, the decreased *N200* amplitude in Ds results essentially from a weaker *N2b* component that is thought to reflect the transition from a purely automatic cognitive process reflected by MMN to a covert orienting. This interpretation is more in agreement with the fact that automatic functions are usually preserved in depression. The orienting system of Näätänen has been based upon experiments on the auditory system. The equivalent posterior attention system of Posner is based on the visual system. The plausible claim of a distinct, nonmodality-specific posterior orienting structure supposes that common points are found between the two systems based on auditory and visual data respectively.

The top–down, feed-forward processes representing expectancy, anticipation, and preparation can be characterized as inferential. Inference is at the very base of elaborated cognitive strategies. The *frontal lobes* are supposed to play a major role in these functions. Could a depressive syndrome be considered in terms of frontal lobe dysfunction? A number of symptoms of frontal lobe dysfunction— disruption of higher cognitive functions, disturbed affective responses, stereo-typed motor behavior, indifference to external events and withdrawal from social interactions (Goldman-Rakic, 1984; Levine, Leven, & Prueitt, Chapter 9 in this volume)—could be considered to characterize depression. A functional deficit of frontal lobes in Ds seems to be confirmed by electrophysiological recordings. Small amplitude of *PN*, of nonspecific frontocentral components of N200 (Ban-quet et al., 1987) and of CNV (Timsit-Berthier et al., 1987) support this assump-tion. Yet controlled processes are still present, as indicated by abnormally pro-longed frontal negativities consecutive to emission of behavioral responses (Baribeau-Braun & Lesèvre, 1983). Furthermore, there is certainly no trace of behavioral incongruency in depression. Therefore, these perturbations of frontal functions could reflect rather a deficiency in motivational-emotional afferences from the hypothalamus and limbic system to the frontal lobes than a specific deficit of the frontal lobes per se. These signs should be placed in a larger context of dominant *inhibition*. Therefore, although frontal dysfunction is plausible, the term "frontal syndrome" seems inadequate.

Frontal lobes could be involved in the symptomatology of depression at a more subtle level than in a lesional frontal syndrome. There are two, interrelated, although distinct, subsystems in the frontal lobes (Levine et al. Chapter 9 in this volume and Levine, 1986). The orbitofrontal inferomedial system receives hypo-thalamic and limbic afferents. The dorsolateral system is bidirectionaly related to the different cortical areas. The frontal lobe is classically involved in temporal integration of goal-directed behavior. It plays a role of executive controller (Baddeley, 1986). Indeed the two prefrontal subsystems are in an ideal position to integrate motivational and cognitive information, and further to serve as a relay for transfers of information automatically processed at a subcortical level, in particular the hippocampus and the hypothalamus, to cortical control systems. Some ERPs reflect purely automatic processes (*MMN*), some others controlled processes (*PN*), and some both controlled and automatic ones (*P300*). Most of them have nonspecific components located in the frontocentral area, which seem more specifically to reflect activity of the frontal lobes. ERPs could, therefore, constitute an ideal tool to chart this "unexplored continent." Moreover, evidence has been presented for an anterior attention system involved in detection of signals and focal attention, regardless of their sources, and including, according to brain blood flow or metabolic studies, not only the cingulate gyrus but also lateral superior frontal areas.

Thus, the psychological construct of attention could very closely reflect, in its different dimensions, the motivation factor we seek to explore. The conse-quences of attention system impairment on more cognitive functions remain largely unresolved. It certainly affects *declarative* memory and higher-controlled cognitive functions, but there is some evidence, in these results, that *procedural* memory and automatic processes are not seriously disturbed. The inferential functions could be supported by top–down, feed-forward processes. Hence, there is a possibility that deficit in automatic and/or controlled phasic attention and also alertness play an important role in more controlled processes of anticipation and preparation that seem to be more directly supported by alertness.

Motivation can certainly not be confounded with attention. In particular the two types of factors can be dissociated in detection tasks performed under scopolamine and analyzed in the framework of *signal detection* theory: Stimulus sensitivity is decreased, reflecting decreased attention or vigilance, but there is no change in motivation or control of response output. Yet we have seen how a defect in motivational-emotional systems seems to match with attentional deficits. This suggests that motivational-emotional systems, just as attentional systems, act as modulators of cognitive structures (not necessarily the same), facilitating the flux of information when normally activated and conversely inhibiting it when hypoactivated. Hence, the flow of neuronally coded information could be modulated by self-generated emotional-motivational inputs in a way similar to the modulation of this flow by external inputs. Perturbations in information transfer could be both the origin (top–down automatic feedback) and the consequences (top–down controlled feed-forward) of these attentional and motivational deficits.

The most arduous problem concerns the interpretation of *psychomotor retardation* (Widlöcher, 1983). Does it result uniquely from a deficit in attention and preparation processes, or does it relate to specific alterations? In other words, is it a diffuse retardation affecting all processing stages as a whole, or is it a specific deficit of some stages, motor ones in particular? The fact that RTs to rare stimuli are as slow in Ns as in Ds is not necessarily in favor of an absence of specific motor retardation in Ds, because the counterperformance of Ns has been interpreted as a result of inadequate preparation. This hypothesis of inadequate preparation does not seem to hold for Ds who apparently perform the task without any strategy of anticipation or preparation. Therefore, a specific motor slowing down is plausible in Ds, but most probably it constitutes only a sign in a larger psychomotor *retardation or inhibition* syndrome. A paradigm manipulating specifically different stages of motor response—response selection, motor programming, and response release—should help answer this question.

To proceed further in interpretation, one could, on the basis of what is known from animal experiments as well as human neuropsychology and pharmacology (cf. Hestenes, Chapter 7 in this volume; Hestenes, 1987) attempt to give an integrated explanation of these different deficits in terms of neurotransmitter system alterations. Unfortunately there is little chance that most depressions result from the perturbation of just one neurotransmitter system, although there is some evidence of specific types of depressions responding better to specific neurotransmitter precursors or agonists. The *monoamine* neurotransmitter group seems more specifically implicated in the pathology of depression. In particular dysfunctions of the frontal *catecholaminergic* noradrenaline (NA) and dopamine (DA) systems replicate the frontal syndrome. It is, therefore, tempting to try to bridge the gap between neurobiology and behavior by means of the electrical intermediary link of ERPs, and, thus, we will briefly try to relate what is known about the pharmacology of depression with our scant knowledge about the biochemical bases of ERPs.

At least three neuromediators are involved in eliciting sPSPs (Libet, 1984), which we have presented as the building blocks of ERPs:

1. Acetylcholine (ACh) through its *muscarinic receptor* produces a sEPSP. Implications of cerebral cholinergic systems in learning, memory, and cognitive processes in general have been documented in the work of Deutsch (1973) and confirmed by the pathology of Alzheimer's disease, which features a major deficit in the cholinergic system and memory. There is some evidence suggesting that the *P*300 could be cholinergic-dependent.

2. NA and DA induce sIPSPs through alpha 2 receptors. Furthermore, DA acts also as a *neuromodulator,* inducing a D1-mediated contingent synaptic activation that potentiates amplitude and duration of ACh-induced sEPSPs. Brain stem nuclei send monoamine projections to the forebrain and more diffusely to cortical areas. Neurons of these systems make "loose" contacts with postsynaptic neurons, suggesting more diffuse activation and slower dynamics of the supported functions.

From these considerations, models of ERPs, and CNV in particular, have been constructed (Marczinski, 1978). Activation (not necessarily corresponding to negative shifts) could be mediated by the cholinergic system and modulated by DA. Inhibition (not necessarily corresponding to positive shifts) could be mediated by the NA system. The NA and DA systems are dynamically related and also related to the serotonin system; thus, not only a deficiency but also an imbalance between them could explain ERP variations in Ds (Smith, 1989; Timsit-Berthier, 1987; Van Praag, Korf, & Lakke, 1975). This imbalance could also account for the bipolarization of symptomatology between "blunted" (dopamine deficit) and "impulsive" (serotonin deficit) types.

There is also evidence of a nonspecific involvement of NA and DA systems in attention, learning, and memory. Catecholamines are involved in the *motivational aspect* of behavior and probably mediate self-stimulating activity in the Olds phenomenon. They are also responsible for an attentional set. In particular animal studies indicate that NA cells play a role in changes of arousal and vigilance. The NA system has a dominant distribution in the right hemisphere. The lesions of this hemisphere, particularly near the frontal pole, lead to a bilateral depletion of NA (Robinson, 1985). Confirming this hypothesis, the omission of a warning signal before a target deteriorated the performance of patients with right parietal lesions, whereas patients with left parietal lesions were not (Posner & Presti, 1987). DA agonists improve attention capacities of hyperkinetic children. Nevertheless diffuseness of monoamine action does not support the hypothesis that their synaptic modulation directly mediates specific associative learning. They could rather foster the systems' ability to engage their storage mechanisms in specific learning situations (Libet, 1984).

Diffuse projections of the NA system to the entire cortex may facilitate *synchronization* of the activity of distant modules. Supporting this view, animal experiments and human neuropsychological studies have shown the involvement of the NA system in memorization of *complex associations,* whereas simple associations were maintained independently of NA deficit. On the neuronal level, NA induces a decrease of spontaneous action potentials along with an increase in stimulus-evoked action potentials. In terms of information theory, this could be construed as an increase of *signal to noise ratio.* One can, therefore, suppose that the NA system plays an important role not only in attentional and memorization processes but also in information transfers. This disturbance of information transfers is one of our interpretations of defects in depression.

Thus, a deficit of NA–DA systems could account for both phasic orienting and tonic focal attention troubles that were encountered in our patients, and also for blocking of information transfer between processing levels. If this hypothesis is true, disorders in learning complex association should also have been encountered. However, it is difficult to conclude whether probability context was normally learned, because it does not result from a complex association or because it corresponds to an early acquired automatic complex process.

NA deficits are not the only possible perturbations in Ds. Indeed there exist very tight interactions not only between NA and DA systems, but also between these systems and the serotonin system. They interact not only on the level of target structures, in particular nucleus accumbens and striatum, but also at the level of the nuclei supporting the monoamine systems: raphe dorsalis (serotonin) and ventral tegmentum (DA). Thus, it is difficult to suppose an alteration of one system without a reactional modification of the paired system. In the recent study already mentioned (A. Pierson et al. in prep.), the "blunted" and "impulsive" types of depression differed not only on psychological and ERP grounds but also in their reactions to an inhibitor of serotonin reuptake, the impulsive group reacting much more favorably to this therapy, a phenomenon that has been observed in many other studies of serotonin agonists. Finally there is a hypothesis that makes of the DA system a kind of terminal pathway or final outcome explaining the action of various kinds of neurotransmitters. This would explain why all types of antidepressants potentiate the action of DA agonists (Maj, 1987) and perhaps why antidepressants, whatever their mechanism of action, all seem to have the same efficacy.

CONCLUSIONS

The motivational perturbation of the depressive syndrome seems to be most clearly correlated with the "intervening" psychological construct of attention. This implies common determinants for the two factors, in particular on the level of the *energetic resources* engaged in the tasks. However, there are well-founded reasons not to confound the two processes. More subtle cognitive processes involved in learning, such as task automatization (contextual conditioning) and inferences (top–down, feed-forward processes) are also affected. We submit the hypothesis that these defects result essentially from lack of top–down information transfers between processing levels or systems. Conversely more primitive and automatic bottom–up transfers seem to be preserved. It is plausible that the perturbations of these cognitive processes and information transfers are related to attentional and/or motivational deficits. Indeed the automatic processes that do not rely upon these attentional-motivational resources remain largely normal. The frontal lobes, by their structure, function, and connectivity, seem ideally suited to be at the center of the connecting system between cognitive and motivational-emotional systems. Thus, we started with the very vague hypothesis of a perturbation of right hemisphere functions in depression. Our results suggest very specific perturbations of the frontal lobe functions and/or hypothalamic–hippocampal systems. Frontal lobes, by their dorsal and ventral subsystems, lie at the intersection between cognitive and motivational systems. Their deficit and/or the deficit of the hypothalamic–hippocampal systems could explain why automatic cognitive processing is preserved, without being able to "break through" in the controlled or attended domain, to induce inferential processes.

Monoamine systems defects that seem to be dominantly implicated in our patients could account for the absence of implementation of tonic (NA) and phasic (DA) aspects of attention and, thus, the absence of modulation of cognitive processes, more directly supported by the ACh system.

It would be tempting to consider top–down mechanisms, demonstrated in this article to be essential processes of cognitive functions, as a particular class of very general feedback or loop systems of the brain. These feedback systems can be retrieved at more peripheral stages of information processing. At the peripheral nervous system level, they combine in different proportions sensory and motor aspects:

1. In the most studied sensory systems of vision and hearing, the main inward sensory pathways are associated with outward circuits aimed at adapting receptor systems (lens and external ciliated cells). These feedback pathways, thus, allow for an adaptation of the receptors to specific inputs, as a function of higher processing levels.

2. In the striate skeletal muscles, the outward motor command pathway is complemented by an inward circuit that informs the brain on the degree of

stretching and tension in the muscles implicated in the movement. Here also the functional significance of this loop is to permit a fine adaptation of muscle contractions to peculiarities of each movement that cannot be forecast in the general motor plans.

In the first example, the dominant path is receptive, and the ancillary one is motor. In the second, the reverse is true. In our information-processing feedback loops, there are apparently no receptors or effectors involved. Top–down processes may well remain localized between two cognitive processing stages. Nevertheless the feed-forward, top–down processes, which include in their dynamics several stimuli in a longer-range strategy, plausibly include as an essential feature of anticipation and preparation processes long-range adaptations of receptors and muscles similar to that presented in the examples of receptor and muscle systems.

REFERENCES

Baddeley, A. D. (1986). *Working memory*. Oxford, UK: Oxford University Press.

Banquet, J. P., Baribeau, J., & Lesevre, N. (1984). Learning of "single trial" and "contextual" information processing in an odd-ball paradigm. In R. Karrer, J. Cohen, & P. Tueting (Eds.), *Brain and information: Event related potentials* (pp. 162–165). New York: New York Academy of Sciences.

Banquet, J. P., El Massioui, F., & Godet, J. L. (1986). ERP–PT chronometry and Learning in normal and depressed subjects. In W. C. Mc Callum, R. Zappoli, & F. Denoth (Eds.), *Cerebral psychophysiology: Studies in event-related-potentials* (Suppl. 38, pp. 94–96). Amsterdam: Elsevier.

Banquet, J. P., & Grossberg, S. (1987). Probing cognitive processes through the structure of event-related potentials during learning: an experimental and theoretical analysis. *Applied Optics, 26,* 4931–4946.

Banquet, J. P., & Guenther, W. (1985). Intuitive statistics and related memory models. In *Cognitiva 85* (pp. 49–56). Paris: Cesta-Afcet.

Banquet, J. P., Guenther, W., & Smith, M. (1987). Probability processing in depressed patients. In R. Johnson, Jr., R. Parasuraman, & J. W. Rohrbaugh (Eds.), *Current trends in event-related potential research* (Electroenceph. Clin. Neurophysiol. Suppl. 40, pp. 645–650). Amsterdam: Elsevier.

Banquet, J. P., & Lesèvre, N. (1980). Event-related potentials in altered states of consciousness. In H. H. Kornhuber & L. Deecke (Eds.), *Motivation, motor and sensory processes of the brain: Progress in brain research* (pp. 447–453). Amsterdam: Elsevier.

Banquet, J. P., Renault, B., & Lesevre, N. (1981). Effect of task and stimulus probability on evoked potentials. *Biological Psychology, 13,* 203–214.

Banquet, J. P., Smith, M. J., & Renault, B. (1990). Bottom–up versus top–down: An alternative to the automatic-attended dilemma? *Behavioral and Brain Science*, 13, 201–288.

Banquet, J. P., Smith, M. J., Spinakis, A., & El Ouardirhi, S. (1989). Probability learning and memory: A connectionist approach. In L. Personaz & G. Dreyfus (Eds.), *Neural networks: From models to applications* (pp. 63–70). Paris: I.D.S.E.T.

Baribeau-Braun, J., & Lesèvre, N. (1983). Event-related potentials in depressed patients during choice reaction time tasks. In J. Mendlewicz & H. M. Van Praag (Eds.), *Advances in Biological Psychiatry, 13,* 211–223. Basel: Karger.

Broadbent, D. E. (1970). Stimulus set and response set: Two kinds of selective attention. In D. Mostofsky (Ed.), *Attention: Contemporary theory and analysis* (pp. 51–60). New York: Appleton-Century-Crofts.

Carpenter, G. A., & Grossberg, S. (1987). ART 2: Self-organization of stable category recognition codes for analog input patterns. *Applied Optics, 26,* 4919–4930.

Caspers, H., Speckman, E. J., & Lehmenkulher, A. (1980). Electrogenesis of cortical DC potentials. In H. H. Kornhuber & L. Deecke (Eds.), *Progress in brain research: Motivation, motor and sensory processes of the brain, electrical potentials, behavior and clinical use* (Vol. 54, pp. 3–17). Amsterdam: Elsevier-North Holland.

Coles, M. G. H., Gratton, G., Bashore, T. R., Eriksen, C. W., & Donchin, E. (1985). A psychophysiological investigation of the continuous flow model of human information processing. *Journal of Experimental Psychology: Human Perception and Performance. 11,* 529–553.

Coles, M. G. H., Gratton, G., & Donchin, E. (1988). Detecting early communication: Using measures of movement-related potentials to illuminate human information processing. *Biological Psychology, 26,* 69–89.

Courchesne, E. (1978). Changes in P3 waves with event repetition: Long-term effects on scalp distribution and amplitude. *Electroencephalography and Clinical Neurophysiology, 45,* 754–766.

Courchesne, E., Hillyard, S. A., & Galambos, R. (1975). Stimulus novelty, task relevance, and the visual evoked potential in man. *Electroencephalography and Clinical Neurophysiology, 39,* 131–143.

Damen, E. P. J., & Brunia, C. H. M. (1987). Changes in heart rate and slow brain potentials related to motor preparation and stimulus anticipation in a time estimation task. *Psychophysiology, 24,* 700–713.

Desmedt, J. E. (1980). *P*300 in serial tasks: An essential post-decision closure mechanism. In H. H. Kornhuber & Deecke (Eds.), *Motivation, motor and sensory processes of the brain: Electrical potentials, behavior and clinical use.* Amsterdam: Elsevier-North Holland.

Desmedt, J. E., & Debecker, J. (1979). Slow potential shifts and decision P350 interactions in tasks with random sequences of near-threshold clicks and finger stimuli delivered at regular intervals. *Electroencephalography and Clinical Neurophysiology, 47,* 671–679.

Deutsch, J. A. (1973). The cholinergic synapse and the site of memory. In J. A. Deutsch (Ed.), *The physiological basis of memory* (pp. 59–76). New York: Academic Press.

Dimond, S. J., & Beaumont, J. G. (1973). Difference in the vigilance performance of the right and left hemisphere. *Cortex, 9,* 259–265.

Donald, M. W., & Young, M. J. (1982). A time course analysis of attentional tuning of auditory evoked response. *Experimental Brain Research, 46,* 357–367.

Donchin, E. (1981). Surprise! . . . surprise? *Psychophysiology, 18,* 493–513.

Donchin, E., Ritter, W., & McCallum, W. C. (1978). Cognitive psychophysiology: the endogenous components of the ERPs. In E. Callaway, P. Tueting, & S. Koslov (Eds.), *Brain event-related potentials in man* (pp. 349–341). New York: Academic Press.

Donchin, E., Heffley, E., Hillyard, S., Loveless, N., Maltzman, C., Ökman, A., Rösler, F., Ruchkin, D., & Siddle, D. (1984). The orienting reflex and *P*300. In R. Karrer, J. Cohen, & P. Tueting (Eds.), *Brain and information: Event-related potentials* (Vol. 425, pp. 39–57). New York: New York Academy of Sciences.

Duncan-Johnson, C. C., & Donchin, E. (1977). On quantifying surprise: the variation in event-related potentials with subjective probability. *Psychophysiology, 14,* 456–467.

El Massioui, F., & Lesèvre, N. (1988). Attention impairment and psychomotor retardation in depressed patients: an event-related potential study. *Electroencephalography and Clinical Neurophysiology, 70,* 46–55.

Flor-Henry, P. (1988). EEG spectral analysis in Psychopathology. In Giannitrapani & Murri (Eds.), *The EEG of mental activities* (pp. 182–200). Basel: Karger.

Gaillard, A. W. K. (1977). The late CNV: Preparation versus expectancy. *Psychophysiology, 14,* 563–568.

Giard, M. H., Perrin, F., Pernier, J., and Peronnet, F. (1988). Several attention-related wave forms in auditory areas: topographic study. *Electroencephalography and Clinical Neurophysiology 69,* 371–384.

Goldman-Rakic, P. S. (1984). Modular organization of prefrontal cortex. *Trends in Neuroscience, 7,* 419–424.

Grossberg, S. (1975). A neural model of attention, reinforcement and discrimination learning. *International Review of Neurobiology, 18,* 263–327.

Grossberg, S. (1976a). Adaptive pattern classification and universal recoding I: Parallel development and coding of neural feature detectors. *Biological Cybernetics, 23,* 121–134.

Grossberg, S. (1976b). Adaptive pattern classification and universal recoding II: Feed-back, expectation, olfaction and illusions. *Biological Cybernetics, 23,* 187–202.

Grossberg, S. (1978). A theory of human memory: Self-organization and performance of sensory-motor codes, maps, and plans. In R. Rosen, & F. Snell (Eds.), *Progressive and theoretical Biology* (Vol. 5). New York: Academic Press.

Grossberg, S. (1980). How does a brain build a cognitive code? *Psychological Review, 87,* 1–51.

Grossberg, S. (1982a). Processing of expected and unexpected events during conditioning and attention: A psychophysiological theory. *Psychological Review, 89,* 529–572.

Grossberg, S. (1982b). *Studies of mind and brain: Neural principles of learning, perception, development, cognition, and motor control.* Boston: Reidel-Dordrecht.

Grossberg, S. (1984). Some psychological and pharmalogical correlates of a developmental, cognitive and motivational theory. In R. Karrer, J. Cohen, & P. Tueting (Eds.), *Brain and information: Event-related potentials.* New York: New York Academy of Sciences.

Grossberg, S., & Stone, G. O. (1986). Neural dynamics of word recognition and recall: Attentional priming, learning and resonance. *Psychological Review, 93,* 46–74.

Günther, W., Moser, E., Mueller-Spahn, F., Oefele, K., Buell, U., & H. Hippius. (1986). Pathological cerebral blood flow during motor function in schizophrenic and endogenous depressed patients. *Biological Psychiatry, 21,* 889–899.

Halgren, E., Squires, N. K., Wilson, C. L., Rohrbaugh, J. W., Babb, T. L., & Crandall, P. H. (1980). Endogenous potentials generated in the human hippocampal formation and amygdala by infrequent events. *Science, 210,* 803–805.

Hansen, J. C., & Hillyard, S. A. (1984). Effects of stimulation rate and attribute cueing on event-related potentials during selective auditory attention. *Psychophysiology, 21,* 394–405.

Heilman, K. M., Watson, R. T., & Valenstein, E. (1985). Neglect and related disorders. In K. M. Heilman & E. Valenstein (Eds.), *Clinical neuropsychology* (pp. 243–293). New York: Oxford.

Hestenes, D. (1987). How the brain works, the next great scientific revolution. In C. Ray Smith (Ed.), *Maximum entropy and Bayesian spectral analysis and estimation* (pp. 173–205). Boston: Reidel-Dordrecht.

Hillyard, S. A., Hink, R. F., Schwent, V. L., & Picton, T. W. (1973). Electrical signs of selective attention in the human brain. *Science, 182,* 177–180.

Johnson, R., Jr. (1986). Triarchic model of *P300* amplitude. *Psychophysiology, 23,* 367–384.

Johnson, R., Jr., & Donchin, E. (1982). Sequential expectancies and decision making in a changing environment: an electrophysiological approach. *Psychophysiology, 19,* 183–199.

Jouvent, R., Hardy, P., et Bouvard M. (1987). L'hétérogénéité de l'humeur dépressive: Construction d'une échelle polydimensionnelle. [Heterogeneity of depressive Mood: Construction of a Multidimensional scale.] *L'Encéphale, 13,* 233–237.

Karis, D., Fabiani, M., & Donchin, E. (1984). P300 and Memory: Individual differences in the von Restorff effect. *Cognitive Psychology, 16,* 177–216.

Kramer, A., Schneider, W., Fisk, A., & Donchin, E. (1986). The effects of practice and task structure on components of the event-related brain potentials. *Psychophysiology, 23,* 33–47.

Kutas, M., & Hillyard, S. A. (1980). Reading senseless sentences: Brain potentials reflect semantic incongruity. *Science, 207,* 203–205.

Kutas, M., & Hillyard, S. A. (1984). Brain potentials during reading reflect word expectancy and semantic association, *Nature, 307,* 161–163.

Kutas, M., McCarthy, G., & Donchin, E. (1977). Augmenting mental chronometry: the *P*300 as a measure of stimulus evaluation time. *Science, 197,* 792–795.

Levine, D. S. (1983). Neural population modelling and psychology: A review. *Mathematical Biosciences, 66,* 1–86.

Levine, D. S. (1986). *A neural network theory of frontal lobe function. Proceedings of the Eighth Annual Conference of the Cognitive Science Society, Amherst: MA.* Hillsdale, NJ: Lawrence Erlbaum Associates.

Libet, B. (1984). Heterosynaptic interaction at a sympathetic neuron as a model for induction and storage of postsynaptic memory trace. In G. Lynch, J. L. McGaugh, & N. Weinberger (Eds.), *Neurobiology of learning and memory* (pp. 405–430). New York: Guildford.

Luria, A. R. (1973). *The working brain.* New York: Basic Books.

Maj, J. (1987). *Repeated treatment with antidepressant drugs and functional changes of catecholamine receptors on the behavioral level.* Paper presented at the Sixth International Cathecolamine Symposium, Jerusalem.

Marczinski, T. J. (1978). A parsimonious model of mammalian brain and event-related slow potentials. In D. A. Otto (Eds.), *Multidisciplinary perspectives in event-related brain potential research* (pp. 626–634). Washington, DC: U.S. Government Printing Office.

McCallum, W. C., Curry, S. H., Cooper, R., Pocock, P. V., & Papakostopoulos, D. (1983). Brain event-related potentials as indicators of early selective processes in auditory target localisation. *Psychophysiology, 20,* 1–17.

McCarthy, G., & Donchin, E. (1981). A metric for thought: a comparison of *P*300 latency and reaction time. *Science, 221,* 77–80.

Munson, R., Ruchkin, D. S., Ritter, W., Sutton, S., & Squires, N. K. (1984). The relation of *P3b* to prior events and future behavior. *Biological Psychology, 19,* 1–29.

Näätänen, R. (1990). The role of attention in auditory information processing as revealed by event-related potentials and other brain measures of cognitive functions. *Behavioral and Brain Sciences, 13,* 201–288.

Näätänen, R. (1982). Processing negativity: an evoked-potential reflection of selective attention. *Psychology Bulletin, 92,* 605–640.

Näätänen, R., & Gaillard, A. W. (1983). The orienting reflex and the N2 deflection of the ERPs. In A. W. K. Gaillard & Ritter (Eds.), *Tutorials in event-related potential research: Endogeneous components* (pp. 119–142). Amsterdam: North-Holland.

Näätänen, R., Gaillard, A. W. K. & Mantysalo, S. (1978) Early selective attention effect on evoked potential reinterpreted. *Acta Psychologica 42,* 313–329.

Näätänen, R., & Picton, T. W. (1986). N2 and automatic versus controlled processes. In W. C. McCallum, R. Zappoli, & F. Denoth (Eds.), *Cerebral psychophysiology: Studies in event-related potentials* (EEG suppl. 38, pp. 169–186). Amsterdam: Elsevier.

Näätänen, R., Simpson, M., & Loveless, N. E. (1982). Stimulus deviance and evoked potentials. *Biological Psychology, 14,* 53–98.

Neville, H. J., Kutas, M. Chesney, G., & Schmidt, A. L. (1986). Event-related brain potentials during initial encoding and recognition memory of congruous and incongruous words. *Journal of memory and language, 25,* 75–92.

Peterson, S. E., Fox, P. T., Rosner, M. I., Mintum, M., Raichle, M. E. (1988). Positron emission tomographic studies of the cortical anatomy of single-word processing. *Nature, 331,* 585–589.

Picton, T. W., Campbell, K. B., Baribeau-Braun, J., Proulx, G. B. (1978). The neurophysiology of human attention: A tutorial review. In J. Requin (Ed.), *Attention and performance VII* (pp. 429–467). Hillsdale, NJ: Lawrence Erlbaum Associates.

Pierson, A., Partiot, A., Ammar, S., Dodin, V., Loas, G., Jouvent, R. (in prep.). ERP differences between anxious-impulsive and blunted-affect depressive patients. In R. V. Frenchell (Ed.), *Biological markers of depression: State of the art.* Excerpta Medica. Amsterdam: Elsevier.

Posner, M. I., & Presti, D. E. (1987). Selective attention and cognitive control. *Trends in Neurosciences, 10,* 13–17.

Pribram, K. H., & McGuinness, D. (1975). Arousal, activation, and effort in the control of attention. *Psychophysiological Review, 2,* 116–149.

Renault, B. & Lesevre N. (1978). Topographical study of the emitted potential obtained after the omission of an expected visual stimulus. In D. Otto (Ed.), *Multidisciplinary perspectives in event-related brain potential research* (pp. 202–208). Washington, DC: U.S. Government Printing Office.

Renault, B., Ragot, R., Lesevre, N., & Remond, A. (1982). Brain event-related potentials: their onset and offset as indices of mental chronometry. *Science, 216,* 1413–1415.

Ritter, W., Simson, R., Herbert, G., Vaughan, H. G., Jr., & Friedman, D. (1979). A brain event related to making a sensory discrimination. *Science, 203,* 1358–1361.

Ritter, W., Simson, R., Vaughan, H. G., Jr., & Macht, M. (1982). Manipulation of event-related potential manifestation of information processing stages. *Science, 218,* 909–911.

Robinson, R. G. (1985). Lateralized behavioral and neurochemical consequences of unilateral brain injury in rats. In *Cerebral lateralization in nonhuman species* (pp. 135–156). New York: Academic Press.

Rohrbaugh, J. W., Syndulko, K., & Lindsley, D. B. (1976). Brain wave components of the contingent negative variation in humans. *Science, 191,* 1055–1057.

Roland, P. E. (1985). Cortical organization of voluntary behavior in man. *Human Neurobiology, 4,* 155–167.

Rolls, E. T. (1987). Information representation, processing, and storage in the brain: Analysis at the single neuron level. In J. P. Changeux & M. Konishi (Eds.), *The neural and molecular bases of learning* (pp. 503–540). New York: Wiley.

Rosler, F., Hasselman, D., & Sojka, B. (1987). Central and peripheral correlates of orienting and habituation. In R. Johnson, Jr., J. W. Rohrbaugh, & R. Parasuraman (Eds.), *Current trends in event-related potential research* (EEG Suppl. 40, pp. 336–372). Amsterdam: Elsevier.

Roth, W. T. (1973). Auditory evoked responses to unpredictable stimuli. *Psychophysiology, 10,* 125–138.

Ruchkin, D. S., Johnson, R., Jr., Mahaffey, D., & Sutton, S. (1988). Toward a functional categorization of slow waves. *Psychophysiology, 25,* 339–353.

Ruchkin, D. S., & Sutton, S. (1983). Positive slow wave and *P300*: Association and dissociation. In A. K. W. Gaillard & W. Ritter (Eds.), *Tutorials in ERP research-endogenous components* (pp. 233–250). Amsterdam: North Holland.

Ruchkin, D. S., Sutton, S., Kietzman, M. L., & Silver, K. (1980a). Slow wave and *P300* in signal detection. *Electroencephalography and Clinical Neurophysiology, 50,* 35–47.

Ruchkin, D. S., Sutton, S., & Mahaffey, D. (1987). Functional differences between members of *P300* complex: *P3e* and *P3b*. *Psychophysiology, 24,* 87–103.

Ruchkin, D. S., Sutton, S., Mahaffey, D., & Glaser, J. (1986). Terminal CNV in the absence of a motor response. *Electroencephalography and Clinical Neurophysiology, 63,* 445–463.

Ruchkin, D. S., Sutton, S., & Stega, M. (1980). Emitted *P300* and slow wave event-related potentials in guessing and detection tasks. *Electroencephalography and Clinical Neurophysiology, 49,* 1–14.

Sams, M., Alho, K., & Näätänen, R. (1984). Short-term habituation and dishabituation of the mismatch negativity of the ERP. *Psychophysiology, 21,* 434–441.

Simson, R., Vaughan, H. G., & Ritter, W. (1977). Scalp topography of potentials in auditory and visual discrimination tasks. *Electroencephalography and Clinical Neurophysiology, 42,* 528–535.

Smith, M. J. (1989). *Rôle de la dopamine dans les troubles cognitifs du ralentissement psycho-moteur dépressif: Apport de trois études électrophysiologiques.* Paris: M.D. Thesis. [Role of Dopamine in cognitive deficits of depression: Results of three electrophysiological studies.]

Snyder, E., & Hillyard, S. A. (1976). Long-latency evoked potentials to irrelevant, deviant stimuli. *Behavioral Biology, 16,* 319–331.

Squires, K. C., Wickens, C., Squires, N. K., & Donchin, E. (1976). The effect of stimulus sequence on the wave form of cortical event-related potentials. *Science, 193,* 1142–1146.

Squires, N. K., Squires, K. C., & Hillyard, S. A. (1975). Two varieties of long-latency positive waves evoked by unpredictable auditory stimuli in man. *Electroencephalography and Clinical Neurophysiology, 38,* 387–401.

Sternberg, S. (1969). The discovery of processing stages: extension of Donders' method. In W. G. Koster (Ed.), *Attention and Performance II, Acta Psychologica, 30,* 276–315.

Sutton, S., Braren, M., Zubin, J., & John, E. R. (1965). Evoked potentials correlates of stimulus uncertainty. *Science, 15,* 1187–1188.

Tecce, J. J. (1972). Contingent negative variation (CNV) and psychological processes in man. *Psychological Bulletin, 77,* 73–108.

Timsit-Berthier, M., Mantanus, H., & Ansseau, M. (1987). Contingent negative variation in major depressive patients. In R. Johnson, Jr., J. W. Rohrbaugh, & R. Parasuraman (Eds.), *Current trends in event-related potential research* (EEG Suppl. 40, pp. 762–771). Amsterdam: Elsevier.

Timsit-Berthier, M., Mantanus, H., Poncelet, M., Marissaux, P., & Legros, J. J. (1987). Contingent negative variation as a new method to assess the catecholaminergic systems. In V. Gallai (Ed.), *Maturation of the CNS and evoked potentials* (pp. 762–771). Amsterdam: Elsevier.

Van Praag, H. M., Korf, J., & Lakke, J. P. W. F. (1975). Dopamine metabolism in depression, psychoses, and Parkinson's disease. *Psychological Medicine, 5,* 138–146.

Walter, W. G., Cooper, R., Aldridge, V. J., McCallum, W. C., & Winter, A. (1964). Contingent negative variation: an electric sign of sensory-motor association of expectancy in the human brain. *Nature, 203,* 380–384.

Widlöcher, D. J. (1983). Psychomotor retardation: Clinical, theoretical, and psychometric aspects. In H. G. Akiskal (Ed.), *The psychiatric clinics of North America,* (Vol. 6, pp. 27–40). Philadelphia: Saunders.

Wilkins, A. J., Shallice, T., & McCarthy, R. (1987). Frontal lesions and sustained attention. *Neuropsychology, 25,* 359–366.

Willner, P. (1983). Dopamine and depression: a review of recent evidence. *Brain Research Review, 6,* 211–224.

Woods, D. L., & Elmasian, R. (1986). The habituation of event-related potentials to speech sounds and tones. *Electroencephalography and Clinical Neurophysiology, 65,* 447–449.

Zarifian, E. (1979). Le dopa et les agonistes dopaminergiques dans la depression [Dopa and dopaminergic agonists in depression]. *L'Encephale, 5,* 665–670.

7
A Neural Network Theory of Manic-Depressive Illness

David Hestenes
Arizona State University

Neural network theory holds great promise for a new, biologically based conceptual framework for psychiatry. This article lays the groundwork for a network theory of manic-depressive illness and related psychiatric disorders. Pertinent empirical evidence and principles of neural network theory are reviewed in support of the following proposal.

Information is represented in the brain by neural activity patterns. Pattern formation in distinct modules of the brain is coordinated by a central monoamine control system. For each module, the monoamines regulate pattern stability, enhancement, mixing, matching, and switching. Many psychiatric disorders can be attributed to various malfunctions of the monoamine regulatory mechanisms. Specifically manic-depressive illness is attributed primarily to a malfunction of gain control on inputs to the nucleus accumbens. The accumbens functions as a gate through which the limbic system influences behavioral output. The gate is regulated dually by dopamine input from the ventral tegmentum and serotonin input from the raphé dorsalis.

Among the clinical implications of the theory, possibilities for control of mania and depression with monoamine precursors are discussed at length, including original case histories of two sisters with manic-depressive illness. As a prophylaxis against mania, the older sister has been successfully treated with L-tryptophan for ten years. The younger sister's case illustrates the clinical potential of the theory for interpreting symptoms and suggesting therapy.

Biological psychiatry is based on the premise that the concept of mind is simply a way of characterizing general functions of the brain, therefore, mental illnesses are to be regarded as neurobiological malfunctions and treated accordingly. The neurosciences have accumulated overwhelming empirical evidence

209

correlating psychological and neurobiological functioning. However, a satisfactory theoretical link between psychology and neurobiology is yet to be established. A premise of this article is that the necessary theoretical mind–brain link can be supplied only by a neural network theory. Network theory is still in its early childhood, and the brain is complex, so it might be thought that the theory is far from providing insight into mental illness. On the contrary, a whole system of general principles about brain structure and function has already emerged from network theory, and this article aims to show how it can be used to construct a theoretical foundation for biological psychiatry.

Perhaps the most fundamental question about brain function is "How is information represented in the brain?" Network theory proposes a general answer that, although not indubitable, is a most plausible working hypothesis. The answer can be expressed as a general principle of brain function: "Information is represented in the brain by neural activity patterns in brain modules." This is to be understood as a generic principle applying to information of every type, including visual, auditory, somatic, motor, and cognitive. Thus, network theory reduces general issues about information processing in the brain to more specific issues about pattern processing. The various types of mental disorders are, therefore, to be conceived as specific kinds of breakdown in pattern processing. This provides the beginnings of a new conceptual framework for psychiatric science. Our task will be to elaborate this framework with additional facts and principles to achieve genuine insight into the causes and treatments of mental illness. The first step is to identify the relevant biological variables.

Psychopharmacological research and clinical experience have firmly established that the three brain monoamines (dopamine, noradrenaline, and serotonin) play prominent roles in the major mental disorders. Even so, improvements in psychiatric drug therapy have relied heavily on trial-and-error methods. To do better, it will be necessary to understand the functions of the monoamines in a normal working brain and how these functions break down. Fortunately there has been considerable recent progress toward that end. Anatomical, physiological, and behavioral research have been converging toward the conclusion that the monoamines serve to modulate and integrate the activities of the various brain components (Clark, Geffen, & Geffen, 1984; Foote & Morrison, 1987; Iversen, 1984; Koella, 1982, 1984). That already explains why monoamine malfunctions have such global mental effects. Much research is still needed to discover the details of monoamine modulation, but it is evident that the monoamines operate synergistically, so they can be fully understood only as parts of a general modulatory system with a few specialized subsystems.

The main concern of this article is to develop a theory of the central monoamine control system as a foundation for psychiatric science. Section 1 identifies dopamine and serotonin as control variables for a behavioral control subsystem. Manic-depressive illness is attributed to control malfunctions localized in the nucleus accumbens. Huntington's, Parkinson's, and Tourette's diseases are attributed to similar control malfunctions in the striatum. This theory is unique in asserting that serotonin is at least as significant as dopamine in the etiology of manic-depression and the related diseases.

Principles of neural network theory are applied in section 2 to characterize the monoamine control variables more specifically as modulators of pattern processing, with the following conclusion: Noradrenaline modulates selective attention and long-term memory storage by pattern enhancement. Serotonin modulates pattern stability, matching and switching. Hallucinations, delusions, and obsessive-compulsive behavior result from malfunctions of serotonin modulation. The theory holds great potential for further elaboration and refinement, including well-defined directions for experimental and theoretical research.

A second part of this article is concerned with clinical implications of the first part. Its main emphasis is on the importance of serotonin in the interpretation and control of manic-depressive illness and on the use of monoamine precursors in therapy. Original case studies of two sisters with manic-depressive illness are presented. In regard to precursor treatment, the studies are of clinical interest even apart from the theory. The first study reports on the *successful use of L-tryptophan as a prophylactic against mania for ten years*. This case is of special interest, because the period of nearly continuous treatment with tryptophan is believed to be the longest one reported in the literature, no negative side effects of the treatment have appeared, and there is a dearth of such published reports in the literature. As an alternative or adjunct to the standard lithium treatment, tryptophan prophylaxis has not yet been adequately evaluated by clinical tests. This study along with its theoretical and empirical rationale provide ample reason to conduct such tests.

The final case study illustrates application of the theory to a detailed analysis of the course and treatment of a manic-depressive illness. Although no firm conclusions can be drawn from the study, many issues are raised that are worthy of further research.

PART I: CENTRAL MONOAMINE FUNCTIONS
AND MALFUNCTIONS

The Locus of Manic-Depressive Disorders

The catecholamines and serotonin have been clearly implicated in mania and depression since Kety (1971) and Prange (1974) suggested that *serotonergic action opposes excitatory action of the catecholamines*. As a generalization about behavioral effects, this "opposition principle" appears still to have some validity. However, at the physiological level, the situation is more complicated.

Behavioral and psychological effects of the two catecholamines, dopamine (DA) and noradrenaline (NA), are difficult to separate by pharmacological manipulation, because they share the same precursor (tyrosine) and synthesis pathway. Nevertheless it now appears doubtful that NA plays a primary role in mania, although it probably plays a role in some types of depression and other forms of mental illness.

Accumulated evidence that dopamine plays a major role in mania as well as schizophrenia and depression has been ably reviewed by Swerdlow and Koob (1987). They advocate a unified model for mental illness based on established facts about neuroanatomy. Their model can be criticized on many accounts. However, one central feature of the model seems secure, namely their identification of the nucleus accumbens (NAC) as the anatomical locus of manic-depressive illness. This identification can be supported by evidence from many other sources. The critical step is determining the normal function of the NAC.

Anatomical evidence in mammals shows that there is a direct pathway from the limbic system through the NAC to the pallidum, which is now believed (e.g., Horak & Anderson, 1984) to be the motor output module for the basal ganglia (Fig. 7.1). This suggests that the NAC functions as a gate through which the limbic system exerts control over behavioral output. That suggestion is strongly supported by evidence that DA input from the ventral tegmentum (VT) facilitates the passage of limbic signals through the NAC. In other words, DA input functions as a gain control parameter that opens the NAC gate and closes it by turning

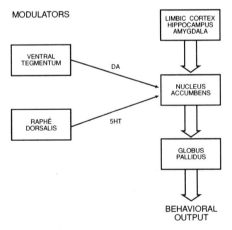

FIG. 7.1. The *execution pathway* for control of motivational/volitional behavior. The nucleus accumbens functions as a "gate" through which motivations and intentions, expressed as signals from the limbic system, gain control over motor output through the pallidum. The gate is opened by DA signals from the ventral tegmentum whereas a fairly tonic 5–HT signal from the raphé dorsalis helps to close it. Malfunctions of this gating mechanism are presumed to produce mania and depression.

off. A number of experiments have shown that stimulation of the NAC with DA agonists induces hyperactivity in animals (Anden, 1977; Taylor & Robbins, 1984), whereas, DA antagonists reduce activity. Further evidence for gating is reviewed by Mogensen (1984). To this may be added the fact that observed behaviors correlated with recordings of VT activity in freely moving cats (Jacobs, 1975) are at least compatible with the gating hypothesis. Only the most direct evidence for gating is still lacking.

With the NAC gating model in hand, it is reasonable to attribute the enhanced motor activity induced by amphetamines and other DA agonists to increased DA transmission from the VT that facilitates the execution of "impulses" or "urges" generated by the limbic system. Likewise it appears that the hallmarks of hypomania and mania, such as pressured speech and impulsive behavior, can be attributed to excessive DA gain in the NAC.

On the other hand, when the DA gain is too low, the subject will have difficulty initiating motivated behaviors and expressing interest or emotion. This is characteristic of a particular kind of depression that has been labeled "anhedonic" (Wise, 1982). It is a depression of activity rather than a feeling of sadness. For that reason, some psychiatrists refer to it as *psychomotor retardation* and do not regard it as a true depression (Mendels & Frazer, 1974; Willner, 1983). The subjective impression of an inability to experience pleasure associated with anhedonia may well be due to a broader influence of the VT. As indicated in Fig. 7.2 (but omitted from Fig. 7.1), the VT projects to all major components of the limbic system as well as the NAC; this includes the amygdala and septal-hippocampal complex in addition to prefrontal and limbic cortex. If the VT regulates gain throughout the limbic system as it does in the NAC, then insufficient gain would depress activity of the entire limbic system as well as behavioral output.

Thus, we arrive at the hypothesis that manic-depressive disorders and probably unipolar anhedonic depressions are due to malfunctions of gain regulation by the VT, with a critical locus in the NAC. This hypothesis is supported by a whole series of experiments showing that NAC/DA gain is crucial for the maintenance of rewarding behaviors, including intercranial self-stimulation as well as cocaine and amphetamine (Fibiger & Philips, 1987). There is, however, much more to the story.

Previous discussions of NAC gating have neglected the powerful influence of serotonin (or 5–hydroxytryptamine, 5–HT) input from the raphé dorsalis (RD). The RD projections to the NAC are comparable in density and extent to those from the VT. Indeed the concentration of 5–HT in the NAC is about the same as in the RD, and electrical stimulation of the RD exerts a strong, long-lasting inhibition on NAC activity. Moreover, evidence that 5–HT transmission plays a role in behavioral inhibition (reviewed by Soubrié, 1986) is quite as strong as the evidence that DA transmission plays a role in behavioral facilitation. All this

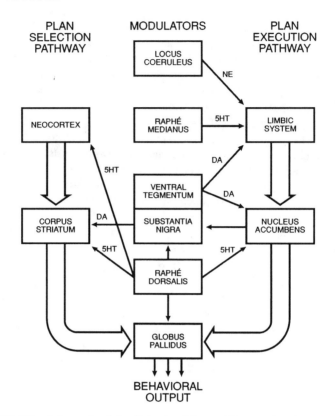

FIG. 7.2. Schematic of the *Behavioral Control System* showing principal components and connections. The system has two major pathways, one for the organization and selection of behavioral plans, the other for motivational/volitional control over plan execution. Activity in both pathways is modulated by dense, distributed DA and 5–HT inputs. Of course many details, including all feedback loops, have been omitted.

suggests that the RD input has an inhibitory effect on NAC activity that opposes the facilitatory effect of VT input. This hypothesis is a useful rule of thumb, although we shall see that it is certainly an oversimplification.

If an increase in RD input can compensate for excessive DA gain in the NAC, then it should be possible to control mania by increasing 5–HT transmission. That implication has been confirmed in several studies demonstrating the successful treatment of mania with the 5–HT precursor tryptophan (Prange et al., 1974; Chouinard, Young, & Annable, 1985). Additional support comes from a variety of animal studies on behavioral effects of the DA agonist amphetamine. Amphetamine induces dose-dependent locomotor activity that is enhanced by the drug PCPA, a depletor of brain 5–HT, and the effect is reversed by administering the 5–HT precursor 5–HTP (Mabry & Cambell, 1973). Amphetamine-induced activity is also enhanced by reducing 5–HT transmission with lesions destroying at least 60% of the RD projections to the NAC (Green & Harvey, 1974). In other experiments, amphetamine has been shown to induce stereotyped behavior by increasing DA activity in the striatum. The threshold for this effect is lowered by reducing the available 5–HT in striatum and raised by increasing the available 5–HT (Weiner, Goetz, Westheimer, & Klawans, Jr., 1973). This suggests that Parkinsonian symptoms due to decreased DA function in the striatum should be exacerbated by treatment with 5–HT precursors 5–HTP and tryptophan. The truth is more complex. Precursor treatment has been found to increase Parkinsonian tremor in some patients but reduce tremor in others (Dray, 1982).

The function of the NAC and its relation to the striatum can be better understood by placing it within the context of a larger "Behavioral Control System" (Fig. 7.2). The anatomical components and connections in Fig. 7.2 are well established, although their functions are poorly understood. Our first concern is with gross functional organization of the system, which is not so controversial. Assuming that the NAC pathway operates as described previously, its function can be recognized as the initiation and/or execution of goal-directed behavior. Call it the *Plan Execution Pathway*. The organization and selection of behavioral plans to achieve a specific goal must occur at another locus, one with direct access to the necessary motor and sensory information. As Fig. 7.2 suggests, there is little doubt that the striatum plays a central role in this activity, operating in concert with the thalamus, cerebellum, and other modules not represented in the figure (DeLong, Alexander, Mitchell, & Richardson, 1986). Thus, the striatum lies in a behavioral *Plan Selection Pathway*. The point is that separate pathways for execution and selection of behavioral plans exist, and they converge at the pallidum where final decisions are broadcasted by the release of "GO signals" to the spinal column (Bullock & Grossberg, 1988; Horak & Anderson, 1984).

The next thing to notice is the pattern of connections that the modulating nuclei (modulators) make with the two pathways. The figure has been arranged to reveal symmetries in the pattern. There are two modulators with 5–HT output, the raphé medianus (RM) and the RD, and two modulators with DA output, the substantial nigra (SN) and the VT. It is noteworthy that each modulator projects preferentially to targets sharing some common function, most likely to help coordinate their activities. The RM projects to limbic components, whereas the RD projects to motor components.

The VT regulates gain in the execution pathway, whereas the SN regulates gain in the selection pathway (Iversen, 1984). The projection from the NAC to SN provides a means for coordinating the gains and, hence, the outputs through both pathways.

The RD regulates flow through the two pathways in two ways: indirectly through its projections to the VT and SN, and directly through its projections to the NAC and striatum (Fig. 7.2). The RD projections to VT and SN serve to inhibit DA output, as has been established by microinjections of 5–HT and 5–HT blockers directly into the SN as well as by lesion studies (Dray, 1982). This is clearly a mechanism for 5–HT regulation of DA gain in VT and SN simultaneously. Antelman and Chiodo (1984) reviewed evidence that this is the mechanism through which DA response to stressful stimuli is mediated. In accordance with evidence we consider later, the locus ceruleus (LC) signals the presence of stressful stimuli, inhibiting the RD and, thus, disinhibiting the NAC and SN in preparation for a vigorous behavioral response. Lesions of the RD connections to the VT and SN eliminate DA responses to stressful stimuli.

The second means for RD/5–HT regulation of the Execution and Selection Pathways is by direct action on the information processing mechanisms in the NAC and the striatum. Considering the anatomical contiguity and similarity of NAC and striatum (Groves, 1983) it is reasonable to assume that they employ similar physiological mechanisms. This leads to many illuminating and potentially fruitful inferences by comparing what is known about each of them. In particular, corresponding malfunction of NAC and striatum mechanisms should have corresponding clinical manifestations. Concerning DA gain control malfunctions, it is well known that Parkinsonian symptoms due to the suppression of DA gain in the striatum by neuroleptics can be alleviated by cholinergic antagonists. Neurological research has determined that the striatum has cholinergic interneurons where this compensatory drug action takes place. By analogy, it is to be expected that mania due to excess DA gain in the NAC can be reduced by cholinergic agonists, and this has been confirmed for physostigmine (Janowsky, El-Yousef, Davis, & Sederke, 1970). Evidently the low striatal DA gain in Parkinson's disease corresponds to the low NAC/DA gain in anhedonic depression. Similarly the excess NAC/DA gain in mania corresponds to excess striatal DA gain in Huntington's chorea and in Tourette's syndrome.

Tourette's syndrome consists of multiform motor and phonic tics and stereotypic actions (Cohen, Shawitz, Caparlo, Young, & Bowers, 1978). The premovement cortical potentials associated with volitional movements are absent when the tics occur, supporting the view that the syndrome originates in the aberrant release of simple motor programs from the striatum (Cummings & Frankel, 1985). The fact that the DA antagonist Halperidol dramatically suppresses the syndrome in most cases points to a malfunction of DA gain control (Butler, Koslow, Seifert, Caprioli, & Singer, 1979). Furthermore, because of undesirable side effects, long-term treatment with Halperidol is not feasible; however, the α-adrenergic agonist clonidine hydrochloride has been found to be almost as effective. At low doses, clonidine stimulates LC autoreceptors to reduce LC firing (Cohen, Detlor, Young, & Shawitz, 1980). According to our previous considerations, this should disinhibit the RD/5–HT pathway and so reduce the DA gain in striatum. This proposed mechanism for the therapeutic action of clonidine should be tested.

There is empirical evidence for an indirect effect of striatal RD/5–HT input on DA gating. Impairment of 5–HT function correlates with a weaker response to treatment with the DA precursor L–DOPA in Parkinson patients as well as to the severity of Huntington's chorea (Dray, 1982). The physiological mechanism for this 5–HT influence on gating remains to be elucidated. Some clues to the mystery of 5–HT function will emerge in the next section.

Network Theory of Monoamine Functions

In the preceding section, manic-depressive illness was attributed to a malfunction in the modulation of a behavioral control network. However, the illness is often accompanied by cognitive and/or sensory impairments as well. To see how that might come about, we strive in this section for a deeper understanding of mono-amine control systems in the brain.

The various neurotransmitters can be classified into two general types, fast and slow, according to rate of receptor response (Strange, 1988). The response time for fast receptors is on the order of milliseconds, whereas, for slow recep-tors, it is on the order of hundreds of milliseconds, seconds, or longer. Only the fast receptors are fast enough to accommodate the known rate of information processing in the brain. On this evidence alone, therefore, it is reasonable to conclude that the slow receptors perform a modulatory function. The fast trans-mitters are either excitatory or inhibitory. Glutamate is the principal excitatory transmitter in the brain, whereas GABA (γ-aminobutyric acid) is the principal inhibitory transmitter. The slow transmitters are not so simply classified, as each transmitter has several different receptor types with a variety of modulatory effects that are still only imperfectly understood. The class of slow transmitters includes the monoamines (dopamine, noradrenaline, serotonin, acetycholine— with muscarinic receptors), and a number of neuropeptides. Our attention here will be limited to the monoamines, as they are most strongly implicated in mental illness and their anatomical organization is indicative of global brain state control functions.

The gross anatomy of the "central monoamine system" consists of several widely branching, ascending pathways issuing from a few groups of nuclei centrally located in the brainstem and midbrain. We have already mentioned the DA pathways to frontal cortex and the limbic system from the VT and to the striatum from the SN, as well as the two 5–HT pathways from the RD and RM nuclei. There are also two NA pathways, a "dorsal NA bundle" originating in the locus coeruleus (LC) and a "ventral NA bundle," which is of lesser interest here. We shall focus on the RD and LC, because they clearly play major roles in modulating cortical processing. We shall apply neural network theory in an effort to ascertain the nature of their modulatory functions. But first we need to review the relevant neurobiological facts that severely constrain the possibilities. Most of these facts have been obtained from animal experiments. However, the general

RD and LC properties appear to be invariant across mammalian species, so the conclusions almost certainly apply to humans.

Besides its subcortical projections indicated in Fig. 7.2, the RD innervates the entire neocortex, although with some variations among cortical regions with different functions (Foote & Morrison, 1987). The modulatory function suggested by extensive and diffuse arborization of individual RD neurons is supported by direct observations of RD activity in awake and freely moving animals (Jacobs, Heym, & Steinfels, 1986):

1. The RD neurons have a slow regular output suggesting a tonic function.
2. The output varies with the state of behavioral arousal, decreasing during slow-wave sleep and vanishing during paradoxical sleep.
3. The effects are slow to start and terminate.
4. Responses to afferent inputs are nonspecific and stereotyped.
5. RD activity is coupled to activity in the LC.

The following properties of the LC are well-established (Aston-Jones, Foote, & Bloom, 1984):

1. Like the RD, the LC innervates the entire neocortex, although preferentially in different layers.
2. At a cellular level, NA modulates the activity of a target neuron by eliminating its spontaneous firing and facilitating its response to other inputs.
3. The LC neurons fire as a group and so influence modules throughout the brain almost simultaneously.
4. The LC discharge increases phasically in response to novel, aversive, or rewarding stimuli. However, signal propagation in LC axons is slow, requiring up to 400 ms to reach the entire neocortex.
5. The LC has a tonic baseline activity that, along with the RD activity, decreases in slow-wave sleep and vanishes in REM sleep.

These properties strongly suggest the interpretation of the LC/NA output as a *vigilance control* variable that sensitizes the entire brain for response to significant stimuli. In other words, the LC controls a specific kind of *selective attention*. This function is also reasonably attributed to the subcortical projections of the LC to the hippocampus and the cerebellum.

The LC is believed to have terminals on the RD causing the RD output to track the LC response to significant stimuli (Trulson & Jacobs, 1979a). The LC and RD outputs increase in phase. Considering the facilitating action of the LC, this suggests a compensatory reaction of the RD to prevent hyperexcitation. The LC does not interact directly with any DA neurons. Indeed the subcortical targets of the DA and NA pathways do not overlap, and in cortex their targets are preferentially in different layers (Lindvall & Björklund, 1984). We have already noted, however, that the LC interacts indirectly with DA neurons through the RD.

Although the previous facts suggest a type of attentional control function for the LC/NA system, they do not explain how it works, and the function of the RD/5-HT system is still a mystery. We can go further by invoking some general principles of brain design. We know that the neocortex is partitioned into modules dedicated to such diverse functions as visual, auditory, and motor processing (Mountcastle, 1978). Since the RD evidently treats all modules alike, we might be able to explain RD function in terms of general principles without reference to specialized details of brain structure.

Seven general principles of brain design that have been extracted from research in neural network theory are listed in Fig. 7.3 (Grossberg, 1982; Hestenes, 1987). No doubt most of the principles look plausible enough as generalizations of empirical knowledge about the brain, but they are much more than that. They can be given precise mathematical formulations from which a wealth of mathematical implications and insights can be derived. This is not the place for a mathematical treatment, so we will be content with a qualitative discussion of the principles and some of their implications.

The first four principles are most relevant to present concerns. The first needs no further comment, but the others require some explanation. Each module is a two-dimensional layer of interacting units called *nodes*. Each node is a lumped system of interacting neurons and interneurons that produce a coherent output

---

Architectural Principles

- The brain has a *modular structure*.

- Each module is a two-dimensional *competitive-cooperative net* dedicated to a specific processing function.

Functional Principles

- Active representation: Information is represented in a module by *stable activity patterns*.

- *Competitive selection:* Ambiguities and inconsistencies among module inputs are resolved by competition.

- *Associative learning:* Information is stored in modifiable synapses that encoded correlation between pre- and postsynaptic activities.

- *Opponent processing* for rapid switches in pattern selection.

- *Resonant coding and recognition:* New information is compressed and encoded by adaptive resonances. Recognition is a resonant matching process.

FIG. 7.3.   General Principles of Brain Organization and Function

through the axons of one or more neurons. For example, primary visual cortex is a module in which cortical columns may be regarded as nodes.

In network theory, the internal state of a node is represented by a single variable called the *activity* of the node. The function of the node is described by mathematical equations for computing the activity from inputs to the node. The internal state of a module with N nodes is represented by an *activity pattern* $\{x_1, x_2, \ldots, x_N\}$, where x_i is the activity of the ith node. The meaning of information represented in an activity pattern depends on the module and its connections to the rest of the brain. A pattern could represent an array of visual features in visual cortex or a muscle synergy in motor cortex.

The interactions among nodes within a single module are called *lateral interactions*. If the mutual interactions between two nodes are excitatory, they *cooperate* in forming a pattern by reinforcing one another's activity. However, if the interactions are inhibitory, the nodes *compete*, with the more strongly activated node tending to suppress the other's activity. Thus, a module with both excitatory and inhibitory lateral interactions is said to be a *cooperative-competitive* network or net. Such networks have been found empirically throughout the brain, but mathematical analysis has revealed the following deep reason for their existence: Subject to some provisos on the nature of the interactions, it has been proved mathematically that a balance among cooperative and competitive interactions is essential for the accurate and stable representation of information in activity patterns. It is with great confidence, therefore, that the second principle in Fig. 7.3 can be asserted as a general principle of brain design.

Now consider the fourth principle in Fig. 7.3. Cooperative-competitive nets have some remarkable information processing capabilities. It is well known, from both empirical and theoretical studies, that such nets can contrast enhance input patterns. Moreover, when "sharply tuned," the competition is so strong that only a few nodes can survive as winners. This is a fundamental mechanism for neural code compression in pattern recognition (Grossberg, 1987), and it is an important way of implementing the *competitive selection principle* (Fig. 7.3). The similarity of this principle with Darwin's principle of natural selection is seen as more than accidental when competition is recognized as a characteristic of all self-organizing systems.

Having clarified the first few principles in Fig. 7.3, we can combine them with the facts about LC/NA action to draw some important conclusions about LC function. When the LC is activated by a significant stimulus, it will increase the output of active nodes in all cortical modules and, therefore, by lateral interaction, more strongly depress inactive nodes. This will sharpen active patterns but, more importantly, stabilize them by giving them a "competitive edge" against the erosive effects of competing inputs. Here we have a more specific formulation of the vague function of "selective attention" suggested earlier. The most important functions of this "attentional processing mode" may be to facilitate retrieval and enhance learning of significant associations. Note that the NA "vigilance signal" tends to enhance and stabilize active patterns in all modules at the same time whereas increasing the strength of signals transmitted between them. This will certainly strengthen associations among these patterns according to the *associative learning principle* (Fig. 7.3). The strengthening of associations among simultaneously active patterns makes sense, because some of them are likely to have significant relations to the activating stimulus. Moreover, there is experimental evidence that NA can accelerate associative learning by potentiating changes in synaptic plasticity (Kasamatsu et al., 1984).

Note that the slow onset of the vigilance signal allows time for the significant patterns to set up. Furthermore, the vigilance signal simultaneously enhances the activity patterns in many different modules and, thus, promotes the learning of complex associations among the patterns. Without such a coordinating signal, the synchronous activation of patterns in more than two modules would be unlikely, so only simple paired associations could be learned. This seems to be just what is needed to explain the results of animal experiments showing that lesions of the locus coeruleus have no effect on the learning of simple tasks but make the learning of complex tasks impossible (Iversen, 1984). A similar result was obtained from learning tests on normal human subjects after the administration of clonidine, which, as we noted earlier, reduces LC/NA activity. The clonidine had no effect on free recall of word lists, digit span, or short-term memory; however, it markedly impaired the learning of verbal paired-associates, especially of novel associations (Frith, Dowdy, Ferrier, & Crow, 1985). Further evidence comes from studies on patients with Korsakoff's disease for which there is anatomical evidence of damage to the NA system, typically preceded by alcohol abuse (McEntee & Mair, 1984). Korsakoff patients can learn simple tasks, but performance of complex tasks, such as discrimination learning, is dramatically impaired; they have retrograde amnesia back to (but not before) the onset of the disease; they have a variety of perceptual deficits consistent with impaired attention, including longer discrimination times and smaller orienting responses that habituate less quickly. Overall, Korsakoff patients have a limited ability to compare and integrate *successive* stimulus items.

The information processing functions of selective attention and memory consolidation attributed to LC/NA activity certainly do not exhaust the functions of NA in brain. Disorders of NA activity are implicated in major depressive illness, but they most likely occur in the subcortical ventral NA bundle that projects heavily to the hypothalamus, the major organ for internal body state regulation. Unfortunately the vast literature on the subject has still not resolved the basic question as to whether depression is associated with NA hyperactivity (Gold, Goodwin, & Chrousos, 1988) or hypoactivity (Van Praag, 1983). Be that as it may, in the light of our other considerations, it does not appear likely that disorders of NA activity play a primary role in manic-depressive illness, although some may well be induced by drug treatments of the illness.

Returning now to the difficult problem of ascertaining RD/5–HT function, we follow the suggestion of network theory that the RD must be involved in some way in modulating pattern processing. One possibility that presents itself immediately is *lateral gain control*. This is to suggest that RD input to each module modulates the relative strengths of excitatory and inhibitory lateral interactions throughout the module. In the absence of direct physiological evidence, we can only evaluate this hypothesis by its consequences. Our general principles imply that a *lateral gain parameter* will do at least two things: It will regulate the following: (a) the stability of pattern formation, and (b) the sharpness of competitive pattern selection. This opens new possibilities for explaining a number of mental disorders as breakdowns in pattern formation due to malfunctions of lateral gain control.

The thought disorder that often appears in mania and schizophrenia finds a natural explanation as due to instabilities in pattern formation. The particular symptoms of the disorder will depend on which module breaks down. Thus, instabilities in the selection of plans (represented by activity patterns) for speech output can produce frequent, sudden switches in meaning even in midsentence, as often observed. Moreover, when the influence of intended meaning on the selection of words and phrases is weakened, the selection will fall under the control of overlearned associations, with tendencies for punning and free association. Alternatively perceptual confusion will result from an inability to decide among multiple interpretations of sensory stimuli. Hallucinations may result from the arbitrary selection of unlikely interpretations of stimuli, although this type of hallucination might better be classed as a delusion.

Hallucinations produced by hallucinogenic drugs like LSD are of a different type. These drugs are known to inhibit RD/5–HT transmission, and current evidence strongly indicates that this is the mechanism for their hallucinogenic effects (Jacobs & Trulson, 1981; Jacobs, 1984). A loss of lateral gain control may indeed be involved. In the early stages of LSD action, simple geometric forms appear with characteristic cobweb, spiral, and funnel forms. Ermentrout and Cowan (1979) showed mathematically that the shapes in these visual hallucinations can be attributed to the logarithmic mapping of the visual field into the visual cortex, and they arise from instabilities of pattern formation in visual cortex that appear when the cooperative/competitive strength ratio reaches a critical value. This illustrates the potential power of mathematical theory for detailed explanations of brain function and malfunction.

Instabilities in pattern formation from sensory input may be responsible for the "florid" nature of the LSD perceptual experience, but hallucinations, like dreams, also have a component that is independent of sensory input. Dreams can be regarded as byproducts of normal perceptual mechanics (Hobson, 1988). Modules involved in perception receive "top–down" inputs representing expectations as well as "bottom–up" sensory inputs. Gestalt psychology as established that each percept is a fusion of inputs from both channels. Expectations are needed to resolve ambiguities in the sensory input. However, if the top–down gain is too strong, the top–down inputs can override the sensory inputs altogether, so the percepts are simply a readout of internally generated expectations. This undoubtedly occurs in dreaming and probably also in LSD hallucinations. Since the RD transmission is turned off when REM sleep begins and is significantly reduced when LSD hallucinations appear, 5–HT probably modulates the relative gains of bottom–up and top–down inputs. One can speculate that a similar reduction in gain control at the highest levels of processing (in the frontal cortex?) may result in the top–down readout of plans or expectations that are self-confirming because of insufficient "reality check" with bottom–up inputs. In other words, the same kind of gain control malfunction that produces hallucinations in one module may produce delusions in a different module.

The Gestalt mixing of top–down and bottom–up inputs in perception can be regarded as a process of unconscious inference that combines past experience with present data in constructing a percept. However, neural network theory provides a deeper insight. Grossberg (1980) suggested that Gestalt mixing is part of a pattern matching process that is essential to code development and utilization in neural networks. A percept can accordingly be regarded as a state of resonant activation among different network modules indicating a consistent encoding (interpretation) of sensory input. The underlying theoretical idea is called the *principle of resonant coding and recognition,* in Fig. 7.3, where it is listed last, because it presumes all the other principles. Among its many theoretical and experimental implications (Grossberg, 1984b), the principle leads to specific predictions about pattern matching and switching events that are supported by evoked potential experiments (Banquet & Grossberg, 1987). This opens up the possibility of a sound theoretical basis for the use of evoked potentials in psychiatric research and evaluation. Our previous considerations strongly suggest that the pattern matching process is modulated by tonic RD/5–HT input and that malfunctions in this matching produce hallucinations and delusions. Our considerations also suggest that the other monoamines are involved as well. Grossberg (1984a) applied the opponent processing principle (Fig. 7.3) to develop a class of specific models for rapid pattern switching called gated dipoles. The gated dipole has the potential for explaining some of the paradoxical effects of monoamine action, such as the fact that DA agonists often reduce hyperactivity in adolescents whereas they usually increase it in adults. One thing appears certain, the development and testing of specific mathematical models for the mechanisms of pattern matching and switching is essential to the understanding of neural networks in general and the modulatory actions of the monoamines in particular.

Having gained some insight into the potential of neural network theory for explaining the mechanisms underlying the processes of perception and misperception, let us return to the empirical question of identifying the monoamine variables in psychosis. This question has been investigated in an enormous literature on the psychotimimetic effects of drugs (Hollister, 1978). The drugs inducing psychological states most similar to clinical psychosis are LSD and amphetamine, the principal representatives of two families of drugs with such effects. With sufficient doses, both drugs can produce delusions and hallucinations within a setting of clear consciousness, that is, without the thought disorder and disorientation that accompanies the psychotimimetic effects of other drugs, although thought disorder can be induced by higher doses. We have already reviewed evidence that the mechanism of LSD action is a reduction of RD/5–HT transmission. On the other hand, according to our considerations in the preceding section, the euphoric effects of amphetamine (speed) should be attributed to increased dopamine transmission. With increasing doses, amphetamine induces stages similar to hypomania, mania, and ultimately in some people, paranoid psychosis (Snyder, 1972). For this reason, it has been supposed that psychosis involves DA (and possible NA) malfunction. One problem with this conclusion is the fact that neuroleptics, which are known to reduce DA activity, do not alleviate psychotic symptoms. Another is the fact that the onset of amphetamine psychosis occurs much later than the reduction in DA transmission. It appears that the issue has been resolved by Trulson and Jacobs (1979b, 1979c), who showed that amphetamine also reduced 5–HT activity. Although this effect is smaller than the DA reduction, it is cumulative with each dose, and the net reduction is between 40 and 67 percent over 10 days. Furthermore, the onset and offset of behavioral effects (model psychosis) in cats correlates perfectly with large changes in 5–HT transmission. We conclude, therefore, that reduced cortical 5–HT activity is the major factor, and possibly a sufficient factor, in all model psychoses, including dreaming. Surely it must be a major factor in clinical psychoses, although that remains to be demonstrated.

It should be clear by now that network theory suggests (reveals?) relations among different psychiatric disorders by attributing them to malfunctions of a common system of pattern processing mechanisms. As another example, let us consider *obsessive-compulsive disorder* (OCD), regarded since Freud as the prototypical psychiatric disorder. Once thought to be rare, OCD has recently been estimated to afflict as much as 2% of the population at one time or another (Robins et al., 1984). OCD is a disorder of the will. *Obsessions* are persistent, recurrent, and repugnant thoughts that invade consciousness against an individuals will. *Compulsions* are senseless and frequently bizarre ritualistic behaviors that individuals feel must be performed to prevent overwhelming anxiety. In prescientific societies, the afflicted was thought to be possessed by outside agents that which doctors attempted to exorcise. Freud proposed that the will was controlled by unconscious repressed motives, which the psychoanalytic method aimed to elucidate. Despite a voluminous literature, all forms of psychiatric theory for OCD were ineffective until a breakthrough in drug therapy within the last two decades (Salzman & Thaler, 1981).

From the viewpoint of network theory, OCD is evidently a disorder of the competitive pattern selection mechanism, with inappropriate patterns repeatedly winning the competition for expression as thoughts and/or behaviors. If 5–HT modulates the competition as suggested previously, then drugs affecting 5–HT transmission should be effective in treating OCD. Indeed treatment with the 5–HT precursor tryptophan (3–9g/day) was shown to be effective in seven cases (Yaryura-Tobias & Bhagavan, 1977), whereas a combination of lithium and tryptophan has been shown to augment clomipramine treatment (Rasmussen, 1984). Clomipramine is a potent 5–HT reuptake blocker, and this is almost certainly the mechanism by which it reduces OCD symptoms (Flament, Rapaport, Murphy, Berg, & Lake, 1987; Zohar, Insel, Zohar-Kodouch, Hill, & Murphy, 1988). In an exceptionally thorough study, Zohar and Insel (1987) demonstrated the agents that bind to $5-HT_1$ receptors can acutely affect OCD symptoms. By the way, LSD has equal affinity for $5-HT_1$ and $5-HT_2$ receptors, with the highest $5-HT_2$ binding levels in the caudate and layer IV of cerebral cortex (Peroutka, 1988).

As to the anatomical locus of OCD, the fact OCD and Tourette's syndrome have clinical similarities and frequently occur together within families suggests that they share a common neurological mechanism (Cummings & Frankel, 1985), which, according to our previous considerations, is likely to be located in the striatum. Recently PET scans of acutely symptomatic OCD patients have revealed unusually high metabolic rates localized in the left orbital gyrus of the prefrontal cortex and bilaterally in the caudate nucleus of the striatum (Baxter et al., 1987). This suggests deficient integration of orbital-caudate activities, perhaps by a malfunction of 5–HT modulation similar to the one proposed in hallucinations. Lesions of the orbital-caudate connections in animals result in perserverative interference with switches in behavior (Alexander, DeLong, & Strick, 1986). All this raises the challenge of developing a network model of orbital-caudate interactions to account for OCD and related disorders. This is likely to require an understanding of modulatory mechanisms for pattern processing in the entire striatum and the NAC, thus, bringing us back to the considerations of the preceding section with a richer perspective.

PART II: CLINICAL IMPLICATIONS

Monoamine Precursor Control of Mania and Depression

According to the *gating theory of manic-depressive illness,* in Section 1, the illness is due to malfunction of a signal gating mechanism in the nucleus accumbens under the dual control of dopamine and serotonin inputs. Mania occurs when the gating gain is too high, due possibly to excessive dopamine input or to hypersensitivity of dopamine receptors. Anhedonic depression occurs when the gating gain is too low. DA gain is modulated both directly and indirectly by serotonin input. Obviously this implies that optimal drug therapy for manic-depressive illness must control *both* dopamine and serotonin variables. The clinical question is how?

Although a single mechanism is held to be the locus of manic-depressive illness, there are many ways it might malfunction. For example, there might be receptor supersensitivity at the sites of transmitter action or malfunctions of feedback mechanisms regulating the basal output level of the modulating neurons and many other possibilities. Consequently manic-depressive illness undoubtedly has many subtypes that perhaps should be treated differently. However, there is one malfunction that might be the most common and is certainly the easiest to treat, namely monoamine transmitter depletion due to insufficient precursor availability. The illness resulting from this type of malfunction is best described as benign, because it can be completely "cured" simply by increasing precursor availability; no brain components are defective or damaged. No such category of benign mental illness is recognized in general psychiatric practice, but the possibility has immense implications, which are explored in the following.

Benign types of bipolar and unipolar illnesses are likely to be common, because plausible precipitating causal factors can be identified, and they are commonly occurring. Extensive evidence shows that monoamine transmission stores can be significantly depleted by stress (Anziman & Zacharko, 1982) as well as by diet (Wurtman, 1988). Stress elevates the transmission rates of dopamine, noradrenaline, and (probably as a compensatory reaction) serotonin. Under continued stress, transmission rates eventually fall, because transmitter replenishment cannot keep up with depletion. Serotonin is especially susceptible to deletion, because the normal dietary concentrations of its precursor tryptophan is lower than that of tyrosine, the precursor of both dopamine and noradrenaline. Consequently a suitable combination of stress and diet can maintain or even increase dopamine levels whereas reducing serotonin levels to produce the kind of imbalance conducive to mania. Alternatively other combinations of stress and diet can reduce dopamine as well as serotonin depletion and so produce depression.

A strong dependence of monoamine transmitter stores and transmission rates on the concentrations of precursors circulating in the blood has been well documented (Wurtman, 1988; Fernstrom, 1983). The monoamine precursors compete with other, large neural amino acids (LNAA: primarily phenylalamine, leucine, isoleucine, and valine) for passage through the blood–brain barrier. Accordingly the precursor transmission rate through the barrier varies directly with precursor blood concentration relative to the total concentration of the other LNAA. The brain transmitter levels are so sensitive to the blood precursor levels that they may vary significantly even with a single meal.

These well-documented results provided a strong, scientific justification for *monoamine precursor treatments* of bipolar and unipolar illness (Van Praag, 1986). Such treatments aim to raise brain levels of serotonin and/or dopamine by direct administration of their precursors in purified form. Tryptophan treatment works best, because the rate limiting enzyme in serotonin synthesis, tryptophan hydroxylase, is not ordinarily saturated. In contrast, tyrosine hydroxylase is more commonly saturated, so tyrosine therapy has a more limited usefulness.

Three major variants of monoamine precursor treatments are of clinical interest: (a) treatment of mania with a combination of tryptophan and, for a limited period, a dopamine antagonist that does not antagonize serotonin; (b) tryptophan prophylaxis against mania, perhaps in combination with lithium in some cases; (c) treatment of depression with a combination of tryptophan and tyrosine, especially if the depression has an anhedonic component. Examples of all these treatments are discussed in subsequent sections, including suggested doses and therapeutic strategy. A brief discussion of the current clinical status of each treatment is in order here.

Depression.   Association of depression with low CNS serotonin turnover has been one of the most consistent findings in psychiatric research (Van Praag, 1986). This does not necessarily imply a malfunction of the serotonergic system, however. For, if elevation of serotoneric output over the basal level is a compensatory mechanism to insure processing stability under increases in catecholamine (NA and DA) outputs, then low serotonin activity would be a consequence of low catecholamine activity. This would explain the fact that, by itself, tryptophan is not a very good antidepressant. In some cases, low catecholamine activity may be due to depleted transmitter stores, in which case tyrosine treatment should work. A combination of tyrosine and tryptophan has been advocated as an especially promising treatment for depression by one of the leading researchers in the field (Van Praag, 1988). Large-scale tests are needed to see if it is effective for a substantial fraction of depressives. When the treatment works, the depression should be classified as benign.

Mania.   Clear evidence that tryptophan is effective against mania was cited earlier. Although such evidence has often been cited in the literature, tryptophan is seldom used in treating mania, because it has the reputation of a "weak antimanic agent," and stronger agents are preferred. Be that as it may, the facts tell us that tryptophan is raising the serotonin level, and the theory tells us that this should be helpful. Indeed, in the proposed benign type of illness, it will directly eliminate the proximate cause of the illness. Accordingly it seems advisable to include tryptophan in any treatment of mania, even if the tryptophan appears to be ineffective by itself. Theory suggests that the optimal treatment should be some combination of tryptophan and a dopamine antagonist. However, this entails the danger of suppressing the dopamine activity too severely and so inducing anhedonic depression. Such drug induced depression may in fact be a common aftereffect of mania treatment. Fortunately a simple remedy suggests itself, namely tyrosine treatment. As a hedge against depression, it may be a good idea to prescribe tyrosine routinely after neuroleptic treatment for mania.

Mania is often accompanied by some kind of psychosis, so it is of clinical interest to know if the psychosis indicates a subtype of the illness that deserves special treatment. Our consideration in the second section that the appearance of psychosis along with mania is especially indicative of subnormal serotonin activity and, hence, a need for tryptophan.

Tryptophan prophylaxis.   Even if tryptophan is only a weak antimanic agent, that may be enough to prevent the development of mania, so tryptophan might be at least as effective as lithium in prophylaxis. Ample evidence is now available to justify large-scale clinical tests of this possibility. If indeed the prophylactic efficacy of tryptophan is comparable to that of lithium, there is little doubt about which should be the treatment of choice. Tryptophan prophylaxis is safer, more convenient, and more flexible. It hardly amounts to more than a regular dietary supplement. There is no danger of overmedication. Blood levels need not be monitored. Occasional lapses do not seriously disrupt the prophylactic effect. Doses can be adjusted by the patient without consulting a doctor. The main drawback is expense.

Without prophylaxis, a single manic episode is likely to be followed by another in the overwhelming majority of cases (Goodwin & Jamison, 1984). The average time between the first and second episode is three to four years, and subsequent episodes almost always follow, separated by successively shorter time intervals. Evidently some genetic mechanism is at work. One possibility is a problem in monoamine metabolism or unusual sensitivity to variations in precursor availability that are tolerated by everyone else.

Everyone is more or less susceptible to monoamine variations induced by stress and diet. This suggests that the distinction between reactive and endogenous illness is not so sharp as commonly supposed. The main difference may be that the precipitating factors of stress and diet may not be as obvious in the so-called endogenous case. Monoamine precursor treatment may work for both endogenous and reactive types. In that case, both types should be classified as benign. Thus, the class of benign mental illnesses may be quite large.

The main conclusion from all this is that tryptophan should be widely used to combat mania and depression, not to mention hyperactivity in children. It should always be helpful when serotonin levels are low, because the serotonin synthesis pathway is unsaturated. The main caution is to watch out for competition between tryptophan and tyrosine.

A Case of Tryptophan Prophylaxis

As a prophylactic against mania and depression, Marie has taken L–tryptophan (TRY) regularly for ten years. Her case history provides valuable information about the design and effectiveness of the treatment. Marie's first manic episode occurred at age twenty-two. She has exceptional artistic talent that had led her to

Paris to study sculpture at the time. Her studies were going well, but she took a part-time job, and her living conditions were such that the combination subjected her to severe stress. That may be what precipitated her episode. She was hospitalized in Paris for about ten days until she was well enough to return with a relative to the United States. For the next week, without drugs, she was in a hilarious hypomanic state that her family did not understand. Then she fell into uncontrollable mania characterized by severe delusions, so she had to be hospitalized. She was diagnosed as manic-depressive and kept in the hospital for a month, where she was first treated with antipsychotic drugs and then put on lithium carbonate (900mg/day). She remained on lithium for three months. During this time, her effective level was intolerably low, too low for her to function artistically.

Despite the ample reasons for clinical investigations of TRY prophylaxis discussed in the preceding section, only one other trial has been found in a literature search. Beitman and Dunner (1982) reported a single case of successful TRY prophylaxis followed for eleven months. The adjustable daily TRY dose (2–2.67g) found effective in that case is consistent with the conclusions following for Marie's case.

Marie's psychiatrist was a "self-acknowledged" expert in lithium therapy. He had been director of a country clinic in Los Angeles where he had supervised the treatment of hundreds of people with affective disorders. When asked how lithium works, he gave the stock reply that the mechanism is unknown, but the drug's effectiveness had been proven in extensive clinical tests. That settled the matter for him, but Marie's father was unsatisfied. The drug was clearly not "doing the job" in this case. As an experienced research scientist, he was suspicious of any drug treatment that could not be rationalized by some hypothesis (however tentative) about the mechanisms for the drug action and information about relations to the actions of other drugs. So he directed his research skills to an intensive review of the research and clinical literature on manic-depressive illness. After two months, he returned to the psychiatrist with a thoroughly documented proposal to replace lithium by tryptophan. He had found evidence that lithium may achieve its therapeutic effect primarily by enhancing serotonin transmission (by any one of several possible mechanisms). Although that evidence was inconclusive, it was supported by evidence showing that tryptophan and lithium have similar behavioral effects, in particular in alleviating depression and reducing impulsive behavior. A comparable review documenting tryptophan's therapeutic action was published only recently by Young (1986). Young's review, therefore, serves as an up-to-date justification for Marie's treatment, which began seven years earlier.

To his credit, Marie's psychiatrist enthusiastically endorsed the TRY alternative to lithium therapy when its rationale was explained to him. Indeed he began experimenting widely with TRY in his clinical cases, with favorable results including several successful treatments of hyperactive children. After a year and half, he declared that TRY was his "treatment of choice." He prefers not to use other drugs until he is sure that TRY was not effective. Unfortunately he never got around to putting his observations to controlled test, so they remain anecdotal and of questionable value to other clinicians. "Anecdotal" seems to describe the current clinical status of TRY therapy in general, perhaps because pharmaceutical companies see no reason to support research on a substance that cannot be sold as a drug. Ironically the depressive condition of Marie that stimulated the TRY therapy might better have been treated with tyrosine, for reasons given later in the case study of Marie's sister.

If Marie's problem was really inadequate central serotonin production, as proposed, then precursor treatment with TRY should be as effective as lithium and free of lithium's drawbacks. The transition from lithium to TRY was made cautiously to reduce the possibility of reversion to mania. In retrospect, the caution was probably unnecessary. First, Marie was given a TRY dose of 2g/day for 10 days to improve her sleep. Then her lithium dose was reduced from 900mg/day to 600mg/day. Within two days, her depression disappeared almost completely. She remained in good spirits for a week, then depression returned after a night with little sleep. Her TRY dose was raised from 2g to 4g that night, and the effect was striking. She went to sleep immediately, awakening after 9 hours to her best day in the four months since treatment began, a day that was notable for the patience and concentration she displayed as well as her sunny disposition. A week later, her lithium was dropped entirely.

The following prophylactic plan was adopted and has been followed, more or less, for the ten years since. Marie's daily bedtime TRY dose was varied up and down over the range 0g, 2g, 4g, and 6g as needed to maintain stable sleep pattern and control any hypomania that appears. The idea is that mania develops slowly over a period of many days, during which sleep disruption, excessive talkativeness, and exuberance are easily recognized signs. Experience suggests that 4g to 6g TRY doses suffice to prevent mania. Marie's dosage has varied over the years. The average has been between 1g and 2g per day, which by comparison with the normal average daily TRY intake of about 1.5g amounts to hardly more than a dietary supplement. Frequently, especially when she was under stress from work or school, Marie became moderately hypomanic before the end of her period, so for several days before her period she often took 4g and occasionally 6g per day. During the last two years, she has settled on 2g doses as most effective (in agreement with the conclusion of Young, 1986).

Individuals vary widely in their sensitivity to TRY (Moeller, Kirk, & Flemming, 1976). A dose of 2g of TRY at bedtime is usually sufficient for Marie's sleep, unless the day has been particularly stressful. She reports that, one-half hour later, she gets a feeling like something spurting or rising into her head. This fills her with a sense of ease, a sense of relief that she can finally sleep. She reports a definite switch from a verbal mode of conscious thought to a visual mode consisting of vaguely defined shapes. She insists that this switch is necessary for her to get to sleep. Once she gets to sleep, she usually sleeps soundly.

Tryptophan does not solve Marie's sleep problem entirely. The time of sleep onset tends to shift to an hour later each day and will continue to shift around the clock unless interrupted by a night with little sleep. This has been carefully documented with records over many months. She has adjusted pretty well to her irregular sleep pattern.

Marie's TRY intake has been kept as conservative as is consistent with its prophylactic function to avoid conceivable long-term complications. No such complications have been reported in the literature or observed in the ten years of Marie's treatment. Evidently tryptophan prophylaxis is the safest possible long-term therapy in biopsychiatry.

Marie has usually avoided 6g doses, because she claims it gives her a headache the next day. She may be right that this is due to vitamin B–6 depletion (because she takes so much tryptophan). She insists that the problem is solved by two B–complex tablets (including 100mg B–6) and that this is superior to B–6 alone. Her claim that the B–complex makes her feel better is consistent with reports in the literature that B–6 may have an antidepressant effect. Another reason for conservative TRY intake should be mentioned. Most of the excessive TRY is metabolized in the liver through the kynurenic pathway, which not only depletes B–6 but, when overstimulated, may deflect TRY from other important targets (Young, 1986).

Marie's numerous brief hypomanic and depressive episodes provide some evidence for the efficacy of TRY prophylaxis. Stronger evidence for the anti-manic action of TRY is found in a second manic episode that she experienced five years after the first. She had returned to school for a degree in nursing. The nursing program proved to be extremely stressful for her. During the second semester, she ran out of her supply of TRY. After three weeks without TRY, she began a delusional manic episode. After two days in this condition, she was given a one-time dose of 50mg chlorpromazine to calm her down and then 6g/day TRY for several days. Her recovery was remarkably rapid. By the third day, she was back in school, and she successfully completed the semester after dropping the most stressful courses. She has not had another manic episode in the five years since. However, she finally decided to give up nursing as it was too stressful.

The classification of this second episode as manic is questionable. It is justified primarily by the fact that, for two weeks prior to its sudden onset, she exhibited hypomanic ideation, restlessness, and sleep loss. The dominant features of the episode itself were deep depression and fear accompanying the delusions rather than manic activity. The episode might better be characterized as an acute depressive reaction to stress. Perhaps that is why the TRY treatment was so successful.

Marie has continued to have frequent mood swings, like her fraternal grand-mother, she is especially susceptible to a depressive reaction after a few days of continuous stress, but she has learned to recognize the danger signals and cope quite well. She has developed a mature insight into her problem and consequently into the problems of others. She has become a caring and loving adult.

Analysis of an Illness

The second case study is broken into three stages consisting of two manic episodes separated by an intermediate depressed period. The study is included to illustrate the potential of the theory in clinical practice and raise some specific issues for further research. It contains more detail than the usual clinical report for the benefit of readers without clinical experience as well as to enable detailed comparison with other cases.

The study should be read with the theory of Part I in mind. The theory asserts that the illness is due to some combination of disturbances in two brain state control variables: dopamine and serotonin. Moreover, it suggests that the symptoms of delusions and paranoia derive primarily from a serotonin malfunction—the main issue in the study the extent to which these hypotheses are in accord with the clinical data. A secondary issue is the use of the monoamine precursors, tryptophan and tyrosine, to help control variables. Finally the study reports some clear effects of stress on the illness and some unique effects of drug and precursor treatment.

No definitive conclusions can be drawn from a single case study like this. The best it can do is stimulate more definitive research.

STAGE 1: TRYPTOPHAN IN MANIA CONTROL

Eight years after Marie's first manic episode at age 22, her sister Susan had a similar episode at age 19. The sisters share many other similarities. In retrospect, it is evident that both had long periods of depression before their episodes. Susan was also away from home at college and subject to more than ordinary academic stress when her episode occurred. From the beginning, however, her treatment was influenced by the knowledge of Marie's experience. Her parents were experienced and had Marie to help; so it was unnecessary to hospitalize Susan during treatment. They were able to monitor her 24 hours a day when necessary. They kept a detailed record that reveals various effects of the drugs in the treatment. We now turn to an analysis of that record and its implications.

A chronology of the episode, treatment, and recovery is charted in Fig. 7.4. Three sets of variables are charted in the figure. Before discussing the day by day chronology, a discussion of how the charts are to be interpreted is in order.

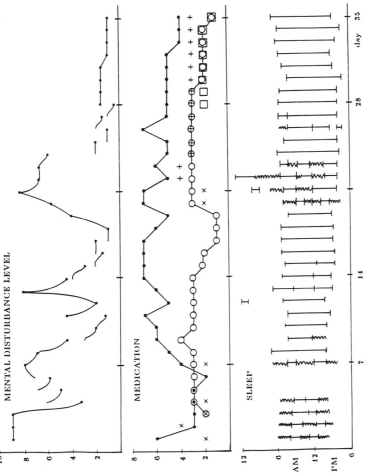

FIG. 7.4. *Chronology of a Manic Episode.* See text for explanation on the Mental Disturbance Scale, the dot indicates end of day and the connecting lines indicate variations during waking hours. Medication doses are represented by the following code and scale: ● = tryptophan (1g units); ○ = thiothixene (10mg units); × = chlorpromazine (25mg units); + = lithium carbonate (300mg units); □ = benztropine mesylate (1mg units).

233

Medication

The medication chart in Fig. 7.4 gives the daily dose of each of the relevant medications: TRY–thiothixene (TX, brand name: Navane)—lithium, and chlorpromazine. The benztropine (brand name: cogentin) dose to reduce extrapyramidal side effects is recorded only after day 28.

The TRY was administered as one dose close to bedtime, except on several days when 5g was given at bedtime and 2g was given at noon to keep the daytime blood level up. A large dose at bedtime is crucial to raising serotonin levels in the brain and assisting sleep. TRY is rapidly absorbed in the digestive tract and its effect is noticeable within one-half hour. Blood concentration reaches a maximum (up to 30 times normal level) in about two hours. This high concentration increases the amount passing through the blood–brain barrier. At low concentrations, competition with other circulating amino acids significantly inhibits the passage of TRY into the brain, so a large dose is the surest way to achieve the desired result. Normally no more than one percent of plasma TRY gets converted to serotonin in the brain (Fernstrom, 1983).

Marie's experience and experience reported in the literature show that 6g/day TRY is effective against mania, although 12g distributed throughout each day may be more effective by suppressing the brain intake of tyrosine to produce dopamine.

Sleep Assessment

The sleep chart in Fig. 7.4 gives a sleep line for each day starting at the time Susan went to bed and ending when she got up. The solid line indicates steady sleep. The occasional crossbar indicates a short interruption to go to the bathroom, but such interruptions often went unrecorded. The wiggly lines indicate completely disrupted sleep. The sleep lines are quite accurate for the first four weeks and especially for nights with severe sleep disturbance, because Susan was monitored the entire night. By the end of the fifty week, when sleep was consistently good, only bedtime and rising time were recorded, thus, the actual sleep time is undoubtedly somewhat less than that recorded on the chart.

Mental State Assessment

Various mood inventories are commonly used to assess the affective state of a patient. However, they do not work well during the manic episode, because patient self-reports are unreliable, and behavioral indicators of mood are deceptively dependent on what has been going on in the immediate environment. Accordingly Susan's expressions of mood from deep fear to happiness and delight are not directly represented in Fig. 7.4, although they were observed to correlate fairly well with the mental state assessment when they were clearly noticeable.

Attention span is an important indicator of a patient's mental state that is easy to evaluate qualitatively. Gross changes in attention span were noted in evaluating Susan's state, but no record of this is included in Fig. 7.4, because these changes are presumed to depend on both of the measured variables. Thus, attention span is regarded as a secondary variable in the present case, useful as a check on the primary observations.

The mental disturbance chart in Fig. 7.4 is a composite of distinct observation on two separate scales, the impulsivity scale of Table 7.1, and the delusion scale of Table 7.2. The choice of these two scales was strongly influenced by theory suggesting that impulsivity and delusions are due to independent disturbance in neurotransmission, the first being due primarily to excessive dopamine activity, whereas the second is due primarily to insufficient serotonin activity.

The choice of scales was also influenced by recollections of Marie's experience and observations of Susan's. It is important to note that a behavior variable and a perception variable is being measured. On general grounds alone, one might anticipate that behavior and perception may be regulated by different variables, although the theory in Part I suggests that serotonin contributes to the regulation of both, whereas dopamine contributes only to the behavior. Some sort of impulsive behavior is characteristic of manic and hypomanic states, almost by definition. The perceptual disorder most prominent in the episodes of both Marie and Susan was delusion, so a scale was developed to measure it. This scale has the virtue of being more specific than other scales commonly used for mental state assessment.

The calibration of both scales is based on empirical observations of Susan's experience. The scales are of course ordinal rather than metrical. Susan was observed to move up and down through the states indicated by the scales in the order given. The extremes of the scales were easiest to identify. The intermediate states on the delusion scale were determined by interpolation. The highest level on the delusion scale, an inability to recognize and respond to others, was never approached by Susan, but it was approached by Marie in her first manic episode. Ballistic behavior output, as the top of the impulsivity scale, was easy to identify in Susan's behavior once it had been suggested by theory. In the shaky category

TABLE 7.1
Impulsivity Scale.

8	—	*Ballistic*—emits sudden, forceful, and inappropriate behaviors.
6	—	*Impulsive*—difficulty sitting still, constant need to get up and move about for no apparent reason.
4	—	*Agitated*—constant wringing of hands, cracking knuckles, tapping feet, and so on.
3	—	*Shaky*—mild tremors.
2	—	*Clear* of agitation.

TABLE 7.2
Delusion Scale.

10	—	Unable to recognize and respond to others.
9	—	Impaired sense of body and self.
8	—	Delusions about present reality, objects imbued with symbolic meaning, mystical and spiritual powers.
7	—	Delusions about the nature of illness (e.g., "I am the white witch").
6 5	— }	Apparent regression of mental functioning to an earlier age.
4	—	Delusions about past events, especially the onset of the episode.
3	—	Delusions dissolving into metaphors.
2	—	Clear of delusions, but energy and concentration weak.
1	—	Realistic, energetic, but incapable of sustained concentration such as in reading.
0	—	Well, normal functioning.

at the low end of the impulsivity scale, it is difficult to distinguish primary agitation from side effects of medication.

The lowest part of the scale (in Table 7.2) is not concerned with either delusion or agitation, but it proved to be needed for the composite mental state scale in Fig. 7.4. More information about the scales will be given as the chronology is discussed.

Chronology

The chronology in Fig. 7.4 begins with the evening of day 1, when Susan was brought home for treatment. The onset of her mania was several days earlier. She had been hospitalized the day before as a danger to herself after police had found her raving in the park at 2:00 a.m. Her parents had noted clear signs of hypomania three weeks before when she had returned home from college for two days. She exhibited pressured speech and would not allow anyone else to speak without interruptions. Her parents were concerned but not alarmed, because she had not had a manic episode. She was given 4g TRY the first night, and her hypomania was noticeably lower the next day. She was instructed to take 2g each night for the next 10 days when she returned to school. Her boyfriend agreed to monitor this and note signs of hypomania. However, none of this was carried out, as Susan absolutely refused to consider tryptophan after she left home. Her parents were not informed that anything was amiss, and her friends tried to deal with her increasingly unusual behavior until it got out of their control, and she ran away to the park where she was found many hours later. Thus, there was perhaps a month of hypomania before the sudden transition to a manic state. The long onset time without treatment may have increased the severity of the episode.

At the height of the episode, during days 2 and 3, Susan suffered a variety of delusions about self and body triggered by incidental events. For example, on seeing a bright blue sponge in the kitchen, she began to speak to herself as a blue sponge; she insisted on wearing blue clothes, and she was obsessed with blueness for half a day. At one time, she evidently felt some discomfort in her left eye; on looking in a mirror, she pointed to the eye and cried out in distress that it was "bulging;" thereafter she was greatly distressed by the poor condition of eyes on her old stuffed animals. On another occasion, she claimed that she had become "very small;" measurement of her height marked on a door frame showed her full five-feet seven inches, but she pointed at the mark and cried, "See, I'm shrinking!" When refusing her TRY at night, she cried "I have Druid in my mind! I want control over my own mind!"

During the mornings of days 2 and 3, Susan took a bath every 15 minutes or so–undressing, splashing about briefly, dressing fully again—about 20 baths each morning. The similarity of this activity to obsessive-compulsive disorder (OCD) suggests, in accordance with theory, that it stems from a disorder of serotoneric modulation in the striatum. This possibility is supported by the fact that TRY treatment can be effective against OCD (Yaryura-Tobias & Bhagavan, 1977).

Susan's high agitation level was exhibited in its purest form in ballistic release of behaviors after she had been put in bed to sleep. She would suddenly sit bold upright and announce, for example, "I am going hunting with a friend of mine." When asked "Who?" she replied "Gandolf" (a fictional creature whom she had reified). Then she would get up forcefully and walk out the door. The term ballistic seems appropriate to describe this kind of event, because it is clear that an entire action pattern ("get up and walk") is suddenly and forcefully released. The action pattern had sufficient impetus to maintain itself for about half a minute. Then, when it was suggested that Susan return to bed, she turned around and did so without objection.

The disruption of sleep by agitation during the first two days is evident (see Fig. 7.4). Note the high correlation between sleep disturbance and high mental disturbance, demonstrated throughout the figure.

Susan accepted 6g TRY before she left the hospital for home on day 1. However, she vigorously objected to TRY for more than a week thereafter. The available TRY came in large, half-gram pills; thus, it was difficult to get her to swallow several grams. As there was still some uncertainty about what is the optimal treatment, it was decided to go with 3g doses for a while. Thus, Susan's vigorous objections initiated a dosage experiment. Her objection was understandable. She associated the TRY with her sister's illness, so to take it would be an admission that she has the same problem. In her delusional state, she associated the white tryptophan with death and the "white witch."

Systematic treatment of Tx began on day 3, and the dose was distributed over the whole of day 4. The improvement during day 4 was rapid and spectacular. By evening, her delusions seemed to be dissolving into metaphors. Whereas, in the morning, she referred to herself as the white witch, in the evening, she joked about the white witch as a symbol of her mania. In the evening, Susan was happy, vibrant, and witty, but the disturbed sleep that followed signaled that victory was not to be so easy.

Susan's mental state regressed during the next three days for no apparent reason. On day 7, Susan reiterated, "I am the white witch" and spoke of suicide often. By this time, it was clear that the Tx was not solving the problem by itself, so the TRY dose was increased. Improvement followed immediately, including a stabilization of sleep as soon as the TRY dose reached 5g. The disruption of sleep on day 10 was due to a late visit by Susan's boyfriend. Susan reported vivid dreaming each night during these and subsequent days, which suggests that the serotonergic system was not fully recovered, because REM sleep occurs only when the serotonergic system is off.

To get Susan to take her full dose of TRY during this period, several devices were tried, including powdering or chopping up the TRY and mixing it with apple sauce. Marie's experience with various ways of ingesting the unpalatable TRY was most helpful.

TRY appeared to be reducing a delusion; so the decision to increase the Tx dose to day 9 was promptly reversed. No delusions at all were evident on day 11. Susan was happy, appeared to have a normal attention span, and wrote some poetry. Her parents remarked that she seemed better than normal.

A second rapid regression occurred on day 13 for no apparent reason. The only change in medication was the inadvertent omission of the 2g noontime TRY dose on day 13. It seemed unlikely that that could be sufficient to cause the regression. However, in the absence of an alternative explanation, that was taken as pretext for keeping the TRY dose at 7g for the next several days. On review of the data later, it was realized that a significant stress factor was operative at the time that could well have caused the regression. With perhaps a precursor on Sunday, the regression occurred on Monday after Susan's boyfriend returned to school. The two of them had been exceptionally close for company during the weekend, although he had returned from school on the weekend for the sole purpose of visiting her. Their relation was strained, because he was upset over her treatment, or rather what he imagined the treatment to be. He remained very upset for several weeks until his questions and fears were resolved in a long conversation with Susan's father. In the meantime, he was unfortunately only a source of stress for Susan.

After the regression on day 13, improvement was steady for the next 5 days. Late in the morning of day 16, she swept suddenly into her father's office to announce "the white witch has been banished from the neuron forest!" She was very happy (but not euphoric) all the rest of the day, and she had her best sleep yet that night. Day 18 was even better, as she initiated her own activities and engaged in sustained, vigorous dancing. During this period Susan came to associate TRY with "life" instead of "death," and thereafter she amiably accepted her prescribed TRY dose without objection.

The tryptophan had evidently eliminated the delusions and full recovery appeared to be at hand; thus, reduction of the Tx dose was started on day 15. Unfortunately the reduction was too rapid. A third regression began on day 19 with agitation and irritability. On day 20, deterioration progressed steadily from agitation through delusion to ballistic behavior. It was like plummeting into a deep hole. Evidently an excess of dopamine that had been blocked by the Tx was still "waiting in the wings" and rushed in when the blockage was removed. This is not necessarily evidence against the ability of serotonin to suppress mania. It only suggests that serotonin is ineffective against large, local concentrations of the catecholamines. It may be, however, that, in a more normal state, the serotonergic system helps prevent the build up of such concentrations.

On day 24, three days after the full dosage of Tx was restored, the agitation and delusions vanished overnight. This marked the end of the mania and the beginning of recovery.

In an effort to stabilize Susan's state so the Tx could be reduced without another setback, lithium was introduced on day 21, and then 8 days later the reduction of Tx began again, this time proceeding more cautiously. The TRY was also reduced, because lithium is known to potentate its action. For the next three weeks, Susan's state was one of amiable lassitude, without enthusiasm or initiative.

Only two good days after the Tx dose had been reduced to zero, mild agitation set in again on day 46 (Fig. 7.5). The TRY dosage was increased immediately to see if it could help. The next day the agitation increased anyway, and that evening a crisis set in. Susan's boyfriend visited for only an hour. He was literally sick with worry over her state and her treatment. To Susan, he seemed stiff and unresponsive. He told her that she was getting the wrong treatment, that she needed counseling for depression. He complained that he was powerless to help. In a bid for control, he threatened to abandon her. She was hesitant and confused; it was time for bed, so he left.

If ever there was a stress vector, this was it. Susan's agitation level shot up immediately, and it stayed there, for two nights and a day, before it began to wane. Tx was started again to combat it. This was a powerful lesson in the biological effects of stress. Nevertheless no delusions appeared, and the agitation never reached the ballistic level.

The conflict with Susan's boyfriend was completely resolved on day 50, to the enormous relief of both of them. Even so, Susan's agitation continued throughout the next two days. Her affect was very flat. She often failed to respond to questions, even when they were repeated. "My head is all stuffed up" was her daily complaint. At one time she said, "It's not that I have racing thoughts. I have no thoughts. It's Scarey!" It was conjectured that her condition was due mainly to an enhancement of the fairly large TRY dose by the lithium. This combination had not been tried before. Accordingly the TRY dose was reduced to 2g. By the third day thereafter, the improvement was obvious. In the morning,

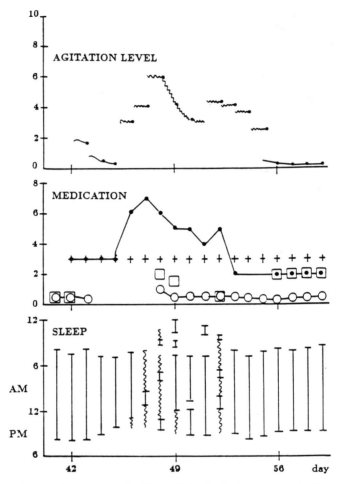

FIG. 7.5. *Chronology of a Stress Episode.* Scales same as in Fig. 7.4. However, the mental disturbance during this period was best described as agitated with no apparent delusions.

Susan spent two hours reading adult literature, something she had not done in a long time.

On day 53, it was recognized that much of Susan's agitation was of extrapyramidal origin rather than primary. The first clue actually appeared on day 49. Susan was prevented from sleeping by spontaneous, vigorous leg spasms, just like running in place, although she was lying in bed. Let us give this unusual effect the descriptive name *locomotor spasm,* because it will reappear more prominently in Susan's second manic episode. The spasms abated after two hours. They appeared again three nights later and continued throughout the night.

The problem was solved the next day after a 3mg dose of benztropine. For this reason, the benztropine dose is recorded in Fig. 7.4 beginning on day 28. Susan's residual tremors were gradually eliminated in three days by the 3mg/day benztropine dose.

In retrospect, the whole treatment of the manic episode could probably have been improved considerably. Perhaps the mania could have been curtailed completely within a week by a daily dose of 6g TRY and 30mg Tx. Then the Tx should have been eliminated slowly over the next several weeks or so with or without introducing lithium. On the other hand, more was learned from the clumsy procedure that was actually followed. Surely the treatment of mania with the combination of tryptophan and some neuroleptic deserves more clinical study.

STAGE 2: TYROSINE TREATMENT OF DEPRESSION

When it was clear that Susan's mental state had stabilized after the severe stress episode was over on day 56, her Tx dose was gradually reduced and ended (along with benztropine) on day 73. Her lithium treatment was terminated on day 86, and she was placed on a steady TRY maintenance schedule of one 2g TRY dose at bedtime every other day. Of course the single concentrated dose was intended to maximize transfer from the blood–brain barrier.

By day 105, it was clear that Susan had been in a steady state of moderate depression since her stress episode ended on day 56. She was not functional enough to return to a regular program of study at college. She was not interested in taking a job of any kind. She spent most of each day with her mother and evening with both parents. During this two month period, she exhibited the following symptoms:

1. *Anhedonia.* She displayed little interest or excitement about any external events. She seemed neither sad nor glad about anything.

2. *Lack of initiative.* She initiated no projects of her own and had great difficulty getting started on assigned tasks. On the other hand, she readily followed her mother's lead in activities. If anything, she was overly cooperative.

3. *Withdrawn.* She seemed lacking in sensitivity to external stimuli. She often failed to attend to questions, even when repeated several times. Her answers to questions were uninformative and without elaboration. She seldom initiated a conversation.

4. *Timidity.* At one time, she expressed fear of crossing a busy street on her own, even where there was a red light. Evidently she recognized her own slowness to react.

These symptoms are characteristic of a particular type of depression that, as noted in Part I, should perhaps not be regarded as true depression but rather as *psychomotor retardation*. It was noticed that Susan's symptoms are strikingly similar to side effects of the dopamine blocker droperidol in normal individuals (Clark, Geffen, & Geffen, 1986). That suggested that her depression was due to subnormal catecholamine activity as an aftereffect of her earlier thiothixene treatment for mania. Subnormal catecholamine activity can result from reduced transmitter stores, which in turn suggests that the transmitter synthesis pathway is not saturated. Accordingly it should be possible to raise catecholamine stores and reduce depression directly by intake of the catecholamine precursor tyrosine. On the basis of this argument, it was decided to give Susan a two-week tyrosine treatment. The key hypothesis of depleted catecholamine stores received surprising confirmation almost immediately.

Medication and Side Effects

The schedule of treatment is charted in Fig. 7.6. To optimize plasma concentration and consequently transfer through the blood–brain barrier, the tyrosine was administered in a single dose at least one-half hour before breakfast. The plasma concentration reaches a maximum in two hours and remains significantly elevated for roughly eight hours (Glaeser, Melamed, Growden, & Wurtman, 1979). A similar plasma concentration profile applies to tryptophan. Consequently the morning tyrosine dose and evening tryptophan dose will not interfere significantly with one another.

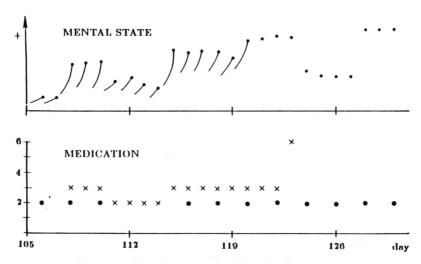

FIG. 7.6. *Chronology of a Tyrosine Episode.* See text for explanation of the mental state scale. Medication key: • = tryptophan (1g units); × = tyrosine (1g units).

The original plan was a daily three gram dose; however, on the third day, Susan finally let it be known that side effects were bothering her. In her visual field, she was experiencing unusual brightness and sharpness of details. She laid in her bed late in the morning examining cracks in the wall she had never noticed before. This result is striking for two reasons. First, normal subjects report no such side effects even from a single dose of 9 grams (Glaeser et al., 1979). Second, normal subjects report those same side effects from the dopamine agonist methylphenidate (Clark, Geffen, & Geffen, 1986), although our observations in section 2 suggest that the side effects are due in part, at least, to noradrenaline agonism (see also Segal, 1985). Anyway this is strong evidence that Susan's catecholamine stores had been depleted.

The side effects disappeared when the dose was decreased to 2g/day, and they did not reappear when the dose was raised back to 3g/day or even increased to 6g the last day of treatment. This suggests that the synthesis pathway had been brought back close to saturation, and the brain brightness computation mechanisms had adjusted to the higher catecholamine levels. As a check to see that the pathway remained saturated, Susan was given a one-time dose of 4g more than a month later on day 145, and no side effects were observed.

Mental State Assessment

No sleep chart (like the one in Fig. 7.4) is included in Fig. 7.6, because, throughout the period in question, Susan's sleep pattern was regular and undisturbed, although long (about 10 hr/day). The mental state chart in Fig. 7.6 was constructed from daily logs of Susan's activities kept by her father. The logs are rich in interesting observations, but the chart is intended only to indicate a general trend in mental functioning. The scale on the chart is ordinal only. It was constructed by comparing daily logs in pairs with respect to exhibited initiative, responsiveness, interest, and pleasure. Days that did not differ by at least one notable event were judged about equal. The tails attached to some of the points serve to indicate an improvement in state through the day. Evenings were always better than mornings, but the difference was more noticeable in the beginning part of the treatment.

The most significant features of the chart are the obvious jumps in mental state. The presence of these jumps was confirmed through independent evaluation by Susan's mother, who was kept blind to the tyrosine treatment until after the fact.

A positive effect was evident from the first day of tyrosine treatment. Particularly noteworthy are the four-day regressions beginning on days 111 and 124 when the doses were reduced. In the latter case, there was a spontaneous recovery without medication. This suggests that an equilibration process was at work, with several days required for the brain to adjust to the new levels of precursor loading. The generally higher level of functioning beginning on day 128 persisted throughout the months thereafter. The tyrosine treatment was terminated after 16 days, because Susan had objected to it in principle from the beginning. Undoubtedly the dose was too low, and the period of treatment was too short to gain its full benefit. Nevertheless the evidence is sufficient to suggest that tyrosine may be useful in treating anhedonic depression (or psychomotor retardation), especially soon after neuroleptic treatment for mania. Extensive clinical trials will be necessary before firm conclusions can be drawn.

Although Susan was functioning fairly well in most respects after the tyrosine treatment, one perplexing symptom remained, a very severe writer's block. Before her episode, Susan had avidly maintained a diary and enjoyed writing poetry. After the neuroleptic treatment, however, all spontaneity was gone, and she could hardly commit a single word to paper even after hours of suggestions and prodding by her parents, despite the fact that she truly wanted to write letters to her boyfriend and make up incomplete writing assignments from school. Her skillful performance in several different kinds of parlor games showed that her intelligence was in no way impaired. Rather she lacked initiative in ideation and action.

Susan denied the existence of any writer's block, insisting that her only problem was a lack of interest that would disappear as soon as she returned to college and her boyfriend. As she had been stable for several months and was functioning reasonably well, her parents relented in her wish to return to college, hoping that she would soon get fully back to normal by natural means. However, that hope was not realized, and Susan flunked her next semester, because she was unable to complete her assignments. Naturally this severely strained the relation with her boyfriend, who was frustrated by his inability to understand her problem and help. In all, her psychomotor retardation persisted for nine months after the neuroleptic treatment was terminated. Evidently it would have been better to intervene with some antidepressant, if not with tyrosine.

STAGE 3: A SECOND LOOK AT MANIA

As a prophylactic against mania, Susan was maintained on 2g TRY every other day for five months after the Tx and lithium were terminated. Encouraged by her boyfriend, Susan discontinued this a month after she returned to college. In the summer, after the semester was over, her depression lifted only to be replaced by a state bordering on hypomania. She lived with her sister Marie during the summer but spent most of her time with her boyfriend, so a continuous record of her behavior is not available. Marie reported that, on two occasions, she observed that Susan was clearly hypomanic, so she gave her 4g TRY, and Susan was back to normal the next day. Friends of Susan reported that they were exhausted by her unrelenting talkativeness late in the summer.

Susan's parents were able to see her for only a couple of weeks before she returned to college for the fall semester. At the time, she exhibited high energy, cheerfulness, and amiability but appeared to be under control, although the confused state of her bedroom suggested that all was not right during the summer. She easily agreed to reinstate her TRY prophylactic schedule and was advised to increase the TRY at the slightest sign of hypomania. Although her parents had not been adequately informed at the time about Susan's problems during the preceding semester and the summer, they were uneasy about her return to college.

As a precondition for her return, Susan's father required that she complete the written assignments for an English course that had been interrupted by her first manic episode. She exceeded this requirement immediately by producing, within a few hours, nearly 30 pages of poetry showing wit, imagination, and a sensitivity to subtle turns of language. The writer's block of some months earlier had been replaced by an extraordinary fluency. It was almost too easy.

The day Susan prepared to leave for college, there appeared the first of several symptoms signaling her impending manic episode six weeks later. She adamantly insisted on taking two huge carloads of "essential" goods to clutter up her dorm rooms. This showed an *impaired ability to make choices,* even easy choices, not just hard ones. The impairment was clearly a month later when she returned home for a weekend with a stack of nearly 20 books she had just checked out of the library. The selection of books was miscellaneous in the extreme, devoted to topics that hardly fell within her more peripheral interests. However, she expressed enthusiasm for every one of them. It was as if she had wandered through the library stacks excited by every book that chanced to fall within her gaze.

Another clear symptom was Susan's *excessive sociability.* Everywhere she went, she addressed perfect strangers without the slightest hesitation, as if they were long standing friends, and there were no restraints on what she might say about her own thoughts and feelings. This behavior endeared her to shy freshmen in her dorm but made her appear peculiar to others. Susan had difficulty getting along with her roommate and sensed that others were treating her as peculiar. Her teachers noted erratic behavior in class. One day she would repeatedly disrupt the class with inappropriate remarks, whereas, on another day, she would dominate class discussion with astute and cogent observations. A crisis emerged when Susan's performance on midterm exams was far below her expectations. She was so distressed that her advisor sent her to the school psychiatrist, who observed that she was hypomanic and suggested that she should be on lithium. Susan was infuriated and frightened by the psychiatrist's remarks. Fortunately she called home and was fetched home immediately.

When Susan returned home that evening still in a high state of distress, a striking feature of her distress was that it would suddenly vanish when conversation was switched to some neutral topic, and it would reappear just as suddenly when the precipitating events were mentioned. This is consistent with the idea of switching between "cognitive channels" with different emotional (DA) gains. Susan was given 3g TRY to calm her down and help her sleep. Less than an hour later, when she was in bed with her concerned parents nearby, her distress was so extreme that she began thrashing about violently, exhibiting the same kind of locomotor spasm that appeared during treatment for her first manic episode. Her parents held her down and consoled her for ten minutes until the attack abated. Only later, after similar incidents, was it realized that the locomotor spasm was probably activated by the TRY dose. Susan was calm the next day and seemed okay the next few days, but it was decided that she should withdraw from school.

The transition to Susan's second manic episode occurred in the evening of the day she was withdrawn from school. It is likely, therefore, that the stress of the withdrawal, including the separation from friends and activities she loved, was a major contributing factor. Another factor was TRY. Susan was given a 3g TRY dose when she was put to bed at 9:00 p.m. At 11:00 p.m., she was discovered outside her bedroom compulsively clipping a hedge in the dark. She insisted she was gardening and nothing could persuade her to stop. Finally her father and grown brother forcibly carried her, kicking and fighting, into the house. Once inside, she scrambled to an empty corner of the living room, grabbing a small chair for protection and crouching defensively with her back to the wall. For the next half hour, surrounded by her parents and brother, she directed at her parents an intense stream of complaints, criticisms, jeers, insults, and invective such as never before had issued from the lips of this gentle young lady. She was finally induced to take another 2g TRY dose in the hope that would help calm her down. It did the opposite. After escaping to her bedroom, where she was left alone for a while, she suddenly dashed out of the house and down the back alley at 1:00 a.m. In her room, she had shredded a favorite coat and several dresses. Her father and brother followed in pursuit and caught up with her within 30 minutes, because she travelled in a predictable direction. She kept them at a distance with belligerent words and gestures. She continued to walk belligerently and aimlessly through the streets of the city for the next four hours, with her brother following for protection. Finally arrangements were made to have her picked up and taken to a psychiatric hospital for treatment with antipsychotic drugs.

Susan's second episode was quite different than the first. The first was predominated by delusions, whereas the second was predominated by an unremitting anger. Evidently the TRY exacerbated the anger, and it may even have triggered the switch to mania. The exacerbation of anger by TRY has been noticed by others (e.g., Yaryura-Tobias & Bhagavan, 1977), although it has not been explained. In accordance with our theory, the likely mechanism is this: Anger is expressed (in part) by a signal from the amygdala to the accumbens. Although TRY administration increases serotonin synthesis, it decreases the firing rate of the raphé dorsalis in proportion to the dose (Trulson & Jacobs, 1976). This disinhibits the DA gain signal from the ventral tegmentum and so potentates the amygdala "anger signal" as well as its transmission through the accumbens. The strong DA gain sustains the anger as well as its behavioral expression, evidently for many hours in Susan's second episode. This is further evidence of the important role for serotonin in the gain control of limbic inputs to the accumbens as well as for a stress-dependence of the gain control mechanism. Thus, we come to a paradoxical conclusion: Although TRY may trigger or exacerbate mania under stressful conditions by reducing serotonin transmission, it may nevertheless contribute to mania control in the long run by increasing serotonin synthesis.

Nevertheless Susan's second episode was handled with thiothixene (Tx) in much the same way as the first episode, and it was decided to put Susan on lithium, because there was some doubt that TRY prophylaxis could work for her. Early in the month, before her episode, Susan took 2g TRY doses on alternate days, but, with no one around to guide her, she failed to realize the need to increase the dose to at least 2g everyday. Furthermore, during the week before her episode, she switched to ½g TRY daily, a dose that is too small to affect her brain serotonin level significantly. Thus, the TRY doses were too low to conclude that TRY cannot effectively protect Susan against mania. The need for a larger dose is also shown in the case reported by Beitman and Dunner (1982), where an increase in the daily TRY dose from 2g to 2.67g was sometimes needed to prevent hypomania.

Susan's recovery from the second manic episode did not go smoothly. A brief chronicle of the difficulties is instructive. Susan's mania was suppressed by the neuroleptic Tx within a few days after its onset (day zero). On day 15, she returned home from the hospital where she was maintained on 30mg Tx/day for the next week. During this week, her mind was clear, but she suffered pronounced *akathisia,* a restless urge to keep moving about that sometimes appears as a side effect of neuroleptic treatment. Standard treatment with benzetropine failed to alleviate the akathisia. The akathisia remained at a moderate level whereas the daily Tx dose was reduced to 15mg on day 22, 10mg on day 28, 5mg on day 31, and zero on day 34. On day 33, Susan had her first sleep without early awakening (before 6:00 a.m.). Her akathisia vanished, and she was mentally clear and calm without irritability. However, this blessed state lasted for only a couple of days. The reduction in Tx had been too soon and/or too fast.

During the next three days, an increasing tendency to cry appeared, and her sleep deteriorated. By day 37, Susan had degenerated into a state of *extreme emotional lability,* bursting into tears frequently over the most trivial thoughts or remarks, dwelling obsessively on the loss of her boyfriend and her school, given to occasional sudden expressions of frustration (but not really anger). This state persisted through a sleepless night into the evening of the next day, when her TRY dose was increased in an attempt to combat it. She had been receiving a steady TRY dose of 3g/day since day 3, although there was no clue that this had any effect on the treatment.

At 8:15 p.m. on day 38, Susan was given 5g TRY to improve sleep and alleviate depression. By 10:00 p.m., she had become extremely disturbed and fearful. A sudden chill kept her shivering for at least one-half hour, although her body was heaped with blankets. During this period, she was convulsed by two locomotor spasms of about ten seconds duration. Her fear and crying had increased by 11:00 p.m., and she said it feels like a manic episode is coming. However, there was no sign of manic impulsivity or hyperactivity. Susan expressed a deep sense of being *alone,* even with the continuous presence of her father. Qualitatively the experience appeared to be similar to the second episode of her sister Marie. As an emergency measure, Susan was given a 2mg dose of the benzodiazapine lorazepam at 11:30 p.m., and she was asleep soon after midnight.

There can be no doubt that the fears, chills, and locomotor spasms were released by the large TRY dose, because they appeared within the two hours required for the TRY to reach its maximum blood concentration. Nevertheless they are not necessarily to be regarded as adverse effects of the TRY. Instead it may be supposed that the TRY unmasked an instability already present in the system. We have already noted that the TRY reduces the firing rate of the raphé nuclei and so reduces the threshold for dopamine gain in the accumbens and striatum. This may have allowed stray dopamine to produce the adverse effects, dopamine left around from the rapid removal of the dopamine blocker Tx within the previous week. At any rate, the correlation between the singular effects of the TRY and the unblocking of dopamine is an important clue. Also it should be noted that the chills and perhaps the fears were probably released by reducing the activity of the raphé medianus (rather than the raphé doralis), because it projects to the hypothalamus where serotonin contributes to the regulation of body temperature.

Despite her frightening experience after the 5g TRY dose, Susan insisted the next day that the TRY gave her a calm feeling. Indeed, after waking at 9:00 a.m., she was tired and weepy until about 2:00 p.m., when the effect of the lorazepam (10-hour half life) wore off. Thereafter she was much better, no more weeping or obsessive talk. That evening she was given 4g TRY without a repeat of the singular adverse effects on the previous night. She slept little that night, although she remained calm and peaceful.

Susan's emotional lability returned the next morning, although she was amiable and happy the next evening. Then it was decided to reinstate 10mg Tx/day and begin treatment with the antidepressant desipramine (brand name norpramin). Again Susan slept little despite 4g TRY.

The next week was miserable for Susan as anticholinergic side effects (such as blurred vision) increased with increasing doses of desipramine until they became intolerable, and the desipramine was discontinued. For the next month (days 47 to 74), Susan was kept on a daily dose of 10mg Tx and 2g TRY, except for four days when the Tx was reduced to 7mg with slightly worse results. Susan felt good for the first week of this period, but thereafter she was clearly depressed, crying frequently (especially in the morning) and making a variety of vague somatic complaints. She was completely dependent on others to plan and initiate her activities for the day. As no progress was being made with this treatment, it was decided to try another antidepressant nortriptyline (brand name pamelor).

The nortriptyline was introduced slowly with a 20mg dose on each of the first three days. On the third day, the Tx was reduced from 10mg to 7mg, and Susan again had locomotor spasms within an hour after taking 2g TRY. Here is additional evidence that the spasms are caused by unblocked dopamine, as the Tx reduction was the only change in medication from the preceding two days. Nevertheless the TRY treatment was discontinued for an indefinite period thereafter to avoid any further interactions of the TRY with other medications.

As the nortriptyline dose was increased to 75mg during the next five days, Susan developed a severe psychosis, which will be instructive to discuss in some detail. For the last two days, she was continually feeling her head between the temples, complaining of pain or pressure there, as if there were a big rock on her head and a big bubble inside her head. Several times each day she complained of a brain hemorrhage, asserting that the bubble had burst so blood and brains were streaming out of her ears and trickling down her cheeks. Each time she was easily persuaded that this was an illusion generated by side effects to her medication. She was very suggestible.

Susan's dreams during the night of the fifth day provided dramatic examples of the integration of somatosensory perceptions into dreams (Hobson, 1988). Suddenly awakening from a vivid nightmare, she exclaimed, "Dad, they're taking me for a CAT scan. The plates in my head are loose!" When told that there are no plates, she felt her head with her hands and said, "Oh, it was a dream!" She awakened from a second nightmare clutching her throat and crying, "I'm swallowing my brain!" Again she readily accepted reassurance to the contrary and returned to bed calmly. The next morning, in clear consciousness while she was attentively watching and evidently comprehending a television movie, she calmly asserted that she could *visually see* her body with bleeding head laid out before her. She insisted that the image was visually real and reported that it vanished when she closed her eyes. That evening she was utterly confused, staring at the television without reacting. Again she complained about her head and swallowing her brains. She asked, "When I go to the bathroom, I lose pieces of myself, don't I?" When told to dress for bed, she started putting her pajama pants over her jeans. The nortriptyline was discontinued that night, and the improvement the next morning was dramatic. The delusions and hallucinations were gone, although some paranoia was evident for the next five days. She repeatedly complained that social workers and the government had her signature and social security number, and they were going to use this to lock her up.

This psychotic episode of Susan's has the earmarks of an amphetamine psychosis (Snyder, 1972) or a bad LSD trip: It involved the following: (a) paranoid ideation, (b) high suggestibility, and (c) somatic hypersensitivity distorted into delusions and hallucinations, although the subject had a clear consciousness and was aware of the unreality of the experience. Theory in Part I suggests that this kind of psychosis is likely to be the result of a disturbance of the serotonergic system. That is consistent with neuropharmacological evidence that nortriptyline facilitates serotonin and noradrenaline transmission by blocking transmitter reuptake with an insignificant effect on dopamine transmission. Here we have the cleanest evidence associating psychosis with serotonin rather than dopamine. However, it also suggests that nortriptyline does something other to the serotonergic system than altering reuptake, that the nortriptyline may in face trigger the same serotonergic mechanism that is involved in amphetamine psychosis (Trulson & Jacobs, 1979c). Indeed it is known that manic-depressives often respond adversely to tricyclic antidepressants. Here we have a clue that may help us find an explanation for that perplexing fact.

After the nortryptyline was discontinued, Susan's daily Tx dose was increased to 30mg. However, many depressive symptoms remained; thus ten days later, a third antidepressant, amoxapine (brand name Asendin), was introduced. The amoxapine was increased gradually over three weeks before the normal therapeutic dose of 150mg/day was reached. During this period, Susan exhibited increasing psychomotor retardation until she had difficulty even with eating and dressing herself. This effect was undoubtedly due to excessive dopamine blocking by the combination of amoxapine and Tx. Amoxapine is unique among antidepressants in its dopamine blocking action. As expected, therefore, Susan's retardation was rapidly reduced by terminating the Tx treatment altogether. Although Susan evidently tolerated the amoxapine better than the other two antidepressants, it too was discontinued a few days later when signs of possible tardive dyskinesia appeared. One evening, about an hour after her amoxapine dose, Susan was observed to pucker her lips involuntarily. The amoxapine was discontinued the next day, but two days later Susan had several spells when, in the midst of a normal conversation, she lost control of her articulators for a few seconds and emitted completely garbled phrases. When asked, at the time, to stick out her tongue and hold it steady, she was unable to comply, although she could do it a couple of days later. Tardive dyskinesia rarely strikes anyone as young as Susan, but the symptoms just described suggest some risk in continuing Susan on amoxapine.

Fortunately this chapter in Susan's saga was brought to a quick and happy end after three miserable months seeking help from antidepressants. Considering the success of Van Praag (1981, 1983) in treating severe depression, it was decided to repeat the monoamine precursor treatment employed after Susan's first manic episode. The treatment began after a week on lithium alone to clear out residual effects of the amoxapine. The daily does consisted of 4g tyrosine in the morning and 3g tryptophan before bed. The tyrosine was administered in two 2g doses separated by two to three hours to prolong the peak in tyrosine blood concentration. Within three days, there was obvious improvement in Susan's ability to function, and the rapid improvement continued for two weeks until Susan seemed perfectly normal and able to resume normal activities of work and school. The treatment was terminated after a month, as there appeared to be no further gains to be made. Besides, the most likely cause of Susan's depressed state was a drug-induced depletion of her catecholamine stores, which suggests that only limited precursor treatment is needed to replenish the stores.

The results of this monoamine precursor treatment were striking enough to be worth describing in more detail. During the week before the treatment began, the following observations were made about Susan. First, she exhibited symptoms of psychomotor retardation very similar to those described earlier in connection with her first treatment. Theory suggests that this indicates subnormal dopamine transmission, possibly due to depleted dopamine stores. Second, Susan exhibited the depressive symptoms of frequent crying and obsessive preoccupation with negative experiences in the past. Third, she exhibited cognitive deficits in processing complex spatial and temporal patterns. Thus, she had difficulty completing household tasks or following instructions, because she evidently lost track of what she was doing. Similarly her reading was impaired. She could read aloud with expression that showed that she understood what she was reading, but she could recall hardly anything that she had read a few minutes earlier. Theory suggests that this is due to a noradrenaline deficit in modulating memory consolidation. All of these symptoms disappeared within two weeks of precursor treatment, and Susan was once again engaged in avid reading on her own. Incidentally a single 4g dose of tyrosine on the first day of treatment did not elicit the psychophysical brightening and sharpening effects reported in Susan's first treatment.

In retrospect, it appears that the monoamine precursor treatment might have been safely introduced on day 33, when the Tx treatment was terminated, so that Susan (and her family) might have been spared three months of misery. Indeed it might be that most cases of depression occurring soon after acute treatment with neuroleptics could be eliminated, if it were standard practice to provide a two-week monoamine precursor treatment immediately after neuroleptic treatment is terminated. Certainly there is ample reason to investigate this issue clinically.

CONCLUSIONS

This article has proposed a new theoretical framework for biological psychiatry founded on principles of neural network theory. In the present, initial stage of development, the theory must be regarded as speculative in many respects, so its implications should be regarded as hypotheses to be evaluated empirically. The theory needs to be expanded, refined, revised, and tested before it can provide a reliable guide to clinical practice. However, it is already sufficiently developed to produce provocative questions for theoretical and empirical research. A good theory is as valuable for the questions it raises as for the answers it supplies.

In outline, the theoretical framework is formed by the following general hypotheses, all of which have some empirical support:

1. All psychological functions, including perception, emotion, cognition, learning, memory, and motor control, are modes of neural activity pattern processing.

2. Pattern processing in the various brain modules is coordinated by a central control system. The control variables include the monoamines (dopamine, noradrendaline and serotonin), probably acetylcholine, and possibly others. These variables modulate pattern formation, stabilization, mixing, matching, and switching in each module.

3. Manic-depressive illness and related mental disorders are malfunctions of the modulatory mechanisms for pattern processing. The particular symptoms of a disorder depend on the nature of the malfunction and the specific module(s) in which it occurs.

Schizophrenia can also be incorporated in this general framework, although it may involve more than disorders of modulatory mechanisms.

Besides its general framework, the theory includes a host of more-or-less empirically grounded assumptions about neuroanatomy, modulatory mechanisms, the functions of various brain modules, and so on. The assumptions already suffice for nontrivial implications about the etiology and treatment of manic-depressive illness, but more specificity is needed. Perhaps the greatest important need is for specific models of pattern matching and switching mechanisms that are consistent with known neurophysiological facts. That is an essential prerequisite to the modeling of drug actions on the modulatory mechanisms as well as for extending the qualitative theory to quantitative models.

As to clinical applications of the theory, ideally they should proceed something like this: The theory determines the significance of the various symptoms. Thus, symptoms such as hyperactivity, excessive sociability, somatic delusions, paranoia, or compulsions are each attributed to some specific type of modulatory malfunction in one or more specific modules that, once identified, can be targeted for appropriate, corrective drug treatment. Being neurally based, the theory will eventually interpret the results of more refined diagnostic tools such as tomography, evoked potentials, and metabolic measures. In the meantime, we have much to learn.

ACKNOWLEDGMENTS

A first draft of this article was written while the author was a Visiting Scholar at the Center for Adaptive Systems, Boston University. The congenial atmosphere and intellectual interplay at the Center contributed significantly to the development and critique of ideas in the article. Thanks especially to Carol Yanakakis and Denise Jackson for their invaluable assistance in preparing the manuscript.

REFERENCES

Alexander, G. E., De Long, M. R., & Strick, P. L. (1986). Parallel organization of functionally segregated circuits linking basal ganglia and cortex. *Annual Review of Neuroscience, 9,* 357–381.

Anden, N. E. (1977). Functional effects of local injections of dopamine and analogs into the neostriatum and nucleus accumbens. *Advances in Biochemical Psychopharmacology, 16,* 385–339.

Antelman, S. M., & Chiodo, L. A. (1984). Stress: Its effect on interactions among biogenic amines and role in the induction and treatment of disease. In L. L. Iversen, S. D. Iversen, & S. H. Snyder (Eds.). *Drugs, neurotransmitters and behavior (handbook of psychopharmacology, Vol. 18)* (pp. 279–341). New York: Plenum.

Anziman, H., & Zacharko, R. M. (1982). Depression: The predisposing influence of stress. *Behavioral and Brain Sciences, 5,* 89–137. *Behavioral and Brain Sciences* (1985) 8: 368–378.

Aston-Jones, G., Foote, S. L., & Bloom, F. F. (1984). Anatomy and physiology of locus coeruleus neurons: Functional implications. In M. Zeigler & C. Lake (Eds.), *Norepinephrine* (pp. 92–116). Baltimore/London: Williams & Wilkes.

Banquet, J. P., & Grossberg, S. (1987). Probing cognitive processes through the structure of event-related potentials during learning: an experimental and theoretical analysis. *Applies Optics, 23,* 4931–4946.

Baxter, L. R., Phelps, M. E., Mazziota, J. C., Guze, B. H., Schwartz, J. M., & Selen, C. E. (1987). Local cerebral glucose metabolic rates in obsessive-compulsive disorder. *Archives of General Psychiatry, 44,* 211–218.

Beitman, B. D., & Dunner, D. L. (1982). L–tryptophan in the maintenance treatment of bipolar II manic-depressive illness. *American Journal of Psychiatry, 139,* 1498–1499.

Bullock, D., & Grossberg, S. (1988). The VITE model: A neural command circuit for generating arm and articulator trajectories. In J. A. S. Kelso, A. J. Mandel, & M. F. Shlesinger (Eds.), *Dynamic patterns in complex systems* (pp. 305–326). Singapore: World Scientific.

Butler, I. J., Koslow, S. H., Seifert, W. E., Caprioli, R. M., & Singer, H. (1979). Biogenic amine metabolism in Tourette Syndrome. *Annuals of Neurology, 6,* 37–39.

Chouinard, G., Young, S. N., & Annable, L. (1985). A controlled clinical trial of L–tryptophan in acute mania. *Biological Psychiatry, 20,* 546–557.

Clark, C. R., Geffen, L. B., & Geffen, G. M. (1984). Monoamines in the control of state dependent cortical functions: Evidence from studies of selective attention in animals and humans. In R. Badler (Ed.), *Modulation of sensorimotor activity in behavioral states* (pp. 487–502). New York: Alan R. Liss.

Clark, C. R., Geffen, G. M., & Geffen, W. B. (1986). Role of monoamine pathways in control of attention: Effects of droperidol and methylphenidate in normal adults. *Psychopharmacology, 90,* 28–34.

Cohen, D. J., Detlor, J., Young, J. G., Shaywitz, B. A. (1980). Clonidine ameliorates Gilles de la Tourette Syndrome. *Archives of General Psychiatry, 37,* 1350–1357.

Cohen, D. J., Shawitz, B. A., Caparlo, B., Young, J. G., & Bowers, M. B. (1978). Chronic multiple tics of Gilles de la Tourette's Disease. *Archives of General Psychiatry, 35,* 245–250.

Cummings, J. L., & Frankel, M. (1985). Gilles de la Tourette Syndrome and the neurological basis of obsessions and compulsions. *Biological Psychiatry, 20,* 1117–1126.

DeLong, M. R., Alexander, G. R., Mitchell, S. J., & Richardson, R. T. (1986). The contribution of basal ganglia to limb control. In H. J. Freund, B. Cohen, & J. Noth (Eds.), *Progress in brain research* (Vol. 64, pp. 161–174). Elsevier Science.

Dray, A. (1982). Serotonin in the Basal Ganglia. In Osborne (Ed.), *Biology of serotonergic transmission* (pp. 335–361). New York: Wiley.

Ermentrout, G. B., & Cowan, J. D. (1979). *Biological Cybernetics, 34,* 137–150.

Fernstrom, J. D. (1983). Role of precursor availability in control of monoamine biosynthesis in brain. *Physiological Review, 63,* 484–546.

Fibiger, H. C., & Philips, A. C. (1987). Role of catecholamine transmitters in brain reward systems: implications for the neurobiology of affect. In J. Engel & Oreland (Eds.), *Brain Reward Systems and Abuse* (pp. 61–74). New York: Raven Press.

Flament, M. F., Rapaport, J. L., Murphy, D. L., Berg, C. J., & Lake, C. R. (1987). Biochemical changes during clomipramine treatment of childhood obsessive-compulsive disorder. *Archives of General Psychiatry, 44,* 219–225.

Foote, S. L., & Morrison, J. H. (1987). Extrathalamic cortical modulation. *Annual Review of Neuroscience, 10,* 67–95.

Frith, C. D., Dowdy, J., Ferrier, I. N., & Crow, T. J. (1985). Selective impairment of paired associate learning after administration of a centrally-acting adrenergic agonist (clonidine). *Psychopharmacology, 87,* 490–493.

Glaeser, B. S., Melamed, E., Growden, J. H., & Wurtman, R. J. (1979). Elevation of plasma tyrosine after a single oral dose of L–tyrosine. *Life Sciences, 25,* 265–272.

Gold, P. W., Goodwin, F. K., & Chrousos, G. P. (1984). Clinical and Biochemical Manifestation of Depression. *New England Journal of Medicine, 319,* 347–353, 413–420.

Goodwin, F. K., & Jamison, K. R. (1984). The natural course of manic-depressive illness. In R. M. Post, J. C. Ballenger (Eds.), *Neurobiology of mood disorders* (pp. 20–37). London: Williams & Wilkins.

Grahame-Smith, D. G., & Green, A. R. (1974). The role of brain 5–hydroxytryptamine in the hyperactivity produced in rats by lithium and monoamine oxidase inhibition. *British Journal of Pharmacology, 52,* 19–26.

Green, T. K., & Harvey, J. A. (1974). Enhancement of amphetamine action after interruption of ascending serotonergic pathways. *Journal of Pharmacology and Experimental Therapeutics, 190,* 109–117.

Grossberg, S. (1980). How does the brain construct a cognitive code? *Psychological Review, 89,* 1–51.

Grossberg, S. (1982). *Studies of mind and brain.* Dordrecht: Reidel.

Grossberg, S. (1984a). Some normal and abnormal syndromes due to transmitter gating of opponent processing. *Biological Psychiatry, 19,* 1075–1118.

Grossberg, S. (1984b). Some psychological and pharmacological correlates of a developmental, cognitive and motivational theory. In R. Karrer, J. Cohen, & Tueting (Eds.), *Brain and information: Event related potentials.* New York: NY Academy of Science.

Grossberg, S. (1987). Competitive learning: from interactive activation to adaptive resonance. *Cognitive Science, 11,* 23–63.

Groves, P. M. (1983). A theory of the functional organization of the neostriatum and the neostriatal control of voluntary movement. *Brain Research Review, 5,* 109–132.

Heninger, G. R., Charney, D. S., & Sternberg, D. E. (1984). Serotonergic function in depression. *Archives of General Psychiatry, 41,* 398–402.

Hestenes, D. (1987). How the brain works: The next great scientific revolution. In G. R. Smith & G. J. Erickson (Eds.), *Maximum entropy and Bayesian spectral analysis and estimation problems* (pp. 173–205). Dordrecht: Reidel.

Hobson, A. (1988). *The dreaming brain.* New York: Basic.

Hollister, M. E. (1978). Psychotomimetic drugs in man. In L. L. Iversen, S. D. Iversen, & S. H. Snyder, *Handbook of psychopharmacology* (Vol. 11, pp. 389–424). New York: Plenum.

Horak, F. B., & Anderson, M. E. (1984). Influence of globus pallidus on arm movements in monkeys, II. Effects of stimulation. *Journal of Neurophysiology, 52,* 305–322.

Iversen, S. D. (1981). *Behavioral Pharmacology* (2nd ed.). New York: Oxford University Press.

Iversen, S. D. (1984). Cortical monoamines and behavior. In L. Descarries, T. R. Reader, & H. H. Jasper (Eds.), *Monoamine innervation of cerebral cortex* (pp. 321–349). New York: Alan R. Liss.

Jacobs, B. L. (Ed.). (1984). *Hallucinations: Neurochemical behavioral and clinical perspectives.* New York: Raven Press.

Jacobs, B. L. (1985). Overview of the activity of brain monoaminergic neurons across the sleep–wake cycle. In Wauquier (Ed.), *Sleep: Neurotransmitters and neuromodulators* (pp. 1–12). New York: Raven Press.

Jacobs, B. L., Heym, J., & Steinfels, G. F. (1986). Physiological and behavioral analysis of Raphé unit activity. In L. L. Iversen, S. D. Iversen, & S. H. Snyder (Eds.), *Drugs, neurotransmitters and behavior* (pp. 343–391). New York: Plenum.

Jacobs, B. L., & Trulson, M. E. (1981). The role of serotonin in the action of hallucinogenic drugs. In B. L. Jacobs & Gelperin (Eds.), *Serotonin neurotransmission and behavior* (pp. 366–400). Cambridge, MA: MIT Press.

Janowsky, D. S., El-Yousef, M. K., Davis, J. M., & Sederke, H. J. (1970). Antagonistic effects of physostigmine and methylphenidate in man. *American Journal of Psychiatry, 130,* 1370–1376.

Kasamatsu, T., Itakura, T., Jonnson, G., Heggelund, P., Pettigrew, J. D., Nakai, K., Kazushiga, W., Kupperman, B. D., & Ary, M. (1984). Neuronal plasticity in cat visual cortex: A proposed role for the central noradrenaline system. In L. Descarries, T. A. Reader, & H. H. Jaspers (Eds.), *Monoamine innervation of cerebral cortex* (pp. 301–319). New York: Alan R. Liss.

Kety, S. S. (1971). Brain amines and affective disorders. In Ito & McIsaac (Eds.), *Brain chemistry and mental disease* (pp. 237–263). New York: Plenum.

Koella, W. P. (1982). A modern neurobiological concept of vigilance. *Experientia, 38,* 1426–1437.

Koella, W. P. (1984). The organization and regulation of sleep. *Experientia, 40,* 309–408.

Lindvall, O., & Björklund. (1984). General organization of cortical monoamine systems. In L. Descarries, T. R. Reader, & H. H. Jasper (Eds.), *Monoamine innervation of cerebral cortex* (pp. 9–40). New York: Alan R. Liss.

Mabry, P. D., & Cambell, B. A. (1973). Serotonergic inhibition of catecholamine-induced behavioral arousal. *Brain Research, 49,* 381–391.

McEntee, W. J., & Mair, R. G. (1984). Some behavioral consequences of neurochemical deficits in Korsakoff psychosis. In L. R. Squire & Butlers (Eds.), *Neuropsychology of memory* (pp. 224–235). New York: Guilford Press.

Mendels, R., & Frazer, A. (1974). Brain biogenic amine depletion and mood. *Archives of General Psychiatry, 30,* 447–451.

Moeller, S., Kirk, L., & Flemming, K. (1976). Plasma amino acids as an index for subgroups in manic-depressive psychosis: Correlation to effect of tryptophan. *Psychopharmacology, 49,* 205–213.

Mogenson, G. J. (1984). Limbic-motor integration with emphasis on initiation of exploratory and goal-directed locomotion. In L. Descarries, T. R. Reader, & H. H. Jasper (Eds.), *Monoamine innervation of cerebral cortex* (pp. 121–137). New York: Alan R. Liss.

Mountcastle, V. B. (1978). An organizing principle for cerebral functions: The unit module and the distributed system. In G. M. Edelman & V. B. Mountcastle (Eds.), *The mindful brain*. Cambridge, MA: MIT Press.

Peroutka, S. J. (1988). 5–hydroxytryptamine receptor subtypes. *Annual Review of Neuroscience, 11*, 45–60.

Prange, W., Jr., Wilson, I., Lynn, C., Alltop, L., & Strikeleather, R. (1974). L–tryptophan in mania: contribution to a permissive hypothesis of effective disorders. *Archives of General Psychiatry, 30*, 56–62.

Rasmussen, S. A. (1984). Lithium and tryptophan augmentation in clomipramine-resistant obsessive-compulsive disorder. *American Journal of Psychiatry, 141*, 1283–1285.

Robins, L. N., Helzer, J. E., Weissmann, M. M., Orvaschel, H., Gruenberg, E., Burke, J. D., & Regier, D. A. (1984). Lifetime prevalence of specific psychiatric disorders in three sites. *Archives of General Psychiatry, 41*, 949–958.

Salzman, L., & Thaler, F. H., (1981). Obsessive-compulsive disorder: a preview of the literature. *American Journal of Psychiatry, 138*, 286–296.

Segal, M. (1985). Mechanisms of action of noradrenalin in the brain. In B. E. Will, P. Schmitt, & J. C. Dalrymple-Alford (Eds.), *Brain plasticity, learning and memory* (pp. 235–239). New York: Plenum.

Snyder, S. H. (1972). Catecholamines in the brain as mediators of amphetamine psychosis. *Archives of General Psychiatry, 27*, 169–179.

Soubrié, P. (1986). Reconciling the role of central serotonin neurons in human and animal behavior. *Behavioral and Brain Science, 9*, 319–364.

Strange, P. G. (1988). The structure and mechanism of neurotransmitter receptors. *Biochemical Journal, 249*, 309–318.

Swerdlow, N. R., & Koob, G. F. (1987). Dopamine, schizophrenia, mania and depression. *Behavioral and Brain Science, 10*, 197–245.

Taylor, J. R., & Robbins, T. W. (1984). Enhanced behavioral control by conditioned reinforcers following microinjections of d–amphetamine into the nucleus accumbens. *Psychopharmacology, 84*, 405–412.

Trulson, M. E., & Jacobs, B. L. (1976). Dose-response relationships between systemically administered L–tryptophan and the Raphé unit activity in the rat. *Neuropharmacology, 15*, 339–344.

Trulson, M. E., & Jacobs, B. L. (1979a). Raphé unit activity in freely moving cats: Correlation with level of behavioral arousal. *Brain Research, 163*, 135–150.

Trulson, M. E., & Jacobs, B. L. (1979b). Long term amphetamine treatment decreases brain serotonin metabolism: Implications for theories of schizophrenia. *Science, 21*, 1295–1297.

Trulson, M. E., & Jacobs, B. L. (1979c). Chronic amphetamine administration to cats: Behavioral and neurochemical evidence for decreased serotonergic function. *Journal of Pharmacology and Experimental Therapeutics, 211*, 375–384.

Van Praag, H. M. (1981). Management of depression with serotonin precursors. *Biological Psychiatry, 16*, 291–310.

Van Praag, H. M. (1983). In search of the mode of action of antidepressants, 5–HTP/tyrosine mixtures in depressions. *Neuropharmacology, 22*, 433–440.

Van Praag, H. M. (1986). Monoamine precursors in the treatment of psychiatric disorders. In R. J. Wurtman & J. J. Wurtman (Eds.), *Nutrition and the brain* (Vol. 7, pp. 89–138). New York: Raven Press.

Van Praag, H. M. (1988). Commentary. *Integrative Psychiatry, 5*, 246–248.

Warburton, D. M. (1987). Drugs and the processing of information. In S. M. Stahl, S. D. Iversen, & E. C. Goodman (Eds.), *Cognitive neurochemistry* (pp. 111–134). New York: Oxford University Press.

Weiner, W. J., Goetz, C., Westheimer, R., & Klawans, H. L., Jr. (1973). Serotonergic and anti-serotonergic influences on amphetamine-induced stereotyped behavior. *Journal of Neurological Sciences, 20,* 373–379.

Willner, P. (1983). Dopamine and depression: A review of recent evidence. *Brain Research Reviews, 6,* 211–224.

Wise, R. A. (1982). Neuroleptics and operant behavior: The anhedonia hypothesis. *Behavioral and Brain Sciences, 5,* 39–87.

Wurtman, R. J. (1988). Nutrients affecting brain composition and behavior. *Integrative Psychiatry, 5,* 226–257.

Yaryura-Tobias, J. A., & Bhagavan, H. N. (1977). L–tryptophan in obsessive-compulsive disorders. *American Journal of Psychiatry, 134,* 1298–1299.

Young, S. N. (1986). The clinical pharmacology of tryptophan. In R. J. Wurtman & J. J. Wurtman (Eds.), *Nutrition and the brain* (Vol. 7, pp. 79–87). New York: Raven Press.

Zohar, J., Insel, T. R., Zohar-Kodouch, R. C., Hill, J. L., & Murphy, D. L. (1988). Serotonergic responsivity in obsessive-compulsive disorder. *Archives of General Psychiatry, 45,* 167–172.

Learned Helplessness, Memory, and the Dynamics of Hope

Samuel J. Leven
Radford University and For a New Social Science

A neural network model describing stereotyped depressive behavior is presented. Based on animal and human research, the model suggests a mechanism for engendering depressive behavior that is *tripartite:* such behavior can be caused by cognitive deficits, state-dependent memory episodes, or affective process. The model belongs broadly to the Grossberg paradigm and follows a suggestive model in Leven (1987, 1988).

Starting from Grossberg (e.g., 1987), Levine (1986), and Leven (1987, 1988), a network model of learned helplessness (Seligman, 1975), based on viscerally tuned (Aggleton & Mishkin, 1986), affectively tuned (Lang, 1988; Zajonc, 1980), and semantic (Schank, 1982) memory is described. Monoamine (VanPraag, 1986), peptide-opioid (Roberts, Polak, & Crow, 1984), and GABAergic (Petty, 1986; Scatton et al., 1986) messengers play critical roles in information storage, retrieval, and processing.

The approach is couched in terms of a control theory (Hyland, 1987), and suggests the utility of network representations of stereotypical behaviors. It seeks to extend current "wiring models," beginning to describe system-wide and local brain activity not of solely electrical origin (Eccles, 1986; Fuxe et al., 1988).

INTRODUCTION: HELPLESSNESS
AND ITS DISCONTENTS

The problem is clearly one of triadic . . . relations . . . and is almost . . . unspecifiable in finite and unambiguous terms without the proper calculus . . . We have, at present, no theory to account for those abductions which have permitted our evolution, ensured our ontogenesis, and preserved our lives. The question remains: What's in the brain that ink may character? (McCulloch, 1965, p. 397)

Three broad theories of the genesis and extinction of "learned helplessness" have duelled in the psychological and psychophysiological literature. Each proclaims and integrated view and each suggests, politely, that the other approaches do not meet the data squarely.[1] I shall suggest that not only are the three "helplessnesses" mutually *supportive,* but they can be instrumental in understanding the roles of the new psychopharmacology and new neural network approaches to gross human behaviors.

The persistent suggestion of a *trilogy* of brain function and human faculties (Hilgard, 1980; Levine, 1986), which runs from Bruner (1984) to MacLean (1970) and from Lang (1988) to Arnold (1984), will play a critical role in this new view (see Fig. 8.1). In taking *learned helplessness* (Seligman, 1975) as a case study, the proposed method may demonstrate that many of the gross behaviors for which we have sought single explanations require an *integrated* approach.

Further, this demonstration will suggest that the interaction of brain regions joins physiological and affective states to cognitions. These interactions produce information states (Marr, 1982) that get stored; they lead to memory.

Memory, it will be suggested, represents a match of cues; some matches represent conditioning (Tulving's *procedural memory*), some context or emotion (*episodic* memory), and some logical organization (*semantic* memory). We shall follow Mishkin, Malamut, and Bachevalier (1984) and Arnold (1984) in arguing that each type of memory represents neural architectures. However, all of the electrical network is mediated and paralleled by a *chemoarchitecture* that shares in the representational process (Fuxe et al., 1988; Changeux, 1986) and a *paracrine* chemical remote-signaling process from the periphery (Bergland, 1985).

This work suggests that the only effective vehicle for coping with such complex, dynamical processes, in describing helplessness or any other phenomenon, is neural network technology (see the chapters in this volume by Levine, Leven, and Prueitt; Grossberg, Levine, and Schmajuk; and Ricart). Further, helplessness may be seen more clearly in light of the three architectures and signaling processes, and in light of an effective way of examining one of them in detail.

McCulloch (1965) framed the response of the last generation of neural network theorists to most chemical mediation of synaptic response when he spoke of obvious neurochemical effects on brain nets as *gremlins* that " . . . defy dimensional analysis. Energy, time, and length are not their measure" (p. 374).

---

[1]Note the caveats in Weiss and Simson (1986) and Minor, Pelleymounter, and Maier (1988).

The task the group led by Grossberg and Levine undertake is to quantify chemical gremlins.

Of Wires, Chemicals, and Helplessness

The problem of understanding the interaction of transmitters, modulators, and hormones in a largely "wired" environment requires us to employ modeling tools. As Halbreich (1987) suggested, the interaction of any class of neurochemical and neuroelectrical process "cannot be isolated from other biological and psychosocial parameters, and they have to be studied and viewed in the larger perspective of the multidimensional integrative activity which regulates mood and behavioral processes" (p. 4).

In other words, the neural *system* involves homeostatic, self-adjusting, and plastic processes. Their complexity and interdependence is such that the *integrative activity* involved in the generation of human behavior requires extensive models (Lynch & Baudry, 1988). In fact, Gilbert's (1984) suggestion that three apparently competing theories—stress-based, affect-based, and appraisal-based—may be *complementary* will be supported.

I shall argue, as Black et al. did, that the level of neurotransmitter plays a critical role in the construction of memory processes. These processes will be tied to known producers of the various modulators and suggest that environment, affect, and expectations play critical roles in the representation of information in the brain. In particular, we shall find that stress and frustration are central in the production of some of these neurochemicals—and that success in aggressive settings performs a similar function.

Next we consider the finding that learned helplessness, in animal experimentation and social settings, induces classic depressive symptomatology. In particular, we shall tie these results to transmitter outcomes.

A plausible sequence of behavior and response will be presented that describes a dynamical process of expectation, action, outcome, appraisal, and physiological result. This "loop," we shall find, can be entered at any point (Levine et al., Chapter 9 of this volume; Hyland, 1987; see Fig. 8.1).

A network will be constructed to demonstrate the plausibility of these findings in one case—and to demonstrate further possibilities for the employ of neuropharmacological data in neural modeling. Here the work will follow Grossberg (1980, 1988) and Leven (1987, 1988). The results suggest practical extension of our own work—and seek to stimulate similar research that seeks to marry models with data, to *improve the question-asking process.*

Finally, work by Pribram (in press), Gray (1982), and Gilbert (1984) will lead to the suggestion that there is a potential for reversing helplessness. Seligman's (1975) and Maier, Sherman, Lewis, Terman, and Liebeskind's (1983) accounts of this "emergence" process will serve as guides.

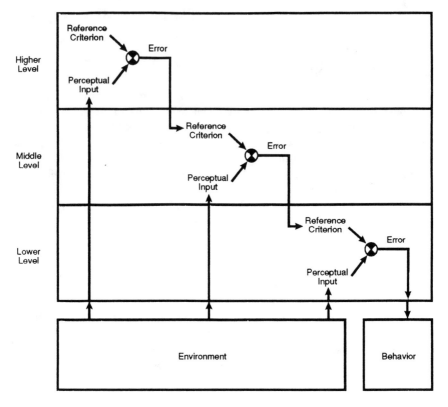

FIG. 8.1. A "control theory" model of behavior. (Reprinted from Hyland, 1987, with permission of the Psychonomic Society)

THE CONSTRUCTION OF MEMORY
—A MODERN PERSPECTIVE

A useful model of learned helplessness requires an effective understanding of brain process to meet Halbreich's plaint. A revised analytical engine with which to view neural behavior is required; it will be based on the presentation of Changeux (1986). Neurochemical "messengers" will be described and their characteristics described generally. Then known data about brain region performance in helplessness will be compared. Finally, as suggested by Hestenes (Chapter 7 of this volume), a match will be sought to existing neural network models. As Changeux (1986) noted:

A straightforward consequence of the coexistence of multiple messengers in a given neuron is an increase of its abilities to communicate with other cells and . . . itself. (A) large repertoire of chemical species multiples its coding facilities. (p. 384)

Further, he noted, coreleased chemical signals provide *two distinct modes* of communication. The *synaptic* mode involves concentrated, fast-acting transmitters (e.g., GABA and ACTH) that have very short delay (0.3 msec at the synapse) and quick reversibility. The *endocrine* mode described chemical action-at-a-distance, requiring transport times between emission and target as long as several minutes and involving low concentrations of modulators (peptide hormones). These communications take place both *among* and *within* neurons. Further, as Iversen (1986) pointed out, some compounds may play *multiple roles,* doubling as fast-acting local signalers and slow-acting messengers-at-a-distance. We shall find this "mixed function" is critical to the model.

One can distinguish among functional and topological relationships played by messengers. *Divergent and independent* contact occurs when distant endocrine mode transmission results in a widely diffused signal reaching apparently unrelated receptors, as in "stress response" adrenal transmissions (Swanson, 1986). Local contacts can involve *convergent and interacting* paths in which many infrasynaptic (*homosynaptic*) or intersynaptic (*heterosynaptic*) signals interact with other chemical messengers in a "soup" (Iversen, 1986; see Figure 8.2).

Some of these coreleased signals play a role *presynaptically,* acting as auto-inhibitors (receptor self-regulators) and cross-inhibitors (neighbor regulators). A modulating role involves the chemical signal as *degradative enzyme,* reducing the rate of weakening of another signal. Another *postsynaptic* role involves "receptor–receptor interactions"—here receptor signals cooperate or compete (mutually inhibit each other).

Beyond these chemical signals, recall the role of *electrical coupling.* Changes in electric potential may regulate receptor properties, intraneuronal environment (likelihood of release of chemical signal), and regulating channel opening through electrical field effects.

From a computational viewpoint, the many different signals present in the neural environment offer the opportunity for many more *neuronal states* than even the most progressive current network models (e.g., Grossberg & Kuperstein, 1989) allow. Each receptor can be viewed as representing an analog information state, as can electrical channel-opening and -closing, and local homosynaptic and heterosynaptic signal levels (see Fig. 8.3). The acknowledged inclusion of electric field effects even gives rise to the possibility that group signaling could produce broader electrical information states (Pribram, in press); this lies beyond the scope of this chapter.

A generalized model of neuronal action can be presented. Multiple traditional "neurotransmitter" sources (e.g., producers of catecholamines or GABA) coexist with more recently discovered "neuromodulators" (e.g., hormones or peptides). Their release is mediated by gross numbers of receptors, current receptor

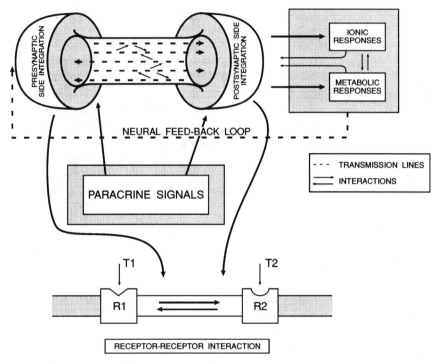

FIG. 8.2.   The complexity of neuronal signalling. (Reprinted from Fuxe
et al., 1988, with permission of Springer-Verlag)

states, local chemical signal levels, amounts of available messenger-at-a-distance, and electrical field levels. Of course, these differ by brain region, external stimuli, and quality of self-regulation (Changeux, 1986; Shepherd, 1988).

Why is such detail necessary for description of as gross behavior as learned helplessness?

We shall argue below that the different representational states embodied in memory (Arnold, 1984) and behavior (Pribram, in press) are mediated by divergent processes (see Leven, 1988). Whereas neural net researchers have begun to model electrical information storage and transmission effectively (e.g., Grossberg, 1980; Kohonen, 1988), comparable analyses of neuromodulator-based representation are in their infancy (Gazzaniga, 1988), as Ricart (Chapter 5 of this volume) notes also. Yet the evidence is becoming overwhelming that, as Black et al. (1988) wrote:

> molecular mechanisms . . . mediate the long-term storage of functionally important neural information in response to external stimuli. Depolarization induced by presynaptic signals regulates the steady-state levels of postsynaptic transmitter mRNA, probably by altering gene readout. . . . Information about the external

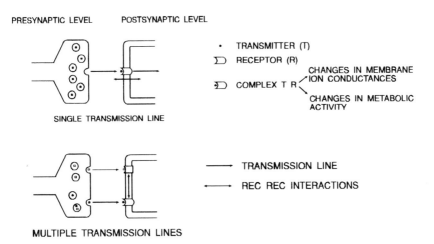

PRESYNAPTIC LEVEL   POSTSYNAPTIC LEVEL

•   TRANSMITTER (T)

RECEPTOR (R)

COMPLEX T R
- CHANGES IN MEMBRANE ION CONDUCTANCES
- CHANGES IN METABOLIC ACTIVITY

SINGLE TRANSMISSION LINE

———→ TRANSMISSION LINE

←——→ REC REC INTERACTIONS

MULTIPLE TRANSMISSION LINES

CHEMICAL TRANSMISSION AT LOCAL CIRCUIT LEVEL

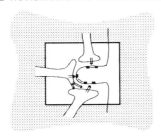

MULTIPLE TRANSMISSION LINES (⇒) WITH A LOCAL CIRCUIT MICROENVIRONMENT (☐) OF ELECTRONIC AND BIOCHEMICAL INTERACTIONS

FIG. 8.3. A model of basic neuron function. (Reprinted from Fuxe et al., 1988, with permission of Springer-Verlag)

world is thereby stored through the very mechanism that serves neuronal intercommunication. (p. 13)

Such a mode of information storage could explain findings that permanent learning takes place in the CNS, outside the blood-brain barrier (Martinez, 1986). It may even be supportive of the much richer view of nervous system performance advocated by Pribram (in press).

This chapter will confine itself below to advancing representational models toward inclusion of biochemical storage and retrieval media. It is beyond its scope to explore "dendritic processing" and "holonomic memory" models (but see Pribram, in press, and Rall & Segev, 1988). Further, one should not presume to model mRNA transcription and protein production processes themselves.

Although both of these are beyond this current writ, they remain central issues in any serious revision of neural network theory.

Preliminaries: Toward a Realistic Classic Transmitter Model

Carpenter and Grossberg (1989) sought to include neurochemical information processing in network modeling (vide Grossberg, 1980). This progressive work embraces much that was understood about neurotransmitters in the last generation. Following Dale's principle (Eccles, 1986), the Carpenter-Grossberg view allows for a single transmitter, a single vesicle (storing and distributing transmitter), and a single receptor. As has been discussed above, the current state of knowledge about chemical messenger processes is substantially different—in ir implications for neural network models profound (see Fig. 8.4).[2]

Compare the current understanding of neural representation processes with the Carpenter-Grossberg improvement on traditional network theory. Their adaptive resonance extension applies a Dale-style neuron to search processes. They offer three hypotheses tied to a mathematical model of traditional neurotransmission (Carpenter & Grossberg, 1989):

> *ART SEARCH HYPOTHESIS 1:* Intracellular transmitter u_{ij} is released at a rate jointly proportional to the presynaptic signal S_i and a function of the postsynaptic activity x_j . . .
>
> *ART SEARCH HYPOTHESIS 2:* The nonspecific mismatch/reset signal quickly removes transmitter v_{ij} from the extracellular space . . .
>
> *ART SEARCH HYPOTHESIS 3:* Offset of an input leads to a nonspecific signal that restores intracellular transmitter u_{ij} up to its maximal level z_{ij}. (p. 204)

Such a model asserts that a *single signal* stimulates release of a *single transmitter* directed at a *single site*—and that uptake (removal) and homeostasis (restoring) of the neuromodulator is engineered by *single* processes. Yet many of its underlying principles are fully applicable in a network model that contemplates the broader processing capacities discussed above.

A model is called for that allows simulation of the many other representation possibilities of neurochemical signaling. The proposal that follows is merely an opening volley. The Carpenter–Grossberg terms should be revised to reflect

---

[2]Eccles (1986) noted that belief in a single mechanism for storage, modification, and transmission of neural modulatory chemicals was held firmly through most of the last decade. Hence, recent advances in understanding of messenger processes are not incorporated even by such far-sighted theorists as Kohonen (1988) and Grossberg (1988). Carpenter and Grossberg (1989) acknowledge that they present "a highly simplified model of the chemical synapse" (p. 203). They also (on p. 201) mention their own work in progress on "slow learning," a key element of the new pharmacology (see also Hestenes, Chapter 7 of this volume).

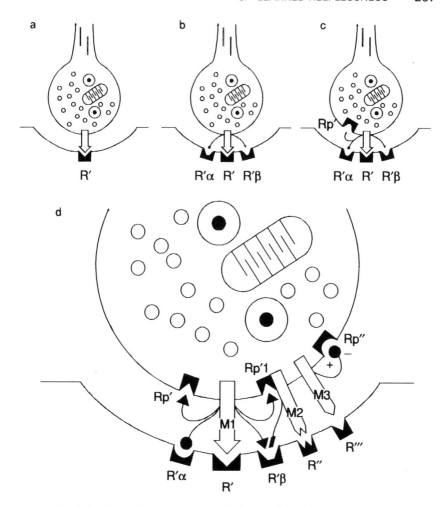

FIG. 8.4. A post-Dale set of transmission models: (a) one transmitter, one postsynaptic receptor; (b) one transmitter, multiple postsynaptic receptors; (c) transmitter acting on presynaptic as well as postsynaptic receptors; (d) multiple compounds released at the same nerve ending—main interactions are represented by signs. (Reprinted from Eccles, 1986, p. 11, with permission of Elsevier Science Publishers)

chemical messenger coexistence and the varieties of interprocess and interregional communication. Begin by replacing earlier beliefs about neural signaling with a model of "classical transmitters," a class that will seem familiar. One must add neuropeptides to the mix, later.

Vesicle storage u_t is based on a series of conditions: its previous chemical quantitative state u_{t-1} *(is it below firing threshold τ_t because of recent firing?)*;

informational state (has feedback from messengers v produced reset?); current electrical impulse state S (is it firing or not?); distance/effectiveness Δ (is impulse intensity diminished by distance from soma below threshold τ_Δ?); and inhibition by neighbors β (within the synapse) above threshold τ_β. How, as a practical matter, do these terms interact (as well as the model can represent; see Fig. 8.5)?

Synaptic boutons can mutually inhibit each other by intrasynaptic signals—they *compete* chemically by sending messenger to each other's postsynaptic receptors. They lie downstream on an electrical "wire," whose efficiency varies (if *unmyelinated*, uninsulated)—the further away from the soma, center, the less powerful the signal. After firing, the bouton must be replenished before having sufficient resources to be fired. All of these conditions affect the readiness and stimulus state of each bouton.

Similarly, neighboring boutons can produce chemical messengers that are identical or complementary. The first condition is obvious: two vesicles u_{i1} and u_{i2} *fire messenger* v_i toward the same receptor (Fig. 8.6a). Simply sum the amount v_i that arrives from all sources at the receptor to see whether, in the absence of other conditions, the threshold for receptor response, τ_r, has been

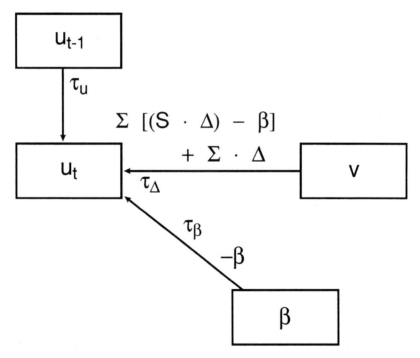

FIG. 8.5. A preliminary model of neuron-signal interactions; see text for details.

reached (signaling the effective receipt of the information). Alternatively v_i can be *gated* by output from neighboring vesicles: the message is either *amplified* (multiplicatively increased) or *diminished* (multiplied by a factor less than 1). Thus, v_i may be facilitated or inhibited by v_j, the neighbor's chemical message.

These responses are all regulated by presynaptic receptors, p_i, which respond to three sets of signals in the extracellular chemical environment (Fig. 8.6b). One type of message received by receptors is the available *message in the extra-cellular space*. This can include remaining signals v_i and v_j at time t_1 that were sent at time t. Why should such signals remain in the environment? Some are *excessive:* like any system, boutons can be induced to refire far more often and in greater quantities than the system ordinarily requires (e.g., under stress, as we shall see). These messages are clearly directed from u to p and are successful in reaching their target receptors. But the excess, sensed by receptors serving u, produces *a homeostatic* down-regulating response—less v is produced by u, as in Fig. 8.6.

A second message received by r_i (see Fig. 8.6) is produced at p'_i, the postsynaptic receptor. Such a signal refers to s_p, the sensitivity of the receptor to signals v. If there has been a rapid change in signals v received at the receptor, then p is likely to seek a homeostasis-preserving change back toward previous levels. Receptor sensitivity can also be affected by the presence of gating (ampli-fying or diminishing) v_j—which can affect the regulation of u by p.

Lastly, presynaptic *and* postsynaptic receptors are affected by what Bergland (1985) and Fuxe et al. (1988) called *paracrine* signals, $\mathcal{P}$. These messages derive from *peripheral* neurons and play a critical role, as we shall explore, in pain sensitivity (Melzack & Wall, 1988). Thus, although we have previously consid-ered the hierarchy of signals to include only *brain-based* signals, critical infor-mation about *physiological state* emerges from neurochemical processes that may lie beyond the spinal cord, at fingertips and elbows. And there is substantial evidence (Lynch & Baudry, 1988; Martinez, Weinberger, & Schultheis, 1988) that complex information processing and learning occur in such remote neuron groups.

Consider postsynaptic receptor processes and message-passing. A prolonged shortage of messengers v at receptor p can lead to two varieties of *up*-regulation, or effort at restoring previous levels. First, the *quantity* or *density* of p_i's can increase (or decrease, in response to a surplus). If more postsynaptic receptors exceed threshold t_p and accept v_i's message, then a reduction in signal intensity and quantity might be balanced by increases in receivers. This is a common receptor response.

Second, as mentioned above, receptor sensitivity s_p can respond to a shortage of messenger v_i. The net affect again is balance: less message is passed, but less is required by the receptor in order to register information.

One problem with the adjustments considered—increases in sensitivity and delay at p and increases in firing by u—is that they are relatively *short-lived*.

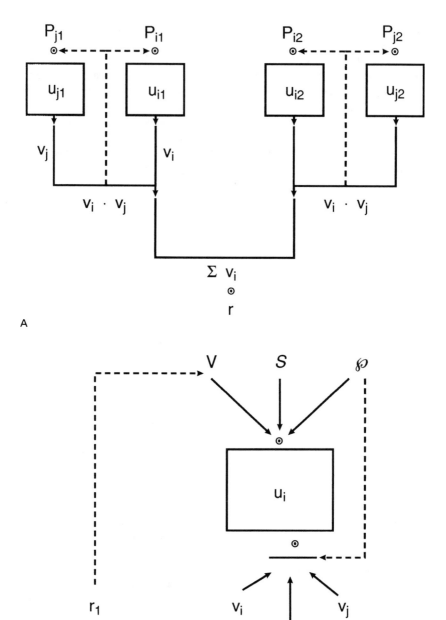

FIG. 8.6. A model of some neuronal processes. (a) Same-receptor interactions; (b) Response to extracellular influences. See text for details.

That is, after a short time, the systems tend to return to their previous density, sensitivity, and firing rate. This response is imagined by researchers to be *exhaustion* of the capacity to maintain those changes (Kandel & Schwartz, 1985).

A less well-understood adjustment takes place both at p and at r—receptor *binding*. This longer-term (sometimes permanent) process is a frequent device for studying effects of electrical or chemical stimulation of target receptors. Hippocampal learning is likely to be generated by long-term potentiation of hippocampal sites (Lynch & Baudry, 1988). However, Dunn (1986) cautioned: "binding sites . . . may include more than one type of receptor, and even binding sites with no biological significance" (p. 190). He emphasized the difficulty of controlled study.

The phenomenon of intraneuronal calcium regulation is central, on the other hand. Zucker (1989) and others have built an extensive model of Ca control of current in neurons, release, and reuptake. They have emphasized the role of externally derived Ca as central to electrical signal production S, both in rate (tS) and intensity (S)—and have produced useful models of Ca availability.

The understanding of corelease of transmitters by Kandel and his group (e.g., Castelucci et al., 1986) has led to a broader view of the process of learning. Whereas others (e.g., Dunn, 1986) emphasized that mRNA transcription is clearly not the sole mechanism for learning, Kandel's group point to a complex process, involving both neuronal messengers (e.g., serotonin) and calcium channel regulation. The central role of chemical messengers, Kandel's group found, is the activation of receptors; the role of Ca is storage of protein formation results and electrical (S) regulation.

In fact Alkon (1989) demonstrated that "spread of electrical and possibly chemical signals from one postsynaptic site to another—without activity or firing" (p. 47) is characteristic of storage, based on calcium and potassium ion flows that produce protein storage. These processes result in "collateral" pathways, based in sensitivity to individual synaptic signals. Alkon's DYSTAL system is a neural network emulating this work.

There are, therefore, three sets of signals (see Fig. 8.7). They are considered to derive from three disparate sources: local production (both electrical S and chemical V), endocrine production (suffusing most brain areas from the hypothalamic-pituitary-adrenal axis), and paracrine (extrabrain) production. We shall shortly have reason to build on this model to produce an analytic view of memory formation and learned helplessness.

Ingredients for a Model

How can such complex processes be rendered in a model? *Slowly.* There are many complexities involved. For example, our work contemplates only a small piece of the *results* of Zucker's (1989) work on Ca and axonal signaling. Parsimony and computational complexity are limitations.

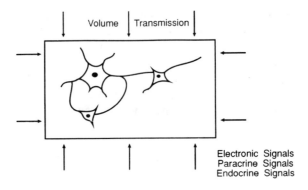

	Speed of transmission	Degree of divergence	Segregation ("safety" of the transmission)	Plasticity	Preferential information processing
Wiring transmission: Neuron-linked electrochemical transmission	High	Low to moderate	High	Low to moderate	Elementary elaboration Short-term action
Volume transmission: Humoral ("open") electrochemical transmission	Low	High to very high	Low	High to very high	Holistic elaboration Long-term action

FIG. 8.7.   The three sets of signals—electronic, paracrine, and endocrine—and their implications. (Reprinted from Fuxe et al., 1988, with permission of Springer-Verlag)

However, as computing and scientific knowledge increase, the challenge Halbreich (1987) presented becomes a serious (and yet nearly tractable) task for network modelers. Only in the context of extensive models can interactions among various elements of the complex neurochemistry and neurophysiology be considered. Moreover, only in such an environment can needed new theories of computing appear (Winograd & Flores, 1986), from Alkon's low-level DYSTAL to higher-order visions.

Following, evidence will be considered for a theory propounded, somewhat differently, by Tulving, Pribram, and MacLean, among others, that there are *three characteristic ways of learning and knowing.* Some supporting results suggest, further, that *these ways are tied to physiological subsystems.* Each of these subsystems may have its own *electrical, chemical,* and *physiological connectivity.* These, on this view, offer unique modes of storage and response to information, but are *heavily interconnected* in a broad *neural environment.*

In fact we may find that these three subsystems produce insights into reconciling apparently conflicting data and theory. We shall consider the three commonly accepted (but outwardly mutually antagonistic) views of learned helplessness in the context of three systems; we shall find the views are in fact complementary and supportive of each other. Models based on rat performance and *hermissenda* performance should not be ignored in discussions of human behaviors, but they should be considered in light of the complexity of the human neural system.

This discussion will be broadened after presentation of that evidence. For now, a research model can be offered that accommodates theorizing about an extensive system in a highly interactive environment.

Interneuron Learning and Communication Including Neuropeptides

Recall, for a moment, the preceding figures. These represent the *conceptual neurons* of the model. Figure 8.8 demonstrates a fundamental difference between "fast" and "slow" transmitters (Stinus, Kelly, & Winnock, 1984; Iversen, 1986). Note that there are *two classes* of neural transmission. These classes

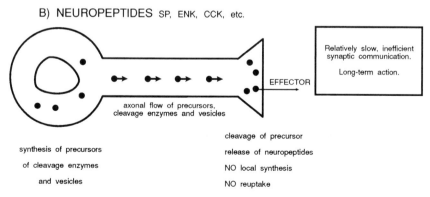

FIG. 8.8.   Fast and slow transmitters in action. (Reprinted from Stinus et al., 1984, with permission of Oxford University Press)

follow different rules (neuropeptides have no reuptake T nor local synthesis and local production/regulation). They operate at different rates of effectiveness (dB_{ik}) and messenger decay δ. Production of neuropeptide messenger does not occur near the synapse, as in bouton output B. Instead, its production, at ribosomes (in amounts $\mathcal{R}$) in hypothalamus, is affected by extracellular "peptide killer" peptidases (in amounts $\mathcal{P}$). Further, it is transmitted long distances, along chemical pathways, throughout the brain (see Nieuwenhuys, 1985).

Beyond cooperating in a traditional, largely additive way or competing by simply diminishing the amount of effective messenger available, neuropeptides have a *modulating* effect (measured as *m* in our model). Peptides can block all interaction at receptors or can multiply the effects of a small amount of another messenger on a receptor (Prange, Whybrow, & Loosen, 1988).

What distinguishes this model from previous views are, thus, two modern discoveries. First, as we have seen, in the coexistence of several messengers in the same neuron, which are even accessible to the same receptors. Second is the discovery, equally recent, that many peptides that had been found elsewhere in the body (as products of pituitary, etc.) are available at synapses, either as products transported from outside the blood brain barrier or as products of ribosome synthesis.

As DeWied (1987) observed, the new finding of neuropeptides "suggests an extraordinarily complex synaptic communication [involving] an additional neuromodulator influence . . . to maintain homeostasis and to facilitate adaptive processes" (p. 94). This suggestion requires us to seek the impacts of chemical and electrical transmission in the context of neurophysiology. They shall produce insights on mood and context dependence.

To be certain, the capacity of hundreds of calcium channels to store information is considerable. The fact that this learning is based on information derived from the ends of the body (paracrine), from internal physiological states (endocrine), and from local computation at hundreds of nearby boutons, and from receptor feedback, is awesome.

One should inquire how specific brain structures respond to separate sets of information. We shall find, at the end of the next section, that the recognition of multiple colocalized messengers and modulating effects of neuropeptide changes the questions we ask, the models we construct, and even the answers we obtain about gross human behaviors.

HELPLESSNESS: A "THREE-SIDED DOOR" ON BEHAVIOR

Three *mutually exclusive* accounts of a standard experimental model for depression, learned helplessness, will be introduced. We shall find validity in each theory's claim for behavioral and psychophysiological accuracy. Three correct theories may be combined to produce a more generalizable model of help-lessness. Finally this model may fit the views of broader mental function pro-pounded (separately) by Tulving, by MacLean, and by Pribram. Although those three researchers do not agree fully either, we shall find many of their commonly held attitudes help guide us to another general view. This will lead of course to an application and conclusion.

Seligman (1975) asserted the following:

> when organisms experience events . . . in which the probability of the outcome is the same whether or not the response of interest occurs, learning takes place. Behaviorally, this will tend to diminish [efforts] to control the outcome; cognitively, it will produce a belief in the inefficiency of responding . . . ; and emotionally, when the outcome is traumatic, it will produce heightened anxiety, followed by depression. (pp. 46–47)

Seligman isolated three disturbances caused by perceived uncontrollability. A *motivational disturbance* derives from the failure to obtain relief. A *cognitive disturbance* emerges from the loss of the belief that causes produce effects. Finally, an *emotional disturbance* is produced in response to uncontrollable trauma that does not respond to escape or fight behaviors. Consider this theory as Seligman One.

Later Seligman "reformulated" his hypothesis, turning to an "attributional" hypothesis (Miller & Seligman, 1982):

> People who attribute the causes of their helplessness to stable factors expect to be helpless whenever the original situation recurs. . . . People who attribute the causes of their helplessness to global factors expect to be helpless even when the situation changes. . . . People who make internal attributions . . . exhibit low self-esteem and feelings of worthlessness. (p. 152)

A "depressive attributional style" involves making internal, stable, and global attributions for failure, and making external, unstable, and specific attributions for success. Call this approach, in which attributional style produces self-efficacy or helplessness, Seligman Two.

In the first instance, thus, Seligman suggested that the *experience of unex-pected, consistent failure* produces an accurate perception that effort-in-context is useless. Seligman One is an approach to overwhelming problems that undermine our drive to extinguish frustration, our satisfaction with our ability to reach goals, and our understanding of *directionality,* that causes have effects and vice versa. When these problems occur, an emotional "short circuit" occurs, and depression is the most likely conclusion.

In the second case, Seligman attended to the approaches people take to prob-lems. Seligman Two maintains that two classes of approaches exist, as Weiner (1986) asserted: one class sees failures as unlikely and impersonal, while the other group anticipates failure and believes individuals are the cause of failure. A member of the first group sees success as the presumable result of his or her continuing competence and hard work; a member of the second finds success a lucky, uncontrollable outcome.

The easiest way to distinguish Seligman One from Two is to focus on *content* in the first view and *context* in the second. If one is in fact *helpless,* his response may be sad; but it is *appropriate* to the circumstances (a reasonable result). If, on the other hand, one *expects* to be ineffective and refuses to accept his own competence, then his response is *inappropriate* and *out of context.*

A third view of helplessness has been propounded, for many years, by Weiss. He has maintained that *anxiety* and *stress* in helpless situations *induce depression.* In this model (Glazer & Weiss, 1976), a struggle takes place between the motivation to escape and the frustration and anxiety that obtains from seeking to master the unsolvable. The result of such conflict is stress, which produces, as Weiss and Simson (1986) wrote: "(a) deficits in motor activity . . . , (b) deficits in appetitive behavior . . . , (c) deficits in grooming behaviors . . . , and (d) disturbance of sleep."[3]

Whereas Seligman One is *affective,* and Seligman Two is *cognitive,* Weiss' conflict/anxiety model is *visceral,* a drive-based, *automatic* function of the simple motivation to avoid discomfort. The three models pose different questions. Seligman One asks in effect, "How would you feel, if you lost control?" Seligman Two poses the question, "What happens when you look for failure, and find it?" Weiss and his colleagues ask, "How should I respond when I need to act, but can't?" The questioners do not always listen to each other.

One cannot be surprised to find that the three models can be viewed as three different *neurophysiological models* as well. We shall explore these differences and discover common ground below.

However, some agreements among the theories are clear now. All three theories acknowledge the role of stress in presenting the helpless state. All require the perception of helplessness to be achieved and a sense of frustration to be suffered; all accept the result of the condition to be depressed affect. These agreements suggest the nature of behavior as *integrated* but with different structures and tendencies.

Three Views of Helplessness' Neurobiology and Neurochemistry

We shall investigate experimental results that support each of the three arguments. Although the physical brain structures are simpler to describe, the more elegant experiments have involved manipulation of neurochemical pathways that connect them. These studies will support each of the views.

---

[3]Minor, Pelleymounter, and Maier (1988) have produced evidence supportive of Weiss and Simson's view, as discussed following.

At one time or another, many brain structures and chemical systems have been proposed as critical to depression or its analog, helplessness. The motivation of most current research is the success of antidepressant drug treatments. Messenger systems on which these drugs work include the monoamines (noradrenaline [NA], dopamine [DA], and serotonin [5-HT], acetylcholine [ACh], and gamma-aminobutyric acid [GABA]. Some attention is now being paid to peptides as central causes, but the five messengers listed are most often discussed in helplessness and depression (Willner, 1985).[4]

Each of these messengers has characteristic paths through neural structures and centers of concentration. The effectiveness of chemical experimental manipulation may tell as much about the roles of these brain regions as they do about their own importance to regulation of affect and behavior.

> Weiss and Simson (1986) review evidence that changes within noradrenergic systems of the brain played a major role in producing or mediating stress-induced behavioral depression . . . indicating that stress-induced behavioral depression was caused by a large decrease in the concentration of noradrenaline in the locus ceruleus (LC)." (pp. 192–193)

After exposing an experimental group to uncontrollable shock, they observed reduced activity and lower NA levels among the "helpless." Many other neurochemicals (which we shall discuss below) remained at similar levels after control. This reduced activity level gradually reversed over three to four days; by the end of that time, increased production of NA (through its precursor, tyrosine hydroxylase) restored normal levels. Normal NA production was correlated with normal behavior.

Weiss and Simson were able to *reverse* helplessness through control of NA depletion in locus ceruleus (an extension of the brain stem). Subjects shocked sufficiently to become helpless performed normally in the presence of the artificially preserved NA. The authors stated that whereas pargyline (an NA-preserving drug) had no effect on behavior of the nonpunished controls, it reversed depressive behaviors.

Fig. 8.9 displays Weiss' explanation of the vehicle by which NA-depleted LC leads to behavioral depression. As stress occurs, boutons are forced to fire quickly (presumably by *a* radical increase in electrical impulse *s*). Meanwhile production of NA lags, understandably; yet whatever NA is available is released. Finally, the massive depletion leaves a shortage of NA within LC.

Without sufficient NA messenger, receptors α_2 are stimulated less. As a result, less motivating signal is available to LC signal destination (which we shall detail below). The loss of message produces lower motivated behavior levels, at a time of alarm.

---

[4]Use of the term messenger is discussed above, in the section entitled "Preliminaries: Toward a Realistic Classic Transmitter Model."

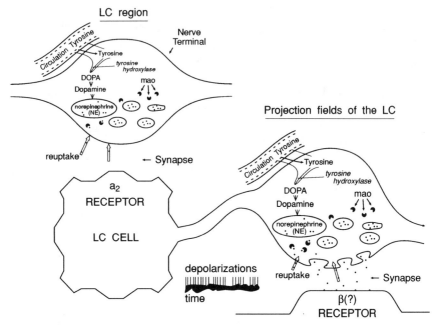

FIG. 8.9. Weiss' model of neurochemical production of helplessness.
(Reprinted from Weiss & Simson, 1986, with permission of John Wiley
and Sons)

Further proving the central role NA in LC plays in helpless behavior, Weiss'
group established that providing an *agonist* (a messenger *m* that *modulates*
strongly the effects of NA) can reverse the effects of helplessness training. Also,
a down-modulator of NA (an *m* that reduces effectiveness) can induce helpless
behavior, when applied to LC receptors. Lastly, a drug that prevents reuptake (T)
of NA also prevents helpless effects, by keeping sufficient quantities available to
receptors.

Hestenes (Chapter 7 of this volume) suggests that NA releases from LC
constitute *vigilance control,* a gating mechanism that responds to such significant
stimuli as novel events. He considers the wide innervation of LC throughout the
brain as a signal from NA, "Attend to what you perceive."

Clearly the broad connectivity by NA paths from LC is suggestive of a central
role for recognition of pattern changing. This role of "calling attention" may be
crucial to certain types of learning. Its limbic efferents' job, Gray (1982) wrote,
is "to tag certain stimuli . . . as 'important' " (p. 460); its hypothalamic
efferents' task is "priming hypothalamic motor systems (especially those involved in fight and flight behavior) for rapid action when required" (p. 460).

Central to the point of Weiss' argument is this strong connection between LC
and the fight/flight complex. Note, first, the excitatory NA connections from LC

to limbic structures (Gray's SHS) and the hypothalamus. Direct stimulation of hypothalamus leads to high arousal and motivation levels (fight/flight response). Simultaneously, however, high LC output may sufficiently excite the limbic system to *inhibit* the high activation response. This is the "freezing" response that Weiss produced: high arousal and high inhibition, producing frustration, anxiety, and finally depression (see Fig. 8.10).

Maier and his colleagues (Minor et al., 1988) pointed to the relationship between locus ceruleus, ascending dorsal tegmental bundle (ADTB), and superior forebrain. An NA pathway connects these regions; depletion of pontine nucleus and locus ceruleus NA results in sharply reduced forebrain NA levels. Gray (1982) and others maintain that the LC-ADTB-FB circuit mediates filtering or gating of stimuli.

Maier's group found that helplessness training produced NA depletion. The performance change that Minor et al. (1988) discovered, both from shock and from ADTB lesions, was contrary to the original experimental Seligman results:

Choice errors resulted from an inability to ignore the irrelevant cue. Thus, while learned helplessness theory predicts that exposure to inescapable shock should interfere with the formation of response-outcome interactions, the actual difficulty appeared to arise at an earlier stage of information processing, perhaps at an attentional level. This deficit . . . is not easily accommodated by the learned-helplessness hypothesis. (p. 136)

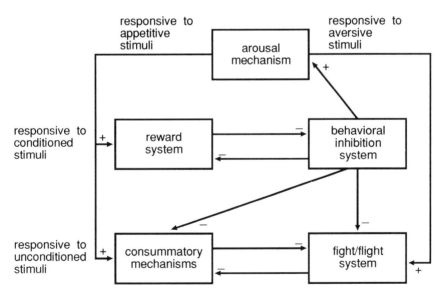

FIG. 8.10. A possible network representation of the Weiss "freezing" hypothesis. (Reprinted from Gray, 1987, with permission of Cambridge University Press)

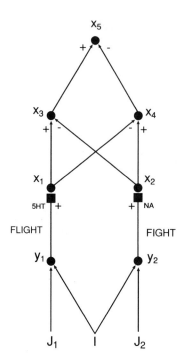

FIG. 8.11. An example of a gated dipole. In this case, J_1 and J_2 are inputs to opponent channels representing flight and fight respectively. Square synapses have transmitters that become depleted with repeated use. The greater signal at J_1 than at J_2 balances greater depletion of NA than of 5HT, causing "deadlock" at x_5 in which neither channel wins. (Adapted from Grossberg, 1980, with permission of The American Psychological Association; cf. chapters in this volume by Grossberg et al., Levine et al., and Ricart)

The argument that Maier and his coworkers advanced differs from the Weiss and Simson approach. Whereas Weiss has considered stress as causing a "freezing" effect from underproduced NA acting *within* the LC, Maier's alternative view is based on asserted LC effects on forebrain. In the first case, low inhibitory LC activity permits limbic processes; in the second, low LC activity prevents systematic cortical filtering of irrelevant stimuli through exaggerated NA stimulation of forebrain.[5] In the first, *drive levels* are reduced; in the second, confusion is induced.

Fig. 8.11 shows another possible network representation of the Weiss-Simson helplessness hypothesis. Note that the decision mechanism is stimulated by reward (locus ceruleus NA) and inhibited by punishment mediated by limbic serotonergic (5–HT) pathways. The decision mechanism appears to be a classic Grossberg dipole, in which one channel "beats" the other—but in this case, *both channels may remain equally effective*. The failure of one signal to succeed over the other is predictable because of our understanding of complex messenger systems—and yields the "freezing" outcome.

In the network of Fig. 8.11, the choice between alternative acts J_1(NA, fight) and J_2 (5-HT, flight) is made at x_5. As NA depletion is normally assumed to take place at a faster rate, inhibiting limbic J_2 should "beat" J_1. This assumption is

---

[5]Minor et al. (1988, p. 143) discussed this conflict differently.

based on the notion that fleeing is usually preferred to fighting as an evolutionary strategy.

The reuptake of NA is substantially lower than the reuptake of 5-HT, presumably for other evolutionary reasons (one ought to be prepared to fight, almost always). However, the J_2 signal is sufficiently strong that, despite NA activity and stimulus to J_1, no fight takes place—and no flight either.

After a time, NA production to u_2 sinks low enough so that x_2 can no longer fire. That is of course the depressive outcome of helplessness. This failure produces reduced choosing of alternatives—and poorer *accuracy* of choices actually made.

The Maier version requires that we add a layer of processing to model the failure of frontal filtering. A parameter ought to be introduced to represent high attentional demands—in other words, *arousal, A*. Another mechanism must emulate the ability to filter irrelevant information (i.e., data that does not help limit processing to finding clearly novel or clearly recognizable cues). Call this device *gain control, G*. The resulting model is highly reminiscent of the ART model of Carpenter and Grossberg (1987, 1989).

In Fig. 8.12, *A* is the excitation derived from the helpless state. How exciting (how large) *A* is depends on the importance or stressfulness of the environment.

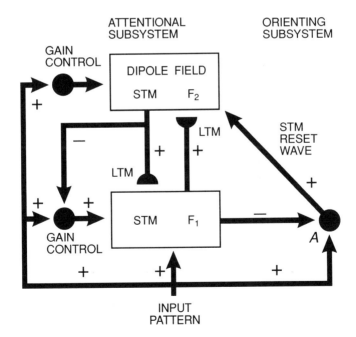

FIG. 8.12. An adaptive resonance network. Its interpretation in the context of learned helplessness is described in the text. (Reprinted from Carpenter & Grossberg, 1987, with permission of Academic Press)

The environmental input I is perceived at a level F_1. Interpretation takes place at cortical F_2, as an existing category for I is recognized (and appropriate behavior is "ordered") or a new category emerges (and new plans can be required). When a mismatch between F_1 and F_2 occurs, a mechanism similar to TOTE (Miller, Galanter, & Pribram, 1960) feeds back instructions to extinguish the failed match possibility and reduce the number of possible matches (uncertainty). When G is too low, however, *old mismatches can continue,* and *correct categorizations fail to emerge.* In this model, the helpless person suffers long response latencies—he cannot "make up his mind."

Are the two models inconsistent (as Minor et al. suggested)? No, they are not necessarily. Either problem could emerge from a failure of *self-regulation* (i.e., inability to maintain stable NA levels in the face of stress). In fact Kraemer (1986) found that stressed monkeys were incapable of sustaining amounts of NA appropriate to the time of day. This problem might well be dependent on adequate adaptability of postsynaptic receptors (the rate-limiting P).

In fact, one can combine the two models. In Fig. 8.13, the input stimulus I is involved in a *system:* LC levels may affect hippocampal *or* forebrain areas. The arrangement here in fact follows a suggestion by Grossberg (1988) that ART may output to a field of dipoles.

Work by Henn (1987) suggests reconceptualization of the Maier and Weiss findings. Instead of finding strong NA connections to LC in helpless animals, Henn's group found that the area most affected by training was the hippocampus. Breeding generations of animals, some "immune" to helplessness and others very helpless, they considered NA and 5-HT pathways in studying helplessness.

Their findings suggest (Henn, 1987) that "there may be a very specific anatomical pathway which mediates the change" (p. 259) to helplessness. They suggest that a model circuit can be offered (see Fig. 8.14). The LC sends NA signals to the hippocampus, which plays a critical role in influencing (largely *through 5-HT circuitry*) the hypothalamus, septum, and frontal neocortex. Their notion is that distorted β-receptor levels allow abnormal cortisol production levels, producing depression by allowing hyperresponsiveness in the hypothalamus-pituitary-adrenal axis to corticotropin (ACTH) (cf. Gold et al., 1988, p. 67 ff.).

Henn's work suggests three significant phenomena requiring study. First, gross behaviors are engendered by *systems* and not *modules* (e.g., Fodor, 1984). Anatomical and experimental studies have revealed interactions between hypothalamic nuclei and cerebellar regions. These connections, which are direct (i.e., not by way of LC or other intermediaries, show that "cerebellar nuclei communicate directly with hypothalamic centers [giving evidence of] influence on somatic and visceral functions" (Haines et al., 1984, pp. 209–211).

Second, information is not merely mediated by receptor action (as in "Dale's principle" models) but is *generated by receptor computation and transmission.* In fact β receptors respond to environmental stressors (depletion of estrogen,

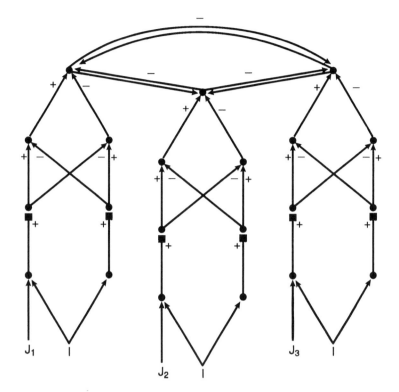

FIG. 8.13. One possible detailed architecture for the F_2 level in Figure 12. J_i are inputs to several competing gated dipoles, each also receiving a tonic input I to both channels. The left channel of the ith dipole represents processing of the ith input, whereas the right channel represents offset of that input. The output nodes $x_{i,5}$ compete in an on-center off-surround network. (Adapted from Levine & Prueitt, 1989, with permission of Pergamon Press)

decrease of corticosteroids) by increasing in number and sensitivity (Duman & Enna, 1987).

This next suggestion produces a final hypothesis for the Weiss–Maier–Henn helplessness. The response R of receptors is based on presence of extracellular messenger v (e.g., cortisol), includes a distance/effectiveness (concentration and decay) measure Δ, as well as r, the existing number of receptors in the environment. Only when such parameters are included can the *effective signal NA + corticosteroid* be calculated.

Last, Henn's work is consonant with earlier, classic formulations on chemical mediation of depression (see Willner, 1985). These first systematic hypotheses involved dopaminergic causation, then monoamines (including 5–HT and NA). The accumulation of evidence based on some depressions being induced by

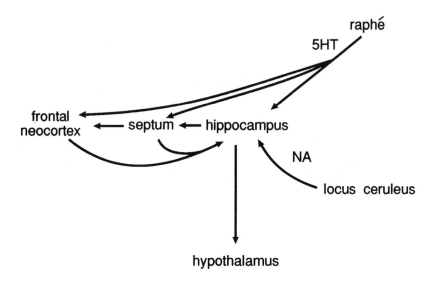

FIG. 8.14. A model circuit, including both NA and 5-HT pathways, mediating the change to helplessness. (Adapted from Henn, 1987, with permission of Raven Press)

reserpine (a reducer of NA, DA, and 5–HT) and reduced by iproniazid (their enhancer) supports this approach (Gilbert, 1984). Further, antidepressant drugs, such as monoamine oxidase inhibitors have proved successful by reducing reuptake of monoamines (Iversen & Iversen, 1981)—thus, making more of these substances available for messenger function.

The successful application of dexamethasone suppression tests to *Weiss*-helpless rats confirms that the *HPAC axis* (hypothalamus-pituitary-adrenal cortex) is involved in helplessness. However, some writers stress the role of corticosteroids as more central than that of monoamines (e.g., Haracz, Minor, Wilkins, & Zimmerman, 1988). Even in confirmatory findings on monoamine causality, therefore, there is the suggestion that the phenomenon requires complex explanation.

In fact *interregional* phenomena are critical to integrated helpless behaviors. The triune model may provide explanations of otherwise difficult data.

Helplessness is a loss of willingness to perseverate, to accept negative outcomes on the way to a goal. Furthermore, the failure to learn about the environment that helpless subjects display (Seligman, 1975) is mirrored by Isaacson's (1982) report that "animals with hippocampal lesions develop a perseverative mode of responding secondary to the inability to solve the problem" (p. 213). Environmental cues become meaningless: incentives lose their allure, and context produces confusion.

This disoriented helplessness, we propose, may be similar to the Seligman

One phenomenon. Affect disappears as the subject learns, quite appropriately, that he or she has no control and does not grasp the context. Ultimately self-esteem and effort after goals are the victims.

Roberts et al. (1984), working from a broad model of neural function similar to the one we have championed, considered the production of "modality specific engrams" generated in limbic areas by "attachment of environmental significance" (pp. 239–240). Amygdalar and hippocampal structures convolve sensory and semantic information with "an affective component."

The "engine" for this information processing, Roberts' group proposes, is *peptide and opiate modification* of LC NA signals, ACh from stria terminalis, and DA from brainstem. They suggest that *transmitter-specific interactions* take place: basolateral nucleus processes NA with local VIP, CCK, and neurotensin, whereas amygdala processes DA with CCK and 5–HT with somatostatin and substance *P* (among others). Further, *peptide signaling* is almost totally efferent—hippocampus signals cingulate cortex with neurotensin and septum with VIP, CCK, and met-enkephalin.

The Seligman One phenomenon (control orientation) has bee tied to opiate responses. Earlier work by Maier et al. (1983) explored opiate responses to uncontrollable stress and found a strong parallel with learned helplessness effect when they discovered the following:

(1) Exposure to inescapable shock produces decreased responsivity on analgesimetric measures if the organism is given a brief reexposure to the shock;
(2) This pain inhibition is strongly influenced by the degree of control the organism has over the stressor;
(3) Experience with controllable shock before uncontrollable shock prevented the usual analgesic effect;
(4) This effect is reversed by opiate antagonists and is cross-tolerant with the analgesic effects of morphine;
(5) The analgesic effects of inescapable shock seem unrelated to its associative effects. Its relation to activity is unknown, but a simple cause-effect relation is contradicted.

Perhaps the central point Maier et al. (1983) made is that the *standard* explanations (associative—Seligman Two—and activity—Weiss) are not adequate to explain opiate-related helplessness. This *third* helplessness is supported by the kindling (seizure) literature. Post, Weiss & Rubinow (1988) pointed out that *repeated* opiate administration (emulating the effects of the stressor corticotropin-releasing factor or CRF) produces *increased* motor activity—the system becomes desensitized to constant stresses. On the other hand, *intermittent* opiate introduction decreases motor activity, as the system becomes sensitive to the presence of a stress response.

Evidence suggests that actual seizures tend to produce higher continuing quantities of somatostatin in amygdala (Post et al., 1988). They find plausible the interaction of opiates and somatostatin in helplessness involving "depressive pseudodementia," cognitive postseizure failures, and other motor and mood deficits.

Effects of antidepressants on opioids is further supportive of a role in depression for limbic regions. Agren and Terenius (1988) reported that hippocampal met-enkephalin levels decreased after chronic desipiramine treatment—but that cerebral cortex levels *remained the same.*

These studies clarify the finding of Bandura, Cioffi, Taylor, and Brouillard (1988) that opiate levels increased on the presence of *cognitive* (Seligman Two) stresses. Bandura's team required college students to face difficult mathematical problems. The determined, by pretest, that one group perceived itself "less self-efficacious" than another—and then showed that the less confident group was more sensitive to pain. This proves, they suggested (Bandura et al., 1988), the following:

> Perceived coping inefficacy was highly stressful and autonomically arousing. Subjects who perceived themselves as unable to exercise control over cognitive demands experienced a high degree of stress. . . .
> [After] self-efficacy beliefs are instilled, simply approaching environmental demands in a self-inefficacious frame of mind may produce some opioid activation anticipatorily. (p. 486)

Does the failure to perform adequately instill *attributions* of a sense of failure (Weiner, 1986; Ortony, Clore, & Collins, 1988)? On the contrary, the Bandura group was asked to *rate itself,* a behavior doomed to require a context-bound response (Leven, 1988). The self-rating process induced an inevitable affective response—not the detached appraisal process of Seligman Two. The opiate release was most likely a response a la Roberts et al. (1984) to a threatening and mood-affecting context.

This model may support Simonov's (1983) notion of an "information theory of emotions":

> . . . depending on [the] stage in the organization of behaviour, the excitation of emotionally positive and emotionally negative structures may enter the neural elements of the motor system, transforming itself into the reaction of approach or avoidance.
> . . . Only integration of the [need] excitation and . . . the mechanism generating a positive emotion, can ensure conditioning. With any other correlation of the converging excitations, . . . the activation of the negative emotion mechanisms leads to the defense reaction of avoidance. . . . (pp. 181–182)

Simonov's suggestion (see Fig. 8.15) is that traditional models of even simple conditioning require that we add to conditioned (CS) and unconditioned (US) stimuli other variables representing *functional state* (FS), *need* (N), and *emotion*

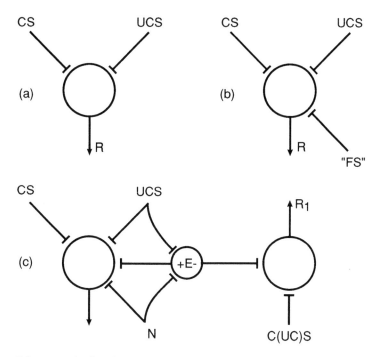

FIG. 8.15.   A tripartite model of "emotional conditioning". (a) Classical conditioning (CS-US → Response); (b) State-dependent learning (FS = functional state); (c) Integration of emotion (E) and appraised need (N). (Adapted from Simonov, 1983, with permission of MIR Publishers)

(E). These variables are akin to others we have discussed previously. Need can be matched to arousal (A), functional state to the array of variables describing such longer-term brain states as attitudes (or *cognitions,* to be discussed later), and emotions to levels of affective transmitters (e.g., peptide and opiate action in the limbic system).

Clearly the roles that "higher" functions play in conditioning are not only supportive of an "affective helplessness" but also of a "cognitive helplessness." Beyond this next step, broader questions can be posed.

Last, consider a model of Seligman Two, cognitively mediated helplessness. Petty (1986) showed that one antidepressant (desipramine) applied intracranially reversed helplessness only when injected into frontal neocortex. His results were remarkable:

[Although] the cure for learned helplessness would appear to involve a cortical serotonergic locus, its prevention involves a GABAergic component in several brain areas. . . The anatomical direction of the pathway implicated in the reversal of helplessness [is] frontal cortex to hippocampus to septum. . . . The prevention of learned helplessness is . . . related to the GABA system. (pp. 63–64)

Petty's "cure," involving cortical serotonin pathways, GABA in hippocampus, and serotonin in septum, is illustrated in Fig. 8.16.

How do we distinguish between prevention and cure in studying information pathways? Recall that 5–HT is "upwardly" afferent, like all monoamines. It signals from lower brain areas to limbic system and cortex (Iversen, 1984).

GABA neurons, on the other hand, are cortically *intrinsic* (Hendry, 1987). They constitute many cortical cell types: basket, chandelier, and others that terminate nonselectively and permeate the entire cortex. In as complex and segmented an environment as cortex, Hendry maintained, GABA neurons constitute the informational "glue," tying to hippocampus with excitatory CCK and inhibitory SRIF. Thus, the common cortical language bears different "accents' based on its cotransmitter.

A central function of GABA afferents is inhibitory (Willner, 1985). GABA

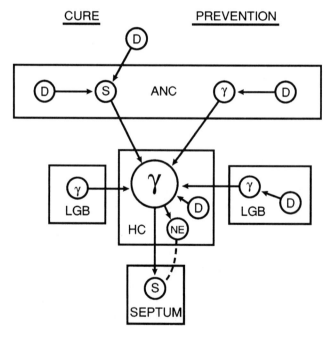

FIG. 8.16.   Proposed neurochemical pathways involved in the prevention and cure of learned helplessness in rats: *D* = desipramine; *S* = serotonin; *NE* = noradrenaline; α = GABA; ANC = anterior neocortex; *LGB* = lateral geniculate body; HC = hippocampus. (Reprinted from Petty, 1986, with permission of Raven Press)

connections seem to modulate DA actions (possibly through competitive binding on CCK receptors).

Yet, despite the GABA pathway Petty described and its ability to prevent helplessness, Willner reported that GABA levels are generally unresponsive to kindling. We may hypothesize that their lack of action is explicable as a manifestation of *cognitive*—not *affective* or *motoric*—helplessness pathways. This meets the suggestion of Gray (1987) that GABA mediates cognitive anxieties through an LC-forebrain nexus.

Petty's notion that frontal cortex (Brodmann's area 10) is the site for extinction of helplessness by a traditional antidepressant offers an insight. Helplessness is not merely a failure of fight-flight systems—it clearly operates on a *series of levels* in neural architecture.

This process of cure by inhibitory messenger suggests that neocortical regions have the capacity to return to homeostasis (i.e., readiness for challenge) with plain reset mechanisms. However, this model does cast doubt on the notion of a deeply embedded mechanism that structures all incoming information and develops a uniform style of expectation.[6]

In fact Scatton et al. (1986) found that even LC NA activity is mediated by GABA, improving production of and sensitivity to NA. GABA receptors, stimulated by increased GABA stimulation, lead to increased synthesis and turnover of NA—but *no 5–HT, ACh, or opiate effects are observed*. Yet, in areas of cortex where 5–HT is plentiful, GABA diminished 5–HT sensitivity and production. The production inhibition takes place at the serotonin-rich anterior raphé: desensitizing takes place in prefrontal cortex and other highly sensitive sites.

Hence, GABA performs two classic antidepressant roles, acting on different classic neurotransmitters at different sites (see Fig. 8.17). These actions are not centered in brainstem or hippocampus. Therefore, centrally distributed GABA acts simultaneously, *at different sites* and with *different mechanisms* to control mood-representing messengers; reduced levels of GABA can lead to monoamine-induced helplessness of both inhibitory 5–HT and excitatory NA. This evidence seems to be pharmacologically convincing that cortically centered processes can act at deeper brain centers: *higher brain activity can control evidence of affect and activity*.

What sense can be made of Seligman Two, in light of Petty's and Scatton's findings? First, not all frontal representations are arcane or unknowable. Second, cognitions have *some* state dependence. Finally, the sense of control is largely chemically mediated.

What we may learn from this exercise is that "reformulated helplessness" still describes the same condition. Helplessness is an *affective* condition, which plays a role in generating distorted cognitions (Segal, 1988). It is a frustrated moti-

---

[6]It is important to note that Petty's work is with rats, which have limited frontal structures.

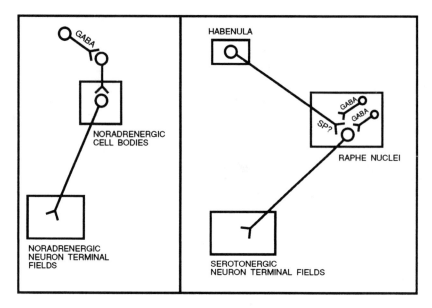

FIG. 8.17.   A schematic view of GABAergnic influence on NA and 5-HT pathways. (Reprinted from Scatton et al., 1986, with permission of Raven Press)

vation, which requires and affective response and, in humans, an attributional process.

Our three models are not as different from each other as their advocates have claimed. Control loss, affect distortion, and attributional flaws all fit into a common model of mind—which we shall now offer.

Mental Process as Structure, Mental Structure as Process

We have found different processes at work in the three models of helplessness: cognitive versus affective versus motivational. We shall find that these categories continue to emerge from the literature—and guide us toward a general model.

MacLean (1970, 1980) introduced the *triune brain hypothesis* to explain the relationship between brain and behavior. He summarized (MacLean, 1980) as follows:

> There exists, so to speak, a hierarchy of three-brains-in-one, or what I call . . . a triune brain. . . .
> It is inferred that each cerebrotype has its own special kind of intelligence, its own special memory, its own sense of time and space, and . . . other functions. Although these three brain types are extensively interconnected and functionally dependent, . . . each is capable of operating somewhat independently. (p. 14)

MacLean outlined brain development as a process involving an ancient, "reptilian" center that contains instinctive and primary motor and very basic sensory functions; a later, "paleomammalian" or "limbic" brain that is the center of emotion and orientation; and the late "neomammalian" center, for planning and higher memory coordination. The three form, he insisted, an "internal world," with the reptilian system "constantly bombarded by impulses," the limbic system forcing us to "apprehend ourselves and the world as an aesthetic continuum," and the neocortex performing "nice discriminations" that "subdivide things into smaller and smaller entities."

MacLean's view of behavioral systems has found only spotty support. However, the notion he popularized, that there are three subsystems within the neural environment that maintain some separation of function, has been more embraced.

The architecture and chemistry of the brain understandably may well give rise to higher level faculties of similar dimension. Tulving (1985) identified the following three memory systems:

Procedural memory enables organisms to retain learned connections between stimuli and responses, including those involving complex stimulus patterns and response chains, and to respond adaptively to the environment. Semantic memory . . . permits the organism to construct mental models of the world . . . that can be manipulated . . . covertly, independently of an overt behavior. Episodic memory . . . [involves] acquisition and retention of knowledge about personally experienced events and their temporal relations in subjective time. . . . (p. 387)[7]

Procedural memory is stimulus- and state-dependent recall that precipitates automatic (or autonomic) response. Semantic memory is standard in these and other models as associative recall of cognition-based items. Tulving's episodic memory is closely tied to models of affective memory that stress the connection to limbic cortex (the site of mapping and time- and experience-bound recall).

Bruner (1984) posited three-stage approaches to learning and creativity. He described how we learn by developing visions of the subject, thus:

Enactive representation . . . is storing one's knowledge in the forms of habits of acting . . . .
 . . . iconic [representation] is storage in images; symbolic [representation is] a symbol system like language. (p. 143)

Bruner referred to these three views as visceral, affective, and cognitive. He also suggested that a creative act "produces effective surprise" in one of three ways:

---

[7]Recent experimental support for Tulving's notion can be found in Mitchell (1989).

(1) Predictive effectiveness. This is exemplified by the discovery of laws . . . which allow the prediction of certain phenomena [e.g.] the speed of falling bodies.
(2) Metaphoric effectiveness . . . connecting domains of experience that were before apart, but with the form . . . that has the discipline of art.
(3) Formal effectiveness [which is] an ordering of elements [so] that one sees relationships that were not evident before, groupings that were before not present . . . . (p. 143)

The view of learning and creativity as extensions of the three processes (motor/habit, affect, semantics) also reinforces the work of Dreyfuss and Dreyfuss (1986). They claimed that we develop skills at *three levels* (calculative rationality, deliberative rationality, and arationality). Their study showed that nonexperts employed *calculative rationality:* they sought and employed context-free cues by precise rules (information processing). Competent thinkers developed hierarchical rule bases and collected a set of facts, a semantic net; they knew when, from "a particular constellation of those elements a certain conclusion should be drawn, decision made, or expectation investigated"—they employ *deliberative rationality.* Finally, Dreyfuss and Dreyfuss determined that experts responded, not even looking for facts or rules: *"When things are proceeding normally, experts don't solve problems and don't make decisions; they do what normally works"* (pp. 24–31)—*they employ arationality.*

This approach can be extended to high-level decision theoretic issues. One view of choice making suggests that the same automatic ("Dantzig"), probabilistic ("Bayesian"), and intuitive ("Godelian") processes I have suggested (Leven, 1988) for learning operate at the highest behavioral levels.[8] These broad behavioral levels of analysis find substantial support.

In neural network modeling, Levine (1986) suggested the applicability of a "three *weltanschauung*" view several years ago. His effort to model frontal function in the light of these categories continues (Levine et al., Chapter 9 of this volume).

These categories are not identical to ones we touched upon earlier, but they suggest a research agenda: to trace these systems.

WHAT THE MAN'S MIND TELLS HIM
ABOUT HIS BRAIN

We conclude with a provisional statement on the structure of mind and the construction of behavior. It is the expression of a research programme, not the results of years of inquiry.

---

[8]See also Suojanen's (1983) pathbreaking work.

The notion of three structures of behavior and knowing, clear to Pribram and MacLean, Marr and Tulving—each in a different way—makes structural and intuitive sense. Levine (1986; see also Levine et al., Chapter 9 of this volume) suggested ways to integrate this notion with quantitative neural network modeling. His blend of common sense and common scientific knowledge has driven the effort outlined here.

We shall briefly construct a three-part theory of structure and behavior for testing and simulation. It will be our ongoing concern to test it.

The three components are: *automaticity,* the development of what Wise (1987) called variable action patterns, form locus ceruleus to ganglia to cortex; *context-sensitivity,* the construing of *sense* from complexity, amygdarlarly, hippocampally, and temporal lobe-based and extending through the higher limbic system (including limbic cortex); and *semantics,* the cortical and neocortical categorizing process, the "accountant within." We tie the Mishkin et al. (1984) "habit memory" and the more limited procedural processes to automaticity. The model promoted by Zajonc (1984) of "affective memory" and the notion of *analogical reasoning* belong to context sensitivity. Last, traditional associative memory models, from spreading activation to Boltzmann machines, fall into the class of semantic models. Table 8.1 suggests a few of the large number of threefold structures proposed in various disciplines.

TABLE 8.1
A Sampling of Three-Fold Models.

Low Level		
	Information Construction: Fuxe	
Electrical	Chemical Trans-mitter	Paracrine Response
	Information Description: Semiotic (Peirce, Eco)	
Icon	Index	Symbol
Intermediate Level		
	Physiological Structure: MacLean	
Reptilian	Neomammalian	Limbic
	Memory: Tulving	
Procedural	Semantic	Episodic
Higher Level		
	Forms of Rationality: Dreyfuss and Dreyfuss	
Calculative	Deliberative	Arational
	Decision Making: Leven	
Dantzig	Bayesian	Godelian

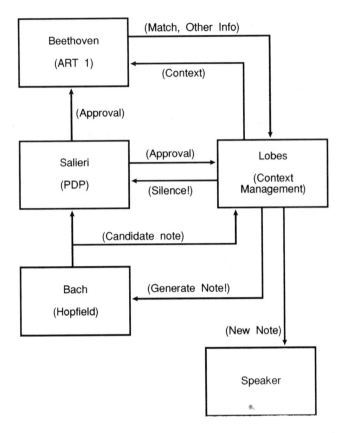

FIG. 8.18.   Structure of a hybrid neural network that composes melo-
dies. (Reprinted from Blackwood et al., with permission of Pergamon
Press)

It is our basic argument that the three operate at different speeds (in the order
we have listed, in descending order), perform recall functions in different ways
(neurochemistry more essential to simple pattern matching in automatic processing, electrical transmission central to semantic), and mediate each other by
massive interconnection. Yet, as Fuster (1980, 1985) and Levine (1986) maintained, it is apparent that prefrontal functions *drive* and *maintain order* among
these *flavors of memory* and *information.*

Can a "society of mind" be effectively modeled?

Elsberry (1989; see also Blackwood, Elsberry, & Leven, 1988) presented a
model of music composition, based on combining automatic (Hopfield), affective (ART), and semantic (Boltzmann/PDP) models of information processing.
Surprise to say, listeners claim his music is "pretty good."

For us to respond systematically to our inner processing requires that we ask daring questions, as Levine, Hestenes, and others in this volume do. Furthermore, it requires us to *try to make mistakes*—because that is the only way we shall ever get it right.

ACKNOWLEDGMENTS

Thanks are due, especially, to Dan Levine—my mentor, partner, friend, and confessor. His encouragement and guidance have been invaluable to this project (many of the *good* ideas are his). My colleagues at the Center for Brain Research and Information Sciences have offered insight and counsel during the latter stages: Karl Pribram, critic and guru; Joe King and Bill Hudspeth, helpful analysts. Wesley Elsberry and Diane Blackwood have participated from the beginning. I am most grateful to my wife Nina for her patience, sacrifice, and affection.

REFERENCES

Aggleton, J. & Mishkin, M. (1986). The amygdala: sensory gateway to the emotions. In J. Plutchik & H. Kellerman (Eds.), *Biological foundations of emotion* (pp. 281–299). New York: Academic Press.

Agren, H. & Terenius, L. (1988). Opioid peptides and mood: neuroendocrine aspects. In D. Ganten & D. Pfaff (Eds.), *Neuroendocrinology of mood* (pp. 273–290). New York: Springer-Verlag.

Alkon, D. (1989). Memory storage and neural systems. *Scientific American 261*(1), 42–50.

Arnold, M. (1984). *Memory and the brain*. Hillsdale, NJ: Lawrence Erlbaum Associates.

Bandura, A., Cioffi, D., Taylor, C., & Brouillard, M. (1988). Perceived self-efficacy in coping with cognitive stressors and opioid activation. *Journal of Personality and Social Psychology, 55,* 479–488.

Bergland, R. (1985). *The fabric of mind*. New York: Penguin.

Black, I., Adler, J., Dreyfuss, C., Friedman, W., LaGamma, E., & Roach, A. (1988). Experience and the biochemistry of information storage in the nervous system. In M. Gazzaniga (Ed.), *Perspectives in memory research* (pp. 3–22). Cambridge, MA: MIT Press.

Blackwood, D., Elsberry, W., & Leven, S. J. (1988). Competing network models and problem solving. *Neural Networks 1,* Supplement 1, p. 10.

Bruner, J. (1984). *In search of mind*. New York: Harper & Row.

Carpenter, G. A., & Grossberg, S. (1987). A massively parallel architecture for a self-organizing neural pattern recognition machine. *Computer Vision, Graphics, and Image Processing, 37,* 54–115.

Carpenter, G. A., & Grossberg, S. (1989). Search mechanisms for adaptive resonance theory (ART) architecture. *International Joint Conference on Neural Networks, 1,* 201–205.

Castelucci, V. F., Schacher, S., Montarolo, P. G., Mackey, S., Glanzman, D. L., Hawkins, R. D., Abrams, T. W., Goelet, P., & Kandel, E. R. (1986). Convergence of small molecule and peptide transmitters on a common molecular cascade. In T. Hokfelt, K. Fuxe, & B. Pernow (Eds.), *Coexistence of neuronal messages: a new principle in chemical transmission* (pp. 83–102). Amsterdam: Elsevier.

Changeux, J.-P. (1986). Coexistence of neuronal messengers and molecular selection. In T. Hokfelt, K. Fuxe, & B. Pernow (Eds.), *Coexistence of neuronal messages: a new principle in chemical transmission* (pp. 373–403). Amsterdam: Elsevier.

DeWied, D. (1987). The neuropeptide concept. In E. R. DeKloet, V. M. Wiegant, & D. DeWied (Eds.), *Neuropeptides and brain function*. Amsterdam: Elsevier.

Dreyfuss, H. L., & Dreyfuss, S. (1986). *Mind over machine*. New York: Free Press.

Duman, R., & Enna, S. (1987). On the relationship between hormones, depression, and neurotransmitter receptor responses to antidepressants. In U. Halbreich (Ed.), *Hormones and depression* (pp. 279–296). New York: Raven.

Dunn, A. (1986). Biochemical correlates of learning and memory. In J. Martinez, Jr. & R. Kesner (Eds.), *Learning and memory: a biological view*. New York: Academic Press.

Eccles, J. (1986). Chemical transmission and Dale's principle. In T. Hokfelt, K. Fuxe, & B. Pernow (Eds.), *Coexistence of neuronal messages: a new principle in chemical transmission* (pp. 3–13). Amsterdam: Elsevier.

Elsberry, W. R. (1989). Integration and hybridization in neural network modeling. Unpublished master's thesis, University of Texas at Arlington.

Fodor, J. A. (1984). *Modularity of mind*. Cambridge, MA: MIT Press.

Fuster, J. M. (1980). *The prefrontal cortex*. New York: Raven.

Fuster, J. M. (1985). The prefrontal cortex; mediator of cross-temporal contingencies. *Human Neurobiology, 4,* 169–179.

Fuxe, K., Agnati, L., Harfstrand, A., Cintra, A., Aronsson, M., Zoli, M., & Gustafsson, J.-A. (1988). Principles for the hormone regulation of wiring transmission and volume transmission in the central nervous system. In D. Ganten & D. Pfaff (Eds.), *Neuroendocrinology of mood* (pp. 1–53). New York: Springer-Verlag.

Gazzaniga, M. (ed.). (1988). *Perspectives in memory research*. Cambridge, MA: MIT Press.

Gilbert, P. (1984). *Depression: from psychology to brain state*. Hillsdale, NJ: Lawrence Erlbaum Associates.

Glazer, H. I. & Weiss, J. M. (1976). Long-term and transitory interference effect: an alternative to learned helplessness. *Journal of Experimental Psychology: Animal Behavior Processes 2,* 191–201.

Gold, P. W., Kling, M. A., Demitrack, M. A., Whitfield, H., Kolageras, K., Loriaux, D. L., & Chrousos, G. P. (1988). Clinical studies with corticotropin releasing hormone: implications for hypothalamic-pituitary-adrenal dysfunction in depression and related disorders. In D. Ganten & D. Pfaff (Eds.), *Neuroendocrinology of mood* (pp. 55–77). New York: Springer-Verlag.

Gray, J. (1982). *The neuropsychology of anxiety*. New York: Oxford University Press.

Gray, J. (1987). *The psychology of fear and stress*. New York: Cambridge University Press.

Grossberg, S. (1980). How does a brain build a cognitive code? *Psychological Review, 87,* 1–51.

Grossberg, S., Ed. (1987). *The adaptive brain*, Vols. I and II. New York: Elsevier.

Grossberg, S. (1988). *Neural networks and natural intelligence*. Cambridge, MA: MIT Press.

Grossberg, S., & Kuperstein, M. (1989). *Neural dynamics of adaptive sensory-motor control: Ballistic eye movements*. Elmsford, NY: Pergamon.

Haines, D., Dietrichs, E., & Sowa, T. (1984). Hypothalamic-cerebellar and cerebello-hypothalamic pathways: A review and hypothesis concerning cerebellar circuits which may influence autonomic centers and affective behavior. *Brain, Behavior, and Evolution, 24,* 198–220.

Halbreich, U. (ed.). (1987). *Hormones and depression*. New York: Raven.

Haracz, J., Minor, T., Wilkins, J. & Zimmerman, E. (1988). Learned helplessness: an experimental model of the DST in rats. *Biological Psychiatry, 23,* 388–396.

Hendry, S. (1987). Recent advances in understanding the intrinsic circuitry of the cerebral cortex. In S. Wise (Ed.), *Higher brain functions* (pp. 241–284). New York: Wiley.

Henn, F. (1987). Models of self-helplessness and melancholia in animals. In U. Halbreich, U. (Ed.), *Hormones and depression,* (pp. 255–262). New York: Raven.

Hilgard, E. (1980). The trilogy of mind: cognition, affection, and conation. *Journal of the History of the Behavioral Sciences, 16,* 107–117.

Hyland, B. (1987). A control theory model of depression. *Psychobiology, 15*, 311–328.

Isaacson, R. (1982). *The limbic system* (2nd ed.). New York: Plenum.

Iversen, L. (1986). Chemical signaling in the nervous system. In T. Hokfelt, K. Fuxe, & B. Pernow (Eds.), *Coexistence of neuronal messages: a new principle in chemical transmission* (pp. 15–21). Amsterdam: Elsevier.

Iversen, S. (1984). Recent advances in the anatomy and chemistry of the limbic system. In M. Trimble, & E. Zarifian (Eds.), *Psychopharmacology of the limbic system* (pp. 1–16). New York: Oxford University Press.

Iversen, S. & Iversen, L. (1981). *Behavioral Pharmacology*, (2nd ed.). New York: Oxford University Press.

Kandel, E. R., & Schwartz, J. H. (Eds.). (1985). *Principles of Neural Science*. New York: Elsevier.

Kohonen, T. (1988). Representation of sensory information in self-organizing feature maps, and the relation of these maps to distributed memory networks. In R. Cotterill (ed.), *Computer simulation in brain science* (pp. 12–25). Cambridge, England: Cambridge University Press.

Kraemer, G. W. (1986). Causes of changes in brain noradrenaline systems and later effects on responses to social stressors in rhesus monkeys: the cascade hypothesis. In R. Porter, G. Bock, & S. Clark (Eds.), *Antidepressants and receptor function* (pp. 216–233). New York: Wiley.

Lang, P. (1988). Fear, anxiety, and panic: context, cognition, and visceral arousal. In S. Rachman & J. Maser (Eds.), *Panic: psychological perspectives*. Hillsdale, NJ: Lawrence Erlbaum Associates.

Leven, S. (1987). S. A. M.: a triune extension to the A. R. T. model. Paper presented at the *Conference on Networks in Brain and Computer Architecture*, Denton, TX, October, 1987.

Leven, S. (1988). Choice and neural process. Unpublished doctoral dissertation, University of Texas at Arlington.

Leven, S. J. & Levine, D. S. (1987). Effects of reinforcement on knowledge retrieval and evaluation. *First International Conference on Neural Networks II*, 269–279.

Levine, D. S. (1983). Neural population modeling and psychology: a review. *Mathematical Biosciences, 66*, 1–86.

Levine, D. S. (1986). A neural network theory of frontal lobe function. *In Proceedings of the Eighth Annual Conference of the Cognitive Science Society* (pp. 716–727). Hillsdale, NJ: Lawrence Erlbaum Associates, 1986.

Levine, D. S. & Prueitt, P. S. (1989). Modeling aspects of frontal lobe damage: novelty and perseveration. *Neural Networks 2*, 103–116.

Lynch, G., & Baudry, M. (1988). Structure-function relationships in the organization of memory. In M. Gazzaniga (Ed.), *Perspectives in Memory Research* (pp. 23–91). Cambridge, MA: MIT Press.

MacLean, P. D. (1970). The triune brain, emotion, and scientific bias. In F. Schmitt (Ed.), *The Neurosciences Second Study Program*. New York: Rockefeller University Press.

MacLean, P. D. (1980). Sensory and perceptive factors in emotional functions of the triune brain. In A. Rorty (Ed.), *Explaining emotions* (pp. 9–36). Berkeley, CA: University of California Press.

Maier, S. F., Sherman, J. E., Lewis, J. W., Terman, G. W., & Liebeskind, J. C. (1983). The opioid/nonopioid nature of stress-induced analgesia and learned helplessness. *Journal of Experimental Psychology: Animal Behavior Processes, 9*, 80–91.

Marr, D. (1982). *Vision*. San Francisco: W. H. Freeman.

Martinez, J., Jr. (1986). Memory: drugs and hormones. In J. Martinez, Jr. & R. Kesner (Eds.), *Learning and memory: a biological view* (pp. 127–163). New York: Academic Press.

Martinez, J., Jr., Weinberger, S., & Schultheis, G. (1988). Enkephalins in learning and memory: a review of evidence for a site of action outside the blood-brain barrier. *Behavioral and Neural Biology, 49*, 192–221.

McCulloch, W. S. (1965). *Embodiments of mind*. Cambridge, MA: MIT Press.

Melzack, R., & Wall, P. (1988). *The challenge of pain* (revised edition). New York: Penguin.

Miller, G., Galanter, E., & Pribram, K. H. (1960). *Plans and the structure of behavior*. New York: Random House.

Miller, S., & Seligman, M. (1982). The reformulated model of helplessness and depression: evidence and theory. In R. Neufeld (Ed.), *Psychological stress and psychopathology*. New York: McGraw-Hill.

Minor, T., Pelleymounter, M., & Maier, S. (1988). Uncontrollable shock, forebrain norepinephrine, and stimulus selection during choice-escape learning. *Psychobiology, 16*, 135–145.

Mishkin, M., Malamut, B., & Bachevalier, J. (1984). Memories and habits: Two neural systems. In G. Lynch, J. L. McGaugh, & N. M. Weinberger (Eds.), *Neurobiology of Learning and Memory*. New York, London: Guilford.

Mitchell, D. (1989). How many memory systems are there? Evidence from aging. *Journal of Experimental Psychology: Learning, Memory, and Cognition, 15*, 31–49.

Nieuwenhuys, P. (1985). *Chemoarchitecture of the brain*. New York: Springer-Verlag.

Ortony, A., Clore, G., & Collins, A. (1988). *The cognitive structure of emotions*. New York: Cambridge University Press.

Petty, F. (1986). GABA mechanisms in learned helplessness. In G. Bartholini, K. Lloyd, & P. Morselli (Eds.), *GABA and mood disorders* (pp. 61–66). New York: Raven.

Post, R., Weiss, S., & Rubinow, D. (1988). Recurrent affective disorders: lesions from limbic kindling. In D. Ganten, & D. Pfaff (Eds.), *Neuroendocrinology of mood* (pp. 91–115). New York: Springer-Verlag.

Prange, A., Whybrow, P., & Loosen, P. (1987). Depression and other mental symptoms in endocrine disorders: an overview. In U. Halbreich, U. (Ed.), *Hormones and depression* (pp. 313–324). New York: Raven.

Pribram, K. (1991). *Holonomy and Structure in Figural Processing: the MacEachran Lectures*. Hillsdale, NJ: Lawrence Erlbaum Associates, in press.

Rall, W., & Segev, I. (1988). Excitable dendritic spine clusters: nonlinear synaptic processing. In R. Cotterill (Ed.), *Models of brain function* (pp. 26–43). Cambridge, England: Cambridge University Press.

Roberts, G., Polak, J., & Crow, T. (1984). Peptide circuitry of the limbic system. In M. Trimble, & E. Zarifian (Eds.), *Psychopharmacology of the limbic system* (pp. 226–243). New York: Oxford University Press.

Scatton, B., Nishikawa, T., Dennis, T., Dedek, J., Curet, O., Zivkovic, B., Bartholini, G. (1986). GABAergic modulation of central noradrenergic and serotonergic neuronal activity. In G. Bartholini, K. Lloyd, & P. Morselli (Eds.), *GABA and mood disorders* (pp. 67–75). New York: Raven.

Schank, R. (1982). *Dynamic memory: a theory of reminding and learning*. Cambridge, England: Cambridge University Press.

Segal, Z. (1988). Appraisal of the self-schema construct in cognitive models of depression. *Psychological Bulletin, 103*, 147–162.

Seligman, M. (1975). *Helplessness*. New York: W. H. Freeman.

Shepherd, G. M. (1988). *Neurobiology* (2nd ed.). New York: Oxford University Press.

Simonov, P. (1983). The reinforcement function of emotions. In E. A. Asratyan & P. V. Simonov (Eds.), *The learning brain*. Moscow: MIR Publishers.

Simonov, P. (1986). *The emotional brain*. New York: Plenum.

Stinus, L., Kelly, A., & Winnock, M. (1984). Neuropeptides and limbic system function. In M. Trimble, & E. Zarifian (Eds.), *Psychopharmacology of the limbic system* (pp. 209–225). New York: Oxford University Press.

Suojanen, W. (1983). Management and the human mind: on the three kinds of contingencies. In R. Bessinger & W. Suojanen (Eds.), *Management and the brain*. Atlanta: Georgia State University Press.

Swanson, L. W., Sawchenko, P. E., & Lind, R. W. (1986). Regulation of multiple peptides in CRF parvocellular neurosecretory neurons: implications for the stress response. In T. Hokfelt, K. Fuxe, & B. Pernow (Eds.), *Coexistence of neuronal messages: a new principle in chemical transmission* (pp. 169–190).

Tulving, E. (1985). How many memory systems are there? *American Psychologist, 40*, 385–398.

VanPraag, H. M. (1986). Monoamines and depression. In J. Plutchik & H. Kellerman (Eds.), *Biological foundations of emotion* (pp. 335–361). New York: Academic Press.

Weiner, B. (1986). *An attributional theory of motivation and emotion.* New York: Springer-Verlag.

Weiss, J., & Simson, P. (1986). Depression in an animal model: focus on the locus coeruleus. In R. Porter, G. Bock, & S. Clark (Eds.), *Antidepressants and receptor function.* New York: Wiley.

Willner, P. (1985). *Depression: a psychobiological synthesis.* New York: Wiley Interscience.

Winograd, T., & Flores, F. (1986). *Understanding Computers and Cognition: a New Foundation for Design.* Norwood, NJ: Ablex.

Wise, S., Ed. (1987). Higher brain functions. New York: Wiley.

Zajonc, R. (1980). Feeling and thinking: preferences need no inferences. *American Psychologist, 3–5*, 151–175.

Zajonc, R. (1984). The interaction of affect and cognition. In K. Scherer, & P. Ekman (Eds.), *Approaches to emotion* (pp. 239–246). Hillsdale, NJ: Lawrence Erlbaum Associates.

Zucker, R. S. (1989). Short-term synaptic plasticity: a review. *Annual Review of Neuroscience, 12*, 13–31.

9 Integration, Disintegration, and the Frontal Lobes

Daniel S. Levine
University of Texas at Arlington

Samuel J. Leven
Radford University and For a New Social Science

Paul S. Prueitt
Georgetown University

Recent neural network modeling supports a partial qualitative view of the pre-frontal cortex developed over decades by Milner, Pribram, Nauta, and other neurobiologists. Two mutually paradoxical effects of frontal damage, namely cognitive perseveration and novelty preference, are explained by weakened gain of signals from motivational regions to sensory regions. Networks embodying such principles as adaptive resonance, synaptic gating, and opponent processing have been shown to simulate these effects. Such motivational-sensory linkage combines with planning and time-sequence organization into a role described by Pribram as that of "executive of the brain." It is suggested that most functions needed for this executive can be modeled by suitable reconcatenation at many hierarchical levels of the same architectures used in our simulations, with two added mechanisms. The additions are the masking field and the avalanche, which serve to link perceptual and motor events across time.

It is conjectured that frontal lobe architectures embody analogies between some functions at the level of perception or movement, and other functions at the level of cognition or belief. Perseveration of movements is analogous to inflexibility of categorizations, whereas ability to change speech parsing with context is analogous to plasticity in the cognitive boundaries of beliefs. The frontal lobes enable (but do not force) their possessors to transcend the tyranny of dichotomous emotional constructs and reach more rewarding syntheses.

OUR MENTAL LIFE: ANARCHIC OR DEMOCRATIC?

The prefrontal area of the neocortex is involved in every imaginable mental activity (and probably a few that are not yet imagined) beyond the lowest levels of complexity. Its connections with the other association areas of cortex, both temporal and parietal, and with the secondary processing areas of cortex for each sensory modality give it a role in the processing of sensory data. Its connections, both directly and via the mediodorsal thalamus, with the limbic system and hypothalamus give it a role in the processing of emotions and internal states. Its connections with midbrain regions such as the ventral tegmentum and substantia nigra (see Hestenes, chapter 7 in this volume) give it a role in the modulation of responses to sensory patterns. Its connections with motor control areas such as the corpus striatum give it a role in the planning of movements.

The literature on functions of the prefrontal cortex in monkeys and humans is vast. Most classical work on this part of the brain (e.g., Jacobsen, 1935; Pribram, 1961; Spaet & Harlow, 1943; Warren & Akert, 1964) deals with cognitive and behavioral effects of prefrontal lesions. (To clarify the boundaries of the brain region considered in this chapter, it consists of the part of the frontal lobes that is association cortex, and excludes the precentral motor cortex. This region is also distinguished as the part of neocortex that is reciprocally connected with the mediodorsal nucleus of the thalamus. However, we shall refer to the region interchangeably as either "prefrontal cortex," "frontal cortex," or "the frontal lobes"—except for one mention of the frontal eye fields that are part of the frontal lobes but not of the prefrontal cortex proper.) More recently, these behavioral data have been supplemented by electrophysiological data from single prefrontal neurons (for example, Fuster, Bauer, & Jervey, 1982; Goldman-Rakic, 1984, 1989; Rosenkilde, Bauer, & Fuster, 1981).

Trying to incorporate a large part of this literature into a good qualitative theory, let alone a quantifiable neural network theory, is a daunting task. Some recent books (for example, Stuss & Benson, 1986) have, therefore, tended to steer clear of general conclusions. Yet conclusions made by earlier investigators have, thus far, stood the test of time. This has encouraged us to embark on a general program of integrating these qualitative ideas into existing neural network theories of other processes; this chapter is a continuation of work in Levine (1986), Leven and Levine (1987), and Levine and Prueitt (1989).

Let us review a few of these functional conclusions. Nauta (1971) stressed the integration of emotional and visceral information about the organism's internal state with sensory information about the environment, thereby enabling decisions to be made (and acted on) about the consequences of events. Fuster (1980, 1985) stressed the integration of behavior into goal-directed temporal sequences. Pribram (1973) included both these types of functions in his designation of the prefrontal cortex as "the executive of the brain."

The primary function of the frontal lobes can be described best by the overused word *integration:* coordinating thoughts, feelings, behaviors, beliefs, and plans into efficient, coherent use of the complex environment that our own expanded mental capacities have created. Of late it has become fashionable to see multiplicity rather than unity in human personalities. Often this multiplicity is considered tantamount to anarchy (Gazzaniga, 1986; Minsky, 1986).

Perhaps the best known multiple mind notion is the triune brain theory (for example, Mac Lean, 1970). From behavioral studies of different brain areas, Mac Lean conjectured that the human brain is divided into three "layers" that arrived at different stages of evolution. The deepest layer is the "reptilian brain," responsible for automatic instinctive behavior—behavior that is sometimes necessary for the organism's survival and sometimes (as in the case of dominance hierarchies) merely part of the species' habitual patterns. Above the reptilian brain is the "old mammalian brain," responsible for emotions such as fear, love, and anger that attend the needs for individual and species survival. Finally, at the top, is the "new mammalian brain," responsible for rational strategies and verbal capacities.

Mac Lean's scheme is quite oversimplified and has received some justified scientific criticism (e.g., Pribram, 1984, pp. 13–17). For example, some of his "old mammalian" areas, like the hippocampus, are well developed in reptiles. Further, lesions of limbic system regions can produce cognitive as well as emotional deficits. Yet his qualitative notion of triunity, his idea that reason and emotion must be supplemented by a third organizing principle of instinct or habit, has been supported by recent data. For example, Mishkin, Malamut, and Bachevalier (1984) summarized evidence that there are separate systems for encoding the reinforcement value of events (centered in the hippocampus and amygdala, parts of Mac Lean's old mammalian brain) and for encoding motor habits (centered in the corpus striatum, part of Mac Lean's reptilian brain). The "habit" system seems to have a memory of specific movements made regardless of their reinforcement value. Our work will suggest that the habit system encodes not only *motor* habits but also *cognitive* habits—obsessions, prejudices, and stereotypes, for example.

Mac Lean described the "three brains" within us metaphorically as a person, a horse, and a crocodile in the same room, communicating badly with each other. However, the miscommunication he described is mitigated by the frontal lobes— when we use them well. Of all the regions of our cerebral cortex, the prefrontal is *both* the area encoding the most complex cognitive associations and the area most directly connected with the "old mammalian" emotional brain (the limbic system and hypothalamus). If anything in our brains bespeaks the benevolent plan of nature, that fact does. At best "the executive of the brain" (Pribram, 1973) is a democratic C.E.O., letting all the "employees" (the reason, emotion, and habit systems) perform their functions but supervising to make sure every system's "needs" are met.

Clearly this "best of all possible worlds" (Voltaire, 1966) does not happen all the time. Even in people without obvious brain damage, the frontal "executive" can at times be either too weak or too strong. Now we turn to the study of such sub-optimal conditions, exaggerated by brain damage or biochemical abnormality.

THE NOVELTY–PERSEVERATION PARADOX

Frontal lesions often lead to perseveration in formerly rewarding behavior after it ceases to be rewarding (Milner, 1963, 1964; Konorski & Lawicka, 1964). In addition, frontal damage leads to deficits in responding to stimuli after a delay (Jacobsen, 1935; Spaet & Harlow, 1943; Stamm, 1964). These delay deficits were at first thought to reflect impairment of short-term memory but were later found instead to illustrate forms of perseveration.

Yet, if novel objects are introduced, frontally lesioned monkeys change their behavior to approach the novel objects more readily than do normal monkeys (Pribram, 1961). How can the same brain lesions lead to increased perseveration if there are changes in reinforcement contingencies, but to decreased perseveration if there are changes in the stimuli presented?

One possible explanation is that the primary locus of damage within the prefrontal cortex is different for the two sets of experiments. The perseverating patients Milner (1964) found were lesioned in the dorsolateral frontal area, whereas the novelty-preferring monkeys Pribram (1961) found were lesioned in the orbital (or ventral) frontal area. These two areas have functional differences for which a complete theory is lacking. (Pribram, 1973, functionally divided the orbital area further into medial and posterior orbital.) In general the dorsal area has reciprocal connections with the secondary sensory cortices, whereas the orbital area has reciprocal connections (some via the mediodorsal thalamus) with the limbic system and hypothalamus. Hence (Fuster, 1980):

> Lesion studies indicate that the cortex of the dorsal and lateral prefrontal surface is primarily involved in cognitive aspects of behavior. The rest of the prefrontal cortex, medial and ventral, appears to be mostly involved in affective and moti-vational functions and in the inhibitory control of both external influences and internal tendencies that interfere with purposive behavior and provoke inappropri-ate motor acts. (p. 74)

However, Levine and Prueitt (1989) simulated both the novelty and perseveration data using a neural network model that ignores subregion differences. They simply modeled frontal damage as the weakening of certain connections. The effects of this weakening were shown to mirror aspects of a "frontal lobe syn-drome" the existence of which is widely accepted, a syndrome that includes both novelty and perseveration effects. The cognitive effects of dorsal damage and the motivational effects of orbital damage were both treated as part of a general defect in the guidance of behavior by motivational influences.

Nauta (1971) emphasized that the frontal cortex integrates sensory information from the neocortex with visceral information from the hypothalamus and limbic system. The lack of such integration, resulting from frontal damage, leads to a variable set of effects that Nauta (1971, p. 182) called "interoceptive agnosia." These effects may include distractibility (see also Grueninger & Pribram, 1969; Wilkins, Shallice, & McCarthy, 1987), lack of foresight, and situationally inappropriate behavior. (There have been clinical reports, for example, of frontal patients urinating in public or telling off-color jokes at funerals.) In general severing of fronto-limbic cognitive-motivational links decreases the influence of reward or punishment on behavior. Therefore, nonaffective influences on behavioral decisions, including *both* entrenched habits and attraction to novelty, are disinhibited. Which of those two is stronger depends on the task involved.

Milner (1963, 1964) compared patients with different brain lesions and normal subjects on the Wisconsin Card Sorting Test. In this test, a subject is given a sequence of 128 cards, each displaying a number, color, and shape, as shown in Fig. 9.1. The subject has to match the card shown to one of four template cards. The experimenter then says whether the match is right or wrong, not giving a reason. After ten correct matches in a row to color, the experimenter (without warning) switches the criterion to shape. Then, if ten correct matches are made in a row to shape, the criterion shifts to number, then back to color, and so on. Most patients with damage to the dorsolateral frontal cortex learned the color criterion

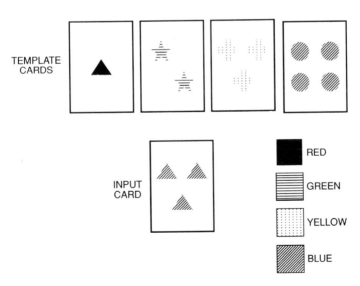

FIG. 9.1.   Cards used in the Wisconsin Card Sorting Test; see text for details.

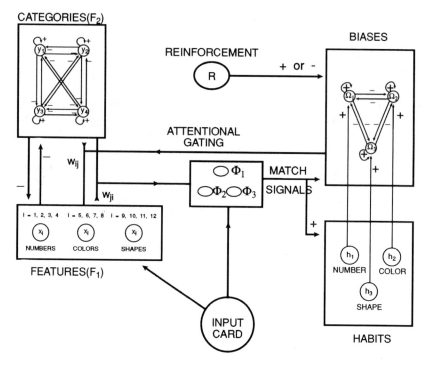

FIG. 9.2. Neural network, based on adaptive resonance theory, used in the simulation of Milner's card sorting data. Frontal lobe damage is modeled by reduced gain of positive and negative signals from the reinforcement node R to the bias nodes Ω_i ($i = 1$ for number, 2 for color, 3 for shape). The bias nodes in turn gate signals from feature to category nodes. Details of interactions between bias nodes, habit nodes, and match signals are in the text. (From Leven & Levine, 1987; reprinted with permission of the IEEE.)

as quickly as normals but never switched to shape after having learned color. Normals and patients with other brain lesions, by contrast, achieved on the average four or five criteria (color, shape, number, color, shape) over 128 trials.

Milner's results were simulated using the neural network of Fig. 9.2. This network builds on the adaptive resonance theory network (ART 1) of Carpenter and Grossberg (1987a), which is designed to classify input patterns. ART 1 includes a field of nodes coding input features and another field of nodes coding categories. A given pattern, treated as a vector of feature node activities, differentially excites category nodes, which competitively inhibit each other. Leven and Levine (1987) added to ART 1 a mechanism for attentional biases within the feature field (cf. Grossberg & Levine, 1975).

In the network of Fig. 9.2, nodes in the field F_1 code individual features (4 numbers, 4 colors, 4 shapes). Nodes in the field F_2 code template cards, each establishing the category of cards "similar" to it. F_1 divides into three "sub-fields" (number, color, and shape). To each subfield corresponds a "habit node" and a "bias node," separate from F_1 and F_2. Habit nodes detect how often classifications have been made, rightly or wrongly, on the basis of the given criterion. Bias nodes are affected by both habit node activities and reinforcement signals (the experimenter's statements of "Right" or "Wrong").

Synaptic strengths z_{ij} and z_{ji} between F_1 and F_2 are large when node x_i represents a feature present in card y_j. Attentional gating from bias nodes selectively enhances F_1-to-F_2 signals; for example, if color bias is high, and shape bias is low, the "one red triangle" node at F_2 is more excited by the "red" node at F_1 than by the "triangle" node. When an input card is presented, the template card whose activity y_j is largest in response to the input is chosen as the one matched. If the card chosen and the input card share a feature (color, shape, or number), a "match signal" is sent to the habit and bias nodes. This signal either excites or inhibits the bias node, depending on the sign of reinforcement.

Fig. 9.3 shows results of our simulations. The parameter α that was varied measures gain of signals (positive or negative) from the reinforcement node to the bias nodes. With high α, the network acted like one of Milner's normal subjects. It reached ten correct responses in a row five times during 128 trials. With low α, the network acted like one of Milner's dorsal frontal patients. It learned the color criterion as rapidly as did the "normal" network, but classified on the basis of color for all remaining trials.

Fig. 9.4 shows an alternative network for simulating the Milner data. In this network, input patterns at F_1 are compared with prototype patterns stored at the synaptic weights from F_2 to F_1, as in the ART networks of Carpenter and Grossberg (1987a, 1987b). In ART, a vigilance parameter is used to determine the degree of match that is recognized by the network. This vigilance parameter can be interpreted as the gain of signals from a preprocessing layer to a node that shuts off reset at the F_2 level. The bias nodes, instead of gating F_1-to-F_2 signals as in Fig. 9.2, selectively modulate contributions of different subfields of F_1 to these vigilance gain signals.

		CRITERION	TRIAL
FIG. 9.3. Simulation results on the network of FIG. 9.2. Trial number listed is the first one on which the network achieved ten correct matches in a row based on the given criterion. (From Levine & Prueitt, 1989; reprinted with permission of Pergamon Press).	$\alpha = 4$ ("Normal")	Color	13
		Shape	40
		Number	82
		Color (again)	96
		Shape (again)	115
	$\alpha = 1.5$ ("Frontally Damaged")	Color	13
		Thereafter, classified by color for all remaining trials	

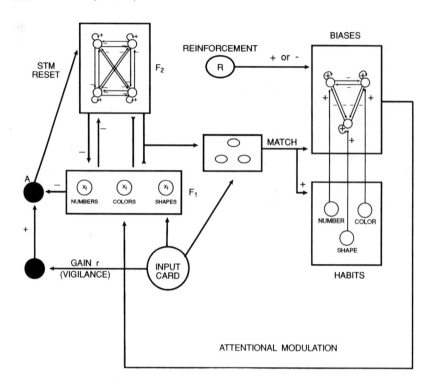

FIG. 9.4.   An alternative to the network of FIG. 9.2 for explaining the card sorting data. If [X] is the total activity at F_1 and [I] the total activity at the input (card) level, the reset node A is inhibited, if and only if [X] > r[I], which is the criterion for match between the input and the active top–down category prototype. As in Carpenter and Grossberg (1987a) when A is activated, reset occurs at F_2, allowing a new category to be tested. When A is inhibited, the input is placed in the active category. Bias nodes, instead of modulating bottom–up synapses as in FIG. 9.2, selectively modulate contributions of different features to overall F_1 activity.

Parts of the network of Fig. 9.4 exhibit some similarities with known properties of various neurotransmitter systems originating in different subcortical regions (cf. Foote & Morrison, 1987; Hestenes, chapter 7 in this volume). The gain from reinforcement to bias nodes is somewhat analogous to the norepinephrine (NE) system originating in the midbrain locus coeruleus (see also Ricart, chapter 5 in this volume). The NE system projects diffusely to the neocortex and appears to enhance responses to rewarding, aversive, or novel stimuli. Likewise the more localized connections between bias nodes and feature nodes in Fig. 9.4 show some analogy with the acetylcholine system originating in the nucleus basalis of the forebrain. At this stage, detailed anatomical ascription is premature, but the analogies are suggestive enough to drive the next stage of research on these models.

Separation of habit and reinforcement loci is compatible with macaque monkey data showing that memories of motor responses and memories of the reinforcement values of events are encoded in interacting but separate neural systems (Mishkin et al., 1984; Mishkin & Appenzeller, 1987). Perseveration of specific movements, as opposed to decision criteria, could be modeled using positive feedback from habit nodes to bias nodes to feature nodes without involvement of a category layer.

As for novelty preference, Pribram (1961) compared normal and frontally lesioned rhesus monkeys in a scene with several junk objects. In the first step of the experiment, the monkey is presented with one cue, a junk object placed over one of twelve holes drilled in a wooden board. A peanut has been placed under this cue. After a certain fixed number of trials in which the monkey first lifts the cue and is, thus, rewarded, a second (novel) junk object is introduced while the board is hidden from the monkey's view. This object is placed over another of the twelve holes. Again the reward (peanut) is placed under the novel cue. This same process is repeated until all the holes are covered with junk objects. Each time the peanut remains under the same (novel) cue until the animal finds the peanut a certain number of times.

Fig. 9.5 shows Pribram's results. The number of repetitive errors (liftings of the familiar object) before the monkey first selects the novel object is shown for both normal and frontally damaged ("frontal") subjects. In general frontal animals make fewer errors than normals, being more attracted to the novel object.

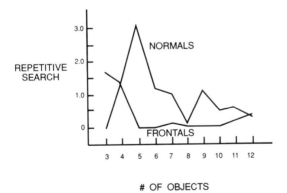

FIG. 9.5. Experimental data on frontally damaged versus normal rhesus monkeys in a scene with up to 12 junk objects. The graph shows how often, on the average, the monkey approaches the previously rewarded object before reaching a criterion number of consecutive responses to the novel one. (From Pribram, 1961; reprinted with permission of Academic Press.)

(Frontal animals remained variable in their responses, however, even after the first approach to the novel object.) The greater attraction to novelty on the part of frontals is most pronounced over the middle range of cues. The performance of the frontal animals was worse if there were very few cues, and the performance of the normals improved with very many cues.

We shall return later in the chapter to a qualitative explanation of the effects at the extreme ends of the graph in Fig. 9.5. However, first we shall discuss a network Levine and Prueitt (1989) simulated, which explains the novelty effects described in the middle range of that graph. Hence, we must first explain attraction to novelty in any animals (brain damaged or normal). To do so, let us briefly review the neural network notion of *gated dipole*. Gated dipoles are devices, using habituating chemical transmitters, for comparing current values of stimulus or reinforcement variables to recent past values of the same variables. In this way, reactions to novel or unexpected events are more enhanced than reactions to familiar or expected events, other things being equal.

Grossberg (1972a, 1972b) first introduced gated dipoles in a model of avoidance conditioning. Suppose an animal receiving steady electric shock presses a lever that turns off the shock. Later, in the same context, the animal's tendency to press the lever is increased. How can a motor response associated with the *absence* of negative reinforcement (shock) become itself positively reinforcing? If I touch the back wall of my room and do not get shocked, my tendency to touch that wall is not increased. Hence, absence of shock has no intrinsic reward value and must become (transiently) rewarding by contrast with an ongoing positive shock level.

Fig. 9.6 shows a schematic gated dipole with its equations. The synapses marked with squares have a chemical transmitter that tends to be depleted with activity, as indicated by the $-yz$ terms in the differential equations for those z values, where z denotes the amount of available transmitter. Other terms in those equations denote new transmitter production. The amount produced is greatest when the transmitter is much less than its maximum (in this case, .5).

In Fig. 9.6, the input J represents shock, for example. I is nonspecific arousal to both channels y_1-to-x_1-to-x_3 and y_2-to-x_2-to-x_4. While shock is on, the left channel receives more input than the right channel; hence, transmitter is more depleted at z_1 than at z_2. However, the greater input overcomes the more depleted transmitter, so the left channel activity x_1 exceeds the right channel activity x_2. This leads, by feedforward competition between channels, to net positive activity of the left channel output node x_3. However, for a short time after shock ends, both channels receive equal inputs I, but the right channel is less depleted of transmitter than the left channel. Hence, the right channel activity x_2 now exceeds x_1 until the depleted transmitter recovers. Competition now leads to net positive activity of the right channel output node x_4. Whichever of x_3 and x_4 has positive activity either excites or inhibits x_5, thereby enhancing or suppressing a particular motor or cognitive response.

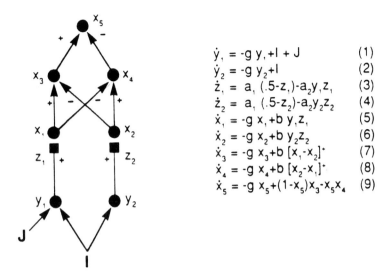

$$\dot{y}_1 = -g\, y_1 + I + J \qquad (1)$$
$$\dot{y}_2 = -g\, y_2 + I \qquad (2)$$
$$\dot{z}_1 = a_1\,(.5 - z_1) - a_2 y_1 z_1 \qquad (3)$$
$$\dot{z}_2 = a_1\,(.5 - z_2) - a_2 y_2 z_2 \qquad (4)$$
$$\dot{x}_1 = -g\, x_1 + b\, y_1 z_1 \qquad (5)$$
$$\dot{x}_2 = -g\, x_2 + b\, y_2 z_2 \qquad (6)$$
$$\dot{x}_3 = -g\, x_3 + b\, [x_1 - x_2]^+ \qquad (7)$$
$$\dot{x}_4 = -g\, x_4 + b\, [x_2 - x_1]^+ \qquad (8)$$
$$\dot{x}_5 = -g\, x_5 + (1 - x_5)x_3 - x_5 x_4 \qquad (9)$$

FIG. 9.6. Schematic gated dipole with two competing channels (representing, for example, "fear and relief," if the input J is electric shock, or "on and off," if J is a given sensory stimulus) and its system equations. I is a nonspecific arousal input to both channels. Synapses with depletable transmitter, as shown by Equations (3) and (4), are indicated by filled-in squares. See text for details. For any real number u, the symbol u^+ denotes max $(u, 0)$. (From Levine & Prueitt, 1989; reprinted with permission of Pergamon Press).

Characteristic output of one gated dipole is graphed in Fig. 9.7. As that figure indicates, while the input J is on, x_3 is activated. After J is shut off, x_4 is activated for a period of time, with somewhat less intensity than was x_3 earlier.

More recently (Grossberg, 1980; Levine & Prueitt, 1989), gated dipoles have been generalized from the reinforcement domain to the sensory domain. In the sensory domain, a gated dipole consists of "on cells" and "off cells" responding to the presence or absence of a particular sensory stimulus. On cells and off cells for different stimuli are joined into a *dipole field*.

Fig. 9.8 shows a dipole field used to model Pribram's data. Two dipole channel pairs are shown, one corresponding to an old cue and one to a novel cue. The nodes $x_{1,5}$ and $x_{2,5}$ of the dipoles represent tendencies to approach the given cues. Inhibitory links between these nodes and a node $x_{3,5}$ coding some other cue in the environment, denote competition between attractions to different cues. The cue with largest $x_{1,5}$ at a given time is approached.

The network of Fig. 9.8 incorporates two competing rules. There is a net positive output at $x_{i,5}$ for each of the cues that have been presented. However, for the novel cue, the on channel is less depleted than for the old cue, so that, in the absence of reward, the net output is greater for the novel cue than for the old cue.

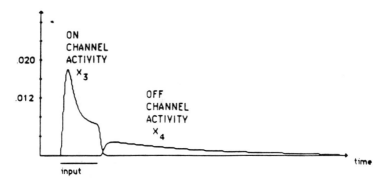

FIG. 9.7. Typical time courses of the channel outputs x_3 and x_4 in a single gated dipole. (From Levine & Prueitt, 1989; reprinted with permission of Pergamon Press).

Hence, competition among $x_{i,5}$ nodes favors those corresponding to novel cues, all else equal. Also, however, the reward node is excited when the monkey finds the peanut. Each $x_{i,5}$ connects with the reward node via modifiable synapses; these synapses learn which cues have been rewarded. Hence, competition among $x_{i,5}$ nodes favors those with strong links to the reward node, all else equal.

The equations defining the network of Fig. 9.8, for all variables except $x_{i,5}$ and the reward node u, are exactly those shown in Fig. 9.6, except that, for the ith cue and for each r (up to 4 as relevant), x_r, y_r, and z_r are replaced by $x_{i,r}$, $y_{i,r}$, and $z_{i,r}$. To connect $x_{i,5}$ in a competitive network with other $x_{j,5}$ nodes, we replace Equation (9) (from Fig. 9.6) by the following:

$$dx_{i,5}/dt = -gx_{i,5} + (1 - x_{i,5})(\alpha u z_{i,5} + x_{i,5}) - cx_{i,5}\left(x_{i,4} + \sum_{j \neq i} x_{j,5}\right) \qquad (9')$$

In (9'), the coupling factor α between reward and sensory loci is assumed to be large in normal animals and small in frontally damaged animals.

The synaptic strength $z_{i,5}$ between the reward node and $x_{i,5}$ for a given cue obeys the following equation:

$$dz_{i,5} / dt = -f_1 z_{i,5} + f_2 u x_{i,5} \qquad (10)$$

with f_1 and f_2 positive constants. Reward node activity obeys the following equation:

$$du / dt = -gu + r \qquad (11)$$

where r represents actual reward input.

Levine and Prueitt (1989) simulated equations (1)–(8), (9'), (10), and (11). Typical graphs of their simulations are shown in Fig. 9.9. The critical variable is again the gain α of signals from the reward locus to sensory loci. If α is high, as in a normal monkey, the output $x_{i,5}$ of the channel for the previously rewarded cue is the larger. If α is low, as in a frontally damaged monkey, the output $x_{2,5}$ of the novel cue is larger.

It remains to provide qualitative explanations for the effects at the extreme ends of the graph in Fig. 9.5. The better performance of normal animals with large numbers of cues may be explained by the formation of a higher-order category. The animal, instead of thinking "object X is rewarding," has learned the rule "whichever object is new is rewarding." Learning of such an abstract

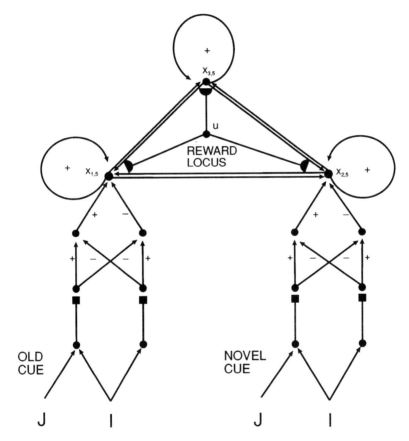

FIG. 9.8. Dipole field, with two of the gated dipoles shown, used to model Pribram's data. One dipole corresponds to an old cue and one to a novel cue. Competition among output nodes $x_{i,5}$ is biased by [1] modifiable connections with u, giving an advantage to previously rewarded cues; and [2] transmitter depletion at "square" synapses within dipoles, giving an advantage to novel cues. Which of [1] or [2] is stronger depends on the gain of reward signals to the $x_{i,5}$s. (From Levine & Prueitt, 1989; reprinted with permission of Pergamon Press).

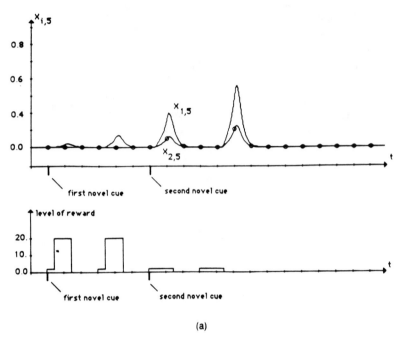

(a)

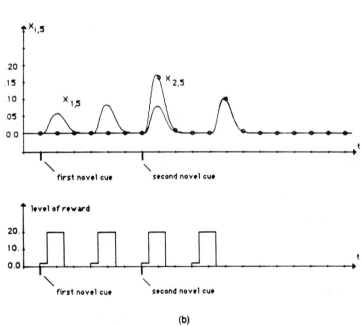

(b)

rule may depend on an intact frontal cortex (see Pribram, 1973; Dehaene & Changeux, 1989).

A simplified mechanism that can account for some of this behavior, however, is shown in Fig. 9.10. The network of Fig. 9.7 is extended so that the coefficient α of Equation (9') is no longer constant but is instead the dynamically changing activity of an additional node. This node is in turn inhibited by all of the sensory nodes $x_{i,5}$, resulting in a new equation as follows:

$$d\alpha/dt = -f\left(\sum_{1}^{n} x_{i,5} \right) + (k - \alpha)I \qquad (12)$$

where f is a monotone increasing function, I is a tonic arousal input, and k is the maximum activity of node α. Equation (12) says that increasing the number of cues present, other things being equal, increases "background arousal," which tends to reduce the influence of reward on the competition between cues. Hence, as in frontally lesioned animals, the influence of novelty is disinhibited.

The worse performance of frontal animals with small numbers of cues in Pribram's experiment might be explained by faulty segmentation of the perceptual environment. In the early stages of the experiment, the monkey may not isolate the junk object cues mentally from the rest of the scene. Such segmentation also is likely to include higher cortical functions; hence, frontally damaged monkeys could be slower than normal monkeys to separate the junk objects from the scene, a precondition for discrimination *between* these objects.

Alternatively this effect might be explained by involvement of the habit system utilized in Fig. 9.2 but not included in Fig. 9.8. With few cues, positive feedback from habit nodes could tend to reinforce attraction to previously rewarded cues, which would perseverate for longer in frontally damaged than in normal animals. With an increase in the number of cues, the habits of approach to several previously rewarded cues would compete with each other so that no single habit predominates. This in turn would disinhibit the approach to novel cues that is also enhanced by frontal damage.

The frontal lesion effects described in this section are similar to some effects of schizophrenia, as Goldman-Rakic (1989) described. Of course such a state-

---

FIG. 9.9. Simulation results on the dipole field network of FIG. 9.8. $x_{1,5}$ denotes approach to the first cue presented, and $x_{2,5}$ to the second cue presented. Dark vertical tick marks show first presentation times of novel cues. The bottom graph (labeled "level of reward") denotes the value of the reward node activity u: (a) in the "normal monkey" network, α = 2. When both cues are present, $x_{1,5} > x_{2,5}$, so the previously rewarded cue is chosen (and not rewarded); (b) in the "frontal monkey" network, α = .1. When both cues are present, $x_{2,5} > x_{1,5}$, so the novel cue is chosen (and rewarded). (From Levine & Prueitt, 1989; reprinted with permission of Pergamon Press.)

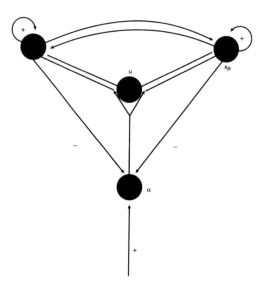

FIG. 9.10. Architecture embodying Equation (12), where the coupling coefficient α between reward and cue approach nodes is itself a node activity. The node α, which modulates synapses between each $x_{i,5}$ and the reward node u, is in turn inhibited by each $x_{i,5}$ and excited by a tonic arousal input I. (From Levine & Prueitt, 1989; reprinted with permission of Pergamon Press).

ment must be made cautiously, because "schizophrenia" is not a single disorder but an array of symptoms, ranging from paranoid delusions to flatness of affect, that can occur in varying combinations in different individuals (Astrachan et al., 1972). Nevertheless, one characterization of schizophrenic behavior is that it tends to be dominated by immediate stimulation rather than weighing such stimulation with past information and internal drives (Salzinger, 1971); this is reminiscent of the novelty preference resulting from frontal damage. Other data shows that schizophrenics, like frontal patients, are deficient in shifting hypotheses on cognitive tasks after errors (Pishkin & Williams, 1976). Goldman-Rakic (1989) reviewed preliminary evidence that some schizophrenics can be treated with norepinephrine agonists; this is compatible with the hypothesis that norepinephrine is involved in affect-based selective attention.

OBSESSIONS VERSUS COMPULSIONS;
BELIEFS VERSUS PLANS

The behavior of frontally damaged patients on the Wisconsin Card Sorting Test is also reminiscent in some ways of obsessive-compulsive disorder (OCD) (Khanna, 1988; Luxenburg et al., 1988; Rapoport, 1989). OCD was once thought to be rare but is now believed to afflict up to two percent of the population. As Rapoport (1989) described, this disease

316

manifests itself through obsessions (recurrent, persistent ideas, thoughts or impulses that are experienced, at least initially, as intrusive and senseless) or compulsions (repetitive, purposeful behaviors—perceived as unnecessary—that are performed in response to an obsession, or according to certain rules or in a stereotyped fashion.) (p. 83)

Recent work hints that OCD is based on some biochemical, and at times structural, abnormalities. In particular, Luxenburg et al. (1988) showed, using tomography, that the disorder is often accompanied by damage to the caudate nucleus and excess metabolic activity of the prefrontal cortex. The caudate is a motor control area that is part of a feedback loop with the frontal cortex (see the pathway described in Fig. 9.11). This provides some clues to the motor, or

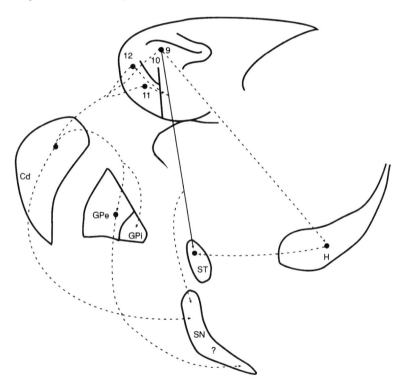

FIG. 9.11.   Schematic map of some neural pathways involved in responding to stimuli after a delay. Lines between structures do not imply direction of the pathway. Areas 9 and 10 are in motor cortex. Areas 11 and 12 are dorsal and ventral prefrontal cortex respectively. Other abbreviations: Cd = caudate; GP = globus pallidus (the motor output area of the basal ganglia); SN = substantia nigra (the main source of midbrain dopamine inputs); ST = stria terminalis; H = hippocampus. (From Rosvold & Szwarcbart, 1964; reprinted with permission of McGraw-Hill Book Company).

compulsive, side of obsessive-compulsive disorder. About twenty percent of the patients with OCD also exhibit motor tics: involuntary movements such as eye-blinks or grimaces. Further, many of the compulsive behaviors resemble in-stinctual species-specific patterns found in other animals, particularly birds.

Hence, obsessive-compulsive or perseverative behavior suggests uncontrolled activity of Mac Lean's reptilian brain. Yet this behavior has a cognitive compo-nent as well: it is as if the reptilian habit system has bound the reasoning and semantic systems to its own service. In fact, whereas an OCD sufferer may have an innate biochemical tendency to the disorder, the *focus* of the person's obses-sion (whether it is bodily dirt, religious rituals, or lucky numbers, for example) seems to be heavily influenced by early training. Similarly the perseveration of Milner's frontal patients is *conditioned* perseveration in the sense that learning is strong enough to determine which cognitive habit develops (but not strong enough to overcome that habit later on).

Rapoport (1989) mentioned a drug that has been effective in the treatment of OCD. This drug is called clomipramine (CMI) and previously had been used as an antidepressant. The reason for CMI's effectiveness against obsessive-com-pulsive symptoms—which is *not* shared by other antidepressants—is uncertain, but Rapoport believed that this drug acts by blocking reuptake (removal from the synapse) of the neurotransmitter serotonin. CMI also has some effect on the transmitter dopamine, which is important in reward circuits.

Serotonin is one of the important transmitters in the frontal lobes, and neurons that respond to serotonin are particularly concentrated in the basal ganglia. (The fronto-caudate connection itself is not serotonergic but may be modulated by serotonin from other, nearby synapses.) Hestenes (chapter 7 in this volume) adduces some evidence that serotonin is involved in a range of functions that could broadly be called pattern matching or reality testing. The principle of adaptive resonance (Carpenter & Grossberg, 1987a, 1987b) involves the com-parison of two sets of patterns, or one set of patterns and one set of synaptic weights, at two interacting brain loci. These loci could be, for example, the feature and category regions (possibly located at primary and secondary areas of visual cortex) shown in Figs. 9.2 and 9.4; or they could be sensory and moti-vational areas, as are activated in Pavlovian conditioning (see Grossberg, Levine, & Schmajuk, chapter 2 in this volume); or they could be a frontal region generating desired motor behavior, based on expected reinforcement, and a cau-date region generating actual behavior, based on motor plans with "a life of their own" regardless of reinforcement. In all these cases, Hestenes conjectures, serotonin pathways regulate how much mismatch between the two patterns is tolerated. In the adaptive resonance network of Fig. 9.4, for example, the vig-ilance connection could either be serotonergic or have its gain modulated by a serotonergic input.

Serotonin inhibitors such as LSD can produce hallucinations by causing a judgment that two patterns (say, in imagination and in the real world) match when the amount of actual match is relatively small. By an analogous mechanism, obsessions and compulsions could involve proceeding with previously conceived motor plans or previously held beliefs in spite of insufficient match with the areas calculating their reinforcement value.

Rapoport stated that OCD is responsive to a specific drug when it is resistant to psychotherapy. Her clinical observation is undoubtedly sound, but a word of caution must be stated here. If a condition is described as "biochemical," this frequently leads people to conclude that verbal suggestion, or a supportive human environment, will have no effect on this condition. The example of learned helplessness (Leven, chapter 8 in this volume) makes it abundantly clear that this conclusion is false; rather the relationship between human behavior and biochemistry is one of continuous feedback, and verbal suggestions profoundly affect our neurochemistry. Hence, the possibility exists of supplementing drug treatment for OCD with future, more refined techniques of psychotherapy.

Now what part of the brain can we expect to mediate the effects of verbal statements? What area receives inputs from cortical auditory processing areas and passes them on to subcortical motivational and motor plan centers? Why, of course the prefrontal cortex. Indeed Milner (1964) and Luria and Homskaya (1964) found that frontal patients frequently can express in speech what is incorrect about their behavior on cognitive tasks but that such speech has no effect on changing their behavior. More recently, Gorelick and Ross (1987) and Ross and Stewart (1987) pinpointed cortical areas (some of them frontal) whose damage results in various kinds of *aprosodia,* or mismatch between speech content and external affect.

In the last, most speculative section of this chapter, we shall return to an inquiry of how speech can perform such a regulative role through higher-level reasoning processes. Levine (1986) suggested that, to allow associations to develop rapidly to stimuli in flexible contexts, the connections between those frontal areas (mainly dorsal) with sensory cortical connections and other frontal areas (mainly orbital) with limbic connections should be diffuse and nontopographic. That suggestion is supported by the anatomical finding (Barbas, 1986) that projections to the frontal lobes from the limbic cortex were more diffuse than projections from the sensory areas of the neocortex.

ORGANIZATION OF GOAL-DIRECTED SEQUENCES
ACROSS TIME

Numerous investigators (see Nauta, 1971; Fuster, 1980; and Stuss & Benson, 1986, for summaries) have implicated the frontal lobes in the forming of strategies for goal-directed behavior. This general function seems to involve the coordination of subsystems involved in integrating motivational with cognitive information (as simulated herein) with other subsystems that link past events or

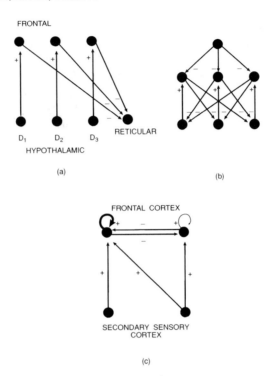

FIG. 9.12. Some possible architectures for different frontal lobe functions: (a) Each hypothalamic drive locus D_i could have a frontal representation that in turn inhibits a reticular nonspecific arousal locus. Motivationally significant inputs would then cause reduction in distractibility, hence in attention paid to other inputs; (b) part of secondary sensory cortex is shown as an on-center off-surround subnetwork that is *unlumped,* that is, excitatory and inhibitory cells occupy separate nodes (Ellias & Grossberg, 1975). The frontal cortex inhibits the inhibitory cells in that subnetwork. (c) another on-center off-surround network at the frontal cortex itself could have nodes encoding sequences of one or more sensory events. Here two such events, S_1 and S_2, are multiply represented. Frontal nodes encoding longer sequences, which receive more inputs from the sensory level, are assumed also to have stronger self-excitation (shown by a darker arrow at the S_1S_2 node than at the S_2 node). This leads to bias toward longer sequences and, hence, increased attention to plans. (Adapted from Levine, 1986, with permission of Lawrence Erlbaum Associates.)

actions across time (Fuster, 1980, 1985) and anticipate future events or actions (Ingvar, 1985; Gevins et al., 1987).

Levine (1986) proposed some network hypotheses for how the motivational and the timing functions of the frontal lobes could be coordinated. As shown in Fig. 9.12, it was conjectured that different, interacting subsystems of the frontal cortex could supply inhibition of the reticular activating (nonspecific arousal) system; inhibition of inhibitory cells in secondary sensory cortical areas, enabling greater attentional focus on a smaller number of cues; and selective activation of areas coding longer rather than shorter sequences of stimuli or movements, so that events can be linked across time.

The process of Fig. 9.12(c) is particularly important. It is based on the notion that goal-directed behavior depends on the cortical encoding of *chunks*, or sequences of either stimuli or movements. The chunking idea was discussed in Grossberg (1978) and further developed in the masking field architecture of Cohen and Grossberg (1987), an example of which is shown in Fig. 9.13. (Masking fields may also provide more detailed explanations for the cognitive

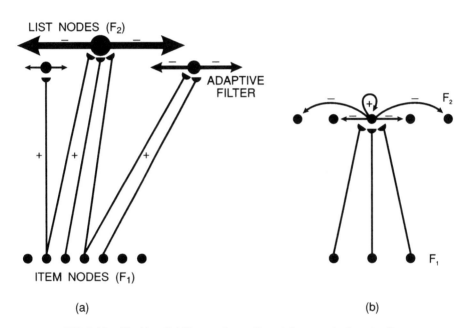

LIST NODES (F_2)

ADAPTIVE FILTER

ITEM NODES (F_1)

F_2

F_1

(a)   (b)

FIG. 9.13.   Masking field interactions; F_1 and F_2 are as in the adaptive resonance networks, but F_1 nodes are interpreted as coding items in sequences and F_2 as coding sequences. (a) Cells from F_1 to F_2 grow randomly along positionally sensitive gradients. The nodes in the masking field F_2 grow so that larger item groupings, up to some optimal size, can activate nodes with broader and stronger inhibitory interactions. Thus, F_1-to-F_2 connections and within-F_2 interactions both exhibit self-similarity. (b) Interactions within the masking field F_2 include positive feedback from a node to itself and negative feedback from a node to its neighbors. Long-term memory traces at the ends of F_1-to-F_2 pathways adaptively tune the filter defined by these pathways to amplify the F_2 reaction to item groupings that have previously succeeded in activating their target F_2 nodes. (From Cohen & Grossberg, 1987; reprinted with permission of The Optical Society of America.)

regrouping and perceptual segmentation processes that we have used to explain the data at the extreme ends of the graph in Pribram, 1961.)

The masking field architecture incorporates a rule described by Grossberg (1978) as follows: "*Self-Similar Coding Rule:* Other things being equal, higher-order chunks have greater STM (short-term memory) activity and longer duration than lower-order chunks" (p. 325). This means that chunk representations compete in an on-center off-surround field, with a competitive advantage to the "higher-order" ones that encode longer sequences. Hence, the response to a given stimulus is biased in favor of actions that are potentially appropriate to the whole sequence of preceding stimuli as well as the immediate one. Such architectures have particularly been used in simulations of context-dependent speech parsing (Cohen, Grossberg, & Stork, 1987).

The role of the prefrontal cortex in goal direction and in suppression of distractibility suggests that this part of cortex is the most probable locus for masking field anatomies, if any exist in the brain. Their existence is also partially supported by single-cell data. Fuster et al. (1982), working in the dorsal frontal cortex, and Rosenkilde et al. (1981), working in the ventral frontal cortex, recorded from cells during the performance of rewarded discrimination tasks with delays. These authors found different groups of cells responding to different aspects of the task (visual stimuli, delay periods, rewards, and movements). Moreover, they found a columnar organization, reminiscent of that of primary sensory areas of cortex, whereby cells in nearby locations tend to have similar firing properties during the task.

However, the masking field only answers part of the timing question. How do such higher-order and lower-order chunks arise in the first place? To answer that, we must extend previously discussed network notions of category formation. Many commonly used neural network models of categorization (Carpenter & Grossberg, 1987a, 1987b; Edelman, 1987; Rumelhart, Hinton, & Williams, 1986; Rumelhart & Zipser, 1985) involve a layer that codes individual input features and another layer that codes *spatial patterns* of feature node activities. In order to model prefrontal functions, we must extend this categorization notion to *space–time patterns* (see also Dawes, 1989).

Indeed the difference between time-dependent and time-independent pattern processing is one of the two most cogent functional distinctions between the prefrontal cortex and other multimodal association areas like the temporal and parietal cortices.[1] Grossberg and Kuperstein (1986), in their model of saccadic eye movements, located *target position maps* in the parietal cortex and *target position sequences* in the frontal eye field. Although the frontal eye field lies just

---

[1]The other cogent distinction is of course the prefrontal area's greater ability to process emotional inputs. Leven (1987) challenged traditional models in economics and other social sciences, which posit actors with static preferences and a paucity of internal dynamics. Does this mean that *homo economicus* has temporal and parietal lobes but lacks frontal lobes?

outside the boundaries of the prefrontal cortex, it is similar enough to the prefrontal cortex in its structure and connections that it might be studied as a microcosm of the region (Fuster, personal communication).

Hence, categorization networks like adaptive resonance (Carpenter & Grossberg, 1987a, 1987b), back propagation (Werbos, 1974; Rumelhart et al., 1986), competitive learning (Rumelhart & Zipser, 1985), or Darwin II (Edelman, 1987) do not require frontal lobes. A network of this type could exist in the brain with the lower layer located in an area of cortex coding a single sensory modality, for example, and the higher layer in parietal or temporal association cortex. Or it could even have both layers located in cortices for a single modality, at primary and secondary regions. We suggest that a form of some such architecture, modified to include time sequencing, also exists with the lower layer at parietal cortex and the higher layer at prefrontal cortex. (Although any of the networks mentioned here could probably be used as the basis of such a sequence-categorization model, we base our proposed architectures on the adaptive resonance network, because it seems to have the greatest potential for extension to include context effects; see Levine, 1989, for discussion.)

Results of Pinto-Hamuy and Linck (1965) and Brody and Pribram (1978) indicate that the primary representation of motor sequences does not require frontal lobes either. In particular Pinto-Hamuy and Linck showed that prefrontal lesions affect the learning and performance by monkeys of flexible movement sequences (such as pressing three panels but in any order) but have relatively little effect on invariant movement sequences. Hence, we conjecture that the frontal lobes exert some higher-order controls on a learned sequential performance network located elsewhere, most probably in the corpus striatum of the basal ganglia (cf. Gerfen, 1989). These higher-order controls allow for development of complex classification rules among possible sequences (cf. Dehaene & Changeux, 1989) and tracking of place within a sequence (cf. Pribram, 1991, Lecture 10).

One possible architecture for learned sequential performance is discussed in Grossberg (1978, pp. 265–266). Grossberg's network, shown in Fig. 9.14, was built on his own previous and widely known idea of an *avalanche,* a network for performance of a ritualistic sequence of motor acts. The network shown here extends the avalanche to include sensitivity to external feedback. The nodes v_{i1} in that figure are active in succession, but external events can alter the exact timing of their firings or even interrupt the sequence altogether. Frontal lobe control of this circuit, we believe, is exerted mainly through the arousal locus; more detailed architectures mediating such frontal influence, to be integrated with this figure, are the subject of work in progress by Levine and Bapi (1990).

The lack of distinction between sensory and motor representations in Fig. 9.14 may seem strange but could be a good approximation, if the motor nodes are encoding *anticipated* movements. These planned movements could be stored in the caudate nucleus, whereas sensory events are stored in the various sensory

INPUT

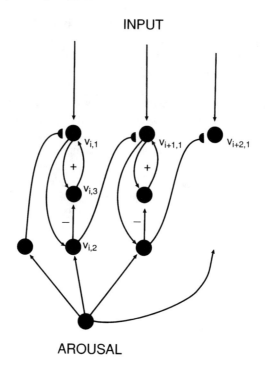

AROUSAL

FIG. 9.14.   Minimal network for learned sequential performance with modulation by arousal. The sensory or motor representations $v_{i,1}$ are activated in succession. Each $v_{i,1}$ has corresponding to it a $v_{i,3}$ to keep it reverberating in short-term memory as long as needed and a $v_{i,2}$ (influenced by an arousal source) to shut off its reverberation. $v_{i,2}$ also activates the next stage $v_{i+1,1}$ of the sequence. (Adapted from Grossberg, 1978, with permission of Academic Press.)

cortices. The prefrontal cortex, which has feedback connections with both sensory cortex and caudate, would then contain "copies" of both types of representations.

Fig. 9.15 shows one possible method for combining the categorization function of the ART network with the sequencing function of the network in Fig. 9.15. Just as in ART the prototype pattern for a category is learned at a set of synaptic weights from the active category node to the feature nodes, so do the sensory events or motor acts in a sequence (chunk) become encoded as a set of top–down weights in this network.

HIGHER-ORDER SYNTHESIS AND SELF-ACTUALIZATION

If parsimony operates in the human central nervous system, the same architectures (masking fields or their equivalent) that favor higher-order over lower-order chunks in sensory or motor space could have analogs in another layer of the frontal cortical hierarchy that encodes beliefs or concepts. What might the self-similar coding rule mean in the realm of beliefs? A belief that incorporates the insights of larger parts of one's personality should tend to dominate beliefs that satisfy only a small part of one's personality. For example, a world view that meets one's needs for both security and excitement is preferable to a world view that provides only security or only excitement. Hence, when the prefrontal cortex is operating effectively, there should be a tendency to prefer "synthetic" rather than "either–or" beliefs.

Synthetic approaches to resolving cognitive dissonance characterize those human beings that Maslow (1968, 1971) described as the most mentally healthy (i.e., integrated). Maslow placed such notions under the umbrella term *self-actualization*. His description of the self-actualized person includes the ability to combine concepts that are commonly regarded as opposites, such as masculine and feminine, organized and spontaneous, serious and playful, and (perhaps most importantly for readers of this book) rational and emotional.

What else is involved in self-actualization? Maslow (1971) said that "self-

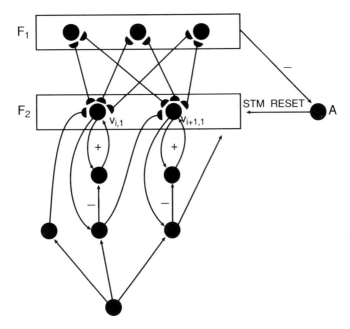

FIG. 9.15.   Minimal synthesis of part of the sequential network of FIG. 9.14 with the adaptive resonance network of Carpenter and Grossberg (1987a). Each $v_{i,1}$ is a node of the input level F_1. The nodes at F_2 learn categories of activity vectors at F_1. During learning, if the input pattern at F_1 mismatches the pattern of synaptic weights from F_2 to F_1, node A causes short-term memory reset, leading to testing of a new category at F_2.

actualization means experiencing fully, vividly, selflessly, with full concentration and total absorption" (p. 45). It is, he stressed, a state that we all reach sometimes (in "peak experiences") but few reach regularly. However, the drive toward such a state is universal, and people tend to feel frustration in its absence.

The idea that self-actualization is a *primary drive* along with those for food, drink, sex, and safety begins to suggest ways to understand it mechanistically. What could be going on biologically when an apparently functioning individual says to himself or herself: "I feel less than I could be?" The frustrated individual feels *less than complete*. The ideal of completeness has a history far older than Maslow: the Hebrew word *shalom,* for peace, originally meant "completion."

The neural network modeling literature contains a notion of *pattern completion*. This idea has so far chiefly been used in the sensory domain (Grossberg, 1974; Kohonen, 1984). If a significant part but not all of a familiar pattern, like the letter A, is in view, the eye and brain together reconstruct the rest of this pattern. The tendency toward completion depends on the degree of familiarity of the context. For example, one of the authors (D.S.L.) often can accurately "fill in" a blurred or partially occluded road sign in Boston, where he lived for eight years, but not in Kansas City, where he has spent only a few hours.

Self-actualization may, therefore, be analogous to pattern completion at another (higher) level of processing. In this case, a "pattern" should be an entire environment as perceived by a person, including perceptions from the internal organs (*interoception*) as well as from the traditional five senses (*exteroception*).

Are there, somewhere in the prefrontal cortex, "superpatterns" of neural activity with varying degrees of completeness that include both actual and anticipated events, all with sensory and visceral components? The aforementioned single-cell data on behaving monkeys by Fuster et al. (1982) and Rosenkilde et al. (1981) enhance the likelihood of this suggestion. So do some human electroencephalographic data. Gevins et al. (1987) looked at EEG recordings from people before the performance of either an accurate or an inaccurate movement. They found one EEG component in the parietal lobe that occurred before either type of movement, and another component in the frontal lobe that occurred only before an accurate movement.

Now if such a "superpattern" is incomplete—say, if a person is in a situation but not currently achieving the satisfaction he or she would wish from the situation—how can one know the course of action that will complete the pattern? I mean "know" not in a purely rational sense but in a sense that combines reason and intuition. Nauta (personal communication) said that we often decide that one plan is better than another on the basis of objective reasoning, but reject the first plan because thinking about it *makes us sick*. He meant literally sick, via one of the pathways connecting the brain to the heart, endocrine glands, and digestive organs through the autonomic nervous system. Again (see Nauta, 1971), frontal lobe damage blocks such "interoceptive censorship of plans."

On lower cognitive levels, such as reading a blurred road sign in a familiar or unfamiliar city, the perception of a potential complete pattern is heavily dependent on learning. Learned patterns, such as cultural beliefs and mores, also play a major role at higher cognitive levels. However, there is also evidence of a strong innate component to perceptual pattern completion. Infants, for example, try to track a moving object visually after it has gone behind an opaque screen (Bower, 1971). This indicates that the infant has a neurally stored belief in the continuity of motion, even when such continuity is not directly observed. Might the innate drive toward self-actualization be due to an analogous hard-wired mechanism on higher hierarchical levels of the brain?

The non-self-actualized or mentally incomplete state is often characterized by someone choosing one of two opposites—deciding to be strong as opposed to being generous, for example, as if the two were irreconcilable. Seemingly the two opposite concepts have been learned by two competing channels of a gated dipole (see Fig. 9.6), probably somewhere in the limbic system. Such dichotomous constructs (Kelly, 1955) characterize people's mental life more often than not. These constructs tend to be highly stable and yet, because of the sense of "incompleteness" described previous, not fully satisfying.

The lesser satisfactions that people settle for (Thoreau's "quiet desperation") are reminiscent of the nonoptimal equilibrium states that frequently occur in dynamical systems describing artificial neural networks (for example, Hopfield, 1982; Cohen & Grossberg, 1983; Rumelhart et al., 1986). The optimal state is typically interpreted as the global minimum of some energy surface and the nonoptimal equilibria as local minima of the same energy, as shown in Fig. 9.16. In a variant of this scheme, the nonoptimal state may actually be an equilibrium only for part, and not for all, of the network.

The problem of how to move from a "comfortable" local minimum to a more "risky" global minimum will be important in future applications of neural networks to psychotherapy. It has been approached in artificial networks by a variety of techniques; the best known is called *simulated annealing* and involves the application of noise to the network (Kirkpatrick, Gelatt, Vecchi, 1983).

Simulated annealing can have its uses in increasing mental integration, through therapies of the primal-scream variety or through unsettling events that cause shifting of perspective. However, perhaps more lastingly effective therapies can be based on use of the frontal-caudate serotonin-sensitive links discussed earlier in this chapter. Recall the suggestion of Hestenes (chapter 7 in this volume) that serotonin adjusts the amount of mismatch that will be tolerated between patterns at different levels of the brain. Leven (1988) constructed a triune theory of human personality in which the main differences between individuals relate to how much they are satisfied with partial solutions to problems. How this mismatch vigilance can be affected not only by drugs but by speech (the words of the therapist, the social environment, or even the client's silent speech to himself or herself) is a source of many years of open problems. Yet, as the work of Luria and Homskaya (1964) and others quoted in this chapter makes

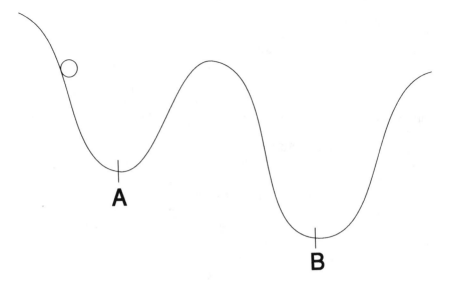

FIG. 9.16.   Path of the variables in many neural networks is analogous
to the path of a ball bearing along a curve (representing the system
"energy function"). Like the ball bearing, the system eventually
reaches a local minimum state of the energy (either *A* or *B*), but may
not reach the global minimum energy or "optimal" state *B*. (From
Rumelhart & McClelland, 1986; reprinted with permission of MIT
Press).

clear, the architecture of the frontal lobes and their connections is a key to
understanding the answers.

Thus far, we have discussed pattern matching and vigilance primarily in the
context of adaptive resonance (ART) networks (Carpenter & Grossberg, 1987a,
1987b), because ART seems to us especially amenable to modulation by additional nodes. However, these concepts might also be compatible with other
neural network classification architectures, such as back propagation (Rumelhart
et al., 1986). Back propagation networks have been criticized on grounds of
reliance on an external teacher, but the layered network that Rumelhart et al.
simulated is, like most neural networks to date, intended to be analogous to only
a small part of the brain at best, and the "teacher" can represent a different part
of the brain. When reward or punishment comes in the form of primary reinforcers like food, sex, or physical pain, or secondary reinforcers like money that
have become strongly conditioned to the primary ones, our "teacher" is in the
limbic system or hypothalamus. When reinforcement is less direct, some prefrontal area may itself be the teacher. This is particularly true in the case of
beliefs or ethical conduct, where the frontal lobes could provide a "conscience."

Hence, the commonly drawn distinction between supervised and unsupervised learning schemes (e.g., Duda & Hart, 1973; Levine, 1991) is somewhat

less sharp than it is often made out to be (cf. Dawes, chapter 12 in this volume). Although back propagation networks have usually produced error signals by comparing an output pattern with a fixed target pattern, the same architecture can probably be generalized to one producing an error signal based on a less rigid criterion. Another network architecture that embodies a more flexible error criterion is the learning system with an *adaptive critic* (Barto, Sutton, & Anderson, 1983).

The problem of synthesizing two sides of a "gated dipole" construct involves transfer of control between levels in a hierarchy. Again such a control transfer would appear to be mediated by a vigilance parameter measuring the degree of mismatch to be tolerated between two patterns in two different, specified brain regions. The pattern classification network of Carpenter and Grossberg (1987a, 1987b) always comes to a decision as to which of several categories an input pattern belongs to, regardless of the ambiguity in the arriving information. This is a desirable property in some contexts but not in others. Levine (1989) suggested a potential extension of their architecture that prevents the network from obliterating information about ambiguity itself. The network proposed in that article, shown in Fig. 9.17, includes two separate vigilance parameters, one for "certain match" and one for "possible match." If "possible match" occurs to more than one category but certain match to none, control is transferred to a different level. (Another neural network approach to *recording* rather than *resolving* ambiguity was developed by Rumelhart and Zipser, 1985.)

By a mechanism like that of Levine (1989), the limbic reinforcement system or the parietal spatial perception system can communicate with the frontal "executive of the brain" (Pribram, 1973). The message includes not only the pattern itself but a statement like "I can't make sense of this; you decide." The frontal executive can then either make an out-and-out decision or selectively change the gain at lower-level nodes to resolve the ambiguity. Pribram (1991) reviewed evidence that frontal damage interferes with the ability to switch between different resolutions of an ambiguous percept, such as the Necker cube.

Consideration of ambiguity suggests another overarching function for the prefrontal "executive." Processing at lower levels involves a large amount of inhibition, much of which wipes out incoming information. The prefrontal cortex seems to be involved in restoring at a higher level the information that was previously wiped out. Again this has applications to psychotherapy: Lower-level inhibition is analogous, for example, to the Freudian notion of repression. The stronger the repressed ideas were before they were inhibited, the more likely is the prefrontal cortex to derepress them; this necessitates information flow to the prefrontal cortex from all previous levels, which in fact occurs. For example, if a limbic gated dipole had allowed "strength" to defeat "generosity" on the basis of a difference in activations of, say, .55 to .45, the frontal cortex would be exercised to find a new synthetic approach that restores generosity without losing strength. The planning function of the prefrontal cortex suggests that, through its

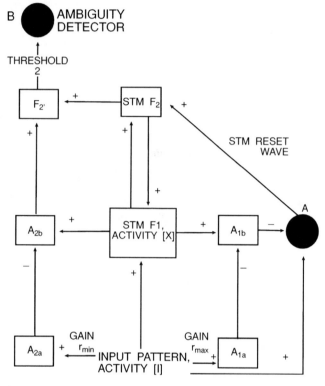

FIG. 9.17. Ambiguity detection architecture. In the ART 1 model of Carpenter and Grossberg (1987a), an input and a category prototype are considered to match if total STM activity $[X]$ divided by input pattern activity $[I]$ be larger than some vigilance value r. In this modification of ART 1, r is replaced by two values, r_{max} for "certain" match and r_{min} for "possible" match. A_{1b} is activated, if $[X]/[I] > r_{max}$ and turns off STM reset. A_{2b} is activated, if the same ratio is above r_{min}. Each category node at F_2 has a copy at $F_{2'}$ that is activated by combined signals from the corresponding F_2 node and from A_{2b}. The "ambiguity detector" fires if two or more $F_{2'}$ nodes are active. (From Levine, 1989; reprinted with permission of the Society for Computer Simulation.)

feedback connections to other areas, it does not just passively receive the repressed information but actively solicits it.

The ideas discussed in this section give a sense of the difficulties involved in the neural modeling of higher-order synthesis and complex rule formation. Difficulties such as these prompted Fodor and Pylyshyn (1988), to argue for some inherent weaknesses of connectionist (that is, neural net) approaches, particularly to semantic modeling. Fodor and Pylyshyn stated that connectionist networks can create essentially arbitrary links between nodes representing different events or concepts. Moreover, they say, strong connection between two nodes does not reflect logical or constitutive relationship between the two sets of concepts these nodes represent.

Fodor and Pylyshyn's article has become a manifesto for those who feel that, in the most complex knowledge representation tasks, connectionist architectures must be supplemented by rule-based heuristics from traditional artificial intelligence. However, we who seek to understand natural neural networks or design artificial ones should see these authors' challenge not as an indictment of our outlook but rather as a call for further innovation along lines that are already developed. There is much merit to their argument, and that is why our brains find it hard to be rational (or, better yet, "rationally emotional"). However, difficulty should never be confused with impossibility. After all, Fodor and Pylyshyn reached their conclusions through the use of their own frontal lobes, which process a dizzying array of events and interconnections, not all of which make logical sense. The frontal lobes, while building on previous layers that do connect concepts rather haphazardly, somehow make order out of these concepts without totally suppressing the lower layers.

We hope that our neural network analysis contributes to the dialogue on how such awesome tasks might be performed. Although still far short of proposing a "wiring diagram" for the frontal lobes and their interconnections, we have made some bold suggestions about some of the types of neural architectures that anatomists and physiologists should look for in those areas. The richness of the prefrontal cortex's reciprocal connections with other cortical and subcortical areas (Goldman-Rakic, 1989) and of its innervation by different monoamine transmitter systems (Descarries, Reader, & Jasper, 1984) is beginning to be matched by a corresponding richness of theoretical structures.

REFERENCES

Astrachan, B. M., Harrow, M., Adler, D., Brauer, L., Schwartz, A., Schwartz, C., & Tucker, G. (1972). A checklist for the diagnosis of schizophrenia. *British Journal of Psychiatry, 121,* 529–539.

Barbas, H. (1988). Pattern in the laminar origin of corticocortical connections. *The Journal of Comparative Neurology, 252,* 415–422.

Barto, A. G., Sutton, R. S., & Anderson, C. W. (1983). Neuron-like elements that can solve difficult learning control problems. *IEEE Transactions on Systems, Man, and Cybernetics, 13,* 835–846.

Bower, T. G. R. (1971, October). The object in the world of the infant. *Scientific American,* 30–38.

Brody, B. A., & Pribram, K. H. (1978). The role of frontal and parietal cortex in cognitive processing: Tests of spatial and sequence functions. *Brain, 101:* 607–663.

Carpenter, G. A., & Grossberg, S. (1987a). A massively parallel architecture for a self-organizing neural pattern recognition machine. *Computer Vision, Graphics, and Image Processing, 37,* 54–115.

Carpenter, G. A., & Grossberg, S. (1987b). ART 2: self-organization of stable category recognition codes for analog input patterns. *Applied Optics, 26,* 4919–4930.

Cohen, M. A., & Grossberg, S. (1983). Absolute stability of global pattern formation and parallel memory storage by competitive neural networks. *IEEE Transactions on Systems, Man, and Cybernetics, 13,* 815–826.

Cohen, M. A., & Grossberg, S. (1987). A massively-parallel architecture for learning, recognizing, and predicting multiple groupings of patterned data. *Applied Optics, 26,* 1866–1891.

Cohen, M. A., Grossberg, S., & Stork, D. (1987). Recent developments in a neural model of real-time speech analysis and synthesis. *Proceedings of the First International Conference on Neural Networks* (Vol. IV, pp. 443–454). San Diego: IEEE/ICNN.

Dawes, R. E. (1989, June). The parametric avalanche: Bayesian estimation and control with a neural network architecture. International Joint Conference on Neural Networks. Washington, D.C. (Vol. II, p. 759).

Dehaene, S., & Changeux, J.-P. (1989). A simple model of prefrontal cortex function in delayed-response tasks. *Journal of Cognitive Neuroscience, 1,* 244–261.

Descarries, L., Reader, T. R., & Jasper, H. H. (Eds.). (1984). *Monoamine innervation of cerebral cortex.* New York: Liss.

Duda, R. O., & Hart, P. E. (1973). *Pattern classification and scene analysis.* New York: Wiley.

Edelman, G. (1987). *Neural Darwinism.* New York: Basic.

Ellias, S. A., & Grossberg, S. (1975). Pattern formation, contrast control and oscillations in the short-term memory of shunting on-center off-surround networks. *Biological Cybernetics, 20,* 69–98.

Fodor, J. A., & Pylyshyn, Z. W. (1988). Connectionism and cognitive architecture: a critical analysis. In S. Pinker & J. Mehler (Eds.), *Connections and symbols* (pp. 3–71). Cambridge, MA: MIT Press.

Foote, S. L., & Morrison, J. H. (1987). Extrathalamic cortical modulation. *Annual Review of Neuroscience, 10,* 67–95.

Fuster, J. M. (1980). *The prefrontal cortex.* New York: Raven.

Fuster, J. M. (1985). The prefrontal cortex: mediator of cross-temporal contingencies. *Human Neurobiology, 4,* 169–179.

Fuster, J. M., Bauer, R. H., & Jervey, J. P. (1982). Cellular discharge in the dorsolateral prefrontal cortex of the monkey during cognitive tasks. *Experimental Neurology, 77,* 679–694.

Gazzaniga, M. (1986). *The social brain: discovering the networks of the mind.* New York: Basic.

Gerfen, C. (1989). The neostriatal mosaic-striatal patch-matrix organization is related to cortical lamination. *Science, 246,* 385–388.

Gevins, A. S., Morgan, N. H., Bressler, S. L., Cutillo, B. A., White, R. M., Illes, J., Greer, D. S., Doyle, J. C., & Zeitlin, G. M. (1987). Human neuroelectric patterns predict performance accuracy. *Science, 235,* 580–584.

Goldman-Rakic, P. S. (1984). Modular organization of prefrontal cortex. *Trends in NeuroSciences, 7,* 419–424.

Goldman-Rakic, P. S. (1989). Circuitry of primate prefrontal cortex and regulation of behavior by representational memory. *Handbook of physiology—The nervous system, V,* pp. 373–417.

Gorelick, P. B., & Ross, E. D. (1987). The aprosodias: further functional-anatomical evidence for the organisation of affective language in the right hemisphere. *Journal of Neurology, Neurosurgery, and Psychiatry, 50,* 553–560.

Grossberg, S. (1972a). A neural theory of punishment and avoidance. I. Qualitative theory. *Mathematical Biosciences, 15,* 39–67.

Grossberg, S. (1972b). A neural theory of punishment and avoidance. II. Quantitative theory. *Mathematical Biosciences, 15,* 253–285.

Grossberg, S. (1974). Classical and instrumental learning in neural networks. In R. Rosen & F. Snell (Eds.), *Progress in theoretical biology* (Vol. 3, pp. 51–141). New York: Academic Press.

Grossberg, S. (1978). A theory of human memory: self-organization and performance of sensory-motor codes, maps, and plans. In R. Rosen & F. Snell (Eds.), *Progress in theoretical biology* (Vol. 5, pp. 233–374). New York: Academic Press.

Grossberg, S. (1980). How does a brain build a cognitive code? *Psychological Review, 87,* 1–51.

Grossberg, S., & Kuperstein, M. (1986). *Neural dynamics of adaptive sensory-motor control: ballistic eye movements.* Amsterdam: Elsevier/North-Holland.

Grossberg, S., & Levine, D. S. (1975). Some developmental and attentional biases in the contrast enhancement and short-term memory of recurrent neural networks. *Journal of Theoretical Biology, 53,* 341–380.

Grueninger, W. E., & Pribram, K. H. (1969). Effects of spatial and non-spatial distractors on performance latency of monkeys with frontal lesions. *Journal of Comparative and Physiological Psychology, 68,* 203–209.

Hopfield, J. J. (1982). Neural networks and physical systems with emergent collective computational abilities. *Proceedings of the National Academy of Sciences, 79,* 2554–2558.

Ingvar, D. (1985). Memory of the future: an essay on the temporal organization of conscious awareness. *Human Neurobiology, 4,* 124–136.

Jacobsen, C. F. (1935). Functions of the frontal association area in primates. *Archives of Neurology and Psychiatry, 33,* 558–569.

Kelly, G. (1955). *The psychology of personal constructs.* New York: Norton.

Khanna, S. (1988). Obsessive-compulsive disorder: is there a frontal lobe dysfunction? *Biological Psychiatry, 24,* 602–613.

Kirkpatrick, S., Gelatt, C. D., Jr., & Vecchi, M. P. (1983). Optimization by simulated annealing. *Science, 220,* 671–680.

Kohonen, T. (1984). *Self-organization and associative memory.* Berlin: Springer-Verlag.

Konorski, J., & Lawicka, W. (1964). Analysis of errors of prefrontal animals on the delayed-response test. In J. Warren & K. Akert (Eds.), *The frontal granular cortex and behavior* (pp. 313–334). New York: McGraw-Hill.

Leven, S. J. (1988). *Choice and neural process.* Unpublished doctoral dissertation, University of Texas at Arlington.

Leven, S. J., & Levine, D. S. (1987). Effects of reinforcement on knowledge retrieval and evaluation. In M. Candill & C. Butler (Eds.), *Proceedings of the First International Conference on Neural Networks* (Vol. II, pp. 269–279). San Diego: IEEE/ICNN.

Levine, D. S. (1986). A neural network theory of frontal lobe function. *Proceedings of the Eighth Annual Conference of the Cognitive Science Society* (pp. 716–727). Hillsdale, NJ: Lawrence Erlbaum Associates.

Levine, D. S. (1989). Selective vigilance and ambiguity detection in adaptive resonance networks. In W. Webster (Ed.), *Simulation and AI—1989* (pp. 1–7). San Diego: Society for Computer Simulation.

Levine, D. S. (1991). *Introduction to neural and cognitive modeling.* Hillsdale, NJ: Lawrence Erlbaum Associates.

Levine, D. S., & Bapi, R. S. (1990, June). *Networks modeling the involvement of the frontal lobes in learning and performance of flexible movement sequences.* International Joint Conference on Neural Networks, San Diego, CA. (Vol. II, pp. 759–764).

Levine, D. S., & Prueitt, P. S. (1989). Modeling some effects of frontal lobe damage: novelty and perseveration. *Neural Networks, 2,* 103–116.

Luria, A. R., & Homskaya, E. D. (1964). Disturbance in the regulative role of speech with frontal lobe lesions. In J. Warren & K. Akert (Eds.), *The frontal granular cortex and behavior* (pp. 353–371). New York: McGraw-Hill.

Luxenburg, J. S., Swedo, S. E., Flament, M. E., Friedland, R. P., Rapoport, J., & Rapoport, S. (1988). Neuroanatomical abnormalities in obsessive-compulsive disorder detected with quantitative X–ray computed tomography. *American Journal of Psychiatry, 145,* 1089–1093.

Mac Lean, P. D. (1970). The triune brain, emotion, and scientific bias. In F. Schmitt (Ed.), *The neurosciences second study program* (pp. 336–349). New York: Rockefeller University Press.

Maslow, A. H. (1968). *Toward a psychology of being.* New York: Van Nostrand.

Maslow, A. H. (1971). *The farther reaches of human Nature.* New York: Viking.

Milner, B. (1963). Effects of different brain lesions on card sorting. *Archives of Neurology, 9,* 90–100.

Milner, B. (1964). Some effects of frontal lobectomy in man. In J. Warren & K. Akert (Eds.), *The frontal granular cortex and behavior* (pp. 313–334). New York: McGraw-Hill.

Minsky, M. (1986). *The society of mind.* New York: Simon & Schuster.

Mishkin, M., & Appenzeller, T. (1987, June). The anatomy of memory. *Scientific American,* 80–89.

Mishkin, M., Malamut, B., & Bachevalier, J. (1984). Memories and habits: two neural systems. In G. Lynch, J. McGaugh, & N. Weinberger (Eds.), *Neurobiology of learning and memory* (pp. 65–77). New York: Guilford.

Nauta, W. J. H. (1971). The problem of the frontal lobe: a reinterpretation. *Journal of Psychiatric Research, 8,* 167–187.

Pinto-Hamuy, T., & Linck, P. (1965). Effect of frontal lesions of performance of sequential tasks by monkeys. *Experimental Neurology, 12,* 96–107.

Pishkin, V., & Williams, W. V. (1976). Cognitive rigidity in information processing of undifferentiated schizophrenics. *Journal of Clinical Psychology, 33,* 625–630.

Pribram, K. H. (1961). A further experimental analysis of the behavioral deficit that follows injury to the primate frontal cortex. *Experimental Neurology, 3,* 432–466.

Pribram, K. H. (1973). The primate frontal cortex—executive of the brain. In K. H. Pribram & A. R. Luria (Eds.), *Psychophysiology of the frontal lobes* (pp. 293–314). New York and London: Academic Press.

Pribram, K. H. (1984). Emotion: a neurobehavioral analysis. In K. R. Scherer & P. Ekman (Eds.), *Approaches to emotion* (pp. 13–38). Hillsdale, NJ: Lawrence Erlbaum Associates.

Pribram, K. H. (1991). *Brain and Perception: Holonomy and structure in figural processing.* Hillsdale, NJ: Lawrence Erlbaum Associates.

Rapoport, J. L. (1989, March). The biology of obsessions and compulsions. *Scientific American,* 83–89.

Rosenkilde, C. E., Bauer, R. H., & Fuster, J. M. (1981). Single cell activity in ventral prefrontal cortex of behaving monkeys. *Brain Research, 209,* 375–394.

Ross, E. D., & Stewart, R. S. (1987). Pathological display of affect in patients with depression and right frontal brain damage—an alternative mechanism. *Journal of Nervous and Mental Disease, 175,* 165–172.

Rosvold, H. E., & Szwarcbart, M. K. (1964). Neural structures involved in delayed-response performance. In J. Warren & K. Akert (Eds.), *The frontal granular cortex and behavior* (pp. 1–27). New York: McGraw-Hill.

Rumelhart, D. E., Hinton, G. E., & Williams, R. J. (1986). Learning internal representations by back propagation. In D. E. Rumelhart & J. L. McClelland (Eds.), *Parallel distributed processing* (Vol. 1, pp. 365–422). Cambridge, MA: MIT Press.

Rumelhart, D. E., & McClelland, J. L. (Eds.). (1986). *Parallel distributed processing* (Vol. 1, p. 287). Cambridge, MA: MIT Press.

Rumelhart, D. E., & Zipser, D. (1985). Feature discovery by competitive learning. *Cognitive Science, 9,* 75–112.

Salzinger, K. (1971). An hypothesis about schizophrenic behavior. *American Journal of Psychotherapy, 25,* 601–614.

Spaet, T., & Harlow, H. F. (1943). Problem solution by monkeys following bilateral removal of the prefrontal areas. II. Delayed reaction problems involving use of the matching-to-sample method. *Journal of Experimental Psychology, 32,* 424–434.

Stamm, J. S. (1964). Retardation and facilitation in learning by stimulation of frontal cortex in monkeys. In J. M. Warren & K. Akert (Eds.), *The frontal granular cortex and behavior* (pp. 101–125). New York: McGraw-Hill.

Stuss, D. T., & Benson, D. F. (1986). *The frontal lobes.* New York: Raven.

Voltaire (1966). *Candide; or optimism: a new translation, backgrounds, and criticism* (R. M. Adams, Trans. & Ed.). New York: Norton.

Warren, J., & Akert, K. (Eds.). (1964). *The frontal granular cortex and behavior.* New York: McGraw-Hill.

Werbos, P. J. (1974). *Beyond regression: new tools for prediction and analysis in the behavioral sciences.* Unpublished doctoral dissertation, Harvard University.

Wilkins, A. J., Shallice, T., & McCarthy, R. (1987). Frontal lesions and sustained attention. *Neuropsychologia, 25,* 359–365.

10

Familiarity and Novelty: The Contributions of the Limbic Forebrain to Valuation and the Processing of Relevance

Karl Pribram
Radford University

> The idea that study of the brain and other biological subjects is useful for philosophy has been resisted more strongly in relation to questions of value than in any other aspect of human thinking and behavior. Nevertheless there are insistent reasons for further consideration of the process of valuing. Recent studies have shown that the achievement of satisfaction of various sorts of need is accomplished by activity in specific parts of the brain. (Young, 1987, p. 173)

INTRODUCTION

This chapter reviews neurobehavioral data on distinctive brain systems that determine how events are processed as familiar or novel. These processes are initiated and terminated by an orienting reaction that signals the boundaries of an episode. Within an episode, familiarity is based on processing relevance, novelty on restructuring currently irrelevant events. The amygdala and hippocampal systems are critically implicated: Amygdalectomized animals are deficient in processing currently relevant (i.e., reinforcing or deterrent), hippocampectomy results in deficient processing of currently irrelevant events.

These deficiencies in familiarization following *amygdalectomy* become manifest in species shared behaviors such as the "four Fs": feeding, fighting, fleeing, and sex. Experimental results are reviewed that show that the basis for the deficiencies in familiarization is a failure to properly process the visceroautonomic, temperature, and pain dimensions of stimulation. The pathways for this type of stimuli, classified as "protocritic," are shown to reach the frontolimbic forebrain in contrast to those for "epicritic" stimuli that reach the parietal convexity.

Hippocampectomy leads to inadequacy in processing currently irrelevant (i.e., nonreinforced) aspects of a situation, which compose the context within which relevant stimuli are processed. This leads to a processing deficiency when changes in circumstances change context, as in discrimination reversal tasks. Innovation depends on processing such changes in context. A model is presented that ascribes efficiency to the processing of changes in context (and, therefore, content) to a hippocampal system contribution to a parallel distributed brain procedure (in a Hopfield or Boltzmann-like network).

THE AMYGDALA

Sometimes our perceptions are ambient, enhancing span by freely sampling sensory input and categorizing it. However, for the most part, our perceptions become directed by our interests. Interests are frequently initiated by imbalances in neurochemical states such as those leading to eating or sexual behavior. As often, however, we maintain interest in something that has become familiar and comfortable, especially when small changes in the familiar are brought about. The interests of gourmets, of connoisseurs of wine and of the arts, of readers of novels and of comic strips, of aficionados of soap operas and of popular and classical music, and even the dedicated efforts of computer programmers are determined by incremental changes in what has become familiar. In short, we are interested in perceptions relevant to our motives and memories, and these interests can change what it is that we perceive (Bruner, 1957; Hastorf & Knutson, 1954).

There is a close relationship between motive and memory. Lecture 7 of Pribram (1991) reviewed the role of reinforcing events in enhancing processing span. (A reinforcer is defined as any sensory event that increases, a deterrent any sensory event that decreases, the probability of recurrence of behavior that becomes associated with it.) Reinforcers as used in animal experiments ordinarily address appetites (motives) and lead to changes in brain chemistry that, when subsequently activated, constitute memory. The effectiveness of such reinforcers is a function of deprivation as well as the schedules (programs) of presentation of the reinforcers.

The sensory processing that leads to reinforcement and deterrence is considerably different from the more familiar "information processing" discussed in Pribram (1991), Lectures 1–7. This chapter describes distinct anatomical systems that connect receptors to distinct parts of the brain, brain systems involved in the reinforcement and deterrence process. Studies of these brain systems, identified as processing a *protocritic* dimension of experience, have provided insights into what makes a sensory event novel and interesting, relevant and reinforcing. The next sections review some of the critical experimental results that led to these insights.

THE AMYGDALA SYSTEM

In order to analyze the complex of effects produced by total resection of the temporal lobe that were reviewed in Pribram (1991, Lecture 7), surgical techniques were developed to make possible restricted resections of the medially lying amygdala and hippocampus of monkeys (Pribram, 1954, 1958). When resections were restricted to the amygdala and adjacent pole of the temporal lobe, the marked taming of the monkeys, which had followed resection of the entire temporal lobe (Brown & Schaefer, 1888), was reproduced in its entirety (Pribram & Bagshaw, 1953). Once again, as in the case of resection of the posterior convexity of the lobe, it was then necessary to find out just what the resulting behavioral change signified.

First it was determined that not only were the monkeys tamed, but also they put everything in their mouths, gained weight, and increased their sexual behavior—all effects that had also followed total temporal lobectomy. These changes in behavior were summarized under the rubric of the "four Fs": fighting, fleeing, feeding, and sex (Pribram, 1960).

Historically these apparently disparate behaviors were classified together as drives and instincts (terms still used to describe the processes underlying such behaviors in the psychoanalytic literature). More recently, these terms have, however, come into disfavor (see, e.g., Beach, 1955), and ethologists have substituted the category "species-specific" behavior for instinct, because these behaviors can be shown to have a common genetic component. However, this substitution loses much of the meaning of the older terminology: Human language is species specific but not "instinctive" in the earlier sense. My preference is to retain the concept of "instinct" as descriptive of the four Fs: What these behaviors have in common is that they are *shared* by practically all species. What makes the study of geese and other birds so often interesting is that we recognize our own behavior in the descriptions provided by ethologists (see, e.g., Lorenz, 1969). It is, therefore, "species-shared" behaviors that are of interest in tracking the effects of amygdalectomy.

In our own work, these apparently disparate behaviors were shown by careful analysis to be influenced by a common mechanism. It is worth summarizing the highlights of this analysis, because identifying a common mechanism operating in apparently disparate behaviors is a recurring problem in behavioral neuroscience, as it is in behavioral genetics, where it involves identifying genotypes from phenotypical behaviors. Qualitative and quantitative determinations were made in each of the four Fs with the following results.

In a social hierarchy, fighting and fleeing were both diminished *provided there was a sufficiently skillful antagonist* (Rosvold, Mirsky, & Pribram, 1954). As in the study reported by Brown and Schaefer (1888), when a monkey was returned to the social colony after amygdalectomy, he "voluntarily approaches all persons—and fellow monkeys indifferently." Furthermore, having just interacted with his fellow monkey and perhaps having been trounced, "he will go through the same process, as if he had entirely forgotten his previous experience" (pp. 310–311).

This behavioral change was dramatically demonstrated when a lighted match was displayed to those monkeys. They would invariably grab the match, put it into their mouth, dousing the flame, only to repeat the grab when the next lit match was presented. This behavior could be elicited for a hundred consecutive trials unless either the monkey or the experimenter became bored or tired before the session was ended (Fulton, Pribram, Stevenson, & Wall, 1949).

The increases in feeding and sexual behavior that follow amygdalectomy were shown to be due to a failure in stopping the behavior once it had begun. For instance, as reported by Brown and Schaefer (1888), monkeys with such resections appear to be indiscriminate in what they pick up, put in their mouths, and swallow. However, when tests were performed, and a record was kept of the order in which the food and nonfood objects were chosen, it turned out that the order of preference was undisturbed by the brain operation; only now the monkeys would continue to pick up additional objects beyond those that they had chosen first (Wilson, 1959). In fact amygdalectomized animals may be a bit slow to start eating but continue eating far past the point when their controls stop eating (Fuller, Rosvold, & Pribram, 1957).

The fact that amygdalectomy impairs the stop—the satiety—mechanism might suggest that amygdalectomized monkeys are hungrier or have greater appetite. This is not so, however. When deprived of food for from 24 to 72 hours, amygdalectomized monkeys do not eat more rapidly than they did before deprivation, whereas of course their control subjects do (Weiskrantz, 1956).

After amygdalectomy, the effectiveness of food as a reward is diminished. Ordinarily a change in the amount of reward given changes its effectiveness. After amygdalectomy, changes in amount have much less effect than they do when control subjects are used (Schwartzbaum, 1960).

These disturbances in *feeding* after amygdalectomy were shown to be due to connections with the satiety mechanism centered in the ventromedial region of the hypothalamus. For instance, a precise relationship was established between the amount of carbachol injected into the amygdala and the amount of feeding (or drinking) once it had been initiated (Russell, Singer, Flanagan, Stone, & Russell, 1968).

This modulation of a stop mechanism was also shown responsible for changes in *fighting* behavior. Fall in a dominance hierarchy after amygdalectomy was, when it occurred, related to the amount of aggressive interaction between the dominant and submissive animals in the group. After amygdalectomy, such interactions were overly prolonged, leading to a reorganization of the dominance hierarchy. It was as if the amygdalectomized monkeys approached each interaction as novel. Prior experience, which modulated the behavior of the control subjects, seemed to have little influence after amygdalectomy. This finding characterizes many of the experimental results to be described shortly.

Analyses of the effects of amygdalectomy and electrical stimulations of the amygdala on avoidance (*fleeing*) behavior brought a similar conclusion. Escape behavior is unaffected, and sensitivity to shock is not diminished (Bagshaw & Pribram, 1968). Nor is there a change in generalization gradient to aversive stimulation (Hearst & Pribram, 1964a, 1964b). What appears to be affected primarily is the memory aspect of avoidance—the expectation based on familiarity with the situation that aversive stimulation will occur. Such expectations are ordinarily referred to as "fears" that direct and constrain perception.

The theme recurs when the effects of amygdalectomy on *sexual* behavior are analyzed. The hypersexuality produced by the resections is found to be due to an increased territory and range of situations over which the behavior is mainfest. Ordinarily cats perceive unfamiliar territory as inappropriate for such behavior (see Pribram, 1960, for review).

The finding that the amygdala is involved in a process that ordinarily operates to stop ongoing behavior also led to a series of studies on its role in the orienting reaction. Orienting not only stops ongoing behavior but directs perception to the orienting stimulus. A series of studies (to be reviewed shortly) showed that only the visceroautonomic components of orienting were affected by amygdalectomy and that the habituation of the behavioral components of orienting was dependent on the occurrence of these visceroautonomic responses.

Two related processes are involved in these effects: (a) Amygdalectomy affects a particular dimension of perceptual experience, and (b) this dimension is crucial to the process of familiarization.

A Disturbance of Perception

To begin, an experiment was undertaken to determine whether the marked taming observed to follow amygdalectomy is due to the fact that the resection impairs the perception of the threat or whether the observed change is due to an impaired ability or inclination to respond to the perceived threat. The so-called split brain is the ideal preparation to determine whether the observed change is sensory or motor. In this preparation, the hemispheres are severed from one another by sectioning the corpus callosum and anterior commissure (the large tracts that connect the two cerebral hemispheres), and the optic chiasm is cut so the visual input from each eye will go only to the hemisphere on the side of that eye.

When monkeys whose brains had been split in this fashion were given an amygdalectomy on one side only and then examined with one eye occluded with an opaque contact lens, their responses were specific according to the side being tested. When the unoccluded eye was on the side of the amygdalectomy, the monkey was tame; when the unoccluded eye was on the unoperated side, the monkey behaved normally fearful, avoiding all potentially threating objects such as snakes and humans (Barrett, 1969; Doty & Nagrao, 1973).

Interestingly, when touched, the monkeys retreated from the tactile stimulation irrespective of the side stimulated; tactile stimuli are conveyed to both sides of the brain, and no attempt had been made to isolate the tactile input to each hemisphere. Even after bilateral amygdalectomy, the threshold for initiating escape behavior by tactile stimuli remained unchanged (Bagshaw & Pribram, 1968). Furthermore, another set of experiments along the same lines showed that generalization remains unchanged after amygdalectomy (Hearst & Pribram, 1964a, 1964b). By contrast, amygdalectomy markedly altered avoidance of the stimulus when a signal indicated that this to-be-avoided stimulus would appear in four seconds (Pribram & Weiskrantz, 1957).

Two conclusions can be drawn from these experiments: (a) The change in behavior that follows amygdalectomy has to do with how the monkeys perceive stimuli and not with a change in the monkeys' motor processing apparatus, and (b) the perceptual process that is involved has to do not with sensing or categorizing (threshold and generalization gradients remain unchanged) but with some other memory-based process.

Equi-valence: The Evaluation of Perceptions

The nature of this other process became evident during the following experiments. When monkeys are trained to select the larger of two circles and then tested to see whether they will select the larger of two squares, unoperated controls selected the larger of the squares with no hesitation. After amygdalectomy, transferring the selection to the new pair is severely impaired: Larger is no longer perceived as an independent dimension common to the pair of circles and the pair of squares (Bagshaw & Pribram, 1968). This change in perception is not due to any change in the monkeys' ability to discriminate between cues or between reinforcing events: Generalization gradients remain unaltered by amygdalectomy in both a food reinforcement and a footshock deterrence procedure (Hearst & Pribram, 1964a, 1964b). The effect of resection is that larger fails to be perceived as equivalent, of equal value for the purposes at hand.

This disruption of valuation was demonstrated in another similar experiment. In this experiment, the monkeys were trained to select the lighter of two, gray, square panels embedded in a medium-gray background. On test trials, panels of different shades of gray were substituted, but the monkeys were still to choose the lighter shade. Control monkeys did just this. The amygdalectomized monkeys, however, hesitated and then selected either of the new panels on a random basis. They perceived the situation as novel, which it was, but failed to perceive it on the basis of the history of reinforcement that placed a value on the relation "lighter of the two shades." It is this relation that made the original and substitute panels equi-valent, i.e., of equal value (Schwartzbaum & Pribram, 1960).

Protocritic Processing: A Comfort–Discomfort Dimension

The answer to the question "What process underlies the valuation (appraisal) of a perception?" was gained by considering and pursuing what appears to be a most extraordinary fact: Pain and temperature sensibility are coupled in a single pathway in the spinal cord. (Considerable effort has gone into analyzing the physiology of various submodalities of somatic sensory processes; see Kenshalo, 1968, for review). This coupling becomes evident when the spinothalamic tract of the cord is surgically severed in order to alleviate intractable pain or abnormal sensations accompanying a phantom limb. The temperature as well as the pain sense is abolished below the level of the transection. A similar effect is produced by the disease syringomyelia: A loss of pain and temperature sensibility ensues after the interruption of fibers from the dorsal root of the cord (the channel for sensory input) across the midline to ascend in the spinothalamic tract. The disease consists of a degenerative enlargement of the spinal canal, which occupies the center of the cord; the degeneration interrupts the crossing pain and temperature fibers.

Again what could be the common denominator uniting this odd couple? The answer to this question is not known, but a hint comes from the fact that, in warm-blooded animals, keeping a constant temperature is basic to the entire metabolic process (Brobeck, 1963). When the basal temperature begins to fall, muscular contraction (activity), feeding, resting (slowing down respiration), and piloerection (ruffling the fur) prevent further temperature loss. When the basal temperature rises, the organism pants, skin blood vessels dilate, sweating occurs, drinking ensues, and the organism may repair to a cooler place. These mechanisms operate to keep the organism within a metabolic "comfort" range.

Comfort–discomfort appears to be the dimension that characterizes the odd couple: The answer to the question "What process underlies valuation?" is that temperature-pain sensibility makes an associated sensory input desirable or undesirable.

On this basis, the hypothesis was formulated (Pribram, 1960) that perhaps the comfort–discomfort dimension might also be responsible for the fact that resections of the amygdala affects all four Fs. Effects on fleeing and fighting would be due to interference with the pain-discomfort pole of the dimension; effects on feeding and sex would be due to interference with the temperature-comfort pole. The fact that sexual processes have something to do with comfort can be readily appreciated, but the connection with temperature sensibility appears more remote. There is, however, the well known connection between sexual attraction and olfaction and, in a theory attributed to Faraday, between olfaction and temperature (Pfaffman, 1951). Faraday proposed that the nose forms an infrared—heat—chamber and that odors depend on selective radiation through a monomolecular stereochemical film of odorant absorbed on the olfactory receptor surface (see also Beck & Miles, 1947).

The effects of amygdalectomy on the pain-discomfort pole of this couplet have been reviewed earlier in this chapter. To test the hypothesis that temperature as well as pain is processed by the forebrain systems of which the amygdala is a critical part, electrodes were implanted in the amygdala and in the pathways leading from it. Electrodes were also implanted in control sites such as various portions of the parietal cortex, where major portions of the sensory tracts from skin and muscle receptors terminate. The monkeys were trained on a temperature discrimination task using a visual task as a control. Electrical stimulation of the amygdala and related structures, but not of the parietal cortex, produced a marked disruption of performance on the temperature task leaving performance on the visual task intact (Chin, Pribram, Drake, & Greene, 1976).

The distinction between the type of sensory input that reaches the cortex of the posterior cerebral convexity, including that of the parietal lobe and that reaching the amygdala and associated limbic cortical formations can best be understood in terms of earlier observations on the functions of the very small fine fiber system of peripheral nerves that serve what is called in neurology "slow pain," because its conduction time is long compared to that which conveys the sharp effects of pin prick, touch, and pressure. Experiments performed by severing a peripheral nerve and describing the sensory experience as the nerve regenerates were performed by Head (1920) early in the century. Initially all the fibers of the regenerating nerve are of the same size, but, as time goes on, some of the fibers become larger, whereas others remain small. For each sensory (and motor) nerve, a specific fiber size spectrum develops, a spectrum that depends on the particular location innervated (Quilliam, 1956; Thomas, 1956). While the fibers are all the same size, stimulation of the innervated area produces a diffuse, unpleasant sensation that is hard to locate and describe accurately. Normal sensibility is restored with the reconstitution of the normal fiber size spectrum. Head (1920) labeled the abnormal nonlocalizable sensation *protopathic,* because it is primitive and pathological. He called the normal sensation *epicritic,* because it displays what neurologists refer to as a local sign: an experience critically located in space and time.

Those aspects of the somatic sensory process that are epicritic are relayed to the parietal portion of the cortex of the posterior cerebral convexity. The termination of the pathways of those aspects of somatic sensation that do not show local sign were until recently unknown. In the past three decades, anatomical studies have traced multisynaptic pain pathways to the amygdala and related limbic cortical structures (Morin, Schwartz, & O'Leary, 1951). This fact plus the results of the temperature discrimination experiments described earlier make it likely that those aspects of sensation that do not display "local sign" involve the amygdala and related limbic cortex. The effects of the electrical stimulation of the amygdala interfered with discrimination of these dimensions of pain and of temperature, and there is no pathological sensibility involved; therefore, the term protocritic rather than protopathic is used to describe these nonepicritic aspects of somatic sensation that characterize the comfort–discomfort dimension.

In humans, the protocritic dimension of experience is measured by administering tolerance techniques such as those described by McGuinness (1972) and McGuinness and Cox (1977). In these procedures, the subject is asked to turn up a sensory stimulus such as a light or tone until its intensity reaches the upper limit of tolerance. Tolerance level is found to vary independently of threshold that is determined by asking the subject when a sensory stimulus becomes perceptible.

To summarize, the brain systems that are involved in somatic sensibility are divided into two, major parts: (a) an epicritic system based on touch and pressure that transmits local sign (i.e., the sensation can be critically localized in time and space), and (b) a protocritic system based on pain and temperature sensibility that processes a nonlocalizable dimension of the experience.

In the spinal cord, the pathways for the protocritic experiences of pain and temperature appear to be inseparable. In the brainstem and thalamus, the sites from which pain (deterrents) can be elicited are intermingled with those that are involved in producing reinforcement: the repeated pressing of a panel in order to receive electrical brain stimulation (Olds & Milner, 1954; Olds, 1955). Furthermore, low frequency (10–20 Hertz) stimulation in these sites produces analgesia (Liebeskind, Guilbaud, Besson, & Oliveras, 1973; Liebeskind, Mayer, & Akil, 1974), and when such stimulations are produced in humans, sensations of cooling accompany the analgesia (Richardson & Akil, 1974).

The forebrain termination of the protocritic pathways is the amygdala and related limbic cortex. The forebrain termination of the epicritic system is the parietal portion of the cortex of the cerebral convexity.

The two distinct sets of brain systems, an epicritic and a protocritic, both operate on the perceptual process. The epicritic systems of the cerebral convexity serve *comprehension* and *categorizing* that *enhance processing span;* the *protocritic* limbic systems *constrain processing* on the basis of its *value,* its *relevance* to the organism.

Familiarization as Consolidation of Memory, Dependent on Protocritic Processing

A percept becomes relevant only when it is pertinent, germane to something familiar. In this section, the evidence is reviewed to show that behavioral habituation serves as an indicator of familiarity and that habituation occurs as a result of visceroautonomic activity. What is oriented to or novel depends on prior experience. However, as detailed, the prior experience must either have been repetitiously experienced or to have induced a visceroautonomic reaction to become familiar.

It is of course clear from the host of other studies relating brain and behavior reviewed earlier that not all memory processes critically depend on the occurrence of visceroautonomic responses. The learning of motor skills, perceptual categorizing, rote memorization, and so on are examples where the memory mechanism operates on the basis of simple repetition. Still it is equally clear that there are occasions when memory is dependent on a "booster" that places a value on the experience. It is this booster process in which the amygdala is involved (Pribram, Douglas, & Pribram, 1969).

Familiarity is a feeling regarding a valued experience. In the clinic, patients who have a lesion in the region of the amygdala (and the adjacent horn of the hippocampus) describe experiences that are called "jamais vu" and "deja vu"— the patient will enter a place such as his living room and experience a "jamais vu," a *feeling* of "never having seen," of complete unfamiliarity. Others will come into a place they have never been and *feel* that they have "already seen," are already ("deja") completely familiar with it.

In the laboratory, familiarity has been shown to be related to reinforcement history. Monkeys were trained to select one of two cues on the basis of a 70% reinforcement schedule (i.e., selection of one cue was rewarded on 70% of the trials, and selection of the other cue was rewarded on 30% of the trials). Then the cue that had been most rewarded was paired with a novel cue. Monkeys who had their amygdalas removed selected the novel cue. Familiarization by virtue of previous reinforcing experience had little effect on monkeys who lacked the amygdala (Douglas & Pribram, 1966). These monkeys were performing in a "jamais vu" mode.

An extensive series of experiments was then undertaken to discover what might be the physiological basis for this deficiency in the familiarization process. The problem was found to center on the fact that ordinarily a novel or a reinforcing event produces a visceroautonomic reaction: A galvanic skin response due to a slight increase in sweating, a brief increase in heart rate, a change in respiratory rate, are some of the readily measurable effects. After amygdalectomy, the visceroautonomic reactions to novel or reinforcing events fail to occur (Bagshaw & Benzies, 1968; Bagshaw & Coppock, 1968; Bagshaw, Kimble, & Pribram, 1965; Kimble, Bagshaw, & Pribram, 1965; Koepke & Pribram, 1967a, 1967b; Pribram, Reitz, McNeil, & Spevack, 1979).

These visceroautonomic responses are in fact elicited by electrical excitation of the amygdala and the related limbic cortex of the medial portions of the frontal lobe, anterior insula, and temporal pole (Kaada, Pribram, & Epstein, 1949; reviewed by Pribram, 1961). Changes in blood pressure, heart and respiratory rate, gut and pupillary responses as well as gross eye, head, and body responses are elicited. An entire mediobasal motor system involving the anterior portions of the limbic forebrain has been delineated. As in the case of the classical precentral motor system discussed in Pribram (1991, Lecture 6), the mediobasal motor process operates as part of a feedback circuit that alters the peripheral structures from which signals for perceptual processing originate. (In this case, it is the protocritic dimension of processing that is involved.)

The relationship between visceroautonomic responsivity and familiarization was firmly established in the experiments (described earlier) in which control subjects rapidly habituated both visceroautonomic and behavioral responses to novel stimuli (within 3 to 10 trials), whereas monkeys with their amygdalas resected failed even to show the visceroautonomic effects. These monkeys failed to habituate their *behavioral* responses, showing the visceroautonomic responses to be necessary for rapid habituation: Visceroautonomic activity serves to boost the memory process.

In another series of experiments, McGaugh (reviewed by McGaugh & Hertz, 1972) showed that amygdalectomy impaired memory consolidation in rats. In a task in which control rats remember not to jump into a mildly electrified grid having once done so, amygdalectomized rats jumped readily. Further, it was shown that the amygdalectomy impaired adrenal visceroautonomic activity elicited by the behavioral task in normal subjects. Memory becomes consolidated when there is an event that arouses visceroautonomic activity. Behavioral habituation, familiarization, is, thus, likely due to the consolidation of memory of events experienced in a visceroautonomically arousing situation.

Habituation is fragile. The process is readily disrupted by head injury or by distraction. Some of the factors govering distractibility such as proactive and retroactive interference are well known. Amygdalectomy and resections of forebrain systems related to the amygdala have been shown to increase susceptibility to distraction (Douglas & Pribram, 1969; Grueninger & Pribram, 1969; see also Levine, Leven, & Prueitt, chapter 9 in this volume). More on this will appear shortly, in the sections on relevance and episodic processing.

In summary, the familiarization process is initiated (and terminated) by a stop to prior ongoing processing, an interrupt (an orienting reaction) that begins (and ends) an episode within which the protocritic attributes of stimuli become processed. This leads to valuation of the perception in terms of its relevance to the organism. Often the perceptual process is constrained, the organism becomes habituated, by this evaluation of relevance.

Innovation: The Processing of Novelty

What happens to sensory stimuli that become momentarily irrelevant through habituation? Do they fail to influence perception and behavior? Many observations and experiments indicate that momentarily irrelevant sensory events, called *S delta* in operant behaviorism and *negative instances* in mathematical psychology, continue to shape the course of learning and in general to guide behavior.

In the process of achieving sensory discriminations, behavior toward the nonreinforced aspects of the situation becomes extinguished in steps (see, e.g., the review by Pribram, 1986) as these aspects become habituated and perceived as currently irrelevant. Should the situation change as when another aspect is reinforced (as in the experiments reviewed in Pribram, 1991, Lecture 7), the "irrelevant" cues are again noticed ("spontaneous recovery"). In fact they have been influential throughout the procedure serving as context, the "ground" within which a "figural" content becomes processed. (See Dawes, chapter 12 in this volume, for another slant on the recovery of irrelevant events in memory.) The first part of this chapter has been concerned with the processing of content into context; the following part concerns the processing—and reprocessing—of context per se.

Whenever a situation changes, an orienting reaction occurs, and previously habituated perceptions become dishabituated (Sokolov, 1963). The orienting reaction signals the perception of novelty, the perceived change in the situation. What is of interest here is that perceived change can be generated internally—as when an organism becomes hungry. In such instances, the perception of novelty—restaurant signs begin to populate the landscape—depends on making relevant what had become irrelevant. Effort is expended; attention is "paid;" the familiar is experienced innovatively.

There is a great deal of confusion regarding the perception of novelty. In scientific circles, much of this confusion stems from the confounding of novelty with information. Shannon and Weaver (1949) introduced measures of information in terms of bits that reduced the amount of uncertainty in communication. Berlyne (1969) and others then suggested that bits of information and novelty were equivalently arousing, calling them collative variables. However, as will be detailed, novelty, in the sense used here, neither increases nor reduces the amount of uncertainty: Rather it is due to a rearrangement of what is familiar. The skill in writing a novel resides not in providing information in the sense of reducing the amount of uncertainty in communication. Rather the skill lies in portraying the familiar in novel ways, that is, in new combinations. If the structure of a novel depended on providing information, *Reader's Digest* would not be in business. Nor is there a reduction in the amount of communicable uncertainty involved in the composition or production of a great piece of music. It is the arrangement and rearrangement of a theme that challenges composer and conductor, the manner in which to structure repetition: "repetition, ah, there's the rub," exclaimed Bernstein (1976), in his comparison of musical composition to natural language.

A definitive experiment that draws the distinction between novelty and information (in Shannon's sense) was performed by Smets (1973). Smets used some of the same indicators of arousal as those used in our monkey experiments. He presented human subjects with a panel upon which he flashed displays equated for complexity (difficulty in discrimination), differing either in the *number of alternatives* (bits) or in the *arrangement* of analyzable attributes (orientations of lines) of a pattern. Very little visceroautonomic activity was induced by varying the number of alternatives; by contrast, the changes in arrangement evoked *pronounced* reactions.

THE HIPPOCAMPAL SYSTEM

Innovation depends on an initial step, a process by which the familiar drops into background as current events arouse and habituate. However, these earlier events remain available for renewed processing, should demand arise. The floor, walls, and doors of a classroom are familiar objects; we are not aware of them. We walk through the door when class is over, failing to notice what we are perceiving while engaged in a discussion following the lecture. However, should an earthquake rearrange things, we become instantly aware of swaying floor and walls and head deliberately for the safety provided by the door's frame.

In the laboratory, the process of familiarization is called extinction, and is demonstrated by a discrimination reversal procedure. Monkeys are trained to select one of two cues by consistently being rewarded on only one of the cues. After criterion performance (90% or better on 100 consecutive trials) is reached, the reward is shifted to the other cue. Ordinary monkeys, after a few trials, stop selecting the now nonrewarded cue and proceed to select the now rewarded cue. The shift in behavior accelerates as the reversal is repeated. Response to the currently nonrewarded cue has been extinguished but is rapidly reinstated once the situation demands it (Pribram, Douglas, & Pribram, 1969).

Hippocampectomy (i.e., removal of the entire hippocampal gyrus, hippocampus, and its surrounding subiculum and entorhinal cortex) radically alters this course of behavioral events. The hippocampus, a phylogenetically ancient cortex, is the other major anatomical structure lying within the medial portion of the temporal lobe. As might be expected, extinction (conceived as an extension of habituation) of the response to the now-reinforced cue remains intact after hippocampectomy. Nor does the slope of acquisition of the currently appropriate response differ from that of the control monkeys. What does occur is that a long series of trials intervenes between extinction and acquisition during which the monkeys select cues at random, thus receiving a reward approximately 50% of the time, that is sufficient to keep them working (Pribram, Douglas, & Pribram, 1969). There is no obvious event that pulls them out of this "period of stationarity;" quite suddenly the hippocampectomized monkeys resume the acquisition of more rewarding behavior. What goes on during the period of stationarity, and what prolongs this period for monkeys who have had their hippocampal gyrus resected?

Explanation must rely on inference, as there are currently no techniques for directly assessing what goes on during the period of stationarity. What is clear is that innovative rearrangement of the association between cue and reward has occurred and that this rearrangement must be perceived before it can be acted upon. Rearranging must be processed efficiently and appears to take effort (Pribram & McGuinness, 1975; Pribram, 1986).

Cognitive Effort: Efficiency in Processing Novelty

Removal of the hippocampal gyrus has also been shown to reduce the efficiency with which recombinations of analyzable stimulus attributes are processed. In an experiment in which we used a modified decision theory procedure, hippocampectomized monkeys were shown to be inordinately biased toward caution as compared with their controls (Spevack & Pribram, 1973). This result is the opposite from that obtained following resections of the inferotemporal cortex (cf. Pribram, 1991, Lecture 7). Novelty entails risk, and it demands processing effort.

In the experiment in which we paired a novel cue with a cue that had previously been reinforced, monkeys with resections of the hippocampal gyrus performed as well as controls when the pairing was made with the cue that had been reinforced on 70% of the trials during the training procedure. However, when the novel cue was paired with the cue that had been reinforced only 30% of the time, the monkeys with resections of the hippocampal gyrus chose the novel cue more often than did control monkeys. The processing of the previously less relevant cue had been inefficient when compared with that of controls (Douglas & Pribram, 1966). It can be important on a subsequent occasion to have processed not only what arouses interest but also the context within which interest is experienced (latently learned).

The results of an additional experiment supports the conclusion that, in the absence of a hippocampal gyrus, processing of the nonreinforced aspects of a situation becomes inefficient and that ordinarily such processing demands effort (in psychiatry, this has been termed "listening with the third ear"). In one experiment, monkeys had to choose a consistently rewarded cue from a set of nonrewarded cues. The number of nonrewarded cues influenced the performance of control monkeys but not the performance of monkeys who had had their hippocampus resected (Douglas, Barrett, Pribram, & Cerny, 1969).

However, the most critical evidence that the hippocampus is ordinarily involved in processing the nonreinforced rather than the reinforced aspects of a situation comes from an experiment in which we recorded electrical activity from the hippocampus while monkeys were performing discrimination tasks. In a go/no-go situation, the electrical activity (specifically the amount of theta rhythm) was distinctly different during the go and no-go trials. When the cues were then presented simultaneously, and the monkey had to select the consistently reinforced cue, we were greatly surprised to find that the hippocampal electrical activity was identical to that recorded on the no-go trials of the previous task (Crowne, Konow, Drake, & Pribram, 1972). Again, as in the case of the electrical activity recorded from the inferotemporal cortex (cf. Pribram, 1990b, Lecture 7), it is as if these systems were processing "don't look there" rather than "look here."

Extinction is, thus, the key to understanding the operations of both the posterior inferotemporal and hippocampal systems in pattern perception. These systems are connected via the entorhinal and subicular cortex. In fact theta rhythms have been recorded to directly reflect extinction (Gray, 1970, 1972).

Extinction entails a win-*shift* strategy. First, the organism has learned that a particular stimulus constitutes the "figure," the content within a context. When he must shift his responses to a novel figure, a novel content, the original stimulus becomes a part of ground, context. These shifts are not limited to instrumental responding. The effects are also observed when eye movements are recorded (Bagshaw, Mackworth, & Pribram, 1970a, 1970b, 1972).

Responding to context entails the risk of distraction and processing overload. Signal detection theory has developed techniques to measure perceptual risk, the bias with which an organism approaches a situation. Using these techniques, both inferotemporal and hippocampal resections were shown to shift bias, albeit in opposite directions (Pribram, Spevack, Blower, & McGuinness, 1980; Spevack & Pribram, 1973). Hippocampal resections shift bias toward caution; inferotemporal damage shifts bias toward risk.

Other investigators (see reviews of Amsel, 1986, and Gray, 1982a, 1982b), using rats, have also demonstrated that hippocampectomy influences behavior in situations in which nonreinforcement plays an important role, especially when the now nonreinforced cues had been previously reinforced (frustrative nonreward). According to these authors, the first step in discrimination learning is to anticipate reinforcement (for responding to either cue) and then to differentiate their responses to reinforced and nonreinforced cues. According to the results of our primate studies reviewed previously, the amygdala is essentially involved in both of these initial steps. Hippocampectomy does not interfere with these primary aspects of learning (as example, go/no-go alternation, also called patterned alternation, remains intact after resections of the hippocampal formation in both monkeys and rats). By contrast, when a previously reinforced cue becomes "context" (i.e., the unreinforced element in a discrimination), hippocampectomized monkeys and rats fail to respond to changes in the number or position of these cues.

Taken together, the effects of amygdalectomy and hippocampectomy produce an organism deficient in processing events to compose a context in which they are relevant. At times such processing entails expending effort to efficiently recombine familiar, and, thus, currently ignored, events into contextual configurations that are perceived as novel.

Relevance, Distraction, and the Limbic Forebrain

A patient with a bilateral resection of his amygdala and hippocampus dramatically demonstrates these effects on familiarizing and innovating. When interviewed, this patient appears normal; he answers questions readily and solves adequately the problems presented to him. The patient can accurately remember anything that happened before surgery had been performed on his brain. Furthermore, he can perform perceptual and motor skills that, through repetitive practice, he has learned since surgery. In fact he shows no evidence of forgetting in any of the tasks presented to him. This is no different from what is found when monkeys with hippocampal resections are tested in this fashion. In one experiment, we trained monkeys in a visual discrimination, used them for other purposes, and then examined their retention 2 *years* later. Unoperated controls performed the first 100 trials at 80%–85% correct. Hippocampectomized monkeys performed at 92%–96%.

Once interrupted and distracted, however, the patient fails to recall that the interrogation had taken place and even fails to remember having seen the interrogator. In order to perform a daily task such as grocery shopping, he must carry a list (a common procedure for all of us, but we are not totally lost as to what to do should we lose our list). In a procedure characterized by many such interruptions administered as "novel" stimuli, the patient failed to remember the contents of what he had experienced. Freed, Corkin, and Cohen (1987) noted that:

> when the . . . procedure was modified in a manner that required [him] to focus on novelty, HM's . . . performance was above chance. These data suggest that HM's performance may reflect a heightened [unconsciously determined] response on his part to the [to us] novel stimuli that [for him act as] distractors [unless specifically attended]. (p. 470)

Just as in the case of the monkeys described earlier, unless he is instructed to focus on the novel stimuli, they act as distractors and, thus, fail to become integrated into configurations that have relevance. As noted, irrelevancies are not overtly remembered. Only relevancies become familiar and provide the context from which novelties become constructed.

Familiarization and innovation occur within a processing space, an episode. Episodes provide the context within which perceptions are valued on the basis of their relevance to the memory-motive structure of the organism (cf. Killeen, chapter 4 in this volume). Context (processing space) and content (stimuli sampled) interact in a reciprocal fashion. The nature of this interaction has been determined by using another set of tasks that have been called one-trial learning or *trial unique tasks* (Nissen, 1951; Mishkin, 1973). Resections of the various anatomical structures that compose the limbic forebrain and its related frontal cortex and basal ganglia disrupt performance of these tasks, whereas resection of the cortex of the posterior cerebral convexity do not. (Conversely resections of the cortex of the posterior cerebral convexity disrupt *sensory discrimination tasks* dependent on stimulus sampling, whereas resections of the structures composing the frontolimbic forebrain do not.)

There are two basic forms of trial unique tasks, and there are also variations on these forms and combinations. The basic tasks are delayed response and delayed alternation. In the delayed response task, a reward is hidden within sight of the monkey, an opaque screen is lowered and then raised after a period of 5 to 15 (or more) seconds, and the monkey is then allowed to find the reward. In the delayed alternation procedure, rewards are hidden behind the opaque screen in two sites identical in appearance. The screen is raised, and the monkey is allowed to find the reward. The screen is lowered for a period of 5 to 15 seconds and then raised, once more allowing the monkey to find the remaining reward. In order to find the reward on this trial, the monkey must adopt a win-shift strategy (i.e., the monkey must shift its response to the site other than the one in which it found the reward on the previous trial). For subsequent trials, the reward is alternately hidden in the two locations while the screen is down.

Using the delayed response procedure, it was found that the distraction produced by the interference of the screen was the factor critically responsible for the disruption produced by resections of structures within the frontolimbic forebrain. When the delay was produced by darkening the test chamber instead of by lowering and raising a screen, monkeys with frontolimbic resections performed as well as their controls (Malmo, 1942; Pribram, 1961; Pribram, Plotkin, Anderson, & Leong, 1977).

The difficulty produced by resections within the frontolimbic forebrain on the delayed alternation task has also been shown to be due to interference. When the delay between trials was the same irrespective of which location was baited, monkeys with frontolimbic resections failed the task; when the delay between trials was made unequal (e.g., 5 seconds when the left location was baited, 15 second when the right location was baited), monkeys with such resections performed as well as their controls (Pribram & Tubbs, 1967; Pribram, Plotkin, Anderson, & Leong, 1977). It is well known that similarity is a powerful determinant of both proactive and retroactive interference. More on this is discussed in Pribram (1991, Lecture 10) in relation to the frontal cortex.

The delayed alternation task has two forms: a go-right/go-left, and a go/no-go version. These versions have been used to explore possible functional differences in various anatomical subdivisions of the frontolimbic forebrain (see Pribram, 1986, 1987, for review).

A modification of the delayed response task, called the indirect form or the delayed matching from sample procedure, has also proved useful, because it minimizes the spatial aspect critical to performance of the classical task. It has been further modified into a hybrid with delayed alternation. This hybrid is the delayed nonmatching from sample procedure. In both of these modifications, the monkey is shown a cue, then a screen is lowered for some seconds, and, when it is raised, the monkey confronts two cues, one of which is the previously shown sample. In the match from sample procedure, selecting the sample is rewarded; in the nonmatch from sample, selecting the novel cue is rewarded.

These modifications of the delay procedures also contain elements of sensory discrimination tasks. They have, therefore, proved useful in analyzing the functional relationships between the limbic and convexal portions of the temporal lobe of the brain. Just as the limbic part of the lobe is divided into amygdala and hippocampal formation, so also is the convexal cortex of the temporal lobe divided into an anterior (polar) and a posterior part that are functionally distinct (Pribram & MacLean, 1953; Pribram & Bagshaw, 1953; Iwai & Mishkin, 1968). When objects are used in the nonmatching from sample procedure, resections of the anterior portion of the convexal cortex and of the amygdala produce severe deficits in performance, whereas resection of the posterior part of the inferotemporal cortex and of the hippocampal formation do not (Spiegler & Mishkin, 1981). Mishkin interpreted his results to indicate that the anterior inferotemporal cortex and amygdala are involved in object–reward associations, which is consonant with the results of the series of experiments on the amygdala described earlier.

Resections of the posterior portions of the inferotemporal cortex do not produce deficits in object–reward association; even with match and nonmatch to sample procedures, the difficulty that is produced is best interpreted as a difficulty in stimulus sampling, for a number of reasons. First, in contrast to the effects of anterior inferotemporal resections, the deficit is proportional to the difficulty of the task (see Pribram, 1984, for review, and also Mishkin, 1966). Second, as described in Pribram, 1991, Lecture 7, when the monkeys had to choose one object out of a set of objects, the techniques of stimulus sampling theory accounted quantitatively for differences in performance of the monkeys with the resections and their controls.

There are indications that still another factor is involved in sampling, a factor dependent on the functions of the hippocampal formation. Sampling, as shown in Wilson (1987) and Wilson and DeBauche (1981), proceeds as follows: Generalization gradients sharpen, and this sharpening involves the setting of a baseline, an adaptation level. Once a baseline has been set, the nonreinforced aspects of the stimulus array must be gated (filtered) out, sharpening the focus of the reinforced aspect. In stimulus sampling theory, this is accomplished one element at a time—and monkeys have been shown to learn visual discriminations in just this fashion (Blehart, 1966; Pribram, 1984). However, as described earlier, hippocampal resections have been shown to interfere with the monkeys' processing of these nonreinforced components of a situation, a result in many respects similar to that obtained after inferotemporal cortical resections in the multiple object study. Based on these results, a hypothesis can be formulated to the effects that it is likely that relevance (from Latin *relevare,* to lift up) is often due to perceiving these nonreinforced, filtered events "in a new light." This hypothesis is basic to the model that is discussed in the last section of this chapter.

THE BOUNDARIES OF AN EPISODE

The importance of the amygdala and hippocampal formation in determining the boundaries of an episode is attested by the results of another set of experiments. Kesner and DiMattia (1987) presented series of cues to animals to allow them to become familiar and then paired the initial, intermediate, and final cues of the series with novel cues in a discrimination. When similar tasks are administered to humans, they recall the initial and final cues of the series more readily than they recall the intermediate ones. These are termed primacy and recency effects. Unoperated monkeys showed both effects in Kesner and DiMattia's experiments. However, after amygdalectomy, monkeys failed to show either a recency or a primacy effect, whereas the effects of hippocampectomy influenced especially the primacy effect. If the series is taken to be an episode, the effects of amygdalectomy can be considered to impair the demarcation of an episode. As described in Pribram (1991, Lecture 10), after resections of the far frontal cortex, ordering within an episode become deficient.

These data also aid in understanding a hitherto unexplained result of hippocampectomy: Hippocampectomy produces deficits on spatial alternation but not on the go/no-go form nor on delayed response. Perhaps spatial alternation is more dependent on primacy than is delayed response. The fact that spatial cues are especially potent distractors (Douglas & Pribram, 1969) makes it plausible that they serve better in tasks depending on recency, such as delayed response, than in tasks where the subject's own responses in the form of kinesthetic stimuli serve as cues. As described earlier, hippocampal recordings indicate that even in spatial tasks, the hippocampal theta rhythm reflects the no-go aspect of the task, thus the earlier (more primary) cue in the sequence of responding.

To summarize, four distinct but interrelated processes are involved in perceiving an object as relevant. Each of these processes has been related to the functions of a separate system whose forebrain component lies in the temporal lobe of the brain.

1. The *cortex of the posterior convexity* of the lobe is involved in *stimulus sampling*.
2. The role of the *amygdala* of the medial portion of the lobe is to provide context by furnishing *a familiar base*.
3. *Associations between objects* and visceroautonomically arousing, *reinforcing events* are mediated by the *cortex of the anterior (polar) convexity of* the lobe.

4. The *hippocampal formation* furnishes the opportunity for *perceiving novelty* in processing the *nonreinforced aspects* of the situation.

The following relationships between these processes have been established. When novelty is experienced, sampling increases. In the absence of sampling, selection depends solely on object-reinforcement associations that leads to stereotypy. In the absence of such associations, processing depends solely on the processing of novelty, which, as was shown by eye movement and other experiments, can lead to much irrelevant exploration.

A MODEL FOR EPISODIC PROCESSING

William James (1950) noted that values color perceptions. Coloration can be effected, he stated, either by operating through a separate brain system or by utilizing the same pathways as those that organize perception. As we know now, both of James' possibilities are realized. The neuropsychological research reviewed in this chapter indicate that the limbic formations of the medial portion of the temporal lobe—amygdala and hippocampus—are critically involved in valuing perceptions. Valuation was shown to color percepts by way of inputs that deter or reinforce behavior. These inputs are routed to the brain via a separate set of protocritic systems based on pain and temperature sensibility. Both amygdala and hippocampus are reciprocally connected with hypothalamic and mesencephalic brain stem nuclei. These in turn exert widespread influence on the forebrain (see Bloom, Lazerson, & Hofstadter, 1985, for review) and are, therefore, ideally situated to value the processes involved in perception.

Computational models of such processes rely heavily on changing "values" or "weights" of connections (synapses) on the basis of error signals. Errors result when the output layer of the model generates something other than what a "teacher" is prepared to accept.

Such computations were undertaken to model the learning process. They are, however, also relevant to modeling the cognitive aspects of perception, because these aspects are largely due to learning. A computational model of brain processes that operate to value perceptions is, therefore, feasible.

When Hopfield (1982) described his network, and Hinton and Sejnowski (1986) proposed the "Boltzmann" engine as a model of learning, the proposals immediately struck a responsive chord with the author. As described, he had considered the functions of the hippocampus and related systems in terms of the concept of cognitive "effort," effort conceived as a measure of the degree of efficiency with which processing is proceeding (Pribram & McGuinness, 1975, 1989; McGuinness & Pribram, 1980; Pribram, 1986). The concept of efficiency is the basis of the second law of thermodynamics as formulated by Boltzmann. The thermodynamically based models should, therefore, in some fashion be able to describe formally the functions of the amygdala and hippocampus and related systems.

The potential for modeling is greatly enhanced by a modification of the Hopfield model that is developed mathematically in Appendix D of Pribram (1991) and is outlined here. The original model described energy minima as Hamiltonians. As noted, in our own work (Barrett, 1969), we also initially modeled brain functions in terms of Hamiltonians created by interference patterns: The cortex was conceived to be operating as an interferometer.

The current modification (see Pribram, 1990, 1991, Lecture 2) in terms of the holonomic brain theory deals with a Hilbert space of Gabor elementary functions in which Hamiltonian operators are the vectors. Correlations are carried out by taking the inner products of the vectors. The Gabor functions are considered to be quanta of information, entropy minima, not energy (intensity) minima. In the brain, these functions describe "channels," the functional receptive fields of neurons.

The Gabor channel is capacity limited, it describes the minimum uncertainty, the minimum entropy with which a unit of information can be transmitted. The holonomic brain theory generalizes the Gabor relation to construct a multidimensional manifold. This manifold makes available the potential for minima via a least action principle. The manifold is entropic, its entropy defined as potential information. In keeping with the thermodynamic model, maximum efficiency is attained not by pushing each Gabor relation to its unique minimum but by modifying the ensemble of Gabor relations (e.g., by altering band width; see Caelli & Hubner, 1983) until the *ensemble* computes with maximum efficiency.

Efficiency, as the term is used here, is a communication engineering concept. Whenever values are to be assigned to a process in a quantitative fashion, two attributes must be present: a reference and a unit of incrementation (von Neumann & Morgenstern, 1953; Pribram, 1960). For instance, if we wish to describe the amount of heat in terms of temperature, we need a reference such as that provided by phase changes of water (the freezing and boiling points at appropriate atmospheric pressure) and also a unit of incrementation such as the degree Celsius, which divides the range between the freezing and boiling points into 100 equal units (centigrades). For the model of efficiency proposed here, an episode within which equivalence is achieved by familiarization can serve as the reference. The reference is demarcated by a destabilizing interrupt of prior ongoing processing and ends with the next interrupt, which initiates a different processing episode. As reviewed, there is considerable evidence that the amygdala system is integral to this type of processing.

The temporary stability that defines an episode as a processing reference also determines the inner shape (the structure of redundancy) of a processing "holoscape." The holoscape of isovalent contours connecting equivalent polarizations in the network of postsynaptic microprocesses is unique to the episode. Thus, when one is hungry, one notices restaurant signs by virtue of processing described by one particular contour map of the holoscape; when one needs to mail a letter, mailboxes are attended by virtue of processing described by another such contour map (Zeigarnik, 1972).

As the same distal stimulus situation may be involved, the difference in emphasis is due to the operation of the "mind's eye," a difference produced by the episode currently "motivating the perceptual process" (see, e.g., Bruner & Postman, 1949; Hastorf & Knutson, 1954). Despite considerable controversy regarding the experiments, the results produced the "new look" in perception in the 1950s.

In the experiments of Rothblat and Pribram (1972) and Nuwer and Pribram (1979), the same four cues (red square, green square, red diamond, green diamond) were shown to monkeys, but, in different episodes, color or form was reinforced. In these experiments, brain electrical activity reflected the previously reinforced cue (the effects of which were still "occupying" his brain and possibly his thoughts), whereas his behavior was correctly reflecting current reinforcing contingencies. These findings demonstrate the existence of operations (of the mind's eye) independently of expressed behavior. Further, these experiments show that the cortex of the temporal lobe and not the primary sensory systems is critical to this operation. Posner (1973) showed how such mind's eye effects can be obtained in humans even in the absence of eye movement.

In terms of the holonomic brain theory, the holoscape of contours describing isovalent junctional polarizations would appear considerably different under the condition "mail a letter" from that mapped under the condition "hungry." Different configurations of values would display different hills and valleys on the polarization contour map. A simpler example would be attending to the color or to the form of a scene as in our monkey experiment. The pattern of isovalent contours produced by receptive fields responding to color and the pattern responding to form would be different, much as when one asks all those in a classroom to briefly raise their hand, if they wearing a red sweater and then asking those who are wearing glasses to raise theirs.

With regard to the units of incrementation (values given to polarizations of junctions in the dendritic microprocess), these units must describe the "distances" between isovalent contours. In the holonomic brain theory, the minimum entropy for the band width defined by these isovalent contours serves as the unit of measure on these distances. This results in an entropic domain where the distance between isovalent contours is set in terms of the distances between the minimum uncertainty attainable in each channel.

In such a process, what characterizes innovation? In the intact organism, habituation of the visceroautonomic components of an orienting reaction occurs within three to ten repetitions of the orienting stimulus. The orienting, distracting stimulus has perturbed a stable organization of redundancies (an organization sometimes referred to as an apperceptive mass) that rapidly restabilizes. After restabilization, there continue to be mild cyclic fluctuations of these components with irregular periods measured in minutes. Originally we thought these stabilities described states of equilibrium (Piaget, 1970; Pribram, 1958, 1969). The advent of Prigogine's descriptions of stabilities far from equilibrium offered a much richer model: Perturbations of equilibrium states could only lead to a return to equilibrium; perturbations of states far from equilibrium would lead to the potential for novel constructions (McGuinness, Pribram, & Pirnazar, 1990).

The thermodynamic considerations put forward by Prigogine (1980) regarding stabilities far from equilibrium were intriguing. The results of the experiments performed in our laboratory that delineated the effects of amygdalectomy and resections made in related systems were conceived as destabilizing the organism (Pribram, 1969, 1980; Pribram, Reitz, McNeil, & Spevack, 1979). The destabilization was related to an inability to properly process the structure of redundancy (Pribram, Lim, Poppen, & Bagshaw, 1966; Pribram & Tubbs, 1967; Pribram, 1969, 1987).

There is, thus, the potential for understanding the contributions of the medial temporal lobe systems in terms of two computational models derived from thermodynamics: the creation of stabilities in the Boltzmann model that is perceived as familiarization and the efficiency with which novelty can emerge by way of recombinant processing, (i.e., restructuring—far from equilibrium—of the redundancies, inherent in these stabilities (see Pribram, 1986, for review).

An essential characteristic of stabilities far from equilibrium is that they are "attractive" (i.e., they operate as "attractors" toward which the process tends; cf. Killeen, chapter 4 in this volume). Thus, the "episode," characterized by its temporary stability far from equilibrium, can act as an attractor during learning—in experimental psychology terms, it acts as a reinforcing process. In the holonomic brain theory, this process is mediated by the protocritic (pain and temperature) system.

Often the neuropsychological system is actually operating close to equilibrium, and perturbation is handled by a return to equilibrium: The distraction of an orienting reaction is either ignored or incorporated into the ongoing process through repetition or familiarization. However, if the perturbation is great, a reaction we ordinarily call emotionally upsetting can result in turbulence, and a new stability has to be achieved. When, as in the holonomic brain theory, the process is conceived to be composed of continuous functions (e.g., as manifolds described by the Lie algebra), vortices can develop in the turbulent systems. Thus, an often realized possibility is to be "hung up" in the turbulence, but, because this is a state far from equilibrium, one can deliberately seek alternate constraints in order to change the state.

Ashby (1960) described an interesting and powerful method for dealing with turbulence that leads to "catastrophic" restabilizations ("step functions"). In his computational model, stability was achieved by adding to the computation, numbers taken from a list of random numbers. Randomicity provides maximum variance, the widest spread of possible consequences (Miller, 1956). In a system with such a probability distribution, there is also maximum possibility (potentiality) for new organization to develop. As in Prigogine's model, one cannot predict just how the system will restabilize because of the randomness injected into the turbulent system.

Ashby's and Prigogine's models have many things in common with the more recently developed thermodynamic models. Maximum efficiency in processing is achieved by a heuristic in which the addition of noise is important to preclude premature closure onto an overriding attractor.

However, as described in Pribram (1991, Lecture 10), there is in intact organisms an alternative processing mode that leads to innovation that does not involve a catastrophic reaction. This mode utilizes equivocation, the sum of noise and redundancy. To achieve novel recombinations, the options provided by the mind's eye must be exercised. This is accomplished by selectively attending the variety of possibilities in a scene or alternatively through "envisioning" by virtue of memories of previous scenes, as Beethoven did in composing although deaf. These options are provided by redundancies that enhance efficient processing of information and, therefore, constitute "structured" entropy (Shannon & Weaver, 1949; Gatlin, 1972). The isovalent contour maps of the holoscape describe the neural nature of this entropic structure.

Hinton and Sejnowski (1986) developed a "hill climbing" routine that moves an element in a stepwise manner over such a contoured terrain. Processing proceeds perpendicular to the contours. In their model, "climbing" is actually down a mountain and is accomplished by random steps, until the bottom of the mountain is reached, when the "elasticity" of the process contracts the "line of climb" into the shortest path. This "moment of truth" may well describe the consolidation of an episode in memory (McGaugh, 1966; McGaugh & Hertz, 1972).

Hinton and Sejnowski's model can be usefully modified with respect to the data reviewed in this chapter and in Pribram (1991, Lecture 7). The process can be described as a matter of sharpening generalization gradients until *separation* between domains is achieved. The "moment of truth" is when the separation occurs. Hill "climbing" is replaced by a stepwise "steepening" of the gradient—by actually changing the shape of the hill, the generalization gradient.

In summary, the weightings (values) of polarizations of the junctional microprocess are conceived to be structured by the effects of previous experience through the process of habituation of relevant, and the extinction of irrelevant, experiences. Perturbation, internally or externally generated, produces an orienting reaction. Continuation of the perturbing event (e.g., repetition) leads to habituation and then, if processing allows stability to be regained, to extinction. Innovation demands that the extinguished experience become reactivated. Efficiency in innovating is enhanced not only by adding randomness to the process but also by adding the structured variety produced by prior experience. A formal description of these processes is given in Appendices F and G by Yasue, Jibu, and Pribram in Pribram (1991), and a proposal for how these processes are implemented is provided in Pribram (1991, Lecture 10).

REFERENCES

Amsel, A. (1986). Daniel Berlyne memorial lecture: Developmental psychobiology and behavior theory: Reciprocating influences. *Canadian Journal of Psychology, 40*, 311–342.

Ashby, W. R. (1960). *Design for a brain: The origin of adaptive behavior* (2nd ed.). New York: Wiley.

Bagshaw, M. H., & Benzies, S. (1968). Multiple measures of the orienting reaction and their dissociation after amygdalectomy in monkeys. *Experimental Neurology, 20*, 175–187.

Bagshaw, M. H., & Coppock, H. W. (1968). Galvanic skin response conditioning deficit in amygdalectomized monkeys. *Experimental Neurology, 20*, 188–196.

Bagshaw, M. H., Kimble, D. P., & Pribram, K. H. (1965). The GSR of monkeys during orienting and habituation and after ablation of the amygdala, hippocampus and inferotemporal cortex. *Neuropsychologia, 3*, 111–119.

Bagshaw, M. H., Mackworth, N. H., & Pribram, K. H. (1970a). Method for recording and analyzing visual fixations in the unrestrained monkey. *Perceptual and Motor Skills, 31*, 219–222.

Bagshaw, M. H., Mackworth, N. H., & Pribram, K. H. (1970b). The effect of inferotemporal cortex ablations on eye movements of monkeys during discrimination training. *International Journal of Neuroscience, 1*, 153–158.

Bagshaw, M. H., & Pribram, K. H. (1968). Effect of amygdalectomy on stimulus threshold of the monkey. *Experimental Neurology, 20*, 197–202.

Barrett, T. W. (1969). The cerebral cortex as a diffractive medium. *Mathematical Biosciences, 4*, 311–350.

Beach, F. A. (1955). The descent of instinct. *Psychological Review, 62*, 401–410.

Beck, C. H., & Miles, W. R. (1947). Some theoretical and experimental relationships between infrared absorption and olfaction. *Science, 106*, 511–513.

Berlyne, D. E. (1969). The development of the concept of attention in psychology. In C. R. Evans & T. B. Mulholland (Eds.), *Attention in neurophysiology* (pp. 1–26). New York: Appleton-Century-Crofts.

Bernstein, L. (1976). *The unanswered question*. Cambridge, MA: Harvard University Press.

Blehart, S. R. (1966). Pattern discrimination with rhesus monkeys. *Psychological Reports, 19*, 311–324.

Bloom, F. E., Lazerson, A., & Hofstadter, L. (1985). *Brain, mind, and behavior*. New York: Freeman.

Brobeck, J. R. (1963). Review and synthesis. In M. A. B. Brazier (Ed.), *Brain and behavior, Volume II* (pp. 389–409). Washington, DC: American Institute of Biological Sciences.

Brown, S., & Schaefer, E. A. (1888). An investigation into the functions of the occipital and temporal lobes of the monkey's brain. *Philosophical Transactions of the Royal Society of London, 179*, 303–327.

Bruner, J. S. (1957). Neural mechanisms in perception. *Psychological Review, 64*, 340–358.

Bruner, J. S., & Postman, L. (1949). On the perception of incongruity: a paradigm. *Journal of Personality, 18*, 206–223.

Caelli, T., & Hubner, M. (1983). On the efficient two-dimensional energy coding characteristics of spatial vision. *Vision Research, 23*, 1053–1055.

Chin, J. H., Pribram, K. H., Drake, K., & Greene, L. O., Jr. (1976). Disruption of temperature discrimination during limbic forebrain stimulation in monkeys. *Neuropsychologia, 14*, 293–310.

Crowne, D. P., Konow, A., Drake, K. J., & Pribram, K. H. (1972). Hippocampal electrical activity in the monkey during delayed alternation problems. *Electroencephalography and Clinical Neurophysiology, 33,* 567–577.

Doty, R. W., & Nagrao, N. (1973). Forebrain commissures and vision. In R. Jung (Ed.), *Handbook of sensory physiology, Volume VII/3B,* (pp. 543–582). Berlin: Springer-Verlag.

Douglas, R. J., Barrett, T. W., Pribram, K. H., & Cerny, M. C. (1969). Limbic lesions and error reduction. *Journal of Comparative and Physiological Psychology, 68,* 437–441.

Douglas, R. J., & Pribram, K. H. (1966). Learning and limbic lesions. *Neuropsychologia, 4,* 197–220.

Douglas, R. J., & Pribram, K. H. (1969). Distraction and habituation in monkeys with limbic lesions. *Journal of Comparative and Physiological Psychology, 69,* 473–480.

Freed, D. M., Corkin, S. & Cohen, N. J. (1987). Forgetting in H. M.: a second look. *Neuropsychologia 25,* 461–471.

Fuller, J. L., Rosvold, H. E., & Pribram, K. H. (1957). The effect on affective and cognitive behavior in the dog of lesions of the pyriform-amygdala-hippocampal complex. *Journal of Comparative and Physiological Psychology, 50,* 89–96.

Fulton, J. F., Pribram, K. H., Stevenson, J. A. F., & Wall, P. (1949). Interrelations between orbital gyrus, insula, temporal tip and anterior cingulate gyrus. *Transactions of the American Neurological Association,* pp. 175–179.

Gatlin, L. (1972). *Information theory and the living system.* New York: Columbia University Press.

Gray, J. A. (1970). Sodium amobarbital, the hippocampal theta rhythm and the partial reinforcement extinction effect. *Psychological Review, 77,* 465–480.

Gray, J. A. (1972). Effects of septal driving of the hippocampal theta rhythm on resistance to extinction. *Physiology and Behavior, 8,* 481–490.

Gray, J. A. (1982a). *The neuropsychology of anxiety.* Oxford, UK: Oxford University Press.

Gray, J. A. (1982b). Precis of the neuropsychology of anxiety: An enquiry into the functions of the septo-hippocampal system. *The Behavioral and Brain Sciences, 5,* 469–484.

Grueninger, W. E., & Pribram, K. H. (1969). Effects of spatial and nonspatial distractors on performance latency of monkeys with frontal lesions. *Journal of Comparative and Physiological Psychology, 68,* 203–209.

Hastorf, A. H., & Knutson, A. L. (1954). Motivation, perception, and attitude change. *Psychological Review, 56,* 88–97.

Head, H. (1920). *Studies in neurology, Volumes I and II.* London: Oxford University Press.

Hearst, E., & Pribram, K. H. (1964a). Facilitation of avoidance behavior by unavoidable shocks in normal and amygdalectomized monkeys. *Psychological Reports, 14,* 39–42.

Hearst, E., & Pribram, K. H. (1964b). Appetitive and aversive generalization gradients in amygdalectomized monkeys. *Journal of Comparative and Physiological Psychology, 58,* 296–298.

Hinton, G. E., & Sejnowski, T. J. (1986). Learning and relearning in Boltzmann machines. In D. E. Rumelhart, & J. L. Mc Clelland (Eds.), *Parallel distributed processing* (Vol. 1, pp. 282–317). Cambridge, MA: MIT Press.

Hopfield, J. J. (1982). Neural networks and physical systems with emergent collective computational abilities. *Proceedings of the National Academy of Sciences, 79,* 2554–2558.

Iwai, E., & Mishkin, M. (1968). Two visual foci in the temporal lobe of monkeys. In N. Yoshii & N. A. Buchwald (Eds.), *Neuropsychological basis of learning and behavior.* Osaka, Japan: Osaka University Press.

James, W. (1950). *Principles of psychology* (Vols. I and II). New York: Dover.

Kaada, B. R., Pribram, K. H., & Epstein, J. A. (1949). Respiratory and vascular responses in monkeys from temporal pole, insula, orbital surface and cingulate gyrus. *Journal of Neurophysiology, 12,* 347–356.

Kenshalo, D. R. (1968). *The skin senses.* Springfield, IL: Charles Thomas.

Kesner, R. P., & DiMattia, B. V. (1987). Neurobiology of an attribute model of memory. In A. N. Epstein & A. Morrison (Eds.), *Progress in psychobiology and physiological psychology* (Vol. 12, pp. 207–277). New York: Academic Press.

Kimble, D. P., Bagshaw, M. H., & Pribram, K. H. (1965). The GSR of monkeys during orienting and habituation after selective partial ablations of cingulate and frontal cortex. *Neuropsychologia, 3,* 121–128.

Koepke, J. E., & Pribram, K. H. (1967a). Habituation of the vasoconstriction response as a function of stimulus duration and anxiety. *Journal of Comparative and Physiological Psychology, 64,* 502–504.

Koepke, J. E., & Pribram, K. H. (1967b). Effect of food reward on the maintenance of sucking behavior during infancy. *Proceedings of the 75th Annual Convention, APA,* pp. 111–112.

Liebeskind, J. C., Guilbaud, G., Besson, J. M., & Oliveras, J. L. (1973). Analgesia from electrical stimulation of the periaqueductal gray matter in the cat: behavioral observations and inhibitory effects on spinal cord interneurons. *Brain Research, 50,* 441–446.

Liebeskind, J. C., Mayer, D. J., & Akil, H. (1974). Central mechanisms of pain inhibition: studies of analgesia from focal brain stimulation. In J. J. Bonica (Ed.), *Advances in neurology: Vol. 4, Pain.* New York: Raven.

Lorenz, K. (1969). Innate bases of learning. In K. H. Pribram (Ed.), *On the biology of learning* (pp. 13–94). New York: Harcourt, Brace, & World.

Malmo, R. B. (1942). Interference factors in delayed response in monkeys after removal of frontal lobes. *Journal of Neurophysiology, 5,* 295–308.

McGaugh, J. L. (1966). Time-dependent processes in memory storage. *Science, 153,* 1351–1358.

McGaugh, J. L., & Hertz, M. L. (1972). *Memory consolidation.* San Francisco: Albion.

McGuinness, D. (1972). Hearing: Individual differences in perceiving. *Perception, 1,* 465–473.

McGuinness, D., & Cox, R. J. (1977). The effect of chronic anxiety level upon self control of heart rate. *Biological Psychology, 5,* 7–14.

McGuinness, D., & Pribram, K. H. (1980). The neuropsychology of attention: Emotional and motivational controls. In M. C. Wittrock (Ed.), *The brain and psychology* (pp. 95–129). New York: Academic Press.

McGuinness, D., Pribram, K. H., & Pirnazar, M. (1990). Upstaging the stage model. In C. N. Alexander & E. J. Langer (Eds.), *Higher stages of human development* (pp. 97–113). Oxford, UK: Oxford University Press.

Miller, G. A. (1956). The magical number seven, plus or minus two, or some limits on our capacity for processing information. *Psychological Review, 63,* 81–97.

Mishkin, M. (1973). Cortical visual areas and their interaction. In A. G. Karczmar & J. C. Eccles (Eds.), *The brain and human behavior* (pp. 187–208). Berlin: Springer-Verlag.

Morin, F., Schwartz, H. G., & O'Leary, J. L. (1951). Experimental study of the spinothalamic and realted tracts. *Acta Psychiatrica et Neurologica Scandinavica XXVI, 3 and 4.*

Nissen, W. H. (1951). Phylogenetic comparison. In S. S. Stevens (Ed.), *Handbook of experimental psychology* (pp. 347–386). New York: Wiley.

Nuwer, M. R., & Pribram, K. H. (1979). Role of the inferotemporal cortex in visual selective attention. *Electroencephalography and Clinical Neurophysiology, 46,* 389–400.

Olds, J. (1955). Physiological mechanisms of reward. In M. Jones (Ed.), *Nebraska Symposium on Motivation* (pp. 73–142). Lincoln, NE: University of Nebraska Press.

Olds, J., & Milner, P. M. (1954). Positive reinforcement produced by electrical stimulation of septal area and other regions of rat brain. *Journal of Comparative and Physiological Psychology, 47,* 419–427.

Pfaffman, C. (1951). Taste and smell. In S. S. Stevens (Ed.), *Handbook of Experimental Psychology,* (pp. 1143–1171). New York: Wiley.

Piaget, J. (1970). *Structuralism.* New York: Basic.

Posner, M. I. (1973). Coordination of internal codes. In W. G. Chase (Ed.), *Visual information processing* (pp. 35–73). New York: Academic Press.

Pribram, K. H. (1954). Toward a science of neuropsychology (method and data). In R. A. Patton (Ed.), *Current trends in psychology and the behavioral sciences* (pp. 115–142). Pittsburgh: University of Pittsburgh Press.

Pribram, K. H. (1958). Comparative neurology and the evolution of behavior. In G. G. Simpson (Ed.), *Evolution and behavior* (pp. 140–164). New Haven, CT: Yale University Press.

Pribram, K. H. (1960). The intrinsic systems of the forebrain. In J. Field, H. W. Magoun, & V. E. Hall (Eds.), *Handbook of physiology: Neurophysiology II* (pp. 1323–1344). Washington: American Physiological Society.

Pribram, K. H. (1961). Limbic system. In D. E. Sheer (Ed.), *Electrical stimulation of the brain* (pp. 563–574). Austin, TX: University of Texas Press.

Pribram, K. H. (1969). The neurobehavioral analysis of limbic forebrain mechanisms: revision and progress report. In D. S. Lehrman, R. A. Hinde, & E. Shaw (Eds.), *Advances in the study of behavior* (pp. 297–332). New York: Academic Press.

Pribram, K. H. (1980). Cognition and performance: the relation to neural mechanisms of consequence, confidence, and competence. In A. Routtenberg (Ed.), *Biology of reinforcement: facets of brain stimulation reward* (pp. 11–36). New York: Academic Press.

Pribram, K. H. (1984). Brain systems and cognitive learning processes. In H. L. Rothblat, T. G. Bever, & H. S. Terrace (Eds.), *Animal cognition* (pp. 627–656). Hillsdale, NJ: Lawrence Erlbaum Associates.

Pribram, K. H. (1986). The hippocampal system and recombinant processing. In R. Isaacson & K. H. Pribram (Eds.), *The hippocampus* (Vol. IV, pp. 329–370). New York: Plenum Press.

Pribram, K. H. (1987). Subdivisions of the frontal cortex revisited. In E. Brown & E. Perecman (Eds.), *The frontal lobes revisited* (pp. 11–39). New York: IRBN Press.

Pribram, K. H. (1990). Prolegomenon for a holonomic brain theory. In H. Haken & M. Stadler (Eds.), *Synergetics of competition* (pp. 150–184). Berlin: Springer-Verlag.

Pribram, K. H. (1991). *Holonomy and structure in figural processing: the MacEachran lectures.* Hillsdale, NJ: Lawrence Erlbaum Associates.

Pribram, K. H., & Bagshaw, M. H. (1953). Further analysis of the temporal lobe syndrome utilizing frontotemporal ablations in monkeys. *Journal of Comparative Neurology, 99,* 347–375.

Pribram, K. H., Douglas, R. J., & Pribram, B. J. (1969). The nature of nonlimbic learning. *Journal of Comparative and Physiological Psychology, 69,* 765–772.

Pribram, K. H., Lim, H., Poppen, R., & Bagshaw, M. H. (1966). Limbic lesions and the temporal structure of redundancy. *Journal of Comparative and Physiological Psychology, 61,* 365–373.

Pribram, K. H., & MacLean, P. D. (1953). Neuronographic analysis of medial and basal cerebral cortex, II. *Journal of Neurophysiology, 16,* 324–340.

Pribram, K. H., & McGuinness, D. (1975). Arousal, activation and effort in the control of attention. *Psychological Review, 82,* 116–149.

Pribram, K. H., & McGuinness, D. (1990, in press). Attention and para-attentional processing: Event related brain potentials as tests of a model. *Annals of the New York Academy of Science.*

Pribram, K. H., Plotkin, H. C., Anderson, R. M., & Leong, D. (1977). Information sources in the delayed alternation task for normal and "frontal" monkeys. *Neuropsychologia, 15,* 329–340.

Pribram, K. H., Reitz, S., McNeil, M., & Spevack, A. A. (1979). The effect of amygdalectomy on orienting and classical conditioning in monkeys. *Pavlovian Journal, 14,* 203–217.

Pribram, K. H., Spevack, A., Blower, D., & McGuinness, D. (1980). A decisional analysis of the effects of inferotemporal lesions in the rhesus monkey. *Journal of Comparative Physiology and Psychology, 94,* 675–690.

Pribram, K. H., & Tubbs, W. E. (1967). A comparison of the effects of medial and lateral cerebral resections on conditioned avoidance behavior of monkeys. *Journal of Comparative and Physiological Psychology, 50,* 74–80.

Pribram, K. H., & Weiskrantz, L. (1957). A comparison of the effects of medial and lateral cerebral resections on conditioned avoidance behavior of monkeys. *Journal of Comparative and Physiological Psychology, 50,* 74–80.

Prigogine, I. (1980). *From being to becoming—time and complexity in the physical sciences.* San Francisco: Freeman.

Quilliam, T. A. (1956). Some characteristics of myelinated fiber populations. *Journal of Anatomy,* *90,* 172–187.

Richardson, D. E., & Akil, H. (1974). Chronic self-administration of brain stimulation for pain relief in human patients. *Proceedings of the American Association of Neurological Surgeons,* St. Louis.

Rosvold, H. E., Mirsky, A. F., & Pribram, K. H. (1954). Influence of amygdalectomy on social interaction in a monkey group. *Journal of Comparative and Physiological Psychology, 47,* 173– 178.

Rothblat, L., & Pribram, K. H. (1972). Selective attention: input filter or response selection? *Brain Research, 39,* 427–436.

Russell, R. W., Singer, G., Flanagan, F., Stone, M., & Russell, J. W. (1968). Quantitative relations in amygdala modulation of drinking. *Physiology and Behavior, 3,* 871–875.

Schwartzbaum, J. S. (1960). Changes in reinforcing properties of stimuli following ablation of the amygdaloid complex in monkeys. *Journal of Comparative and Physiological Psychology, 53,* 388–396.

Schwartzbaum, J. S., & Pribram, K. H. (1960). The effects of amygdalectomy in monkeys on transposition along a brightness continuum. *Journal of Comparative and Physiological Psychology, 53,* 396–399.

Shannon, C. E., & Weaver, W. (1949). *The mathematical theory of communication.* Urbana, IL: University of Illinois Press.

Smets, G. (1973). *Aesthetic judgment and arousal.* Leuven, Belgium: Leuven University Press.

Sokolov, E. N. (1963). *Perception and the conditioned reflex.* New York: MacMillan.

Spevack, A., & Pribram, K. H. (1973). A decisional analysis of the effects of limbic lesions in monkeys. *Journal of Comparative and Physiological Psychology, 82,* 211–226.

Spiegler, B. J., & Mishkin, M. (1981). Evidence for the sequential participation of inferior temporal cortex and amygdala in the acquisition of stimulus–reward associations. *Behavioral Brain Research, 2,* 303–317.

Thomas, P. K. (1956). Growth changes in the diameter of peripheral nerve fibres in fishes. *Journal of Anatomy, 90,* 5–14.

von Neumann, J., & Morgenstern, O. (1953). *Theory of games and economic behavior.* Princeton: Princeton University Press.

Weiskrantz, L. (1956). Behavioral changes associated with ablation of the amygdaloid complex in monkeys. *Journal of Comparative and Physiological Psychology, 49,* 381–391.

Wilson, M. (1987). Brain mechanisms in categorical perception. In S. Harnad (Ed.), *Categorical perception* (pp. 387–417). New York: Cambridge University Press.

Wilson, M., & DeBauche, B. A. (1981). Inferotemporal cortex and categorical perception of visual stimuli in monkeys. *Neuropsychologia, 19,* 29–41.

Wilson, W. H. (1959). The role of learning, perception, and reward in monkey's choice of food. *American Journal of Psychology, 72,* 560–565.

Young, J. Z. (1987). *Philosophy and the brain.* Oxford, UK: Oxford University Press.

Zeigarnik, B. V. (1972). *Experimental abnormal psychology.* New York: Plenum.

III APPLICATIONS OF GOAL DIRECTION IN ARTIFICIAL NEURAL SYSTEMS

11 Knowledge-Representation Networks: Goal Direction in Intelligent Neural Systems

Claude A. Cruz
Plexus Systems

A natural or artificial intelligent system does not passively and stereotypically react to environmental stimuli. Instead such a system participates in a cycle of event-driven action selection and execution. The behavior of the system is driven by a set of time-varying goals that serve as an intentional "context" or "orientation" to guide its action-selection process.

Present-day artificial intelligent systems are based on "symbolic" computation in which both the system's knowledge and its internal state are represented by a set of abstract symbols that are transformed according to a set of formal rules. AI systems cannot access the semantics (meaning) of these symbols.

Neural networks are a well-suited substrate for semantic computation. Such networks provide an efficient, low-level associative processing mechanism whose operation is adaptive (and, thus, flexible) and massively parallel (and, thus, rapid). Neural nets possess numerous useful attributes, such as distributed asynchronous graded processing, which are difficult to achieve by other means.

This chapter describes "Knowledge Representation Networks," a knowledge representation and processing system that is embodied in an artificial neural network. This system embeds "knowledge entities" in an architecture consisting of crosscoupled sensory and motor hierarchies. Flow of activation mediates a set of "inference mechanisms" as well as an "attention" control mechanism. The behavior of such a net is jointly determined by the network's external inputs and its current internal state. The latter component may include internally generated signals that act as goal-setting drives.

Since the 1960s, the subfield of computer science known as "artificial intelligence" (AI) has sought to capture certain human cognitive functions in the form of computer programs. These efforts have met with considerable success in specific types of problems, most notably in certain game-playing programs. However, AI has failed to even approach its initial promise of success in replicating the human functions that constitute "commonsense reasoning." There is no indication that evolution of today's AI techniques will successfully meet this challenge.

Prior to the emergence of AI, such early computer science pioneers as John von Neumann and Marvin Minsky were deeply interested in the workings of biological nerve-nets. Their hope was that computers would serve as a means for capturing the basic information-processing properties of nerve-nets. For a variety of technical and political reasons, these early efforts were shunted aside in favor of the nascent AI approach. In the early 1980s, the field of "artificial neural networks" (ANNs, for brevity) sprang phoenix-like from its ashes to again become a contender with AI in the search for artificial intelligent systems.

This chapter describes an ANN-based knowledge-processing system that is patterned on an organism interacting with its environment (Cruz, Hanson, & Tam, 1987, May). The knowledge-representation approach used in the Knowledge Representation Networks system (KRN) embodies a particular view of the physical world as well as a view of the manner in which an organism must interact with that environment. This view also leads to a rationale for why neural networks may be a particularly effective medium for constructing and using a "world model."

As a prelude to discussion of the KRN system, we will trace the roots of the knowledge-representation approach on which it is based. These include four sets of considerations:

1. Identification of those aspects of the world that must be represented.
2. Clarification of how an organism interacts with its environment.
3. Identification of two fundamentally different information-processing approaches.
4. Characterization of a supportive implementation medium (neural nets) for this representation scheme.

MODELING THE EXTERNAL WORLD

In order to interact with its environment in an intelligent way, an organism must be able to internally represent the time-varying state of that world. External entities and situations must be recognizable; specific actions must be reliably repeatable, and appropriate responses must be associated with specific triggering conditions.

Fortunately for us, the world contains some regularities. This is true of the entities that populate the world as well as holding for the laws that govern the interactions among these. Let us define and discuss some terms that we will use throughout this chapter.

We are able to recognize *entities* (objects, conditions, or events) by their characteristic *features* (attributes, or properties). Entities possess certain characteristic, time-invariant attributes (as well as other attributes that are unique to each entity). More specifically, each feature of an entity has an associated range of permissible *feature-values* (e.g., Macintosh apples have a "color" feature that takes on a range of values that we know as "red"). These static properties make it possible to recognize various instances of the members of a given class of object (e.g., different apples).

Entities may be linked by *relationships*. For example, a "table" is defined by a set of essential components (constituent subobjects) that exist in certain spatial relations to one another. Relationships make it possible for us to define and detect complex entities. Thus, for example, an adept chess player is able to discern meaningful spatiotemporal configurations of pieces, for which specific countermoves are appropriate. These configurations are defined through sequences of spatial relationships between the pieces on the board.

Relationships are defined by conjunctions of relative values of corresponding features of entities. For example, to say that one building is "taller" than another is to say that the value of the feature "height" for one is larger in magnitude than the value of that same feature for the other building. Relationships need not deal only with such concrete features as the spatial dimensions of an object; they can also involve more abstract features. For example, to say that a person is "smarter" than another involves a (rather subjective) comparison of the "intelligence" of those individuals. Likewise to say that John and Peter are "brothers" is to say that they share the same values for the attributes "father" and "mother."

The static notion of entities is complemented by the dynamic notion of *events*. Events consist of conjunctions of time-derivatives of feature-values; that is, events are signaled by clusters of *changes* in the feature-values of one or more objects. For example, during an event in which an apple is cut, the "shape" feature of that object changes from an initial value of "round." (This example also points out that such changes can often not be easily described in formal terms; this point will be discussed further. The important point, though, is that an object's feature-values change during an event in which it is involved).

When an event occurs, it can lead to other events; the first event is "coupled" to the others. This coupling may take the form of a direct causal relationship, or it can be an indirect correlation. The mechanisms that effect the coupling operate by transferring the feature-value changes of one event to feature-value changes in the dependent events. As an example, consider two billiard balls at rest on a table. One is hit on a collision course toward the other. The hit-induced acceleration of the first ball constitutes the first (causal) event. When this ball hits the second, the latter is accelerated from its initial stand-still. This is the second (caused) event. In this example, the "acceleration" and "velocity" feature-values of the two balls are coupled by the physical laws that govern collisions.

In responding to events, entities can cause other events to occur. Entities are usually capable of executing various *actions* or *operations* (i.e., of producing various kinds of output activity). Each of these actions produces specific changes in the feature-values of the objects of that action. For example, voluntarily raising one's arms alters the spatial coordinates of that arm. If we view the execution of an action as an event, then that event can cause other events to occur.

To summarize, it appears that a system that can model physical reality must be capable of representing three primitive types of concepts:

1. *Features,* which characterize entities (objects, conditions, or events).
2. *Relationships,* which act as connectives in defining complex features.
3. *Operations* or generalized actions with which an entity may respond to events.

In constructing a system of this type, the choice of low-level implementation medium may be important. This may explain why our brains are not based on the biological equivalent of clockwork. Several characteristics of neural nets recommend them as a powerful mechanism for building and manipulating an internal (mental) model of external reality. These include the following:

1. Much of neural information-processing appears to be based on "association," or the linkage of individual pieces of knowledge into more complex groups (Anderson & Bower, 1973; Kohonen, 1984). Neural nets perform precisely this kind of associative processing. Computers were developed for numerical, logical, and symbolic processing, and cannot efficiently perform associative operations.

2. An intelligent system may do many things at once, while satisfying temporal constraints on operation precedence and timing. It may concurrently process sensory information, produce motions, plan actions to pursue its goals, and so on (Grossberg, 1988; Willwacher, 1982). ANNs provide an ideal mechanism for such distributed parallel processing. Each "module" of a complex net is effectively an independent processor, capable of performing a repertoire of tasks. In contrast, most computers (including AI "symbolic processors") do one thing at a time, in serial fashion.

3. An intelligent system must be able to deal with incomplete, incorrect or inconsistent information. Such information is often described as "fuzzy", and is formally described using "fuzzy logic". Such a logic is based on continuous-valued quantities, rather than on discrete quantities.

Neural nets are capable of performing operations on analog (continuous-valued) information as well as on discrete information. Neural nets are not confined to making black-and-white "YES/NO" decisions but can perform "fuzzy" processing (Kosko, 1987).

4. Knowledge is acquired largely by undergoing *experiences*, many of which are difficult or impossible to accurately describe. Standard AI is based on "symbolic" processing, which in turn depends on formal descriptions of entities, events, and so on. Adaptive ANNs can use *learning* to acquire knowledge through experiences, without the need for formal description. In this sense, they are capable of "semantic" (i.e., meaning-based) processing, not just symbolic processing.

Beyond these general characteristics, neural nets support the various information processing operations needed for intelligent processing. As an approximation, we may separate the overall functions of an intelligent system into three components:

1. "Sensory" processing of the input signals to a system, which involves spatiotemporal pattern recognition and transformation.
2. "Motor" processing of the output signals from a system, which involves the orchestrated production of spatiotemporal patterns.
3. The production of system "behavior" in which motor processing is driven by sensory processing and internal goal-setting.

Each of these functions is based on two activation-pattern operations: pattern transformation and pattern learning. Each is mediated by flow of activation across network links.

In performing "sensory" input processing, an ANN-based system can learn to recognize generalized instances of newly encountered entities and events. Such a system can add to and reorganize its collection of recognition "templates" for entities and events. We cite the following examples:

1. An intelligent system must be able to detect the presence of specific entities or conditions. Each such detection should have an associated "strength of belief" measure that reflects the likelihood of that detection's correctness. A net's continuous-valued node activation levels can efficiently encode this measure. Through its adaptiveness, a neural-net-based system can add to and re-organize its store of "recognition templates" as it encounters novel entities and circumstances.

2. Events can cause other events. There is often a "degree of causality" that reflects how strongly an event favors (or inhibits) other events. Causality is a property of event pairs and should, thus, be associated with interevent links. A

net's positive or negative link weights nicely capture this notion of causality. Adaptive neural-net links make it possible for a system to alter its beliefs about the causal relationships between events based on the system's observation of these relationships.

3. Several events can work in concert to affect the likelihood of another (dependent) event. Their individual degrees of causality must be combined to yield an overall causality. That is, it must be possible to integrate several pieces of evidence, each of which may individually substantiate or contradict a hypothesis. This is well modeled by the summation of (weighted) inputs that network nodes perform. More generally, the "fuzzy processing" capabilities of a neural net can support a variety of evidence-combining methods (e.g., Bayesian or non-Bayesian, plausible-inference methods, etc.).

In performing "motor" output processing, an ANN-based system can learn to produce new sequences of actions and can modify the execution time course of those actions. This may be done using "feedback" sensory-input signals so that the correct execution of an action can be ensured.

A system's behavior usually consists of sequences of actions. These actions must be executed in some order and often with specific timing relationships. Neural nets may be used to implement "handshaking" signals between actions. Furthermore, a net's dynamics (activation-level decay rate, etc.) provide a convenient means for generating action-timing signals. Adaptive network links provide a means for altering the manner in which a set of actions are "chained together."

An ANN-based system can modify its responses to its detection of particular objects and events so as to usually produce responses that are appropriate to the current circumstances. Such a system can also "learn" the consequences of its actions and can use this information to modify its behavior.

To produce behavior, a system must use event detection to trigger responses in the form of associated actions. Such coupling can be easily achieved through network links leading from event-detection nodes to action-triggering nodes. The weights on such links can effectively represent how appropriate each of several possible actions is in response to a given event. If these links are adaptive, then a system can change its response to a given event; that is, an intelligent system can alter its behavior based on its past experiences.

In the course of behavior production, an intelligent system can be guided by its "expectations" of what events should result from the execution of a given action. These expectations consist of associations between an action and its expected results. They provide a potent mechanism for monitoring the correct execution of an action, from inception to completion. Neural network links provide a ready means for expressing these associations. If these links are adaptive, then a system can learn "sensorimotor maps," which encode what results to expect in the course of executing an action.

AN INTELLIGENT SYSTEM IN ITS ENVIRONMENT

When an organism is placed in an environment, we propose that the following cycle of interaction occurs:

1. An event occurs in the environment.
2. The system detects this external event (through a sensory "transduction" process), causing an internal event (i.e., a state change) within the system.
3. The internal event (together with the system's internal state, such as its current goals) causes selection and execution of a system response.
4. Execution of this response produces events (changes) in the environment.
5. The preceding cycle repeats itself.

This cycle is very like that which governs the behavior of a state machine. Such a machine possesses some number of possible internal states and has state transitions and output signals that are controlled by a set of transition "rules." These rules involve the machine's current state (and perhaps its past states), together with current input signals received from the environment.

Step 2 consists of the organism's perception of an environmental stimulus signal. Step 3 is the means whereby the organism produces a response to that stimulus. The organism's behavior is mediated by the set of all stimulus/response pairs (associations) that its nervous system contains. These associations encode the "rules" that determine what the organism will do in a given set of circumstances. Note that these associations may be fixed, or they may be alterable (through learning, or "reprogramming").

An organism's actions are not intentionally neutral—they are designed to help fulfill the organism's current needs, or goals, in the face of a changing environment (Granit, 1981). Goal-directed behavior is driven by a "motivation" function, which establishes the current goals of a system and evaluates progress toward fulfillment of these goals.

The view presented here is that an organism's actions are chosen based on a conjunction of its current (and perhaps its past) processing state, its current goals, and its current environmental inputs. The goals are effectively a subportion of the total internal state; they provide a "context" that selects a goal-relevant subset of the organism's total set of possible actions. We have already seen that execution of an action can modify the organism's current state. Analogously execution of an action can alter the organism's current goals. Diagrammatically a goal-driven organism operates as shown in Fig. 11.1.

Note that, in this scheme, the organism's goal(s) are really just a particular component of its overall internal state. Apart from localization of the goal information to particular structure(s) within the organism's nervous system, there is no way to differentiate goal information from other state information.

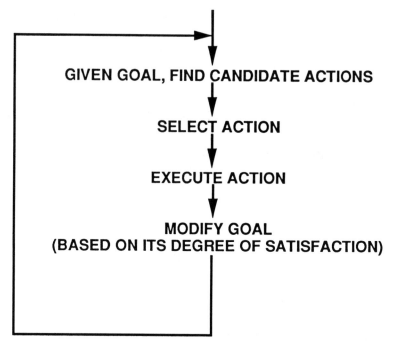

FIG. 11.1.   Goal-Oriented Action

The preceding goal-driven processing cycle can be implemented by a system structured as in Fig. 11.2. Here incoming sensory information is analyzed for known patterns by a "feature extraction" subsystem. A motivation or goal-setting subsystem provides signals that "orient" the system toward specific behavioral modes (e.g., feeding, constraint-satisfaction, etc.). Together the current goals and processed inputs are used to select a sequence of appropriate actions for execution.

The "planning" subsystem can vary widely in complexity. At one extreme, actions may be selected through a rigid set of unconditional stimulus/response associations. At the other extreme, an elaborate, internal "what if" modeling capability may be used to pick a sequence of actions based on their expected (learned) consequences. The output of the planning process is a sequence of action-triggering commands, each of which is then carried out by an "action execution" subsystem. The latter may range in complexity from rote production of triggered output signals to a hierarchy of "closed-loop" action controllers, each of which may use sensory feedback to monitor the progress of an evolving action.

Goal-oriented action may be conceptually decomposed into three distinct functions: an (internal-) "state update" function, a "goal-update" function, and an "output production" function (see Fig. 11.3).

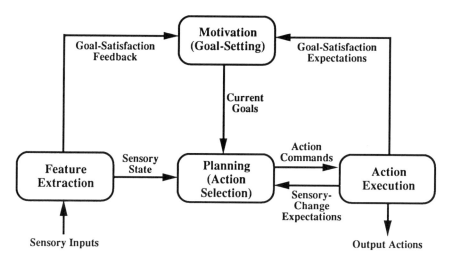

FIG. 11.2.   Goal-Oriented System

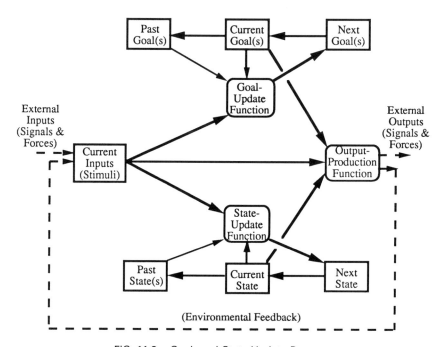

FIG. 11.3.   Goal- and State-Update Process

The organism's state-update function produces the organism's behavior. This function subsumes a number of subfunctions, including sensory processing and output selection (which drives the output-production function).

Organisms vary considerably in the degree of sophistication of their state-update functions. For example, organisms vary in their sensory modalities and in their methods for representing and transforming information derived from these information "input channels." They also differ widely in their decision-making or response-selection methods. For example, simple "hard-wired" nervous systems can only generate a narrow set of responses to a narrow set of conditions (e.g., trophic responses). At the other end of the complexity spectrum, primates are able to plan their actions using mentally manipulated models of the external world.

The goal-update function is responsible for generating and modifying the organism's motivational state. This may include both tonic and phasic signals, originating both exogenously and endogenously. For example, general level of arousal as well as generation of various "appetite" levels may be classified as slowly varying (tonic), internally generated (endogenous) signals. In contrast, the quenching of an appetite signal by a satisfying input (e.g., the quenching of thirst through signals that reflect cell-compartment osmolarity) constitutes a fairly rapid (phasic) externally driven (exogenous) signal.

Although goal signals are a subset of total internal state, they occupy a privileged role: They orient the organism toward particular behaviors, favoring the production of particular potentially goal-satisfying actions. Goals, thus, serve as a framework within which other state information (e.g., sensory inputs) is interpreted in light of their goal-satisfying potential. Goals act as an intentional "context" for sensorimotor processing.

As we have already noted, the organism's current outputs (actions) are generally selected and executed using the net's current state, its current goals, and its current external inputs. Note that actions can be triggered by a subset of these three inputs, such as the initiation of volitional actions (rather than stimulus–response actions) based on goals and current state. Note also that the execution of actions can (and often does) make use of external inputs (sensory inputs and external forces) as well as internal state information (e.g., proprioceptive inputs). In control-theoretic terms, this makes it possible for organisms to execute motor actions in "closed-loop" fashion rather than in "open-loop" mode. The output-production function generates the organism's motor activities.

We would like to construct an artificial intelligent system that is organized as in Figs. 11.2 and 11.3. Such a system should possess the following characteristics:

1. It should be goal-driven (to satisfy the needs of the system, as reflected in internal "motivation" or "drive" state variables).
2. It should be flexible (to cope with operation in a variable world).

3. It should be adaptive (to benefit from its experiences in that variable world).

4. It requires "understanding" (so that the system can pattern its behavior on its own experiences rather than on external descriptions of the world, such as inflexible and brittle "programs").

SYMBOLIC VERSUS SEMANTIC KNOWLEDGE REPRESENTATION

The notion of representation is central to a discussion of information processing. Through representation, we set up equivalences between entities and our mental models (concepts) of them. We propose that two basically different representation schemes are possible: symbolic and semantic representation.

In *symbolic* representation, one assigns a symbol (or referent) to stand for (or point to) a description of the represented entity. Such a scheme separates the definition of an entity from its referent, coupling the two through an arbitrary association. There need be no particular relationship between the nature of the represented entity and the form of its representation. In fact, when a programmer writes a symbolic program, the meaning of the program's symbols exists only in the programmer's head (in the form of an interpretation that he or she assigns to those symbols). A symbolic processor cannot use this "meaning" in its operations.

In *semantic* representation, entities are not really represented at all, at least in the usual sense of establishing arbitrary associations between distinct entities (concept and referent). Instead the *meaning* (or semantic content) of a concept is mapped onto the *structure* of an internal "analog" (or "image") of that entity. In a real sense, instantiation of a concept constitutes a "re-presentation" of its previous instances, all of which produce similar internal "images."

Instantiation of a concept may take the form of a particular spatial pattern of neural-net activation. Through the operation of localized learning mechanisms, this activation pattern may be captured as a coincident spatial pattern of localized network changes—an "engram," or "trace," of that concept. The meaning of a concept is captured in the connections (associations) between the analog of that concept and the analogs of other related concepts.

To make this a bit more clear, imagine that we are learning what an "apple" is. Our senses allow us to perceive ranges of color, shape, and so on. When we look at an apple, its physical properties (red, yellow, or green color; round to oval shape, etc.) cause activity in specific locations within our sensory nervous system. These locations are fixed by the nature of our sensory machinery; they are not arbitrarily determined.

We propose that the "meaning" of the concept "apple" resides in the properties (geometry, intensity, etc.) of the activation pattern associated with "apple."

In contrast with a symbolic processor, which *cannot use* the meaning of the symbols that it manipulates, a semantic processor *cannot avoid using* the meaning of its knowledge entities in performing its operations.

The notion of "data" is appropriate in a symbolic processing system, where it represents the descriptions (data structures) associated with symbols (referents). Data is, thus, the contents of a static storage medium, which is accessed and modified by active procedures.

"Knowledge" describes the constituent entities of a semantic processing system (hence, the term "knowledge entity," or "KE"). KEs do not exist in isolation but are linked to all related KEs. These links constrain the possible inferences in which a KE may participate and are established when the KE is added to a knowledge base. Because interKE links are (active) inference paths, KEs are not separate (passive) entities. In effect an item of knowledge includes not only a definition of that item but also how and under what conditions that item may be used.

We usually think of inference as a logic-based process involving deduction or induction. We will adopt a more general definition of "inference" as any process that alters the state of activity of knowledge entities in a semantic processing system. By this definition, combining various pieces of sensory evidence to conclude that we are looking at an apple qualifies as an inference. So does our decision to eat the apple, because we are currently hungry. So does our formulation of a plan for acquiring the apple, including the control of our movements in reaching for it.

Although this may seem an overly broad definition, it lends a unity to the various hierarchical processes that cooperate in the pursuit of a goal. Several inference mechanisms may cooperatively and simultaneously operate on knowledge. Each of these has a particular role in a knowledge-processing system, and yet each may be based on a common low-level mechanism (i.e., flow of activation in a neural net).

COMPUTATION VERSUS MODELING

"Computation" is a formal (rule-governed) process in which "operators" (sequences of formal transformation rules) are applied to "tokens" (symbols) to produce other tokens. At bottom, symbolic computing is mediated by an interpreter (e.g., a Turing machine) that applies formal rules to update the computer's active token set. The interpreter determines which rules are applicable at any given time, selects one rule at a time for application, and applies that rule to the set of currently instantiated tokens.

Tokens are added to the active token set (or "instantiated") as a consequence of executing rules. Once a token has been instantiated, it may participate in the triggering of rules through a rule-matching process. That is, a rule is deemed applicable, if and only if the token space currently contains all of the tokens that are called for in that rule's "antecedent" clause (its triggering token-pattern-match template). When the match-condition of a rule is satisfied, the rule is "fired;" that is, the sequence of actions that it spells out are executed. This changes the set of currently instantiated tokens, and the rule pattern-matching cycle begins anew.

Contemporary computer science, including the subfield of artificial intelligence, is based on formal descriptions. Such descriptions use symbols, or "place-holder" labels attached to descriptive data, to represent the entities of interest. The nature and structure of these symbols need not (and usually does not) have any intrinsic relationship to the entities to which they refer. Thus, there is no necessary link between the symbols and the semantic content (or meaning) of what they represent.

Formal descriptive systems have sets of rules for forming legal combinations of symbols. In various logics, for example, the basic "rules of the game" are called axioms and are assumed to be a true and essential part of the descriptive system. Legal combinations of symbols are called "well-formed formulas" or "valid expressions." If a given initial set of propositions is assumed to be true, then any further propositions that are formed by applying legal rules to the initial propositions are also taken to be true.

In order to relate such a formal descriptive system to the real world, there must exist a set of equivalences between symbols and entities in the world. There must also be a set of equivalences between formal expression-transformation rules and physical laws. Thus, the process of logical inference is substituted for physical causality. These equivalences constitute an interpretation of the formal system's symbols and expressions. This interpretation is established by the user of the formal system and effectively exists only in his or her mind. The predictive power of a formal description is limited by the degree of detail and fidelity that are explicitly captured in that description.

In *modeling* (or building an "analog" of) a real-world system, the modeler assembles a set of physical entities that are analogs of their counterparts in the modeled system. The model's components are governed by physical laws that capture the qualitative (and perhaps quantitative) behavior of their real-world counterparts. Further, because the real-world system and its model are (or should be) governed by the same laws, they behave in a similar fashion. Thus, by observing how the model behaves, we can project how the real-world system should also behave.

In our usage of the term, the "analog" of a given entity must satisfy the following constraints:

1. There is a structural correspondence between the components of the modeled entity and the components of its analog. Any state that the entity may assume has a counterpart state for its analog.

2. There is a well-defined range of values that the entity's state variables may assume and a well-defined range of values assumed by the corresponding state variables of the analog.

3. If there are functional relationships between particular state variables of the entity, then there are qualitatively (and perhaps quantitatively) similar relationships between the corresponding state variables of the analog.

These constraints are needed to ensure that an analog captures the basic behavior of the entity that it models. This in turn allows the analog to be used to predict (at least qualitatively) the behavior of the modeled entity under given conditions.

The use of an analogical representation system facilitates an intelligent system's acquisition of a "world model" through learning. One of the more interesting functional capabilities of neural networks is that they often incorporate a learning mechanism through which the transfer-function of the network elements may change over time in response to an element's processing history. Thus, the following events can occur in an analogical representation based on neural nets:

1. An event in the environment causes coupled changes in two or more environmental variables.

2. Through the analogical representation, this environmental coupling is reflected in a coupled change in the corresponding variables of the analog. This coupling is realized as coupled changes in state variables of the neural net (e.g., node activation levels).

3. The neural net's learning mechanism can use these changes to locally alter the behavior of specific network elements. That is, a local learning mechanism can alter the degree of coupling between those analog state variables that correspond to the coupled environmental variables. If such learning causes the analog's behavior to more closely mimic the environment's behavior, then the previous sequence will result in the desired "world model."

Through learning, a system can construct (analogical) representations of objects, events, and relationships, that occur in its environment. The representation is analogical; thus, the system can "replay" its experience of those entities, using a kind of mind's eye (or "mind's ear," etc.). Likewise, for motor activity, the system can effectively internally replay sequences of motor commands and their execution. Finally the associations between entities detected and actions taken may also be replayed. In a sophisticated intelligent system, all of these operations can be performed mentally, without causing actual output activity from the system. This can be very useful in intelligently planning actions.

Fig. 11.4 depicts the overall structure of a simple "event-driven" intelligent system. The system may have goal-setting motivational inputs, but it has no

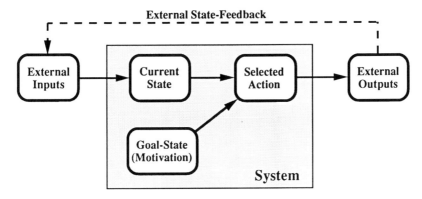

FIG. 11.4.   Event-Driven System

capability for selecting responses to stimuli by projecting the consequences of its actions.

In contrast, Fig. 11.5 schematizes a system that has such planning capabilities. Here the system has two operating modes. In the "execute" mode (conceptual "switch" position shown by solid lines), actual external stimuli are processed, and output actions are executed. In the "projection" mode (conceptual "switch" position shown by dashed lines), possible actions may be internally replayed, causing activation of expected sensory inputs ("expectations") that those actions have become associated with in the past. These hypothetical sensory inputs can then participate in another round of action selection. Once an action is found that satisfies the system's current goal, the "switches" may be put back in the "execute" position for actual production of the selected action.

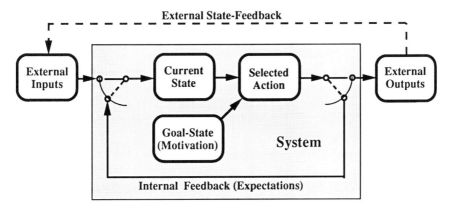

FIG. 11.5.   Expectation-Driven System

NEURAL NETS AS A SUBSTRATE FOR INTELLIGENCE

Artificial neural networks are built on abstractions of the salient information-processing properties of nerve nets: ANNs are much-simplified models of their biological counterparts. We may view neural nets as a low-level information-processing mechanism.

There currently exist many different neural-net models. These differ from one another in their topology (i.e., interelement connectivity pattern), and in the behavior of their constituent network elements. For the present purpose, we simply seek "common denominators" across these models.

At bottom, neural networks are *pattern processors* (Grossberg, 1988): They operate on patterns of network state information that may be distributed across some number of network elements. We may distinguish two basic classes of pattern-processing operations:

1. Pattern *transformation*, in which the signal-processing properties of a net induce specific changes in a currently instantiated activation pattern (i.e., the current pattern is transformed into another pattern). This includes two subfunctions of particular functional significance:

   a. Pattern *recognition*, in which the occurrence of a pattern causes activation of a node(s) that is associated with (or "represents") that pattern.

   b. Pattern *production*, in which the occurrence of a pattern (which may involve activity in one or in many nodes) causes activation of another associated pattern.

2. Pattern *learning* (for adaptive networks), which involves the transfer of pattern information between short-term and long-term memory. This may be further decomposed into two inverse operations:

   a. Pattern *storage*, in which the occurrence of an activation pattern (in the net's "short-term memory," such as node activation levels) lastingly changes the network's processing characteristics (which are determined by the net's "long-term memory," which includes parameters such as synaptic strengths and node firing thresholds).

   b. Pattern *recall*, in which activation of a particular pattern, together with the net's current long-term memory contents, causes activation of another associated pattern. This constitutes a readout of long-term memory information by the initial "access" activation pattern.

Artificial neural networks and standard computers have several important functional differences. Fig. 11.6 graphically compares neural nets and digital computers.

Most computers have a "von Neumann" architecture, in which a central processing unit accesses a program and data, both of which reside in the ma-

	Computers	ANNs
Basic Operations	Rich set of logical, arithmetic and symbolic operators	Small set of basic"fuzzy" pattern-recognition, manipulation and production operators
Nature of Data	Complex data structures (lists, database records, images, etc.)	Simple network activation patterns
Processing Method	Sequential set of operations, performed under centralized control	Parallel set of (many) operations, performed under distributed multiple streams of control
Processing Environment	Fixed, predictable data relationships and rules of data manipulation	Variable, unpredictable data relationships and rules of interaction ("real-world")
System Behavior	Fixed and exhaustively specified (through program covering all operational contingencies)	Variable (through net adaptation) system behavior refined in the course of normal system operation
Interface to Environment	Single comparatively slow input/output data stream, produced under centralized control	Many simultaneous real-time input and output signals, produced under distributed control

FIG. 11.6.   Computers vs. ANNs

chine's memory. The computer performs logical or arithmetic operations on one item of data at a time, following a single, sequential thread of instructions contained in a program.

A program's processing state is encoded in the system's memory, which is a passive repository whose contents are manipulated by the system's (single) processor. The rules governing the system's behavior are encoded in a precisely-defined program, which exhaustively specifies the system's responses to all conditions that it may encounter.

In comparison, an ANN's state is encoded in two places: in node activation levels (short-term memory), and in link weights (long-term memory). Flow of activation across links can alter link weights (through "learning"), and link weight changes affect flow of activation; thus, ANN memory is active.

Each network node has memory, but each is also a simple processor. Both memory and processing are, thus, distributed throughout the net. A neural net contains no explicit "program." Instead the network topology and node/link parameters determine the net's behavior. Whereas a standard computer's activities are orchestrated by its serial instruction fetch-and-execute cycle, an ANN's behavior is mediated by parallel flow of activation.

Neural-net elements (nodes and links) can be assembled into a variety of pattern-processing circuits. Much of the effort in developing the KRN system centers on the design of its underlying neural-net circuitry. A few examples of this circuitry will be presented after the KRN architecture is described.

KNOWLEDGE REPRESENTATION NETWORKS (KRN)

From our previous considerations, it appears that an intelligent system needs internal representations for a few types of primitive "knowledge entities" (KEs): (a) *features* to represent entities (objects, conditions, or events); (b) *relationships* to act as connectives in defining complex features; and (c) *operations* to represent the actions that the system may execute. Each such knowledge entity is the internal representation of an external entity, of an interentity relationship, or of an action.

The knowledge representation network architecture appears in Fig. 11.7. This organization incorporates several major principles:

1. Sensory processing (event/entity recognition) takes place in a *feature hierarchy,* which operates on input from various sensory modalities (input channels). Features encode declarative knowledge in the network.

2. Motor (action-execution) processing occurs in an *operation hierarchy,* which produces coordinated low-level activity under the direction of high-level commands (distributed motor control). Operations encode procedural knowledge in the network.

3. Crosscoupling between these hierarchies produces "rule-like" behavior. Active features ("IF" conditions) trigger operations ("THEN" responses). Crosscouplings from operations to features activate *expectations* of which features should be activated by execution of that operation.

4. A KRN net has a *static* structure. That is, no nodes or links are added to or deleted from the net subsequent to its creation. Flow of activation through the net

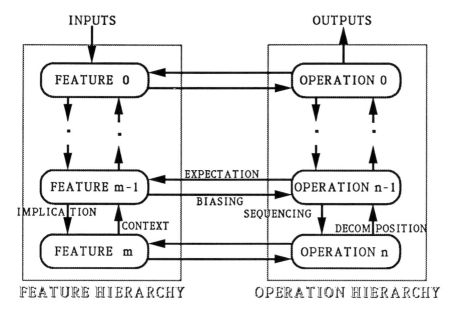

FIG. 11.7.   The KRN Architecture

creates a *dynamic* structure atop this static structure (through localized activation of portions of the overall net).

5.   At any given instant, many simultaneous operations may occur in a KRN net. This is possible, because a KRN net is itself composed of a massively parallel low-level processing mechanism (a neural network).

6.   In keeping with the use of a distributed processing medium, KRN's adaptiveness is mediated by a local learning mechanism.

Significance of the KRN Architecture

The KRN system is interesting, because it is explicitly designed to operate effectively in a real-world environment, and because its structure is in many ways similar to that of advanced biological nervous systems (sensory processing, from raw inputs to increasingly abstract features; driving motor processing, from high-level commands to primitive motor acts). These attributes are directly mirrored in the set of primitive KRN knowledge entities (features, relationships, and operations) and in the six KRN inference mechanisms.

Unlike extant AI systems, KRN is based on *semantic* rather than *symbolic* processing; KRN inferences make use of the *meaning* of knowledge entities, as defined by the connections (associative relationships) between those knowledge entities.

KRN is unusual in its use of neural nets as a low-level implementation medium. Such nets provide a high-performance parallel processing mechanism that readily lends itself to KRN's distributed real-time processing architecture. In addition, the adaptiveness of neural nets makes it possible for a KRN net to modify its own contents based on interactions with its environment. This is essential in functions such as the automatic addition of feature recognition templates for newly encountered entities or conditions.

Neural nets also enforce relatively uniform processing across an entire KRN net. All KRN functions, be they feature recognition, or operation execution, or rule-like triggering of operations by features, are based on only two fundamental neural-net processes: *flow of activation* (which mediates all inferences) and *association* (which mediates adaptive changes in the network). This uniformity allows a KRN net to be built as a set of functional modules, which can then be assembled to form the entire system. The uniformity of processing also permits efficient low-level implementations of KRN.

The KRN Knowledge Entities

A KRN network consists of a set of "knowledge entities," or "KEs," each of which has its own time-varying "state of activation." In representing the world à la KRN, there is a need for three primitive types of knowledge entities: *features, relationships,* and *operations.*

Features represent generalized events: the presence of specific objects in a net's environment or the occurrence of some specific condition of the environment. Loosely speaking, features represent sets of simultaneously active subfeatures. For example, at the lowest level of sensory processing, features represent clusters of simultaneously present sensory data entering the net (such as those caused by the net's perception of a particular object—say, an apple—in its environment).

Features may be defined in terms of other (more basic) subfeatures forming a feature hierarchy. As a simple example, we can define a recognition template for the concept "apple" in terms of the attributes of apples:

In Fig. 11.8, activation flows over links in the direction indicated by the arrowheads. The arcs labeled "AND" and "OR" represent conjunctions and disjunctions of active features respectively. These may be "fuzzy" operators rather than Boolean (binary) operators. Thus, an object that sufficiently closely satisfies the attributes that define a "Pippin apple" may cause partial activation of the node that represents that concept. We should also note that the nodes and links in this diagram represent entire neural-net circuits, not single elements.

This representation scheme suggests a natural metric for gauging the degree of similarity between two entities: Similar entities have similar representations. That is, presentation of similar entities will cause patterns of activity with similar spatial and temporal structure. Similar entities share many active features. Such

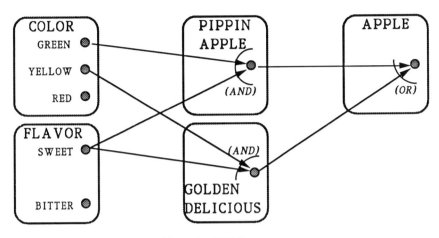

FIG. 11.8.   KRN Features

entities should activate many of the same portions (features) of a KRN net. In addition, the relative degree of activation of each feature should be similar for the two entities.

Each KRN feature may have three distinct forms of usage: *deductive, declarative,* and *interrogative* modes. Implementation of each of these usage modes depends upon proper ANN circuit design of the KRN "feature" knowledge entities. (To date, ANN circuits have only been tested for the deductive and interrogatory modes.)

In a deductive usage, the presence of a feature (i.e., the presence of a specific object, event, or condition) is deduced on the basis of its defining subfeatures. For example, when presented with an object of the class "fruit having oblong shape and yellow color," one may deduce that the object is probably a banana.

In this data-driven operating mode, activation flows from lower toward higher levels of the KRN feature-definition hierarchy. This resembles the "forward-chaining" inference mechanism often used in rule-based AI systems. In the preceding example, highly active value nodes "oblong" (for subfeature "shape") and "yellow" (for subfeature "color") jointly activate the "banana" feature node (and perhaps, to a lesser extent, the features defining other, similar fruits).

In the declarative mode of usage, an assertion is made and causes a feature to become active. Through flow of activation from higher toward lower levels of the feature hierarchy, defining subfeatures become active. For example, we may (tentatively or conclusively) decide that a partially obscured object is a banana. In making this assertion (by activating the "banana" node), the defining subfeatures of the concept "banana" are also activated (i.e., the nodes for "oblong" ("shape") and "yellow" ("color") also become active. Note that, in this usage, activation flows in a direction opposite to that of a deductive stage.

Finally the interrogative usage of a feature definition complements its deductive usage. The interrogative usage guides the acquisition of subfeature values that are needed to confirm or disconfirm a conclusion that may be reached through deductive activation of a feature.

As an example, we may interrogatively consider ("ask") whether or not an object in our view is a "banana." For this to be true, the object in question must have appropriate feature values ("yellow color", etc.). When the feature node "banana" is activated in the interrogative mode, attention is focused on the defining subfeatures for that concept. This enables the deductive-mode flow of activation from those specific feature value nodes to the "banana" feature node. If all of those required value nodes are active, then the "banana" node should also become active, confirming that the object is indeed a "banana." The converse also holds. Note that this attention mechanism is analogous to the "backward-chaining" inference mechanism used in AI.

Relationships are the second basic type of KRN knowledge entity. This notion is considerably more complex than that of a feature in that it involves a comparison between corresponding subfeatures (aspects) of two separate features (entities).

Relationships are fundamental knowledge entities because of their role in defining "complex" features—features whose constituent subfeatures satisfy pairwise constraints. For example, the concept "TABLE" may be defined as a "TABLETOP" "ABOVE" "LEGS," with subfeatures "TABLETOP" and "LEGS" appropriately defined and connected by the relationship "ABOVE." This relationship is itself defined through a comparison of the "HEIGHT" attribute (subfeature) of "TABLETOP" and "LEGS," as schematized in Fig. 11.9.

Operations are the third basic type of KRN knowledge entity. Through operations, a KRN net can alter its own internal state or the state of its environment. Operations are generalized actions that the net can execute.

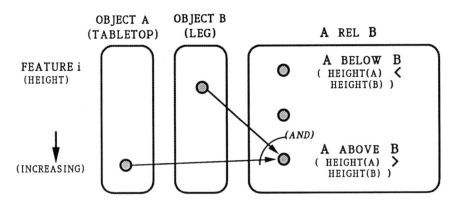

FIG. 11.9.   KRN Relationships

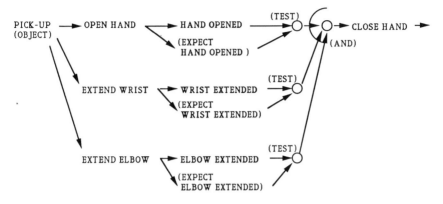

FIG. 11.10.   KRN Operations

Operations can be defined hierarchically; an operation may be expressed as a sequence of suboperations. As an example, consider Fig. 9.10, which portrays the actions required to pick up an object.

Here we see that a high-level command ("pick-up object" can be expressed as a sequence of sets of subactions ("open hand . . . extend shoulder," followed by "close hand"). Each of these subactions can in turn be further decomposed down to a set of primitive actions. At each level of this hierarchy, each subaction can trigger and control execution of its own subactions. Each suboperation can use feedback of local state information to perform its suboperations in "closed-loop" fashion (i.e., a suboperation can use such information to guide its proper execution).

The KRN Inference Mechanisms

In KRN, inference refers to any change in the state of a knowledge entity that leads to a change in the state of another KE. The processes by which KEs interact are referred to as "inference mechanisms." The KRN architecture provides for six, distinct, coactive, cooperative inference mechanisms, each performing a different function.

Two of these inference mechanisms operate up and down the feature hierarchy:

1. The (feature-) "implication" inference mechanism, which is an evidence-combining, data-driven mechanism analogous to forward chaining.

2. In the opposite direction, the (feature-) "context" inference mechanism allows the current state of the net's higher levels to bias its lower-level activity. This is essential in some tasks (e.g., disambiguation of a Necker cube's orientation).

Two operate up and down the operation hierarchy:

3. The "(operation-) decomposition" inference mechanism expresses higher-level operations as sequences of lower-level suboperations.

4. In the opposite direction, the "(operation-) sequencing" inference mechanism permits detection of when (if) an operation is complete (based on completion of its suboperations).

Two operate across the two hierarchies:

5. The "(operation-) biasing" inference mechanism permits the firing of operations by active features. This gives the network "rule-like" behavior.

6. The "(feature-) expectation" inference mechanism allows operations to be executed in "closed-loop" fashion. It isolates features that should be activated by an operation. If these become active, the operation is executing properly; otherwise corrective measures are needed.

This set of inference mechanisms results from the organization of a KRN net as crosscoupled feature and operation hierarchies. Although each of these mechanisms is mediated by flow of activation through corresponding neural-net circuits, their different directions of flow of activation lead to logically distinct functions.

Evidential Reasoning: The "Implication" Inference Mechanism

In the physical world, the occurrence of events can imply the upcoming occurrence of specific other events. In KRN, this mode of inference is called *implication* and is analogous to forward chaining in AI systems. This inference mechanism is mediated by flow of activation from active KRN features to other features located higher in the feature hierarchy.

Through implication, the occurrence of events cast votes for or against the likelihood of occurrence of other (dependent) events. Each such vote carries a weight, because the KRN implication mechanism is implemented using continuous-valued neural-net variables and variable network link weights. The result is a plausible-inference mechanism akin to the "certainty factors" often used in rule-based expert systems (e.g., EMYCIN).

As an example of the implication mechanism, assume that we are attempting to identify a fruit that we know is definitely very oblong and that may be yellow or green or brown in color. Given this, it is quite likely that the fruit is a banana. This is due to the following fact that: (a) An oblong shape is strongly characteristic of bananas and not of most other fruits, and (b) we know with a high degree of certainty that our unknown fruit has this trait.

In the KRN model of this situation, there is a link with a large, positive link weight between the "oblong" value-node of the "shape" feature and the "banana" value-node (class member) of the "fruit" feature (class). This corresponds to (a) previous. In addition, the "oblong" node is highly active, corresponding to (b) previous. The product of this high activation level, times the large positive link weight, transmits a large scaled activation to the "banana" node, moving it strongly toward (or even over) its firing threshold.

Biasing Perceptions: The "Context" Inference Mechanism

The KRN system contains a means for performing inferences "in context." That is, conclusions reached (features activated) up to the present time can enter into the system's current decision making. This feature is needed for sensory processing in which the current state of the KRN net is important. As an example, this mechanism is important, selecting one of the two equally possible interpretations of a wire-frame Necker cube.

KRN links directed from features to other features lower in the feature hierarchy are called context links. Such links propagate activation from current active conclusions (features) to possible future conclusions at a lower level. In so doing, the current features bias the possible future activation of those lower-level features.

Positive context links drive the dependent features toward activation, making it easier for future evidence to cause their activation. Conversely negative context links make it more difficult for future evidence to fire the dependent features.

ORGANIZED ACTIVITY: THE "OPERATION DECOMPOSITION" INFERENCE MECHANISM

In a KRN network, operations (actions) are defined hierarchically. A hierarchical structure is used to define operations as sequences of suboperations. The selection of a KRN operation requires the issuing of a command to execute that operation. This is done by activating a command node for that operation. Once an operation is selected, it must be decomposed into its defining suboperations. The lowest level of the operation hierarchy produces the primitive outputs of the net.

The preceding process is called "operation decomposition." The KRN links used to accomplish this are, thus, referred to as operation-decomposition links.

These links are directed from KRN operation nodes to lower-level operation nodes.

Rule-Like Behavior: The "Operation Biasing" Inference Mechanism

At each level of the operation-decomposition hierarchy, relevant state information (feature values) may participate in selection of the next operation to be executed. Such KRN state-feedback links are called "operation-biasing" links.

In a simple system, activation of a given feature may suffice to trigger (cause decomposition of) an associated operation. This crosscoupling between the feature and operation hierarchies implements "rule-like" behavior: Active KRN features are analogous to satisfied IF-clauses in a production system, and active KRN operations are analogous to THEN-clauses selected for firing.

As an example, this mechanism is useful in the production of a specified sequence of operations. Suppose that each of these operations has an associated command (trigger) node and that successful completion of each operation causes the production of an associated activation pattern (a "completion flag") in the feature hierarchy. Then operations can be chained together by having the completion flag of one cause activation of the command node for the next. In effect this scheme uses sensory feedback to guide the execution of operations. In control theory, this is referred to as a "closed-loop" operation-execution mode.

Actions in Variable Environment: The "Expectation" Inference Mechanism

There is a second KRN inference mechanism that operates between the two hierarchies: "expectations." Through expectations, a network can project which state changes (active features) can be expected, or anticipated, as a result of selecting and executing a particular operation. Specific deviations from the expected feature pattern can be used to trigger remedial actions.

One of the principal values of learning is in the establishment of such expectations. This is essential to the human capacity for the use of a "world model" in guiding actions. As an example, a person who is hurt by grasping something hot learns to associate that action with pain. The release of the offending object is found to eliminate the pain. When this association between action (releasing one's grasp) and effect (cessation of pain) is learned, it becomes an expectation. Thereafter, the release of painful objects from one's grasp may become "hard-wired" through associations.

In KRN, expectations are mediated by links directed from operations to features. Thus, when an operation is selected (becomes active), flow of activation through expectation links causes activity changes in feature nodes.

Ordering Actions: The "Operation Sequencing" Inference Mechanism

In hierarchically decomposing an operation, there is a need for a "hand-shaking" mechanism to provide synchronization between sets of suboperations. This is the purpose of the "operation-sequencing" inference mechanism.

Operation decomposition works by allowing an active feature to trigger a set of subfeatures (i.e., operations at a lower level of the operation hierarchy). An operation is completed when all of its suboperations are completed. Thus, determination of the operation's completion is dependent on determination of each suboperation's completion. The individual completion signals must, thus, flow back up the operation hierarchy. This is done through the operation-sequencing mechanism.

What is "Attention?"

The KRN inference mechanisms cause changes in the activation state of ANN circuits that embody the net's knowledge entities (features, relationships, and operations). Flow of activation in the net is also used to modulate the operation of the inference mechanisms. This function is referred to as "attention."

The notion of attention appears repeatedly in studies of cognition (Crick, 1984; Rumelhart, McClelland, & PDP Research Group, 1986). The term has a number of different common meanings, such as the following:

1. In attending to an event, we focus on its associated sensations (e.g., the taste, texture, etc. of a banana split). This allows us to quickly recognize that event or realize that we have not previously experienced it.

2. We are able to recall what previously experienced sensations should be like. That is, we call up our expectations of the event. This provides a learned recognition template for the event.

3. We attend to a sensation, an action or a piece of knowledge that we wish to learn. This helps us remember that item for future use.

4. In executing a novel or difficult motion, we attend to or "concentrate on" the sensations (somesthetic feedback signals) that should occur during the motion. This lets us smoothly follow the space–time trajectory of the motion and helps us detect and correct deviations from its proper course.

Just as attention is important in the cognitive sciences, it also plays a large role in artificial intelligence:

1. Production rule-based expert systems typically do not allow any arbitrary (IF . . . THEN) rule in the system's rule base to become active at an arbitrary time. Instead specific subsets of the rule base are made eligible for "firing,"

based on the current processing state of the system. That is, the system only attends to those rules that are currently eligible.

2. Within the current rule set, at any given moment, the antecedent (IF-clause) of several rules may be satisfied, making the associated consequents (THEN-clauses) eligible for execution. Usually only one such consequent may be executed at a time. The system attends to the time-varying contents of this "conflict set" in order to choose its output operations.

3. In "frame-based" AI systems, conceptually related aspects of an entity or situation are grouped together into "frames." These data structures allow the system to easily focus on (attend to) its total knowledge about that entity or situation. The result is a greatly narrowed (and, thus, accelerated) search process.

In a knowledge processing system, the system's state (i.e., the current contents of its working memory) is changed by one or more inference mechanisms. A particular system's control mechanisms determine when and how to select and apply inference mechanisms to working memory. The system's "knowledge base" (or, more narrowly, its "rule base") may also contain "metaknowledge" (that is knowledge about how to apply knowledge) to guide the inference process.

As an example, an expert system may consist of one or more domain-specific rule bases (e.g., for performing diagnostic tasks in particular medical specialties), forward- and backward-chaining inference mechanisms, working memory, and a user interface.

We see that, in both natural and artificial intelligent systems, a control system is needed to guide the operation of the inference mechanisms. The control system typically includes one or more forms of attention, as we have defined it.

The preceding variety of roles for attention suggest that the latter consists of a set of distinct (but possibly related) mechanisms and is not a single, monolithic phenomenon. We propose that these meanings share a common denominator: attention is a *control mechanism* that serves two basic functions: (a) It gates the flow of local state information through a neural net, and (b) it gates the transfer of information from short-term memory (STM) into long-term memory (LTM).

"Gating" involves the control of one signal (the information "carrier") by another (the "modulator"). The roles of carrier and modulator are not equivalent; the modulator can impress information on the carrier signal, but the carrier does not usually affect the modulator. The idea of neuromodulation is a major theme of several articles in this volume, particularly those of Grossberg, Levine, & Schmajuk, chapter 2; Hestenes, chapter 7; Levine, Leven, & Prueitt, chapter 9; and Ricart, chapter 5.

Gating is not restricted to all-or-nothing modulation of signal flow. Several variants are possible: (a) it may either facilitate or impede the transfer, corresponding to an "enabling" or a "disabling" signal; and (b) it may do so either completely or to some degree, acting as an "discrete" or as a "graded" signal.

There are, thus, four possible types of gating: (a) an discrete disable signal ("complete block"), (b) a graded disabling signal ("partial block"), (c) a graded enabling signal ("partial pass"), and (d) an discrete enable signal ("complete pass").

In a system such as KRN, different neural functions call for different types of gating. Different ANN circuits are needed to implement different combinations of the previous possibilities (e.g., direct excitation vs. release from inhibition).

The following discussion describes some of the roles of attention in controlling inference processes (which operate on the contents of a system's short-term memory). However, attention mechanisms are also probably needed for control of long-term memory. For example, the transfer of information from short-term memory to long-term memory may be gated by a global "now-print" signal. Such a signal would determine when long-term memory should be added to or changed.

Attention is usually viewed as a very selective phenomenon. However, it can also play a role as a global processing modulator. The general level of arousal of a nervous system can affect its local information processing. For example, a global rise in the firing threshold for all nodes in a net would ensure that only strong input signals are attended to.

KRN uses several distinct attention mechanisms in support of its inferencing activities. We will describe one of these: *feature focus,* which works in conjunction with the implication inference mechanism.

As has already been described, the KRN implication inference mechanism activates features whose defining lower-level subfeatures are active. The feature-focus attention mechanism helps to focus the gathering of evidence in support of the implication mechanism.

Fig. 11.11 shows how an apple may be detected, based on the attributes of an object undergoing classification. In this example, consider each possible fruit class as a hypothetical identity for an object that is being classified. Each such category has an associated recognition circuit (an "encoder," to be described later).

Each of these will be active to a degree that reflects the degree of match between its recognition template and the current feature activity levels. (Assume that the object is green and sweet, fitting the template for Pippin apples better than that for Golden Delicious apples).

Feature focus works by "sampling" the defining nodes for a feature (i.e., by enabling the flow of activation from defining to defined feature nodes). For example, activation of the Pippin apple encoder depends on highly active "GREEN COLOR" and "SWEET FLAVOR" encoders.

Highly active features enable flow from their defining features to a greater degree than do less-active features. The Pippin template is very active; thus, it

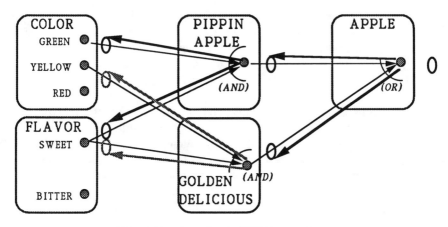

FIG. 11.11.   Attention in KRN Feature Focus

"passes" the activation levels of the "GREEN COLOR" and "SWEET FLA-VOR" encoders, with little or no attenuation. The loop and arrow controlling flow from each of these is, thus, shown schematically with dark lines. The net result of this arrangement is to quickly confirm (or refute) an active hypothesis. Here the network will quickly determine whether or not the object under scrutiny is a Pippin apple.

Neural Network Implementation of KRN

The utility of a system such as KRN cannot be evaluated theoretically, apart from the system's ability to predict phenomenological observations at an appropriate level. The applicable level of prediction may range from gross psychological observations at one extreme to details of neural-net dynamical behavior at the other.

KRN is not intended as a faithful model of actual neurobiological circuits. Rather it represents an effort to identify and artificially mimic at least some of the major processing functions underlying intelligent behavior.

In an effort to retain the benefits of a parallel adaptive low-level processing mechanism, these high-level functions are cast in terms of various neural-net circuits. Note that this latter objective differentiates KRN from a standard artificial intelligence approach, in which the choice of low-level implementation mechanism is deemed to be irrelevant.

The construction and evaluation of KRN requires a large set of theoretical and experimental machinery. First, one or more neural-net models must be defined as the "building blocks" from which the KRN circuits are constructed. Then specific neural-net circuits must be designed to embody each of the high-level KRN mechanisms. Finally a set of technological tools must be used to build and exercise the resulting complex neural network. We will quickly sketch each of these three activities in the context of a KRN implementation.

Parallel Associative Networks (PAN): A Low-Level Mechanism

The work done on KRN, thus far, makes use of the "parallel associative networks" (or "PAN") neural net model (Cruz, Hanson, & Tam, 1987). More commonly used paradigms, such as Hopfield- or back-propagation nets, are too restrictive in their structure and capabilities, and are not sufficiently sparing in their use of network elements.

Some portions of a KRN net are similar to well-known network models. For example, the circuits used to embody KRN "features" resemble an ART network (Grossberg, 1988). In general, however, the design of a KRN net requires a model that can subsume a wide range of network topologies and whose basic network elements possess sufficiently rich dynamical behavior. The PAN model was developed to satisfy these needs.

PAN is not tied to any particular network topology (pattern of node/link connections). The network elements may be assembled into whatever configurations are desired. All PAN nodes perform essentially the same function; however, their detailed behavior can be customized by specifying the values of a set of node parameters. A similar statement holds for PAN links. The features of this model were selected to satisfy projected applications processing requirements whereas allowing considerable efficiency in network emulation (on a parallel digital machine).

The PAN model consists of a set of discrete-time difference equations (which approximate a corresponding set of differential equations). Each PAN node has three parameters: a "threshold" τ, a "gain" G, and a (short-term-memory) "decay constant" δ.

A node sums all of the effective (i.e., scaled) activation levels reaching it from its population of source nodes. The number and identity of these source nodes may vary from one sink node to the next. (Some nodes may receive inputs from many other nodes, whereas others may have few—or even no—inputs).

The node's ("firing"-) threshold is subtracted from this sum. If the resultant value is negative, then it is "clipped" to zero. (No node may have a negative-valued activation level.) Note that, if a node's threshold is negative, then the node's output may be active even in the absence of external input signals. Such a spontaneously active "pace-maker" node is useful in many ANN circuits.

To the preceding difference is added the product of the node's current activation level, times that node's activation-decay constant. Thus, a node's present activation level $A(t)$ depends on its level $A(t - 1)$ during the immediately preceding time step. In the absence of further input signals, a node's activation level

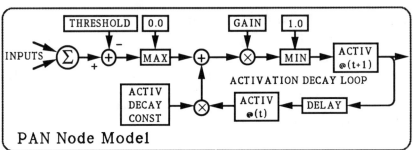

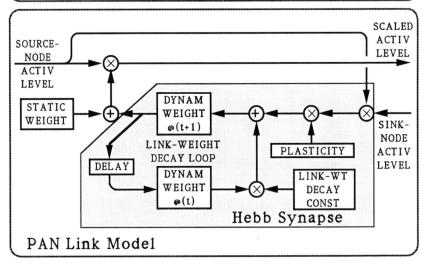

$$A_i(t+1) = \min[1.0 \, , \; G_i \times (\, \delta_i \times A_i(t) + \max[0.0 \, , \; \sigma_i(t) - \tau_i \;] \,) \,]$$

$$\sigma_i(t) = \sum_{j \in \Omega_i} (\, w_{ij} + \Delta w_{ij}(t) \,) \times A_j(t)$$

$$\Delta w_{ij}(t+1) = \Delta_{ij} \times \Delta w_{ij}(t) + \lambda_{ij} \times A_i(t+1) \times A_j(t)$$

FIG. 11.12.   The Parallel Associative Networks Model (PAN)

will exponentially decay toward 0, at a rate determined by the node's activation-decay constant.

The preceding aggregate quantity is multiplied by the node's gain, and, if the result exceeds 1.0, it is clipped to 1.0. (A node's activation level cannot exceed 1.0. At this level, a node's output is said to be "saturated.") A node's gain is reflected in the slope of the linear portion of its output function and allows adjustment of how sensitive the node is to a given level of input signal. For example, a high-gain node that receives a very small input signal may attain its maximum ("saturated") output level of 1.0. Conversely a low-gain, low-threshold node that receives a very large input may nonetheless only produce a small output.

In the PAN model, activation is multiplicatively scaled as it flows over the link from source node to sink node. Link weights λ can be either positive or negative. (For zero-valued link weights, no activation can traverse the link.) Positive link weights are associated with "excitatory" links; activation flowing over these links is positive after scaling and tends to drive the sink node toward its firing threshold. Links with negative weights are "inhibitory" in that they feed negative-valued scaled activation to the sink node, driving it away from threshold.

PAN link weights are composed of two components, one "static" (w) and the other "dynamic" (Δw). These are summed to yield an effective link weight. The static component does not vary with time (hence, its name); it is a link parameter, not a variable. The dynamic component is controlled by a simple ANN adaptive mechanism (or learning model) called the "Hebb synapse." This mechanism increases the strength of a link in which source-node activity frequently and promptly leads to sink-node activity.

The Hebb synapse is the simplest learning model that will capture correlated activity between source and sink nodes (such as that due to a causal relationship in the signals driving the source and sink). It is computed by multiplying the current sink-node activation level, times the previous source-node level, times a link "plasticity" parameter (λ). This parameter may vary from link to link, and it determines how quickly a given link "learns."

To the resulting product is added another product, given by the current dynamic weight component Δw times that link's link-decay constant Δ. The latter parameter determines how quickly a link "forgets" and may vary from one link to another.

Based on this model, the dynamic component of links joining uncorrelated nodes may decay to zero. As indicated earlier, this would prevent any subsequent flow of activation over those links; in effect those links would have dissolved. The added static weight component is used to ensure that a connection is always available where its need is anticipated. (In practice, these static components are often very small but are nonzero in value.)

SOME EXAMPLES OF KRN ANN CIRCUITRY

Much of the effort in designing the KRN system is expended in devising appropriate neural-net circuits for the various KRN knowledge entities and inference mechanisms. To motivate some of these design issues, we will describe a handful of the relevant circuits.

KRN "feature" KEs are represented by "encoder" circuits (assemblies of artificial neural net nodes and links). This term reflects the fact that such circuits "encode" multinode patterns of network activity in the activity of smaller ensembles of nodes (usually single nodes). An encoder's output becomes active, if all required input-feature values are active (present)—hence, the analogy between encoders and IF-condition detectors in a rule-driven AI system.

Encoders perform a "fuzzy" match between current inputs and the encoder's recognition template. They exhibit tolerance for input values within a satisfactory range rather than demanding one exactly matched set of input values. This function resembles that performed by "instars" in Grossberg (1988).

A set of encoders may be driven by the same set of input features. For example, in our "fruit-sorting" net of Fig. 11.8, encoders corresponding to distinct types of "apples" all draw input from nodes (or circuits) representing the possible values of the feature's "color," "flavor," and so on.

For a given input-value vector, each encoder in such a set may become active to a different degree (reflecting the degree of match between that input and the recognition template embodied in each encoder). Interencoder competition is used to maximize the activity of the single encoder that best matches the current input feature values.

Encoders are embodied in "minicolumn" circuits. A group of competing minicolumns may be assembled into a "column" circuit, whose inputs are shared by the constituent minicolumns.

In the column circuit illustrated following, we see two minicolumns. Assume that the afferent sources A_{k-1}, A_k, and A_{k+1} become active in unison, perhaps because of a new input presented to the network. Further, because of their

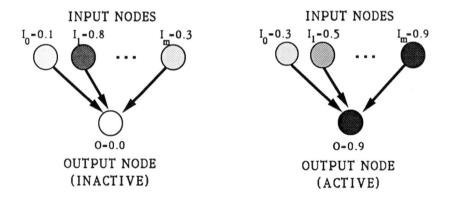

RECOGNITION TEMPLATE (IDEAL INPUT PATTERN) =
(0.25, 0.5, $\cdots$, 1.0)

FIG. 11.13. Encoder Circuit

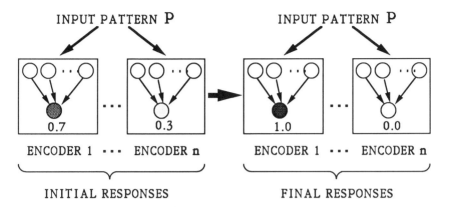

FIG. 11.14. Interencoder Competition

nonzero activation-decay constants (δ), afferent-summing nodes Σ_i and Σ_{i+1} begin to integrate their respective inputs.

In addition, because of the nonzero firing thresholds of output nodes O_i, and O_{i+1}, both of these nodes remain at their initial output values of 0, and because Σ_i and Σ_{i+1} receive somewhat different inputs, arriving via links having different link weights, one of Σ_i or Σ_{i+1} will reach the threshold of its respective O-node first.

Assume that O_i wins this competition. Whichever O-node fires first will provide some (perhaps small) input signal to shared inhibitory node I. Now, because of the latter node's high gain, the output of the inhibitory node will be large and will strongly inhibit *all* Σ-nodes in this column. This prevents any O-node other than O_i from firing. In addition, because of its nonzero activation-decay constant, it will remain active for some time after fires.

The net result of all this activity is that node O_i "recognizes" and perhaps becomes adaptively "allocated" to represent the pattern-driving the afferent sources.

In the KRN system, operation knowledge entities are implemented using "decoder" circuits. These circuits decode, or translate, the state of individual network nodes into larger patterns of activity. Thus, the function of decoders is complementary to that of encoders. Decoders are analogous to the "outstars" described in Grossberg (1988).

Decoders produce a given output activity pattern across a set of output nodes. In producing specific network state transitions, decoders act like the THEN clauses of rule-driven AI systems. The level of decoder-input activity scales the decoder's output activity vector. That is, a more-active decoder input produces an output vector with proportionately larger component activity levels.

A KRN network produces behavior (i.e., a coordinated stream of output

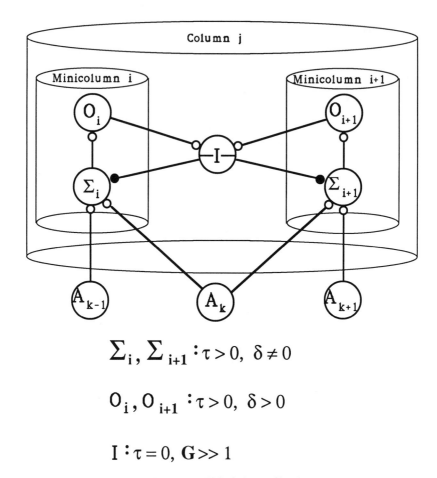

$$\Sigma_i, \Sigma_{i+1} : \tau > 0, \ \delta \neq 0$$

$$O_i, O_{i+1} : \tau > 0, \ \delta > 0$$

$$I : \tau = 0, \ G \gg 1$$

FIG. 11.15. KRN Column Circuit

signals) through a stimulus/response operating cycle. Encoders are cascaded into decoders to form a "fuzzy" state machine that operates as follows:

1. Encoders detect ("stimulus") patterns in the current network state. That is, encoders that are matched by current input signals become active.
2. The output nodes of encoders also serve as the input nodes of decoders. Thus, active encoders trigger activity in associated decoders.
3. The output nodes of active decoders produce a sequence of output activation patterns ("responses"). These output patterns may then be fed back as new inputs to the network. That is, active decoders can change the activity levels of features, which may in turn feed back into encoders. The preceding three steps can then be repeated so that the net produces a sequence of output patterns.

Note that this system is not stimulus-bound, in that external stimuli entering the system are not the sole determinant of the system's behavior. Instead the network's time-varying current state *and* the external stimuli jointly determine the behavior. This provides a natural means for incorporating contextual information in generating response patterns so that the system's past processing can bias its responses to current stimuli. It also provides a mechanism for including internally generated signals, such as various "drives" or "appetites," in current processing.

Sensorimotor Maps

The output of an intelligent system ultimately takes the form of *purposive behavior;* that is, such a system selects and executes actions that are intended to satisfy the system's current goals. An intelligent system is able to *learn* which actions are useful in attaining a given goal.

To pursue this further, we introduce the notion of a *sensorimotor map.* Such a map consists of associations between the current and possible goal states of a system (as reflected in the activation state of its feature nodes) and the actions that the system can execute (through activation of operation-triggering nodes). The associations that are built into a sensorimotor map through learning may later be used in selecting appropriate responses to system goals and current circumstances.

Consider Fig. 11.17, which depicts a paired sensory and motor hierarchy at two consecutive times.

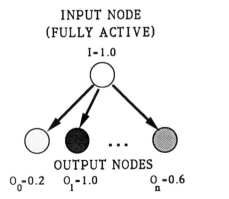
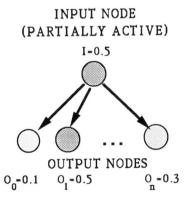

INPUT NODE (FULLY ACTIVE)
$I-1.0$

OUTPUT NODES
$O_0-0.2 \quad O_1-1.0 \quad O_n-0.6$

INPUT NODE (PARTIALLY ACTIVE)
$I-0.5$

OUTPUT NODES
$O_0-0.1 \quad O_1-0.5 \quad O_n-0.3$

PRODUCTION TEMPLATE (IDEAL OUTPUT PATTERN) =
$(0.2, 1.0, \cdots, 0.6)$

FIG. 11.16. KRN Decoder Circuit

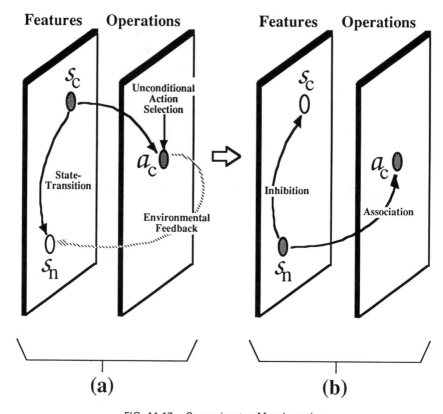

FIG. 11.17.   Sensorimotor Map Learning

Here the system starts in (current) state s_c. Assume that some means exists for unconditionally selecting and "firing" an operation a_c (perhaps through something as crude as random selection). At the moment that a_c is fired, a local learning mechanism may take a "now print" of active nodes s_c and a_c, strengthening the (directed) link between them. (This may be accomplished through a simple correlation-based mechanism, such as a gated Hebb synapse.)

Through environmental feedback (i.e., changes in the state of the environment), a_c causes a transition $s_c \Rightarrow s_n$ in the system's feature state. Once s_n becomes active, two things may occur—see part (b) of Fig. 11.17:

1. First, the learning mechanism may again be enabled, building a directed association from s_n to a_c.
2. Through local competitive mechanisms such as lateral inhibition, activation of s_n may lead to quenching (deactivation) of s_c.

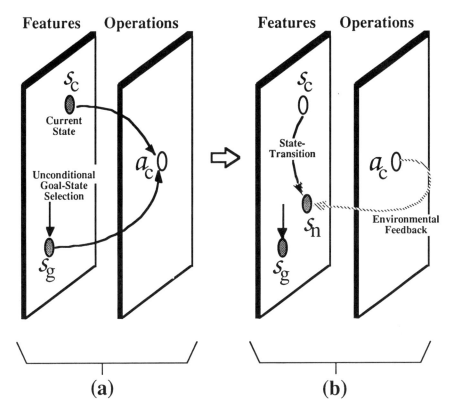

FIG. 11.18.   Sensorimotor Map Usage

The purpose behind this chain of events is illustrated in Fig. 11.18. Through the preceding "experimental" learning activity, the system builds a representation (encoded in point-to-point associations) for how specific operations, in specific circumstances, alter the state of the system's features. Now, given a particular starting feature state s_c and a desired goal state s_g, the system can use its sensorimotor knowledge to pick an operation that will move its current state toward its goal state.

In part (a) of Fig. 11.18, the system begins in state s_c, and a separate component of the system asserts goal state s_g. (This may be done by a "motivational" or "orienting" subsystem.) The conjunction of these inputs selects operation a_c for firing (i.e., that particular combination of goal state and current state gives a_c a competitive advantage over other candidate operations).

Once a_c fires, environmental feedback causes a state transition from s_c to s_n (which is hopefully closer to s_g than was s_c). Features s_n and s_g jointly select

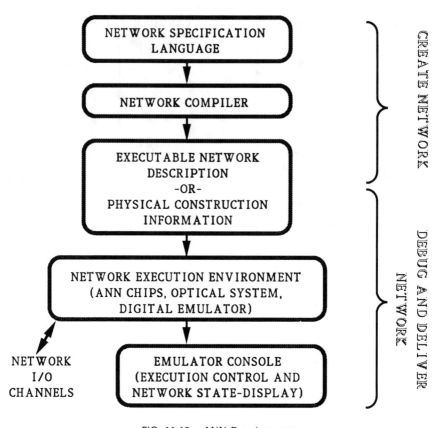

FIG. 11.19.   ANN Development

another operation, and this cycle continues until the current state approximates s_g sufficiently closely.

NETWORK DESIGN TOOLS

In developing an artificial neural network, one must create networks specifically designed for a particular function. Although neural nets may be made adaptive, their overall signal-flow organization must be correctly matched to the processing requirements of a given application. Neural self-organization should be viewed as a functional "fine-tuning" mechanism, not as a means for self-determination of a network's high-level organization.

A network design may range in complexity from a single, small, stereotypically connected net to a large hierarchical or heterarchical assembly of nonhomogeneous subsystems. The design of a network involves the definition of a set of functional units, linked by a set of signal-flow pathways (i.e., a set of functional "centers" or "areas" interconnected in specific afferent and efferent relationships). In particular, this requires the following: (a) selection of the appropriate types of network elements (node/link models), and (b) definition of the appropriate organization ("topology") for these elements.

Network development requires the ability to create large and complex nets, and to exercise them efficiently. In addition, some neural-net applications demand nets that are driven by external data sources and that in turn drive external output devices. This is especially true of a neural-net architecture such as KRN, which is intended to exist in and interact with the external world.

In designing, constructing, and testing a complex system, a contemporary engineer has many powerful tools at his or her disposal. Similarly implementation of complex ANN systems requires a good deal of auxiliary machinery. A complete ANN "development system" contains three major components (see Fig. 11.19): (a) an environment for network creation (a network "compiler" or "assembler"), (b) an interactive network analysis and debug (design validation) tool, and (c) one or more vehicles for efficient network emulation.

There exist many examples of the preceding neural-net tools; the availability of such machinery is an essential enabling step in the development of complex neural networks such as KRN. As an example, Cruz et al. (1987) describe some of the tools that have been used in elaborating KRN networks.

STATUS AND CONCLUSIONS

Implementation of the KRN system is presently underway but is not yet complete. Most of the work done to date has focused on the KRN feature hierarchy. However, preliminary implementation has also been done for the operation network and in connecting features to operations to produce network behavior.

Several variants of the encoder circuit have been designed and tested (initially using the Computational Network Environment developed at IBM and now being recreated on a Macintosh II PC). These circuits implement the KRN implication and context inference mechanisms as well as an integral attention mechanism to permit "feature focus," as described previous. The resulting "minicolumn" circuits have been grouped into larger "columns," which serve as competing feature detectors. This functionally appropriate arrangement is reminiscent of cortical organization and connectivity (Amari & Arbib, 1982; Ballard, 1985; Braitenberg & Braitenberg, 1979; Takeuchi & Amari, 1979). Several uses have been found for the dynamics of the parallel associative network model (Cruz et al., 1987), which is being used to construct the KRN circuits.

Considerable effort is being expended on construction of the ANN tools that are necessary for the design and emulation of a KRN net. These include an ANN descriptive design language, an network compiler, a network emulation engine, and—in anticipation of the heavy computational burden imposed by large neural nets—parallel digital ANN accelerator hardware.

Knowledge representation networks constitutes an approach to intelligent information processing that is quite different from that of mainline artificial intelligence. In many respects, these approaches are complementary to one another. Hopefully further insights from the cognitive and neural sciences will help guide both approaches toward their common goal of true synthetic intelligence.

REFERENCES

Amari, S., & Arbib, M. A. (Ed.). (1982). *Competition and cooperation in neural networks*. New York: Springer-Verlag.

Anderson, J. A., & Bower, G. H. (1973). *Human associative memory*. Washington, DC: Winston.

Ballard, D. (1985, January). *Cortical connections and parallel processing: Structure and function* (Tech. Report No. 133). University of Rochester, Department of Computer Science.

Braitenberg, V., & Braitenberg, C. (1979). Geometry of orientation columns in the visual cortex. *Biological Cybernetics, 33,* 179–186.

Crick, F. (1984, July). Function of the thalamic reticular complex: The searchlight hypothesis. *Proceedings of the National Academy of Science of the USA, 81,* 4586–4590.

Cruz, C. A., Hanson, W. A., & Tam, J. Y. (1987, May). *Knowledge representation networks (KRN): Processing knowledge through flow of activation* (Rep. No. G320–3498). IBM Palo Alto Scientific Center.

Cruz, C. A., Hanson, W. A., & Tam, J. Y. (1987). Computational network environment. *Proc. of IEEE First International Conference on Neural Networks, 3,* 531–538.

Granit, R. (1981). *The purposive brain*. Cambridge, MA: MIT Press.

Grossberg, S. (Ed.). (1988). *Neural networks and natural intelligence*. Cambridge, MA: MIT Press.

Kohonen, T. (1984). *Self-organization and associative memory*. New York: Springer-Verlag.

Kosko, B. (1987). Adaptive inference in fuzzy knowledge networks. *Proc. of IEEE First International Conference on Neural Networks, 2,* 261–268.

Rumelhart, D. E., McClelland, J. L., & the PDP Research Group. (1986). *Parallel distributed processing, 1–2*. Cambridge, MA: MIT Press.

Takeuchi, A., & Amari, S. (1979). Formation of topographic maps and columnar microstructures in nerve fields. *Biological Cybernetics, 35,* 63–72.

Willwacher, G. (1982). Storage of a temporal pattern sequence in a network. *Biological Cybernetics, 43,* 115–126.

12 Perfect Memory

Robert L. Dawes
Martingale Research Corporation

This chapter approaches the subject of memory from the point of view that the purpose of memory is behavioral rather than simply for the storage of sensory patterns. Although most would agree on the purpose, it must be acknowledged that, so long as memory models in neural networks continue to resemble little more than correlation matrices, their relationship to cognition will be as a book is related to its reader.

As the theory of short-term memory (STM) dynamics for neural networks matures, the lack of maturity of long-term memory (LTM) models becomes a major problem. Existing memory models are based either on correlation learning or on error minimization, and in neither case is there any fundamental understanding of what a memory *ought* to do. Without this understanding, we can clearly see the differences between memory models, but we cannot evaluate those differences objectively.

In this chapter, we utilize the results of certain observations on causality of operators on Hilbert resolution spaces to investigate and develop a new theory of memory and learning for neural networks and cognitive systems. These observations suggest a new definition of a perfect memory operator on Hilbert resolution space that captures a more realistic role for memory in the context of its effect on the behavior of dynamical systems. This behavioral role emerges from the close relationship between causal operators and the theory of dynamical systems and modern control, from which the Kalman filter and the Luenberger observer were born. Implementation of a perfect memory in the real world, thus, becomes an embedding problem in which the operator must be factored through an appropriate state space, because realizable systems must be "memoryless" in a mathematically defined sense.

411

The theory and design of neural network architectures have made great strides since the introduction of Rosenblatt's Perceptron and Widrow's Adaline in the 1940s and 1950s. Grossberg's use of Lyapounov functions to describe the dynamics and stability of neural networks, and Hopfield's physical insights linking network dynamics to Ising spin models of ferroelectric ceramics, have started an avalanche of new theoretical and modeling work. Commercial products are beginning to appear, and VLSI implementation is under way. Yet there is still a major theoretical shortcoming that may severely limit the usefulness of these products: the structure of the learning law.

All extant learning laws are of two basic types: (a) error minimization, and (b) correlation averaging. In the first category are the delta rule, the generalized delta rule, the Boltzmann machine and Cauchy machine, and the Perceptron. In the second category are the Hebb rule, the Lernmatrix, Drive Reinforcement, differential Hebbian, shunting Grossberg, and all methods using sums of outer products of sample patterns (Kohonen, 1984; Hopfield, 1982; Kosko 1986, 1987). There are supervised and unsupervised methods in each category. Some learning laws (e.g., the Bienenstock and Bear–Cooper–Ebner models) and some network paradigms (e.g., Grossberg–Schmajuk, Levine–Prueitt, and our own Parametric Avalanche) employ both of these two basic types.

The distinction between supervised and unsupervised learning algorithms is a valuable one but is somewhat misleading. All learning methods are supervised, but some get their supervision extrinsically through an action by the user/tutor, and the rest get their supervision intrinsically through a built-in "drive" to minimize error or maximize entropy or correlate signal pairs. In every case, the environment that supplies the signals always dictates the future states of the memory (unless it fails to function as a memory), so that every learning algorithm is governed by its environmental "fate."

It is difficult to evaluate the mechanisms of memory without understanding the purpose for memory in adaptive systems. Some insight into this purpose begins with the observation that physically realizable dynamical systems are always both causal and anticausal; that is, their current outputs are determined without reference to either the future (causality) or to the past (anticausality). In systems theory, such operators are called "memoryless" operators (cf. Feintuch & Saeks, 1982, p. 16).

Let us emphasize this point: A memoryless system can only count on its current state and inputs to determine its subsequent state and outputs. Physical influences are constrained to act within a space–time light cone that means, for terrestrial purposes, that physical forces do not act across time. If it is to have the *appearance* of memory, a physically realizable system must employ some mechanism for etching the present data into a time invariant form, so that, when it gets to the future, it will have a record of the past in its then current state. It is the use of this record in the current state that gives a memoryless system access to the past, but it is important to realize that this access is indirect, and it is only as true as the record is time invariant. It is also important to consider the mechanisms by which a system may access the future, but we shall reserve that discussion for another time (in the future, to be sure).

What, therefore, is the role of memory in cognition, control, and goal direction, and how can one memory model be compared to another in that context? It is not enough to rate memory mechanisms by the traditional measures such as "capacity" and "longevity" without linking those measures to their role in promoting the cognitive function of the memory. Is capacity alone responsible for the fact that a garden snake can survive longer than an optical disk in the path of a rototiller? Does longevity make a stone tablet intelligent?

What we need is a theory of memory that is expressed in the context of active dynamical systems (as opposed to passive stationary filters) and that provides the analytical tools to characterize and to quantify those elements of memory and learning that relate to the intelligence or cognitive ability of the system. What we offer here is a theory of "perfect memory" as the idealized mechanism of memory and learning in adaptive, cognitive systems. Like the perfect circle, it can serve as the possibly unrealizable ideal around which the cartwheel of autonomous robotics may turn.

We present the ideas first in heuristic form, to make them accessible to the interdisciplinary variety of practitioners of neural networks. However, we are sensitive to the need for substance, the lack of which has damaged the progress and credibility of other approaches to machine intelligence; therefore, we also present some of the mathematics in sufficient detail to serve as a foundation for further work.

Our ultimate objective is to stimulate the development of a synthesis of the concepts of neural networks with the powerful and beautiful—but technically rather difficult—theory of dynamical systems that has been presented in Feintuch and Saeks (1982). We have the overwhelming sense that a successful extension of that theory from its roots in automata to its flower in cognition will bring decisive breakthroughs in our understanding of the nature of intelligence.

HEURISTICS

The language of dynamical system theory has precise mathematical definitions and consequences, some of which we shall present later. However, because the detailed development tends to stretch the background of well-trained engineers, not to mention the fear and loathing that it may engender in biologists, cognitive scientists, computer scientists, and psychologists (etc.), it is appropriate in this interdisciplinary field to give a heuristic exposition.

A cognitive system, whether natural or artificial, is a kind of "system," which, heuristically speaking, is a black box that absorbs inputs (stimulus), some of which may be under our control, and that produces outputs (behavior) that we can observe and measure. These inputs and outputs are signals, usually with vector values. That is, they are vector valued functions of the time variable. (In the next section, when we become more technical, a scalar-valued signal will be reduced to a mere point in an infinite-dimensional vector space called a Hilbert space in which each instant of time corresponds to one of the infinitely many coordinate axes. A vector-valued signal will then be an n–tuple of such points in a product of Hilbert spaces.)

Every system "is" nothing more or less than a relationship between the input signals and the output signals, but this is not to be oversimplified. For example, in most interesting systems, the relationship is one-to-many. That is, one input signal will in general produce a different output signal each time that same input is presented. This is certainly the case with cognitive systems, but it is also true of dumb devices like computers and their memories: If I get the same answer back every time I enter "DIR C:", I would suspect a problem somewhere, especially if I had created some new files in the mean time. However, this variability presents so many analytical complications that it is difficult to know how to tie anything down in a general theory of dynamical systems.

Mathematicians, engineers, and other nonmystics generally like their functional relationships to be one-to-one or at worst many-to-one. So when they are asked to explain an object that may do many things when placed in identical external conditions, they will invent "hidden" variables and label them with clever names, saying, "These are the 'state' variables." Then they will explain that the reason the outputs were different, although the inputs were the same, is because the initial states were different in the two experiments so that, voilá, no two outputs result from the "same" experiment. Although this may at first sound decidedly mystical (and it is), the results are scientific in that the predictions are replicable by the average post-doc.

An alternate explanation would be to point out that, once you have performed an experiment on a system (i.e., presented it with an input signal and measured its output signal), it now "has" a different history than it had before the experiment. Therefore, it is impossible to perform the same experiment on a single system twice from an identical starting point. A little reflection will reveal that, by the time this approach is quantified, it will be practically indistinguishable from the "state variable" approach previous. That is, the purpose for the state variables is to allow us to artificially extract a system from its captivity on a single world line and analyze its behavior against a variety of inputs.

These considerations are central to the problem of memory in a dynamical system. We have indicated previous that the concept of memory is closely related (in a contrary fashion) to that of causality and its reverse-time partner, anti-causality. That is, if a system is anticausal, then memory is something that it has none of, except perhaps through indirect means, just as a causal system does not have any "memory" of the future. Mathematicians express these ideas in the following way: A causal system has the property that, whenever two input signals are identical prior to time t (for any time t), then the output signals must also be identical prior to time t. After all, if the outputs were to differ prior to time t, the only influence in the input signal that could "cause" it to happen would have to come after time t. Likewise an anticausal system is one with the property that, whenever two input signals are identical after time t (for any time t), then the output signals must also be identical after time t. In other words, past differences in the inputs cannot generate future differences in the output.

Let us be very clear about the implications of all this for cognitive systems. Suppose you were to walk into a room to find a man sitting in a chair. You introduce yourself and initiate a conversation, asking a few questions from a list you had prepared. He acknowledges your presence, tells you his name and answers your questions, and nothing seems amiss. You leave the room. Then thirty minutes later you walk into the same room and find the same man sitting in the same chair. You introduce yourself and ask the same questions. He acknowledges your presence, tells you his name and gives exactly the same answers to your questions. He is not annoyed by your return visit. He does not even make any remarks about having seen you before.

Such behavior is indicative of damage to the hippocampus, which is known to be essential for the retention of episodic memory, although its specific role is still a mystery. A person with this kind of damage does not respond differently, if the external initial states (i.e., exclusive of whatever may be going on in his brain) for two experiments are substantially the same except for the wall-clock time, and if the input streams are also substantially the same after the start of the experiment. Of course the two input streams are substantially different prior to the starts of the two experiments because, of necessity, the input signal for the second experiment contains a copy of itself at the earlier time of the first experiment. That difference may seem minor to someone who is accustomed to performing experiments on inanimate objects, but it is the essence of adaptive, intelligent, cognitive systems to prevent you from repeating an experiment in which "all other things are equal."

How much difference must there be in two situations before a cognitive system is able to take notice? So far as mathematical system theory is concerned, if a system is not anticausal, or if it is not causal, then it is of interest only as an example of one that cannot be implemented. Little else is said about it. However, a system that is not anticausal is one that has at least a little bit of memory. That is, there are at least two input signals, $f(t)$, and $g(t)$, and there is a time t' such that $f(t) = g(t)$ for $t > t'$, *but the corresponding output signals are not the same after* t'. Given this inch of insight, why not go the whole mile? What is the most memory a system could have?

We define a "perfect memory" as a system that is maximally nonanticausal. That is, a perfect memory is one that is attentive to the slightest differences between any two, possible input signals and produces different outputs forever after.

One might object that there are some cognitive functions in which such a memory would be quite undesirable. For example, biological systems often exhibit "selective attention" that screens out "irrelevant details." We counter that "irrelevance" is a judgment that is only accessible to hindsight and that in fact the ability to make such a judgment at all is evidence that the irrelevant details are not screened out but rather that their effect on the future is, at least temporarily, small. A future change of context could transform an irrelevant detail into a new course of history.

Implementation of any system with memory, perfect or otherwise, requires solving a certain problem involving the construction of an appropriate "state space" for the system. In practical terms, this simply means that one must provide a recording medium and a recording mechanism that will etch the input into a time-invariant form while the input occurs, so that some "trace" of it will be available in some future present to affect that present's future. In mathematical terms, this is what Feintuch and Saeks called a "lifting" problem (cf. Feintuch & Saeks, 1982), and evidently a satisfactory mathematical solution is not yet available. Such a solution would constitute not just a theory but a method of learning for any system with memory.

TECHNICAL BACKGROUND

In this background section, we review a little of the machinery that is used to define causality, anticausality, and memorylessness of operators on Hilbert space. We shall not bother to use the definitions that apply to linear operators, as they will be of little use in the field of neural networks. We draw heavily from Feintuch and Saeks (1982).

Sobolev Spaces

The technical exposition will assume a familiarity with at least the basic elements of Hilbert spaces. It simply cannot be summed up in a few words. The unprepared reader who wishes to press on may want to substitute a mental picture of ordinary n-dimensional Cartesian vector space, which is a special kind of Hilbert space. Each "axis" of the space represents a time at which a sample of a signal is measured, and the value of the signal becomes the coordinate of the point representing the signal in that space. In Cartesian n-space, the signal is sampled in discrete time; in Hilbert space, it is sampled continuously. It is common for inadequately educated engineers and practitioners of "AI" to claim that finite dimensions are enough, because that is all we have to compute with anyway. To them we suggest some remedial Kailath, especially Kailath (1968, 1970).

Given that, a Sobolev space is a special kind of Hilbert space that is intimately related to the theory of distributions (generalized functions, e.g., the Dirac delta function). The norm, or energy, of a functional member of the Sobolev space includes the L^2 norms of the functional itself plus those of several of its distributional derivatives, the number depending on the order of the Sobolev space.

Although Sobolev spaces are very exotic places to do analysis, they turn out to be infinitely more realistic than the Lebesgue spaces or mere finite-dimensional Cartesian spaces. This is because the members of the functional Sobolev spaces all have a certain degree of continuity, which makes them eminently more practical as models for physical processes. All physical processes are accompanied by at least a small amount of inertia (interpreted as bounded bandwidth for electromagnetic signals), and this will have important implications for causal and memoried operators.

The theory of distributions provides a way to take the derivative of functions regardless of their continuity. In particular it provides a definition of derivative that applies to members of certain Hilbert spaces like $L^2(R)$, which are not even functions at all but equivalence classes of functions. In general the derivative of a member of L^2 lies in a larger space (called $H^{-1}(R)$) which contains L^2. However, there is a maximal subspace of L^2, all of whose derivatives lie in L^2, and it is called H^1. It is a Sobolev space. Its members have the property that both their *zero*th derivatives and their first derivatives have finite energy in the sense of the L^2 norm. More generally, H^k is the Sobolev space of members of L^2 whose first k derivatives have finite L^2 norm. $H^0 = L^2$. Similar considerations apply to vector valued functions (and distributions). The expanded notation $H^k(R,R^n)$ represents the Sobolev space of square integrable functions on $R \rightarrow R^n$ whose first k derivatives have finite $L^2(R,R^n)$ norm.

There is a theorem, called the Sobolev lemma (cf., Yosida, 1974, p. 174), that guarantees that, if $f \varepsilon H^k(R)$, then f is (equivalent to) a function that has n-1 continuous derivatives. In particular, if $k > 0$, then f itself is (equivalent to) a continuous function.

Let n be nonnegative, and, for each real number, t, define an operator P_t on $H^k(R)$ by $P_t f = g$, where

g is identical to f when restricted to the time interval $(-\infty, t]$, and

the sum of the L^2 norms (energies) of the first k derivatives of g in (t, ∞) is minimized.

Example 1. If $k = 0$, then $g(s) = P_t f(s)$ can be obtained by simply truncating f to the right of t—for example, $g(s) = f(s)$, for $s < t$, and $g(s) = 0$, for $s > t$.

With a little effort, one can demonstrate that P_t is a projection operator for each $t \varepsilon R$ that projects any trajectory or signal $f(t)$ onto its PAST (hence, the use of the letter "P"). Further, there is a complementary family of operators $F_t = I - P_t$ associated with P_t that project signals onto their future.

Note that, if $k > 0$, truncation is not a projection operator on $H^k(R)$, because in particular the result need not be continuous. This is extremely important in discussing the causality and memory of operators, because, as discussed in the next section, these concepts are only definable in relation to a particularly complete family of these projections called a resolution of the identity. Among its more peculiar consequences is that a causal operator on Sobolev space, which is heuristically not supposed to employ information from the future to create current effects, can actually operate entirely on the future to obtain current effects, so long as the information that it draws from the future is nothing more than could be predicted from the past. We think that we are the first to make this fascinating observation, which indicates a distinct advantage for Martingale theory over Markov theory in the design of systems that can anticipate the future evolution of their environment.

Causality and Memory of Operators on Sobolev Space

When one defines causality of operators on a Hilbert space H (including the Sobolev spaces H^k), one begins with a *resolution of the identity* operator I, consisting of a family $P = \{P_t / t \ \varepsilon \ R\}$ of projection operators on H satisfying

(i) $P_{-\infty} = 0$
(ii) $P_{\infty} = I$
(iii) $P_s P_t = P_{min(s,t)}$

plus a continuity condition (cf. Feintuch & Saeks, 1982). It is precisely by means of such a resolution of the identity that one is able to identify some feature of the abstract elements of H as the part that evolves with "time," even if it were not already made explicit as it is in the functional members of $H^k(R)$. Typically one chooses for P_t the projections that were described in the previous section (except typically no one has considered the Sobolev spaces). This represents the minimum knowledge of the future given the level of distributional inertia in the system.

Definition. The pair (H,P) is called a Hilbert resolution space.

Example 2. Trajectories of dynamical systems can be represented as functions $u \ \varepsilon$ $H^k(R,R^n)$, where the norm of u is given by a more general quadratic form than simply the sum of the L^2 norms of the first k derivatives of u. In the simplistic case of a vehicle moving under its own power in the absence of external fields, all the energy is contained in the kinetic energy (i.e., the L^2 norm of du/dt is all that counts). In that case, a family of projection operators can be given by the following:

$$P_t u(\tau) = u(\tau), \qquad\qquad\qquad \text{if } \tau < t,$$
$$\text{or } = u(t) + (\tau - t)u'(t), \qquad \text{if } \tau > t.$$

According to the Sobolev lemma, if $n = 3$, and $k > 3/2$, then $u'(t)$ exists (as an ordinary function).

We are now ready to define causality of an operator.

Definition. Let A be an operator (not necessarily linear) on a Hilbert space H, and let $\{P_t: t \ \varepsilon \ R\}$ be a resolution of the identity on H. Then A is *casual* relative to $\{P_t\}$, provided that, for all t and every pair, $f,g \ \varepsilon \ H$,

$$P_t f = P_t g \Rightarrow P_t A f = P_t A g.$$

If the Hilbert space were $L^2(R)$, this would translate into a statement that, for all times t, whenever two input functions are equal (almost everywhere) prior to time t, then their outputs from the operator A will be equal up to time t. In other words, nothing in the output of A prior to time t will be affected by varying only the future values of its input. The interpretation is a little more difficult when H is a Sobolev space, as we indicated earlier.

An *anticausal* operator on H is one that allows no information from the past to influence the future. The precise definition is obtained from the one previous by replacing each occurrence of P_t by $F_t = I - P_t$. An operator that is both causal and anticausal is called *memoryless*. In finite dimensions (i.e., when time proceeds through only a finite number of discrete steps), causal operators are lower triangular matrices; anticausal operators are upper triangular, and memoryless operators are diagonal matrices. The situation is not quite so easy in infinite dimensions, but, as an example, the Hilbert–Schmidt operators are among the memoryless operators.

Definition. A *memory* operator is an operator A that is NOT anticausal. That is, there exists some time t and some pair of inputs, f and g, such that

$$F_t f = F_t g, \text{ and } F_t A f \neq F_t A g.$$

F_t is the projection that looks at the future and ignores the past; therefore, this says that the operator A has at least a little bit of memory storage ability, if, for some time t, there are two input functions whose only differences are in the past, yet A can send them in different directions in the future.

Perfect Memory

Clearly there is more one could do with such a portentious definition. What makes one operator have a *better* memory than another, for example? Toward this end, we suggest the following.

Definition. An operator M is a *perfect memory*, provided that it is causal, and it always maps distinct initial trajectory segments into distinct terminal trajectory segments; that is, for all $t \ \varepsilon \ R$ and for all $f,g \ \varepsilon \ H$, the following occurs:

$$P_t f = P_t g \Rightarrow P_t M f = P_t M g, \text{ and}$$
$$P_t f \neq P_t g \Rightarrow F_t M f \neq F_t M g.$$

Theorem. If M is a perfect memory, and there exists t, f, and g such that $F_t f = F_t g$, and $P_t f \neq P_t g$, then M is a memory operator.

The proof is immediate. The qualifying condition only guarantees that the situation is not vacuous.

We can also accommodate the solipsist philosophy that admits no possibility of direct knowledge of any world outside the world of thought, with the following.

Definition. An operator W is a *weak perfect memory*, provided that, for all $t \, \varepsilon \, R$ and all $f, g \, \varepsilon \, H$,

$$P_t Wf = P_t Wg, \text{ or } F_t Wf \neq F_t Wg.$$

This says that either the initial segments (Past) of two memory traces are identical or their terminal segments are different. Equivalently it is not possible in a weak perfect memory for two input functions to produce memory traces that are distinct up to some time t and identical thereafter. It is easy to show the following.

Theorem. Every perfect memory is a weak perfect memory.

Proof. Let M be a perfect memory. An equivalent statement of the definition of perfect memory is that it is causal, and

$$F_t Mf \neq F_t Mg, \text{ or } \text{NOT}\{ P_t f \neq P_t g \}.$$

However, the latter half of this disjunction (after cancelling the double negation), together with the definition of causality, implies $P_t Mf = P_t Mg$. Thus, M is a weak perfect memory.

THE REALIZATION PROBLEM

The realization problem for a causal system A with memory concerns the construction of a recording medium S and a recording method r so that the memory of A can be represented in the present "state" of its recording medium. Mathematically this problem is stated as an operator factorization problem. That is, the operator A is a mapping of the Hilbert resolution space (H, P) into itself, and the realization problem is to find a "state space" S and two families of mappings $\{r_t \, \mathbf{!} \, t \, \varepsilon \, R\}$ and $\{f_t \, \mathbf{!} \, t \, \varepsilon \, R\}$ such that $r_t : H \rightarrow S, f_t : S \times H \rightarrow H$, and the following:

$$\text{(a) } r_t = r_t P_t$$
$$\text{(b) } f_t = (I - P_t)f_t$$
$$\text{(c) } (I - P_t)A = f_t(r_t, I - P_t)$$

In words, consider the following: (a) r_t records only the past inputs into the state of the system, (b) the readout function f_t affects only the future, and (c) the future output of the system is determined only by the current state and the future input.

There is a trivial state decomposition for every operator, namely $S = H$, $r_t(u) = P_t(u)$, and $f_t(u, v) = (I - P_t)(u)$. However, obviously this may be much larger than is needed for a particular operator in a particular domain. For example, the following standard differential system defines a bounded linear operator A mapping $u \ \varepsilon \ L^2(R)$ to $y \ \varepsilon \ L^2(R)$:

$$(d/dt) \ x(t) = Dx(t) + Bu(t), \ x(0) = x_0 \ \varepsilon \ R^n,$$
$$y(t) = Cx(t).$$

Although $L^2(R)$ is infinite dimensional, A admits an n–dimensional state space, namely R^n, and A factors through R^n as the composition of the following two operators:

$$r_t(u) = e^{Dt}x_0 + \int_0^t e^{D(t-s)}Bu(s)ds,$$

and

$$f_t(x,v)(t') = C\left[e^{D(t'-t)}x + \int_t^{t'} e^{D(t'-s)}Bv(s)ds \right], \qquad \text{if } t' \geq t,$$

$$\text{or} = 0, \qquad \text{if } t' < t.$$

If the range of r_t is dense in S for all t, then the system A is controllable (in S), because there is an input $u \ \varepsilon \ H$ that will drive $r_t(u)$ arbitrarily close to any desired state $x \ \varepsilon \ S$ at any time t. Likewise A is observable, if there exists an "observer" $L: H \times H \to S$ such that, for all $u \ \varepsilon \ H$, $r_t(u) = L(f_t(r_t(u),u), (I - P_t)u)$. That is, A is observable, if the state of A at time t can be uniquely determined from observing the future output and the future input of the system.

Let us now suppose that the universe is neatly divided into two interacting systems, A and M, and that they exchange signals through the functions $u \ \varepsilon \ H$ and $y \ \varepsilon \ H$, as in the previous example, such as follows:

$$u \to A \to y$$
$$\uparrow \qquad \quad |$$
$$\underline{\qquad} M \longleftarrow$$

We might suppose that, for any time t, there is a class of signals $y \ \varepsilon \ H$ such that $(I - P_t)My = 0$ (i.e., for which M has no future beyond time t). We might then distinguish between operators M that are "animate" and those that are not by investigating whether M operates so as to generate control signals u for which the time of entry of $P_t y$ into the fatal region of H is maximized in some sense, thus, maximizing the "survival" of M. Causality would no doubt require that this class of fatal signals be buffered by a neighborhood of signals that drive the state of M into a region identified with "pain." Enlargement of this buffer zone would presumably enhance the survivability of M. This would require M to be a memory system in order that future responses to a signal segment that once lay outside the buffer zone can be altered to improve their survival value.

These considerations provide a quantifiable system theoretic approach to a behavioristic theory of memory and learning. How this approach should be developed is a question that future research will seek to answer. Our definition of perfect memory and the results that will follow will constitute a new theory of memory that is intimately related to the role of memory in adaptation of cognitive systems. Furthermore, the solution of the realization problem will constitute the corresponding theory of learning. Our contribution is that we have given a precise and meaningful formulation to the problem in a mathematical setting where a solution can be found.

CONCLUSIONS AND FORECAST

The Hilbert space theory of systems and control (cf. Feintuch & Saeks, 1982; Kalman, Falb, & Arbib, 1969) is a powerful analytical toolbox that has already produced important practical methods for system identification, estimation, and optimal control, such as the Kalman–Bucy filter. It is remarkable that, although considerable work has been done on causal and memoryless operators, no one appears to have developed any volume of results on operators whose forte is to be as "nonanticausal" as possible, such as our perfect memory. Such operators would not necessarily exhibit all of the properties commonly associated with cognition, but it is clear that cognition is not possible without the behavioral correlates of an approximately perfect memory.

Foundations

Future investigations should expand upon the definitions and results presented previous to develop foundations for properly posing and solving the realization problem. Until the problem is precisely stated, it will not be possible to obtain the desired theory of learning. The solution will no doubt involve the "lifting" problem Feintuch and Saeks described, and it may turn out to be identical to it in the context of nonlinear systems. The pace of progress in memory and learning, as in any other area, is directly linked to the precision with which the problem itself is understood.

Sobolev Space Models

We perceive that there are important implications of causality and anticausality for operators on Hilbert resolution spaces in the case when the underlying Hilbert space is a Sobolev space, for reasons that have been expressed previous. We have carried out some analysis in this setting, but we have not yet fully explored the consequences of the "inertia" of the system on memory and storage mechanisms. An investigation along these lines should formulate the Cauchy problem for several of the appropriate resolution space structures and derive the structure of the resolution of the identity from the variational form of the problem. The implications of this structure for the predictability of causal operators and the memory of anticausal operators can then be developed and interpreted in the context of neural networks, genetics, and perfect memories.

Stochastic Filtering Theory

For the past two years, this author (Dawes, 1989) has been engaged in the theoretical development and the application of a new neural network architecture called the *parametric avalanche,* which implements an adaptive continuous Bayesian estimator (a generalization of the Kalman–Bucy filter). This architecture employs BOTH types of learning laws identified in the introductory remarks to obtain what appears to be a Doob–Meyer decomposition (cf. Kallianpur, 1980) of the observed martingale process into an innovations process and a predictable process. (We say "appears to be," because it is an informal conjecture at this point.) Obtaining the innovations process has required that we devise a constructive mechanism, based on Kalman filtering theory as presented in Kailath (1968, 1970) and in Ho and Lee (1964), for recording the observation history and using it to actually predict the observation. This new constructive mechanism is based on the wave mechanics of the nonlinear Schroedinger equation in a neural lattice and has been called the "quantum neurodynamics" (QND).

The QND theory has been incorporated, together with Kailath's "innovations method" for stochastic filtering, to design a new neural network architecture called the parametric avalanche, or PA for short. (A patent application covering the PA and the QND has been filed.) The PA is a two-layer recurrent network that implements a generalized Kalman–Bucy filter, or, more correctly, a continuous-time Bayesian estimator, by constructing a memory for associative spatiotemporal patterns. In order to allow for the storage of the "evolution equations" for a large class of dynamical systems, the classifier layer of the PA is hard-wired to propagate the wavefunctions of the nonlinear Schroedinger equation, under the control of a potential field that responds associatively to the output of the input layer. These wave packets define a probability distribution over a state space that has been associatively coded by a Hebbian learning law. The output of the classifier layer is then fed back to the input layer, where it is decoded into an estimate of the current observation. That estimate is subtracted from the current observation so that the output of the input layer is a suboptimal "innovations process" of the observation. The observation model that is in the feedback synapses of the input layer is learned by a delta rule learning law in which the desired output of the input layer is zero.

We have shown that the PA can be quite elegantly employed as a Luenberger observer in a robust asymptotic tracker. This is because the suboptimal innovations process, in addition to controlling the evolution of the Schroedinger wave-packets, will also directly control the evolution of the observed system. Thus, the internal model is complementary to the observed system in the sense that the estimation error is minimized by driving the internal model and the external system together. The PA, thus, enjoys a continuous range of behavior between passive observer and adamant controller, depending on the ratio of the inertias of the observed system and the Schroedinger wave-packet. In fact, when used as an adamant controller, the PA control module can right and balance an inverted pendulum from any angle between $+/- 80°$ from the vertical *without prior training and in the presence of severe disturbances.*

However, we have not thoroughly explored the mathematical connections between our architecture and the concept of a perfect memory. Until this point, the perfect memory concept and the parametric avalanche have been independent ideas. However, it is clear that there is a strong connection that deserves more detailed investigation. In particular it appears that a constructive Doob–Meyer decomposition, which will probably be accomplished by a cascade of PA modules, may actually constitute a mechanism for the embedding of a perfect memory into a memoryless operator.

ACKNOWLEDGMENT

I am grateful to Dr. Richard Saeks for introducing me to the Hilbert space theory of dynamical systems and for his enthusiastic and helpful conversations over the past several years. But my inadequate understanding and interpretation of subjects that he knows so well should reflect discredit only to myself.

REFERENCES

Dawes, R. (1989). Quantum neurodynamics and the parametric avalanche (Technical Report MRC/NASA–89004). Allen, TX: Martingale Research Corporation.

Feintuch, A., & Saeks, R. (1982). *System theory: A Hilbert space approach.* New York: Academic Press.

Ho, Y. C., & Lee, R. C. K. (1964). A Bayesian approach to problems in stochastic estimation and control. *IEEE Transactions on Automatic Control, AC–9,* 333–339.

Hopfield, J. (1982). Neural networks and physical systems with emergent collective computational abilities. *Proceedings of the National Academy of Sciences, USA, 79,* 2554–2558.

Kailath, T. (1968). An innovations approach to least-squares estimation, Part I: Linear filtering in additive white noise. *IEEE Transactions on Automatic Control, AC–13,* 646–655.

Kailath, T. (1970). The innovations approach to detection and estimation theory. *Proceedings of the IEEE, 58*(5), 680–695.

Kallianpur, G. (1980). *Stochastic filtering theory.* New York: Springer-Verlag.

Kalman, R. E., Falb, P. L., & Arbib, M. A. (1969). *Topics in mathematical system theory.* New York: McGraw-Hill.

Kohonen, T. (1984). *Self-organization and associative memory.* New York: Springer-Verlag.

Kosko, B. (1986). Differential Hebbian learning. In J. Denker (Ed.), *Neural networks for computing. AIP Conference Proceedings, 151,* 277–282. New York: American Institute of Physics.

Kosko, B. (1987). Bidirectional associative memories. *IEEE Transactions on Systems, Man and Cybernetics, SMC–18,* 49–60.

Yosida, K. (1974). *Functional analysis.* New York: Springer-Verlag.

Author Index

(Italics denote pages on which complete references appear)

Subject Index